THE COLLEGE COST BOOK

1992

Twelfth Edition

College Entrance Examination Board
New York

The College Scholarship Service (CSS) is an activity of the College Board concerned with improving equal educational opportunity. The CSS, through the determination of financial need, assists in the equitable distribution of financial assistance to students. Its services are offered to students and their parents, to secondary schools, to noncollegiate sponsors of financial aid programs, and to all institutions of postsecondary education.

The College Board is a nonprofit membership organization committed to maintaining academic standards and broadening access to higher education. Its more than 2,700 members include colleges and universities, secondary schools, university and school systems, and education associations and agencies.

This publication contains material related to Federal Title IV student aid programs. While the College Board believes that the information contained herein is accurate and factual, this publication has not been reviewed or approved by the U.S. Department of Education.

Copies of this book may be ordered from your local bookseller or from College Board Publications, Box 886, New York, New York 10101-0886. The price is $14.95.

Editorial inquiries regarding this book should be addressed to the College Scholarship Service, The College Board, 45 Columbus Avenue, New York, New York 10023-6992.

Photo credits: page 4, left, University of New Mexico; page 4, right, and page 26, Bill Sublette and the University of Virginia Alumni Association; pages 64-66 and 70-71, Monkmeyer Press; pages 20 and 37, Hugh Rogers.

Library of Congress Catalog Number: 80-648095

International Standard Book Number: 0-87447-409-4

Printed in the United States of America

Contents

Preface

This book starts out from a simple premise: without advance planning, almost no one can afford to pay for college. But with planning, *anybody* can. It's true for families whose children are already high school juniors and seniors—and even truer for families whose children are still quite young.

You may have doubted that education or training after high school is within your family's reach. *That's probably not true.*

You may have assumed that there's nothing you can do to help yourself or improve your chances of finding the outside help you need. *That's definitely not true.*

This book is designed to help students and their families meet college costs. If you're worried about your family's ability to pay future educational expenses, early planning *can* help. The *purpose* of planning is twofold:

- to get as much mileage as you can out of your own resources, and
- to secure the additional outside help—the "financial aid"—you may need.

Planning ahead to meet college costs involves several different kinds of activities. This book will:

- show you how to estimate the full costs of attending the colleges you're considering,
- help you to estimate what share of those costs you and your family will probably be expected to bear,
- prove that you can make time work *for* you in covering your share of the costs,
- describe different ways that families can make their costs more manageable,
- help you estimate your own probable need and eligibility for financial aid,
- explain the various types and sources of financial aid available and what you need to do to apply, and
- assist you in developing a personal financing plan and timetable for gathering the resources *you* need.

Next to buying a home, the money that you and your family pay toward college costs may well be the largest financial investment you ever make in your lifetime. You owe it to yourself to investigate all your options beforehand, and then to manage that investment as carefully as you would any other.

The author gratefully acknowledges the contributions of the many individuals who assisted in the development of the 1992 edition of *The College Cost Book*. Data in Part II were compiled by the editorial staff of Guidance Publishing under the direction of Dorothy Siegfried, using information compiled through the College Board's Annual Survey of Colleges. The book was edited by Renée Gernand.

Lisa Bartl, Larry Coles, Janet Hansen, Hal Higginbotham, Jack Joyce, Sheila Kokidko, Jean Marzone, and Adriano Sverko provided valuable assistance in various aspects of research and statistical analysis.

At the time this book went to press, several aspects of financial aid delivery for academic year 1992-93 had not yet been finalized. As is always the case in times of change, it is very important that students seeking aid for the fall of 1992 take steps, early on, to ensure that they fully understand and comply with all application requirements.

To improve your chances of getting the help you need, you must know *what* you have to do, *when* you have to do it, and *how* to do it right—the first time. Missed deadlines, incomplete or inaccurate answers, and messy or illegible forms can hurt you. *If you have any doubts at all about which forms to file or which questions to complete, contact the financial aid offices at the colleges to which you are applying.*

Kathleen Brouder
Director
CSS Information Services and Associational Affairs
The College Scholarship Service

Part I.
Paying for
college

1. What does college cost?

Some of the best things in life may be free, but unfortunately, college isn't one of them.

In fact, it costs even more than you may think. High as the prices may seem to the family that's facing them, the truth is, they represent only part of the real costs. Only a very few colleges charge you the *full* costs of providing an education.

Public colleges and universities receive large operating subsidies from state and local taxes. Most independent or private colleges and universities meet at least some of their operating expenses through endowments, contributions from graduates, and government or foundation grants. Virtually all of them invest money and use the return to help pay for their activities. The influx of federal and state institutional aid for research, facilities, and special programs is an important part of most colleges' operating budgets, helping to hold down the amounts that must be charged to students and their families.

However, all of this may not be much consolation to students and parents like you who actually have to find a way to pay the bills. Average annual costs of attendance continue to climb for virtually every postsecondary educational option, from commuting to a low-cost community college to living on campus at a high-cost private institution.

The purpose of this book is to help you plan to meet college costs. Because every family's personal and financial circumstances are different, each family's plan for meeting college costs will be different, too. The worksheets in Chapter 10 follow three sample students from different family and financial backgrounds—Andrea, Beth, and Carlos—as they plan to meet college costs. Space is also provided for you to make some preliminary plans.

Your first step in planning is to learn what college costs. Part II of this book lists the average student expenses at over 3,000 colleges and universities

for the 1991-92 academic year (AY). The average expenses at different kinds of colleges are listed in Chapter 10.

The components of college costs

Regardless of where you enroll, your expenses include both direct educational expenses *and* living expenses, and typically consist of five parts:
- tuition and fees
- books and supplies
- room and board
- personal expenses
- transportation

Many students have additional expenses not covered under any of these categories, such as costs arising from medical care or a disability. Be sure to include these extra expenses in estimating the costs of attending the particular colleges you're considering.

Don't let the costs scare you! As this book explains, you may not have to pay the whole amount yourself, *and* there are ways of making more manageable the part you do have to pay.

Tuition and fees

Tuition is the charge for instruction. Fees may be charged for services such as the library, student activities, or the health center. The amount of tuition and fees charged by a particular college depends on many factors, but the most significant factor is what kind of college it is.

Because they receive funds from taxes, tuition and fees at public institutions are generally the lowest, particularly for legal residents of the state or district in which they are located. Most two- and four-year public colleges charge higher tuition for nonresidents, however. This "out-of-state" tuition (or "out-of-district" tuition, in the case of two-year com-

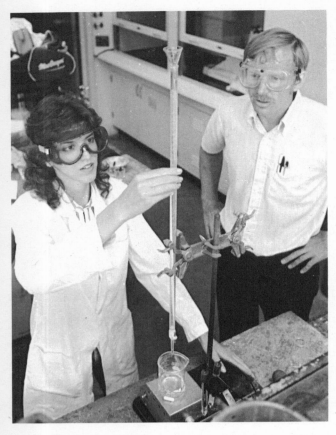

The budget for maintaining, staffing, and operating college facilities is met by federal and state aid, endowments, and investments in addition to charges to students.

munity colleges) often can make the cost of attending a public institution as high as the cost of attending many private institutions. (In rare instances, religiously affiliated colleges may add a surcharge for students who are not members of that religious group.) Tuition at private colleges is usually much higher than at public institutions because private colleges must charge a larger percentage of the real costs. Tuition at proprietary or profit-making institutions (such as many trade and technical schools) is usually set at a level to recover all of their operating costs plus a profit.

The tables in Part II of this book show the tuition and fees charged to most first-time, full-time students. Part-time charges, usually set by credit or semester hour, may work out to be higher per unit. Tuition and fees for upperclassmen and graduate or professional students may also vary.

Books and supplies

Every college student has to buy books, pencils, paper, and other supplies. The amount you spend for books

and supplies will vary only slightly by type of institution but is generally related to the curriculum or courses you select. In some academic fields, for instance, students may have to spend a good deal more than the averages cited in Part II of this book.

Art students, for example, may need more extensive supplies such as canvasses, paints, brushes, and clay. Engineering students may need calculators or slide rules. Students in the sciences may have additional expenses for lab work. Computer science students may need to buy more computer time, or even purchase personal computers. In some programs, the textbooks are more expensive simply because the "information explosion" causes rapid changes in the field.

Room and board

Room and board means basic living expenses for food and housing. Regardless of the kind of institution you choose, you will have to consider these expenses.

You may choose to live in a dormitory on campus or in other college-operated housing located near campus (such as college-owned apartments). Although some private two-year colleges have college-operated housing available, most public community colleges do not.

Or you may want to live in privately owned housing, such as an apartment or rooming house near campus. At many large colleges and universities where on-campus housing is limited, students often live in dormitories for the first year or two and then shift to off-campus private housing.

Or you may choose to live at home with your parents and commute to campus.

The terms "resident student" and "commuter student" can be confusing. In this book, students who live in dormitories or in off-campus, college-owned housing away from their families are called "resident students" (not to be confused with the term "legal resident" used in the discussion of tuition and fees). "Commuter students" are those who live at home with their families. Many colleges have additional budget categories designed to cover students who live off campus in private housing; information about estimated expenses for such students is available in college catalogs and financial aid bulletins. Students who live off campus in private housing generally have expenses that are more like the resident budgets in this book than the commuter budgets.

Colleges with their own housing typically charge residents on a nine-month basis for room rental and most meals, excluding holiday and vacation periods. The room and board charge is built into the student expense budget. Colleges also expect that students living in privately owned, off-campus housing have a similar level of expense (although this is sometimes estimated as somewhat higher or lower than the college's own room and board costs, depending on the local housing market).

Commuter students, on the other hand, are generally assumed to have somewhat lower expenses than resident students because they do not have to pay for housing. However, families should remember that they will still need to buy food for the student and pay for other normal living expenses. For example, if classes start early in the morning and go on until late at night, commuter students will need to buy at least one meal a day, and possibly additional snacks, in the student union or coffee shop. Therefore, the estimated cost of food and other expenses at home is usually built into commuter student expense budgets for financial aid purposes. Take these costs into account in your planning.

Personal expenses

No matter what kind of institution you choose, you will have some personal expenses for such things as clothing, laundry, toiletries, recreation, medical insurance and care, and perhaps incidental furnishings for your dormitory room. This is an area in which you can economize, but colleges usually estimate that students spend at least $900 to $1,200 per academic year on such items.

Transportation

All students spend some money for travel. Resident students who live on or near campus must travel to get there at the start of the academic year and return home at the end; most also go home at least once during the year. If you plan to live at college but expect to travel home frequently, your transportation costs may be considerably higher than the averages shown in this book or reported by individual colleges. Include estimated travel costs in your planning. For financial aid purposes, colleges often budget students for two round-trips home per year by the lowest-cost means of travel possible.

Commuter students who travel to and from campus daily also have travel expenses, whether they use public transportation or a private car. The costs of gasoline and daily parking can add up quickly, so estimate carefully. These costs, too, are built into student expense budgets by colleges for financial aid purposes.

Total expense budget

The total expense budget for a particular college is determined by adding up these five categories of expenses. "Tables, sample cases, and worksheets" in Chapter 10 reflect sample total expenses for resident and commuter students. For your own estimates, remember to consider any additional costs that might result from medical bills or other extraordinary personal expenses.

The total budgets at public colleges are lower than those at private colleges largely because tuition and fees tend to be lower at the former. There is not, however, a lot of difference in the other costs. So don't rule out a private college because of its higher tuition. Private institutions often have more financial aid resources that can help you make up the difference between costs and financial aid. *The greater your overall expense, the greater is the possibility of your demonstrating need for financial aid.*

Questions and answers about college costs

Q All of these costs look greater than anything we can afford. How can we possibly manage to pay for college?

A First, you may be eligible for some financial aid to help you meet part of the costs. What *you* pay for college is not necessarily what the price tag says. Second, you may be able to cut your costs and stretch your resources, as described in later chapters, but be prepared to contribute *something*. In very rare cases, parents are judged too poor to contribute anything toward the costs, but even then, the student himself or herself would be expected to contribute something out of summer job earnings. Third, remember that you and your family are already paying some of these expenses right now—your food, clothing, and personal expenses, for example.

That's not to say that your expenses as a member of the household aren't putting a strain on the household budget; they may well be. If you can manage it now, however, ask yourself seriously if your family can't manage it for another two or four years.

Q With college costs so high, as well as the rising cost of living in general, shouldn't I just look for the cheapest alternative?

A Not necessarily. Higher cost colleges often have more financial aid to help families bridge the gap between the costs and what they can afford to pay.

Q How do I know that the costs at a particular college won't keep going up during the years I'm enrolled?

A You don't. In fact, they probably *will* continue to rise. However, your family's income will probably rise, too. Whether your family's ability to pay will increase at the same rate as college costs depends on a lot of factors, including the overall state of the economy.

2. How much will you be expected to pay?

You should regard your family as the first—and probably primary—source of funds for education. Virtually all colleges, government agencies, and private student aid programs expect you to pay *something* toward college costs, according to your ability. Financial aid often makes up the difference between the costs of attendance and what a family can afford to pay. You may not have to pay as much as the prices listed in a college's catalog if you are eligible for financial aid. Thus, estimating how much your family can reasonably be expected to pay toward educational expenses is a major part of understanding financial aid—and a critical aspect of goal setting.

Whether your family's share of the total costs amounts to 5 percent or 100 percent, you have a better chance of achieving the goal if you know how much you are aiming for.

To help them evaluate a family's financial strength, most college financial aid administrators and aid sponsors use a set of formulas that take into consideration income, assets, expenses, family size, and other factors. Here's how it works.

Evaluating a family's income

A family's total income for the previous calendar year is added up. Parents' wages and all other income (such as dividends, social security, or welfare benefits) are included, but not all of this income can be used to pay for college. For most families, the largest part of its annual income must be used to provide for basic living expenses—housing, food, medical care, clothing, and so forth.

In evaluating a family's financial strength, aid administrators also take into account other demands on the parents' income, such as taxes or unusually large medical or dental bills. Even the costs of working must be taken into consideration—clothing, transportation, meals away from home, and so forth. Elementary and secondary school tuition payments for other children may also be considered.

After all these family expenses are taken into account, the amount remaining to a family for other uses is quite a bit smaller than its original income. This remaining amount is called "available income." A family would be expected to use some of this remaining income to help pay college costs. The more available income a family has, the more would be expected of them.

Evaluating a family's assets

A family's assets are considered, too, because a family with assets is in a stronger financial position than a family with similar income but no assets. All of the assets are added up—equity in a home or other real estate, the value of a business or farm, cash, savings and checking accounts, stocks and bonds, and so forth.

In the same way that a family can't be expected to spend all its income on education, neither is it expected to use all its assets to pay for college. The system "protects" a portion of parents' assets for their use in retirement. The amount parents are allowed to protect gets larger as the age of the primary wage earner increases, because an older worker has fewer years to save for retirement than a younger one. The system also "protects" a substantial portion of family assets tied up in a business or farm, since a business or farm is also a source of income. If it were all used up to pay for college, there would be nothing left to generate income in the future.

Even when the various allowances are subtracted from total assets, a family is not expected to convert all its remaining assets into cash for college—only a portion called "income supplement from assets."

Available income (the discretionary part of a family's annual income) is added to the income supplement from assets to get a dollar amount called "adjusted available income." Not all the adjusted available income is tapped for educational expenses, only a percentage. A family with a higher adjusted available income is expected to pay a greater share of college costs than is a family with a lower adjusted available income.

If more than one family member is attending college at the same time, the amount parents are expected to pay is divided by the number attending, in order to find the expected contribution per student. This means that sometimes a family is not eligible for aid when the first child goes to college, but becomes eligible in subsequent years when a younger brother or sister starts college.

Evaluating a student's ability to pay

A student is usually expected to contribute toward college expenses, too, from savings and summer earnings. Colleges usually expect a freshman to contribute at least $700 a year from summer job earnings, as well as a large portion of any savings or other assets they may have. Upperclassmen are often expected to contribute even more from summer and part-time jobs—upwards of $900 a year at most colleges, and more than that at many.

Estimating your expected family contribution

Your family's "share" is the sum of what your parents can contribute from their income and assets *and* what you can contribute from your earnings, savings, and so forth. In the financial aid process, this amount is also referred to as the "expected family contribution":

> What parents can contribute from income
> + What parents can contribute from assets
> + What a student can contribute from income
> + What a student can contribute from assets
> _____
> = Expected family contribution.

If you're simply curious about what magnitude of expense this represents, the Parents' Contribution table in Chapter 10 gives you a sense of what is

Table 2.1. Sources for educational expenses

Resources	Percentage of students having resource	Percentage of students receiving $1,500 or more from resource
Parents' assistance	79%	53%
Pell (Basic) Grant	23	7
Supplemental Educational Opportunity Grant	7	1
State scholarship or grant	16	4
College scholarship or grant	22	10
Other scholarship or grant	11	3
Stafford Loan (GSL)	23	14
Perkins Loan	8	2
College loan	6	3
Other loan	6	4
College Work-Study Program	10	1
Part-time job on campus	21	1
Part-time employment	22	1
Full-time employment	2	1
Savings from summer work	56	7
Other savings	32	6
Student's spouse	2	*
Other government aid	3	2
Other aid	3	1

Note: Asterisk indicates less than 1 percent.
Source: *The American Freshman: National Norms for Fall, 1990* (Los Angeles: American Council on Education and University of California at Los Angeles, 1990).

expected of *parents* at different income and asset levels, assuming they meet the specifications as to age, family size, and other characteristics. Pick the combination of annual income and asset figures that most resembles your own, add a $700 first-year student earnings expectation, and you will have a *very* crude approximation of how your family's share might work out.

You can make a much closer estimate of what might be expected of you and your family by fully completing the worksheets in Chapter 10. By subtracting your expected family contribution from the average costs of attendance at different kinds of colleges, you can get a sense of your remaining financial need. (In addition, computer software, such as the College Board's *College Cost Explorer*, can be helpful when you're trying to determine how to pay for college. It provides detailed information about costs at 2,700 colleges and also explains how expected family contribution is calculated and then translated into eligibility. Check to see if your guidance office or library has a copy of *College Cost Explorer* for you to use.)

You are usually eligible for financial aid equal to the amount of your demonstrated financial need. (Whether you are able to obtain all of the financial aid you're eligible for depends on a variety of factors, such as the availability of funds in any given year.)

Setting a goal

Your estimate of your expected family contribution—be it 5 percent or 100 percent of college costs—should be your goal. Your plan should be organized to help you achieve, or even exceed, that goal. If the goal seems too *big* in relation to your household budget, don't panic! Chapters 3 and 4 give some ideas about ways to finance your share of the costs. If your goal seems too *small* in relation to actual college costs, don't worry! Chapters 5 and 6 demonstrate how financial aid can bridge the gap. Whatever your goal, write it down on a piece of paper and refer to it occasionally. *Writing goals down on paper helps to make them real.*

Special note on independent (self-supporting) students

So far the discussion has focused on students who are dependent on their parents for financial support. If you are truly financially independent of your parents, you are called an "independent," or "self-supporting," student. This does not mean that your resources are always sufficient to pay your direct educational costs as well as living expenses (for yourself and your family).

What it *does* mean is that, in considering your need for financial aid, colleges and other aid providers assume that your parents will not provide you with any support. (Some colleges will expect parents to supply *information*, however, regardless of the student's dependency status.)

Your ability as a self-supporting student to contribute toward college costs is evaluated on the basis of your own income, assets, and expenses. Expenses are typically higher than a dependent student's because self-supporting students must provide for maintenance and living expenses year-round. You may also have extra expenses, such as child care, which may be considered in the student expense budget developed by a college for self-supporting financial aid applicants. Because they do not get help from

their parents and because their expenses are usually higher than dependent students' expenses, self-supporting students often have a greater financial need. (They may also be expected to contribute more toward their own educational expenses. For instance, a single, self-supporting student with no dependents is expected to come up with a minimum of $1,200 from summer earnings, as compared to the $700 to $900 minimum expectation of dependent students.)

Who is considered self-supporting and who is not? There are certainly many students who really are self-supporting, such as younger students who no longer have financial support of their parents, or older students with families of their own. The problem is defining what really constitutes self-supporting status.

At the time this book went to press, it was assumed that for the 1992-93 academic year, the federal definition of independence, as outlined in the Higher Education Amendments of 1986, will be used to determine eligibility for the Pell Grant, Stafford Loan, and campus-based programs. This definition, however, is subject to congressional amendment. Most state, institutional, and private aid sponsors are expected to use a similar definition.

Under the new definition, if you are receiving federal aid for the first time, you are *automatically* considered to be self-supporting if:
- you are at least 24 years old by December 31 of the award year (e.g., by December 31, 1992, for the 1992-93 award year),
- you are a veteran of the United States Armed Forces, regardless of age,
- you are an orphan or a ward of the court, or
- you have legal dependents of your own *other than* a spouse.

You *may be* considered self-supporting if:
- you are a single undergraduate *and* were not claimed as an income tax exemption by your parents or guardians for the two calendar years preceding the award year (e.g., 1990 and 1991 for the 1992-93 award year) *and* can demonstrate total resources of at least $4,000 per year in both years (from sources other than parents), conditions subject to verification prior to disbursement, *and* you'll first receive aid in the fall of 1992,
- you are married *and* can demonstrate, prior to disbursement, that you will not be claimed as an income tax exemption by your parents or guardians for the first year of the award year (e.g., the 1992 tax year for the 1992-93 award year),
- you are a graduate or a professional student *and*

can demonstrate, prior to disbursement, that you will not be claimed as an income tax exemption by your parents or guardians for the first year of the award year (e.g., the 1992 tax year for the 1992-93 award year), or

■ you are determined to be self-supporting by financial aid administrators exercising professional judgment on the basis of unusual circumstances not covered by any of the statutory criteria.

Even if you meet the federal criteria for self-supporting status, however, you may be required to submit parents' financial data as part of the aid application process at some colleges. Some colleges may also ask you to provide additional documentation of your income and expenses if you claim self-supporting status. Also, some states and private sponsors may use different definitions than the federal government for determining self-supporting status. Contact the financial aid offices at the colleges from which you are seeking help if you think you may qualify as a self-supporting student and wish further information.

The Higher Education Act is scheduled for reauthorization in 1991 or 1992, and many aspects of federal student aid programs, including eligibility criteria, could be affected. Many observers believe that the definition of independent student status will be altered in the Reauthorization.

Questions and answers about how much you will be expected to pay

Q We have special expenses that aren't talked about in this chapter that affect our ability to pay (for example, a handicapped child who requires special medical care or education). Does anybody take this into account?

A Colleges try to take into account the unique circumstances of each applicant. In Chapter 6, where applying for financial aid is discussed, you will learn about ways in which you can make sure that the colleges you're considering at least understand your situation fully. Whether they will be able to give you extra help depends on a variety of factors, one of the most important being how much money they have available to help students in any given year.

Q We live in a big city and the rents for apartments are very high. Does the need analysis system take this into account?

A The formulas do take housing costs into account, along with food, clothing, and other family living expenses. Financial aid administrators at some colleges also may consider the high cost of living in your particular residential area.

Q I've calculated our expected family contribution, and it's more money than we can possibly afford. How can we pay this out of our current earnings?

A You aren't necessarily expected to pay it out of your current earnings alone. The next chapter will explain that no matter how large that expectation may appear to you, it can be made smaller if you break it into monthly amounts. The earlier you start planning, the more choices you have about how to finance your share of the costs.

3. How to make time work for you

If you had estimated how much you may be expected to pay toward college costs, you may wonder how you can possibly squeeze that much out of current income.

In fact, you probably *can't* squeeze it all out of current income. Few people are wealthy enough to pay cash for houses, cars, or major appliances. Most of us save or borrow, sometimes both, to finance the purchase of "big-ticket" items. In fact, we may not even be able to figure out whether we can afford something until we see how it breaks down in terms of monthly payments.

The more time you give yourself, the more choices you will have about how to finance your share. If you still have several years left before enrollment, you have many more options than families who are facing enrollment within the next year or two. But even if you were to enroll next month, you would still have some choices.

What does "expected family contribution" actually mean?

Your expected family contribution is *not* a prediction of how much extra cash you actually have on hand, or even an assumption of how much you "ought to" be able to pull from current income. Rather, the expected family contribution is a measure of your family's overall capacity to absorb some portion of educational expenses, and you can cover your share in any number of ways.

If you start early enough, you may be able to *save* your entire share, and more. One of the advantages of starting early is that you *earn* interest toward your goal. If you start late, you may have to *borrow*. The downside is that you're *paying* interest, not earning it. You could use a combination of saving *and* borrowing—or even "leverage" your money by borrowing against your own savings. The toughest way to cover your share of educational expenses, though, is to force

them into your current household budget. Some families do it, but it's not easy.

Financing the parents' contribution

Students can get summer or part-time jobs to help finance their portion of the expected family contribution. Accommodating the parents' portion, or "par-

Table 3.1. Relationship of family income to parental contribution (1991-92 Congressional Methodology)

Annual family income	Net income (after tax)	Parents' contribution (annual)	Percentage of total	Percentage of net
$ 5,000	$ 4,218	$ 0	0.0%	0.0%
10,000	8,435	0	0.0	0.0
15,000	12,450	0	0.0	0.0
20,000	15,918	220	1.1	1.4
25,000	19,385	980	3.9	5.0
30,000	22,853	1,740	5.8	7.6
35,000	26,320	2,610	7.5	9.9
40,000	29,788	3,700	9.3	12.4
45,000	33,255	5,120	11.4	15.4
50,000	36,215	6,510	13.0	18.0
55,000	39,384	8,000	14.5	20.3
60,000	42,584	9,500	15.8	22.3
65,000	45,784	11,010	16.9	24.0
70,000	48,984	12,510	17.9	25.5
75,000	52,184	14,010	18.7	26.8
80,000	55,384	15,520	19.4	28.0
85,000	58,584	17,020	20.0	29.0
90,000	61,784	18,530	20.6	30.0
95,000	64,837	19,970	21.0	30.8
100,000	67,787	21,350	21.4	31.5

Note: Estimated parents' contributions in Tables 3.1-3.4 assume four family members; one family member in college as an undergraduate; older parent (age 45) is employed; the other parent is not employed; income only from employment; no unusual circumstances; standard deductions on U.S. income tax; asset neutrality (assets equal to Asset Protection Allowance).

Table 3.2. Parents' contribution related to monthly net income (1991-92 Congressional Methodology)

Annual family income	Monthly net income (after tax)	Amount of monthly net required to pay parents' contribution
$ 5,000	$ 352	$ 0
10,000	703	0
15,000	1,038	0
20,000	1,327	18
25,000	1,615	82
30,000	1,904	145
35,000	2,193	218
40,000	2,482	308
45,000	2,771	427
50,000	3,018	543
55,000	3,282	667
60,000	3,549	792
65,000	3,815	918
70,000	4,082	1,043
75,000	4,349	1,168
80,000	4,615	1,293
85,000	4,882	1,418
90,000	5,149	1,544
95,000	5,403	1,664
100,000	5,649	1,779

Table 3.3. Financing parents' contribution (PC) under four different scenarios: percentage impact on monthly budgets

Annual family income	Expected parents' contribution	Percentage of gross income required each month to finance PC			
		Pay from current income (0-4-0)	Borrow in full (0-4-10)	Borrow and save (4-4-4)	Save in full (8-4-0)
$ 20,000	$ 220	1.1%	0.4%	0.4%	0.3%
25,000	980	3.9	1.4	1.3	1.2
30,000	1,740	5.8	2.1	1.9	1.7
35,000	2,610	7.5	2.7	2.4	2.2
40,000	3,700	9.3	3.4	3.0	2.7
45,000	5,120	11.4	4.2	3.7	3.3
50,000	6,510	13.0	4.8	4.3	3.8
55,000	8,000	14.5	5.4	4.8	4.3
60,000	9,500	15.8	5.8	5.2	4.7
65,000	11,010	16.9	6.2	5.5	5.0
70,000	12,510	17.9	6.6	5.8	5.3
75,000	14,010	18.7	6.9	6.1	5.5
80,000	15,520	19.4	7.2	6.3	5.7
85,000	17,020	20.0	7.4	6.6	5.9
90,000	18,530	20.6	7.6	6.7	6.0
95,000	19,970	21.0	7.7	6.9	6.2
100,000	21,350	21.4	7.9	7.0	6.3

ents' contribution," in the current household budget can be much harder, simply because the amount represents a large portion of annual income, as Table 3.1 illustrates.

At any point on the chart, you can see that the expected parents' share would require a pretty large percentage of income—*if* you were trying to take it all out of current income. At the $45,000 annual income level, for example, the expected parents' contribution would require *11.4 percent* of gross income, and a whopping *15.4 percent* of net (after-tax) income. As Table 3.2 demonstrates, that translates into a pretty big chunk of the monthly household budget.

You don't have to finance your share that way. You can if you want to and are able to, but spreading the expense out over time has a much smaller impact on your monthly budget. This is true whether you save, borrow, or both.

By way of illustration, consider these four very different scenarios for financing the *same* parents' contribution:

■ Pay the entire contribution out of current income during the four years of enrollment.

■ Borrow the full amount of the same contribution, starting at the point of enrollment and spreading repayment out over the four years of enrollment and the 10 years following graduation.

■ Save some of the amount during the four years preceding enrollment, and then borrow the balance, with repayments spread out over the four years of enrollment and the four years following graduation.

■ Save the full amount in the eight years preceding and the four years of enrollment.

The four approaches yield the same parents' contribution, but their respective effects on a household's monthly budget differ. Table 3.3 displays parents' contributions as constant percentages of total (pre-tax) income under each of the four scenarios.

To get a feel for how the percentages in Table 3.3 work out in dollar terms, see Table 3.4.

Look at the $45,000 annual income band again. Paying the parents' contribution entirely from current income would require modifying consumption by approximately $428 a month. Spreading the expense over time by any of the other scenarios could reduce the effect on the monthly budget by more than half.

Table 3.4. Financing parents' contribution under four different scenarios: dollar impact on monthly budgets

		PC in monthly scenarios			
Annual family income	Expected parents' contribution	Pay from current income	Borrow in full	Borrow and save	Save in full
$ 20,000	$ 220	$ 18	$ 7	$ 7	$ 5
25,000	980	81	29	27	25
30,000	1,740	145	53	48	43
35,000	2,610	219	79	70	64
40,000	3,700	310	113	100	90
45,000	5,120	428	158	139	124
50,000	6,510	542	200	179	158
55,000	8,000	665	248	220	197
60,000	9,500	790	290	260	235
65,000	11,010	915	336	298	271
70,000	12,510	1,044	385	338	309
75,000	14,010	1,169	431	381	344
80,000	15,520	1,293	480	420	380
85,000	17,020	1,417	524	468	418
90,000	18,530	1,545	570	503	450
95,000	19,970	1,663	610	546	491
100,000	21,350	1,783	658	583	525

The other important point about Tables 3.3 and 3.4 is that it is *never too late* to plan. If you were to enroll tomorrow and hadn't yet saved any money, you could still make time work for you by borrowing. The differences in the monthly payouts between the borrowing, saving, and borrowing/saving options in Tables 3.3 and 3.4 are nowhere near as large as the difference between all three of them and the pay from current income options.

However, when you are actually at the point of determining what your family should do, analyze the total *costs* associated with each option. Depending on the length of time you will be making loan payments, the amount of interest you will be paying, the rate of inflation, and the general state of the economy, some borrowing options may be a lot more expensive than others.

NOTE: The values in Tables 3.3 and 3.4 are calculated by a computer model using standard annuity formulas to create a monthly "outlay" computed as a constant percentage of family income. The model also assumes a 7 percent yield on investments, an 11 percent interest rate on borrowed money, and 5 percent annual increases in income and parents' contributions over the period of years associated with each scenario. Note that the model is designed to compare the relative effects of various financing scenarios on a monthly household budget. It cannot be used to compare the relative *costs* associated with those scenarios; borrowing, for instance, typically costs more than saving (except when inflation is high). Furthermore, the model deliberately fixes the monthly outlay as a constant percentage of income for comparison purposes, and thus Tables 3.3 and 3.4 cannot be used as amortization tables.

Questions and answers about making time work for you

Q My child will start college in less than a year. Isn't it too late to start saving?

A It is *never* too late to make plans. First of all, check your current finances to ensure you're getting as high a rate of return as possible. Second, take steps to make sure that you are creditworthy. If you are going to have to borrow, make sure that your credit history is accurate and that you have not exhausted your borrowing capacity. Third, look at the next chapters for some ideas about ways to finance your share—and reduce your costs. Fourth, investigate financial aid. Remember, even if your child *does* start college next year, he or she will be enrolled for four or more years. You don't just have one year to plan ahead; you have several.

Q Is it wise to borrow for education?

A Borrowing is an honorable way of paying for education; many students *and* parents take out loans to cover college costs. The important thing is not to get in over your head. Chapters 5 and 6 describe some current loan programs designed to help students and parents cover expenses, and Chapter 7 includes consumer advice about responsible borrowing.

Q How do I actually start saving for future educational expenses?

A The worksheets in Chapter 10 will help you estimate probable future college costs and what might be expected of your family toward paying those expenses. Once you have set an overall goal, break it down into annual, monthly, or even weekly goals.

The next chapter describes a variety of approaches to financing your share of the costs. If you have many resources already, you may wish to consult your financial adviser to make sure that your savings and investment programs are achieving your objectives.

4. Making the most of your own resources

Are you concerned that your family can't come up with enough cash to cover the contribution a college believes you should be able to make? What if a college can't give you any aid or can't give you enough to meet your need fully? What if you decide to attend college late in the year, and financial aid has already run out by the time you apply for admission?

Remember that colleges and most other student aid sponsors regard the student and his or her family as the primary source of funds for meeting the cost of education or training after high school. (There are rare instances where parents are considered unable to contribute anything whatsoever toward college costs, but even then, the student would be expected to contribute something from savings and summer earnings.)

This chapter will review some of the strategies that students and families have used to meet their share of college costs. Not all of these ideas will be applicable to your unique family situation, of course, but perhaps one or two will provoke some creative thinking. (Several commercial and not-for-profit organizations' programs are described in this chapter. Their inclusion is intended to illustrate the wide and growing array of options available to families in meeting college costs but does not imply any endorsement whatsoever.) The next chapter will describe how financial aid—grants and scholarships, loans, and jobs—can cover the gap between your best efforts and the costs of attendance.

If there is a "silver lining" to the combination of rising costs and declining aid resources, it is that colleges are working harder than ever not only to contain the costs but also to develop new mechanisms to assist students and families in meeting the costs. This chapter also describes some of the ways that colleges are trying to help families finance education after high school. Not all of these approaches will be available at the particular colleges you're consider-

ing, but they're worth asking about. Make sure that you review the lists in Part II of this book; you'll find the names of many colleges that offer special kinds of help to families in financing educational expenses.

Strategies for stretching your resources

Many students and families have used a variety of strategies for getting the most out of the resources they *do* have for meeting college costs. Some of these ideas may work for you, and some may make you angry! This section describes some possible strategies for getting more mileage out of family resources. Remember, the point is to do your share, *not* necessarily to cover the whole expense.

Rearranging your personal finances

Few families can cover their expected share from current earnings only, never mind bridge the gap that could be created by insufficient financial aid resources. To minimize the impact on your household budget when the time comes to start paying college bills, you should start planning as early as possible.

For instance, you might want to think about how your current assets can be resources for paying educational bills. Ask yourself, What are they worth now? What are they most likely to be worth when I want to use them? You may want to talk to your banker, a financial adviser, or an investment specialist about the best way of "saving" for college, given your financial situation. These professionals can offer you advice on financial planning for college based on your present situation, how much time you have left to save, and the risks involved in selecting certain financing alternatives.

The long-range approach

The earlier you start, the more time you have to arrange your personal finances to the greatest advantage. Families with young children, for instance, should think about creating a regular savings plan against the day when their children start college. Starting earlier rather than later really does make a difference. Deposited funds accrue interest, and the effect of compounding can be astonishing over a long period of time.

Many banks, savings and loan organizations, credit unions, investment firms, and other financial institutions market programs designed to help families accumulate resources for their children's future education. Under some programs, families make regular deposits to a savings account at interest rates that increase with the amount of the balance in savings; other programs provide for one-time or periodic payments into various kinds of investment funds or other financial products. Sometimes counseling and financial planning services are included as part of the program.

The Tax Reform Act of 1986 changed some of the rules governing ways in which families can accumulate money for college. Consumer guides to the tax law are widely available in bookstores, and you can also pose questions directly to the local office of the Internal Revenue Service (IRS). Or you may want to seek the help of a professional adviser, such as a Certified Financial Planner (CFP), a Certified Public Accountant (CPA), or a tax attorney. In any case, carefully investigate all the features of the programs offered by banks and investment firms. There is considerable variety in the safety, the yield, and the requirements of college savings programs and products now on the market. Shop around before you invest your hard-earned dollars.

More immediate options

Even if you have to start paying bills within the next year, it is worth your time to talk to your banker about your current savings and investment arrangements. Banks, savings and loan associations, credit unions, and investment firms never have been more eager for your money or have offered so many varieties of plans. The family with several thousand dollars in a 5 percent savings account is almost certainly not getting the most mileage out of its money.

No college expects you to sell the family homestead to pay for education, but some colleges *are*
becoming quite explicit about their expectations of families with assets. You may find that a college financial aid office wants to know your net return on investments, for instance. Others may suggest that you refinance the mortgage on your home. Others may inquire about the contribution that other members of the extended family (such as grandparents) might make to a student's educational expenses. Such observations from colleges may startle or even anger you, but they reflect a renewed emphasis on the family's central responsibility for financing education or training after high school.

There are some respects in which the family homestead has taken on potential new importance in paying educational expenses. Under the Tax Reform Act of 1986, the consumer interest deduction is being phased out over a period of five years, effective December 31, 1986. One important exception is interest on indebtedness securing a taxpayer's principal residence or a second residence, up to the amount of the original purchase price plus improvements. (Taxpayers can't take out home equity loans on the appreciated value to make consumer purchases and deduct the interest, except in strictly limited cases where loans are to be used for education, medical expenses, or home improvements. Make sure you understand how the IRS rules are applied before you act.)

Many banks are marketing new loans and lines of credit based on home equity. Some of the new programs are geared specifically to educational expenses. As with most financial services, there is considerable variation in the terms of such programs, so you will want to shop both widely and cautiously. Make sure you understand all the implications of using your home this way, not just the tax-related ones.

Here are some other ideas.

Parent loan program

The Education Amendments of 1980 created a new financial resource for families—the Parent Loans for Undergraduate Students (PLUS) Program. (The Stafford Loan Program—formerly the Guaranteed Student Loan or GSL Program will be described in the next chapter.) Parents may borrow up to $4,000 a year to a total of $20,000 for each dependent child. The interest rate is pegged to the Treasury or T-bill rate plus 3.25 percentage points up to a maximum of 12 percent. Repayment begins within 60 days after disbursement and may extend up to 10 years. The federal government subsidizes the interest rate so that it is more favorable than many other borrowing options; the government also guarantees repayment of the loans in the event of death or disability.

Because repayment generally must begin within 60 days, PLUS loans are primarily assistance in meeting the cash-flow problems caused by college bills. (Some lenders may permit parents to defer payments on interest and principal while their children are still in college; terms and conditions vary widely.) Parents, rather than students, are the borrowers under this program, and they may borrow without regard to demonstrated financial need. Some parents borrow under the PLUS program to meet all or part of the expected parental contribution, while others may borrow to make up the difference between costs and their contribution plus available financial aid.

PLUS loans are widely available through many banks, credit unions, savings and loan associations, and programs like CollegeCredit™, sponsored by the College Board. About 256,000 PLUS loans were made to parents in 1989-90.

There is a similar program for self-supporting undergraduate students and graduate and professional students called Supplemental Loans for Students or SLS. (Dependent undergraduates may also be permitted to borrow under SLS at their aid administrators' discretion; a student might be allowed to borrow under SLS if the parents can't get a PLUS loan, for example.) An estimated 688,000 students borrowed under SLS in 1989-90.

Supplemental loans

Some banks, credit unions, and other organizations have created special educational loan programs with more favorable interest rates or other features that make the loans more attractive than other consumer borrowing options. Parents rather than students are usually the borrowers under such programs, and eligibility relates more to demonstrated creditworthiness than demonstrated financial need. Some programs are offered by commercial entities, while others are sponsored by nonprofit organizations. You may want to investigate the loan possibilities available in your community. Colleges' financial aid offices are often good sources of information about supplemental loans and alternative financing vehicles.

A variation on commercial loans is a line of credit against which checks can be made directly to the college; interest is charged only when and if checks are written. The Edu-Check™ program, sponsored by

Mellon Bank in Rockville, Maryland, which has branches in the mid-Atlantic states, is available to parents and students in Maryland, Pennsylvania, and Delaware. Edu-Check™ has an elective life insurance policy, and monthly repayment may be made by check or through a draft from a Mellon checking account.

The ExtraCredit™ Loan Program, sponsored by the College Board in New York City, permits creditworthy individuals (generally parents) to borrow variable amounts for each child enrolled in college per each academic year. ExtraCredit loans are available to families, regardless of state of residency, provided their children are enrolled at participating colleges and universities. (Contact the College Board or your financial aid office for details.)

Under the Family Education Loan (FEL) Program, the Massachusetts Educational Financing Authority in Boston lets parents and students (from any state) jointly borrow up to 100 percent of the costs of attendance (minus any financial aid) at 52 participating Massachusetts colleges and universities on a 15-year, fixed-interest-rate basis; borrowers who secure their loans with a home mortgage option may be able to take advantage of the tax deductibility of interest payments.

Nellie Mae, a not-for-profit organization in Braintree, Massachusetts, offers EXCEL™, a supplemental loan offered in cooperation with participating colleges to creditworthy parents, who may borrow up to $20,000 annually ($80,000 maximum); repayment schedules range from 4 to 20 years, and borrowers can opt for a fixed or variable rate.

SHARE is a supplemental loan program operated by Nellie Mae in cooperation with the Consortium on Financing Higher Education (COFHE), a group of 32 high-cost, selective institutions; parents of students enrolled in participating colleges can borrow up to $20,000 per year for all four years and take up to 20 years to repay at an interest rate that's adjusted monthly; a one-year renewable option is also available. The TERI Supplemental Loan Program is a privately administered program under which students and their parents can borrow $2,000 to $20,000 annually at a variable interest rate to attend a participating college or university; the program is operated by The Education Resources Institute, a not-for-profit organization in Boston.

There are also two relatively new loan programs directed at students, rather than their parents. The Alliance Education Loan Program at the Bank of

Boston will lend from $2,000 to $20,000 per academic year to undergraduate or graduate degree candidates at accredited colleges and universities. While no collateral is necessary, the creditworthiness of the applicant (and cosigners, if necessary) is taken into account. The interest rate is variable, and payment can extend up to 15 years. The student borrower pays only interest while enrolled but must begin repayment of principal and interest 45 days after leaving school.

PLATO℠: The Classic Student Loan is a program of University Support Services, a not-for-profit organization in Herndon, Virginia, dedicated to assisting students and their families who do not qualify for need-based aid or who need additional assistance to meet the costs of education. Qualified applicants may borrow from $1,500 up to the total cost of attendance not to exceed $25,000 per year, with a cumulative maximum of $100,000. PLATO provides several unique features, including the ability to borrow for a prior period of enrollment as well as present costs. The repayment term is 15 years with no prepayment penalty. Student borrowers may defer principal payments for up to four years while in college.

If you plan to borrow funds under *any* program, subsidized or unsubsidized, commercial or nonprofit, make sure you understand exactly what your obligations are before you assume the responsibilities. (Chapter 7 has consumer advice about borrowing.)

Combination savings/loan plans

This approach to financing a child's education is becoming more widely available. Under such plans, a participating bank will "leverage," or multiply, a customer's balance to give a family a line of credit for meeting college costs that is, in effect, a long-term loan, with the interest on savings offsetting to a substantial degree the interest on the loan. An example is the Collegeaire® plan offered by Students' Financial Services in Atlanta.

Terms and conditions of these and similar programs can vary considerably from sponsor to sponsor, so prospective users will want to shop around. Inquire about the availability of programs at banks in your community.

College-sponsored financing programs

Many institutions of higher education participate in a tuition budgeting plan that permits families to spread out their payments over a longer period of time. Some colleges finance the programs themselves, while others participate in commercially available options.

Because of the interest, insurance, and service fees involved in such programs, a family will typically end up spending more money than if the charges had been paid outright. However, for families with cash-flow problems or insufficient reserves, as well as for families who prefer to preserve their capital, such programs can be very helpful. Information about the options available at a particular college usually can be found in its catalog or financial aid bulletin; if you don't find it, ask.

Many colleges have created loan programs out of their own resources to assist students and parents. Some of the approaches are quite innovative. Beloit College in Wisconsin, for instance, has created a "moral obligation" scholarship program in which students receive funds that carry a moral, but not a legal, repayment obligation. Such an approach would permit students to repay their scholarships when they are out of college and working; since there would be no legal obligation to repay, the payments to the college as a nonprofit educational institution would be, in effect, tax-deductible gifts (provided that the donors itemize their deductions, in accordance with the requirements of the Tax Reform Act of 1986).

Other institutions lend money to students or parents under plans with competitive interest rates and other features that make the programs particularly attractive. For example, The "Higher Education Loans to Parents," or HELP Program, at Lafayette College in Pennsylvania, loans qualified parents up to $5,000 a year on a low fixed-interest-rate basis and an eight-year repayment term. A unique feature of the program is that the college pays the interest while the student is enrolled, and repayment on the principal is deferred until after graduation.

Under the "flexible financing" program at Dickinson College in Pennsylvania, borrowers can choose between plans with fixed or variable interest rates, depending on the amount they want to borrow. The College of Wooster in Ohio makes a wide array of options available to parents, including loans, credit lines, and installment payment plans, while the University of Pennsylvania's Penn Plan offers several different flexible financing plans.

Don't assume that you can always find financing plans or tuition installment plans at every college and university. Some public institutions, for instance, are prohibited by state law from extending credit to anyone. However, they may be able to direct you to commercial budgeting or installment plans offered by outside companies. Information about programs designed to help you manage educational expenses at a particular college can usually be found in the college's catalog or financial aid bulletin.

Insured tuition installment and budgeting plans

Some insurance companies have offered insured tuition budgeting programs to families for many years. Under the Insured Tuition Payment Plan offered by Knight Insurance, for example, a family makes monthly payments to an FDIC-insured money market account (on which it earns interest), and the company makes payments to the college for tuition, room, and board. (Write Knight Tuition Payment Plans, 855 Boylston Street, Boston, Massachusetts 02116 for information.) Tuition Management Systems, Inc., works with individual colleges and universities to offer several different deferred payment services to smooth out tuition and room and board expenses. These include interest-free Monthly Payment Options (eliminating the burden of paying each semester's expenses in one large payment), supplemental nonneed-based loans and credit lines, federally backed loans and optional payer life insurance. (For information, write Box 335, Newport, Rhode Island 02840.)

Insurance features on plans like these generally guarantee that the tuition will continue to be paid in the event of a parent's death or total disability. Some colleges offer variations on plans like this, financed through their own resources.

In evaluating these approaches to stretching your resources, get all the facts before you sign any contracts, promissory notes, or loan agreements. You should evaluate both what you pay and what you get back to ensure that you are getting the best possible deal.

Strategies for cutting costs

In the absence of sufficient personal resources and financial aid, one obvious approach to financing a college education is to reduce the overall costs. There are many different ways to cut expenses, and your personal situation and ambitions will determine whether any of these approaches can work for you.

Reducing the time involved in earning a degree

By reducing the length of time involved in earning a degree, you can reduce the overall costs. (Reducing the amount of time you spend in education or training may also reduce your "forgone income," or the amount of money you could otherwise have earned if you were employed.) There are several approaches to cutting time and thus cutting costs.

For instance, many colleges award advanced placement and/or academic credit to students who can demonstrate proficiency in college-level studies through examinations such as those sponsored by the Advanced Placement (AP) Program and the College-Level Examination Program (CLEP) of the College Board. Credit-by-examination means the number of courses required to earn a degree is reduced, so the overall costs are cut. As you investigate colleges, you may want to ask about credit-by-examination policies.

Some colleges also grant advanced placement and/or academic credit to students who can demonstrate proficiency because of prior independent study and "life experience." A student might demonstrate particular competencies or skills, for example, by compiling a portfolio that documents prior learning experiences. College requirements for documenting prior learning tend to be quite rigorous, but if you can meet them, you can reduce both your time and your financial investment. (You may find that the approach is less commonly available than credit-by-examination options. You may also find that some colleges offering such opportunities restrict their use to older, "nontraditional" students who have spent several years working or raising a family.)

Some students also compress the time required to earn their degrees by taking more courses than the average student and/or attending summer school. (Obviously, attending summer classes will cut down on your ability to work during the summer to earn money for college.) Some students successfully complete a bachelor's degree in less than four years, thus reducing their overall costs, but this clearly requires a high degree of motivation. You may want to ask colleges you're considering whether it's possible to earn a degree in less than four years, since some colleges have policies limiting the number of credits a student can carry per semester.

Sometimes students can earn some college credit without actually attending classes, thus reducing transportation and possibly some living expenses. (This approach would also allow a student to work and save for full-time attendance later.) Check with the colleges you're considering if this appeals to you.

Reducing indirect costs

Living at home instead of on campus has helped many students reduce their overall costs. Some students live at home and commute to campus for the entire course of their studies, while others alternate between living in college housing (or off-campus private housing) and living at home with their families. Other students elect to attend a local, lower cost college (such as a community college) for the first two years and then transfer to a higher cost public or private college to complete their degrees.

Dormitory residents at some colleges have also discovered that savings can be achieved in the choice of college-sponsored meal plans. Investigate carefully the options open to you before you select a particular meal plan.

Some students work in return for room and board. For example, the Student Housing Exchange in Boston seeks to match students who can give 15 to 20 hours a week in household services to families who provide room and board in return. Information about similar opportunities is often available through a college's placement or student affairs office.

Students at many colleges have banded together to provide services for each other that can reduce both their direct educational expenses and their living expenses. The range of student-sponsored services is enormous and well worth investigating as part of your college-search process. Secondhand bookshops enable students to reduce textbook expenses. Food co-ops enable residents in private, off-campus housing to cut their food bills and still get adequate nutrition. Daycare programs provide help to students with dependents of their own. Revolving emergency loan funds can provide short-term financial assistance. Housing referral services or guides can help students to locate private housing, while tenant organizations protect and advocate their rights with landlords. Entertainment programs are specifically designed to provide free or low-cost recreation to students living on a budget.

College administrators, too, have instituted programs at many institutions, usually in conjunction with the student affairs or financial aid offices. The financial aid office may conduct workshops on money management, for instance, or the student activities office may issue guides to low-cost housing and shopping in the community. As the effects of rising costs and declining aid begin to be felt more widely, the number and range of such programs to help students live on a tight budget can be expected to grow.

Guaranteed or stabilized tuition plans

You can expect increases in tuition charges at least once, and probably annually, during your enrollment in a particular college. A few colleges guarantee their tuition for four years at the time of enrollment, at no obligation to the student. Under other plans, families can prepay tuition for four years in one lump sum and escape subsequent tuition increases.

Taking advantage of such programs could reduce your overall expenses, although you may want to consider whether you can get a return on your investments that's equivalent to or better than the rate of tuition increases, while still having the use of your money. For families who do not have enough disposable income to pay the entire sum at once, some colleges offer a borrowing option whereby payment is made in monthly installments over a period of years. However, with the gradual phaseout of consumer interest deductibility, you may want to make some calculations to ensure that this option still makes financial sense for you.

Strategies for working your way through college

Working your way through college is certainly possible, but it's not easy, particularly if you want to attend college on a full-time basis. The problems include both money and time. Educational and living expenses are sufficiently high to make it difficult to earn enough money to cover them fully while maintaining a full course load, but here again, there are a variety of approaches to working your way through. One or more of them may work for you. An estimated half of all college students now hold jobs of some sort.

Part-time employment

Some students find that they can earn enough money through part-time employment to meet their costs. Many students work part-time while enrolled full-time, and find that a part-time job does not hamper their studies. The College Work-Study Program described in Chapter 5 provides employment opportunities for many students with demonstrated financial need. Other students work in jobs, on or off campus, that they find themselves.

Some colleges have made a special commitment to helping students pay some of their educational expenses through working. For example, Cornell University in New York has two distinctive programs that assist students in meeting their educational costs. The Cornell Tradition, a loan forgiveness fellowship program, recognizes students committed

To find out about employment opportunities, contact the job placement office or consult the job bulletin board.

to the work ethic and service. In addition to working during the academic year, Tradition Fellows receive awards that reduce the amount of their student loans up to $2,500 per year. Since the program's inception, over $8 million has been awarded in recognition of student work and service; in 1990-91, nearly 600 students were recognized. Through the Summer Job Network, students are referred to career-related summer jobs, many of which have been identified or created by alumni. In 1990, students earned over $1.1 million and 438 students were placed in jobs through the Network.

At Babson College in Massachusetts, students are helped to own and operate their own businesses, both to earn needed funds and develop hands-on business skills. A student Chamber of Commerce serves as a forum for exchanging ideas and sharing skills, while the Babson Entrepreneurial Exchange links students with alumni and nonalumni business people.

Some colleges have instituted special programs to help students find part-time employment. For

instance, Johns Hopkins University in Maryland developed a job program in cooperation with the local business community. The University of Texas at Austin has a 24-hour job hotline that students can call to get information about part-time job opportunities.

You should begin lining up summer job prospects as soon as you are old enough to work. You might also think about acquiring and cultivating skills that will be useful in finding part-time jobs to help finance your education. As you investigate colleges, you may want to inquire about the availability of part-time jobs on and off campus. Admissions recruiters, financial aid counselors, and job placement counselors may be able to give you some clues about the kinds of jobs most frequently available. If you're visiting a college, pick up copies of the student newspaper as well as local newspapers to check out the want ads.

You might be able to tailor some of your precollege courses or summer job experiences to improve your chances in the job market once enrolled. For example, if there's a typically heavy demand for term paper typists at the college you're aiming for, it may be worth your while to take an elective course in typing and acquire a portable typewriter. If there are usually openings on campus and in the community for experienced waiters and waitresses, that might be useful to know when you're looking for summer and part-time jobs in high school.

Unless you have truly unusual and marketable skills, part-time work is not likely to earn you enough money to cover all your expenses, but, depending on your overall costs and your family's ability to contribute toward your education, plus financial aid, you may be able to cover the difference through part-time employment.

Cooperative education

Some students have found that alternating periods of full-time employment and full-time enrollment works best for them. Many colleges have even formalized such arrangements through cooperative education programs. In cooperative education programs, students alternate semesters of academic enrollment with semesters of full-time employment, usually in jobs directly related to their field of study. In addition to helping them finance their studies, cooperative education programs give students a chance to develop concrete job skills and experience that enhance their employability after graduation. About

1,000 colleges and universities across the country offer some form of cooperative education opportunities; inquire about the possibility at the colleges you're considering.

Deferred enrollment

Some students take a year or two off before going to college to get some money in their pockets. Some colleges have formalized this, too—it's called "deferred enrollment." You're accepted, but you don't actually start going to college until the following year. You might keep this in mind as a question to ask about the various colleges you investigate.

Employee fringe benefits

Some students decide to work full time and attend college part time at their employer's expense. Many employers offer educational opportunities as fringe benefits. Sometimes workers are reimbursed, in whole or in part, for successfully completed course work; other programs pay tuition expenses up front. (Check with the Internal Revenue Service for the most current tax treatment of employee educational expense benefits.)

Keep in mind, too, that some unreimbursed educational expenses may be considered tax deductible. However, under the Tax Reform Act of 1986, they can be deductible only if they meet specific criteria and only to the extent that aggregate miscellaneous itemized deductions exceed 2 percent of your adjusted gross income. Check with the IRS for more information.

Managing your time if you work

There have not been many studies of students who combine work and school. The information that does exist, however, tends to show that students who work part time do not usually seem to suffer academically for the time they put into their jobs. Some studies have indicated, in fact, that students who work part time achieve higher grade-point averages than their nonemployed fellow students. For most students who work, the discipline required to juggle their responsibilities and manage their time effectively pays off in academic work, too. (At the same time, some colleges try to minimize the necessity of part-time work for some groups of students, particularly freshmen, in order to ease their transition into college life.) Some students also like the opportunity to develop employment experience in anticipation of job hunting after graduation.

Questions and answers about making the most of your resources

Q My parents have scrimped and saved for my college education, but because we have savings, we won't have as much eligibility for financial aid. Aren't we being penalized for being thrifty?

A You and your parents *will* be expected to contribute something toward the cost of college from the money you and they have saved, but as subsequent chapters will illustrate, the system *also* takes into account your parents' ages and corresponding need to save for retirement. Remember, too, that a student whose parents have no savings must rely much more heavily on financial aid than you. That family may have a heavier work or loan burden than yours will have to carry. In a time when public appropriations for student aid programs are not keeping pace with increases in college costs, your reduced reliance on financial aid may give you a wider range of choices.

Q Didn't tax reform knock out all the incentives for college saving?

A The Tax Reform Act of 1986 affected many of the "income transfer" strategies that some parents have used in the past to accumulate college savings and shelter some assets from taxation by putting them in their children's names. "Clifford Trusts," for instance, were eliminated entirely, and new restrictions were imposed on "generation-skipping" bequests from grandparents.

The experts still have lots of ideas about how families can build up money for college, with or without tax advantages. The more time you give yourself to study the various ideas, the better off you'll be. The important thing is to take advantage of whatever time you and your family have before enrollment. The loss of a specific tax break that may have existed in previous years is no reason to stop saving for college.

Q Is the interest on educational loans tax-deductible?

A The Tax Reform Act of 1986 initiated a gradual phaseout of the deductibility of consumer interest on all nonmortgage loans, including loans assumed by students and parents to pay for education, such as Stafford Loans (formerly Guaranteed Student Loans) and PLUS loans. However, interest on home mortgages, including second mortgages up to the fair market value of the house, is still deductible, and interest on debt *in excess* of a house's value may still be deductible if used for educational or medical expenses. Always check with the IRS or your tax adviser before making any personal financial decisions on the basis of tax treatment. Laws change and so do regulations.

Since the passage of the Tax Reform Act of 1986, legislation that would *reinstate* the tax deductibility of student loans has often been contemplated, but is not yet enacted. This could change.

5. How financial aid can help

Financial aid is help for meeting college costs: both direct educational costs (such as tuition, fees, and books) and personal living expenses (such as food, housing, and transportation). People are sometimes surprised that students can get financial aid to help them pay for living expenses. Even colleges with comparatively low tuition, such as community colleges, can give qualified students some help in paying for food, rent, commuting, and other personal expenses.

Many students don't realize that financial aid is available to pay for noncollegiate education and training programs, too. If you are thinking about vocational or trade school after high school, financial aid could be a possibility for you.

Who gets financial aid?

While many scholarships are based on criteria other than demonstrated need, most financial aid today is awarded on the basis of need. (Sometimes factors such as academic performance, career plans, or special abilities are considered in addition to demonstrated need.) Chapter 2 explained that "need" is the difference between what it costs to attend a particular college and what you and your family can afford to pay toward those costs. Students are usually eligible for aid equal to the amount of their demonstrated financial need.

Since the amount a family can afford to pay stays the same whether the costs are high or low, you can see that you would be eligible for different amounts of aid at different colleges. In fact, if you get all the financial aid you're eligible for, you could end up paying the same amount at a high-cost college as you would at a low-cost one.

That's a pretty big "if." In 1990-91, more than 5 million students received an estimated $28 billion in various forms of student assistance to help them meet the costs of education or training after high school. Large as that amount may seem, it still wasn't enough to fully meet the need of all the students who could have used some help.

You can improve your chances of getting the outside help you need. Financial aid doesn't just happen to you. You have to take an active part in the process—by identifying all possible sources of assistance for which you might be eligible (the topic of this chapter) and by applying in the right way at the right time (discussed in Chapter 6).

Types of financial aid

There are three types of financial aid generally offered to undergraduate students in college.

Grants and scholarships are sometimes called gift aid, because you don't have to repay them or work to earn them. Grants are usually awarded on the basis of need alone, while scholarship recipients may have to meet criteria other than or in addition to need (academic achievement, for example).

Educational loans are a form of self-help aid. These are usually subsidized by the state or federal government or by colleges themselves and carry lower interest rates than commercial loans. They have to be repaid, generally after you have graduated or left college.

Student employment or work aid is another form of self-help aid. The federal College Work-Study Program is perhaps the best known example of this kind of assistance. Students work, usually 10 to 15 hours a week, to "earn" their aid.

Financial aid comes from a variety of sources: the federal government, the state government, colleges themselves, and a wide range of private organizations.

Most students get a combination of gift aid and

self-help aid from a variety of sources. This is called a financial aid package. The financial aid administrator at the college you attend or apply to will help you put your package together.

Eligibility for financial aid

While each program has its own special criteria, certain basic eligibility requirements are common to almost all programs. For instance, to be eligible for many programs, you must be at least a half-time student (usually defined as six semester hours of courses per semester or the equivalent). In some cases, less-than-half-time students may be eligible for some federal funds but other programs, such as those sponsored by colleges and private organizations, require recipients to attend on a full-time basis, usually at least 12 hours per semester.

You must be enrolled in an eligible program at an eligible institution, according to the aid program's definition. For some federal student aid programs, you can receive aid to attend more than 9,500 eligible institutions, including colleges, universities, and vocational and technical schools. State aid programs are sometimes limited only to accredited colleges and universities. Some programs have restrictions on providing aid to students in certain fields of study (for example, religious studies) or in vocational or technical courses (those that are shorter than six months in duration). Most programs require that you maintain satisfactory academic progress toward a degree or certification and that you be in good standing with the institution you attend.

Federal student aid programs require that a recipient be either a United States citizen, or a noncitizen who is a permanent resident; refugees or persons granted political asylum may be eligible, too. State student aid programs are usually restricted to legal residents of their particular state, although exceptions to this rule do exist, especially in loan programs. College-sponsored and private assistance programs usually require recipients to be citizens of the United States, too, except for a few programs designed for foreign students.

Financial aid from the federal government

Since the 1950s, there has been in the United States a bipartisan national commitment to equalizing higher educational opportunity that remains unpar-alleled anywhere in the world. From the late 1950s onward, there occurred a steady expansion of federal student assistance programs, peaking with the enactment of the Middle Income Student Assistance Act (MISAA) in 1978. Since 1980, however, there has been a slight but troubling erosion in the national consensus about the way to achieve equal opportunity in higher education.

Federal funding of student aid programs has not kept pace with rising college costs in recent years, and there has been a major shift of funds from grant to loan programs in the same time period. These changes can be traced to several factors, including competing demands on the federal budget, the skyrocketing federal budget deficit, increasingly divergent views on the appropriate federal role in higher education, and a continuing struggle between Congress and the administration over the scope and level of student aid funding by the federal government.

In the fall of 1986, Congress "reauthorized" the Higher Education Amendments. The basic structure of federal student aid programs appears to be intact for at least the immediate future, although funding levels are difficult to predict because of annual appropriations battles and the effects of the Gramm-Rudman-Hollings deficit reduction law.

Like all of the programs described in this chapter, these federal programs could be significantly changed by the time you are ready to start college. (In fact, the Higher Education Amendments are up for reauthorization in 1991 or 1992.) Don't be discouraged by this warning, but *do* watch the situation closely and intensify your own efforts to accumulate funds for college.

You may find it heartening to know that Congress has resisted attempts to cut the student aid budget since 1980. For the most current and detailed information about federal programs, you should obtain a copy of the free pamphlet, "The Federal Student Aid Fact Sheet," published by the government and cited in the bibliography at the end of this chapter.

Pell Grant Program

The Pell Grant Program is the largest need-based student aid program. An estimated 3.2 million undergraduates received Pell Grants ranging from $100 to $2,200 for the 1989-90 academic year. The amount a student receives depends on need, the costs of education at the particular college he or she attends, the length of the program in which he or she is enrolled, and whether enrollment is full- or part-time. Graduate students are not eligible, nor are students who have previously received a bachelor's degree.

Supplemental Educational Opportunity Grant Program

The Supplemental Educational Opportunity Grant Program (SEOG) is one of three federal campus-based programs. "Campus-based" means that while the money comes from the federal government, the colleges distribute the money to students who demonstrate need. Recipients must be United States citizens enrolled at least half-time in an undergraduate program at an accredited college or university. Grants of up to $4,000 a year are awarded on the basis of need. About 633,000 students received SEOGs in 1989-90.

Perkins Loan Program

The Perkins Loan Program (formerly called the National Direct Student Loan Program, or NDSL) is another federal campus-based program administered by colleges and universities. Undergraduate and graduate students enrolled at least half-time may borrow up to $4,500 a year for the first two years of undergraduate study, to a total of $9,000 for an undergraduate degree and $18,000 for graduate and professional study (including any amount borrowed as an undergraduate). Approximately 826,000 students borrowed Perkins Loans in 1989-90.

Perkins Loans carry the lowest interest rate of any educational loans (5 percent) and repayment is deferred until a student graduates or leaves school. Nine months after a student leaves school, regular repayments are required over a maximum period of 10 years until the total amount (including interest) is repaid. A minimum monthly payment of $30 is usually required, unless the college agrees to a lower amount.

Repayment can sometimes be further deferred for up to three years for service in the military, the Peace Corps, or approved comparable organizations, or if study is resumed on at least a half-time basis. (In such instances, however, the student does not get another six-month grace period in which to defer payment.) A student who wants to have repayment of a Perkins Loan deferred for any reason must complete a request form and submit it to the college from which the loan was originally borrowed. Perkins Loans are cancelled outright in the event of a student's death or total disability. (See Chapter 7 for more information about borrowing money from this and other programs, including legal requirements and advice.)

College Work-Study Program

The College Work-Study Program (CWSP) is also a federal campus-based program. Participating colleges provide employment opportunities for students with demonstrated need who are enrolled for at least half-time study at either the undergraduate or graduate level. Students are almost always employed on campus, although occasionally jobs are arranged off campus. In assigning work-study to aid recipients, financial aid administrators typically take into account their employable skills, class schedule, and academic progress.

Students are generally paid at least the prevailing federal minimum wage. Students may work as many as 40 hours a week under the program, although 10 to 15 hours is far more typical. The only limitation on College Work-Study is a student's demonstrated financial need.

Examples of on-campus jobs for students are faculty aide, dining hall worker, library assistant, grounds keeper, office secretary, and financial aid peer counselor. About 835,000 students received help under the College Work-Study Program in 1989-90.

Stafford Loan Program

The Stafford Loan Program (formerly called the Guaranteed Student Loan [GSL] Program) permits students with demonstrated need to borrow money for educational expenses from private sources such as banks, credit unions, savings and loan associations, and programs such as the CollegeCredit™ program, sponsored by the College Board. In some states, a public agency also acts as a lender; some colleges also participate in the program as lenders. Organizations can also sponsor programs that provide Stafford Loans. For example, the new CollegeCredit™ program is a coordinated array of subsidized and unsubsidized educational loans available through participating colleges and universities.

Because Stafford Loans are subsidized by the government, the interest rate is lower than most commercially available loans (although higher than Perkins Loans). For new borrowers after July 1, 1988, the interest rate is 8 percent for the first four years of repayment and 10 percent thereafter. Repayment on both interest and principal is deferred until a student graduates or leaves school. In most states, a state government guaranty agency (or a private organization authorized by the state government) insures the loans; in those states where there is no guaranty agency, the federal government insures them, in which case they're called Federally Insured Student Loans. An estimated 3.7 million students borrowed under the Stafford Loan Program in 1989-90.

Although some states permit half-time students to borrow under the Stafford Loan Program, most states require that borrowers be full-time students. Freshmen and sophomores may borrow up to $2,625 a year, and upperclassmen may borrow up to $4,000 annually, to a maximum of $17,250. Limits are lower in some states. Graduate and professional students are currently eligible to borrow a maximum of $54,750, including any undergraduate loans.

If you borrow money under the Stafford Loan Program, you are charged an origination fee or service charge of about 5 percent. Your guaranty agency may also charge you an insurance premium of up to 3 percent. This amount is subtracted from the amount of your loan money before you receive payment.

Stafford Loans are insured against the student's death or total disability, but there are no provisions for cancellation of any part of a loan for other reasons. Under certain circumstances (such as full-time study or service in the military or Peace Corps), repayment can be deferred temporarily. The schedule for repayment is worked out between the student and the lender; the borrower usually has between 5 and 10 years to repay, with the amount of monthly payments and the length of the repayment period depending on the total amount borrowed.

For more information about Stafford Loans, contact the financial aid office at the colleges you're considering, your guidance counselor, or the guaranty agency for your state listed in Part II of this book. (See Chapter 6 for information about applying and Chapter 7 for advice on responsible borrowing.)

Military options

Military service options are a way of paying for education as you go. Service academies offer a college education at no cost to students, while the Reserve Officers' Training Corps (ROTC) programs help pay for your education at participating colleges and universities. (Still another approach is described elsewhere in this chapter under the heading "Assistance from Benefit Programs.")

Service academies

The United States service academies prepare both men and women for careers in the military, merchant

ROTC offers college scholarships with a commitment of military service after graduation.

marine, or coast guard. Students attending one of the academies have all expenses paid by the federal government and receive a monthly stipend for incidental expenses as well. Appointments to the academies (with the exception of the Coast Guard) are made through nominations from members of Congress. If you are interested, contact your senator or congressional representative early in the spring of your junior year in high school. Appointments to the Coast Guard Academy are based on national competition for admission. For more information write:

Director of Admissions
United States Air Force Academy
Colorado 80840-5000

Director of Admissions
United States Military Academy
606 Thayer Road
West Point, New York 10996-1797

Dean of Admissions
United States Naval Academy
Leahy Hall
Annapolis, Maryland 21402

Director of Admissions
United States Merchant Marine Academy
Steamboat Road
Kings Point, New York 11024

Director of Admissions
United States Coast Guard Academy
New London, Connecticut 06320-4195

Reserve Officers' Training Corps

Reserve Officers' Training Corps (ROTC) programs are located at approximately 600 colleges and universities across the country; in addition to the institutions that serve as hosts or extensions, there are about 1,800 other institutions in which an ROTC student can cross-enroll. Graduating high school seniors may qualify for competitive four-year ROTC scholarships that typically cover the costs of tuition, fees, and books, and provide a monthly stipend of $100. Students who receive ROTC scholarships must meet certain physical and academic requirements and agree to accept appointment as commissioned officers in the military after graduation. (A minimum of four years' active and two years' reserve duty is required.)

In addition, some ROTC in-college scholarships may be available for students who decide to join as sophomores or even juniors, as well as for students who originally joined ROTC units as nonscholarship students. The requirements and obligations are somewhat different than for four-year scholarship students.

There are different procedures, requirements, and benefits associated with the ROTC programs operated by the different military services. In addition to ROTC programs, there are also other special programs providing financial assistance for education to students who promise to fulfill a term of military service after graduation; the officer training occurs during summer vacations or after college. A good source for students interested in exploring the various military-related options for college assistance is *How the Military Will Help You Pay for College*, by Don M. Betterton (see bibliography), which describes each service's ROTC program, the service academies, and several other programs available to military personnel who want to continue with their education. The book also contains a comprehensive list of host and cross-enrollment

institutions. Contact the ROTC units at the colleges you are considering, or write:

Air Force ROTC Four-Year Scholarship Branch
Maxwell Air Force Base
Montgomery, Alabama 36112-5001

Army ROTC Scholarship Program
HQ—Cadet Command
Building 56/Scholarship Branch
Fort Monroe, Virginia 23651

Navy-Marine Corps NROTC Scholarship Program
Chief of Naval Education and Training
Code N-1/081
Naval Air Station
Pensacola, Florida 32508-5100
Telephone: (800) NAV-ROTC

Assistance from the Bureau of Indian Affairs

Students who can demonstrate financial need and are registered as being at least one-fourth Native American or Alaskan native of a federally recognized tribe are eligible for assistance through the Bureau of Indian Affairs (BIA). Scholarship assistance may be used at any accredited postsecondary institution. For more information, contact your tribal education officer, BIA Area Office.

Assistance from benefit programs

Benefit programs are not quite the same as financial aid programs, but they provide many students with assistance in meeting college costs.

Assistance for military personnel and veterans

There are several programs designed to help servicemen and women pursue higher education, as well as to assist veterans. Defense Activity for Non-Traditional Education Support (DANTES) permits military personnel to demonstrate job proficiency, qualify for college admission, or earn college-level credits by taking correspondence courses and/or examinations. Each of the services operates programs in which active duty personnel can take courses on an off-duty basis, and you also may be able to translate some of your on-the-job technical training into college credits later on. If you are thinking about enlisting, carefully explore the educational possibilities associated with the various services, including the requirements and obligations of each.

If you think you may want to go to college eventually but are also interested in the military, investigate the major initiative launched on July 1, 1985, called the New G.I. Bill, which replaced the former Veteran's Educational Assistance Plan (VEAP). Although an enlisted service person could use the plan to pay for college work while on active duty, it is more likely that people will use the New G.I. Bill to accumulate benefits for use after discharge. Under the terms of the New G.I. Bill, $100 per month would be automatically deducted from your paycheck during your first year of active duty for a total initial deposit of $1,200 in your "education account." (You can choose not to participate when you enlist, in which case the deduction would not be made.) Depending on how many years you serve on active duty, the government would add between $7,800 and $9,600 more to your account for later use in paying for education.

The New Army College Fund currently offers additional benefits beyond those cited above to men and women who enlist in the army. Men and women serving in the reserves can also participate in New G.I. Bill benefits in return for a service commitment. Because these programs are still new and subject to modification, they may be changed by the time you are ready to go to college; the most current information can be obtained from military recruiting offices.

If you are already a veteran and want to know whether you or your spouse or dependents qualify for educational assistance, contact your local Veterans Administration (VA) office.

Vocational rehabilitation benefits

Since 1977 the federal Rehabilitation Act has prohibited discrimination on the basis of a handicap and has provided for equal participation by handicapped people in programs and activities of postsecondary educational institutions that receive federal funds. The intent of the law is to assure qualified handicapped students of access to educational programs, including financial aid. Many colleges have tried to expand opportunities, particularly in the College Work-Study area.

State vocational rehabilitation agencies in most states can help students with handicaps meet the costs of education or job training after high school. In many states, these agencies are working with groups of financial aid administrators to develop cooperative agreements about financial aid and other assistance for handicapped students enrolled in post-

secondary institutions. In developing an aid package for a handicapped student, the financial aid administrator at the college typically will consider both the amount of assistance and type of services provided by the vocational rehabilitation agency. A handicapped student's expense budget may be larger than a nonhandicapped student's budget, in order to take into account their greater expenditures for such things as special equipment, noninsured and nonroutine medical expenses, assistants or attendants, and special transportation. To find out about special help for handicapped students, contact your state department of vocational rehabilitation.

Financial aid from state governments

Every state has a scholarship or grant program that provides some form of financial aid to eligible students who are legal residents of the state. Eligibility criteria vary from state to state. Most state programs award aid to students with demonstrated need, although a few states have some funds available to assist students who meet criteria other than or in addition to need (such as academic performance). Most programs require that students attend a postsecondary institution within the state. (A few states have reciprocal agreements with other states, meaning that students can use their state grants in other states, but this practice may decline as funds become more limited.) Over 1.6 million students received some form of state grant or scholarship in 1989-90.

Your high school guidance counselor can provide you with additional information about the programs and requirements in your particular state. Part II of this book contains summaries of the major scholarship and grant programs in each of the 50 states, with an address to which you may write for additional information.

Financial aid from colleges

Assistance programs sponsored and administered by colleges and universities themselves are another important resource. College-sponsored financial aid usually comes from one of two sources: tuition revenues and contributions from private donors.

Some scholarships and grants-in-aid are based on demonstrated need, while others are awarded to students who meet criteria other than or in addition to need (such as academic performance, proposed field of study, or special talents or abilities).

Student employment programs are also provided on many campuses to supplement employment provided through the College Work-Study Program. These college-funded job programs usually are not based on financial need but on the special skills of the student employees. Examples include laboratory assistant, business office aide, and dormitory resident adviser. At some colleges, need is also considered in addition to skills and experience.

Short-term and emergency loans usually are available to all students. The repayment period generally is confined to an academic year, and interest is either quite low or not charged at all.

The criteria and application procedures for college programs vary considerably, and your best source of information is the catalog or financial aid bulletin published by the college you're considering. Private colleges often have more college-sponsored aid available to assist students than do public institutions; proprietary or profit-making institutions generally have very little or none at all.

Financial aid from private sources

While aid from the federal government, state governments, and colleges and universities constitutes most of the financial assistance received by students, private student aid programs can offer important assistance. The total amount of funds available through such private programs is comparatively small. For an individual student, however, these programs can mean the difference between attending the college one likes best and the college one can afford. So it's well worth investigating the private programs for which you may be eligible.

There are literally thousands of private student aid programs in the United States that award grants, scholarships, and low-interest loans to students to help them further their education or training after high school. One of the best programs is the National Merit Scholarship Program, which awards over $35 million each year to about 7,800 students. High school juniors compete for these awards by taking the Preliminary Scholastic Aptitude Test/National Merit Scholarship Qualifying Test (PSAT/NMSQT) each October at nearly 20,000 high schools around the country that offer the test.

Eligibility criteria, application procedures, number of awards given annually, and average award amounts vary tremendously from program to program. Some programs base their awards on financial

need, others on need plus other criteria, and still others don't consider need at all. You might qualify because of your:

- academic achievement
- religious affiliation
- ethnic or racial heritage
- community activities
- artistic talents
- leadership potential
- athletic ability
- career plans
- proposed field of study
- hobbies and special interests
- parents' employers or union membership
- parents' membership in a civic or fraternal group.

Since virtually everyone can claim to meet one of these general criteria, some perspective on the subject seems important. Frequently, stories appear in the press about the "millions of scholarship dollars that go begging every year." Strictly speaking, that's true, but that doesn't mean that if *you* go begging for some of them, you'll necessarily get any!

Many of the scholarships are tied to particular colleges and universities, or programs of study within those institutions. For instance, there actually may be an obscure little scholarship fund for students with a particular last name, but it has to be used at the particular college which administers that bequest. That means you have to be admitted to that college before you can claim any of the funds. If that happens to be a college you have been accepted to and want to attend anyway, terrific! But trying to finance your education in this way is a little like using coupons to get a discount on a product you don't really want and would never buy under normal circumstances.

Many of the scholarships have very detailed and restrictive eligibility requirements—you might, for instance, have to live in a certain state or region, attend a particular college, pursue a particular course of study, meet certain high academic standards, and demonstrate financial need. If you don't meet them all, you don't qualify.

Nevertheless, it makes good sense to investigate all possible sources of assistance for which you might be eligible. Check with your guidance counselor, and periodically look for notices on your school bulletin board. If you are not yet a senior, read your hometown newspapers (especially in April, May, and June) for the names of scholarships given to graduating seniors in your area. If you think you might qualify, check with the sponsor.

Contact your church or synagogue to see if either the local unit or national organization offers any student aid programs. Contact local civic and fraternal organizations, religious groups, and veterans' posts; many local, state, and national units sponsor some scholarship programs, especially for members' children.

Ask your parents to check with their employers. Many employers have some form of scholarship or grant aid available to help employees' children meet educational expenses; sometimes these programs are competitive, with awards based on academic achievement, while others are based on demonstrated need alone. Some employer programs are even offered as employee fringe benefits, particularly in educational institutions and nonprofit organizations.

If your parents are members of labor unions or trade and professional associations, they may discover that these organizations have some type of aid available to assist members' children. If one of your parents is a military veteran, you might also qualify for some help.

Investigate programs that may be underwritten by local businesses and industries. Community-based Education Opportunity and Upward Bound programs sometimes can assist you in identifying private sources of aid, too.

Take a few hours to go through books in your library about sources of financial aid. (Some are listed in the bibliography at the end of this chapter.) You could be pleasantly surprised to discover that there is a local, regional, or national scholarship program aimed specifically at someone with your particular experiences, talents, part-time employment history, career plans, or proposed field of study.

Evaluating locator services

Should you use one of the locator or search operations that offer to computer-match students with sources of financial aid, for a fee that can range from modest to hefty? The Student Advisory Committee of the College Scholarship Service (CSS) looked at that question in 1985. Noting that "at least two major studies have suggested that commercial computer search services may be ineffective," the Student Advisory Committee suggested that prospective clients check out a company's claims carefully before spending any money.

The committee also sent out a series of questions to high school counselors and college financial aid administrators and suggested that they might want to share the questions with students or parents to help them evaluate a service. Here are the committee's questions:

- If the company suggests that large amounts of aid currently are not being used, how does it document the statement?

- How many financial aid sources exist in the company's computer file? Does the company maintain its own file of sources, or does it use the file of some other company or service?

- Is there a minimum number of sources provided by the company? Are the listings in the form of scholarships, work, loans, or contests? Do they include federal and state programs for which the student will be considered through the regular financial aid application process?

- How often does the company update its list of aid sources? Does the company check to confirm that the source still exists, and that data concerning application deadlines and eligibility criteria are current?

- Can the student apply directly to the aid sources provided by the company, or must he or she be recommended for consideration by some other person or group? Are there application fees for the sources provided?

- How long will the student have to wait for the information? Will the list of aid sources be received prior to application deadlines?

- What characteristics are used to match students with aid sources?

- How successful have previous participants been in obtaining funds from aid sources identified by the company?

- Will the company refund the program fee if aid sources are incorrectly matched with the student's qualifications, if aid sources no longer exist or fail to reply to the student, or if application deadlines for aid sources have already passed when the information is received?

The committee correctly noted that "positive answers will not, however, guarantee that a student who uses the services actually will receive any funds," and suggested that the "high school guidance office, local library, and college financial aid office and academic departments are excellent resources through which [students] can conduct searches for sources of financial aid at no cost." Several useful publications are included in the bibliography.

Questions and answers about financial aid

Q With fewer scholarship and loan dollars available and jobs so hard to find, is financial aid available only to people with very low incomes?

A No. You don't have to be poor to receive financial aid, but you have to prove you need it. You are eligible for financial aid equal to the difference between college costs (tuition, living expenses, and so forth) and what you and your family can afford to contribute toward those costs.

Q I've done an estimate of my expected family contribution and financial need on the worksheets in Chapter 10. Can I count on getting this much money to help me?

A Not necessarily. You may be eligible for a certain amount, but you may not be able to get all you're eligible for simply because there's not enough to go around. If you've done the estimate, you've got a rough idea of your financial need, but you should be aware of some important limitations on this estimate.

The methods and formulas used in analyzing a family's financial need can and often do change from year to year.

Family situations change. Your family may have unusual personal or financial circumstances that could not be taken adequately into account in these calculations, but would affect your family's ability to pay for education. (An example might be unusually high expenses associated with an illness or a disability.) When the time comes for you to actually apply for financial aid, you can provide more detailed information than you used in completing these worksheets. At that time, you can explain your financial situation in more detail, and note any special family circumstances.

You should be aware that financial aid administrators at colleges can—and often do—adjust the family share calculated by CSS if a change in circumstances or additional information about your situation warrants a revision. This is because a national need analysis system can never accommodate all the special circumstances that make each family's situation unique. For any of these reasons, your expected family contribution and financial need could be different from your current estimate when the time actually comes for you to apply for financial aid. Use the estimates as a tool for planning, but count on doing as much as you can to help yourself.

Q If I am awarded aid, when will I actually get my money?

A You should get your money when you enroll (although not necessarily "on the spot") or at the start of the term or semester for which you enroll. The financial aid officer can tell you exactly when you will receive your award. Note that awards are not necessarily cash grants but may also be in the form of loans and jobs; most students get a combination or "package."

Q I plan to attend school half time, but I'll still need help with expenses. Will going to college part-time lessen my chances of receiving aid?

A In awarding aid, many institutions give priority to full-time students; however, you may be eligible for some aid on a half-time basis. Depending on the priorities and availability of funds at a particular college, half-time students could be eligible for virtually all forms of federal aid. Depending on your financial situation, you could be eligible for a Pell Grant. Ask the financial aid office at the colleges you're considering whether part-time students are given any assistance.

Q Are noncitizens eligible for financial aid?

A In most cases noncitizens are not eligible for tax-supported financial aid (such as federal or state assistance). Usually, however, noncitizens who are permanent residents are eligible, as are some refugees. Some colleges may have limited private funds to assist foreign students. Noncitizens applying to colleges in the United States are encouraged to read "Financial Planning for Study in the United States," a booklet published by the College Board and available through guidance offices and college foreign student advisers.

Q Will I receive special consideration if I have brothers and sisters who are continuing their education beyond high school?

A Generally speaking, yes. Your parents cannot be expected to contribute as much to your college costs if you have brothers and sisters whom they are also assisting.

Q My older brother was turned down for financial aid last year. Is there any point in my trying for financial aid?

A Definitely! College costs, institutional policies, and your family's financial circumstances change from one year to the next. The only way to know for sure whether you're eligible for financial aid is to apply for it. (See the next chapter for details.)

Q My older sister and my next-door neighbor both applied for financial aid at the same school last year. Their house is bigger than ours, and they make more money than our parents, so why did my neighbor get more financial aid than my sister?

A The formulas used to assess family financial strength are designed to treat families in similar circumstances equally. There are many reasons why your neighbor may have received more money than your sister:

1. Although her family has a larger house and a greater total income, they may also owe substantially more money on their home mortgage. If so, they would be able to contribute less to college costs and would be eligible for more aid.
2. The family might have financial circumstances of which you are unaware (more family members, extraordinary medical expenses, and so forth).
3. Your neighbor may have met the criteria for some financial aid award that your sister did not meet. For instance, the college may have been able to award her some aid because of her proposed academic major or because of her past academic achievement.
4. The college didn't have enough money to fully meet the needs of all the students who needed some assistance. Unfortunately, when the overall student need at a college exceeds the funds available, the financial aid administrator has to make difficult choices in deciding how much to give each recipient.

But *you* are not your sister. The only way to find out if you're eligible and how much you can receive is to apply for financial aid.

Q Do I have to pay income tax on my student aid award? How about FICA tax on my earnings from work-study jobs?

A The Tax Reform Act of 1986 included some new provisions related to the taxation of scholarships and fellowships. Under the new law, grants, scholarships, and fellowships *in excess of* the amount needed for tuition and fees plus related expenses must be included in taxable income. The Internal Revenue Service has ruled that this means that amounts of awards used for tuition, fees, and required books, sup-

plies, and equipment are nontaxable, but amounts used for other indirect expenses—such as room and board—are subject to taxation.* (However, remember that even these portions of your student aid package would be taxable only if you make enough money overall that you are required to pay income taxes.) Ask at your financial aid office or local IRS office if you have questions about the taxability of your aid award.

Under current law, students are *not* required to pay social security (FICA) tax on wages they earn in jobs provided by the colleges and universities they attend, such as jobs in the College Work-Study Program. (Jobs with *other* employers are subject to FICA tax withholding.)

Bibliography of aid sources

General

Annual Register of Grant Support: 1991-92. 25th ed. Wilmette, Il.: National Register Publishing Co. $141.00 plus $4.50 shipping and handling. Updated annually. Over 3,000 programs providing grant support in the humanities, international affairs and area studies, special populations, education, urban and regional affairs, social sciences, physical sciences, life sciences, technology, and other areas are listed.

The College Blue Book: Scholarships, Fellowships, Grants, and Loans. 23rd ed. New York: Macmillan, 1991. One of five volumes; $48.00 per volume. Sources of financial assistance are listed for students ranging from high school seniors through those involved in advanced professional programs.

Davis, Dr. Herm and Joyce Lain Kennedy. *The College Financial Aid Emergency Kit (1991-92).* Cardiff, Calif.: Sun Features, Inc., 1991. Pocket guide to scholarships, loans, and other sources of income for college. $5.00.

The Federal Student Aid Factsheet. Washington, D.C.: U.S. Department of Education. 1991. Free. Order from Consumer Information Center, Dept. 506, Pueblo, Col. 81009. Updated annually. Describes financial aid programs sponsored by the federal government.

Financial Aid to Education. New Haven, Conn.: Knights of Columbus, 1988. Free. Information about loans and scholarships for children of members of the Knights of Columbus.

*Department of the Treasury, Internal Revenue Service, Public Affairs Division, News Release IR-87-55, April 13, 1987, page 1.

Keeslar, Oreon, ed. *Financial Aids to Higher Education, 1991-92.* 14th ed. Dubuque, Ia.: Wm. C. Brown Company, 1990. $45.00 plus $2.50 shipping and handling. Updated biennially. Lists more than 3,000 programs specifically for students entering as college freshmen.

Lesko, Matthew. *Getting Yours: The Complete Guide to Government Money.* 3d ed. New York: Penguin U.S.A., 1987. $9.95 plus $2.00 shipping and handling. Many of the federal government programs listed in the Office of Management and Budget's Catalog of Federal Domestic Assistance are summarized here, including grants, scholarships, and fellowships.

Margolin, Judith B. *Financing a College Education: The Essential Guide for the 90s.* New York: Plenum, 1990. $14.95 plus $3.00 postage and handling. Specific and practical advice on paying for college. Includes chapters on government financial aid, private scholarships, building a college nest egg, loans, and bargains.

Need a Lift? 40th ed. Indianapolis: The American Legion, 1990. $2.00 prepaid. Updated annually. Sources of career, scholarship, and loan information for all students, with emphasis on scholarship opportunities for veterans, their dependents, and children of deceased or disabled veterans. Also includes a computerized scholarship search application.

Renz, Loren, ed. *Foundation Grants to Individuals.* 7th ed. New York: Foundation Center, 1990. $40 plus $4.50 postage and handling. Undergraduate and graduate scholarship sources categorized under general and specific requirements. Also includes fellowships, residencies, internships, and grants by U.S. foundations to foreign nationals or citizens, as well as company-sponsored aid programs.

Student Aid Annual, 1991-92. Moravia, N.Y.: Chronicle Guidance Publications, 1991. $19.97 plus $2.00 postage and handling. Financial aid programs for students at undergraduate and graduate levels of study, including those offered by noncollege organizations, labor unions, and federal and state governments. Order #502-A.

Specific populations groups

Blum, Laurie. *Free Money for Graduate School.* New York: Henry Holt, 1990. $34.95 plus $3.00 postage and handling. Lists all known sources of private monies available for graduate students.

Bureau of Indian Affairs Higher Education Grants and Scholarships. Washington, D.C.: Bureau of Indian Affairs. Free. Lists sources of assistance for students who are native American or Alaskan natives of a tribal group recognized by the Bureau of Indian Affairs for certain benefits.

Financial Aid for Minorities in Business and Law. Garrett Park, Md.: Garrett Park Press, 1990. $4.00. Lists financial aid sources for minority student specifically in business. Other books in the Financial Aid for Minorities series cover allied health, education, engineering, science, and mass communications and journalism. $19.90 for the series.

Frankel, Norman, ed. *Grants Register, 1991-93.* New York: St. Martin's Press, 1990. $85.00 plus $1.50 postage and handling. Updated biennially. Lists scholarships and fellowships at all levels of graduate study. Specific awards are included for refugees, war veterans, minorities, and students in unexpected financial difficulties.

Funding for U.S. Study: A Guide for Foreign Nationals. New York: Institute of International Education, 1989. $39.95. Available grant data recommended to foreign nationals and U.S. educational advisers.

Higher Education Opportunities for Minorities and Women. Washington, D.C.: U.S. Government Printing Office, 1989. $4.25. Select listing of opportunities available for minorities and women in higher education, including some information on scholarships, fellowships, and loans.

Johnson, Willis, ed. *Directory of Special Programs for Minority Group Members: Career Information Services, Employment Skills Banks, Financial Aid Sources.* 5th ed. Garrett Park, Md.: Garrett Park Press, 1990. $27.00 prepaid.

Schlachter, Gail Ann. *Directory of Financial Aids for Minorities, 1991-93.* San Carlos, Ca.: Reference Service Press, 1991. $47.50 plus $3.00 postage and handling. 2,200 references and cross-references to scholarships, fellowships, grants, loans, awards, and internships set aside for ethnic minorities.

Schlachter, Gail Ann. *Directory of Financial Aids for Women, 1991-92.* San Carlos, Ca.: Reference Service Press, 1991. $45.00 plus $3.00 postage and handling. Over 2,000 scholarships, fellowships, grants, loans, awards, and internships set aside for women.

Schlachter, Gail Ann and R. David Weber. *Financial Aid for the Disabled and Their Families,1990-91.* San Carlos, Ca.: Reference Service

Press, 1990. $35.00 plus $3.00 for postage and handling. Lists nearly 1,000 scholarships, fellowships, loans, grants-in-aid, and awards established for the disabled.

Fields of study

Arts

Fandel, Nancy A. *The National Directory of Grants and Aid to Individuals in the Arts*. 7th ed. Des Moines, Iowa: Washington International Arts Letter, 1987. $25.95. Lists grants, prizes, and awards for professional work in the United States and abroad. Includes information about universities and schools offering aid to students in the arts.

Athletics

Green, Alan. *The Directory of Athletic Scholarships*. New York: Facts on File, 1987. $29.95 hardcover, $15.95 paperback. No postage and handling if order is prepaid. Comprehensive listing of which sports are played where, and what schools are offering scholarships in those sports. In addition, suggests a strategy for winning grant-in-aid.

Communications

Grants and Awards Available to American Writers. 17th ed. New York: PEN American Center, 1990. $7.50. Updated annually. Lists awards granted to American writers to use in the United States or abroad.

1991 Journalism Career and Scholarship Guide. Princeton, N.J.: Dow Jones Newspaper Fund, 1991. First copy free; additional copies $3.00 each. Updated annually. Information on journalism programs and a section on scholarships and minority grants.

Health

Allied Health Education Directory. 19th ed. Chicago: American Medical Association, 1991. $36.00. Contains a section on financial aid and a listing of allied health education programs.

Medical School Admission Requirements, U.S. and Canada, 1991-92. 41st ed. Washington, D.C.: Association of American Medical Colleges, 1990. $10.00 plus $2.50 postage and handling. Updated annually. Includes suggestions for undergraduate financial aid planning, sources of aid at medical and postmedical school levels, and aid sources for minorities and the disadvantaged.

Scholarships and Loans in Nursing Education 1990-91. New York: National League for Nursing. $10.95 plus $3.00 postage.

History

Grants, Fellowships and Prizes, 1991-92. Washington, D.C.: American Historical Association, 1991. $8.00 to members; $10.00 to nonmembers. Updated annually.

Humanities

Directory of Grants in the Humanities, 1991-92. 5th ed. Phoenix, Ariz.: Oryx Press, 1987. $74.50 plus $7.00 postage and handling. Contains more than 2,500 current funding programs that support research and performance in literature, language, anthropology, philosophy, ethics, sculpture, crafts, mime, etc.

Library education

Financial Assistance for Library Education. Chicago: American Library Association, 1990-91. $1.00 (postage and handling). Updated annually. Lists assistance administered by state library agencies and associations, local libraries, and academic institutions.

Military

Betterton, Don M. *How the Military Will Help You Pay for College*. Princeton, N.J.: Peterson's Guides 2d ed. 1990. $9.95 plus $3.25 postage and handling. Extensive information about scholarship and financial aid opportunities for students going directly to college after high school, including the service academies, ROTC programs, and other special programs, as well as scholarship and tuition-payment programs available to members of the armed forces.

Schlachter, Gail Ann and R. David Weber. *Financial Aid for Veterans, Military Personnel, and Their Dependents, 1990-91*. Biennial. San Carlos, Ca.: Reference Service Press, 1990. $35.00 plus $3.00 postage and handling. Lists 1,100 scholarships, fellowships, loans, grants-in-aid, awards, and internships designed for education, research, travel, training, career development, etc., for individuals associated with the military.

Philosophy

Fellowships and Grant Opportunities of Interest to Philosophers, 1991-92. Newark, Del.: American Philosophical Association, 1991. $7.00 prepaid. Updated annually. This listing is included as a section in the association's *Proceedings and Addresses*.

Psychology

Graduate Study in Psychology and Associated Fields, 1990. Washington, D.C.: American Psychological Association, 1990. $15.50 to members, $19.50 to non-members, plus $2.00 postage. Information about financial assistance and foundations and agencies accepting fellowship applications, as well as information about graduate programs in psychology.

Speech

Student Financial Aid: Speech-Language Pathology and Audiology. Rockville, Md.: American Speech and Hearing Association, 1986. $1.25 prepaid. Mimeographed listing of general information about grants, scholarships, and loans at the graduate level and information about aid for graduate education in the field.

6. Applying for financial aid

If you have estimated your expenses at the colleges that interest you, evaluated your family's financial situation, and concluded that you will need some extra help in meeting educational expenses, then you should apply for financial aid. Even if you are not certain that you will qualify, you should apply—that's the only way to find out if you are eligible. Simply applying for admission to college is not enough. If you think you need financial aid, you *must apply* for aid.

The process of applying for financial aid can be confusing and time-consuming, especially to the first-time applicant. (Yes, you must reapply for aid every year, but it really does seem a lot simpler and less confusing the second time around.) In Chapter 5, you learned about the various types and sources of financial aid. Application requirements differ from college to college (and program to program), but the good news is that you don't really have to file separate applications for each and every one.

In order to improve your chances of getting the aid you need, you must know *what* you have to do, *when* you have to do it, and *how* to do it right—the first time.

The Financial Aid Form and other need analysis documents

For most students, the process begins with the completion of a need analysis document like the Financial Aid Form (FAF), prepared by the College Scholarship Service (CSS). Some students may be asked instead to file other forms, such as the Student Aid Application for California (SAAC), the Family Financial Statement (FFS) published by the American College Testing Program, the Application for Pennsylvania State Grant and Federal Student Aid (APSGFSA) of the Pennsylvania Higher Education Assistance Agency, the Application for Federal and State Student Assistance (AFSSA) of CSX Commercial Services, Inc., SingleFile (SF) of the United Student Aid Funds, or the Application for Federal Student Assistance (AFSA) of the U.S. government.

How do you know *which* form you should file? *Always check with the colleges and programs from which you are seeking aid.* Do whatever they instruct you to do. All forms are *not* alike! Some processors collect more information than others, and some produce reports for colleges and programs in different paper or electronic formats and/or on different schedules.

Many colleges and agencies *require*, or at least *prefer*, a particular document, such as the FAF. When colleges or programs require or prefer one processor's form over another's, it is often because their programs depend on the full set of data or their application-processing systems are set up to use particular kinds of reporting media.

Other colleges and programs may *accept* any one of several forms. So compare the requirements and preferences of all the colleges and programs from which you are seeking help. Chances are good that you will only have to complete one need analysis form to apply for aid from all of the sources—the federal government, your state government, the colleges to which you are seeking admission, and any private scholarship programs from which you are seeking aid.

While you are checking on required need analysis forms, make sure you find out whether a college or sponsor has its own separate aid application that you must complete *in addition* to a need analysis document. Some do; others don't.

Also make sure that you understand the deadlines or preferred filing dates. Students generally file a need analysis form in the late winter or early spring *preceding* the fall term for which help is needed. If possible, send in your form four weeks before the earliest dead-

Applying for aid usually begins with completion of a "need analysis" form. Find out about the forms required by the colleges that interest you, and be sure to meet the financial aid deadlines.

line you need to meet. (Do *not* file before January 1, however.)

Where do you *get* need analysis forms? FAFs and some (but not all) other need analysis forms are generally available through high school guidance offices, college financial aid offices, and many community centers. Sometimes a college will send you a form directly. (If a college asks you to use a need analysis form that is *not* available through the high school guidance office, request one directly from the college.)

If you are using the FAF (or the CSS version of the SAAC), you will be asked for information about your family and finances much like that reviewed in Chapter 2—information about income, assets, family size, unusual expenses, and so forth. Detailed step-by-step instructions are provided.

You should gather your most recent income tax returns, W-2 forms, and other financial records together before sitting down to complete the FAF. (You don't actually have to *file* your income tax return before you complete the FAF, but it's a good idea to at least rough it out; items on the FAF are cross-referenced to the most common federal income tax return documents to make the FAF easier to complete.)

After you have completed *and checked* your FAF, send it to CSS in the preaddressed envelope provided. The information you report is confidential, and is sent only to the colleges, programs, and government agencies that you authorize. You should be aware, however, that the federal government does engage in some comparison of data bases between and among its various programs. Colleges may also ask you later on to verify some of the information that you report on your FAF.

When CSS receives your FAF, it transmits selected data from your form to the federal central processor. The federal central processor computes your need and eligibility according to the federal formulas and sends results back to CSS.

At that point, CSS does two things: it sends your record—in paper or electronic reporting format—to all the colleges, agencies, and programs you originally named, provided you listed them correctly and included the appropriate fee; a copy of your FAF also accompanies the computer-generated reports.

CSS also sends *you* a Student Aid Report (SAR). Your SAR displays information about your eligibility for student aid, including a Pell Grant. Review the information carefully and make any necessary changes directly on the special page provided. *Your SAR is valuable: do not misplace or discard it*. Eventually, you will need to provide it to the college in which you enroll.

CSS will also send you a special "Acknowledgment" page along with your SAR. Study this Acknowledgment carefully, too, to ensure that all the colleges, agencies, and programs to which you are applying received your record. The Acknowledgment may contain special messages to you from those aid sources, such as requests for additional information or a copy of your parents' most recent tax return. You can also use the Acknowledgment to add more colleges and programs.

You may get a request for more information if something on your original application was incomplete or unclear. Make sure that you respond promptly and accurately to such requests.

When colleges and programs receive your need analysis report, they will evaluate your financial need and eligibility and decide how much money you will actually receive. Eventually you will receive award notices from the colleges to which you applied, as well as from your state scholarship or grant program and the federal student financial aid programs. Review all communications carefully, and promptly supply any additional information that may be requested.

Tips on completing a need analysis form

1. *Make sure you know what need analysis form you need to complete*. Usually the FAF will service for all of the colleges and programs from which you are seeking aid, but check to make sure. The most reliable source of information about a particular college's requirements is the catalog or financial aid bulletin published by the college itself. For federal programs, including Pell Grants and campus-based funds, you can simply check off the appropriate box on the FAF or other appropriate document to indicate that you want to be considered for federal assistance. In many states, you can apply for state aid by a similar process; your high school counselor can tell you whether the FAF or FFS can be used to apply for aid in your state. Private student aid programs may or may not require you to complete a need analysis form; you should review their published guidelines for details.

2. *Read the instructions that accompany the form*. If you don't understand them, read them again. Enough said.

3. *Gather your financial records together before you start completing the form*. Because need analysis documents ask questions about your family's financial situation, it is helpful to have such records as the following on hand: your federal income tax returns (IRS 1040 or 1040A or 1040 EZ), state and local income tax returns, W-2 forms and other earnings records (for example, paycheck stubs), current bank statements, current mortgage information, records of medical and dental bills, business or farm records, and records of veteran's benefits and social security payments.

4. *Complete the form accurately, completely, and legibly*. Inaccurate or missing information on your form could cause costly delays in processing your application.

If you are using a document like the FAF, you will see that the form collects both federal questions *and* supplemental information used by many colleges, programs, and state agencies to award aid. If you want to be considered for aid from all sources, make sure to complete all sections of the form. Also, be sure to enclose the appropriate reporting fee to ensure that your record is sent to all of the colleges and agencies that you list.

5. *Provide all information requested*. For instance, if an answer is zero, enter zero. Keep in mind that colleges may subsequently request a copy of your parents' or your own tax return to verify the information reported on your FAF or other need analysis document. Inaccurate information may jeopardize your getting financial aid.

6. *Submit your need analysis form for processing as early as possible AFTER January 1*. If possible, send in your form at least four weeks before the earliest deadline. This may not always be possible if a deadline falls before January 31. In that case, just send in the form as soon as possible after January 1. (If you send in your form *before* January 1, federal rules require that you file another form later reporting your income, and this could, in the end, delay your application.)

7. *When you receive your Student Aid Report (SAR) from your processor, review it thoroughly*. If there are errors in the information, make corrections directly on the special page provided, and mail it back to your processor. In a few weeks, you will get a revised SAR. Handle your SARs with care! You will need to provide your SAR to the college in which you eventually enroll before you can receive any federal aid.

8. *Review your css Acknowledgment carefully, too.* Make sure that your records have been sent to all of the colleges and programs by which you want to be considered. Review any messages contained on your acknowledgment directing you to provide additional information to colleges or programs.

Other applications you may have to complete

Although a need analysis form is the starting point of the process, you also may be required to complete several other documents during the course of applying for financial aid. The advice on completing these applications is basically the same: accuracy, completeness, legibility, and timeliness are all very important.

College applications

Many colleges have their own applications that students must complete in addition to an FAF or other form. When checking the requirements of the various colleges and universities you are considering, make sure you know whether or not you must also complete separate applications for each college. This information, along with information about deadlines, is available in the college catalog or bulletin.

A college's financial aid application is not the same as the admissions application, although you send them in at approximately the same time. You do not need to wait until you have been accepted for admission to apply for financial aid. In fact, if you *do* wait, you could find that the money is all gone. Follow the rules specified by the college in its catalog or other materials.

Stafford Loans

If you are applying for a Stafford Loan (formerly a Guaranteed Student Loan or GSL), you will have to complete a separate application for this program. Applications are available from eligible participating lenders, from colleges, and from guaranty agencies. Fill out the first section of the form with information about yourself; the college financial aid administrator will complete another section that certifies your enrollment (or admission and prospective enrollment), academic standing, cost of education, and other financial aid. After both sections are completed, the application is taken (or sent) to the lender. If the lender agrees to make the loan, the application is sent on to the state guaranty agency or federal government for approval. It

normally takes four to six weeks to completely process an application, so give yourself plenty of time.

If you have difficulty finding a lender who is willing to make a Stafford Loan, check with the college financial aid administrator; he or she may be aware of active lenders. Also, in some cases, the aid administrator can act on behalf of a state lending agency in either approving or in recommending approval of a "loan of last resort." Lenders are prohibited by law from discriminating against loan applications on the basis of race, sex, religion, national origin, marital status, or because an applicant receives public assistance or has exercised consumer rights. However, lenders can limit the number and the amounts of the loans they make. Sometimes they may also attach other requirements, such as being a customer or having a parent who is a customer.

State and state-authorized guaranty agencies can charge an insurance premium on Stafford Loans, and the amount is usually collected by the lender at the time the loan is disbursed to you (not earlier than 30 days before the beginning of the academic term). You will also be required to pay a "loan origination fee," which comes off the top of the loan. See Chapter 7 for advice about borrowing.

State student assistance programs

Some states also have separate applications that must be completed by applicants for state student assistance programs. Your high school counselor, financial aid administrator, or state student assistance agency can tell you whether you need to complete any separate applications. Most states, however, permit a student to use one of the need analysis documents as the application. If you live in such a state, make sure that you file the state-specific FAF or other need analysis document, and follow the instructions carefully for listing the state agency as one of the recipients of information from your FAF.

Private scholarship programs

Many private scholarship programs have their own separate applications that must be completed in addition to the FAF or other need analysis document. Details about the application requirements are provided by the sponsor. Sometimes these additional applications are fairly simple and straightforward; however, some of these programs require students to provide extensive biographical information, high school transcripts, essays, and/or other material as part of the application process.

Federal student aid programs

You do not need to complete a separate application for federal student aid if you are filing an FAF or certain other need analysis forms. Simply follow the directions for adding the federal government to the list of recipients of information from your need analysis document. There is no additional charge for using any of these forms to apply for federal student assistance.

Additional information you may have to provide

In the course of applying for financial aid, you may be asked to provide additional information at various points in the process. For example, most colleges ask students to provide information to assist them in "validating" the data reported on the FAF or other need analysis document. Before actually disbursing money to students, copies of the parents' most recent tax returns may be requested. If different information appears on the tax return, the applicant's aid award may be adjusted. An aid recipient may refuse to provide such information, but the college in turn has the right not to provide money.

One or more of the colleges from which you are seeking aid may also request additional information in order to *verify* the data you reported on your FAF or other need analysis form. Since the 1986-87 academic year, the federal government has engaged in extensive efforts to verify the financial situation of selected applicants for the Pell Grant, Stafford Loan, and campus-based programs. While colleges did not have much latitude in structuring their compliance with the new verification procedures, they did have some choice about whether they would routinely follow up on all applicants or just selected students, as well as about whether they would use individualized letters, customized forms, blank forms, or other mechanisms for collecting information from students.

So don't be surprised or distressed if you receive requests from one or more colleges to report new information or confirm previously reported data. Simply provide the requested information as quickly and completely as possible. If you don't understand what a request means, ask. If you feel as though you are being asked to reconfirm information you already reported, you may be! One of the reasons for the procedure is to make sure that information is as accurate at the point of *awarding* aid as it was at the point of *applying* for it, as well as to correct any errors.

A student who receives funding under the College Work-Study Program will be required to file a federal income tax withholding form (Form W-4) or withholding exemption form (Form W-4E) with the college before he or she can earn any funds.

A student who receives a Perkins Loan will be required to sign a promissory note for each loan advance. A copy of the promissory note and other loan information is provided to recipients in accordance with federal loan disclosure laws. Recipients may also have to provide additional information, such as a list of personal references.

Comply with all requests for additional information promptly, accurately, and legibly. The paperwork may seem like a nuisance, but remember that hundreds or even thousands of dollars are at stake. Don't blow your chances for financial aid by failing to provide the information someone needs to evaluate your situation.

Questions and answers about applying for financial aid

Q Must I be accepted for admission before I apply for financial aid? Must I be admitted before I receive financial aid?

A You should apply for financial aid at the time you apply for admission. Remember, too, that simply applying for admission is not the same as applying for financial aid. To receive aid, you must *apply* for aid; this means that you must file the FAF (or some other need analysis form). In some cases, you may also be required to submit a separate institutional or state application as well. You will not actually receive aid until you have enrolled.

Q Is it necessary for me to apply for financial aid every year?

A Yes. At most colleges you must apply each academic year, but applying is almost always easier the second time around because there is less paperwork and you are familiar with the process.

Q I want to apply for a scholarship only. Do I have to fill out the FAF?

A Check with the sponsor of the scholarship and/or the financial aid office at the institution to which you are applying. Find out what forms should be completed and when they are due.

Q How can I find out what the deadline is for applying for aid at the college I am interested in?

A Look for the deadline in Part II of this book or in the college's catalog. If you cannot find it there, ask the college's financial aid office. Be aware that many institutions have "priority filing dates," which you should meet if you possibly can. After that date, some aid may still be available; check with the financial aid office if you are applying later than the deadline or priority date given.

Q One college I'm applying to *requires* the FAF and another *requires* a different form. Do I have to complete both need analysis forms?

A Contact the financial aid offices at both colleges, explain the situation, and see if both colleges would accept the same form. If neither college is willing to accept the other form, you will have to file both forms.

Q Will I have to file more than one need analysis form for aid?

A Because the FAF is accepted, preferred, or required by most postsecondary institutions, state agencies, and scholarship programs, most families that file an FAF will not be required to complete another need analysis form; however, students may have to complete an additional institutional or state application. Part II of this book lists the forms required by more than 3,100 institutions of higher education. Students should always consult the colleges and programs directly to make sure that they understand exactly what forms are required, and when.

Q My parents are divorced. Who should complete the FAF?

A The parent with whom you lived for the longest period in the last 12 months should fill out the FAF. If you didn't live with either parent, or lived with each parent for an equal number of days, the FAF should be filled out by the parent who provided things such as housing, food, clothes, car, medical and dental care, and college costs.

Q Can a college legally require each of my divorced or separated parents fill out a need analysis document?

A The Pell Grant Program requires information only from the parent with whom you live. However, an aid administrator at a particular college can make his or her own decision about whether to require both parents to file the FAF or other need analysis forms when you are being considered for funds from programs that the institution administers. The current marital status and other obligations of the parent who doesn't have custody would be considered in this situation.

Q My parents are divorced, but the parent who qualifies and who must complete the FAF doesn't want to provide the necessary data. However, the parent who doesn't qualify is willing. What should I do?

A According to criteria established by federal programs, the qualifying parent *must* provide information or the student cannot receive a Pell Grant. However, for purposes of qualifying for aid administered by colleges, the aid administrator at the college may resolve the problem. The administrator may determine, for instance, that there are sufficiently adverse home circumstances that information from the responsible parent cannot be obtained and that information from the other parent is acceptable. This situation should be explained on your form.

Q My parents refuse to file an FAF or other documents. What should I do?

A In order to be considered for financial aid, you must file a need analysis form. However, aid administrators will sometimes consider special circumstances if they are documented by your clergyman, counselor, or social worker. You must realize that resources will be limited because no state or federal funds can be distributed without documented financial need. (You also may be asked to provide a notarized statement of parent nonsupport.)

Q I plan to start college in the fall of 1992. So why do all the forms ask questions about my parents' income from *this* year when I need the money *next* year?

A 1991 is the last complete year for which your parents' income can be verified through tax returns. If your parents' income in 1992 will differ substantially from their 1991 income, explain this situation. The financial aid administrator may be able to take these special circumstances into consideration in making your award.

Q Is there any way that the IRS will find out how we answered questions on the FAF?

A The College Scholarship Service *does not* routinely provide information from the FAF to the IRS.

The CSS will disclose your records only if the IRS subpoenas them as part of an investigation. The information that you provide on the FAF or other need analysis documents is shared only with the colleges and programs you list as recipients because you are seeking financial aid from them.

Q Should I attach receipts? Will anyone ever ask for receipts? Should I attach my IRS Form 1040 to my FAF or other need analysis document?

A No. Don't enclose receipts. However, financial aid offices at colleges to which you apply may ask for documentation of unusually high expenses that occur during the academic year. It is more likely that they will request a copy of your tax returns to verify expenses that occurred in the prior calendar year. More and more colleges are requesting tax returns to validate information reported on documents such as the FAF. Do *not* attach a copy of your tax returns to the the FAF or other need analysis document. If a college or program wants to see your tax returns, send them directly to the address indicated.

7. Credit where credit is due

As costs rise and financial aid resources get tighter, fewer and fewer students will be able to escape the necessity of borrowing some amount of money to complete their education.

Almost half of the student aid dollars available today are in the form of loan dollars, predominantly in the federally backed Stafford Student Loan Program. Other federal loans available to students include Perkins Loans and Supplemental Loans to Students (SLS). (See Chapters 4 and 5.)

Parents, too, are increasingly turning to public and private loan programs to help finance some or all of their "expected contribution." PLUS Loans and private supplemental loans are among the major loan programs aimed at parents of college students. (See Chapter 4.)

Keep borrowing in perspective

The idea of borrowing to pay for college makes some students (and parents) anxious. This is understandable among people who have never borrowed money, or who have had a negative experience with borrowing. But without borrowing, few people could afford houses or cars or major appliances—*or* college. Borrowing is an increasingly common and perfectly appropriate way to finance educational expenses.

If you're worried about your ability to repay a student loan, remember that your education will make you more employable and thus increase your earning power. (Recent U.S. Census data suggest that the average lifetime earnings of college graduates far exceed lifetime earnings for high school graduates.) If you are committed to earning a degree or certificate, you will probably not have difficulty finding a job at the end of that process that will permit you to repay your loan.

At the same time, you should remember that a loan *is* a loan, not a grant. You are legally responsible for repaying student loans (except for a few, very specific conditions that allow you to forgo paying some or all of them).

If you have grave doubts about your ability to do college work, or you're honestly not sure you're interested in education or training after high school, you might want to hold off on borrowing until you have a clearer sense of what you really want. Taking out a large student loan just to "see how you like college" may not be as sensible as taking a course or two at a low-cost institution on a part-time basis, or working for a while to save the first semester's tuition.

If you're sure about your desire for education, but still anxious about borrowing, it may help you to think of your student loan as "credit," rather than as "debt." When someone loans you money, they are extending credit to you—because they believe that you will be willing and able to repay the money, with interest. That makes it a good deal on both sides of the transaction.

And contrary to the headlines, the vast majority of citizens *do* repay their student loans and go on to participate fully in the economic life of the country in a way that justifies the nation's investment in them. Repayment may sometimes leave borrowers with less discretionary money in their pockets than they'd like, but they manage. And if financial setbacks occur, steps can be taken to arrange for temporary relief of student loan payments until a borrower's economic condition improves.

Educate yourself about loans

Your student loan may be the first big legal obligation you've ever assumed. And it may well be the largest single obligation you'll ever take on, short of a home mortgage. Many students borrow during each of their undergraduate years, and then borrow more funds for graduate or professional school as well. Protect yourself by becoming an informed consumer.

Whether you borrow from a government-subsidized loan program or a commercial lending institution, you should take the time to educate yourself about loans *before* you actually have to apply for one. The worst possible time to start learning about loans is when you're in the midst of looking for one!

Learn the language

Know your terms. The amount of money you borrow is called the *principal*. When you pay back a loan, you pay both principal and the *interest*—which is the fee you pay for using someone else's money. Interest is expressed as a percentage.

When you investigate different nonfederal education loans, look for the annual percentage rate (APR). Every consumer loan agreement must disclose the APR in large bold type. The APR will be different from the simple interest rate, because the APR reflects *compounded* interest. Also look carefully at the way interest rates are expressed. A 1½ percent *monthly* interest rate amounts to an 18% *yearly* rate (1.5% x 12). Note that the interest rates for GSL, SLS, and PLUS will always be the same from one lender to the next because the rates are set by law.

How much you pay each month is called the *minimum monthly payment*. Your lender or your financial aid office can help you estimate your minimum monthly payment, which varies by the amount borrowed and the number of years for which you've borrowed it.

The *term* of a loan is how long you have to repay the obligation. This can vary substantially, up to 10 years or more. Some loan programs, such as the Stafford, PLUS, and SLS programs, permit you to *prepay* your loan, or pay it off early; that can save you considerable interest. (In other programs, you may pay a penalty if you pay off early.)

The *grace period* is how long you can wait before you have to *start* repaying; this, too, varies by program. With Stafford Loans, for example, you have a grace period of six months after you graduate, leave school, or drop below half-time status.

An *origination fee* is a charge deducted from a loan to pay for the costs of making the loan; some programs have an origination fee and others do not. Some programs also charge an *insurance premium* to insure your loan, while others may charge an *application fee*, which may or may not be refundable,

depending on whether you qualify for the loan. Read the lender's literature carefully to make sure you understand what costs you may be incurring.

Subsidized loans—such as Stafford Loans, Perkins Loans, PLUS Loans, and Supplemental Loans to Students—are loans backed by a guarantor; they usually have a lower interest rate and/or other more favorable features than *unsubsidized* or *commercial* loans. A *guarantor* (or *guarantee agency*) is an organization that agrees to pay the loan if the student doesn't; state agencies, the federal government, and authorized private organizations are the most typical guarantors for student loans. Some loans are *privately insured* rather than backed by a guarantor.

A *lender* may be a bank, a savings and loan association, a credit union, a finance company, a college or university, a public or quasi-public agency, or a private organization. Check out several lenders before you make a decision about where to borrow.

Even in the case of the government-backed loans, there are some important differences between lenders, such as what kind of *repayment options* they offer. Repayment options can include *graduated repayment*, where payments are smaller in the first few years after you leave school (when earning power is less), and increase later on; and *consolidation*, where you combine multiple loans into a single obligation for smaller monthly payments but a longer repayment term.

Regardless of where you borrow from or from what loan program you borrow, you will have to provide some information about yourself on a *loan application*; this information may be checked before a loan is actually made to you. A *promissory note* is another name for a legal agreement or contract you sign when you borrow money.

A *cosigner* or *cosignatory* is a person who signs for your loan with you. You don't need a cosigner for Stafford or Perkins Loans, but you may be asked for one if you borrow from other loan programs, particularly if you are a minor.

If you *default*, or fail to repay your loan when it comes due, a cosigner is legally responsible for your debt. There are other things that can happen, too, if you default on a loan. Your *credit record* (or *credit history*) will most likely be damaged, which will create problems for you if you want to borrow money for other purchases, like a car or a house (or more education). Your salary may be *attached* (or *garnished*), which means that your employer is legally required to turn over part of your earnings to your lender; your federal income tax refund may also be withheld.

People sometimes default because they don't know that other options are available to them—options that would protect their credit records and help them finance their debt. Under certain circumstances, for example, you may qualify for *deferment*, or temporary postponement of payments (*forbearance*); interest may or may not continue to *accrue* (or add up) during this time.

Evaluate how much you need

Make a realistic but conservative estimate of how much you really *need* to borrow. Remember, you don't have to borrow the maximum amount available. Have you exhausted other alternatives for meeting your expenses? Could you cut your expenses a little, or perhaps work a bit more and borrow a bit less?

Borrowing *more* than you really need just because the yearly or aggregate maximums are higher than your immediate need can be risky. It could impede your eventual ability to repay your loans, or at least reduce your borrowing capacity at a point in the future when you genuinely need more money.

At the same time, borrowing *less* than you really need can be risky, too, particularly if you jeopardize your enrollment. Remember that you will probably be in a better position to manage your financial obligations, including your student loans, once you've secured your degree.

Estimate how much you can repay

Estimating how much debt you can manage becomes more critical every time you borrow (and many students borrow more than once, and from more than one program). Take into account the amounts you've already borrowed, how much more you'll need to complete your education (including graduate or professional school, if that's in your plans), your estimated monthly payments, and starting salaries for the kinds of jobs you're likely to get once you graduate.

According to the U.S. Census Bureau, the average monthly income for persons with a bachelor's degree is $2,109, while monthly incomes for persons with professional degrees average $4,323. Of course, those figures are for all workers with degrees. A somewhat better frame of reference for estimating your own future earnings are the data in Tables 7.1 and 7.2, which highlight *starting* salaries. (If you want to check out the job and salary prospects for the career field you're thinking about, a good place to start is the *Occupational Outlook Handbook* published by the

Table 7.1. Average annual salary of bachelor's degree recipients employed full-time 1 year after graduation, by field of study, 1987

	Average salary of 1985-86 degree recipients in June 1987, current dollars
Total	$20,300
Engineering	26,600
Business and management	21,100
Health professions	22,600
Education	15,800*
Public affairs and social services	17,700
Biological sciences	16,400
Physical sciences, mathematics, and computer sciences	22,500
Psychology	17,300
Social sciences	20,300
Humanities	16,200
Communications	**
Miscellaneous	17,600

*Most educators work 9 to 10-month contracts
**Fewer than 75 respondents
Source: U.S. Department of Education, National Center for Education Statistics, "Recent College Graduates" surveys.

U.S. Department of Labor Bureau of Labor Statistics and available in many public libraries.)

Understand what you're doing

Make sure you know what you're doing before you sign on the dotted line. Sometimes students borrow without even realizing that they're doing it; they fail to read award letters carefully and aren't paying attention when they sign a promissory note. Some students also have borrowed from more than one program on the mistaken assumption that their loan will automatically be consolidated in a single obligation later on; that's not the case, although sometimes it may be possible.

Whether you are considering a subsidized government loan or a commercial loan, you should know the answers to all of these questions before you commit yourself:

- What is the simple interest rate?
- When will you have to begin repayment?
- How large will the monthly payments be, and how long will you be paying back the loan?
- Are there any extra charges involved in borrowing the money? (For instance, you may have to pay an

Table 7.2. Income, earnings, and work activity of persons who held a bachelor's or advanced degree, by field of study: Spring 1984

	Mean monthly income[1]		Mean monthly earnings[2]		Number of months worked during previous 4 months	
	Bachelor's degrees	Advanced degrees	Bachelor's degrees	Advanced degrees	Bachelor's degrees	Advanced degrees
All degree recipients	**$1,841**	**$2,711**	**$1,540**	**$2,341**	**3.08**	**3.35**
Agriculture and forestry.	1,945		1,559		3.25	
Biology	1,559		1,201		2.73	
Business and management	2,381	3,564	2,179	3,192	3.48	3.64
Economics	2,846		2,280		3.36	
Education.	1,290	2,062	1,012	1,695	2.76	3.23
Engineering	2,833	3,308	2,282	2,886	3.38	3.55
English and journalism	1,477	1,945	1,095	1,567	2.66	3.48
Home economics	1,065		525		2.12	
Law		4,060		3,624		3.57
Liberal arts and humanities	1,400	1,720	1,072	1,466	2.87	3.17
Mathematics and statistics	2,116		1,809		3.20	
Medicine and dentistry		4,234		3,797		3.53
Nursing, pharmacy, and health . .	1,424	1,804	1,196	1,610	2.99	2.98
Physical and earth sciences	2,529	2,913	2,068	2,431	3.08	3.21
Psychology.	1,251	2,282	1,166	1,881	2.91	3.28
Religion and theology		1,584		1,211		3.36
Social sciences.	1,610	2,124	1,371	1,745	3.00	3.20
Other	1,840	2,101	1,656	1,717	3.24	3.15

[1] Includes money wages and salary and net income from farm and nonfarm self-employment and all other income.

[2] Includes money wages or salary and net income from farm and nonfarm self-employment.

Note—Data are based on sample surveys of the civilian noninstitutional population. Data not shown where base is less than 200,000 persons.

Source: U.S. Department of Commerce, Bureau of the Census, *Current Population Reports*, Series P-70, No. 11, "Educational Background and Economic Status: Spring 1984." (This table was prepared October 1987.)

origination fee, service fee, or insurance charges up front.)

- Are there any restrictions?
- Can the lender terminate the loan, and under what conditions? Do you have to be notified before cancellation?
- Can you terminate the loan before the contract is up? How much notice must you give the lender? Are there any prepayment penalties, such as additional costs for paying the loan off early?
- Does the loan agreement contain a "balloon clause"—one payment, usually larger than the rest, that is tacked onto the end of the contract? (Sometimes borrowers can't afford to pay this larger sum when the time comes and must get their loans refinanced.)
- Does the contract include a clause allowing wage assignments or garnisheeing? Such a clause allows the lender to ask your employer to take out a specified sum from your monthly earnings and send it to the lender if you default on your loan for any reason, and without any legal procedure. Most banks have eliminated such clauses from their loan contracts, and you should avoid any contract with such a clause.

- What kind of repayment options does the lender offer? Can you count on graduated repayment and/or consolidation options later on?
- Have you borrowed other loans from this lender already? If you plan to borrow under the Stafford Student Loan Program for each of your years in school, it makes sense to borrow from a single lender. That will make it easier for you to manage your obligations when you go into repayment, as well as to request consolidation if you decide you want it.

Before you sign any contract or promissory note, make sure you understand what it is all about. If something is unclear, don't be embarrassed to ask for an explanation. You have the right to seek outside counsel and advice before entering into any binding legal agreement.

Questions and answers about credit where credit is due

Q Our family didn't qualify for need-based aid. Is any help available?

A A PLUS Loan is a possibility, because you don't have to demonstrate financial need. A PLUS Loan is a government-sponsored loan for *parents* of dependent students. Parents at all income levels may apply; these are "signature loans" that require no collateral. You may borrow from any lender approved by the U.S. Department of Education.

If you are creditworthy, you may also be able to qualify for a privately insured supplemental loan. These programs take many forms, from lines of credit and tuition budgeting plans to more conventional installment loans for students and/or parents. (See Chapter 4 for some examples, or ask your financial aid office for suggestions.)

Q My child is taking out a Stafford Loan. May I take out a PLUS Loan, too?

A Yes. In many families, both students and parents help to pay for college. Your child is legally responsible for Stafford Loan repayment, and you are legally responsible for PLUS repayment. (You may also borrow under a supplemental loan program, if you are creditworthy.) In some loan programs, both the student and the parent(s) are actually co-signatories on the loan, and legally share the obligation for repayment.

Q How much should I borrow?

A Ask yourself two questions: How much do I really need, and how much can I eventually repay?

Be realistic. Borrowing more than you need is risky. It could make repayment unnecessarily difficult, or even reduce your future borrowing capacity when you might genuinely need more money.

Borrowing less than you need and jeopardizing your enrollment is also risky. Remember that you will probably be in a better position to repay loans and

assume other financial obligations if you've secured your degree.

Estimating how much debt you can manage becomes more critical each time you borrow. Take into account amounts you've already borrowed, how much more you'll need to complete your education (including graduate or professional school, if that's in your plans), your estimated monthly payments, and starting salaries for the kinds of jobs you're likely to get. (If you're a *parent*, and you're thinking about a PLUS Loan or a privately sponsored supplemental loan, you may want to consider how much you've already borrowed for education as well as for other purposes, how much more you're likely to need to educate other children, other family needs and goals, your current salary and your prospects over the next several years, and how much debt you can handle for a sustained period.)

Q Can I borrow more than once, or from more than one program?

A Yes, many students borrow under the Stafford Loan Program for each year in school; many also borrow from other loan programs.

Keep in mind, though, that each time you borrow from a new loan program, you create a new repayment obligation. Unless you eventually consolidate your loans, you may have separate minimum monthly payments to make on *each* loan program.

Q What is consolidation?

A Once you've entered your grace period or actually started repayment, you may be able to combine your Stafford Loans and most other government-sponsored student loans into one debt. The result is a single monthly payment for the consolidated debt, which is smaller than the total of the separate monthly payments, at least in the initial years. You generally get more time to pay off the consolidated debt, but you'll also pay more in interest.

Investigate consolidation options before you borrow. The option is not available with all lenders.

8. Pulling it all together

Most of this book has been about how you interact with other people and agencies and institutions in the process of planning to pay for college. (That's partly because most of this book has been about getting other people's help for meeting college costs!) You have read about *guidelines*—for estimating costs, for demonstrating need, for determining eligibility. You've learned about *questions* you'll be asked—questions about your income and your assets, your hopes, and your needs. You've heard about *decisions*—how colleges, the federal government, state student assistance agencies, and private scholarship programs make them.

In the end it comes down to the student and his or her family. There are a lot of people who will help you to pull together a personal financing strategy, get financial aid, or offer you advice. But advice is cheap—college isn't. At some point in the process (the earlier the better), you need to develop your own guidelines, ask yourself some questions, and make some personal decisions.

Understanding financial aid awards

Elsewhere in this chapter you'll see a sample financial aid award letter. In mid-spring of your senior year of high school, you will begin to receive notices from financial aid administrators at the colleges to which you applied. Most selective institutions tell you about their admissions and aid decisions at the same time, often around April 15. Other institutions may have a "rolling" admissions schedule—that is, they make admissions decisions as soon as applications are complete—and use either a rolling or a fixed schedule for telling admitted students about their financial aid awards.

Sometimes financial aid administrators will not know exactly how much money is available in the aggregate to help their applicants; uncertainty about state or federal student aid appropriations, for example, can make estimating difficult. Many colleges issue tentative or preliminary award notices in the spring, which are subsequently confirmed in the summer when more information becomes available. In such a circumstance, a college will try to meet its original commitment to a student, but if government funds are reduced, the college may have to adjust the original award offer. The colleges find this process just as frustrating as do families, but in a time of uncertainty, it may simply be unavoidable.

Comparing award offers

If you are considering more than one college, you may want to compare the financial aid awards offered by the colleges. Resist the temptation to look only at the amount of the awards! College A may offer you $1,500 and College B may offer you $3,000. You need to look at the total student expense budgets at College A and College B before you can determine which award comes closer to meeting your need. The smaller award from College A may be all the extra help you need to attend, while the award from College B may not be enough to bridge the gap.

Here are some points to consider in comparing financial aid awards:

- What is the budget that the college used in determining your award offer? Does it coincide with your estimated budget for that college?
- What is the amount determined by the college that you and your family can be expected to pay toward college costs?
- How much of your need is met at each college—costs minus family contribution?
- What portion of each financial aid package is made up of gift aid (scholarships and grants) and

what portion consists of self-help aid (loan and work)?

- Which college would you most like to attend from an educational standpoint? From a financial standpoint, is this college also your best choice? If not, is the aid offered sufficient to permit you to attend?

Accepting a financial aid award

After you have received award letters from the colleges to which you applied and have compared the offers, accept the award at the college you choose by signing the award letter. Complete and return any additional forms that were sent with the award letter. Also notify the other colleges that you are declining their aid offers, so that the funds can be distributed to other students.

If you have any questions about your award, contact the financial aid office at the college. Sometimes revisions in the composition of your award package are possible. For example, you may be able to shift a loan to a work opportunity. You are usually not required to accept the entire financial aid package as offered. If you decide not to accept a part of your aid offer, it may not be possible for the financial aid office to restore that aid later, should you change your mind.

Particularly in a time of declining resources, you should understand that if you need financial aid to meet college costs, you will almost certainly have to accept some of that aid in the form of self-help aid— that is, loans and/or jobs—during the course of your education. Many colleges gradually increase the self-help portion of a student's financial aid package over the four years he or she is enrolled, so you cannot necessarily expect the same package every year, even if your need is the same. For instance, some colleges try to minimize the College Work-Study awards offered to freshmen so that they can devote more time to studying and adjusting to college life, but colleges that do this may replace some of the grant aid in the freshman packages with jobs in subsequent years.

Appealing your award package

If you believe that your financial aid package is insufficient to meet your needs, you may want to contact the financial aid office at the college. Inquire about how your expense budget was put together and how your family contribution and financial need were determined. If there are special circumstances that you think have been overlooked, bring these to the aid administrator's attention. It may be that the aid administrator can take your particular situation into account and adjust your award offer.

After visiting with the aid administrator, if you still feel that you have unmet needs or that you have been treated unfairly, you may want to consider appealing your award. Some colleges have a formal administrative procedure with a review board to hear your appeal. Others have a much less formal process: usually the award decision is reviewed by the aid administrator's superior to see that institutional policies have been followed. Contact the financial aid office to find out what the appeal procedures are, and follow them.

Understand, though, that a college's inability to meet your full need probably reflects nothing more than insufficient funds. There has never been enough aid to fully meet the needs of all the students who could use some extra help, and when this book was written, resources were shrinking, not expanding. You have a right to a full explanation of a college's policies and practices with regard to determining need, eligibility, and priorities for distribution of funds, and a college will probably be happy to provide you with this information. The answers to your questions will not necessarily provide the answers to your financial problems. (You may want to review Chapter 4 for some ideas on getting the most mileage out of your own resources.)

Private scholarships and your aid award package

Thousands of organizations other than colleges and universities and state and federal governments provide scholarships to thousands of students every year. The way that these outside awards "fit" into a financial aid package can sometimes cause confusion—or even bad feelings—among recipients *and* donors. Often students receive outside scholarships *after* they have already received notification about colleges' financial aid awards. If a student's package was designed to meet fully demonstrated financial need, as discussed earlier in this book, then the college *must* make adjustments in the original award to comply with federal regulations that prohibit recipients of federal aid from getting *more* money than they need. Even if their original awards from colleges did not fully meet their demonstrated need, outside scholarship winners sometimes find that their packages are nonetheless reduced; this might occur because the colleges have a policy of reducing packages to maximize limited resources.

Sample financial aid award statement

Drew University
Madison, New Jersey 07940
201/408-3112

FINANCIAL AID AWARD NOTICE

DATE	AWARD PERIOD	STUDENT I.D. NUMBER
04/01/91	1991-1992	123-45-6789

INSTRUCTIONS ▶ PLEASE SIGN & RETURN BY: May 1, 1991

College of Liberal Arts
Financial aid is based on:
Full time enrollment

12	12	credit hours minimum
Fall	Spring	JAN/SU

Total Cost of Attendance	-	Your Total Family Contribution	=	Your Financial Need
$23,092	-	$3,201	=	$19,891

CHECK BELOW ACCEPT REJECT	TYPE OF AID			
	DREW COLLEGE SCHOLARSHIP	$6500.00	$6500.00	$13000.00
	NEW JERSEY STATE TUITION ASSISTANCE GRANT	$1240.00	$1240.00	$ 2480.00
	STATE DISTINGUISHED SCHOLARSHIP	$ 500.00	$ 500.00	$ 1000.00
	will be credited to account:	$8240.00	$8240.00	$16480.00
	COLLEGE WORK-STUDY ELIGIBILITY	$ 650.00	$ 650.00	$ 1300.00
	STAFFORD LOAN (FORMERLY GSL)	$1055.50	$1055.50	$ 2111.00
	TOTAL FINANCIAL AID	$9445.50	$9445.50	$19891.00

DESCRIPTION OF AID

Your State Grant is pending. The State Grant will not be credited to your account until we are notified by the State that it is approved.

The Work Study Program is subsidized by the Federal government and administered by the University. If you choose to accept the work study award, complete and return the enclosed employment form with this signed award notification.

The Stafford Loan is a federally insured loan program at attractive interest rates. You should contact a bank or lending institution in your home area to obtain an application and additional program details. Priority deadline for receipt of loan applications is August 1.

Please see reverse side for terms and conditions of financial aid and explanation of your award notice.

A few years ago, the New England Regional Office of the College Board asked an advisory committee of college financial aid administrators, high school guidance counselors, and foundation personnel to look at some of the problems that were occurring in that particular region of the country. The advisory committee discovered wide differences in colleges' policies regarding financial aid packaging, the percentage of demonstrated financial need met, and how outside awards were treated—a diversity repeated across the country. The committee helped create a pamphlet addressed to high school students who were applying for or had received outside scholarship assistance. Here is some of the good advice included in that pamphlet:

> Organizations other than colleges, universities, and state and federal governments routinely award scholarships to worthy students to help them pay college expenses. These "outside" scholarships come from various sources including business and industry, church and civic organizations, unions, local scholarship boards, or school-related groups. Such scholarships vary in value anywhere from one hundred to several thousand dollars and are often renewable. Students fortunate enough to be awarded both an outside scholarship and financial aid from a university, college, or government source may encounter reductions of or revisions to their institutional aid because of the outside scholarships. And, if federal funds are involved, federal regulations forbid over-awards, thereby requiring institutional adjustments in cases where a student's full need has been met by an institution before knowledge of an outside scholarship. A review of the institution's policy in advance can prevent disappointment or surprise about the nature of the reduction.

Q. *If I receive financial aid from the college I'm planning to attend, and then I am awarded a scholarship from a civic group or business organization, how do I know if the college will change its financial aid award?*

A. The only way to be sure if your financial aid award will be adjusted is to check the policy of the institution you plan to attend. The financial aid officer at the college or university is your best source of information. A quick review of the institution's financial aid materials might also provide the answers. Remember, policies differ

greatly from one institution to another. What may be true for your classmate's college may not be true for yours.

Q. *Is it true that my institutional financial aid can be reduced by as much as the full amount of any outside scholarship I receive? That seems really unfair.*

A. The answer depends primarily on whether or not your institution has already met your financial need (as measured by the institution). The answer: probably yes if your need has been met; probably no if your need has not been met.

Q. *What if I decide to avoid all this and don't report an outside scholarship to my college?*

A. That's a bad idea. Institutional policies and state and federal regulations require that, if you are a candidate for financial aid, you must report your outside scholarships to the financial aid office of the institution you're planning to attend. Remember, the information you and your parents provide about your financial situation and your outside scholarships must be complete and accurate. If it is not, you risk losing your entire financial aid package.

So what happens if a student's need has already been fully met and he or she receives an outside scholarship? The advisory committee noted that different colleges have different ways of handling the situation. Some reduce the gift aid (grants or scholarships) in the institutional offer by the same amount as the outside award. Others reduce the self-help (work and/or loan) portion of the package, while still others adjust both the gift and the self-help portions. If a student's need has *not* been fully met, however, the committee noted that many colleges would apply the amount of the outside award against the student's remaining unmet need, and not reduce the aid packages until the student's need was fully met.

The advisory committee noted that students were still better off receiving outside scholarships even if their institutional awards were reduced, simply because "only a small number of New England institutions will reduce your institutional gift aid by the full value of your outside scholarship," a situation that holds true in most areas of the country. Investigating institutional policies in advance is certainly advisable, as the committee recommended, and high school counselors and college financial aid administrators continue to be good sources of information and advice on this subject.

Your rights and responsibilities

Education or training after high school requires an investment of time, money, and energy. Some people think of students as consumers, and feel that students, like other consumers, have both rights and responsibilities. The federal government has outlined a series of rights and responsibilities that you may want to keep in mind as you develop a personal financial plan and pursue financial aid opportunities.

Student rights

You have a right to receive the following information from a college:

- what financial aid is available, including information about federal, state, and institutional programs
- what the deadlines are for applying for each kind of aid
- what the cost of attendance is, and what the refund policies are if you withdraw
- what criteria the college uses to select aid recipients
- how the college determines your financial need, including how student expenses are figured in your budget
- what resources, such as parents' contribution, other financial aid and benefits, assets, etc., are considered in determining your need
- how much of your financial need has been met
- what aid resources make up your financial package
- what part of the aid received must be repaid and what part is grant aid
- if you receive a student loan, what the interest rate is, what the total amount is that must be repaid, what the procedures are for paying back the loan, how long you have to repay, and when repayment is to begin
- what the procedures are for appealing a financial aid decision if you feel you have been treated unfairly
- how the college determines whether or not you are making satisfactory academic progress, and what happens if you are not.

Student responsibilities

You have a responsibility to:

- review and consider all information about a college's program before you enroll
- pay special attention to your application for student financial aid, including completing it accurately and submitting it on time to the right place. (Errors can delay your getting aid, and intentional misreporting of information is a violation of law subject to penalties under the United States Criminal Code.)
- return all additional documentation, verification, corrections, and/or new information requested either by the financial aid administrator or the agency to which you submitted your application, read and understand all forms that you are asked to sign and keep copies of them, accept responsibility for all agreements signed by you
- if you receive a loan, notify the lender of any change in your name, address, or school status
- if you are assigned student employment, perform in a satisfactory manner the work that is agreed upon in accepting the aid
- know and comply with the deadlines for applying and for reapplying for aid
- know and comply with your college's refund policies and procedures.

Questions and answers about pulling it all together

Q If I accept a college's financial aid offer, how can I be sure of getting the same amount of money next year? How do I renew my award?

A The terms and conditions of your award will be spelled out in your award letter and/or accompanying literature from the aid office. Review this information carefully to make sure you understand exactly what you have to do to maintain your eligibility.

For several reasons, you may not receive exactly the same financial aid package next year. Your parents' income could go up (or down), or the college's tuition and room and board charges could increase. The college may have more or fewer aid dollars to distribute, or government funding could increase or decrease. Factors like these could influence the amount for which you qualify.

It's also possible that the *contents* of your financial aid package may change somewhat, even if its overall value stays approximately the same. Some colleges don't like to give first-year students too much work-study, for example, lest jobs distract them from academics in the critical first year. Others try to minimize loans until students have demonstrated their persistence by successfully completing a year or two.

The important thing to remember is that the financial aid office is there to *help* you. The staff are as anxious to see you make it—academically and financially—as you are. If you're worried about getting help for future years, or have any questions at all about what your package means or what you need to do to maintain your eligibility, call the aid office and *ask*.

Q I decided really late in the school year that I want to go to college in the fall. Is there any chance that I can still get some financial aid?

A It's possible, but you'll have to act quickly!

If you've already initiated the *admissions* application process, call the aid office to find out what you need to do to apply for assistance. If you haven't taken any action whatsoever yet, call the admissions office and explain that you need information about applying for admissions and financial aid.

If you are eligible for a Pell Grant and/or a Stafford Student Loan, you can still apply. However, you are likely to find that you've missed the deadline for state aid, college scholarships, and other programs administered by the college, like Work-Study. (You *may* be able to get consideration for some of these during the second semester.)

Q My parents say they just can't (or won't) come up with the amount of the expected contribution, and the aid offer from the college I like best just doesn't go far enough. What should I do?

A You can call or write the aid office to explain your situation and see if the staff have any suggestions. Some colleges have installment payment programs or tuition budgeting plans that might make it easier for your parents to finance their contribution. You could also investigate PLUS Loans (for parents) or one of the privately sponsored supplemental loan programs.

If you truly have extenuating circumstances that affect your family's ability to contribute to your educational expenses, the aid office *may* be willing to reconsider your application. Just keep in mind that an aid administrator is likely to be more interested in factors that influence your family's *ability* to pay, not its *willingness* to do so.

It's not always easy—for the aid administrator or the family—to tell the difference between ability and willingness. Another child with exceptional needs or continuing medical expenses, or a parent who's lost a job, affect ability. Not wanting to "spend down" a child's educational trust fund, or wanting more grants in order to avoid borrowing, may reflect more on willingness than on ability. Be prepared to answer some questions.

Q I didn't get nearly as much aid as I needed to attend the college I like best. What now?

A You still have options. Find out if your preferred college will defer your enrollment for a year, giving you time to earn some money. Or consider enrolling in a less expensive college for a year or two, and transferring to your preferred college later on.

You could also go to college part-time while you work. Look for an employer that offers tuition payment or reimbursement as a fringe benefit. (As a matter of fact, colleges and universities often give their staffs free or reduced tuition as a benefit of employment. The advantage is, you're already on campus.)

Financial aid checklist

❑ **Develop a list of colleges that interest you** and that seem to match your educational and career goals. You may want to use a comprehensive guide, such as *The College Handbook* or *Index of Majors*, to help you do this. Software packages like College Explorer can also help; see if it's available in your counselor's office, or obtain a copy to use at home.

❑ **Write to the admissions office** at each college on your list for an admissions application form. Remember also to inquire about financial aid opportunities and application procedures. It is best to do this early in the fall of your senior year of high school.

❑ **Make certain you know what need analysis form to file.** (The most commonly used form is the Financial Aid Form (FAF) of the College Scholarship Service.) You can usually get forms from your high school guidance office or a college financial aid office. The documents are generally first available in November, but they should not be filed until after January 1.

❑ **Mail your completed need analysis form as soon after January 1 as possible.** The form should be sent for processing at least four weeks before the earliest financial aid deadline set by the colleges or state scholarship or grant program to which you are applying (but no earlier than January 1). Carefully follow the instructions for filling out the form. Make sure your answers are complete and correct.

❑ **Apply for federal student financial aid.** You can use the FAF and other federally approved forms to apply for federal assistance programs simply by checking the appropriate box on the form. There is no extra fee for this service.

❑ **Apply for a state scholarship or grant.** In many states your need analysis form can also be used to apply for state aid. Your guidance counselor should know whether you can apply in this way or whether you must fill out additional application forms. Find this out well in advance and make certain you file the appropriate forms by the deadlines.

❑ **Supply additional information promptly.** If you or your parents receive requests for additional information about your need analysis form, respond promptly so that there will be no further delay in processing your request for aid.

❑ **Review the acknowledgment you get back.** After submitting your need analysis form, you will receive some type of acknowledgment from the processor. Make certain that all entries on the acknowledgment are correct.

❑ **Review your award letters carefully.** The director of financial aid at each college and scholarship program is responsible for determining a student's need, knowing which funds a student is eligible for, and making a decision about who will receive financial aid and how much. Once that decision is made, you will receive an award letter describing the contents of your financial aid package and outlining any conditions attached to the award.

❑ **Check to see if other financial aid application forms are required** by the colleges to which you are applying and find out the deadline dates for each. Complete these forms as early as possible.

❑ **Check with your guidance counselor, high school library, and public library** for books and pamphlets about other aid sources. Follow the directions for applying. You may qualify for a private scholarship, grant, or loan program because of your:

   academic achievement
   religious affiliation
   ethnic or racial heritage
   community activities
   hobbies or special interests
   organizational memberships
   artistic talents, athletic abilities, or
      other special skills
   career plans or proposed field of study

❑ **Find out if your parents' employers, professional associations, or labor unions** sponsor any aid programs.

❑ **Investigate community organizations and civic,** cultural, and fraternal groups to see if they sponsor scholarship programs at the local, state, or national level. Also check with local religious organizations, veterans' posts, businesses, and industries.

❑ **If you or either of your parents is a military veteran,** you may be eligible for special assistance. Contact the nearest office of the Veterans Administration for information.

❑ **Contact the Social Security Administration** to find out if you are eligible for education benefits from the Social Security Administration if either parent is deceased, disabled, or retired.

❑ **Ask about benefits from vocational rehabilitation or other social service agencies** if you think you qualify for assistance.

❑ **Pay close attention to award notices from state and federal student financial aid programs.** Forward a copy of your federal Student Aid Report to the colleges to which you are applying so that they can take this information into consideration in putting together a financial aid package for you.

❑ **Learn how the payments from each aid source will be made.** Generally, payment of financial aid awards is made at the time you actually enroll. Also find out if there are additional procedures you should be aware of or forms you must fill out in order to receive aid.

❑ **Explore alternatives.** Some colleges offer tuition and/or fee waivers to certain categories of students, such as adults, children of alumni, or family members enrolled simultaneously. If you qualify, you may want to take advantage of this type of discount. (See Part II of this book for lists of colleges that offer tuition and/or fee waivers.) Colleges that offer special tuition payment plans—installment, deferred, or credit card—or tuition discounts for prepayment also are listed in Part II of this book.

❑ **Educate yourself about loans.** Investigate all the options before you borrow, and make sure that you understand the interest rates, repayment requirements, and other terms and conditions for each loan program you're considering. Give yourself plenty of time—at least six weeks—before the start of the semester to have your loan application processed.

❑ **Make a decision about which college to attend on the basis of your education and career goals.** Remember to notify the college whose offer you are accepting and to communicate your decision to other colleges so that the financial aid they reserved for you can be freed for other applicants.

9. Long-range planning: A special message to parents

If your child will not be enrolling in college for several years, or if you have one enrolling now but others coming up. you have more time to plan. This chapter is written especially for you.

If you have not already done so, turn now to the tables in the next chapter showing average costs, or look up the average expenses for a few colleges with which you are familiar. And then think about this question:

When it is time to enroll in college, will you have enough ready cash to cover these expenses, in a single lump-sum payment, at the start of the semester?

Most people don't. Even what is generally regarded as the *least* expensive of the various educational options—living at home and commuting to a nearby community college—requires upwards of $4,600 a year. The budget for students living on campus now averages about $7,000 per year at an in-state public college or university and over $15,000 at a private one. And no one is sure how much higher the costs are going to go.

If your family saves little or no money before enrollment, it will be almost impossible to change your household budget fast enough or radically enough to pay for all your college expenses out of current income alone. People with low or fixed incomes don't have the extra money to spend. Even people with high incomes can't afford to divert large chunks of current income to make big payments once or twice a year. However, if you do the best you can for yourself, you may be able to get enough outside help to cover the difference between what you can afford and what college costs.

The purpose of planning

Remember that the purpose of financial planning to meet educational costs is twofold:

- to get as much mileage as you can out of your own resources, and
- to secure the additional outside help—the "financial aid"—you may need in order to make up the difference between what you can afford and what it costs to attend the college of your choice.

The two objectives are inseparable. The entire financing system for American postsecondary education is based on the assumption that you and your family have the *primary* responsibility for meeting college costs, to the extent of your ability.

You may wonder, Why should we use *our* resources at all if financial aid is available? Why not "plan" to have financial aid pay for it all?

The answer is that the bulk of financial aid awarded in the United States is, and always has been, based on "demonstrated need"; that is, it comes into play only after a family has done as much as it can reasonably be expected to do for itself, according to formulas that are applied to all aid applicants. Also, every dollar that you save in advance is probably one less that your child will have to borrow.

Some students come from families that have few or no resources to contribute toward college expenses. Others come from families that can easily foot the bill for even the most expensive educational options. But most students come from families that fall somewhere between the two extremes.

The Smiths and the Joneses

Imagine two families whose overall income pictures have been very similar over time and whose

The Smiths

Two parents, one working outside the home, older parent aged 45. Two children, one in junior high school, the other starting college in the fall. No unusual expenses; standard U.S. income tax deductions and exemptions

The Smiths have $20,000 in equity in their cooperative apartment. They also have accumulated $20,000 in savings toward their two children's education.

Income before taxes	$36,000
Total assets	40,000
Expected from parents	2,936
First-year costs	$6,500
− Expected from parents	2,936
= Demonstrated need	$3,564
First-year costs	$6,500
− Aid based on need	3,564
− Cash on hand	2,936
= Shortfall	$0

The Joneses

Two parents, one working outside the home, older parent aged 45. Two children, one in junior high school, the other starting college in the fall. No unusual expenses; standard U.S. income tax deductions and exemptions

The Joneses rent their apartment and thus have no home equity, nor do they have savings beyond a few hundred dollars in their checking account.

Income before taxes	$36,000
Total assets	0
Expected from parents	2,689
First-year costs	$6,500
− Expected from parents	2,689
= Demonstrated need	$3,811
First-year costs	$6,500
− Aid based on need	3,811
− Cash on hand	0
= Shortfall	$2,689

*Parental expectations are based on the Congressional Methodology formulas for the 1991-92 academic year. Values are approximate.

children are approximately the same age. The Smiths have been setting aside money on a regular basis for future educational expenses, while the Joneses have tended to spend almost all their disposable income as they've earned it.

It's obvious enough that when the time comes for their respective children to enroll in college, the Smiths will have more money on hand than the Joneses to put toward college costs. But won't the Jones family simply qualify for more financial aid?

Probably yes—but *it may not help them.* Here's why.

Assets, such as savings, *are* considered in the formulas for estimating what constitutes a family's fair share. A family with assets is assumed to be in a stronger financial position than a family without them.

Because the Smiths have more money in the bank, they have a greater ability to pay *now* than do the Joneses—an ability sometimes called liquidity. But their greater liquidity doesn't necessarily mean there's a big difference *over time* in the relative ability

of the Smiths and the Joneses to pay for education. The formulas try to account for both kinds of ability to pay, and use several factors as measures of capacity over time, including current income

When their children are ready to enroll, a little more will be expected of the Smiths than the Joneses, because they have saved, but as the figure illustrates, the similarity in their incomes would largely offset the difference in their assets. There would not be a large difference in what the financial aid system expects of the two families.

The difference is that the Smiths will *have* it—and the Joneses won't.

If the Joneses don't have on hand what the formulas assume they do, they may not have enough to cover their expenses, even *with* the aid. If they haven't *saved* what the system expects from them as a fair share, they will have to *borrow* it. If their capacity to borrow is already overextended, then they may have to choose a college solely on the basis of cost, rather than for educational reasons. In either case, their child will probably have to work more hours and/or borrow more money than would otherwise have been necessary.

The Smiths, on the other hand, will be in a much better position. As the example shows, they may even qualify for some aid, if their fair share falls short of the costs at the colleges they're considering. Because of the family's effort to save over time, their child will probably not have to work as many hours in part-time jobs or borrow as much under student loan programs. Above all, the Smiths will be able to make choices about college based primarily on long-term personal and educational goals, *not* on immediate financial limits.

How to plan

The *basics* are the same for long-range planning as for short-range planning, and have been described earlier in this book: educating yourself about college costs, estimating what you will be expected to pay toward those costs, developing a timetable, choosing strategies to get the most mileage out of your family resources, and finding out about financial aid programs.

The details of your plan to meet college costs will necessarily be very different from a family whose child will enroll within the next few months. If your children are still quite young, time is on your side—a big advantage. On the other hand, you also have the disadvantage of uncertainty about what circumstances will influence both college costs and your ability to pay between now and enrollment. However, you still can—and should—plan.

Setting realistic goals

Setting realistic goals is the first step. A goal is not a wish but a statement of purpose, a description of an objective to be achieved. It should be as concrete and specific as possible.

Reviewing Chapters 1 and 2 will help you:
- learn what college costs today, and
- estimate what share of those costs *you* would be expected to pay if your child were enrolling in the near future.

Once you have done so, you will have to make some *additional* assumptions about what college costs and family expectations will look like when it's time for your children to enroll.

No one is really sure what college will cost in 5 or 10 or 15 years, and the further into the future you look, the murkier becomes the crystal ball. In the short run, at least, the prices charged by institutions for tuition, room, and board are *not* likely to go down, because operating costs continue to rise. Although colleges and universities are working harder than ever to achieve economies in their operating budgets, higher education continues to be very labor intensive. That means that one of their largest continuing expenses is salaries and benefits for employees—faculty members, administrators, librarians, cafeteria and maintenance workers, health service and security personnel, etc.

Does that mean that the costs charged to students and parents will continue to rise at the same rate as they have in recent years? For the last several years, overall increases have averaged 6 to 7 percent, a somewhat slower rate of increase than the double-digit annual increases that characterized the early 1980s.

A family whose children will start college in the fall of 1992 will probably not be too far off in their estimates of total expense if they add 6 or 7 percent *per year* to the 1990-91 averages in Chapter 10. Beyond that, you will have to keep track of annual increases and revise your own projections.

Nor is anyone certain that the formulas for assessing a family's ability to contribute will remain stable over time. However, the basic *principles* embodied in the current methodology have been in place for over 30 years. The same kinds of factors will probably continue to be considered in evaluating a family's financial strength as are discussed in this chapter, although they may be treated or weighted differently. Expectations probably will not be *reduced* in the foreseeable future. On the contrary, more is likely to be expected of families.

If you are trying to make some ballpark estimate of what will be expected of you when the time comes, you might want to complete the worksheets in Chapter 10, estimating what you think your income, assets, etc., will be at the time of enrollment. Subtract that estimate from your estimate of future college costs. Alternately, use current figures for estimating both total costs and family share, and inflate the resulting goal statement by your assumption of annual inflation between now and the point of enrollment.

Update your assumptions and goals annually. Revise your estimates of probable future expenses by incorporating new data about actual college costs and periodic changes in the formulas for assessing family ability to contribute. Keep your eye on changes in other leading economic indicators, too.

Developing a timetable

Developing a realistic timetable is closely related to goal-setting. The amount of time—in months or years—that's left before your children *start* college is an important factor. It represents the period in which you can *save* money and *look* for extra outside help. However, your plans could also include assumptions about the periods of time *during and after* college in which you may *spend* money to repay loans. Developing a timetable also lets you translate big goals into more manageable terms. To save $1,200 in one year you have to put aside $100 a month or $25 a week or $3.50 a day—actually a little less, assuming your money earns some interest.

Review Chapter 3 to prove to yourself that time really *is* on your side. It demonstrates that the longer the time period over which you finance any purchase, the smaller its impact will be on your monthly budget. For most families, the hardest possible way to finance their fair share of college costs—whether that share is 5 percent or 100 percent—is by cramming it into their household budget during the four-year period of enrollment. Don't assume, however, that you can, or should, defer saving with the intention of relying on loans when your children are ready to enroll.

Under some economic conditions, borrowing is certainly a feasible and even sensible way of making major purchases, but planning to borrow may not be your wisest strategy. The farther into the future you look, the harder it is to be sure about credit availability, your borrowing capacity, the state of the economy, etc.

If you are fortunate enough to have many years before your children enter college and considerable discretionary income, consult your financial adviser for recommendations about various savings and investment strategies to achieve your goals for meeting college costs. A lot is going to be expected of you. Even if you don't have much to spare, plan to save as much as you can in advance. Regular, systematic savings—even of small amounts—add up, and compounding of interest multiples your money powerfully.

Strategies for paying your fair share

Deciding how to pay your fair share is the next step, once you've established goals and timetables. Review Chapter 4 for descriptions of many of the options that are available today. Some are used far in advance of enrollment to save money, while others are designed to make the burden more manageable at the time of enrollment. To keep education affordable, many colleges and universities have instituted new financing programs in the last several years.

Not every choice is appropriate for—or even available to—every student and family. But the earlier you start, the more choices you'll have, and the more time to investigate the potential benefits and risks.

The dilemma, of course, is that other concerns and expenses may push college savings to the back burner. In particular, you may not feel as though there's much to be saved at the end of the month, once the basic bills have been paid.

Financial planning to meet college costs *isn't* just for wealthy people. It's true that particular financial accounts or products may be appropriate for (or even available only to) families at higher income levels. But financial planning itself isn't a product. It's a *process*, a way of thinking about how to organize whatever resources you do have—including your own time and energy—to meet college costs. In fact, the fewer financial resources you have, the more you need to plan the most effective way of using those you do.

- If you can afford to invest several hundred dollars a month to cover future college costs, *do it*. You'll need every penny of the principal *and* interest when the time comes.

- If you can carve $50 or $75 a month out of your household budget to save toward future college costs, *do it*. You may not be able to finance the whole amount that way, but you'll be able to manage a good piece of it. If you cover your fair share, then financial aid may be available to cover the rest.

- If your best effort is only $2 or $5 a week, *do it*. Even a few dollars a week in the jar beside the kitchen sink is important, not just in a financial sense, but as a statement of faith in the future. The important thing is to make it *regularly*.

Evaluating savings and prepayment plans

Should you use one of the many new public and private plans that have recently been developed to help families engage in long-term saving for college costs? The answer will be different for each family, depending on its resources and its goals.

To help families assess the strengths and weaknesses of the different options, the College Board issued a set of guidelines, some of which are cited below.*

1. Is there a minimum contribution required to enter the program? Are incremental additions possible?

2. Is there a maximum annual amount that can be contributed? Will any such maximum restrict the accumulation below a realistic projection of future college costs?

3. Can anyone in the family, or an agent of the family, contribute to the plan? Are there exclusions?

4. Can the proceeds from the plan be transferred to another family member if educational plans change?

5. Are there eligibility restrictions to a particular class of institutions, either within a state or within an institutional sector, such as independent colleges? Are there penalties associated with these restrictions?

6. Is the yield from the plan guaranteed? How is it guaranteed? How is the family protected from investment deficits below college cost levels?

7. Is the plan insured? Can the investment be recovered if the plan sponsor ceases to exist?

8. Does the plan cover all college costs, or just tuition?

9. Are there any residency requirements for eligibility? What happens if the family moves during the plan years?

10. Are there age restrictions or time limits on use? Do proceeds from the plan have to be used within a certain number of years after high school?

11. How many years of study are covered by the proceeds? Undergraduate only? Is graduate study possible? Full-time only? Is part-time attendance possible?

12. Are there restrictions as to who might match funds contributed to the plan? Could an employer or state contribute?

13. What are the refund conditions in the event of a student's nonadmission to college, disability, or death?

14. Does the family benefit from any investment surplus over the necessary cost levels, or is that a profit to the sponsor?

15. Will the plan benefits be taxable, either for federal or state taxes? Will any tax accrue to the contributor, plan sponsor, or student?

Finding extra outside help

Will financial aid continue to be available to help families cover the gap between their best efforts and the costs of attendance? Probably, although its form may change over time. Federal funding of student assistance programs has not kept pace with rising costs in recent years, but Congress has consistently resisted proposals to reduce the level of federal support. Many colleges, states, and private organizations actually have increased their support of student aid programs.

There is not very much you can do in advance of your child's senior year in high school about finding financial aid, beyond educating yourself about it (and expressing your continuing support of it to your legislators). The vast majority of federal, state, and institutional programs do not permit you to apply before January 1 of the year in which your child will actually enroll in college.

Private scholarship programs constitute one exception to this general rule. Review the section on private aid sources in Chapter 5. Competition for some of these private awards begins in the junior year of high school, or even earlier. One of the things you *can* do in advance of your child's senior year is check out the terms, conditions, and application procedures of any private aid source for which you think he or she might be eligible.

A closing note

A college education *is* within the reach of every qualified student in the United States. Paying for it is hard—but planning for it makes the paying easier. If you do as much as you can for yourself, chances are you will find the extra outside help—the financial aid—you need to take care of the rest.

The other kind of planning you should do is academic. Watch what courses your children are taking in school, and make sure that they're on a college preparatory "track." This can save time and money in the future—the curricular choices that children make, as early as the seventh grade, can either open doors or close them.

The College Scholarship Service wishes you well in your planning, and looks forward to serving you when the time comes to apply for financial aid.

*The *College Board Review*, spring 1988, No. 147., p.11.

Questions and answers about planning

Q Isn't educational financial planning complicated?

A A little. Certainly some savings and investment programs can be pretty complicated! The more money you have, the more sophisticated are the options that may be open to you, and the more you may want to get professional advice.

The basic principles are simple. Dr. Karl E. Case, a professor of economics at Wellesley College who has done a lot of thinking about how families can prepare themselves to meet future educational expenses, cites three important ideas:

1. if you pay over more years, your payment is lower
2. if you decide to pay early, you will earn some interest on this investment
3. compound interest can yield surprisingly large gains (8% compounded annually doubles your money in nine years).*

Besides, educational financial planning isn't as complicated as figuring out how to pay for college when you *haven't* done any planning at all.

Q What is a "tuition futures" program? Should I join one for my child?

A At the time this book was written, tuition futures—sometimes also called tuition prepayment or guaranteed tuition plans—were provoking lots of discussion. The idea is that parents make *very* early payments to a college, when their children are still quite young. The college's investment program is intended to produce growth over time that will approximate the tuition anticipated at the time of the children's enrollment. The plans do not guarantee that the children will qualify for admission, nor is there any way of ensuring that the children will want to attend that particular institution when the time comes; if a child does not enroll, his or her parents would get a refund of their original investment (but not necessarily of the interest earned). Only a handful of colleges have actually implemented such programs.

Statewide variations on this idea are under consideration in many other state legislatures, although only Michigan has actually implemented a plan. Under the Michigan plan, parents would be able to "prepay" tuition at any of the state's public universities by investing in a state trust fund many years in advance; students who later choose to attend private or out-of-state colleges could receive an equivalent amount.

Other states are developing entirely different approaches, such as the College Savings Bond Program in Illinois that lets families purchase tax-exempt revenue bonds in small denominations and provides an interest subsidy if the proceeds are used for educational expenses at a college or university within the state.

United States Series EE Savings Bonds have been favored by some families for many years because they can be purchased in small increments (and acquired through payroll deductions in many cases). Now, thanks to 1988 legislation, the proceeds may be deductible when used by parents at lower income levels to pay their children's educational expenses.

Before you enroll in *any* savings or investment plan of this or any other type, make sure that you have all the facts. What will happen if your child is interested in colleges not covered by the plan, or decides not to go at all? How much of your investment and interest can you get back? Do you have to pay income tax on the earnings that accumulate in the plan? Can you make small multiple payments over time, or are you restricted to one lump-sum payment? What does the plan or product actually cover? How big is the administrative fee? What risks do you assume? How does one compare with another, especially in terms of both risks and benefits?

Q I've done some calculations, and I don't think we're going to be able to save our full share between now and the time of enrollment. Can we count on loans being available?

A Review Chapter 4 for some insight into the kinds of financing options available today. You'll note that most of the loan programs aimed at parents (as distinct from many of the student loan programs) require a credit check. So it's important that you not arrive at the point of enrollment with your borrowing capacity already exhausted.

Also, don't assume that installment payment plans are necessarily going to be available at all colleges; state laws may even prohibit them at some public institutions. (Remember that installment plans and budgeting plans typically carry some additional costs, too.)

---

*Case, Karl E. "The Office of Family Finance and Planning" (formerly "The Financial Aid Office") in *Educational Financial Planning: A New Concept for the Financial Aid Office*. Columbus, Ga: Southern Association of Student Financial Aid Administrators, 1986, page 34.

10. Tables, sample cases, and worksheets

The first table in this chapter provides average college costs for the 1990-91 academic year. These costs are based on information from all colleges that provided data for two consecutive years. Average tuition and fees are weighted by total undergraduate enrollment; room and board charges for resident students are weighted by the percentage of undergraduates living in college housing. Additional out-of-state tuition and fees are the mean charges reported by public institutions; they are not weighted by enrollment. (Private colleges rarely have additional nonresident tuition and fees.)

All other figures are average student expenses in each category. Average costs for books and supplies are weighted by total undergraduate enrollment; transportation and other expenses for resident students are weighted by the percentage of undergraduates living in college housing; and board, transportation, and other expenses for commuters are weighted by the percentage of undergraduates who commute.

This table is followed by sample expense budgets based on these average 1990-91 costs for resident students and commuters at different types of colleges.

By the time that *you* are ready to enroll in college, these costs will almost certainly be higher, but the patterns will probably be similar.

The table on estimated parents' contribution shows estimates used to determine how much parents would be expected to pay based on income and family size according to the 1991-92 Congressional Methodology. See Chapter 3 for a discussion of how you can use this in your early financial planning.

Sample cases and worksheets

Meet our three sample students—Andrea, Beth, and Carlos—whose family backgrounds, financial situations, and educational goals have been made up from many of the characteristics of students who are facing the choices of a college education and how to pay for it. Following them through the process of determining financial need and applying for aid may help you develop your own financial plan.

All three begin their planning by estimating on Worksheet 1 their probable expenses at the colleges that interest them. Andrea, Beth, and Carlos come from families with very different financial situations. Before they can tell how much they will be expected to pay toward these educational expenses, they need to evaluate their own circumstances in relation to the costs of attending the particular colleges they're interested in. You will see that Worksheets 2-5 have been completed to help in this process. Worksheet 6 is a record of financial aid they are offered.

You can use Worksheets 1-6 provided for your personal plan.

United States by region

New England
Middle States
West (also includes Alaska and Hawaii)
Midwest

Southwest
South

Average student expenses, 1990-91

	Tuition and fees	Add'l out-of-state tuition	Books and supplies	Resident			Commuter		
				Room and board	Trans-portation	Other costs	Board only	Trans-portation	Other costs
National									
2-year public	884	2,076	452				1,520	857	941
2-year private	5,003		436	3,481	472	864	1,280	691	804
4-year public	1,809	2,948	464	3,161	456	1,101	1,459	776	1,086
4-year private	9,391		479	4,153	432	863	1,610	757	938
New England									
2-year public	1,356	2,329	453				1,671	1,051	904
2-year private	7,643		407	4,812	390	593	1,534	647	754
4-year public	2,550	3,276	489	3,654	294	1,030	1,575	926	1,092
4-year private	12,313		486	5,104	333	793	1,605	784	822
Middle States									
2-year public	1,403	2,070	437				1,441	822	784
2-year private	6,440		441	3,970	426	1,034	1,739	653	1,039
4-year public	2,081	2,762	485	3,728	398	958	1,483	659	989
4-year private	9,967		471	4,658	327	825	1,678	685	882
South									
2-year public	712	1,665	464				1,604	1,021	971
2-year private	4,571		445	3,068	474	947	1,496	803	916
4-year public	1,804	2,549	474	2,828	489	940	1,579	941	948
4-year private	7,856		457	3,534	573	850	1,465	774	866
Midwest									
2-year public	1,201	2,265	440				1,546	889	989
2-year private	4,360		466	2,644	455	842	1,237	724	830
4-year public	2,132	2,742	422	2,860	394	1,164	1,355	737	1,121
4-year private	8,800		469	3,447	442	833	1,701	832	1,031
Southwest									
2-year public	599	1,183	436				1,363*	835	849
2-year private	2,904		445	2,796	911*	1,416*	—	985*	1,070*
4-year public	1,176	2,619	462	2,833	654	1,092	1,349	881	1,015
4-year private	6,528		464	3,298	599	989	1,460	887	1,036
West									
2-year public	405	2,666	468				1,474*	691	1,003
2-year private	2,662		418	—	692	602	—	672	533
4-year public	1,398	4,151	497	3,794	533	1,370	1,493	682	1,224
4-year private	9,028		553	4,539	521	1,140	1,525	714	1,037

Sample expense budgets

	Resident	Commuter
2-year public		$4,654
2-year private	$10,256	8,214
4-year public	6,991	5,594
4-year private	15,318	13,175

Note on the table: Calculations are enrollment-weighted and utilize only those institutions for whom two consecutive years' worth of price and enrollment data are available. Institutions do not necessarily provide cost data in all fields. A dash (—) indicates that the number of institutions reporting data on this item was too small to support an analysis. A blank indicates that the data are not generally applicable for the type of institution. An asterisk (*) following an average indicates that while the number of institutions reporting data on this item was large enough to support an analysis, the sample size was marginal.

1991-92 Estimated Parents' Contribution

Net assets	$20,000				$40,000			
Family size	3	4	5	6	3	4	5	6
1990 income before taxes:								
$12,000	$ 0	$ 0	$ 0	$ 0	$ 0	$ 0	$ 0	$ 0
16,000	0	0	0	0	317	0	0	0
20,000	628	41	0	0	928	370	0	0
24,000	1,271	684	134	0	1,538	981	459	0
28,000	1,914	1,327	777	156	2,180	1,591	1,069	479
32,000	2,673	1,977	1,420	798	2,939	2,240	1,679	1,089
36,000	3,592	2,747	2,083	1,441	3,855	3,009	2,341	1,699
40,000	4,686	3,679	2,869	2,107	5,005	3,951	3,130	2,364
44,000	5,982	4,792	3,823	2,897	6,309	5,119	4,112	3,161
48,000	7,044	5,979	4,981	3,856	7,371	6,306	5,308	4,149
52,000	8,161	7,096	6,106	4,971	8,488	7,423	6,433	5,298
56,000	9,364	8,299	7,309	6,174	9,691	8,626	7,636	6,501
60,000	10,567	9,502	8,513	7,377	10,895	9,830	8,840	7,704
64,000	11,771	10,706	9,716	8,580	12,098	11,033	10,043	8,907

Net assets	$60,000				$80,000			
Family size	3	4	5	6	3	4	5	6
1990 income before taxes:								
$12,000	$ 235	$ 0	$ 0	$ 0	$ 763	$ 151	$ 0	$ 0
16,000	845	288	0	0	1,373	816	294	0
20,000	1,456	898	376	0	1,993	1,426	904	314
24,000	2,087	1,509	987	397	2,722	2,053	1,515	925
28,000	2,831	2,147	1,597	1,007	3,600	2,792	2,154	1,535
32,000	3,727	2,901	2,247	1,617	4,665	3,682	2,909	2,177
36,000	4,830	3,809	3,017	2,270	5,958	4,767	3,818	2,935
40,000	6,133	4,943	3,962	3,044	7,261	6,071	4,956	3,849
44,000	7,437	6,247	5,132	3,999	8,565	7,375	6,260	4,999
48,000	8,499	7,434	6,436	5,175	9,627	8,562	7,564	6,303
52,000	9,616	8,551	7,561	6,426	10,744	9,679	8,689	7,554
56,000	10,819	9,754	8,764	7,629	11,947	10,882	9,892	8,757
60,000	12,023	10,958	9,968	8,832	13,151	12,086	11,096	9,960
64,000	13,226	12,161	11,171	10,035	14,354	13,289	12,299	11,163

NOTE: The figures shown are estimated parents' contributions, assuming the older parent (age 45) is employed; the other parent is not employed; income only from employment; no unusual circumstances; standard deductions on U.S. income tax; and one undergraduate family member in college.

Andrea, Beth, and Carlos plan for college costs

Worksheet 1: Estimating student expenses

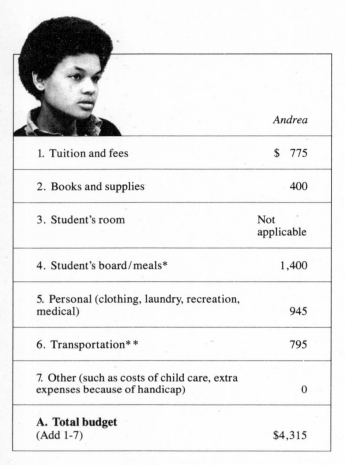

	Andrea
1. Tuition and fees	$ 775
2. Books and supplies	400
3. Student's room	Not applicable
4. Student's board/meals*	1,400
5. Personal (clothing, laundry, recreation, medical)	945
6. Transportation**	795
7. Other (such as costs of child care, extra expenses because of handicap)	0
A. Total budget (Add 1-7)	$4,315

* You will want to consider these expenses to your family if you live at home.

** If you are planning to live on campus, estimate the costs of the round trips you will have to make to your home. Colleges usually estimate a student makes two or three round trips during the year. Students living at home should figure the costs of daily transportation to college.

Andrea Daley, age 18, graduated from high school in June 1991. She planned to live with her family and attend a nearby community college to pursue an Associate of Arts degree in chemistry. She hopes to transfer to a four-year college of engineering when she completes her AA and hopes eventually to become a chemical engineer.

Andrea's father, age 47, earns $16,500 a year as an insurance claims representative; her mother, age 45, earns $8,700 a year as a beautician in a local salon. Her younger brother, age 16, is a sophomore in high school and also hopes to attend college some day. The Daleys have $25,480 equity in their home and $4,950 in a savings account, but no other assets. Andrea earned $700 in 1990 from an after-school job, and has a small savings account of $1,544 into which she's been depositing babysitting earnings and gifts for several years. This year they had unusually high unreimbursed medical and dental expenses of $1,420 because Andrea's brother broke his leg in a soccer game and Mrs. Daley had to have root canal therapy. Even though Andrea planned to live at home with her family and the tuition at the local community college is comparatively low, Andrea and her family worried about how much they could pay toward college.

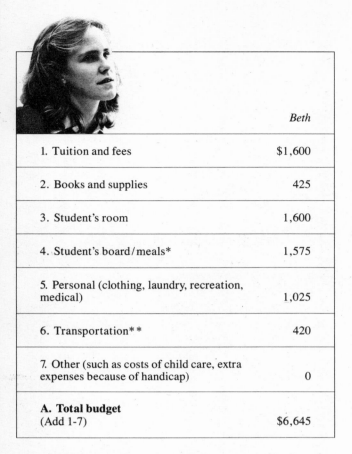

	Beth
1. Tuition and fees	$1,600
2. Books and supplies	425
3. Student's room	1,600
4. Student's board/meals*	1,575
5. Personal (clothing, laundry, recreation, medical)	1,025
6. Transportation**	420
7. Other (such as costs of child care, extra expenses because of handicap)	0
A. Total budget (Add 1-7)	$6,645

* You will want to consider these expenses to your family if you live at home.

** If you are planning to live on campus, estimate the costs of the round trips you will have to make to your home. Colleges usually estimate a student makes two or three round trips during the year. Students living at home should figure the costs of daily transportation to college.

Beth Edwards *is 17 and graduated from high school in June 1991. She hoped to attend the state university to study journalism and planned to live on campus.*

Beth's family was saving hard to make her college plans possible, But two years ago, her father, age 43, died in an automobile accident. Her mother, age 42, does not work outside the home but is kept pretty busy caring for Beth's active 6-year-old sister. The family receives social security benefits (which will be reduced when Beth starts college), but has no other income beyond Beth's part-time and summer employment, which brought in $3,000 last year. The Edwards have $29,225 equity in their home and $7,950 in savings (the remains of the life insurance death benefit). Beth and her mother worried about how much they could pay toward college costs.

	Carlos
1. Tuition and fees	$8,700
2. Books and supplies	430
3. Student's room	1,975
4. Student's board/meals*	1,960
5. Personal (clothing, laundry, recreation, medical)	805
6. Transportation**	410
7. Other (such as costs of child care, extra expenses because of handicap)	0
A. Total budget (Add 1-7)	$14,280

* You will want to consider these expenses to your family if you live at home.

** If you are planning to live on campus, estimate the costs of the round trips you will have to make to your home. Colleges usually estimate a student makes two or three round trips during the year. Students living at home should figure the costs of daily transportation to college.

Carlos Fernandez *is 18 and graduated from high school in June 1991. He hoped to attend a private college to pursue premedical studies; he planned to live on campus.*

Carlos' father, age 57, earns $35,100 annually as a partner in a dry cleaning business; his mother, age 45, does not work outside the home. Carlos has an older brother already in college and a younger sister who plans to go when she completes high school. The Fernandez family has quite a few assets, including $51,700 equity in their home, and $3,100 in the bank. Mr. Fernandez's share of the dry cleaning business is valued at $100,000 and he owes $26,600 on it, for a net worth of $73,400. But living expenses for the five family members are high, and Mr. Fernandez is fast approaching retirement age. The family incurred $2,306 in unreimbursed medical expenses this year, for instance. By the time he graduated from high school, Carlos had already secured two small local scholarships to help meet his first-year expenses. He had also been working part-time for two years and had already saved $1,143. The costs of attending a private college in another state would be high, and the Fernandez family worried about how much they could pay toward college costs.

Worksheet 2: Parents' expected contribution

	Andrea	Beth*	Carlos
A. 1990 income:			
1. Father's yearly wages, salaries, tips, and other compensation	$16,500	$ 0	$35,100
2. Mother's yearly wages, salaries, tips, and other compensation	8,700	0	0
3. All other income of mother and father (dividends, interest, social security, pensions, welfare, child support, etc. *Include IRA/Keogh payments and 401(K) and 403(B) contributions.*)	400	13,800	3,025
4. IRS allowable adjustments to income (business expenses, interest penalties, alimony *paid*, etc.) *Do not include IRA/Keogh payments.*	200	0	0
B. Total income (Add 1, 2, 3 and subtract 4.)	25,400	13,800	38,125
Expenses:			
5. U.S. income tax parents expect to pay on their 1990 income (not amount withheld from paycheck)	1,763	0	3,364
6. Social Security (FICA) tax (7.65% times each salary to a maximum of $3,856 each)	1,928	0	2,685
7. State and other taxes (Enter 8% of B.)	2,032	1,104	3,050
8. Medical and dental expenses not covered by insurance (include insurance premiums) in excess of 5% of B	150	0	400
9. Elementary and secondary school tuition paid for other dependents to a maximum of $4,243 per child.	0	0	1,150
10. Employment allowance. If 2-parent family and both parents work, allow 35% of lower salary to a maximum of $2,300; if 1-parent family, allow 35% of salary to a maximum of $2,300. No allowance for a 2-parent family in which only 1 parent works.	2,300	0	0
11. Standard maintenance allowance (See Table for 11.)	14,930	12,090	15,960
C. Total allowances against income (Add 5, 6, 7, 8, 9, 10, 11.)	23,103	13,194	26,609
D. Available income (Subtract C from B.)	2,297	606	11,516
Assets:			
12. Home equity (total estimated value of your home on the current market minus any unpaid balance on your mortgage)	25,480	29,225	51,700
13. Other real estate equity (value minus unpaid balance on mortgage)	0	0	0
14. Business or farm (Figure total value minus indebtedness and then take percentage shown in table.) If your family is only part owner of the farm or business, list only your share of the net value.	0	0	29,700
15. Cash, savings, and checking accounts	4,950	7,950	3,100
16. Other investments (current net value)	0	0	0
E. Total assets (Add 12, 13, 14, 15, 16.)	30,430	37,175	84,500
Deductions:			
F. Asset protection allowance (See Table for F.)	35,900	23,600	47,900
G. Remaining assets (Subtract F from E.)	–5,470	13,575	36,600
H. Income supplement from assets (Multiply G by 12% if G is $0 or more. If G is negative, use conversion percentage from Table for H.)	–274	1,629	4,392
I. Adjusted available income (Add D and H.)	2,023	2,235	15,908
J. Parents' expected contribution (Multiply I by taxation rate amount given in Table for J.)	$ 445	$ 492	4,093
K. Parents' expected contribution if more than one family member is in college (Divide J by number of family members in college at least half-time.)	—	—	$ 2,047

*Federal need analysis provisions provide a "simple needs test" treatment for families with total Adjusted Gross Income or earned income of $15,000 or less, who file the 1040A or 1040EZ federal income tax return, or do not file taxes. Therefore, if neither Beth nor her parent filed a Form 1040 federal tax return, family assets would not be considered in the "simple needs test," and only Available income ($606 shown in line D) would be used to compute a $121 expected contribution for line J.

Tables used for completion of Worksheet 2

Table for standard maintenance allowance (Item 11)

Family size (including student)	Number in college				
	1	2	3	4	5
2	$ 9,700	$ 8,050			
3	12,090	10,430	$ 8,700		
4	14,930	13,270	11,610	$ 9,960	
5	17,610	15,960	14,300	12,650	$ 9,630
6	20,600	18,940	17,290	15,630	13,980

For each additional family member, add $2,330.
For each additional college student, subtract $1,660.

Table for income supplement from assets when G is negative (When G is $0 or more, use 12%.) (Item H)

If available income (D) is:	Use:
$ 1,333 or less	6%
$ 1,334– 4,000	5%
$ 4,001– 6,667	4%
$ 6,668– 9,333	3%
$ 9,334–12,000	2%
$12,001–14,667	1%
$14,668 or more	0%

Table for business or farm adjustments (Item 14)

Net worth (NW)	Adjustment rate
Less than $1 . . .	$ 0
$ 1– 70,000	$ 0 + 40% of NW
$ 70,001–210,000	$ 28,000 + 50% of NW over $ 70,000
$210,001–345,000	$ 98,000 + 60% of NW over $210,000
$345,001 or more	$179,000 + 100% of NW over $345,000

Table for parents' expected contribution (Item J)

Adjusted available income (Item I)	Total parents' contribution
Less than −$3,409 . . .	−$750
−$3,409 to 8,700 . . .	22% of AAI
$ 8,701 to 10,900 . . .	$1,914 + 25% of AAI over $ 8,700
$10,901 to 13,100 . . .	$2,464 + 29% of AAI over $10,900
$13,101 to 15,300 . . .	$3,102 + 34% of AAI over $13,100
$15,301 to 17,500 . . .	$3,850 + 40% of AAI over $15,300
$17,501 or more	$4,730 + 47% of AAI over $17,500

Table for asset protection allowance (Item F)

Age	Two-parent family	One-parent family
39 or less	$28,000	$20,600
40–44	31,600	23,000
45–49	35,900	25,700
50–54	41,300	29,000
55–59	47,900	33,000
60–64	56,300	37,800
65 or more	62,400	41,300

Worksheet 3: Student's expected contribution

	Andrea *Some savings*	Beth *No assets but part-time employment*	Carlos *Savings plus two local scholarships*
L. Student's 1990 income			
17. Student's yearly wages, salaries, tips, and other compensation	$ 700	$ 3,000	$ 1,200
18. Spouse's yearly wages, salaries, tips, and other compensation	0	0	0
19. All other income of student (dividends, interest, untaxed income, and benefits)	0	0	0
M. Total income (Add 17, 18 and 19.)	700	3,000	1,200
Allowances			
20. U.S. income tax student (and spouse) expect to pay on 1990 income (not amount withheld from paychecks)	0	0	0
21. State and other taxes (Enter 4% of M.)	28	120	48
22. Social security (FICA) tax (7.65% times salary of student and spouse to a maximum of $3,856 per person)	54	230	92
N. Total allowances against student's income (Add 20, 21, and 22.)	82	350	140
O. Available income (Subtract N from M.)	618	2,650	1,060
Resources			
23. Contribution from income (Enter the greater of 70% times *Available income* from line O or $700 for the first year—$900 for any other year.)	700	1,855	742
24. Contribution from assets (multiply the total value of savings and other assets—such as stocks and bonds—by 35%.)	540	0	400
25. Other gifts and scholarships already received	0	0	1,000
Q. Total student resources (add 23, 24, and 25)	$ 1,240	$ 1,855	$ 2,142

Worksheet 4: Total family contribution

	Andrea	Beth	Carlos
J. Parents' expected contribution (Use figure for K instead of J if there is more than one family member in college.)	$ 445	$ 492	$ 2,047
Q. Student's expected contribution from resources	1,240	1,855	2,142
R. Total family contribution (Add J and Q.)	$ 1,685	$ 2,347	$ 4,189

Worksheet 5: Student need

	Andrea *Commuting student (living at home) at an in-state, 2-year public institution*	Beth *Resident student at an in-state, 4-year public institution*	Carlos *Resident student at an independent (private) institution*
S. Total college expense budget	$ 4,315	$ 6,645	$14,280
R. Total family contribution	1,685	2,347	4,189
T. Student need (Subtract R from S)	$ 2,630	$ 4,298	$10,091

Worksheet 6: Financial aid awards

	Andrea
A. Total student budget	$4,315
M. Total family contribution	1,685
N. Demonstrated financial need	2,630
1. Pell Grant	1,100
2. State scholarship	
3. Institutional grant	
4. College Work-Study	800
5. Perkins Loan	500
6. Supplemental Educational Opportunity Grant	230
7. Stafford Loan	
8. Private scholarships	
Total resources for college	$4,315

	Beth
A. Total student budget	$6,645
M. Total family contribution	2,347
N. Demonstrated financial need	4,298
1. Pell Grant	850
2. State scholarship	1,200
3. Institutional grant	
4. College Work-Study	
5. Perkins Loan	
6. Supplemental Educational Opportunity Grant	870
7. Stafford Loan	1,378
8. Private scholarships	
Total resources for college	$6,645

Andrea received a financial aid award offer from the community college that fully met her need. She received a federal Pell Grant and a Supplemental Educational Opportunity Grant, as well as a College Work-Study award (clerking in the campus library) and a Perkins Loan (which she will have to repay once she graduates or leaves school). Although Andrea did not receive any private scholarships, she did identify several for which she might be eligible once she becomes an upperclassman, including some scholarships targeted specifically for engineering students and minority students; she has already started a file on such opportunities.

*The financial aid award offer **Beth** received met her demonstrated need and included aid from a wide variety of sources. She received a Pell Grant from the federal government, a scholarship from her state student assistance agency, and—because her family income is quite low—a Supplemental Educational Opportunity Grant. In addition, like almost all financial aid recipients, Beth will be expected to assume some "self-help aid." In her case, she borrowed a Stafford Loan, which she'll have to repay when she graduates or leaves school.*

	Carlos
A. Total student budget	$14,280
M. Total family contribution	4,189
N. Demonstrated financial need	10,091
1. Pell Grant	
2. State scholarship	1,500
3. Institutional grant	4,566
4. College Work-Study	1,400
5. Perkins Loan	●
6. Supplemental Educational Opportunity Grant	
7. Stafford Loan	2,625
8. Private scholarships	1,000*
Total resources for college	$14,280

*Included in M (above).

Even though **Carlos'** *family had the greatest resources among the three students, he also had the greatest need because the college he wanted to attend had the highest costs. The financial aid award offer he received met his full need. Because his parents' income was higher than the average, he was not eligible for a federal Pell Grant or a Supplemental Educational Opportunity Grant. The college did award him a scholarship from its own scholarship fund, and in addition, he won a scholarship offered each year by his local Chamber of Commerce to a senior who demonstrates exceptional academic apti-*

Your personal plan

Now that you've followed Andrea, Beth, and Carlos through the financial aid application process according to the uniform methodology, here are worksheets for you to complete for your own need analysis estimate. You can begin to make your own plans by filling in Worksheet 1 for the colleges you are considering. You can use the college cost information in Part II of this book, but *remember* that these costs are for the 1991-92 academic year. If you will be starting college in September 1992 you should raise the figures by at least 6 percent. (Some colleges will have a greater increase, others a smaller one.) When you are actually applying for aid, the college catalog or financial aid bulletins forthe colleges to which you are applying are the most authoritative sources of information about costs that will apply to you.

You can begin to get a sense of your need at these colleges by completing your own Worksheets 2-5. These will take you through the steps of estimating parents' expected contribution (Worksheet 2 and table of parents' contribution), estimating your own contribution (Worksheet 3), combining the total family contribution (Worksheet 4), and finding the difference between the contribution and the costs at each of the colleges you are considering (Worksheet 5)—that is, your financial need.

Worksheet 1: Estimating student expenses	College A	College B	College C
1. Tuition and fees	$	$	$
2. Books and supplies			
3. Student's room			
4. Student's board/meals*			
5. Personal (clothing, laundry, recreation, medical)			
6. Transportation**			
7. Other (such as costs of child care, extra expenses because of handicap)			
A. Total budget (Add 1-7)	$	$	$

* You will want to consider these expenses to your family if you live at home.

** If you are planning to live on campus, estimate the costs of the round trips you will have to make to your home. Colleges usually estimate a student makes two or three round trips during the year. Students living at home should figure the costs of daily transportation to college.

See Worksheet 2 for Andrea, Beth, and Carlos, and use the tables following their worksheet to help you estimate parents' expected contribution.

Worksheet 2: Estimating parents' expected contribution	
A. 1990 income:	
1. Father's yearly wages, salaries, tips, and other compensation	$
2. Mother's yearly wages, salaries, tips, and other compensation	
3. All other income of mother and father (dividends, interest, social security, pensions, welfare, child support, etc.) *(Include IRA/Keogh payments and 40(K) and 403(B) contributions.)*	
4. IRS allowable adjustments to income (business expenses, interest penalties, alimony paid, etc.) *Do not include IRA/Keogh payments.*	
B. Total income (Add 1, 2, 3 and subtract 4.)	
Expenses:	
5. U.S. income tax parents expect to pay on their 1990 income (not amount withheld from paycheck)	
6. Social Security (FICA) tax (7.65% times each salary to a maximum of $3,856 per person)	
7. State and other taxes (Enter 8% of B)	
8. Medical and dental expenses not covered by insurance (include insurance premiums) in excess of 5% of B	
9. Elementary and secondary school tuition paid for other dependents to a maximum of $4,243 per child	
10. Employment allowance. If 2-parent family and both parents work, allow 35% of lower salary to a maximum of $2,300; if 1-parent family, allow 35% of salary to a maximum of $2,300. No allowance for a 2-parent family in which only 1 parent works.	
11. Standard maintenance allowance (See Table for 11.)	
C. Total allowances against income (Add 5, 6, 7, 8, 9, 10, 11.)	
D. Available income (Subtract C from B.)	
Assets:	
12. Home equity (total estimated value of your home on the current market minus any unpaid balance on your mortgage)	
13. Other real estate equity (value minus unpaid balance on mortgage)	
14. Business or farm (Figure total value minus indebtedness and then take percentage shown in table.) If your family is only part owner of the farm or business, list only your share of the net value.	
15. Cash, savings, and checking accounts	
16. Other investments (current net value)	
E. Total assets (Add 12, 13, 14, 15, 16.)	
Deductions:	
F. Asset protection allowance (See Table for F.)	
G. Remaining assets (Subtract F from E.)	
H. Income supplement from assets (Multiply G by 12% if G is $0 or more. If G is negative, use conversion percentage from Table for H.)	
I. Adjusted available income (Add D and H.)	
J. Parents' expected contribution (Multiply I by taxation rate amount given in Table for J.)	
K. Parents' expected contribution if more than one family member is in college (Divide J by number of family members in college at least half time.)	$

Student's expected contribution

Students, too, are expected to contribute toward college costs—from savings, part-time employment, and special benefits received, such as social security or veteran's benefits. If you are applying for financial aid, you will be expected to contribute *at least* $700 from earnings for your first year. If you are unable to earn that much money (or find employment), let the financial aid administrator know. The administrator may be able to accommodate this shortfall through additional loans or work opportunities during the academic year.

Worksheet 3: Student's expected contribution	
L. Student's 1990 income	$
17. Student's yearly wages, salaries, tips, and other compensation	
18. Spouse's yearly wages, salaries, tips, and other compensation	
19. All other income of student (dividends, interest, untaxed income, and benefits)	
M. Total income (Add 17, 18, and 19.)	
Allowances	
20. U.S. income tax student (and spouse) expect to pay on 1990 income (not amount withheld from paychecks)	
21. State and other taxes (Enter 4% of M.)	
22. Social security (FICA) tax (7.65% times salary of student and spouse to a maximum of $3,856 per person)	
N. Total allowances against student's income (Add 20, 21, and 22.)	
O. Available income (Subtract N from M.)	
Resources	
23. Contribution from income (Enter the greater of 70% times *Available income* from line O or $700 for the first year—$900 for any other year.)	
24. Contribution from assets (multiply the total value of savings and other assets—such as stocks and bonds—by 35%.)	
25. Other gifts and scholarships already received	
Q. Total student resources (add 23, 24, and 25)	$

Total family contribution

Use *Worksheet 4: Total Family Contribution* to transfer figures from Worksheet 2 (line J, or line K if there will be more than one family member in college) and from Worksheet 3 (line Q). By adding together these two figures, you can determine your total estimated family contribution.

Worksheet 4: Total family contribution	
J. Parents' expected contribution (Use figure for K instead of J if there is more than one family member in college.)	$
Q. Student's expected contribution from resources	
R. Total family contribution (Add J and Q.)	$

Estimated financial need

Are you potentially eligible for financial aid? Use *Worksheet 5: Student Need* to compare your family contribution with the cost of going to college. Record the student expense budgets at the colleges that interest you. Enter your total family contribution (from line R in Worksheet 4) and subtract it from each of the student expense budgets. If your family contribution is less than the student expense budget, you have financial "need," and you are probably eligible for financial aid equal to this estimate of your need.

Remember that the figure you arrive at in line T is only an estimate, and you should consider this figure to be only a rough approximation of your eligibility for financial aid. Your eligibility for financial aid, and the amount and type of aid you receive, will be determined by the financial aid administrator at each college. The only way you can find out for sure if you are eligible to receive financial aid and how much you might receive is to apply for financial aid!

Worksheet 5: Student need	College A	College B	College C
S. Total college expense budget	$	$	$
R. Total family contribution			
T. Student need (Subtract R from S)	$	$	$

Worksheet 6:
Financial aid awards

	College A	College B	College C
A. Total student budget	$	$	$
M. Total family contribution			
N. Demonstrated financial need			
1. Pell Grant			
2. State scholarship			
3. Institutional grant			
4. College Work-Study			
5. Perkins Loan			
6. Supplemental Educational Opportunity Grant			
7. Guaranteed Student Loan			
8. Private scholarships			
Total resources for college	$	$	$

Glossary

The definitions given here of terms commonly used by colleges to describe their programs, admissions procedures, and financial aid policies are necessarily general. Students should consult the catalogs of specific colleges and financial aid programs to get more detailed and up-to-date descriptions of their programs and procedures.

Accelerated program. A college program of study completed in less time than is usually required, most often by attending in summer or by carrying extra courses during the regular academic terms. Completion of a bachelor's degree program in three years is an example of acceleration.

ACT. *See* American College Testing Program Assessment.

Advanced placement. Admission or assignment of a freshman to an advanced course in a certain subject on the basis of evidence that the student has already completed the equivalent of the college's freshman course in that subject. In some cases the college also grants academic credit for the college-level work that has been completed.

Advanced Placement (AP) Program. A service of the College Board that provides high schools with course descriptions in college subjects and Advanced Placement Examinations in those subjects. High schools administer the examinations to qualified students, who are then eligible at many colleges for advanced placement, college credit, or both on the basis of satisfactory grades.

AFSA. *See* Application for Federal Student Aid.

AFSSA. *See* Application for Federal and State Student Assistance.

American College Testing Program. Sponsor of the ACT, a test battery given in test centers in the United States and other countries on specified dates throughout the year, that includes tests in English, mathematics, reading, and science reasoning. *Also* a federally approved processing agency that provides the Family Financial Statement with which students may apply for financial aid, including federal programs.

Application for Federal and State Student Assistance (AFSSA). A federally approved need analysis form processed by CSX Commercial Services, Inc. (*See also* Need analysis form.)

Application for Federal Student Aid (AFSA). A form distributed by the federal government for use by students applying for Pell Grants and other federal financial aid programs. Any federally approved need analysis form, such as the FAF, can also be used as an application for federal aid at no extra charge.

Application for Pennsylvania State Grant and Federal Student Aid (APSGFSA). A federally approved need analysis form processed by the Pennsylvania Higher Education Assistance Authority. (*See also* Need analysis form.)

Bachelor's degree. The degree given for completing undergraduate college programs that normally take four years. Also called the baccalaureate degree.

Campus-based programs. The three federally funded student financial aid programs that are directly administered by colleges: Supplemental Educational Opportunity Grants Program, Perkins Loan Program (formerly the National Direct Student Loan Program), and College Work-Study Program.

Candidates Reply Date Agreement (CRDA). A college subscribing to this agreement will not require any applicants offered admission as freshmen to notify the college of their decision to attend (or to accept an offer of financial aid) before May 1. The purpose of the agreement is to give applicants time to hear from all the colleges to which they have applied before they have to make a commitment to any one of them.

Certificate. An award for completing a particular program or course of study, sometimes given by two-year colleges or vocational or technical schools.

College-Level Examination Program (CLEP). A service of the College Board that provides examinations in undergraduate college courses so that students and other adults may demonstrate achievement at the first- and second-year college levels. The examinations are used by colleges to award credit by examination to adult applicants who have not attended college (or have not done so recently), students transferring from other colleges, and entering freshmen. They are also used by business, industries, government agencies, and professional groups to satisfy education requirements for advancement, licensing, admission to further training, and other purposes.

College Scholarship Service (CSS). A service of the College Board that assists postsecondary institutions, state scholarship programs, and other organizations in the equitable distribution of student financial aid funds by measuring a family's financial strength and analyzing its ability to contribute to college costs. CSS is a federally approved Multiple Data Entry processing agency. It provides the Financial Aid Form (FAF) with which students may apply for financial aid, including federal programs.

College Work-Study Program. A federally sponsored campus-based program. Participating colleges provide employment opportunities for students with demonstrated need who are enrolled for at least half-time study at either the undergraduate or graduate level. Students are almost always employed on campus, although occasionally jobs are arranged off-campus. In assigning work-study to aid recipients, financial aid administrators typically take into account the recipient's employable skills, class schedule, and academic progress.

Consumer Price Index (CPI). A measure of inflation or deflation at the consumer level, updated monthly by the U.S. Bureau of Labor Statistics. The index is determined by comparing the current price of a "market basket" of goods to the price at which the same "basket" could have been purchased during a given base year. (Currently 1980 is used.) The goods include food, shelter, clothing, transportation, and other items.

Cooperative education. A college program in which a student alternates between periods of full-time study and full-time employment in related work. Students are paid for their work at the prevailing rate. Typically, five years are required to complete a bachelor's degree program, but graduates have the advantage of having completed about a year's practical experience in addition to their studies. Some colleges refer to this sort of program as work-study, but it should not be confused with the federally sponsored College Work-Study Program.

CRDA. *See* Candidates Reply Date Agreement.

Credit by examination. Academic credit granted by a college for a student's having demonstrated proficiency in a subject as measured by an examination.

CSS. *See* College Scholarship Service.

CSX Commercial Services, Inc. A federally approved processing agency that provides and processes an application with which students may apply for financial aid, including federal programs.

CWSP. *See* College Work-Study Program.

Dependent student. A student dependent on his or her parents for financial support. For financial aid purposes, a student is classified as dependent unless the strict definition of self-supporting status is met in all respects.

Early decision. Early decision admission plans are offered for applicants who are sure of the college they want to attend and are likely to be accepted by the college. An early decision admission application is initiated by the student, who is then notified of the college's decision earlier than usual—generally by December 15 of the senior year.

Early Decision Plan (EDP-F, EDP-S). Colleges that subscribe to this plan agree to follow a common schedule for early decision applicants. Colleges may offer either of two plans. A student applying under the first-choice plan (EDP-F) must withdraw applications from all other colleges as soon as he or she is notified of acceptance by the first-choice college. A student applying under the single-choice plan (EDP-S) may not apply to any colleges other than his or her first choice unless rejected by that institution. If a college follows either type of plan, applications (including those for financial aid) must be received by a specified date no later than November 15, and the college agrees to notify the applicant by a specified date no later than December 15.

FAF. *See* Financial Aid Form.

Family contribution. The total amount a student and his or her family are expected to pay toward college costs from their income and assets. The amount is derived from need analysis of the family's overall financial situation. Generally, students are eligible for financial aid equal to their financial need.

Family Financial Statement (FFS). A federally approved need analysis form processed by the American College Testing Program. (*See also* Need analysis form.)

Financial aid award letter. A notice from a college or other financial aid sponsor that tells a student how much aid is being offered. The award letter also usually explains how a student's financial need was determined, describes the contents of the financial aid package, and outlines any conditions attached to the award.

Financial Aid Form (FAF). A federally approved need analysis form processed by the College Scholarship Service. (*See also* Need analysis form.)

Financial aid package. The total financial aid award received by a student. It may be made up of a combination or "package" of aid that includes both gift aid and self-help. Many colleges try to meet a student's full financial need, but availability of funds, institutional aid policies, and the number of students needing assistance all influence the composition of a financial aid package.

Financial need. The amount by which a student's family contribution falls short of covering the student expense budget. Generally, students are eligible for financial aid equal to their financial need.

Gift aid. Student financial aid, such as scholarships and grants, that does not have to be repaid and that does not require a student's being employed.

Independent student. *See* Self-supporting student.

Multiple Date Entry (MDE). This refers to the system by which a student can apply for federal aid using any one of several forms approved by the U.S. Department of Education. Most colleges, states, and private scholarship programs also require students to submit an approved MDE form as part of the application process. (*See also* Need analysis form.)

NDSL. *See* Perkins Loan (formerly National Direct Student Loan Program).

Need analysis. The method for determining how much a family can reasonably be expected to pay toward a student's college education costs. Need analysis is based on the assumption that parents and students have the major responsibility for paying college costs to the extent they are able. Formulas used in need analysis are updated annually to reflect changes in the economy, and are approved by the federal government and most colleges and other organizations that award financial aid.

Need analysis form. The starting point in applying for financial aid. In many cases an approved Multiple Date Entry (MDE) need analysis form is the only form that students need to submit to be considered for all types of financial aid—institutional, state, private, and federal, including the Pell Grant Program. The approved MDE need analysis forms are:

Financial Aid Form (FAF) of the College Scholarship Service

Family Financial Statement (FFS) of the American College Testing Program

Application for Federal Student Aid (AFSA) of the U.S. Department of Education

Application for Federal and State Student Assistance (AFSSA) of CSX Commercial Services, Inc.

Application for Pennsylvania State Grant and Federal Student Aid (APSGFSA) of the Pennsylvania Higher Education Assistance Agency

SingleFile (SF) of the United Student Aid Funds

Student Aid Application for California (SAAC)—CSS or ACT version.

These forms are used by independent students or parents of dependent students to supply information about their income, assets, expenses, and liabilities. This information is used in estimating how much money a family is able to contribute to a student's college expenses according to the Congressional Methodology.

All need analysis forms are *not* alike. While all these forms contain the same *federal* questions, there are other important differences among them. (Some collect additional questions used by colleges and/or states in awarding student aid for instance.) Students should check with the colleges, state agencies, and private programs from which they are seeking aid to determine *which* form is required or preferred.

Open admission. The college admissions policy of admitting high school graduates and other adults generally without regard to conventional academic qualifications, such as high school subjects, high school grades, and admissions test scores. Virtually all applicants with high school diplomas or their equivalent are accepted.

Parents' contribution. The amount a student's parents are expected to pay toward college costs from their income and assets. The amount is derived from need analysis of the parents' overall financial situation. The parents' contribution and the student's contribution together constitute the total family contribution, which, when subtracted from the student expense budget, equals financial need. Generally students are eligible for financial aid equal to their financial need.

Parent Loans for Undergraduate Students (PLUS). A federal program that lets parents of undergraduate dependent students borrow for their children's education expenses directly from banks and other lending institutions. Parents may borrow up to $4,000 per academic year and up to $20,000 for the total undergraduate program of each child. The federal government guarantees the loan against loss due to death, disability, or default, and subsidizes the interest rate. Repayment begins within 60 days after disbursement and may extend up to 10 years. The interest rate is set annually, to a maximum of 12 percent.

Pell Grant Program. The largest need-based student aid program. Congress annually sets the dollar range. The amount received depends on need, college costs, the length of the program of study, and whether enrollment is full- or part-time. Students apply using an MDE need-analysis form or an AFSA form.

Perkins Loan (formerly the National Direct Student Loan or NDSL Program). A federally funded program that provides loans of up to $4,500 for the first two undergraduate years and up to $9,000 for the total undergraduate program. Repayment need not begin until the student graduates or leaves school; service in the military, Peace Corps, VISTA, or comparable organization may carry other special provisions for deferment or cancellation. Repayment terms are favorable, and repayment may be partially or wholly waived for certain kinds of employment.

PLUS. *See* Parent Loans for Undergraduate Students.

Preliminary Scholastic Aptitude Test/National Merit Scholarship Qualifying Test (PSAT/NMSQT). A shorter version of the College Board's Scholastic Aptitude Test administered by high schools each year in October. The PSAT/NMSQT aids high schools in the early guidance of students planning for college and serves as the qualifying test for scholarships awarded by the National Merit Scholarship Corporation.

Reserve Officers' Training Corps (ROTC). Reserve Officers' Training Corps programs conducted by certain colleges in cooperation with the United States Air Force, Army, and Navy. Local recruiting offices of the services themselves can supply detailed information about these programs. Information is also available from participating colleges.

SAAC. *See* Student Aid Application for California.

Scholastic Aptitude Test (SAT). The College Board's test of verbal and mathematical reasoning abilities, given on specified dates throughout the year at test centers in the United States and other countries. It includes the Test of Standard Written English (TSWE), whose questions evaluate the ability to recognize standard written English, the language of most textbooks. Required of substantially all applicants by many colleges and sponsors of financial aid programs.

Self-help. Student financial aid, such as loans and jobs, that requires repayment or a student's being employed.

Self-supporting student. For financial aid purposes, a student who is independent of support from his or her parents.

SEOG. *See* Supplemental Educational Opportunity Grant Program.

SAR. *See* Student Aid Report.

SingleFile (SF). A federally approved need analysis form processed by United Student Aid Funds.

Stafford Loan Program (formerly Guaranteed Student Loan, or GSL, Program). A federal program that lets students borrow money for education expenses directly from banks and other lending institutions (sometimes the colleges themselves). Dependent students may borrow up to $2,625 per academic year when they are freshmen and sophomores, $4,000 when they are juniors and seniors, and up to $17,250 for the total undergraduate program. Students must demonstrate need in order to qualify. The federal government pays the interest while the student is in college. Repayment terms are favorable, and repayment need not begin until the student graduates or leaves school. Deferments for limited periods are available under certain conditions.

Student Aid Application for California (SAAC). A federally approved need analysis form used by California residents applying for aid. There are two versions: CSS SAAC and ACT SAAC.

Student Aid Report (SAR). A report produced by the AFSA processor, or an MDE agency, for the U.S. Department of Education and sent to students who have applied for federal student financial aid. The SAR must be submitted to the college that the student attends to certify his or her eligibility for Pell Grants and other federal financial programs such as the College Work-Study Program, Perkins Loan Program, Supplemental Educational Opportunity Grants, and Stafford Loans.

Student expense budget. The annual cost of attending college that is used in determining a student's financial need. Student expense budgets usually include tuition and fees, books and supplies, room and board, personal expenses, and transportation. Sometimes additional expenses are included for students with special education needs, students who have a disability, or students who are married or have children.

Student's contribution. The amount students are expected to pay toward college costs from their income, assets, and benefits. The amount is derived from need analysis of the student's resources. The student's contribution and parents' contribution constitute the total family contribution, which, when subtracted from the student expense budget, equals financial need. Generally students are eligible for financial aid equal to their financial need. Dependent freshmen are usually expected to contribute at least $700 to their education; more is expected of upperclassmen and of independent students.

Supplemental Educational Opportunity Grant Program (SEOG). A federal program administered by colleges to provide need-based aid to undergraduate students. Grants of up to $4,000 a year may be awarded.

Tuition and fee waivers. Some colleges waive the tuition or tuition and fees for some categories of students, such as adults, senior citizens, or children of alumni. Colleges with such plans are listed in a section following the table of college costs and financial aid.

United Student Aid Funds (USAF). A federally approved processing agency that provides and processes SingleFile, an application with which students may apply for financial aid, including federal programs.

Part II. Information about colleges and universities

1. College expenses and financial aid

Introduction

This section provides detailed lists of expenses and financial aid at 3,200 colleges, universities, and proprietary schools. The data were compiled from information supplied by the institutions themselves on the College Board's Annual Survey of Colleges, 1991-92, during the winter of 1991. The lists are alphabetical by state, and include the information provided by all participating institutions through the end of April 1991. Every effort is made to insure that the data are as complete and accurate as possible. However, students are urged to contact institutions directly to confirm the information.

Institutions were asked to give expense figures for the academic year beginning fall 1991. If the 1991-92 costs were not yet set but a reliable forecast was available, these estimated costs are given with a single dagger next to the institution's name. If these figures were not yet available but the institution provided 1990-91 expenses, these are listed with a double dagger next to the name of the institution.

Details on each category of expenses and financial aid and what these figures can mean to applicants are explained here.

In an effort to collect comparable cost information, the College Board asked institutions to provide data for specifically budgeted items. The figures supplied under each column heading represent the following.

Educational Costs

Tuition and fees

This figure indicates the annual tuition and general fees an institution charges most first-year, full-time students. Colleges were asked to report these costs based on a nine-month academic year of 30 semester hours or 45 quarter hours.

Additional out-of-state/district tuition

This item represents only the *additional* charges made to students who do not meet state or district residency requirements. The figure to the left of the diagonal mark shows additional charges for out-of-state students; the figure to the right shows additional out-of-district charges. These charges added to the tuition and fees in the first column will give you the total tuition and fees for out-of-state and out-of-district students, respectively.

Books and supplies

This figure is the average cost of books and supplies for the normal course load for full-time students. Supplies may be more expensive for students in certain areas of study (art, architecture, or engineering, for example) and institutions did not include these special costs unless the majority of their students are in these fields.

Living costs: Campus residents

Room and board for campus residents

For resident students, room and board includes the charge for living and eating for nine months in facilities operated by or for the college. These are average charges based on double-room occupancy and 21 meals a week in college facilities.

Transportation for campus residents

These figues include typical costs for two round trips between home and campus during the nine-month academic year. If you anticipate more frequent trips between home and campus during the academic year, you should adjust this figure accordingly.

Other costs for campus residents

This column shows typical costs for miscellaneous personal expenses, such as clothing, laundry, entertainment, snacks, medical insurance, and furnishings.

Living cost: Students living at home

Board for students at home

This column shows average costs for dependent students living at home, including three meals a day, seven days a week.

Transportation for students at home

The figures in this column represent the typical costs for daily travel to and from college for students who commute.

Other costs for students at home

This column shows miscellaneous personal expenses for students living at home. These include clothing, laundry, entertainment, and medical insurance.

Financial aid information

Total freshmen enrolled

This is the total freshman enrollment for fall 1990 on which the percentage of freshman students receiving aid is based.

Percentage receiving aid

This figure represents the percentage of enrolled freshmen (preceding column) who received some form of financial aid in fall 1990. The aid could be based on financial need or on other criteria such as talent or athletic ability. The financial aid could be in the form of grants, scholarships, loans, or jobs.

Freshmen judged to have financial need

This column shows the number of freshmen in fall 1990 who were judged to have financial need.

Percent offered aid

This figure is the percentage of freshmen with financial need (preceding column) who were offered aid. The financial aid could be grants, loans, or jobs.

Grants and scholarships

Need-based scholarships

An X in these columns indicates that the college awards scholarships on the basis of financial need combined with exceptional academic ability or talent in music or drama, art, or athletics.

Non-need scholarships

An X in these columns indicates that the college awards scholarships, without regard for financial need, on the basis of exceptional academic ability or talent in music or drama, art, or athletics.

Financial aid deadlines

Priority deadline for financial aid

The priority deadline is the date by which the college prefers you submit your financial aid application. Missing this deadline may mean that most or all financial aid may have already been awarded, but it does not necessarily mean that *all* aid has been given. It is best to meet the college's priority deadline in order to have the best chance of receiving aid if you qualify.

Closing deadline for financial aid

This is the final date by which the college will accept your application for financial aid.

Institutional aid form

An X in this column indicates that the college has its own financial aid form that you will have to complete if you are applying for aid. This requirement is in addition to any standard form listed in the next column and discussed below.

Need analysis document required

This column indicates which of the standard financial aid application forms (listed below) are required, accepted, or preferred by the college. If only one form appears, it is required.

When forms are separated by a slash (/), either form is accepted; an asterisk (*) next to one form means the college prefers that you use this form. For example, "FAF*/FFS" means that the college will accept either the FFA or FFS but prefers the FAF.

When forms are separated by a plus sign (+), both forms are required. For example, APSGFSA + FAF*/FFS means the APSGFSA is required and so is either the FAF or FFS, with the FAF preferred.

Most colleges ask for the same form(s) from both in-state and out-of-state applicants. However, when a college has different in-state and out-of-state need analysis document requirements, the in-state form(s) are listed first followed by a semicolon and the out-of-state form(s). For example, "SAAC; FAF/FFS" means that the college requires the SAAC for in-state students and requires the FAF or FFS for out-of-state students.

These are the forms that appear in this column:

AFSA—Application for Federal Student Aid of the U.S. Department of Education.

AFSSA—Application for Federal and State Student Assistance of CSX Commercial Services, Inc.

APSGFSA—Application for Pennsylvania State Grant and Federal Student Aid of the Pennsylvania Higher Education Assistance Agency.

FAF—Financial Aid Form of the College Scholarship Service.

FFS—Family Financial Statement of the American College Testing Service.

SAAC—Student Aid Application for California. There are two versions: CSS SAAC and ACT SAAC.

SF—SingleFile of the United Student Aid Funds.

In general, the AFSA is listed only for those institutions that require no other need analysis document. Most colleges require that you apply for your state scholarship or grant program, and there may be a state-specific form that you will have to fill out for this purpose. Many colleges also require your parents (or you) to submit a copy of your tax return (IRS form 1040) in addition to the need analysis document(s) listed.

Institution	Tuition and fees	Add'l out-of-state/district tuition	Books and supplies	Costs for campus residents			Costs for students at home		
				Room and board	Transportation	Other costs	Board only	Transportation	Other costs
Alabama									
Alabama Agricultural and Mechanical University	1,298	988/—	500	2,036	990	756	1,242	992	748
‡ Alabama Aviation and Technical College	645	450/—	1,625		1,000	1,300	2,700	1,000	1,000
† Alabama Christian School of Religion	4,335								
Alabama State University	1,268	1,160/—	570	1,991	900	1,200	1,500	1,500	1,200
‡ Athens State College	1,125	1,080/—	400		536	637	1,694	1,086	637
Auburn University									
Auburn	1,596	3,192/—	600	3,200	700	1,000	1,600	700	1,100
‡ Montgomery	1,317	2,634/—	525		525	680	1,575	890	680
† Bessemer State Technical College	885	607/—	550				1,500	900	600
‡ Birmingham-Southern College	8,999		500	3,435	500	500	1,500	600	900
† Bishop State Community College	837	770/—	200				400	200	500
Brewer State Junior College	984	738/—	425				1,000	1,050	800
Central Alabama Community College									
Alexander City Campus	645	450/—	300				1,800	600	500
Childersburg Campus	1,114	557/—	450					150	675
Chattahoochee Valley Community College	1,116	837/—	400				1,795	600	100
Community College of the Air Force	0								
† Concordia College	3,176		550	2,700	1,500	1,775	1,500	750	1,625
Douglas MacArthur State Technical College	912	600/—	300				1,350	600	501
Draughons Junior College	3,925		400						
Enterprise State Junior College	645	450/—	300				1,900	650	535
‡ Faulkner University	4,335		600	2,800	650	1,000	800	704	840
‡ Gadsden State Community College	615	450/—	450	1,545	90	500	1,500	750	500
George C. Wallace State Community College									
‡ Dothan	600	450/—	300				2,000	700	300
Selma	885	608/—	475				1,950		975
‡ Harry M. Ayers State Technical College	610	450/—	400				2,400	1,200	
Hobson State Technical College	1,035	450/—	550				600	875	450
Huntingdon College	6,500		350	3,200	350	400		200	400
International Bible College	2,575		400		350	1,500	1,500	900	1,500
J. F. Drake State Technical College	1,200	690/—	500					550	
‡ Jacksonville State University	1,320	660/—	570	2,228	900	1,200	1,360	1,500	1,200
James H. Faulkner State Junior College	795	600/—	450	1,875	550	800	1,500	950	700
Jefferson Davis State Junior College	900	606/—	525				1,500	300	600
Jefferson State Community College	1,075	743/—	450				2,100	600	525
John C. Calhoun State Community College	798	540/—	500				1,900	700	774
John M. Patterson State Technical College	945	709/—							
‡ Judson College	4,370		600	3,587	500	1,100		600	800
Lawson State Community College	951	606/—	400				1,550	725	700
‡ Livingston University	1,524		500	2,055	400	600	1,500	1,000	600
Lurleen B. Wallace State Junior College	1,068	720/—	300				1,800	600	500
Marion Military Institute	5,680		200	3,460	400	1,375			
Miles College	3,760		400	2,300	500	1,000		500	800
Mobile College	4,730		400	2,800	150	800	1,500	384	320
National Education Center: National Institute of Technology Campus	4,715						2,070	522	1,152
Northeast Alabama State Junior College	766	700/—	400				1,000	750	1,500
Northwest Alabama Community College	1,000	450/—	400				2,700		
Oakwood College	5,925		600	3,486	690	410			410

†Figures are projected for 1991-92. ‡Figures are for 1990-91.

All aid		Need–based aid		Grants and scholarships Need–based				Nonneed–based				Financial aid deadlines		Inst aid form	Need analysis document
Total freshmen	Percent receiving aid	Freshmen judged to have need	Percent offered aid	Acad	Music/drama	Art	Athl	Acad	Music/drama	Art	Athl	Priority	Closing		
1,234	60	723	100	X				X	X		X	5/1	6/1	X	FAF/FFS*/SF;FAF/FFS*/AFSA/SF
								X					none	X	FFS
														X	AFSA
1,137	90							X	X	X	X	4/1	none	X	FAF/FFS*/AFSA/SF
							X	X	X	X	X		none		FAF/FFS*/AFSA
2,824	55	1,359	96	X				X	X	X	X	4/15	none		FFS
								X			X	4/15	none	X	FAF/FFS/AFSA/AFSSA/SF
726	60	480	99	X				X				9/1	none		AFSA
284	68	152	100	X	X	X	X	X	X	X	X	3/15	none	X	FAF*/FFS/AFSA
653	42			X				X	X		X	6/15	none	X	FFS
600	38							X	X		X	8/1	none		FAF*/FFS
								X	X	X	X	7/15	none		AFSA
													none		AFSA
													none		FFS/AFSA
													none		
224	98			X	X		X						none	X	FFS
210	70			X				X					none		AFSA
														X	AFSA
				X				X	X	X	X	4/1	none	X	FAF/FFS*/AFSA
149	90							X			X	5/1	none	X	FFS
3,588	33	738	100					X	X		X	5/1	none		FAF/FFS*/AFSA
													none		FFS
													none	X	AFSA
													none		AFSA
													none		FAF/FFS/AFSA*/SF
183	92	67	100	X	X	X	X	X	X	X	X	6/1	none	X	FAF*/FFS FAF/AFSA
440	75			X									none		AFSA
1,286	45	500	100					X	X	X	X	4/1	none		FAF*/FFS/AFSA/SF
865	60							X	X	X	X	7/1	8/1	X	FFS
								X	X	X	X		none		AFSA
1,114	40			X				X	X		X	5/1	none		AFSA
2,360	21							X			X	5/1	none		FAF*/FFS/AFSA/SF
													none		FFS
135	99	82	100	X	X	X		X	X	X	X	4/1	none	X	FFS
886	85			X	X						X		none		AFSA
405	65							X	X	X	X	4/20	none		FFS
340	70			X	X		X	X	X	X	X	6/1	none		FAF/FFS/AFSA*
													none		FFS
225	84	125	100	X			X	X				4/15	none		FAF*/FFS/AFSA
148	92							X	X	X	X	3/31	none	X	FFS
															FAF/FFS/AFSA*
864	45							X	X	X			5/1		FFS
				X	X		X						none		AFSA
354	90	223	100									4/15	none		FAF

*Preferred need analysis document.

Institution	Tuition and fees	Add'l out-of-state/district tuition	Books and supplies	Costs for campus residents			Costs for students at home		
				Room and board	Transportation	Other costs	Board only	Transportation	Other costs
Patrick Henry State Junior College	1,053	675/—	350						
Reid State Technical College	836	587/—	400						
‡ RETS Electronics Institute	5,310		300				1,700	100	100
Samford University	6,540		430	3,354	700	1,650	1,500	990	1,650
Selma University	2,275		200	1,740		600			600
Shelton State Community College	645	450/—	450				3,000	700	700
Shoals Community College	657	450/—	375				1,500	715	900
Snead State Junior College	774	546/—	450	1,643	540	700	1,500	925	700
Southeastern Bible College	3,790		300	2,623	400	1,200	2,000	850	1,500
Southern Junior College	4,150		325				1,962	421	
Southern Union State Junior College	900	608/—	400	1,800	600	1,100	700	600	600
Southwest State Technical College	990	743/—	400				1,500	300	200
Spring Hill College	10,153		500	4,158	300	900	1,575	200	900
† Stillman College	4,260		400	2,640	300	1,000	1,500	300	1,000
† Talladega College	4,373		500	2,030	800	500	732	800	500
Trenholm State Technical College	1,125	844/—	575				2,350	850	350
Troy State University									
‡ Dothan	1,419	210/—	600				1,890	1,575	1,260
† Montgomery	1,370	720/—	550						
‡ Troy	1,395	697/—	400	2,295	450	600	1,200		
Tuskegee University	6,250		550	3,000	600	1,050	1,300	250	300
University of Alabama									
‡ Birmingham	1,920	1,740/—	570	3,800	750	1,200	2,500	1,500	1,200
‡ Huntsville	2,019	2,019/—	450	3,240	675	1,200	1,800	1,350	900
† Tuscaloosa	1,900	2,810/—	525	3,400	773	1,323	1,600	1,323	1,103
University of Montevallo	1,954	1,830/—	500	2,820	800	1,500	800	900	1,000
University of North Alabama	1,296	552/—	550	2,388	800	1,512	1,288	2,038	2,038
‡ University of South Alabama	1,797	600/—	470	2,595	999	1,023	1,986	1,645	1,023
† Walker College	2,028		500	1,978	800	1,750	2,600	1,100	1,750
† Walker State Technical College	614	450/—	600				2,000	1,284	1,000
† Wallace State Community College at Hanceville	603	450/—	400		250	700		800	700
Alaska									
‡ Alaska Bible College	2,370		250	3,200	120	400	1,800	600	300
Alaska Pacific University	6,330		500	4,050	90	1,200	1,500	750	1,200
† Prince William Sound Community College	1,034	2,626/—	440		882	1,062	2,367	882	1,062
Sheldon Jackson College	5,960		500	4,215	1,400	1,000	2,315	500	1,000
University of Alaska									
† Anchorage	1,270	2,444/—	440		882	1,062	2,367	882	1,062
† Fairbanks	1,660	2,444/—	500	2,690	1,017	1,188	1,350	1,017	1,188
† Southeast	1,226	2,444/—			230	1,000	2,250	630	1,000
Arizona									
American Indian Bible College	2,842		400	2,640	1,100	1,400		1,100	1,400
Arizona College of the Bible	4,370		400		630	1,000	1,750	2,520	1,030
Arizona State University	1,590	5,406/—	500	4,150		2,500	1,600		2,500
Arizona Western College	690	5,340/—	350	2,650	350	952	1,100	924	950
Central Arizona College	570	4,770/570	400	2,420	700	1,500	1,500	700	1,500
† Cochise College	710	3,690/—	500	2,870	1,093	675	1,500	1,093	675
DeVry Institute of Technology: Phoenix	5,015		500				1,839	2,738	1,858
Eastern Arizona College	600	3,124/—	450	2,574	850	800	1,500	850	800
Embry-Riddle Aeronautical University: Prescott Campus	6,310		490	3,540	1,640	1,120	1,500	1,780	1,120

†Figures are projected for 1991-92. ‡Figures are for 1990-91.

All aid		Need–based aid		Grants and scholarships								Financial aid deadlines		Inst aid form	Need analysis document
				Need–based				Nonneed–based							
Total freshmen	Percent receiving aid	Freshmen judged to have need	Percent offered aid	Acad	Music/drama	Art	Athl	Acad	Music/drama	Art	Athl	Priority	Closing		
				X	X	X	X	X	X	X	X	7/15	none	X	FAF/FFS/AFSA*
310	80												none		FAF
72	75												6/15		AFSA
644	80	400	100	X				X	X	X	X	3/1	5/15		FAF*/FFS
75	95											9/15	none		FAF/FFS*
1,690	30			X	X	X	X						none		AFSA
937	50							X	X			6/1	none		FAF/FFS/AFSA*/SF
618	65	410	98					X	X	X	X	4/15	none	X	FFS*/AFSA
16	81			X				X				6/30	9/8		FAF
													none		AFSA
955	49			X	X	X	X					4/1	none		FAF/FFS*
													none		FAF/FFS
273	70	147	100	X				X			X	3/1	none	X	FAF*/FFS/AFSA/SF
250	90	237	97	X	X			X	X			6/15	none		FAF*/FFS/AFSA
266	95			X			X	X			X	4/1	6/10		FAF
571	20			X								8/31	none		FFS
192	15	29	100	X				X				5/1	8/1	X	AFSA
													none		FAF
807	50											5/1	none	X	FAF/FFS/AFSA*/SF
1,454	90			X				X	X		X	3/15	3/31		FAF*/FFS
1,217	29	470	100	X		X	X	X	X	X	X	4/1	6/1		FAF/FFS/AFSA*
821	30							X	X	X	X	4/1	none		FAF/FFS*/AFSA/SF
2,813	28	784	95	X				X	X	X	X	3/15	none		FAF/FFS*
577	57	229	100			X		X	X		X	4/15	none		FAF*/FFS/SF
701	44	270	100	X				X	X	X	X	4/1	none		FFS*/AFSA
1,262	30			X			X	X	X		X	4/1	none	X	FFS
329	64	240	100	X		X	X	X		X	X	7/1	none	X	AFSA
								X				4/15	none		AFSSA
1,111	50							X	X	X	X		none		AFSA
93	67	4	100	X				X	X			5/31	none	X	FAF
49	75			X				X				3/15	none		FAF*/FFS/AFSA
								X					none	X	FAF
106	94	70	100	X			X	X	X		X	4/1	none	X	FAF*/FFS
1,233	34			X				X	X	X	X	5/15	none		FAF*/FFS
				X	X	X			X	X	X	5/1	none		FAF/FFS/AFSA/SF
				X	X	X	X					5/1	none	X	FAF
60	100	42	100	X				X				4/1	none		FFS
13	34	8	100	X	X		X	X	X			4/15	none		FFS
3,536	55	1,200	100	X				X	X	X	X	3/1	none		FAF/FFS/SF
													none		FAF/FFS*
1,700	60	375	100	X	X	X	X	X	X	X	X	4/15	none		FAF/FFS*/AFSA
1,374	45	735	100	X			X	X			X	3/15	none		FFS
719	81							X					none		FAF
474	91							X	X	X	X	4/15	none		FAF*/FFS/AFSA
400	54	114	97	X				X				4/15	none		FFS

*Preferred need analysis document.

Institution	Tuition and fees	Add'l out-of-state/district tuition	Books and supplies	Costs for campus residents			Costs for students at home		
				Room and board	Trans-portation	Other costs	Board only	Trans-portation	Other costs
‡ Gateway Community College	720	3,750/2,820	400						3,228
‡ Glendale Community College	720	3,750/2,820	500						
‡ Grand Canyon University	6,330		570	2,800	585	1,035	1,530	585	1,035
ITT Technical Institute									
‡ Phoenix	11,092		950				1,842	546	1,308
‡ Tucson	11,017		990						
Lamson Junior College	4,275		644						
Mesa Community College	780	4,500/3,570	400					350	
‡ Mohave Community College	490	2,890/—	500				1,500	850	900
National Education Center: Arizona Automotive Institute	7,465								
‡ Navajo Community College	380		450	2,620					
‡ Northern Arizona University	1,540	4,376/—	650	2,534	850	1,300	1,700	525	1,025
† Northland Pioneer College	360	1,890/—	418		400	3,800	1,600	650	1,400
† Paradise Valley Community College	780	3,750/2,820	400				3,256		
‡ Phoenix College	720	3,750/2,820	400				1,000	1,500	800
‡ Pima Community College	528	2,850/—	425				500	1,400	2,000
† Prescott College	7,905		700						
‡ Rio Salado Community College	720	3,720/2,790	400					1,038	800
Scottsdale Community College	780	3,750/2,820	320						
South Mountain Community College	780	3,660/2,730	450						3,900
Southwestern College	4,620		400	2,170	400	950	1,600	950	950
University of Arizona	1,590	5,456/—	590	3,702	550	2,090	2,025	550	1,900
University of Phoenix	5,328		500					500	200
‡ Western International University	3,250		500						500
‡ Yavapai College	590	3,960/—	475	2,440	525	1,050	660	525	800
Arkansas									
Arkansas Baptist College	1,670		600	2,200	860	850	1,100	860	860
‡ Arkansas College	6,400		430	2,810	632	520	1,500	970	654
Arkansas State University									
Beebe Branch	850	570/—	500	1,751	560	500		800	500
‡ Jonesboro	1,410	1,250/—	500	2,310	720	600	1,500	1,100	400
† Arkansas Tech University	1,260	1,200/—	450	2,080	300	860	1,500	700	750
† Capital City Junior College	5,760						1,100		
Central Baptist College	2,025		400	1,700	600	800	1,500	600	800
‡ Crowley's Ridge College	3,184		500	2,200	406	600		406	600
East Arkansas Community College	552	372/168	175				1,200	500	400
‡ Garland County Community College	576	1,152/144	400				2,882	726	750
† Harding University	5,205		500	3,000	800	1,000	1,300	800	1,000
Henderson State University	1,220	1,200/—	400	1,900	200	450	500	400	600
† Hendrix College	7,253		400	2,775	500	625	1,500	562	563
John Brown University	5,490		400	3,060	800	1,300	1,300	600	1,300

†Figures are projected for 1991-92.   ‡Figures are for 1990-91.

Total freshmen	Percent receiving aid	Freshmen judged to have need	Percent offered aid	Need-based Acad	Music/drama	Art	Athl	Nonneed-based Acad	Music/drama	Art	Athl	Priority	Closing	Inst aid form	Need analysis document
				X				X				4/15	none		FFS/AFSA;FAF/FFS/AFSA/ACT SAAC
7,880	25	1,693	100						X	X	X	4/15	none		FFS
476	57	200	95						X	X	X	4/15	none	X	FAF/FFS/SF*;FAF/FFS/APSGFSA/SF*
122	97												9/20		FAF/FFS/AFSA/SF
94	97	88	100										5/1		FAF/FFS/AFSA/SF*
													none		AFSA
13,631	10	4,230	100	X		X		X			X	5/15	none		FAF/FFS*
				X				X				3/1	none	X	FAF/FFS/AFSA/SF*
													none	X	FAF*/FFS/AFSA; FAF*/FFS/AFSA/SF
													none		FFS
2,063	65			X	X	X		X	X	X	X	4/15	none		FAF/FFS
1,370	10			X	X		X	X	X	X	X	4/15	none		FAF/FFS*/AFSA
		916	98	X				X					none		FAF/FFS*/AFSA/AFSSA/SF;FAF/FFS*/AFSA/CSS SAAC/ACT
								X	X	X	X	4/15	none		FFS
5,445	20	1,450	75								X	4/1	none		FFS
37	75			X				X				4/15	none	X	FAF/FFS*/AFSA/CSS SAAC/ACT SAAC/AFSSA/SF;FAF/FFS*/
												4/15	none		FFS
													none		FFS
3,350	18	635	91	X	X	X	X	X	X	X			none	X	FAF/FFS/AFSA*
27	100	12	100									4/15	7/15		FAF/FFS*/AFSA
4,357	60			X	X	X	X	X	X	X	X	3/1	4/1		FAF/FFS/AFSA/SF
													none		AFSA
141	44												none		AFSA
2,524	44			X	X	X	X	X	X	X	X	4/15	none		FAF*/FFS/SF
47	43			X		X		X			X		5/1		FFS
255	93	186	100	X	X	X	X	X	X	X	X	4/1	none		FAF/FFS/AFSA/AFSSA*;FAF*/FFS/AFSA
1,223	60	277	100					X	X		X	4/15	none		FFS
1,485	60			X				X	X	X	X	5/1	none		FFS;FAF/FFS*
1,596	51			X	X		X	X	X		X		none		FFS
150	64												none		FAF/FFS
								X	X		X		none		FFS
103	75			X	X							6/30	none		FFS
549	50			X								4/15	none		FFS
1,507	75								X	X	X		5/1		FFS
746	85	432	99					X	X	X	X	3/1	none	X	FAF/FFS
693	55			X				X	X			4/15	none		FFS
276	76	138	100	X				X	X	X	X	4/1	none		AFSSA;FFS/AFSSA*
234	82	111	99	X				X	X		X	4/1	none		FAF/FFS/AFSA/AFSSA;FAF/FFS/AFSA/AFSSA/

*Preferred need analysis document.

93

Institution	Tuition and fees	Add'l out-of-state/district tuition	Books and supplies	Costs for campus residents			Costs for students at home		
				Room and board	Trans-portation	Other costs	Board only	Trans-portation	Other costs
‡ Mississippi County Community College	648	1,272/144	250				900	853	2,282
† National Education Center: Arkansas College of Technology	5,260		100				2,349	522	1,152
‡ North Arkansas Community College	528	504/192	255				705	933	840
† Ouachita Baptist University	5,270		400	2,270	600	900	1,500	600	900
† Philander Smith College	2,350		400	2,300	400	750		400	750
Phillips County Community College	600	480/168	450				1,350	841	1,925
Rich Mountain Community College	580	1,242/160	300					600	470
Shorter College	1,860		250	2,200	100	200			300
Southern Arkansas University									
‡ El Dorado Branch	720	360/—	400				1,500		450
‡ Magnolia	1,080	630/—	320	2,100	300	600		500	600
‡ Technical Branch	720	360/—	400		500	900		700	800
University of Arkansas									
† Fayetteville	1,598	2,352/—	550	2,925	1,200	900			900
† Little Rock	1,570	2,340/—	500				2,100	800	800
Medical Sciences	1,548	2,352/—	470	4,600	831	1,600		1,080	1,600
† Monticello	1,410	1,820/—	400	1,880	450	800	1,100	900	800
† Pine Bluff	1,355	1,738/—	500	1,940	950	800		800	700
† University of Central Arkansas	1,290	1,260/—	300	2,156	330	660		550	660
† University of the Ozarks	3,420		500	2,310	700	2,200	1,000	1,120	1,200
Westark Community College	672	888/192	400				1,500	600	450
Williams Baptist College	3,110		400	2,220	350	600	860	900	450

California

Institution	Tuition and fees	Add'l out-of-state/district tuition	Books and supplies	Room and board	Trans-portation	Other costs	Board only	Trans-portation	Other costs
Academy of Art College	7,560		2,600	7,000			2,700	200	
‡ Allan Hancock College	118	2,880/—	325				1,500	425	900
American Academy of Dramatic Arts: West	7,175		450					510	1,215
‡ American Armenian International College	10,150		240				1,300		
‡ American River College	100	2,970/—	500					400	1,120
‡ Antelope Valley College	100	2,880/—	384					720	1,340
Antioch Southern California									
Los Angeles	7,500		350						
Santa Barbara	6,750		350						
Armstrong College	6,795		750						1,200
Art Center College of Design	10,785		3,400				4,000	1,300	1,250
Art Institute of Southern California	7,700						5,000	1,000	1,900
Azusa Pacific University	9,700		600	3,650	700	1,250		1,000	
‡ Bakersfield College	120	2,880/—	400	3,415	450	900		750	900
‡ Barstow College	100	2,880/—	500				1,600	450	1,200

†Figures are projected for 1991-92.   ‡Figures are for 1990-91.

Total freshmen	Percent receiving aid	Freshmen judged to have need	Percent offered aid	Need-based Acad	Need-based Music/drama	Need-based Art	Need-based Athl	Nonneed-based Acad	Nonneed-based Music/drama	Nonneed-based Art	Nonneed-based Athl	Priority	Closing	Inst aid form	Need analysis document
		400	100	X				X	X	X	X	4/15	none		AFSSA
344	95	327	100	X				X					none	X	FAF/FFS/AFSA*/SF
547	65							X	X	X	X	5/1	none		FFS
382	80	265	91					X	X		X	5/1	none		FAF/FFS*/AFSA/AFSSA*/SF;FAF/FFS/AFSA/AFSSA*/
218	90											5/1	none		FAF/FFS*
								X	X		X	4/1	5/1		FFS
													none		FFS
59	33	19	100									5/1	none		FAF/FFS*
190	54			X				X	X		X	7/1	none		FFS
478	70	370	100					X	X		X	6/1	none		AFSSA
		189	100					X	X		X	7/15	none		
2,379	66	1,200	100	X	X			X	X	X	X	4/1	none	X	FAF/FFS*;FAF/FFS
1,204	60			X				X	X	X	X	5/1	none		FFS
													5/1		FFS
514	70	403	95	X				X	X		X		none		FFS
879	86			X	X	X	X						none		FFS/AFSA*;FFS/AFSA*/CSS SAAC
2,114	65	1,020	100						X	X	X	4/15	8/1		
249	65	66	100	X				X	X		X	5/1	none		FAF/FFS/AFSSA*
				X				X				6/1	none		
166	82			X	X	X	X					6/1	none		FFS
		750	100	X		X		X			X		none	X	FAF/AFSA/CSS SAAC*/ACT SAAC/SF
				X	X	X	X	X	X	X	X		5/1		CSS SAAC*/ACT SAAC
71	53	48	79		X							7/1	none		FAF
22	100	18	78	X								4/30	5/31	X	CSS SAAC+CSS SAAC;FAF+CSS SAAC
													none		CSS SAAC
1,476	20	850	100	X	X	X		X	X	X		8/1	none	X	CSS SAAC*/ACT SAAC;FAF*/FFS/CSS SAAC/ACT SAAC
													none		FAF
													none		FAF
												3/2	none		FAF/CSS SAAC*/ACT SAAC;FAF
250	60			X		X		X			X	3/1	5/1	X	CSS SAAC;FAF
464	80			X	X		X	X	X		X	3/1	none	X	FFS/AFSA/CSS SAAC*/ACT SAAC/AFSSA/SF;FAF*/FFS/CSS SAAC/ACT SAAC;FAF*/FFS
				X				X				5/1	none	X	CSS SAAC*/ACT SAAC;AFSA/CSS SAAC*/ACT SAAC/CSS SAAC;FFS

*Preferred need analysis document.

Institution	Tuition and fees	Add'l out-of-state/district tuition	Books and supplies	Costs for campus residents			Costs for students at home		
				Room and board	Transportation	Other costs	Board only	Transportation	Other costs
† Bethany Bible College	6,210		550	3,000	600	1,200	1,500	650	1,200
Biola University	9,902		539	4,090	550	1,656	1,712	674	1,656
‡ Brooks College	5,710		1,000	3,580	1,300	1,100	1,100	900	1,100
Brooks Institute of Photography	6,050		3,000					800	1,400
‡ Butte College	155	2,820/—	450					675	800
‡ Cabrillo College	169	2,820/—	384				1,512	600	1,595
‡ California Baptist College	5,445		550	3,350	600	1,200	600	800	500
‡ California College of Arts and Crafts	9,760		600		522	1,314	1,512	612	1,458
† California College for Respiratory Therapy	5,895		365						
California Institute of the Arts	12,250		800	5,100	550	1,500		750	850
† California Institute of Technology	14,310		630	4,358	600	2,439	1,500		1,209
‡ California Lutheran University	9,450		504	4,200	522	1,548	2,100	630	1,548
California Maritime Academy	1,391	3,477/—	525	4,002	500	1,000			
† California Polytechnic State University: San Luis Obispo	1,181	7,380/—	450	3,897	522	1,314	1,512	612	1,458
† California State Polytechnic University: Pomona	1,012	7,380/—	558	4,118	570	1,638	731	684	1,638
California State University									
† Bakersfield	1,067	7,380/—	504	3,476	500	1,110	1,512		1,023
† Chico	1,066	7,380/—	504	3,720	522	1,330	1,512		1,256
† Dominguez Hills	1,027	7,380/—	504		522	1,359	1,512	648	1,359
† Fresno	1,070	7,380/—	504	3,675	428	1,114	1,512	622	1,048
† Fullerton	1,108	7,380/—	504		522	1,548	1,512	700	1,548
† Hayward	1,051	7,380/—	504				1,512	648	1,548
† Long Beach	1,046	7,380/—	558	4,326	576	1,638	1,512	684	1,638
† Los Angeles	1,046	7,380/—	504	4,671	522	1,548	1,512	646	1,548
† Northridge	1,128	7,380/—	504		550	2,450		550	3,000
† Sacramento	1,048	7,380/—	504	4,713	522	1,204	1,512	630	1,148
† San Bernardino	1,068	7,380/—	504		575	1,548	1,512	650	1,548

†Figures are projected for 1991-92.   ‡Figures are for 1990-91.

| All aid | | Need–based aid | | Grants and scholarships | | | | | | | | Financial aid deadlines | | Inst aid form | Need analysis document |
| | | | | Need–based | | | | Nonneed–based | | | | | | | |
Total freshmen	Percent receiving aid	Freshmen judged to have need	Percent offered aid	Acad	Music/drama	Art	Athl	Acad	Music/drama	Art	Athl	Priority	Closing		
170	82			X				X				6/1	none		CSS SAAC
								X	X	X	X	3/2	none		CSS SAAC;FAF
310	52							X					none		CSS SAAC*/ACT SAAC;FAF
				X		X						4/15	none		AFSA*/CSS SAAC/ACT SAAC;FAF/FFS/AFSA*
													none		FAF/FFS/AFSA/CSS SAAC*/ACT SAAC
													none		CSS SAAC*/ACT SAAC
152	89			X				X	X		X	4/15	none	X	CSS SAAC;FAF
95	42	42	100	X		X		X		X		3/2	none	X	CSS SAAC;FAF AFSA
						X				X		2/1	none		FAF/CSS SAAC*
209	70	125	100	X				X				2/1	none		CSS SAAC;FAF/CSS SAAC
332	75	180	100	X	X			X	X	X		3/2	none		FAF/AFSA/CSS SAAC*/ACT SAAC/SF; FAF/AFSA
153	35	37	89	X				X				3/2	none		FAF/FFS/AFSA/CSS SAAC*/ACT SAAC; FAF*/FFS/AFSA/CSS
1,657	15			X		X		X		X	X		3/1		CSS SAAC
2,070	37			X	X	X		X			X	3/2	none		FAF/CSS SAAC*/ACT SAAC
485	63			X	X	X	X	X	X	X	X	3/2	none	X	CSS SAAC*/ACT SAAC;FAF/FFS/AFSA
1,676	33			X	X	X	X	X				3/1	none		CSS SAAC*/ACT SAAC;FAF/CSS SAAC*
363	25							X	X	X	X	4/15	none		CSS SAAC
1,651	33	725	89	X	X	X	X	X	X	X	X	3/2	none		FAF/CSS SAAC*/ACT SAAC
2,099	25			X				X			X	3/2	none		CSS SAAC
742	27			X								3/2	none		CSS SAAC*/ACT SAAC
3,100	33							X	X	X	X	3/2	none		FAF/FFS/AFSA/CSS SAAC/ACT SAAC
1,595	48			X				X	X	X	X	3/1	none		CSS SAAC/ACT SAAC; FAF/FFS/AFSA/CSS SAAC/ACT SAAC
2,949	18			X	X	X		X	X	X	X	3/1	none		CSS SAAC*/ACT SAAC;FAF/FFS/CSS SAAC*/ACT SAAC
1,559	28			X	X	X						3/2	none		CSS SAAC/ACT SAAC; FAF/FFS/CSS SAAC/ACT SAAC
908	30	407	59	X	X	X		X				3/2	none		CSS SAAC

*Preferred need analysis document.

Institution	Tuition and fees	Add'l out-of-state/district tuition	Books and supplies	Costs for campus residents			Costs for students at home		
				Room and board	Transportation	Other costs	Board only	Transportation	Other costs
† San Marcos	1,096	7,380/—	504				1,512	648	1,268
† Stanislaus	1,072	7,380/—	504	3,795	522	1,065	1,512	630	1,165
‡ Canada College	115	3,000/—	490					650	1,450
Central California Commercial College	5,400		475						
‡ Cerritos Community College	100	2,910/—	420					655	998
‡ Cerro Coso Community College	100	2,960/—	480				1,500	580	765
‡ Chabot College	100	3,300/—	750				2,700	750	500
‡ Chaffey Community College	102	3,060/—	450				1,500	900	102
Chapman College	12,975		500	5,004	200	2,000	2,540	600	1,500
Charles R. Drew University: College of Allied Health	2,500		2,268		1,683	2,832	1,440	720	1,460
Christ College Irvine	8,790		525	4,170	525	855	1,740	750	855
Christian Heritage College	6,800		400	3,100	486	1,118	1,100	576	1,332
‡ Citrus College	115	2,880/—	450					640	1,000
‡ City College of San Francisco	100	3,120/—	460					310	1,600
Claremont McKenna College	14,810		500	5,180		800			800
‡ Coastline Community College	104	2,880/—	432				1,512	594	1,386
Cogswell Polytechnical College	6,280		600				1,512	711	1,350
Coleman College	8,093		400					1,000	1,000
‡ College of Alameda	104	2,408/—	350						
‡ College of the Canyons	100	2,880/—	425					250	
‡ College of the Desert	115	3,060/—	325					700	640
‡ College of Marin: Kentfield	106	3,030/—	400					675	
College of Notre Dame	10,165		558	5,100	576	1,638	1,512	684	1,638
‡ College of the Redwoods	100	2,856/—	504	3,620	522	1,119	1,512	648	1,116
‡ College of San Mateo	115	3,000/—	500						
‡ College of the Sequoias	115	2,880/—	350					500	650
‡ College of the Siskiyous	115	2,880/—	504	3,390	200	1,000	1,512	600	1,000

†Figures are projected for 1991-92.   ‡Figures are for 1990-91.

Total freshmen	Percent receiving aid	Freshmen judged to have need	Percent offered aid	Acad	Music/drama	Art	Athl	Acad	Music/drama	Art	Athl	Priority	Closing	Inst aid form	Need analysis document
All aid		Need-based aid		Grants and scholarships								Financial aid deadlines			
				Need-based				Nonneed-based							
367	25			X	X			X	X	X	X	3/2	none		CSS SAAC*/ACT SAAC;FAF/CSS SAAC*/ACT SAAC FAF/CSS SAAC*/ACT SAAC
				X	X							5/10	none		CSS SAAC
													none		AFSA*/CSS SAAC/ACT SAAC/AFSSA
													none	X	FAF/FFS/AFSA/CSS SAAC*/ACT SAAC
1,299	6			X	X	X		X	X	X		5/1	none		AFSA/CSS SAAC*/ACT SAAC;FAF*/FFS/AFSA
9,748	25			X				X				8/1	none		CSS SAAC/ACT SAAC;FAF/CSS SAAC/ACT SAAC
		650	100									5/1	none		FAF/FFS/AFSA/CSS SAAC*/ACT SAAC/AFSSA/SF
276	58	110	100	X				X	X	X	X	3/2	none		CSS SAAC;FAF
20	99	18	100	X				X					2/28		CSS SAAC;FAF/FFS/AFSA/CSS SAAC*/ACT SAAC
														X	FAF/AFSA/CSS SAAC*/ACT SAAC;FAF*/AFSA/ACT
90	85			X	X		X	X	X		X	6/1	none		FAF/CSS SAAC/ACT SAAC;FAF
													none		FAF/FFS/AFSA/CSS SAAC*/ACT SAAC
3,399	36	1,297	100	X	X	X	X	X				3/2	5/21	X	CSS SAAC/ACT SAAC
245	70	153	100					X					2/1		CSS SAAC*/ACT SAAC;FAF*/FFS
5,300	10	88	100										none		CSS SAAC;FAF/CSS SAAC*
13	29			X				X				5/1	none	X	CSS SAAC;FAF*/FFS
331	87												none		FAF*/CSS SAAC
3,373	15												none		CSS SAAC/ACT SAAC
				X				X					none		CSS SAAC;FAF/CSS SAAC*
													none		CSS SAAC
													none		CSS SAAC
77	85	62	100	X				X	X	X	X	3/2	11/1	X	CSS SAAC*/ACT SAAC/AFSSA;FAF/FFS/AFSA/CSS
2,244	50	350	100	X				X		X		4/1	none		CSS SAAC;FAF/FFS/AFSA/CSS SAAC*/ACT SAAC
2,758	26	1,249	100	X	X		X	X				3/2	none	X	CSS SAAC;FAF CSS SAAC*/ACT SAAC
430	25							X				4/30	none		FAF/AFSA/CSS SAAC*/ACT SAAC/SF

*Preferred need analysis document.

Institution	Tuition and fees	Add'l out-of-state/district tuition	Books and supplies	Costs for campus residents			Costs for students at home		
				Room and board	Transportation	Other costs	Board only	Transportation	Other costs
‡ Columbia College	125	2,880/—	500		400	1,000	750	500	700
Columbia College: Hollywood	5,250		550					700	1,800
‡ Compton Community College	106	2,880/—	360						
‡ Contra Costa College	102	2,850/—	504				1,512	630	1,548
‡ Cosumnes River College	100	2,970/—	450					850	2,450
‡ Crafton Hills College	115	2,880/—	440					750	550
‡ Cuesta College	150	2,880/—	360				1,950	540	846
‡ Cuyamaca College	125	3,060/—	433				1,500	590	690
‡ Cypress College	125	3,090/—	500				1,100	750	750
† De Anza College	165	3,195/—	558					684	1,301
Deep Springs College	0		300		1,250	350			
DeVry Institute of Technology: City of Industry	5,015		500				1,839	2,769	1,446
‡ Diablo Valley College	102	2,850/—							
† Dominican College of San Rafael	10,164		558	5,184	576	1,638		684	1,638
Dominican School of Philosophy and Theology	4,815		400			1,800		950	1,800
Don Bosco Technical Institute	3,700		400					450	400
D-Q University	3,040		475	3,076	470	1,475	750	470	1,475
‡ East Los Angeles College	150	3,210/—	385				1,100	576	1,300
‡ El Camino College	100	3,150/—					1,500	600	500
‡ Evergreen Valley College	115	3,000/—	500					650	800
Fashion Institute of Design and Merchandising Los Angeles	9,545	150/—	1,050						
San Francisco	9,545	150/—	975				1,410	612	1,512
† Feather River College	125	3,000/—	600					700	1,200
‡ Foothill College	151	2,970/—	510					700	1,000
‡ Fresno City College	115	2,880/—	500				1,600	900	1,300
Fresno Pacific College	8,356		558	3,484	576	1,638		684	1,638
‡ Fullerton College	115	3,235/—	300						

†Figures are projected for 1991-92.   ‡Figures are for 1990-91.

| All aid | | Need–based aid | | Grants and scholarships | | | | | | | | Financial aid deadlines | | Inst aid form | Need analysis document |
| | | | | Need–based | | | | Nonneed–based | | | | | | | |
Total freshmen	Percent receiving aid	Freshmen judged to have need	Percent offered aid	Acad	Music/drama	Art	Athl	Acad	Music/drama	Art	Athl	Priority	Closing		
419	8			X	X	X		X	X	X		4/30	none		CSS SAAC;FAF/CSS SAAC*
													none		FAF/AFSA*/CSS SAAC
1,070	75			X				X	X	X	X		5/15	X	FAF/FFS/AFSA/CSS SAAC*/ACT SAAC/SF
													none	X	CSS SAAC
				X			X					5/15	none		CSS SAAC*/ACT SAAC;FAF/FFS/CSS SAAC/ACT SAAC
				X				X				5/1	none		FAF/FFS/AFSA*/CSS SAAC
				X				X				5/1	none		FAF/FFS/AFSA/CSS SAAC*/ACT SAAC/AFSSA
1,737	15													X	CSS SAAC;FAF
15,458	15			X	X				X			7/1	none		CSS SAAC
				X	X	X		X	X	X		3/2	none		CSS SAAC;FAF*/CSS SAAC
14	100	14	100					X					none		CSS SAAC
651	81							X					none		FAF
12,820	10			X				X				3/2	none		CSS SAAC;FAF
87	62	58	100	X	X		X	X	X		X	3/2	none	X	FAF/AFSA/CSS SAAC*/ACT SAAC
													none		CSS SAAC
													none		FAF/FFS/AFSA/CSS SAAC*/ACT SAAC
72	70			X									none		CSS SAAC;FAF/AFSA
													none		ACT SAAC
19,134	8							X	X	X	X	6/1	none		CSS SAAC
2,979	20							X				7/1			CSS SAAC*/ACT SAAC
1,382	74											3/2	none	X	FAF/AFSA/CSS SAAC*;FAF/AFSA*/CSS SAAC
													none		FAF/AFSA/CSS SAAC*;FAF/AFSA*/CSS SAAC
364	20	85	71	X				X				3/2	none		FAF/AFSA/CSS SAAC*/ACT SAAC;FAF/AFSA*/CSS SAAC
3,040	11	280	100	X	X	X	X	X	X	X	X	6/15	none	X	FAF/CSS SAAC/ACT SAAC
				X				X	X	X		4/15	none		FAF/FFS/AFSA/CSS SAAC*/ACT SAAC/AFSSA/SF;FAF*/FFS/
142	90			X	X	X	X					1/31	none	X	CSS SAAC*/ACT SAAC;FAF*/ACT SAAC
3,795	3			X				X	X	X	X	7/15	none		CSS SAAC*/ACT SAAC;FAF/FFS

*Preferred need analysis document.

Institution	Tuition and fees	Add'l out-of-state/district tuition	Books and supplies	Costs for campus residents			Costs for students at home		
				Room and board	Trans-portation	Other costs	Board only	Trans-portation	Other costs
† Gavilan Community College	127	3,000/—	550				1,520	648	1,600
‡ Glendale Community College	125	2,880/—							
‡ Golden Gate University	4,812		450				1,500	774	2,268
‡ Golden West College	115	2,880/—	504					630	1,548
‡ Grossmont Community College	115	3,060/—	533				1,500	650	730
‡ Hartnell College	100	2,300/—	530				1,536	594	1,380
‡ Harvey Mudd College	14,910		450	5,890		900			
Heald Business College									
Rohnert Park	5,400		450						
San Jose	5,850		450						
Walnut Creek	6,300		450						
Heald College: Sacramento	5,850		450						
Heald Institute of Technology	6,325		450						
Hebrew Union College: Jewish Institute of Religion	6,000		750						
‡ Holy Names College	8,510		504	4,150	522	1,548	1,512	630	1,548
† Humboldt State University	1,095	7,380/—	504	3,606	479	1,119	1,600	512	1,119
† Humphreys College	4,032		615		2,025	1,200	2,610	810	1,458
‡ Imperial Valley College	100	3,160/—	558					684	1,638
‡ Irvine Valley College	120	2,880/—	480					865	1,386
‡ ITT Technical Institute: Sacramento	6,389		706				2,043	2,000	1,143
‡ John F. Kennedy University	4,770		504					675	
Kelsey-Jenney Business College	5,975								
† Kings River Community College	115	2,960/—	551	1,588	688	1,053	643	688	1,053
La Sierra University	10,050		450	3,351	522	1,314	1,512	612	1,458
‡ Lake Tahoe Community College	106	3,510/—	504				1,512	594	1,386
‡ Laney College	104	2,910/—	432				1,512	600	1,150
‡ Lassen College	110	2,880/—	454	2,400	529	1,304	1,588	624	1,455
LIFE Bible College	4,340		350	2,750		425		200	425
Lincoln University	3,884		400					360	
‡ Long Beach City College	120	2,940/—							
‡ Los Angeles City College	100	3,360/—	400					600	1,500

†Figures are projected for 1991-92. ‡Figures are for 1990-91.

All aid		Need-based aid		Grants and scholarships								Financial aid deadlines		Inst aid form	Need analysis document
				Need-based				Nonneed-based							
Total freshmen	Percent receiving aid	Freshmen judged to have need	Percent offered aid	Acad	Music/drama	Art	Athl	Acad	Music/drama	Art	Athl	Priority	Closing		
4,173	15			X				X	X	X	X	4/15	none		CSS SAAC
												7/1	none		ACT SAAC/SF;ACT SAAC/SF
41	33	8	100	X				X				2/15	none	X	CSS SAAC
				X		X				X		6/30	none		FAF/AFSA/CSS SAAC*/ACT SAAC/SF
4,995	10			X	X	X	X	X	X	X	X	4/1	none	X	FAF/AFSA/CSS SAAC*/ACT SAAC
															CSS SAAC+ACT SAAC; FAF+ACT SAAC
176	78	110	100					X					2/15	X	CSS SAAC*/ACT SAAC;FAF*/CSS SAAC/ACT SAAC
													none	X	FAF/FFS/AFSA/CSS SAAC*/ACT SAAC
		52	100	X								6/1	none	X	AFSA*/CSS SAAC
														X	AFSA
				X				X				6/30	none	X	FAF/CSS SAAC
													none	X	AFSA
				X									none		
99	75	61	100	X	X			X	X			3/2	none		CSS SAAC*/ACT SAAC;FAF*/FFS
849	44			X	X	X		X	X	X		3/2	none		FAF/FFS/AFSA/CSS SAAC*/ACT SAAC/AFSSA/SF;FAF/FFS/
96	60												none		FAF/CSS SAAC*;FAF
1,200	40							X	X	X	X		none	X	FAF/FFS/AFSA*/CSS SAAC/ACT SAAC/AFSSA/SF
															CSS SAAC;FAF*/CSS SAAC
													none	X	SF
				X				X				4/1	none		FAF/AFSA/CSS SAAC*/ACT SAAC
														X	FAF/FFS/AFSA/CSS SAAC/ACT SAAC;FAF/FFS/AFSA
1,622	32	552	100	X	X		X	X	X		X	6/1	none		FAF/FFS/AFSA/CSS SAAC*/ACT SAAC/SF
256	85			X				X				5/1	none		FAF
		100	100	X				X				7/1	none		CSS SAAC
												4/15	none		CSS SAAC
772	85			X				X				7/15	none		CSS SAAC*/ACT SAAC
57	25			X				X				6/1	none	X	FAF/FFS/AFSA/CSS SAAC*/ACT SAAC/AFSSA/SF;CSS SAAC
													none		CSS SAAC/ACT SAAC
6,284	20			X	X	X		X	X	X		5/19	none		CSS SAAC
2,000	20			X	X	X	X						6/12		AFSA/CSS SAAC/ACT SAAC;FAF/AFSA/CSS SAAC/ACT SAAC

*Preferred need analysis document.

Institution	Tuition and fees	Add'l out-of-state/district tuition	Books and supplies	Costs for campus residents			Costs for students at home		
				Room and board	Transportation	Other costs	Board only	Transportation	Other costs
‡ Los Angeles Harbor College	100	3,360/—	400					500	
† Los Angeles Mission College	100	2,688/—	400				1,100	576	1,332
‡ Los Angeles Pierce College	100	3,360/—	504					630	1,548
‡ Los Angeles Southwest College	100	2,910/—	400					606	1,212
‡ Los Angeles Trade and Technical College	100	3,360/—	504				1,512	630	1,548
† Los Angeles Valley College	100	3,360/—	450					600	1,500
† Los Medanos College	102	2,852/—	480				1,700	700	1,550
† Louise Salinger Academy of Fashion	12,688		1,090						
Loyola Marymount University	11,376		558	5,671	576	1,638	1,512	684	1,638
† Marymount College	10,510		558		684	1,638	1,512	684	1,638
† Master's College	6,950		504	3,690	522	1,548	1,512	630	1,548
‡ Mendocino College	106	2,712/—	500					650	1,600
Menlo College	12,390		520	6,030	500	1,650	1,500	700	1,650
‡ Merced College	116	2,880/—	450				1,500	625	1,450
† Merritt College	104	3,020/—	450					240	2,000
Mills College	14,000		420	5,700		1,275	1,184	580	1,330
‡ MiraCosta College	126	2,880/—	450				1,512	450	900
‡ Mission College	122	2,940/—	504				1,557	630	1,483
‡ Modesto Junior College	122	3,060/—	558					684	900
Monterey Institute of International Studies	11,345		500					655	1,400
‡ Monterey Peninsula College	135	2,820/—	432				1,512	594	1,386
† Moorpark College	115	3,150/—	500				1,500	1,000	500
Mount St. Mary's College	10,250		558	4,650	576	1,638	1,512	648	1,638
‡ Mount San Antonio College	129	2,850/—	445				1,557	612	1,175
† Mount San Jacinto College	102	2,880/—	450				1,512	450	1,170
‡ Napa Valley College	100	2,880/—	400				1,512	594	1,250
† National Hispanic University	3,100		500					1,600	
National University	5,535		450					900	450
‡ New College of California	5,850		590					800	2,268

†Figures are projected for 1991-92.   ‡Figures are for 1990-91.

| All aid | | Need-based aid | | Grants and scholarships | | | | | | | | Financial aid deadlines | | Inst aid form | Need analysis document |
| Total freshmen | Percent receiving aid | Freshmen judged to have need | Percent offered aid | Need-based | | | | Nonneed-based | | | | | | | |
				Acad	Music/drama	Art	Athl	Acad	Music/drama	Art	Athl	Priority	Closing		
4,745	14	186	100					X				3/14	none	X	FAF/AFSA/CSS SAAC*/ACT SAAC; FAF/AFSA/CSS
		102	100									8/1	none		CSS SAAC/ACT SAAC
2,500	1			X				X				7/7	none		FAF/CSS SAAC/ACT SAAC/AFSSA
		931	71									7/7	none		CSS SAAC FAF/CSS SAAC*/ACT SAAC;FAF*/CSS SAAC/ACT SAAC
8,560	5											6/12	none		CSS SAAC*/ACT SAAC
4,848	10	1,400	86	X				X				3/2	8/1		FAF/FFS/AFSA/CSS SAAC*/ACT SAAC/AFSSA
25	60												none		FAF/AFSA/CSS SAAC/ACT SAAC
767	63	474	85	X	X	X	X	X	X		X	2/15	none		CSS SAAC*/ACT SAAC;FAF*/FFS/CSS SAAC/ACT SAAC
522	40	186	100	X	X	X	X	X					3/2		FAF/FFS/AFSA/CSS SAAC/ACT SAAC;FAF/FFS/CSS SAAC/ACT
224	90	153	100					X	X		X	3/31	6/15		CSS SAAC;FAF/CSS SAAC
												5/31	11/1		CSS SAAC;FAF
		68	88	X				X				3/2	none		CSS SAAC;FAF
2,273	35							X				6/1	none		CSS SAAC;FAF
1,386	28			X								4/1	none		CSS SAAC
158	67	106	100	X	X	X		X	X	X			2/15	X	CSS SAAC;FAF
4,829	10	370	100					X	X	X		5/16	none		FAF/FFS/AFSA/CSS SAAC*/ACT SAAC/AFSSA/SF
3,341	8	600	67	X				X				5/1	none	X	AFSA/CSS SAAC*/ACT SAAC
2,000	25							X	X	X		3/2	none	X	FAF/FFS/AFSA/CSS SAAC*/ACT SAAC/SF
				X				X					3/1	X	CSS SAAC+FAF;FAF/APSGFSA
								X	X	X	X	3/2	none		CSS SAAC/ACT SAAC
2,493	5											5/16	none	X	CSS SAAC;FAF*/FFS
174	75	142	99	X	X	X		X				3/1	none		CSS SAAC*/ACT SAAC;FAF/FFS/CSS SAAC*
				X		X		X			X	5/26	none		CSS SAAC
5,821	20	371	100	X				X	X	X	X		none	X	FAF/AFSA/CSS SAAC*/ACT SAAC
				X		X	X	X	X	X	X	5/5	none		AFSA
														X	CSS SAAC
													none	X	FAF*/CSS SAAC
51	85											5/30	none		CSS SAAC;FAF/CSS SAAC

*Preferred need analysis document.

Institution	Tuition and fees	Add'l out-of-state/district tuition	Books and supplies	Costs for campus residents			Costs for students at home		
				Room and board	Transportation	Other costs	Board only	Transportation	Other costs
† Northrop University	10,700		800		1,020	2,189	3,060	1,603	2,189
Occidental College	14,784		530	5,216		1,152	1,859	500	1,152
† Ohlone College	100	2,910/—	450				2,400	1,000	1,600
‡ Orange Coast College	131	3,060/—	500					750	
‡ Otis Art Institute of Parsons School of Design	10,050		1,440		480	600		480	600
† Oxnard College	115	3,125/—	500				1,500	450	1,000
Pacific Christian College	5,600		500	5,000	600	1,500	2,000	700	1,500
‡ Pacific Oaks College	8,900		400				1,000	1,200	1,100
Pacific Union College	9,585		555	3,315	570	1,200	1,500	570	1,200
‡ Palo Verde College	100	1,170/—	360						
† Palomar College	115	2,880/—	500				1,512	500	1,281
‡ Pasadena City College	115	2,850/—	400				1,100	225	860
Patten College	3,490		500	3,695	400	1,000	1,500	300	1,450
Pepperdine University	15,230		800	6,070	660	660	2,450	1,450	726
Phillips Junior College									
‡ Fresno Campus	3,616		500						
San Fernando Valley Campus	9,075		750						
Pitzer College	16,282		650	5,002		900			900
Point Loma Nazarene College	8,058		604	3,624	650	2,000	2,000	630	1,458
‡ Pomona College	14,030		550	5,700		850	2,000	700	
‡ Porterville College	120	2,880/—	400					350	630
Queen of the Holy Rosary College	2,500								
‡ Rancho Santiago Community College	115	2,880/—	450				1,512	594	962
† Rio Hondo College	115	2,946/—	400						
‡ Riverside Community College	100	2,880/—	470				1,512	648	1,008
† Sacramento City College	100	3,060/—	420				2,350	495	735
† Saddleback College	140	3,060/—	450					800	1,200
‡ St. John's Seminary College	4,035		500	1,100	500	850			
St. Mary's College of California	11,036		558	5,436	576	1,638	1,512	684	1,638

†Figures are projected for 1991-92.   ‡Figures are for 1990-91.

Total freshmen	Percent receiving aid	Freshmen judged to have need	Percent offered aid	Acad	Music/ drama	Art	Athl	Acad	Music/ drama	Art	Athl	Priority	Closing	Inst aid form	Need analysis document
	All aid	**Need–based aid**		**Grants and scholarships**								**Financial aid deadlines**			
				Need–based				**Nonneed–based**							
114	15	20	90	X				X				5/1	none	X	FAF/CSS SAAC*/ACT SAAC;FAF*/FFS/CSS SAAC/ACT SAAC
398	55	260	100	X				X	X				2/1	X	CSS SAAC;FAF
1,620	7	103	100	X	X	X		X	X	X		7/1	none		FAF/CSS SAAC*/ACT SAAC;FAF/FFS/AFSA/ACT SAAC
		461	83	X	X	X	X	X	X		X	6/1	none		AFSA/CSS SAAC*/ACT SAAC;FAF*/AFSA/CSS SAAC/ACT
				X	X							3/1	none	X	CSS SAAC;FAF
1,825	10											7/1	none	X	CSS SAAC;FAF/CSS SAAC*/ACT SAAC
77	90			X	X			X	X			3/31	none	X	FAF*/FFS/CSS SAAC;FAF*/FFS
				X				X				3/1	none	X	CSS SAAC;FAF
								X	X			3/2	none	X	FAF/FFS/AFSA/CSS SAAC*/ACT SAAC;FAF
													none		CSS SAAC;FAF/CSS SAAC*
4,030	12	450	100	X				X				4/1	none		CSS SAAC*/ACT SAAC;FAF/CSS SAAC*
1,610	15							X	X	X	X	6/24	none	X	CSS SAAC;FAF*/FFS
46	80			X				X					3/2		FAF/AFSA/CSS SAAC*
678	63			X	X	X	X	X	X	X	X	2/15	4/1	X	CSS SAAC;FAF*/FFS
															FAF/FFS/AFSA/CSS SAAC/ACT SAAC
													none	X	AFSA+CSS SAAC
151	47	65	100										2/1		CSS SAAC*/ACT SAAC;FAF*/FFS
							X				X	3/15	none		FAF/CSS SAAC*/ACT SAAC;FAF
370	52	199	100										none	X	CSS SAAC;FAF
1,736	40			X				X				8/1	none		CSS SAAC;FAF*/AFSA/CSS SAAC
3,681	3							X	X	X	X	6/30	none		CSS SAAC;CSS SAAC+FAF
2,660	11			X	X	X	X	X	X	X	X	7/15	none	X	CSS SAAC
3,604	38			X	X	X		X	X	X		4/30	none		FAF/AFSA/CSS SAAC*/ACT SAAC
9,966	35			X	X	X						4/15	none	X	FAF/AFSA/CSS SAAC*/ACT SAAC
18,710	6			X				X	X	X	X	3/1	5/1		FAF/CSS SAAC*/ACT SAAC
												4/30	none	X	AFSA
391	50										X		3/15	X	CSS SAAC;FAF

*Preferred need analysis document.

Institution	Tuition and fees	Add'l out-of-state/district tuition	Books and supplies	Costs for campus residents			Costs for students at home		
				Room and board	Trans-portation	Other costs	Board only	Trans-portation	Other costs
‡ Samuel Merritt College	10,165		504	4,400	900	2,373	1,512	900	2,373
‡ San Bernardino Valley College	115	2,880/—	350				1,350	800	600
‡ San Diego City College	115	2,910/—	460				3,000	1,000	2,000
‡ San Diego Mesa College	115	3,060/—	360					890	935
‡ San Diego Miramar College	105	2,910/—	500					800	1,000
† San Diego State University	1,118	7,380/—	504	3,900	355	1,548	1,512	648	1,268
‡ San Francisco Art Institute	10,100		1,100				2,000	220	765
San Francisco College of Mortuary Science	6,390		500				3,600	1,800	1,200
San Francisco Conservatory of Music	9,400		560				1,570	690	1,640
† San Francisco State University	1,052	7,380/—	550	4,204	522	1,500		750	1,400
† San Joaquin Delta College	150	3,030/—	500				2,000	1,200	1,500
San Jose Christian College	4,611		450	2,460	522	1,314	1,512	612	1,458
‡ San Jose City College	115	3,210/—	500					650	800
† San Jose State University	1,130	7,380/—	504	4,316	600	1,504		630	1,548
† Santa Barbara City College	135	3,000/—	600				2,000	800	1,200
‡ Santa Clara University	10,485		504	5,007	522	1,548	1,512	630	1,548
† Santa Monica College	135	3,360/—	400					585	
† Santa Rosa Junior College	115	2,880/—	558		684	1,638	1,512	684	1,638
Scripps College	14,800		500	6,350		700			2,650
‡ Shasta College	126	2,790/—	434		500	1,200	1,500	500	900
‡ Sierra College	115	2,870/—	500	3,244	300	1,000	1,500	800	1,000
Simpson College	6,338		558	3,480	576	1,638	1,512	684	1,638
‡ Skyline College	115	3,000/—	384				1,300	576	1,332
‡ Solano Community College	108	2,940/—	432				1,595	594	1,386
† Sonoma State University	1,074	7,380/—	504	4,332	258	1,125		462	900
Southern California College	7,788		500	3,500	574	1,445	530	612	1,458
† Southern California Institute of Architecture	9,475		1,400					1,380	

†Figures are projected for 1991-92.   ‡Figures are for 1990-91.

All aid		Need-based aid		Grants and scholarships — Need-based				Grants and scholarships — Nonneed-based				Financial aid deadlines		Inst aid form	Need analysis document
Total freshmen	Percent receiving aid	Freshmen judged to have need	Percent offered aid	Acad	Music/drama	Art	Athl	Acad	Music/drama	Art	Athl	Priority	Closing		
25	80	8	100	X				X				3/2	none	X	FAF/AFSA/CSS SAAC*/ACT SAAC; FAF/AFSA
													none		CSS SAAC*/ACT SAAC;FAF
								X	X	X	X	5/1	none	X	CSS SAAC
												5/1	none		CSS SAAC
												5/1	none	X	FAF/CSS SAAC*/ACT SAAC
5,914	39			X	X		X	X	X	X	X	3/2	none		CSS SAAC/ACT SAAC; FAF/FFS/CSS SAAC/ACT SAAC
27	65									X		4/1	none		FAF/CSS SAAC*/ACT SAAC;FAF
31	85												9/5		FAF/FFS/AFSA/AFSSA
16	63	9	100		X				X			4/1	none	X	FAF/CSS SAAC*;FAF
								X	X			3/1	none		CSS SAAC/ACT SAAC
5,008	11	602	94	X				X	X	X		5/1	8/1		CSS SAAC;FAF*/AFSA
21	80			X	X		X	X	X		X	3/2	none	X	CSS SAAC;FAF/CSS SAAC
8,914	6											7/1	none		CSS SAAC*/ACT SAAC;FAF*/FFS
											X	3/1	none		FAF/FFS/AFSA/CSS SAAC*/ACT SAAC/AFSSA;FAF*/FFS
				X				X				5/15	none		FAF/FFS/AFSA/CSS SAAC*/ACT SAAC/SF
927	53	487	100	X	X	X		X	X		X	2/1	none		CSS SAAC;FAF/CSS SAAC
3,893	23			X	X	X	X	X	X	X	X	5/15	none	X	FAF/CSS SAAC*/ACT SAAC
				X				X	X	X	X	3/15	none		FAF/AFSA/CSS SAAC/ACT SAAC
152	46	83	100	X				X				2/1	3/2	X	CSS SAAC;FAF*/CSS SAAC
3,000	27			X	X	X	X	X	X	X	X	3/2	none		FAF/FFS/AFSA/CSS SAAC*/ACT SAAC
2,035	5							X					3/15		FAF/CSS SAAC*/ACT SAAC
62	96	54	100	X	X		X	X	X		X	3/31	none	X	CSS SAAC*/ACT SAAC/SF;FAF/FFS/SF
6,662	8			X								5/13	none	X	CSS SAAC*/ACT SAAC;FAF
													none		CSS SAAC*/ACT SAAC
635	50			X				X	X			3/2	none		FAF/FFS/AFSA/CSS SAAC*/ACT SAAC
159	80			X	X		X	X				3/2	none	X	CSS SAAC*/ACT SAAC;FAF
41	54			X		X		X		X		3/2	5/31	X	FAF/CSS SAAC*

*Preferred need analysis document.

Institution	Tuition and fees	Add'l out-of-state/ district tuition	Books and supplies	Costs for campus residents			Costs for students at home		
				Room and board	Trans-portation	Other costs	Board only	Trans-portation	Other costs
‡ Southwestern College	134	2,610/—	450				1,512	612	1,458
Stanford University	15,102		765	6,159		1,235			1,235
‡ Taft College	100	2,888/—	250	1,480	505	1,385	1,500	505	1,385
‡ Thomas Aquinas College	10,350		275	4,420	600	700		650	900
† United States International University	9,810		500	4,725	580	1,600	1,500	660	1,320
University of California									
‡ Berkeley	2,020	6,416/—	500	5,580	300	1,394	1,700	300	1,394
‡ Davis	1,780	6,416/—	636	4,741	652	1,876		743	1,876
‡ Irvine	1,875	6,416/—	600	4,969	522	1,352	1,504	612	1,418
‡ Los Angeles	1,686	6,416/—	615	4,850	610	1,330	2,530	2,580	65
‡ Riverside	1,693	6,416/—	655	4,850	400	1,100	1,000	1,200	832
‡ San Diego	1,813	6,416/—	504	5,562	522	1,510	1,512	630	1,520
‡ San Francisco	2,019	6,416/—	949	4,455	630	1,080	1,620	630	1,530
‡ Santa Barbara	1,729	6,416/—	580	4,732	351	1,384	1,512	351	1,384
‡ Santa Cruz	1,892	6,416/—	550	4,787	425	1,315	1,620	425	1,315
University of Judaism	8,260		700	5,800	750	1,680	1,600	645	1,540
University of La Verne	11,165		504	4,500	600	1,000		1,548	648
University of the Pacific	14,480		565	5,100	840	1,050	1,500	840	1,050
University of Redlands	14,130		450	5,370		900			900
University of San Diego	11,440		500	5,750	500	1,580	1,500	900	1,380
University of San Francisco	11,040		500	5,214	600	1,500	1,720	600	1,500
University of Southern California	15,306		594	6,260	580	1,640	1,602	879	1,640
‡ University of West Los Angeles	3,543		250					1,000	1,500
‡ Ventura College	115	3,210/—	430				1,500	225	1,025
‡ Victor Valley College	100	2,820/—	800					2,000	1,500
‡ Vista Community College	100	2,910/—	400						
West Coast Christian College	3,560		493	2,904	510	1,514	1,479	616	1,514

†Figures are projected for 1991-92.   ‡Figures are for 1990-91.

| All aid | | Need–based aid | | Grants and scholarships | | | | | | | | Financial aid deadlines | | Inst aid form | Need analysis document |
| Total freshmen | Percent receiving aid | Freshmen judged to have need | Percent offered aid | Need–based | | | | Nonneed–based | | | | | | | |
				Acad	Music/drama	Art	Athl	Acad	Music/drama	Art	Athl	Priority	Closing		
3,026	23	658	83									4/30	none		CSS SAAC
1,600	60	807	100	X	X	X	X				X		2/1	X	AFSA/CSS SAAC*/ACT SAAC;FAF*/FFS/AFSA
				X				X				8/1	none		CSS SAAC;FFS/CSS SAAC*
64	70	46	100									3/1	9/1	X	FAF*/FFS
148	64							X	X		X	4/15	none	X	FAF/FFS/AFSA/CSS SAAC*/ACT SAAC; FAF*/FFS/AFSA
3,160	41			X				X			X		3/2		AFSA/CSS SAAC*/ACT SAAC/AFSSA; FAF*/FFS/AFSA/CSS
3,294	72	1,273	100	X				X					3/2	none	CSS SAAC*/ACT SAAC
								X	X	X	X	3/2	5/1		CSS SAAC+FAF;FAF/CSS SAAC*
3,636	54			X				X	X	X	X		3/2	X	CSS SAAC;FAF
1,583	51			X				X	X	X	X	3/2	none		FAF/AFSA/CSS SAAC*/ACT SAAC
2,547	41	1,397	100	X				X	X			3/2	5/1		CSS SAAC/ACT SAAC; FAF/FFS
												7/1	none	X	FAF/FFS/CSS SAAC*/ACT SAAC
2,803	43	586	100	X	X	X	X	X	X	X	X		3/2		FAF/FFS/AFSA/CSS SAAC/ACT SAAC*
1,906	48	839	87	X				X				3/2	none		FAF/FFS/CSS SAAC*/ACT SAAC;FAF*/FFS/CSS SAAC/ACT SAAC
20	70	14	100					X				3/2		X	FAF/FFS/AFSA/CSS SAAC*;FAF/FFS/AFSA/CSS SAAC
314	73	136	100	X				X	X			3/1	none	X	CSS SAAC;FAF*/FFS/CSS SAAC
669	63	245	100	X	X		X		X		X	3/2	none	X	CSS SAAC*/ACT SAAC;FAF*/FFS/ACT SAAC
317	86	245	100	X	X	X		X	X	X		3/1	6/30		FAF/FFS/CSS SAAC*/ACT SAAC
880	46	329	100	X			X	X			X	3/1	none		CSS SAAC;FAF*/FFS/CSS SAAC/ACT SAAC
437	68	285	100	X			X	X			X	3/2	none		AFSA/CSS SAAC*/ACT SAAC;FAF
2,361	59	1,272	100	X	X			X	X	X	X	2/15	8/15	X	CSS SAAC*/ACT SAAC;FAF*/FFS
				X									none		AFSA
4,000	15			X	X	X			X	X		3/2	5/1		FAF/FFS/AFSA/CSS SAAC*/ACT SAAC
		480	100	X				X					none	X	AFSA/CSS SAAC*/ACT SAAC
													none		FAF/CSS SAAC
52	85			X	X		X	X	X		X		none		CSS SAAC;FAF

*Preferred need analysis document.

Institution	Tuition and fees	Add'l out-of-state/district tuition	Books and supplies	Costs for campus residents			Costs for students at home		
				Room and board	Trans-portation	Other costs	Board only	Trans-portation	Other costs
West Coast University	8,250		500						
‡ West Hills College	100	2,880/—	500				2,880	600	1,162
‡ West Los Angeles College	100	3,060/—	432				1,512	594	1,386
‡ West Valley College	136	2,940/—	504					648	1,548
Western State University College of Law									
‡ Orange County	9,190		530				1,500	1,584	1,500
‡ San Diego	9,190		530				1,500	2,112	1,664
Westmont College	12,070		450	4,650	750	830	2,000	750	830
† Whittier College	14,532		494	4,966	548	1,450	1,588	662	1,607
Woodbury University	10,236		615	5,200	576	1,638	1,512	684	1,638
World College West	9,800		420	4,300	400	1,400		400	1,400
Yeshiva Ohr Elchonon Chabad/West Coast Talmudical Seminary	2,900		125	2,700					
† Yuba College	115	3,060/—	400	2,670	500	1,100	2,592	800	1,100

Colorado

Institution	Tuition and fees	Add'l out-of-state/district tuition	Books and supplies	Room and board	Trans-portation	Other costs	Board only	Trans-portation	Other costs
‡ Adams State College	1,444	2,342/—	500	2,612	140	1,060	660	140	1,060
‡ Aims Community College	663	3,081/525	265					531	954
‡ Arapahoe Community College	1,092	2,826/—	400				1,750	850	75
Bel-Rea Institute of Animal Technology	4,175		500				1,584	195	1,053
Beth-El College of Nursing	2,906								
‡ Blair Junior College	4,470		400						
† Colorado Christian University	5,205		400	3,190	250	800	700	800	750
Colorado College	13,665		400	3,645	225	900			900
‡ Colorado Institute of Art	7,150		1,000					675	1,250
Colorado Mountain College									
Alpine Campus	1,600	3,150/—	500	3,200	200	900	1,500	400	800
Spring Valley Campus	1,600	3,150/—	400	3,200	200	900	1,500	400	800
Timberline Campus	1,600	3,150/—	350	3,000	200	900	1,500	400	800
† Colorado Northwestern Community College	210	2,460/670	490	2,690	575	1,300	3,120	400	1,300
‡ Colorado School of Mines	3,892	6,272/—	540	3,680	400	1,000	1,575	600	1,000
‡ Colorado State University	2,222	1,316/—	450	3,462		1,850			1,850
Colorado Technical College	5,710		700				800	800	200
Community College of Aurora	992	2,826/—	400						
‡ Community College of Denver	1,098	2,826/—	415				1,115	720	916
Denver Technical College	6,600							750	450
‡ Fort Lewis College	1,420	3,628/—	525	2,840	325	550		325	550
‡ Front Range Community College	1,092	2,826/—	365				875	570	600
‡ ITT Technical Institute: Aurora	5,075		1,250						
‡ Lamar Community College	1,167	1,884/—	385	2,618	436	329	1,600	436	329
‡ Mesa State College	1,432	2,338/—	425	2,932	350	800	650	360	750
‡ Metropolitan State College of Denver	1,321	3,114/—	420				1,469	756	851
‡ Morgan Community College	1,002	2,826/—	400				1,170	630	720

†Figures are projected for 1991-92.   ‡Figures are for 1990-91.

| All aid | | Need-based aid | | Grants and scholarships | | | | | | | | Financial aid deadlines | | Inst aid form | Need analysis document |
Total freshmen	Percent receiving aid	Freshmen judged to have need	Percent offered aid	Need-based Acad	Music/drama	Art	Athl	Nonneed-based Acad	Music/drama	Art	Athl	Priority	Closing		
													6/1		FAF/FFS/AFSA/CSS SAAC/ACT SAAC
													none		AFSA/CSS SAAC*/ ACT SAAC;FAF/AFSA
				X								7/6	none		FAF/CSS SAAC*/ACT SAAC
8,571	15							X			X	5/31	none		AFSA*/CSS SAAC/ ACT SAAC
													none	X	FAF
				X				X				4/30	none	X	AFSA/CSS SAAC/ACT SAAC;FAF
299	70							X	X	X	X	3/1	5/1	X	CSS SAAC*/ACT SAAC;FAF*/FFS
275	79			X	X	X		X	X	X		3/1	none		CSS SAAC;FAF*/FFS
125	76			X				X				6/1	none	X	FAF/FFS/AFSA/CSS SAAC*/ACT SAAC/SF
31	76	24	100	X				X				3/1	none		FAF/FFS/CSS SAAC*; FAF*/FFS/CSS SAAC
3,448	12			X				X				3/2	none		FAF; FAF/FFS/AFSA/CSS SAAC*/ACT SAAC/ AFSSA
565	86	486	100	X				X	X	X	X	4/15	none		FAF/FFS*
				X				X				6/1	none		FAF/FFS*/AFSA/SF
5,940	24							X	X			3/15	none		FAF/FFS*/SF
110	55	82	100					X				8/31	none	X	FAF/FFS/AFSA FFS
610	35	350	100										none	X	FAF/AFSA/SF*;FAF/ AFSA/SF
160	73	70	100	X	X		X	X	X		X	3/1	5/15	X	FAF/FFS*/AFSA/SF
494	53	258	100	X				X			X	2/15	none		FAF*/FFS
505	80			X	X	X		X	X	X			none	X	FAF*/FFS/AFSA
													none		FAF/FFS*
													none		FAF/FFS/AFSA
														none		FAF/FFS/AFSA
167	95			X			X	X			X	5/1	none	X	FFS
366	77	288	100	X	X		X	X	X		X	3/1	none	X	FAF/FFS*
2,126	92							X	X	X	X		none		FAF/FFS/AFSA/SF*
275	45			X				X					none	X	AFSA
													none		FAF/FFS/AFSA*/SF
3,528	28	991	100					X	X	X		6/1	none	X	FFS
													none		AFSA
1,662	32	525	100	X				X	X		X		none		FAF/FFS*
3,200	39	550	89	X				X				5/15	none		FFS
84	80												none	X	SF
423	70	250	100	X		X	X	X		X	X	5/1	none		FFS
													none		FFS
1,700	67	1,400	81	X	X	X	X	X	X		X	3/1	none		FAF/FFS*
270	90			X				X				3/1	none		FAF/FFS*/AFSA

*Preferred need analysis document.

Institution	Tuition and fees	Add'l out–of–state/district tuition	Books and supplies	Costs for campus residents			Costs for students at home		
				Room and board	Trans–portation	Other costs	Board only	Trans–portation	Other costs
† Naropa Institute	7,580		400						
National College	5,472								
† Nazarene Bible College	2,625		475				1,500	720	500
Northeastern Junior College	604	1,794/1,200	300	3,300	720	450	1,410	800	450
‡ Otero Junior College	1,092	1,884/—	350	2,792	600			800	1,200
‡ Pikes Peak Community College	1,037	1,884/—	400						
‡ Pueblo Community College	1,030	2,826/1,884	400						
‡ Red Rocks Community College	1,024	1,884/—	435				1,980	805	855
‡ Regis University	9,860		440	4,580	325	1,415	1,580	695	1,415
† Rocky Mountain College of Art and Design	4,960		1,000				1,906	596	1,067
‡ Trinidad State Junior College	1,204	1,884/—	430	3,340	200	800	1,000	400	900
United States Air Force Academy	0								
University of Colorado									
‡ Boulder	2,256	7,158/—	400	3,340	749	2,106	1,150	749	2,106
‡ Colorado Springs	1,708	3,758/—	454				1,575	794	330
‡ Denver	1,458	4,714/—	450				2,835	765	830
‡ Health Sciences Center	3,465	6,930/—							
University of Denver	12,990		375	4,205		1,200		400	1,200
† University of Northern Colorado	1,915	3,875/—	495	3,370	340	2,270	1,660		485
† University of Southern Colorado	1,667	4,120/—	470	3,370	600	1,240	740	900	1,240
‡ Western State College of Colorado	1,542	3,072/—	400	2,958	300	800	1,300	100	800
Yeshiva Toras Chaim Talmudical Seminary	3,600			3,400					

Connecticut

Institution	Tuition and fees	Add'l out–of–state/district tuition	Books and supplies	Room and board	Trans–portation	Other costs	Board only	Trans–portation	Other costs
Albertus Magnus College	10,120		400	4,930	420	747	1,600	642	774
‡ Asnuntuck Community College	934	1,782/—	400				1,500	1,350	700
Briarwood College	7,925		500		945	1,400	1,900	945	1,400
‡ Bridgeport Engineering Institute	6,350		600						
‡ Central Connecticut State University	1,865	2,370/—	500	3,500	158	1,027	1,550	608	1,027
Connecticut College	16,080		500	5,370		650	1,800		500
‡ Eastern Connecticut State University	1,884	2,372/—	500	3,264	400	1,050	1,500	1,000	600
Fairfield University	12,920		450	5,350	300	900	1,250	700	600
‡ Greater Hartford Community College	934	1,782/—	500						
‡ Greater New Haven State Technical College	1,230	2,596/—	500				1,100	800	600
‡ Hartford College for Women	9,017		600	4,672	400	400	2,500	1,200	700
‡ Hartford State Technical College	1,230	2,596/—	500				1,500	1,500	1,000
‡ Holy Apostles College and Seminary	3,000		600	4,320	400	700		850	550
‡ Housatonic Community College	934	1,782/—	400				1,600	1,100	900
‡ Manchester Community College	934	1,782/—	600						
‡ Mattatuck Community College	934	1,782/—	416				1,100	900	1,192
‡ Middlesex Community College	934	1,782/—	400				3,371	1,900	450
‡ Mitchell College	9,600		500	4,100	500	500	1,100	1,000	500
‡ Mohegan Community College	934	1,782/—	450				550	644	400
‡ Northwestern Connecticut Community College	934	1,782/—	440				680	900	1,000
‡ Norwalk Community College	934	1,782/—	450						
‡ Norwalk State Technical College	1,230	2,596/—	1,050				3,100	2,100	1,600
‡ Paier College of Art	9,060		600					400	600
‡ Quinebaug Valley Community College	934	1,782/—	600				1,880	1,500	1,100
Quinnipiac College	10,350		500	4,960	300	800	1,600	500	800
‡ Sacred Heart University	8,070		400	5,000					
‡ St. Basil's College	5,105		500	3,000		1,500			

†Figures are projected for 1991-92.   ‡Figures are for 1990-91.

| All aid | | Need-based aid | | Grants and scholarships | | | | | | | | Financial aid deadlines | | Inst aid form | Need analysis document |
Total freshmen	Percent receiving aid	Freshmen judged to have need	Percent offered aid	Need-based Acad	Music/drama	Art	Athl	Nonneed-based Acad	Music/drama	Art	Athl	Priority	Closing		
				X				X				3/31	none		FFS
50	85			X				X					none		FAF/FFS/AFSA*/SF
				X				X				6/1	none		FFS*/AFSA
													none		FAF/FFS*
334	60	209	96	X	X						X	5/1	none		FAF/FFS*
1,900	51	962	100	X				X				7/1	none		FAF/FFS/AFSA*/SF
4,790	18							X				3/15	5/1		FAF/FFS/AFSA
276	49	136	100	X				X				6/1	none	X	FFS
61	80	48	100	X		X		X		X		7/31	none	X	FAF/FFS/AFSA/AFSSA/SF*
													none	X	FAF/FFS*/AFSA/SF
3,783	55			X	X	X	X	X	X	X	X	4/1	none		FAF/FFS/SF*
375	30	134	85	X			X	X			X	4/1	none		FFS
				X				X	X	X		3/30	none	X	FAF/FFS*/AFSA/SF
614	57	284	100					X				3/15	none	X	FFS
1,798	60	704	95	X				X	X	X	X	3/1	none	X	FAF/FFS*/SF
723	58			X				X	X	X	X	3/1			FAF/FFS*/SF
								X	X	X	X		4/15	X	FAF*/FFS/AFSA/SF
								X	X	X	X	4/1	none		FFS
															FAF*/FFS/AFSA/AFSSA
98	74			X				X				2/15	none	X	FAF*/FFS
639	20	125	100									6/1	none		FAF
156	55							X				4/30	none		FAF*/FFS/AFSA
				X									none	X	FAF
921	28	257	100					X			X	4/1	none		FAF
449	44	198	100										2/15	X	FAF;FAF*/CSS SAAC
620	45			X				X					4/15		FAF
756	65	350	100										2/1		FAF
957	21	184	73	X				X				8/1	none		FAF
435	56											6/15	none	X	FAF
84	72	42	100					X				3/1	none		FAF*/AFSA
163	32											7/1	none		FAF
													none		FAF
												7/1	none	X	FAF/AFSA*
													none	X	FAF;FAF*/AFSA
		800	63	X		X	X					8/1	none	X	FAF*/FFS
				X								8/15	none		FAF/FFS*
450	58	200	100									3/1	7/15		FAF
1,085	40												none	X	FAF*/FFS/AFSA
412	27	110	100					X				6/15	none	X	FAF
1,766	12	125	68	X				X				4/15	none	X	FAF*/FFS/AFSA
229	30	95	56									3/15	none		FAF*/AFSA
93	39	48	96									5/1	none		FAF
404	18	69	100					X	X				none	X	FAF
686	65	515	100	X				X			X	3/1	none	X	FAF
542	86			X		X		X		X	X	3/1			FAF
													8/1		FFS*/AFSA

*Preferred need analysis document.

Institution	Tuition and fees	Add'l out-of-state/district tuition	Books and supplies	Costs for campus residents			Costs for students at home		
				Room and board	Transportation	Other costs	Board only	Transportation	Other costs
St. Joseph College	10,400		500	4,050		880	1,500	662	824
‡ South Central Community College	934	1,782/—	425				1,600	1,262	1,620
‡ Southern Connecticut State University	1,690	2,370/—	600	3,478	150	710	1,500		1,690
Teikyo-Post University	10,184		550	4,180	400	700	2,700	1,000	700
‡ Thames Valley State Technical College	1,230	2,596/—	500				1,300	1,500	600
Trinity College	16,950		400	4,820		650	1,600	300	650
‡ Tunxis Community College	934	1,782/—	420				2,400	1,000	1,145
United States Coast Guard Academy	0								
‡ University of Bridgeport	11,465		450	5,300	400	400	1,600	600	400
University of Connecticut	3,463	5,710/—	530	4,522	300	1,357	1,800	1,350	829
University of Hartford	13,594		400	5,414	400	412	1,400	1,000	558
University of New Haven	9,570		500	4,700	200	700	1,600	720	700
‡ Waterbury State Technical College	1,230	2,596/—	600						
Wesleyan University	16,830		500	4,990		600		600	
‡ Western Connecticut State University	1,855	2,370/—	600	3,092	200	1,087	1,646	570	1,087
Yale University	16,300		500	5,900	444	1,310			1,310

Delaware

Institution	Tuition and fees	Add'l out-of-state/district tuition	Books and supplies	Room and board	Transportation	Other costs	Board only	Transportation	Other costs
‡ Delaware State College	1,455	1,875/—	400	2,550	750	1,250		500	1,500
Delaware Technical and Community College									
† Southern Campus	1,011	1,404/—					1,500	500	300
† Stanton/Wilmington Campus	1,011	1,404/—	450				1,500	500	300
† Terry Campus	1,011	1,404/—	450				1,500	500	300
‡ Goldey-Beacom College	4,855		400		500	4,100	1,800	800	1,500
‡ University of Delaware	3,126	4,790/—	500	3,300		1,100			1,100
Wesley College	8,055		500	3,800	500	350	1,900	1,600	350
‡ Wilmington College	4,690		600				1,800	2,000	1,500

District of Columbia

Institution	Tuition and fees	Add'l out-of-state/district tuition	Books and supplies	Room and board	Transportation	Other costs	Board only	Transportation	Other costs
American University	13,706		450	6,046	700	600	1,600	700	600
Catholic University of America	11,876		500	5,685	500	1,200	900	600	1,200
† Corcoran School of Art	9,500		1,650		1,144	2,079	800	920	1,963
Gallaudet University	3,784		600	4,610	650	1,200	1,960	300	200
George Washington University	15,027		500	6,356	600	950		600	950
Georgetown University	15,797		575	6,320	350	1,040	810	500	1,040
Howard University	6,405		555	3,300	180	2,250	1,500	967	2,250
Mount Vernon College	12,510		500	6,090		600			600
‡ Oblate College	3,750		500	3,500				200	
Southeastern University	6,625		400				1,000	600	850
Trinity College	10,750		450	6,280	600	800		500	
University of the District of Columbia	800	2,880/—	475					790	1,380

Florida

Institution	Tuition and fees	Add'l out-of-state/district tuition	Books and supplies	Room and board	Transportation	Other costs	Board only	Transportation	Other costs
‡ Art Institute of Fort Lauderdale	7,850		1,000				700	900	750
‡ Barry University	8,690		500	4,700	650	800	700	800	800
Bethune-Cookman College	4,835		405	3,172	255	1,405	1,500	420	780
‡ Brevard Community College	780	780/—	380				1,600	540	580
‡ Broward Community College	750	780/—	480				1,620	1,552	1,080

†Figures are projected for 1991-92.   ‡Figures are for 1990-91.

| All aid | | Need–based aid | | Grants and scholarships | | | | | | | | Financial aid deadlines | | Inst aid form | Need analysis document |
| Total fresh-men | Percent receiving aid | Freshmen judged to have need | Percent offered aid | Need–based | | | | Nonneed–based | | | | | | | |
				Acad	Music/ drama	Art	Athl	Acad	Music/ drama	Art	Athl	Priority	Closing		
120	74	86	100					X				2/1	none	X	FAF
1,763	19							X					none	X	FAF/FFS/AFSA*;FAF/ FFS/AFSA
2,089	30	498	100					X				3/15	none	X	FAF*/FFS/AFSA; FAF*/FFS
129	80							X			X	3/15	none	X	FAF
283	12												3/1		FAF
427	41	174	100									2/1		X	FAF
3,184	20			X				X				7/1	none	X	FAF*/FFS/AFSA
													none	X	FAF*/FFS
2,328	30	1,103	84	X	X		X	X	X		X	2/15		X	FAF
1,277	39	700	89	X				X	X	X	X	3/1	none		FAF*/FFS
520	60							X			X		none	X	FAF
328	18			X				X				4/1	6/1	X	FAF
666	40	275	100										1/15	X	FAF*/FFS;FAF*/FFS/ CSS SAAC/ACT SAAC/ APSGFSA
574	65							X					3/15	X	FAF
1,366	41	557	100										1/15	X	FAF;FAF*/CSS SAAC
								X	X		X	5/1	none		FAF/FFS*
765	33												none		FFS
1,574	25							X			X	7/1	none		FAF/FFS/AFSA*/ AFSSA;AFSSA
406	25											5/30	none		FAF/FFS*
354	60	233	100	X				X			X	4/1	none	X	FAF
2,966	53	1,319	100					X	X		X	3/15	5/1		FAF*/FFS
341	70	256	100					X	X			4/15	none		FAF*/FFS/AFSA
308	39	164	100					X			X	6/1	none		FAF/FFS*;FAF/FFS
1,137	60	440	100	X			X	X			X	3/1	none		FAF
542	80			X	X			X	X			2/15	none		FAF
51	64			X		X		X		X		3/15	6/15	X	FAF
311	66							X				4/15	none	X	FAF
1,166	60	466	100	X				X	X		X	2/1		X	FAF
1,360	65	774	100	X		X						1/10			FAF
				X				X	X	X	X		4/1		FAF
104	38	40	100	X				X	X			3/1	none		FAF*/FFS/AFSA AFSSA;FAF*/FFS/ AFSA/CSS SAAC/ACT
													none		FAF
				X				X				3/1	none		FAF
		300	83					X	X		X	4/15	none	X	FFS
850	51												none		FAF*/FFS/AFSA/SF
533	75			X			X	X	X		X	4/1	none	X	FAF*/AFSA
770	88	630	97	X	X		X	X	X		X	3/1	none	X	FAF/FFS
3,872	24	1,206	100	X	X	X	X	X	X	X	X	5/6	none		FAF*/FFS/AFSA/SF
								X	X	X	X	4/15	none	X	FAF

*Preferred need analysis document.

Institution	Tuition and fees	Add'l out-of-state/district tuition	Books and supplies	Costs for campus residents			Costs for students at home		
				Room and board	Transportation	Other costs	Board only	Transportation	Other costs
‡ Central Florida Community College	840	810/—	350				1,500	240	1,000
‡ Chipola Junior College	668	672/—	375	1,950	700	500	1,400	1,020	500
Clearwater Christian College	4,900		450	3,100	600	640		400	
College of Boca Raton	12,200		400	4,700	800	1,000		200	1,000
‡ Daytona Beach Community College	802	813/—	470				1,568	640	780
Eckerd College	13,040		550	3,210	700	600	1,855	700	600
‡ Edison Community College	750	780/—	350				1,500	876	732
Edward Waters College	3,866		400	3,850	500	750		600	550
Embry-Riddle Aeronautical University	6,310		490	3,200	1,680	1,120	1,500	1,780	1,120
‡ Flagler College	4,550		500	2,840	600	1,200	1,500	800	1,200
‡ Florida Agricultural and Mechanical University	1,366	3,300/—	315	2,480	680	1,050	1,010	680	1,050
‡ Florida Atlantic University	1,403	3,300/—	600	3,345	1,095	780	1,560	1,740	780
Florida Baptist Theological College	1,434		400		1,000	600	1,800	1,000	
Florida Bible College	2,800		350	1,750	484	1,328	1,824	809	1,328
Florida Christian College	3,273		500		350	478	1,500	700	478
‡ Florida College	3,700		450	2,400	1,250	950			
‡ Florida Community College at Jacksonville	780	750/—	450				710	640	990
Florida Institute of Technology	10,635		750	3,465	1,140	1,452	1,600	1,140	1,452
‡ Florida International University	1,358	3,310/—	800	3,382	1,180	1,174	1,720	1,666	1,174
‡ Florida Keys Community College	690	690/—	310				1,200	450	900
‡ Florida Memorial College	4,350		400	2,752		810	1,170	2,140	1,000
Florida Southern College	6,600		300	4,200	600	600	1,950	600	600
‡ Florida State University	1,308	3,310/—	400	3,418	600	850		600	850
‡ Fort Lauderdale College	4,270		450		200	500	1,600	1,075	1,200
‡ Gulf Coast Community College	660	660/—	600				1,625	575	2,150
‡ Hillsborough Community College	780	810/—	510				1,500	1,640	2,690
† Hobe Sound Bible College	3,380		400	2,315	800	2,000	1,350	370	2,000
‡ Indian River Community College	740	740/—	450					350	400
International Fine Arts College	8,220		400		528	1,776		944	1,816
‡ Jacksonville University	7,960		600	3,580		600			600
Jones College	3,600		750					950	1,700
‡ Lake City Community College	720	720/—	300	2,159					
‡ Lake-Sumter Community College	750	750/—	400				1,600	1,000	600
Liberty Christian College	2,315		150	2,300					
‡ Manatee Community College	720	900/—	500					1,000	800
† Miami Christian College	4,930		400	2,760	500	800	1,500	600	500
‡ Miami-Dade Community College	803	1,170/—	920				2,146	2,566	2,726
National Education Center: Bauder Campus	5,325		429					486	1,098
‡ New College of the University of South Florida	1,419	3,300/—	600	3,200	490	2,100	1,664	1,720	2,100
New England Institute of Technology	5,475		265				1,500	850	1,190
‡ North Florida Junior College	653	653/—	250				625	300	1,098
‡ Nova University	6,450		400		1,900	1,200		1,900	1,200
‡ Okaloosa-Walton Community College	630	630/—					1,588	656	900
Orlando College	3,561							900	200
Palm Beach Atlantic College	5,400		400	2,600			1,200		

†Figures are projected for 1991-92.   ‡Figures are for 1990-91.

Total freshmen	Percent receiving aid	Freshmen judged to have need	Percent offered aid	Acad	Music/ drama	Art	Athl	Acad	Music/ drama	Art	Athl	Priority	Closing	Inst aid form	Need analysis document
				X				X	X		X	4/1	none		FAF/FFS*
1,312	60	700	100					X	X	X	X	6/15	none	X	FAF/FFS*/AFSA/SF
													none		FAF/FFS
470	40			X			X	X			X	2/15	none		FAF/FFS*
1,517	50			X	X	X	X	X	X	X	X	5/1	none		FAF
336	75	180	100	X	X	X	X	X	X	X	X	4/1	none		FAF*/FFS
1,542	35							X	X	X	X	6/1	none		FAF/FFS*/SF
													none		FAF/FFS*
817	62	495	85	X				X				4/15	none		FFS
295	68	145	99	X	X	X	X	X	X	X	X	3/15	4/1	X	FAF*/FFS
								X	X		X	4/1	none		FAF/FFS*
757	50	150	83	X				X	X		X	4/15	none		FAF*/FFS/SF
73	70	64	66	X	X							5/1	none		FAF/FFS*
24	31							X	X		X	4/30	none		FFS/AFSA*
55	90				X			X	X			4/1	7/15	X	FFS
204	80	80	100	X	X			X	X		X	5/1	none	X	FAF/FFS*/AFSA/SF
								X	X	X	X	3/1	none	X	FAF*/FFS/AFSA/ AFSSA/SF;FAF*/FFS/ AFSA
640	70	412	100	X				X			X	2/1	none	X	FAF*/FFS/SF
957	35							X	X	X	X	4/1	5/1		FAF*/FFS
548	35										X	5/1	none	X	FAF*/FFS
688	95			X			X	X			X	4/1	none		FAF*/FFS
				X	X	X	X	X	X	X	X	4/15	none	X	FAF
2,600	37	963	100					X	X	X	X	3/1		X	FAF/FFS*
													none		FAF/FFS*
2,203	51	1,275	100	X	X	X	X	X	X	X	X	4/1	none	X	FAF/FFS*/AFSA
2,842	32			X	X	X	X					4/1	none		FAF/FFS
35	51	19	100										none		FAF/AFSA/SF;FAF/ AFSA/CSS SAAC/ACT SAAC/SF
1,026	18	452	95					X	X	X	X		none		FFS*/AFSA
350	81							X		X		7/1	none	X	FAF
456	80			X	X	X	X	X	X	X	X	3/15	none		FAF*/FFS
190	80												none		FFS/AFSA*
694	12			X	X		X	X			X	6/1	none		FAF*/FFS
								X	X	X	X	5/1	none		FAF*/FFS
													none		FAF
				X		X	X	X			X	6/1	none	X	FAF/FFS*/AFSA/SF
													none		FAF/FFS*
9,148	48			X	X	X	X	X	X	X	X	4/15	none	X	FAF*/FFS/AFSA
													none		FAF;AFSA
109	76	70	100	X	X			X			X	2/1	6/1		FAF/FFS*
								X					none	X	FAF
				X				X	X	X	X	7/1	none		FAF/FFS*
596	90	100	100	X				X			X	4/1	none	X	FAF
967	33							X	X			4/1	none	X	FAF/FFS*/AFSA/ AFSSA/SF
510	85							X					none		AFSA/SF
382	90							X	X		X	4/1	6/1		FAF/FFS*/AFSA/ AFSSA/SF

*Preferred need analysis document.

Institution	Tuition and fees	Add'l out-of-state/district tuition	Books and supplies	Costs for campus residents			Costs for students at home		
				Room and board	Trans-portation	Other costs	Board only	Trans-portation	Other costs
‡ Palm Beach Community College	795	699/—	600					997	840
‡ Pasco-Hernando Community College	795	795/—	320				1,500	792	1,409
‡ Pensacola Junior College	797	797/—	375				1,800	400	875
Phillips Junior College: Melbourne	4,745								
‡ Polk Community College	810	900/—	250					800	300
Ringling School of Art and Design	8,950		1,500	4,700	500	500	2,000	500	500
Rollins College	13,900		600	4,295	1,000	500	1,700	400	60
‡ St. John Vianney College Seminary	5,600		520	3,000	900	990			
‡ St. Johns River Community College	630	630/—	320				1,500	600	614
‡ St. Leo College	7,870		400	3,290	850	600		950	
‡ St. Petersburg Junior College	798	801/—	500				2,100	1,015	915
St. Thomas University	8,250		500	4,100	1,000	1,000		1,000	1,000
‡ Santa Fe Community College	720	690/—	800					900	1,200
‡ Seminole Community College	780	660/—	376				1,652	811	885
South College: Palm Beach Campus	3,925		650						
‡ South Florida Community College	795	795/—	600	2,950				1,300	1,000
† Southeastern College of the Assemblies of God	3,300		600	2,800					
Southern College	3,870		450						
Stetson University	10,020		525	4,070	520	765	985	825	1,165
‡ Tallahassee Community College	660	660/—	500					735	920
Talmudic College of Florida	4,500		650	3,000					
† Tampa College	4,550							600	700
† United Electronics Institute	4,950						1,200	750	1,100
‡ University of Central Florida	1,373	3,300/—	440	3,620	1,050	1,050	1,500	1,805	1,050
‡ University of Florida	1,322	3,300/—	510	3,330	390	980	1,500	460	980
University of Miami	14,080		525	5,575	843	832	1,700	895	795
‡ University of North Florida	1,325	3,300/—	450					720	540
‡ University of South Florida	1,401	3,300/—	420	2,750	600		1,500	1,640	
University of Tampa	10,920		550	4,500	945	900	1,940	945	900
‡ University of West Florida	1,321	3,300/—	445	3,450	581	899	1,500	925	477
‡ Valencia Community College	810	990/—	500					1,400	580
Warner Southern College	5,375		425	3,140	420	1,000	1,750	420	1,000
Webber College	5,390			2,730					
Georgia									
‡ Abraham Baldwin Agricultural College	1,170	1,779/—	450	2,055	500	1,050	900	500	1,050
‡ Agnes Scott College	10,450		350	4,180	850	500	1,500	850	500
‡ Albany State College	1,599	2,478/—	520	2,355	325	650	1,550	250	550
‡ American College for the Applied Arts	6,900				560	960			
Andrew College	3,955		450	3,480	700	1,100	850	200	1,100
‡ Armstrong State College	1,413	2,478/—	350	2,850			1,230	625	1,100
Art Institute of Atlanta	7,435		1,500		500	500	1,100	200	500
‡ Athens Area Technical Institute	537	360/—	450					3,174	
Atlanta Christian College	3,620		400	2,600		500			500
Atlanta College of Art	7,450		850		200	900	1,440	475	900
‡ Atlanta Metropolitan College	969	1,779/—	450						

†Figures are projected for 1991-92.   ‡Figures are for 1990-91.

All aid		Need-based aid		Grants and scholarships								Financial aid deadlines		Inst aid form	Need analysis document
				Need-based				Nonneed-based							
Total freshmen	Percent receiving aid	Freshmen judged to have need	Percent offered aid	Acad	Music/drama	Art	Athl	Acad	Music/drama	Art	Athl	Priority	Closing		
				X				X	X		X		none		FAF/FFS*/AFSA/SF
1,966	43			X			X	X			X	6/1	none	X	FAF*/FFS/AFSA/SF
													none		FAF*/FFS
301	52	266		X									none	X	SF
													none		FAF/FFS*
241	70					X				X		3/15	none	X	FAF
391	32	112	100	X	X	X	X	X	X	X	X	3/1	none		FAF
7	30												none	X	FAF;FAF/AFSA*
								X	X	X	X	5/15	none		FAF*/FFS
1,000	75							X	X	X	X	3/1	none	X	FAF*/FFS
2,891	60			X				X	X	X	X	4/15	none		FAF/FFS*/SF
178	81											5/1	none		FAF/FFS
2,253	28			X	X	X	X	X	X	X	X	3/1	5/1		FFS
				X	X	X	X	X	X	X	X	5/1	none	X	FAF/FFS*
													none		FAF/AFSA*
1,441	30			X	X		X	X	X		X		none	X	FAF*/FFS
		292	53	X	X							4/1	none		FAF
367	87	196	100										none		FAF*/FFS/AFSA;FAF/ FFS/AFSA*
		207	100	X	X			X	X		X	3/15	none	X	FAF/FFS*
6,093	18			X				X				6/1	none		FAF/FFS*/AFSA;FAF/ FFS*
490	75			X									none		FAF*/AFSA/AFSSA
													none		FFS
													none	X	AFSA
1,319	36	549	97					X	X	X	X	3/15	none	X	FAF/FFS*
				X				X	X		X	4/1	none		FAF*/FFS
1,961	75	1,575	100	X	X			X	X		X	3/1	none		FAF
288	30			X				X	X		X	4/1	none	X	FAF*/FFS
				X				X	X	X	X	2/15	none	X	FAF*/FFS*
467	70							X	X	X	X	3/15	none		FAF*/FFS
686	44			X				X	X		X		none	X	FAF*/FFS/AFSA/ AFSSA;FAF*/FFS/ AFSA/CSS SAAC/ACT
3,188	37			X	X	X	X	X	X	X	X	4/1	none	X	FAF*/FFS
99	83	56	100	X			X	X			X	4/1	none		FAF/FFS*/AFSA
72	67	27	100					X			X	3/31	7/15		FAF/FFS*/AFSA/SF; AFSA+SF
861	76	600	100	X	X	X	X	X	X	X	X	5/1	none	X	FAF*/FFS/AFSA/SF; FAF*/FFS/SF
127	88	61	100	X	X			X	X			3/1	none		FAF
559	88			X	X		X	X				6/1	none	X	FAF*/FFS
278	70							X				6/1	none		FAF*/FFS/SF
													none	X	FAF*/FFS
410	25			X	X	X	X	X	X	X	X	5/31	none		FAF
													none		FAF/FFS
															FFS
36	65			X	X			X	X			6/1	8/1		FAF
		47	100	X		X		X		X		3/15	none	X	FAF*/FFS
662	25			X	X							8/20	none		FAF

*Preferred need analysis document.

Institution	Tuition and fees	Add'l out-of-state/district tuition	Books and supplies	Costs for campus residents			Costs for students at home		
				Room and board	Transportation	Other costs	Board only	Transportation	Other costs
‡ Augusta College	1,431	2,478/—	430						
‡ Augusta Technical Institute	558	360/—	450						
‡ Bainbridge College	984	1,779/—	450				1,700	1,650	450
Bauder Fashion College	6,010		630		1,000	1,008	1,100	1,000	1,008
Berry College	7,050		500	3,302	400	1,460	1,500	890	1,460
Brenau Women's College	7,242		450	5,658	600	500	1,500	800	500
Brewton-Parker College	3,625		555	2,300		1,000	1,140	500	1,000
‡ Brunswick College	1,074	1,779/—	400				1,600	800	400
Chattahoochee Technical Institute	654		750						
Clark Atlanta University	6,400		600	3,500	600	800			800
‡ Clayton State College	1,338	2,478/—	375				1,500	756	1,038
‡ Columbus College	1,413	2,478/—	612	3,519			1,500	567	567
‡ Columbus Technical Institute	552								
Covenant College	8,050		450	3,380	550	550	1,730	550	550
Crandall Junior College	4,560		25					90	100
‡ Dalton College	970	1,779/—	375					750	1,000
‡ Darton College	1,014	1,779/—	250				1,100	450	600
‡ DeKalb College	1,005	1,485/—	325						
DeKalb Technical Institute	435	360/—	735						
DeVry Institute of Technology: Decatur	5,015		500						
‡ East Georgia College	984	1,779/—	400					700	350
Emmanuel College	3,501		600	2,610	700	900		700	900
Emmanuel College School of Christian Ministries	3,501		600	2,610	700	900		700	900
Emory University	14,780		550	4,532		1,100	1,400	722	1,100
‡ Floyd College	984	1,779/—	250					700	600
‡ Fort Valley State College	1,593	2,478/—	400	2,280	250	600	951	1,150	
‡ Gainesville College	1,002	1,779/—	500					1,535	1,000
‡ Georgia College	1,476	2,478/—	490	2,205	665	1,228		665	1,228
‡ Georgia Institute of Technology	2,052	4,002/—	600	3,660	475	800	1,200	900	800
† Georgia Military College	3,270		450	3,654		900		500	900
‡ Georgia Southern University	1,563	2,478/—	450	2,730	450	600		600	600
‡ Georgia Southwestern College	1,527	2,478/—	600	2,220	400	750	1,400	600	700
‡ Georgia State University	1,812	3,978/—	940				2,070	314	770
‡ Gordon College	1,029	1,779/—	379	2,040	750	700	590	750	700
‡ Kennesaw State College	1,344	2,478/—	450					650	500
† LaGrange College	5,537		800	3,175	1,000	600	1,500	1,000	600
‡ Macon College	978	1,779/—	400				1,500	802	888
Meadows College of Business	2,775								
‡ Medical College of Georgia	1,883	3,312/—	570	3,213	315	1,845	1,700	495	1,125
Mercer University									
† Atlanta	6,597		386				1,607	515	515
Macon	9,425		350	3,666	350	800	1,560	500	800
‡ Middle Georgia College	1,164	1,779/—	425	2,220	280	500	1,500	280	500

†Figures are projected for 1991-92.   ‡Figures are for 1990-91.

| All aid | | Need-based aid | | Grants and scholarships | | | | | | | | Financial aid deadlines | | Inst aid form | Need analysis document |
Total freshmen	Percent receiving aid	Freshmen judged to have need	Percent offered aid	Need-based Acad	Music/drama	Art	Athl	Nonneed-based Acad	Music/drama	Art	Athl	Priority	Closing		
		510	100	X	X	X		X	X	X	X	5/1	none	X	FAF*/FFS/AFSA/AFSSA/SF
1,500	25	450	100					X					none		FAF
229	35											7/1	none	X	FAF*/FFS/AFSA
262	55												none		FAF/AFSA*
403	91	296	100	X	X	X	X	X	X	X	X	4/15	none		FAF*/FFS/AFSA
123	55	46	100	X				X	X	X	X	6/1	none		FAF*/FFS/AFSA/AFSSA
362	96							X	X	X	X	4/1	none	X	FAF
399	50			X				X			X	5/1	none	X	FAF*/FFS/AFSA
1,025	11	200	100	X				X					none		AFSA
690	80	490	100	X	X		X	X	X		X	4/15	5/15	X	FAF*/FFS
869	78	179	100	X				X	X	X	X	4/1	none		FAF
572	37	140	100					X	X	X	X	6/1	none		FAF
															AFSA
159	86	117	100		X	X		X	X		X	3/31	none		FAF*/FFS
													none	X	AFSA/SF
				X				X				8/1	none	X	FAF
		463	100	X				X	X		X	9/1	none	X	FAF*/FFS
												7/1		X	FAF*/FFS
				X				X					none	X	FAF
1,135	81							X					none		FAF
206	18			X				X					none		FAF/AFSA
209	96	201	100	X	X		X	X	X		X	3/15	none		FAF*/FFS/AFSA/AFSSA;FAF*/FFS/AFSA/APSGFSA
				X				X				3/15	none		FAF*/FFS/AFSA/AFSSA;FAF*/FFS/AFSA/APSGFSA
1,112	53	400	100	X				X	X			2/15	4/1		FAF
777	45			X				X				4/30	none		FAF
446	96			X	X		X	X	X		X	4/15	5/1		FAF
705	17							X	X	X		4/15	none		FAF
616	65			X	X	X	X	X	X		X	4/15	none		FAF
1,605	39	800	90	X				X					3/1	X	FAF/SF
													none		FAF
2,728	22			X				X	X		X	3/1	4/15	X	FAF
380	47							X	X	X	X	5/1	none		FAF
1,648	25			X				X	X	X	X	5/1	none		FAF/FFS/AFSA/AFSSA/SF*;FAF/FFS/AFSA/CSS SAAC/ACT
520	42							X	X	X	X	6/22	none	X	FAF*/AFSA/SF
650	15			X	X		X	X	X	X	X	4/15	5/1		FAF*/FFS/AFSA/SF
200	55			X				X	X	X		5/1	none	X	FAF*/FFS/AFSA;FAF*/AFSA
877	25							X				4/1	none		AFSA
151	90							X					none		AFSA
				X				X				3/1	none	X	FAF
				X				X				5/1	none	X	FAF*/FFS
													none	X	FAF*/FFS
352	28							X	X		X	7/1	none	X	FAF*/FFS

*Preferred need analysis document.

Institution	Tuition and fees	Add'l out-of-state/district tuition	Books and supplies	Costs for campus residents			Costs for students at home		
				Room and board	Trans-portation	Other costs	Board only	Trans-portation	Other costs
‡ Morehouse College	6,210		500	4,462		2,500	1,500		1,700
‡ Morris Brown College	6,140		500	3,250	500	600		500	600
‡ North Georgia College	1,494	2,478/—	550	2,190	125	750	1,260	900	700
† Oglethorpe University	10,250		450	4,000	1,500	2,100	1,500	1,500	2,100
Oxford College of Emory University	11,000		500	4,040	350	750		900	1,250
‡ Paine College	5,256		400	2,660	1,525	485			485
‡ Phillips College: Columbus	4,025		200				1,100	873	990
‡ Phillips Junior College: Augusta	4,320								
Piedmont College	3,600		600	3,050	600	900	1,500	800	900
Reinhardt College	3,915		500	3,375	70	1,000	1,200	600	400
Savannah College of Art and Design	7,575		1,200		450	5,550	2,500	225	900
‡ Savannah State College	1,569	2,478/—	450	2,085	350	900		280	500
Savannah Technical Institute	486	288/—							
Shorter College	5,300		400	3,300	300	1,000	1,400	900	1,000
South College	3,925		400				1,584	900	1,053
‡ South Georgia College	1,032	1,779/—	475	2,184	700	900	1,500	500	900
‡ Southern College of Technology	1,431	2,478/—	650	3,065		750	2,000	1,000	750
Spelman College	6,707		450	4,770	650	1,150	1,100	400	1,150
† Thomas College	2,979		650				1,210	880	495
† Toccoa Falls College	5,177		300	3,234	200	600		450	600
† Truett-McConnell College	3,723		450	2,400	400	600		650	600
‡ University of Georgia	2,001	3,312/—	405	2,940		1,245	1,650		1,245
‡ Valdosta State College	1,557	2,478/—	600	2,370	550	500		550	500
‡ Waycross College	1,029	1,779/—	500				1,500	600	900
Wesleyan College	9,850		450	3,900	400	750	2,150	400	550
‡ West Georgia College	1,587	2,478/—	416	2,304	759	945	1,575	1,421	945
Young Harris College	4,140		450	3,105	450	825	1,500	750	525

Hawaii

Institution	Tuition and fees	Add'l out-of-state/district tuition	Books and supplies	Costs for campus residents			Costs for students at home		
				Room and board	Trans-portation	Other costs	Board only	Trans-portation	Other costs
Brigham Young University-Hawaii	2,000		450	3,475		950			850
† Cannon's International Business College of Honolulu	6,473		1,000				2,900	200	1,200
Chaminade University of Honolulu	7,850		475	3,900		800	875	207	800
Hawaii Loa College	8,400		600	4,800	180	800	2,000	180	800
‡ Hawaii Pacific University	4,800		500				800	225	700

University of Hawaii									
Hilo	470	2,160/—	530	3,186	104	892	2,011	207	762
Honolulu Community College	430	2,160/—	427					207	762
Kapiolani Community College	435	2,160/—	427				2,011	207	777
Kauai Community College	430	2,160/—	470				2,213	207	838
Leeward Community College	435	2,160/—	427				2,011	207	792
Manoa	1,387	2,590/—	540	3,186	207	1,342		207	892
Maui Community College	438	2,160/—	427	3,186	207	869	1,911	370	724
West Oahu	850	1,740/—	583				1,341	207	1,710
Windward Community College	440	2,160/—	400				3,500	500	1,000

†Figures are projected for 1991-92.   ‡Figures are for 1990-91.

All aid — Total freshmen	Percent receiving aid	Need-based aid — Freshmen judged to have need	Percent offered aid	Grants and scholarships: Need-based Acad	Music/drama	Art	Athl	Nonneed-based Acad	Music/drama	Art	Athl	Financial aid deadlines: Priority	Closing	Inst aid form	Need analysis document
626	70							X	X		X		4/1	X	FAF
701	95			X			X	X	X	X	X	4/15	6/15	X	FAF*/FFS
644	70	342	100	X			X	X	X	X	X	6/1	none	X	FAF
169	85	66	100	X	X			X	X				5/1		FAF/FFS/SF*
287	78			X				X				4/1	none		FAF*/FFS
156	90				X			X				5/15	none	X	FAF
													none		AFSA
													none	X	AFSA
161	65	75	100	X				X	X	X	X	6/1	7/1		FAF*/FFS/AFSA
				X	X	X	X						5/1		FAF
467	55	400	100			X				X		4/1	none	X	FAF*/FFS/AFSA/AFSSA/SF;FAF*/FFS/AFSA/CSS SAAC/ACT
759	85			X	X		X	X	X		X		8/1		FAF
857	33	157	100					X					none		FAF/AFSA*/AFSSA/SF
232	99	108	100	X	X	X	X	X	X	X	X	4/15	none	X	FAF
180	85							X					none		AFSA
													none		FAF
420	38	230	93	X			X	X			X	3/15	5/31	X	FAF*/FFS/AFSA/SF
400	81			X	X			X	X				4/1	X	FAF*/FFS
111	66			X	X			X				9/1	none		FAF
247	75	165	100					X	X			4/1	none		FAF*/FFS/AFSA/AFSSA
652	95							X	X		X		none	X	FAF*/FFS
3,716	30			X				X				3/1	none	X	FAF/FFS*
1,198	45	600	100	X				X	X	X	X	4/15	none	X	FAF/FFS/AFSA/SF
								X	X	X	X		9/2	X	FAF/AFSA
141	93			X				X	X	X		4/1	none	X	FAF
1,007	59	441	100	X				X	X	X	X	3/15	none		FAF
								X	X	X	X	5/1	none	X	FAF
															FAF
155	9	49	100					X					none	X	FAF*/AFSA
				X				X			X	4/17	none		FAF*/FFS
93	71			X				X			X	4/15	8/1	X	FAF*/FFS
927	14	115	95					X	X		X	3/15	none		FAF*/FFS/AFSA/AFSSA;FAF*/FFS/AFSA/CSS SAAC/ACT
													none	X	FAF
													none		FAF;FAF*/FFS/CSS SAAC
													none		FAF
		50	100	X	X			X	X			3/15	6/1		FAF
1,412	15							X				5/1	none		FAF
		291	87	X				X	X		X	3/1	none		FAF
								X				3/1	none		FAF
								X	X	X		6/1	none		FAF
500	10							X				4/1	none		FAF

*Preferred need analysis document.

Institution	Tuition and fees	Add'l out-of-state/district tuition	Books and supplies	Costs for campus residents			Costs for students at home		
				Room and board	Trans-portation	Other costs	Board only	Trans-portation	Other costs
Idaho									
Boise Bible College	2,856		400	2,450	558	849	1,500	568	371
‡ Boise State University	1,303	2,000/—	400	2,768	550	928	1,300	600	603
College of Idaho	9,982		375	2,710	400	675	1,850		675
‡ College of Southern Idaho	800	1,000/930	400	2,070					
‡ Idaho State University	1,160	2,000/—	400	2,628	315	1,305	1,100	315	2,005
‡ Lewis Clark State College	1,120	1,900/—	458	2,658	731	918	1,500	594	687
‡ North Idaho College	804	1,150/1,000	500	2,464	350	830	1,500	350	830
Northwest Nazarene College	7,260		450	2,490	450	690	1,500	600	600
Ricks College	1,480		550	2,710	1,000	1,000	1,335	700	1,000
‡ University of Idaho	1,166	2,340/—	530	2,620	400	1,515	1,600	450	1,512
Illinois									
‡ Aero-Space Institute	6,025		250				4,000	1,200	
† American Academy of Art	7,100		650						
† American Conservatory of Music	8,000		450					800	1,200
Augustana College	11,175		450	3,666	300	250	600	1,750	1,000
Aurora University	8,770		600	3,405	1,115	1,380	3,405	1,275	850
Barat College	8,719		450	3,300	500	750		750	250
† Belleville Area College	910	2,760/1,380	496				1,500	1,463	1,250
Black Hawk College									
East Campus	1,245	3,540/780	463				1,490	1,165	1,655
Moline	1,245	3,540/780	440				1,470	750	1,525
Blackburn College	7,750		500	1,000	250	800	1,500	50	800
Blessing-Reiman College of Nursing	6,650		250						
Bradley University	9,050		440	3,960	200	1,312	450	600	1,912
‡ Carl Sandburg College	855	4,074/1,667	425				1,600	1,400	500
‡ Chicago State University	1,772	3,141/—	650				1,500	600	1,700
City Colleges of Chicago									
‡ Chicago City-Wide College	820	3,304/1,960	500				2,959	540	1,687
‡ Harold Washington College	820	3,304/1,960	400				1,500	450	1,687
‡ Harry S. Truman College	820	3,304/1,960	550				1,950	500	1,700
‡ Kennedy-King College	820	3,304/1,960	300				1,100	450	1,684
‡ Malcolm X College	820	3,304/1,960	385				1,419	550	1,925
‡ Olive-Harvey College	820	3,304/1,960	270				1,100	450	1,679
‡ Richard J. Daley College	820	3,304/1,960	355					650	1,800
‡ Wright College	820	3,304/1,960	500				2,959	540	1,687
† College of DuPage	945	3,105/1,890	835				1,911	1,393	1,034

†Figures are projected for 1991-92.   ‡Figures are for 1990-91.

All aid		Need-based aid		Grants and scholarships								Financial aid deadlines		Inst aid form	Need analysis document
				Need-based				Nonneed-based							
Total freshmen	Percent receiving aid	Freshmen judged to have need	Percent offered aid	Acad	Music/drama	Art	Athl	Acad	Music/drama	Art	Athl	Priority	Closing		
20	81							X					none	X	FAF*/AFSA
2,092	60			X	X	X		X	X	X		3/31	none		FAF
152	80			X	X	X	X	X	X	X	X	3/1	none	X	FAF*/FFS
826	65			X	X	X	X	X	X	X	X	3/1	none	X	FAF*/FFS/AFSA/ AFSSA/SF;FAF*/FFS/ AFSA/CSS SAAC/ACT
1,410	80			X	X	X	X	X	X	X	X	3/15	none	X	FAF
441	83			X			X	X			X	3/15	none		FAF
818	48			X				X	X	X	X	4/15	none		FAF*/FFS
326	85							X	X	X	X	4/1	none	X	FAF*/FFS
4,301	78												none	X	FAF/FFS/AFSA*/ AFSSA/SF;FAF/FFS/ AFSA*/CSS SAAC/
1,306	65			X	X	X	X	X	X	X	X	2/15	none	X	FAF
58	98	56	100										10/1		AFSA/AFSSA*
144	45								X				none	X	AFSA
32	69							X				6/1	none		FAF*/FFS/AFSA/ AFSSA
487	89			X				X	X	X		4/1	none	X	FAF*/FFS
		145	100	X				X				5/1	none		FAF*/FFS/AFSA/ AFSSA
105	70	68	100	X	X	X	X	X	X	X		3/15	none	X	FAF/FFS*/AFSA/ AFSSA
9,847	50			X				X	X	X	X	6/1	none	X	FAF/FFS/AFSA/ AFSSA/SF*
319	60			X				X			X	6/1	none		FAF/FFS/AFSA*/ AFSSA/SF
2,271	62							X	X	X	X	5/15	none	X	FAF/FFS/AFSA
155	84	96	100	X				X				4/1	none		FAF*/FFS
1,060	82	630	100	X				X	X	X	X	3/1	none		FAF*/FFS/AFSA/ AFSSA/SF
				X	X	X	X	X	X	X	X	5/1	none	X	FAF/FFS/AFSA/SF*
613	75	270	100	X				X	X	X	X	4/15	none	X	FAF/FFS*/AFSSA
				X				X				5/1	none		FAF/FFS/AFSA/ AFSSA*
2,646	42			X								5/1	none		AFSA/AFSSA*
													none	X	FAF/FFS/AFSA/ AFSSA*/SF
													none		FAF/FFS/AFSA/ AFSSA*
													none		AFSA*/AFSSA*;AFSA/ AFSSA*
													none		AFSA/AFSSA*
		585	100										none	X	AFSA/AFSSA/SF
2,266	40			X				X			X		none		AFSA/AFSSA*
21,496	10			X	X	X		X	X	X		6/15	none	X	FAF/FFS/AFSA*/ AFSSA/SF;FAF/FFS/ AFSA*/AFSSA

*Preferred need analysis document.

Institution	Tuition and fees	Add'l out-of-state/district tuition	Books and supplies	Costs for campus residents			Costs for students at home		
				Room and board	Trans-portation	Other costs	Board only	Trans-portation	Other costs
College of Lake County	993	4,271/2,882	300						
College of St. Francis	7,980		400	3,580	340	900	1,500	710	900
‡ Columbia College	5,828		500				1,575	450	1,550
Concordia University	7,328		400	3,603	400	600	1,750	310	600
Danville Area Community College	930	3,210/2,250	750				1,600	1,000	1,400
De Paul University	9,342		480	4,703	660	1,300	1,500	400	1,100
DeVry Institute of Technology									
Chicago	5,015		500				1,839	2,446	1,527
Lombard	5,015		500				1,839	2,431	1,527
‡ Eastern Illinois University	2,114	3,141/—	150	2,476	350	895	1,100	350	895
‡ East-West University	5,360		500				1,200	500	1,800
† Elgin Community College	990	3,109/2,108	500				2,400	1,000	700
Elmhurst College	8,460		500	3,442		2,000	1,400	1,150	1,600
‡ Eureka College	8,675		330	2,985	160	510	1,500	675	295
Gem City College	3,640		400					400	1,800
‡ Governors State University	1,646	3,192/—	450					800	
Greenville College	8,750		400	3,880	500	500	1,685	300	500
‡ Harrington Institute of Interior Design	7,565		875		1,000	2,000		1,000	2,000
Hebrew Theological College	5,080		400	3,900	500	1,800	3,000	350	1,500
† Highland Community College	660	3,355/1,767	450					1,500	1,200
Illinois Benedictine College	8,980		550	3,680		1,430	1,425		1,430
Illinois Central College	960	3,932/2,591	450	2,700			2,700	1,152	2,514
Illinois College	6,600		500	3,250	250	600		700	200
Illinois Eastern Community Colleges									
‡ Frontier Community College	605	3,688/2,095	400				1,500	1,300	800
‡ Lincoln Trail College	605	3,688/2,095	400				1,500	1,300	800
‡ Olney Central College	605	3,688/2,095	400				1,500	1,300	800
‡ Wabash Valley College	605	3,688/2,095	400				1,500	1,300	800
Illinois Institute of Technology	12,690		800	4,350	100	800	1,500	800	1,000
‡ Illinois State University	2,272	3,428/—	456	2,560	390	1,233		796	1,656
Illinois Technical College	4,600		997				1,680	416	210
Illinois Valley Community College	698	3,025/1,950	450				1,600	1,200	1,025
Illinois Wesleyan University	11,115		400	3,695	100	550	800	310	600
‡ International Academy of Merchandising and Design	6,844		450					500	1,500
‡ ITT Technical Institute: Schaumburg	6,923		625						
‡ John A. Logan College	642	2,511/1,655	320				1,320	1,240	550
‡ John Wood Community College	990	3,604/1,080	400				1,000	725	500
† Joliet Junior College	910	2,949/1,884	400				1,577	1,097	1,274

†Figures are projected for 1991-92.   ‡Figures are for 1990-91.

All aid		Need–based aid		Grants and scholarships								Financial aid deadlines		Inst aid form	Need analysis document
				Need–based				Nonneed–based							
Total freshmen	Percent receiving aid	Freshmen judged to have need	Percent offered aid	Acad	Music/drama	Art	Athl	Acad	Music/drama	Art	Athl	Priority	Closing		
								X	X	X	X		none	X	FAF/FFS*/SF
145	86	104	100					X			X	3/1	7/1		FAF/FFS*
				X				X				5/1	none		FAF/FFS/AFSA/AFSSA/SF*
194	81	126	100	X	X			X	X			6/1	none		FAF
													none		FAF/FFS/AFSA/AFSSA/SF*
1,040	57	587	100	X	X	X	X	X	X	X	X		5/1	X	FAF
873	81							X					none		FAF
738	81							X					none		FAF
				X				X	X	X	X	3/31	none	X	FAF/FFS/AFSA/AFSSA/SF*;FAF/FFS/AFSSA/SF*
								X					none		FAF/FFS/AFSA/AFSSA*
2,286	19	302	98					X	X	X	X	7/1	none	X	FAF
258	60	158	100	X	X			X	X			5/1	none		FAF*/FFS/SF
123	90							X	X	X		5/1	none		FAF*/FFS/AFSA/AFSSA;FAF*/FFS/AFSSA
		85	100										none		AFSA*/AFSSA
								X	X	X		5/1	10/1	X	FAF
220	90	218	100	X				X				6/1	none		FAF
132	40	27	100									6/1	none		AFSSA
														X	FAF
720	40			X	X	X	X	X	X	X	X	6/1	none		FAF/FFS/AFSA/AFSSA/SF*
222	91							X	X	X		4/15	none		FAF*/FFS/AFSA/AFSSA
				X			X	X			X	4/15	none	X	FAF*/FFS/AFSA/AFSSA
260	83	197	100	X				X	X			5/1	none		FAF*/FFS
				X	X	X		X					none		AFSSA
657	60			X	X	X	X	X					none		AFSSA
926	60			X	X	X	X	X	X		X		none		AFSSA
2,817	60			X	X	X	X						none		AFSSA
293	96	279	100	X			X					5/1	none	X	FAF
								X	X	X	X	3/1	none	X	FAF/FFS/AFSA*/AFSSA/SF;FAF/FFS/AFSA*/CSS SAAC/
55	85												9/3	X	FAF/FFS
								X	X	X		5/1	none		FAF/FFS/AFSA*/AFSSA
550	85	350	100	X	X	X		X	X	X		3/1	none		FAF*/FFS
108	35							X					none	X	AFSA
102	95												none	X	AFSA
2,012	65	900	100	X								5/1	none		AFSSA
													none		FAF/FFS/AFSA/AFSSA*
2,629	25	1,200	83	X	X	X		X	X	X		7/1	none		FAF/FFS*

*Preferred need analysis document.

Institution	Tuition and fees	Add'l out-of-state/ district tuition	Books and supplies	Costs for campus residents			Costs for students at home		
				Room and board	Trans-portation	Other costs	Board only	Trans-portation	Other costs
Judson College	8,090		450	4,090	200	800	1,800	400	800
† KAES College	4,080		300		200	500	2,400	300	1,000
† Kankakee Community College	825	4,724/398	450				1,100	700	700
Kaskaskia College	848	4,223/1,395	400				900	925	765
Kendall College	7,005		400	4,473	125	900	2,005	300	700
† Kishwaukee College	925	2,413/828	400				1,500	1,150	920
Knox College	12,675		350	3,675	200	600	2,040	200	
Lake Forest College	13,895		475	3,155	250	425		820	425
‡ Lake Land College	1,044	3,175/1,008	100				1,500	1,530	800
Lakeview College of Nursing	4,575		400						
‡ Lewis and Clark Community College	798	3,976/1,842	400				1,830	784	900
Lewis University	8,502		450	3,990	650	1,200	1,700	1,475	1,200
Lexington Institute of Hospitality Careers	4,000		450	2,500	450	1,200		450	1,200
Lincoln Christian College and Seminary	3,600		400	2,470	300	1,530	950	300	1,550
Lincoln College	7,260		350	3,400	200	500	2,100	500	500
† Lincoln Land Community College	913	3,181/1,662	350					1,000	440
Loyola University of Chicago	9,270		535	4,908	714	1,210	1,250	714	1,210
MacCormac Junior College	5,925		600				1,650	444	1,200
‡ MacMurray College	7,650		400	3,170	350	500		350	500
† McHenry County College	906	3,800/2,650	450				1,600	1,160	1,400
† McKendree College	6,751		500	3,430	200	800	250	600	800
Mennonite College of Nursing	6,850		800	2,079	220	550	693	220	550
‡ Midstate College	4,035		600		350	825	800	1,000	725
Millikin University	10,061		375	3,784	200	765	1,848	200	765
Monmouth College	12,450		400	3,350	125	300	1,500	250	
Montay College	5,550		500				1,000	400	1,900
Moody Bible Institute	893		400	3,750	200	500		500	500
‡ Moraine Valley Community College	1,170	3,240/2,310	406				1,500	957	1,234
Morrison Institute of Technology	4,700		500		300	1,200	800	800	1,200
† Morton College	1,080	3,234/2,175	400				1,700	800	900
‡ Mundelein College	8,235		400	3,839	200	1,100	1,000	400	900
NAES College	4,220		250						

†Figures are projected for 1991-92.   ‡Figures are for 1990-91.

All aid		Need-based aid		Grants and scholarships								Financial aid deadlines		Inst aid form	Need analysis document
				Need-based				Nonneed-based							
Total freshmen	Percent receiving aid	Freshmen judged to have need	Percent offered aid	Acad	Music/drama	Art	Athl	Acad	Music/drama	Art	Athl	Priority	Closing		
151	100	113	100	X				X					none		FAF*/FFS
				X				X						X	FAF
				X				X	X	X	X	6/1	none	X	FAF/FFS/AFSA*/AFSSA;FAF/FFS/AFSA*
943	19	313	96					X	X		X	7/1	none		FAF/FFS/AFSA/AFSSA/SF;FAF/FFS/AFSA*/AFSSA/SF
75	62	50	100	X				X				6/1	none	X	FAF*/AFSA/AFSSA/SF
				X			X	X			X	6/1	none	X	FAF/FFS/AFSSA/SF
221	85	146	100	X	X	X		X	X	X		3/1	none		FAF*/FFS/SF
248	58	143	100									2/15	none	X	FAF/FFS/AFSA/AFSSA/SF;FAF/FFS/AFSA/CSS SAAC/ACT
1,491	60							X	X	X	X	4/15	none	X	FAF/FFS*/AFSA/AFSSA/SF AFSA/AFSSA/SF
1,724	52	1,503	100					X	X		X	6/1	none	X	FAF/FFS/AFSA/AFSSA/SF*
494	70	275	100					X	X	X	X	6/1	none	X	FAF*/FFS/AFSA/AFSSA/SF
19	63	14	86	X									none		AFSA/AFSSA*
119	97			X				X				8/10	none	X	FAF/FFS*
927	86			X	X	X	X	X	X	X	X		none	X	FAF/FFS/AFSA/AFSSA*
													none	X	FAF/FFS*/AFSA/AFSSA/SF
1,132	75	876	86	X				X	X	X	X	4/1	none	X	FAF
350	80												none		FAF/FFS/AFSA*
157	92			X	X	X		X	X	X		6/1	none		FAF*/FFS/SF
903	20	300	83					X		X	X	7/1	none	X	FAF/FFS/AFSA/AFSSA;AFSSA+FAF/FFS/AFSA/SF*
145	90	106	100	X	X		X	X	X		X	7/1	none		FAF*/FFS/AFSA/AFSSA;FAF*/FFS/AFSSA
				X				X				4/1	none	X	FFS
145	90	120	100	X				X					9/30	X	FAF/FFS/AFSA/AFSSA*;FAF/FFS/AFSA*/AFSSA
467	87	407	100	X	X	X		X	X	X		6/1	none		FAF
141	86	130	100	X	X	X		X	X	X		3/1			FAF*/FFS
245	2			X	X								none	X	FAF/AFSA/AFSSA*
								X				7/1	none	X	FAF/FFS/AFSA/AFSSA*/SF
112	60	82	100										none		FAF/FFS/AFSA/AFSSA*;FAF/FFS/AFSA*/AFSSA
								X	X	X	X	7/1	none	X	SF
100	87	82	100	X	X	X	X	X	X	X	X	4/1	none		FAF
													none		FAF/FFS/AFSA*/AFSSA

*Preferred need analysis document.

Institution	Tuition and fees	Add'l out-of-state/district tuition	Books and supplies	Costs for campus residents			Costs for students at home		
				Room and board	Transportation	Other costs	Board only	Transportation	Other costs
National College of Chiropractic	7,968		800		900	1,915		1,100	2,100
National-Louis University	7,650		500	4,270	75	1,000	1,800	1,050	1,000
North Central College	9,960		450	3,735	320	1,180	1,500	1,050	1,180
North Park College and Theological Seminary	10,665		475	4,035	550	515	1,500	550	600
‡ Northeastern Illinois University	1,967	3,141/—	445				1,378	467	1,862
‡ Northern Illinois University	2,547	3,428/—	450	2,706	350	1,300	1,400	750	1,300
Northwestern University	14,370		651	4,827		981		945	981
‡ Oakton Community College	628	2,400/2,100	400				1,500	1,100	1,000
Olivet Nazarene University	6,472		450	3,510		900			900
‡ Parkland College	975	3,510/1,860	400				1,800	905	850
Parks College of St. Louis University	7,100		450	3,400	250	800		840	800
Phillips College of Chicago	5,925		250					500	1,000
‡ Prairie State College	1,230	3,210/1,770	550				1,500	900	1,000
Principia College	11,100		450	4,590		975			
Quincy College	8,604		400	3,440	460	620	1,500	460	620
Ray College of Design	7,620		825				1,600	450	1,000
† Rend Lake College	690	3,915/2,629	358				826	1,121	991
Richland Community College	899	4,782/2,990	350					1,000	
Robert Morris College: Chicago	7,350		375				1,125	375	870
Rock Valley College	1,020	4,560/2,640	400					950	1,200
Rockford College	9,400		450	3,400	150	900	1,500	500	900
‡ Roosevelt University	7,470		528	4,800	600	1,456	1,580	600	1,456
Rosary College	9,226		450	4,036	50	900	1,500	500	900
† Rush University	8,125		300		225	1,055		495	1,055
‡ St. Augustine College	4,040		590				1,500	600	700
† St. Francis Medical Center College of Nursing	5,150		490			1,260	1,500	350	1,260
† St. Joseph College of Nursing	2,930		600				1,900	700	1,900
‡ St. Xavier College	8,150		420	3,500	139	757	1,500	643	757
‡ Sangamon State University	1,824	3,126/—	500		750	910	1,500	750	910
‡ Sauk Valley Community College	870	2,310/1,298	350					1,000	900
School of the Art Institute of Chicago	11,550		1,750		450	1,080	2,472	450	1,080
‡ Shawnee Community College	710	2,764/994	300					1,200	
Shimer College	9,000		630			1,200			
† South Suburban College of Cook County	1,224	3,962/2,352	500				1,500	300	700
Southeastern Illinois College	630	2,679/887	500				1,500	1,150	675

†Figures are projected for 1991-92.   ‡Figures are for 1990-91.

All aid		Need-based aid		Grants and scholarships								Financial aid deadlines		Inst aid form	Need analysis document
				Need-based				Nonneed-based							
Total freshmen	Percent receiving aid	Freshmen judged to have need	Percent offered aid	Acad	Music/drama	Art	Athl	Acad	Music/drama	Art	Athl	Priority	Closing		
285	85			X				X				8/1	none	X	AFSA/SF
306	87							X			X	6/15	none		FAF/FFS*
206	83	155	100	X				X	X	X		4/1	none		FAF/FFS*
891	22	408	100	X	X	X		X	X	X		4/1	7/1	X	FAF*/FFS
								X	X	X	X	4/1	none	X	FAF/FFS*/AFSA/ AFSSA/SF
4,992	67	1,119	100	X					X	X	X	3/1	5/1	X	FAF
1,773	63	859	100						X		X		2/15		FAF
								X	X	X	X	6/1	none	X	FAF/FFS*/AFSA/ AFSSA/SF
528	85			X	X	X	X	X	X	X	X	4/1	8/1	X	FAF
2,640	65	1,800	100					X	X	X	X	3/15	none	X	FAF/FFS/AFSA/ AFSSA/SF*
200	60			X				X					none	X	FAF*/FFS
87	98												none	X	FAF/FFS/AFSA/ AFSSA/SF*
								X					none	X	FAF/FFS/AFSA/ AFSSA*
129	70	98	100					X					none	X	FAF
422	93	348	100	X				X	X	X	X		none		FAF*/FFS/AFSA/ AFSSA/SF
357	63	91	100										none	X	FAF/FFS/AFSA*/ AFSSA
2,157	66							X			X		none		FAF/FFS/AFSA*/ AFSSA
1,350	28	289	100	X			X	X			X		none		FAF/FFS/AFSA*/ AFSSA
1,015	95							X					none		FAF*/FFS/AFSA
2,561	49							X	X				none		FAF/FFS/AFSA/ AFSSA
157	80	78	100	X	X	X		X	X	X		4/15	none		FAF*/FFS
194	60			X	X	X	X	X	X	X	X	5/1	none		FAF/FFS*
131	75	90	100	X		X		X			X	5/1	none		FAF
				X				X				4/15	6/15		FAF*/FFS
													none	X	FAF
								X					none		FAF/FFS*/AFSA/ AFSSA/SF;FAF/FFS*/ AFSA/AFSSA FFS
225	34			X	X		X	X	X		X	3/1	8/20		FAF*/FFS
				X				X			X	4/1	none	X	FAF/FFS/AFSA/ AFSSA*
1,600	35							X	X		X	5/1	none	X	FFS
175	73			X		X					X	4/1	none	X	FAF*/FFS/AFSA/ AFSSA/SF
													none		FAF/FFS/AFSA/ AFSSA*/SF
11	80	10	100	X	X	X		X	X	X			7/31	X	FAF
8,612	48	207	92	X			X	X			X	6/1	none		FAF/FFS/AFSA*/ AFSSA
1,046	68	725	69	X	X	X	X	X	X	X	X	9/4	none		FAF/FFS/AFSA/ AFSSA/SF*

*Preferred need analysis document.

Institution	Tuition and fees	Add'l out-of-state/district tuition	Books and supplies	Costs for campus residents			Costs for students at home		
				Room and board	Trans-portation	Other costs	Board only	Trans-portation	Other costs
Southern Illinois University ‡ Carbondale	2,332	3,120/—	450	2,780	659	1,088	1,500	595	1,088
† Edwardsville	1,821	3,065/—	202	3,296	807	825	1,284	1,450	934
Spoon River College	1,050	4,285/1,453	500						
† Springfield College in Illinois	4,924		500		276	3,225	390	1,700	878
State Community College	856	4,620/—	165				1,500	380	1,255
Telshe Yeshiva-Chicago	6,100								
† Trinity Christian College	7,785		450	3,360	700	1,050	2,300	1,450	1,050
Trinity College	8,610		600	3,850	350	900	1,850	350	900
† Triton College	1,115	4,350/2,490	450				1,100	1,020	
University of Chicago	16,212		625	5,685		525	2,453	1,000	525
† University of Health Sciences: The Chicago Medical School	10,409		877					1,800	697
University of Illinois ‡ Chicago	2,790	3,540/—	600	4,272	450	2,380	1,500	900	2,380
‡ Urbana-Champaign	2,846	3,540/—	420	3,652	380	1,212			
‡ VanderCook College of Music	7,886		450	4,220	250	250	600	500	250
† Waubonsee Community College	1,018	3,342/2,364	400				1,350	1,584	900
West Suburban College of Nursing	7,328		350	3,603	200	525	2,000	525	600
† Western Illinois University	2,517	3,960/—	500	2,734		1,600	1,800	830	1,045
Wheaton College	9,548		420	3,800		1,150	1,700		1,150
William Rainey Harper College	930	3,634/2,690	434				1,100	795	1,295

Indiana

Institution	Tuition and fees	Add'l out-of-state/district tuition	Books and supplies	Room and board	Trans-portation	Other costs	Board only	Trans-portation	Other costs
Ancilla College	2,086		400				900	800	600
Anderson University	8,060		500	2,870	400	700	1,500	400	700
‡ Ball State University	2,110	2,760/—	510	2,790	485	995	1,600	1,445	995
Bethel College	7,500		450	2,800	250	650		1,200	650
Butler University	10,500		400	3,840	340	1,260	2,500	340	1,260
‡ Calumet College of St. Joseph	3,585		400				1,545	800	930
DePauw University	12,288		375	4,420	220	670	1,500	490	360
Earlham College	13,479		550	3,726	600	500	1,200		500
‡ Franklin College	8,170		400	2,995	455	800		400	855
George Rogers Clark College	5,110						1,200	400	900
Goshen College	7,720		515	3,275	300	945	1,690	360	945
Grace College	7,302		375	3,318	400	400	1,750	650	625
Hanover College	6,700		450	2,885	250	750	1,800	300	750
‡ Holy Cross College	3,650		416				1,664	1,827	1,261
Huntington College	7,890		440	3,100	1,750	900	1,750	940	900
‡ Indiana Institute of Technology	6,735		400	3,030		2,300	1,850	800	1,500
‡ Indiana State University	2,104	2,952/—	400	2,958					
Indiana University ‡ Bloomington	2,310	4,535/—	445	3,159	292	1,337	1,559	826	1,337
‡ East	1,826	2,723/—	518				1,670	954	928

†Figures are projected for 1991-92.   ‡Figures are for 1990-91.

| All aid | | Need–based aid | | Grants and scholarships | | | | | | | | Financial aid deadlines | | Inst aid form | Need analysis document |
| Total fresh–men | Percent receiving aid | Freshmen judged to have need | Percent offered aid | Need–based | | | | Nonneed–based | | | | Priority | Closing | | |
				Acad	Music/ drama	Art	Athl	Acad	Music/ drama	Art	Athl				
2,658	82							X	X	X	X	4/1	none		FAF/FFS/AFSA/ AFSSA/SF;FAF/FFS/ AFSA/AFSSA/
1,010	68	682	95	X	X	X	X	X	X	X	X	4/1	none		SF
1,180	80							X	X	X			none		FAF*/FFS/AFSA/ AFSSA
73	89			X				X	X	X		5/1	none		FAF/FFS*/AFSA/ AFSSA
300	85	250										7/1	none	X	FAF*/AFSA/AFSSA
152	87	103	100					X	X	X	X	2/15	8/15		AFSSA FAF*/FFS/AFSA/ AFSSA
235	87							X	X		X	5/1	8/20		FAF
													none	X	FAF/FFS/AFSA/ AFSSA/SF*
858	66	525	100					X	X	X	X		2/1	X	FAF
												5/15	11/3		SF
2,542	70	1,000	100					X	X	X	X	5/1	none		SF
5,922	80	3,100	97	X				X	X	X	X	3/15	none		FAF/FFS*
48	81	32	100							X		3/1	6/1		FAF/AFSA*
				X	X		X	X	X		X	8/1	none		FAF/FFS/AFSA/ AFSSA
													4/1	X	FAF
2,093	85	1,322	90					X	X	X	X	3/29	none	X	FAF/FFS*/AFSA/ AFSSA/SF
508	60	425	100					X	X				3/15		FAF
3,792	12	432	85	X				X	X	X		5/1	none	X	FAF
				X		X	X					5/1	none	X	FAF*/FFS
522	87			X	X	X		X	X	X		3/1	none		FAF*/FFS
3,722	60	2,238	100			X		X	X		X		3/1		FAF
								X	X		X	3/1	none	X	FAF*/FFS
666	80	332	100				X	X	X		X	3/1	none		FAF
146	62	99	100	X				X				6/1	none		FAF*/AFSA/AFSSA
611	50	290	100					X	X	X			2/15		FAF
330	74	210	100	X	X			X					4/1		FAF;FAF*/FFS
262	95	220	100	X	X	X		X	X			3/1	none		FAF
													none		AFSA
228	95			X	X	X	X	X	X		X	3/1	none	X	FAF;FAF*/FFS
154	80	132	100					X	X	X	X	4/1	none	X	FAF
322	65	175	100	X				X				4/15	none	X	FAF*/FFS/AFSA
267	38	114	96									3/1	none		FAF+FFS/AFSA/SF; FAF*/FFS/AFSA/SF
128	89	112	100	X				X	X	X	X	3/1	6/1		FAF*/FFS/AFSA/ AFSSA
217	81	118	100	X		X		X			X	3/1	none	X	FAF
2,207	76	1,304	88					X	X	X	X		3/1	X	FAF*/FFS/AFSA/SF
5,356	69	2,018	94	X	X	X	X	X	X	X	X	3/1	none	X	FAF
477	68	211	98	X				X				3/1	none	X	FAF

*Preferred need analysis document.

Institution	Tuition and fees	Add'l out-of-state/district tuition	Books and supplies	Costs for campus residents			Costs for students at home		
				Room and board	Trans-portation	Other costs	Board only	Trans-portation	Other costs
‡ Kokomo	1,812	2,723/—	450				1,100	845	945
‡ Northwest	1,826	2,723/—	499				1,500	1,244	1,076
‡ South Bend	1,826	2,723/—	500				1,800	1,350	1,350
Southeast	1,836	2,723/—	412				1,670	800	1,033
Indiana University—Purdue University									
‡ Fort Wayne	1,839	2,639/—	340				1,391	1,092	865
‡ Indianapolis	2,106	4,151/—	500		300	1,314		1,350	1,314
Indiana Vocational Technical College									
‡ Central Indiana	1,509	1,236/—	438				1,515	1,338	945
‡ Columbus	1,509	1,236/—	460				1,654	1,404	990
‡ Eastcentral	1,509	1,236/—	360					1,188	1,287
‡ Kokomo	1,509	1,236/—	417					1,275	1,350
‡ Lafayette	1,509	1,236/—	550					1,200	1,200
‡ Northcentral	1,509	1,236/—	360					1,188	1,287
‡ Northeast	1,509	1,236/—	396					1,188	1,287
‡ Northwest	1,509	1,236/—	396					1,188	1,287
‡ Southcentral	1,509	1,236/—	500					1,188	1,287
‡ Southeast	1,509	1,236/—	360					1,188	1,287
‡ Southwest	1,509	1,236/—	360					1,188	1,287
‡ Wabash Valley	1,509	1,236/—	396					1,188	1,287
‡ Whitewater	1,509	1,236/—	360					1,188	1,287
Indiana Wesleyan University	7,590		350	3,392	300	300	500	300	500
International Business College	7,490		650						
Lockyear College	3,375		600	3,392				585	400
Lutheran College of Health Professions	4,077		480		640	1,620	1,600	1,200	1,620
Manchester College	8,270		400	3,246	150	600	1,536	150	600
† Marian College	7,584		450	3,104	650	900	1,500	640	900
Martin University	4,830		400				1,500	100	100
‡ Oakland City College	6,426		450	3,150	300	1,200	2,300	300	1,300
Purdue University									
† Calumet	1,940	2,850/—	440				1,500	876	1,081
† North Central Campus	1,908	2,835/—	350				1,410	1,055	925
West Lafayette	2,152	4,612/—	370	3,320	400	900	1,400	450	850
Rose-Hulman Institute of Technology	10,935		500	3,627	300	600	1,850	800	600
‡ St. Francis College	6,599		500	3,300	600	400	1,900	700	500
‡ St. Joseph's College	9,410		350	3,570	320	500		1,560	
St. Mary-of-the-Woods College	9,110		750	3,610	700	875	2,260	1,000	650
St. Mary's College	10,010		500	4,200	263	1,539	1,700	404	1,430
St. Meinrad College	5,413		500	4,064	1,100	900			
‡ Summit Christian College	6,000		350	2,690	180	750	1,250	526	750
Taylor University	9,353		300	3,542	300	600	1,715	700	600
Tri-State University	8,298		459	3,600	388	773	1,400	300	300
University of Evansville	9,150		400	3,560	440	440	1,500	950	450
University of Indianapolis	9,020		460	3,470	380	870		770	2,370
University of Notre Dame	13,505		550	3,575	550	840	1,700	550	840
‡ University of Southern Indiana	1,688	2,408/—	375		500	625	1,100	730	625
Valparaiso University	9,990		500	2,740	350	850	750	725	850
‡ Vincennes University	1,641	2,775/30	400	2,940	425	450	502	840	450
Wabash College	10,700		500	3,665		635	1,240		630

†Figures are projected for 1991-92. ‡Figures are for 1990-91.

All aid		Need-based aid		Grants and scholarships								Financial aid deadlines		Inst aid form	Need analysis document
				Need-based				Nonneed-based							
Total freshmen	Percent receiving aid	Freshmen judged to have need	Percent offered aid	Acad	Music/drama	Art	Athl	Acad	Music/drama	Art	Athl	Priority	Closing		
				X				X				3/1	none		FAF
1,138	40	480	100					X				3/1	none	X	FAF*/FFS
1,769	40							X	X	X		3/1	none	X	FAF
897	40			X	X	X	X	X	X	X	X	3/1	none		FAF
								X	X	X	X	3/1	none	X	FAF
3,078	29							X		X	X		3/1		FAF
2,496	25							X				3/1	none		FAF*/AFSA/SF
1,119	60											3/1	none	X	FAF*/AFSA/SF
				X								3/1	none		FAF*/AFSA/SF
599	45	420	94	X				X				3/1	none		FAF/SF
696	64			X				X				3/1	none		FAF/SF
								X				3/1	none	X	FAF*/AFSA/SF
1,070	34			X								3/1	none	X	FAF*/AFSA/SF
													none	X	FAF*/AFSA/SF
404	70											3/1	none		FAF*/AFSA/SF
400	66			X								3/1	none		FAF*/AFSA/SF
998	60	750	93	X				X				8/31	none		FAF/AFSA*/SF
862	80	595	100	X				X				3/1	none		FAF*/AFSA/SF
619	80											3/1	none		FAF/AFSA/SF
													none	X	FAF
350	80							X				5/1			FAF/AFSA/SF
													none		FAF/FFS/AFSA*
57	46			X				X				4/15	none		FAF*/FFS/AFSA/ AFSSA
340	82	227	95	X	X	X		X				5/1	none		FAF
546	71	220	100	X	X	X	X	X	X	X	X	8/15	none	X	FAF*/AFSA
271	65							X				3/1	none	X	FAF
255	97	140	100	X			X	X	X	X	X	3/1	none		FAF
1,650	41			X				X			X	3/1	none		FAF;FAF*/FFS
1,067	25	675	100					X				3/1	none		FAF
5,801	60			X				X				3/1	none	X	FAF
353	90	295	100					X				12/1	3/1		FAF*/FFS
102	80	92	100	X				X		X	X	3/1	none	X	FAF*/FFS/AFSA
257	75	192	100	X				X	X		X	5/1	none	X	FAF*/FFS/AFSA
307	82	64	100					X	X	X		3/1	none		FAF*/FFS
412	43	182	100	X	X	X						3/1	none	X	FAF
18	100	15	100					X				3/1	none		FAF
79	85			X				X				3/1	none	X	FAF*/FFS
434	75	248	100	X				X				3/1	none		FAF
290	90	241	100					X			X	3/1	none		FAF
528	92	346	100					X	X	X	X	3/1	none		FAF*/FFS
360	78	330	100	X				X	X	X	X	3/1	none	X	FAF
1,801	67	815	100	X							X		2/28		FAF
1,219	52	382	90	X				X	X	X	X	3/1	none	X	FAF*/AFSA
722	79	485	100					X	X		X	3/1	none		FAF*/FFS/AFSA
3,580	60	1,590	75	X	X	X	X	X	X	X	X		3/1	X	FAF
208	90	161	100					X	X	X		3/15	none		FAF

*Preferred need analysis document.

Institution	Tuition and fees	Add'l out-of-state/ district tuition	Books and supplies	Costs for campus residents			Costs for students at home		
				Room and board	Transportation	Other costs	Board only	Transportation	Other costs
Iowa									
American Institute of Business	4,525		600	2,655	465	990	900	840	1,590
American Institute of Commerce	4,579		700					873	1,098
Briar Cliff College	8,760		350	3,147	300	700	1,100	700	700
Buena Vista College	10,900		350	3,110	400	800		500	650
Central College	9,293		550	3,417	550	198	1,920	550	198
‡ Clarke College	8,165		350	2,840	300	600	2,500	300	300
‡ Clinton Community College	1,335	600/—	550				1,500	900	900
Coe College	10,380		450	3,840	450	1,200	1,910	450	1,250
Cornell College	12,350		550	3,970		1,000			
‡ Des Moines Area Community College	1,262	1,120/—	650					1,700	2,000
Divine Word College	5,235		400	1,200	800	800			
Dordt College	7,900		650	2,250	1,000	1,050	1,250	1,050	1,050
Drake University	11,040		475	4,215	300	1,500	1,500	600	1,500
† Ellsworth Community College	1,700	1,500/—	400	2,500		1,800		1,000	1,600
Emmaus Bible College	2,100		200	3,580	600	600	1,250	300	65
Faith Baptist Bible College and Theological Seminary	4,186		300	2,822	800	1,000	1,754	800	1,000
Graceland College	7,850		550	2,650		820			820
Grand View College	7,750		400	2,900	400	625	1,333	543	656
Grinnell College	13,742		400	3,868	1,000	400			400
Hamilton Technical College	4,438						1,400	350	750
Hawkeye Institute of Technology	1,383	1,302/—	700				1,577	975	2,182
‡ Indian Hills Community College	1,208	540/—	375	1,608	1,250	750		1,250	750
‡ Iowa Central Community College	1,560	700/—	400	2,450					
‡ Iowa Lakes Community College	1,280	576/—	375	2,367	660	363		660	363
‡ Iowa State University	1,880	4,280/—	600	2,720	405	2,185	750	1,075	820
Iowa Wesleyan College	8,200		500	3,000	450	400	1,700	500	400
Iowa Western Community College	1,470	675/—	325	1,400	250	825	1,400	635	825
† Kirkwood Community College	1,344	1,200/—	400					1,000	800
Loras College	9,115		300	3,200	400	500	1,100	300	500
Luther College	10,600		600	3,300	400	300	1,700	400	300
Maharishi International University	7,250		400	2,532	450	660	1,556		660
‡ Marshalltown Community College	1,510	1,400/—	400					540	625
Morningside College	9,206		350	2,980	350	720	1,580	350	720
Mount Mercy College	7,750		500	3,050	700		1,800	700	
Mount St. Clare College	7,337		350	3,225	300	600	2,000	400	500
‡ Muscatine Community College	1,335	600/—	550				1,500	900	900
National Education Center: National Institute of Technology Campus	5,140								
‡ North Iowa Area Community College	1,375	615/—	500	2,160	300	900	1,800	600	900
‡ Northeast Iowa Community College	1,400	1,152/—	500				1,800	900	540
‡ Northwest Iowa Technical College	1,392	720/—	519		414	630		1,293	630
Northwestern College	8,050		350	2,800	375	750	1,325	300	750
St. Ambrose University	8,530		500	3,430	575	1,500	2,159	780	927
‡ Scott Community College	1,335	600/—	550				1,500	900	900

†Figures are projected for 1991-92.   ‡Figures are for 1990-91.

All aid — Total freshmen	Percent receiving aid	Need-based aid — Freshmen judged to have need	Percent offered aid	Need-based Acad	Need-based Music/drama	Need-based Art	Need-based Athl	Nonneed-based Acad	Nonneed-based Music/drama	Nonneed-based Art	Nonneed-based Athl	Priority	Closing	Inst aid form	Need analysis document
663	79	394	100					X				4/1	none		FAF/FFS/AFSA/SF*
													none		FAF/FFS/AFSA/SF*
161	94			X	X	X	X	X	X	X	X	3/1	none		FAF/FFS*/SF
269	98	250	100	X	X	X		X	X	X		4/1	none		FAF/FFS*
373	97	302	100	X	X	X		X	X	X		3/1	none		FAF/FFS/SF*;FAF/FFS/AFSA/AFSSA/SF*
147	84	89	100	X	X	X		X	X	X		3/1	none		FAF/FFS/SF
				X			X	X			X	6/1	none		FAF/FFS/AFSA/SF*
288	89	251	100	X	X	X		X	X	X		3/1	none		FAF*/FFS/SF
337	85	245	100	X	X	X		X	X	X		3/1	none		FAF*/FFS/SF
4,921	60			X				X			X	3/1	none		FAF/FFS/AFSA/SF*
5	100	5	100	X								8/31	none		FAF/FFS
303	98	251	100					X	X	X	X	4/1	none	X	FAF*/FFS
805	75	446	100	X				X	X	X	X	3/1	none		FAF/FFS/SF*
615	70			X			X	X	X		X	4/1	none		FAF/FFS*/AFSA/AFSSA/SF
54	65			X				X				5/15	8/1		FAF*/FFS/AFSA
66	70	47	100	X	X			X				2/15	none		FAF/FFS*
254	89	173	100					X	X	X	X	3/1	none		FAF*/FFS/AFSA/AFSSA/SF
													none		FAF*/FFS
343	71	225	100					X				3/1		X	FAF
171	90												none		AFSA
1,255	80			X				X				4/22	6/30		FAF/FFS*/AFSSA/SF
								X	X	X	X	4/1	none		FAF/FFS/AFSA/SF*
1,506	75			X	X	X	X	X	X		X		none		FAF/FFS
709	80			X	X	X	X	X	X	X	X		none	X	FAF/FFS/AFSA/SF*
3,338	65	2,038	100	X	X		X	X	X		X	3/1	none		FAF/FFS/AFSA/SF; FAF/FFS/AFSA/CSS SAAC/ACT SAAC/SF
127	85			X	X	X	X	X	X	X	X	7/1	none		FAF*/FFS
1,123	76	431	87					X			X	5/1	none	X	FAF*/FFS/AFSA/SF
5,588	65			X	X		X	X				3/15	none		FAF/FFS*/AFSA/AFSSA/SF
520	80			X				X	X	X	X		4/15		FAF/FFS*
504	83	403	100	X	X	X		X	X	X		3/1	6/1	X	FAF/FFS*/AFSA/SF
145	80	42	100	X				X				2/28	none	X	FAF
													none	X	FAF*/FFS
252	97	196	100					X	X	X	X	3/1	none		FAF/FFS*/AFSA/SF
167	85	135	100		X	X		X	X	X		3/1	none		FAF/FFS/SF*
63	90			X				X				4/1	8/1		FAF*/FFS/AFSA
				X	X		X	X	X		X	6/1	none		FAF/FFS/AFSA/SF*
													none		AFSA
1,822	58	870	95	X	X		X	X	X	X	X	3/15	none		FAF/FFS/AFSA/SF
1,001	75							X				4/1	none	X	FAF/FFS*
392	78							X				4/20	none	X	FAF/FFS*
289	95	232	100	X	X	X	X	X	X	X	X	4/1	none		FAF/FFS*/SF
242	85	205	100	X	X	X	X	X	X	X	X	3/15	none	X	FFS
				X				X				6/1	none		FAF/FFS/AFSA/SF*

*Preferred need analysis document.

Institution	Tuition and fees	Add'l out-of-state/district tuition	Books and supplies	Costs for campus residents			Costs for students at home		
				Room and board	Transportation	Other costs	Board only	Transportation	Other costs
Simpson College	9,585		500	3,375	200	830			1,950
Southeastern Community College									
‡ North Campus	1,136	532/—	300	2,188				500	
‡ South Campus	1,136	532/—	350				1,350		
† Southwestern Community College	1,440	608/—	468	2,232		800			700
† Teikyo Marycrest University	7,890		500	2,700	600	670	1,500	600	670
Teikyo Westmar University	8,671		500	3,339	300	800	1,740	500	500
University of Dubuque	9,205		450	3,100	400	600	1,200	700	600
† University of Iowa	1,952	4,518/—	560	2,769	400	1,420	1,500	590	1,220
‡ University of Northern Iowa	1,880	2,910/—	450	2,326		1,710	1,280		1,710
‡ University of Osteopathic Medicine and Health Sciences	4,220		1,000					200	
Upper Iowa University	8,540		500	2,860	100	500	660	675	440
‡ Vennard College	4,396		375	2,270	300	600	1,500	200	600
Waldorf College	7,090		460	2,850	370	870	1,350	370	870
Wartburg College	9,640		350	3,080	200	700	1,550	250	600
‡ Western Iowa Tech Community College	1,182	1,107/—	425		150	800		825	660
William Penn College	9,190		400	2,720	460	530	685	1,600	530

Kansas

Institution	Tuition and fees	Add'l out-of-state/district tuition	Books and supplies	Room and board	Transportation	Other costs	Board only	Transportation	Other costs
‡ Allen County Community College	800	1,216/—	150	2,300	440	1,620	1,100	200	1,670
‡ Baker University	6,410			3,200	900		1,750	360	1,100
Barclay College	6,225		300	2,650	350	600	1,500	600	600
Barton County Community College	690	1,260/—	400	2,000	600	1,205	1,500	600	1,205
‡ Benedictine College	7,270		300	3,060	500	1,000	1,500	200	1,000
Bethany College	7,028		450	3,127	1,030	1,200	1,791	1,710	680
Bethel College	7,460		450	2,800	500	900	1,550	710	900
‡ Brown Mackie College	5,885		550				1,500	450	1,008
‡ Butler County Community College	855	1,215/—	400	2,375	400	900	1,500	400	900
Central College	6,050		300	2,900	400	500	1,400	400	500
‡ Cloud County Community College	810	1,110/—	300	2,500	475	875	1,500	475	875
‡ Coffeyville Community College	680	1,420/—	275	2,100	400	900		200	900
‡ Colby Community College	832	1,312/—	300	2,300	300	400		800	400
‡ Cowley County Community College	750	1,140/—	500	2,290	450	500	1,600	750	1,000
† Dodge City Community College	930	1,020/—	350	2,600	170	630	1,080	350	525
‡ Donnelly College	2,300		300						
‡ Emporia State University	1,382	2,122/—	400	2,480	450	909		450	909
‡ Fort Hays State University	1,456	2,122/—	400	2,502			2,500		1,200
‡ Fort Scott Community College	660	1,470/—	400	2,200	450	600	1,250	675	600
Friends University	7,155		550	2,630		2,260			2,260
‡ Garden City Community College	757	1,050/—	400	2,300	400	500	1,110	500	500
Haskell Indian Junior College	90		120		600	989			
† Hesston College	6,000		500	3,150	500	1,000		200	1,000
‡ Highland Community College	810	1,200/—	300	2,600	300	400	800	650	300
‡ Hutchinson Community College	720	1,950/—	440	1,995	660	990	1,650	2,380	990
‡ Independence Community College	750	1,410/—	400	2,300	400	700	800	800	700

†Figures are projected for 1991-92.   ‡Figures are for 1990-91.

Total freshmen	Percent receiving aid	Freshmen judged to have need	Percent offered aid	Need-based Acad	Music/drama	Art	Athl	Nonneed-based Acad	Music/drama	Art	Athl	Priority	Closing	Inst aid form	Need analysis document
288	90	218	100	X				X	X			4/22	none		FAF/FFS/SF*
792	76	469	100	X				X					none		FAF/FFS
454	73			X				X					none	X	FAF/FFS/AFSA/SF
482	75			X	X		X	X	X		X	4/15	none		FAF/FFS/AFSA/SF*; FAF/FFS*
245	90	104	87	X	X	X	X	X	X	X	X	3/1	none		FAF/FFS*/AFSA/SF
246	97							X	X		X	4/1	none		FAF*/FFS/AFSA
125	85			X	X			X	X			3/1	8/1		FAF/FFS/AFSA/AFSSA/SF*;FAF/FFS/AFSA/CSS SAAC/ACT
				X				X	X	X	X		none		FAF/FFS*/SF
3,156	70			X				X	X	X	X		none		FAF/FFS/AFSA/AFSSA/SF*
													none		FAF
158	99	156	100	X	X	X		X				4/20	none		FAF/FFS/AFSA/SF
50	84	44	95	X	X			X					none	X	FAF*/FFS/AFSA
437	97	207	100		X	X	X	X	X	X	X	4/15	8/1		FAF/FFS*/SF
372	89			X	X	X		X	X	X		3/1	none		FAF*/FFS/SF
													none		FAF/FFS
175	93			X	X	X		X	X	X		8/1	8/15		FAF/FFS
605	37							X	X		X		none		FFS*/AFSA
240	91							X	X	X	X	3/1	none		FAF/FFS*
28	51	15	100	X	X			X	X			5/15	none		FFS
699	40							X	X	X	X	3/1	none		FAF/FFS*/AFSA;FAF/FFS*/AFSA/AFSSA
183	90			X	X		X	X	X		X	4/15	none		FAF/FFS*
181	91	138	100	X				X	X	X	X	3/15	none		FAF/FFS*/AFSA;FAF/FFS*
106	57	60	100					X	X	X	X	1/1	none		FAF/FFS*;FAF/FFS*/AFSA
				X			X						none	X	FAF*/AFSA
								X	X	X	X	5/1	none		FFS
135	90	121	100					X	X		X	6/1	none		FAF/FFS*
1,887	73			X	X	X	X	X	X	X	X	4/1	none		FAF/FFS/AFSA
													none		FAF/FFS*/AFSA
								X	X	X	X	6/1	none		FAF/FFS*
827	50			X	X	X	X	X	X	X	X	4/1	none	X	FAF/FFS/AFSA*
													none		FAF/FFS*/AFSA
70	85			X				X				5/1	none		FFS*/AFSA
822	85							X	X	X	X	3/15	none		FAF/FFS*/AFSA/SF
801	70			X	X	X	X	X	X	X	X	3/15	none	X	FFS
1,243	40	500	100	X	X	X	X					5/1	none		FAF/AFSA
													none		FFS
1,063	75			X	X	X	X	X	X	X	X	6/1	none		FAF/FFS*
347	65			X								5/15	none		AFSA
177	90	160	100					X	X	X	X	5/1	none	X	FAF/FFS*/AFSA
1,244	81			X	X	X	X	X	X	X	X	4/1	none		FAF/FFS*
2,101	28	919	64	X	X	X	X	X	X	X	X	3/1	none	X	FAF/FFS*
				X	X	X	X	X	X	X	X		none		AFSA

*Preferred need analysis document.

Institution	Tuition and fees	Add'l out-of-state/district tuition	Books and supplies	Costs for campus residents			Costs for students at home		
				Room and board	Transportation	Other costs	Board only	Transportation	Other costs
‡ Johnson County Community College	840	1,965/—	400					975	700
† Kansas City College and Bible School	2,545		350	2,500	900	1,800	675	900	1,800
‡ Kansas City Kansas Community College	690	1,200/—	350				3,900	1,400	
† Kansas Newman College	6,523		605	3,168	1,125	900		1,535	800
‡ Kansas State University	1,576	3,124/—	600	3,772	325	1,500	900	450	1,500
Kansas Wesleyan University	6,700		500	3,000	400	500	1,500	400	500
‡ Labette Community College	630	1,980/—	300	2,100	350	400	1,200	600	400
Manhattan Christian College	3,300		500	2,434	560	400		500	
McPherson College	7,220		530	3,280	430	1,536	1,950	430	900
Mid-America Nazarene College	5,552		600	3,158	800	1,000	1,500	220	900
‡ Neosho County Community College	550	1,200/—	300	2,085	350	350		350	350
‡ Ottawa University	5,990		400	2,898	700	1,200	1,400	400	700
‡ Pittsburg State University	1,358	2,122/—	450	2,562	500	1,000	1,600	700	1,000
Pratt Community College	800	1,216/—	500	2,490	550	775		550	750
St. Mary College	6,450		500	3,250	490	840	1,900	480	840
‡ St. Mary of the Plains College	6,420		400	3,000	400	1,000		400	1,000
‡ Seward County Community College	660	1,290/—	600	2,100	500	400		800	400
Southwestern College	5,050		400	2,810	350	750	1,680	350	750
Sterling College	6,800		450	3,000	800	600		1,200	
Tabor College	6,800		550	3,000	750	2,500	1,200	750	2,500
University of Kansas									
‡ Lawrence	1,564	3,124/—	500	2,496	443	1,270	1,885	443	1,170
‡ Medical Center	1,362	3,124/—	400				1,500	900	1,440
† Washburn University of Topeka	2,492	1,290/—	450	2,895	640	755		640	525
‡ Wichita State University	1,608	3,124/—	500	2,727	700	700	1,000	700	700
Kentucky									
‡ Alice Lloyd College	270	—/2,970	400	2,364	300	409	1,250	800	409
Asbury College	7,372		495	2,491	750	660	1,282	300	
Ashland Community College	680	1,360/—	400						
Bellarmine College	7,260		600	2,450	440	750	1,100	570	700
‡ Berea College	177		350	2,331	200	742			
Brescia College	5,500		475	3,320	600	900	1,720	600	900
Campbellsville College	4,900		500	2,780	270	720	1,500	810	720
CareerCom Junior College of Business	7,805								
Centre College	10,110		500	3,930	100	500			
Clear Creek Baptist Bible College	2,000			2,100					
Cumberland College	5,296		200	3,076	350	550	1,600	350	550
† Eastern Kentucky University	1,420	2,600/—	450	2,685	250	600	1,700	600	600
Elizabethtown Community College	680	1,360/—	450						
Franklin College	4,200		400					900	900
Georgetown College	6,250	100/—	500	3,286	650	500	1,900	750	
Hazard Community College	680	1,360/—	500						2,600
Henderson Community College	680	1,360/—	450						
Hopkinsville Community College	680	1,360/—	450						2,650
† Institute of Electronic Technology	4,875		100				1,500	500	1,000
Jefferson Community College	680	1,360/—	400				2,000	500	300
Kentucky Christian College	3,250		600	2,950	1,336	1,300	1,670	1,404	890

†Figures are projected for 1991-92.   ‡Figures are for 1990-91.

Total freshmen	Percent receiving aid	Freshmen judged to have need	Percent offered aid	Need-based Acad	Music/ drama	Art	Athl	Nonneed-based Acad	Music/ drama	Art	Athl	Priority	Closing	Inst aid form	Need analysis document
				X				X	X	X	X	4/15	none		FAF/FFS/AFSA/SF*
													none	X	AFSA
3,407	17	841	71				X	X	X		X	4/15	none	X	AFSSA
83	54	45	100	X			X					3/15	none		FFS
3,516	38	1,396	100	X	X	X	X	X	X	X	X	3/15	none		FAF/FFS*
174	97	174	97	X	X	X	X	X	X	X	X	4/15	none		FFS
1,208	42	502	100	X	X	X	X						none		FFS
46	76	40	88	X	X			X				4/1	none		FAF/FFS*
79	91	58	100	X	X	X	X	X	X		X	4/15	none		FAF/FFS*
288	87			X	X		X	X	X		X	3/1	none	X	FAF/FFS*
455	65			X	X	X	X	X	X	X			none		FAF/FFS*/AFSA
133	92	109	100	X	X	X	X					4/1	none	X	FAF/FFS/AFSA/ AFSSA/SF;FAF/FFS/ AFSA/CSS SAAC/ACT
681	69	307	100	X	X	X	X	X	X	X	X	3/15	none		FAF/FFS*/AFSA
353	65							X	X	X	X	5/1	none	X	FAF/FFS*/AFSA
304	18	54	100	X			X	X	X	X	X		none		FAF/FFS*
152	96	138	100					X	X	X	X	4/1	none		FAF/FFS*
													none		FFS*/AFSA
122	83	93	100					X	X	X	X	4/1	none		FAF/FFS*/AFSA/ AFSSA/SF
124	90	98	100	X	X	X	X	X	X	X	X	5/1	none	X	FAF/FFS*
105	100	80	100	X	X		X	X	X		X	4/15	none		FFS;FAF/FFS*/AFSA
3,590	43	1,544	100	X				X	X	X	X	3/1	none		FFS
				X				X				5/1	none		FFS
774	80			X	X	X	X	X	X	X	X	3/15	none		FAF/FFS*
1,598	27	450	96	X				X	X	X	X	3/15	none		FFS
209	100							X			X	2/15	8/31		FAF
253	83			X	X	X		X	X	X		3/15	none	X	FAF;FAF*/FFS/AFSA/ CSS SAAC/ACT SAAC/ AFSSA/APSGFSA/SF
													none	X	FAF
266	89	228	100					X			X	5/1	none		FAF*/FFS/AFSA
384	100	384	100									2/28	none		FAF;FAF/FFS
173	69							X	X	X	X	4/1	5/1	X	FAF;FAF*/FFS
217	85			X	X	X	X	X	X	X	X	4/1	none	X	FAF
													none		AFSA
228	70	129	100	X				X					3/15	X	FAF
23	95			X									none		AFSA
450	85	433	100					X	X	X	X	3/15	none		FAF*/FFS/AFSA
4,471	60							X	X	X	X	4/15	none	X	FAF
981	50							X				4/1	none		FAF
16	95	12	100										none	X	AFSA
386	85	285	100	X	X	X	X	X	X	X	X	4/1	none		FAF
													none	X	FAF
600	55							X			X		none	X	FAF
													none		FAF
130	83												none	X	FAF/FFS
								X				4/1	none	X	FAF
													none	X	FAF*/FFS/AFSA/SF

*Preferred need analysis document.

Institution	Tuition and fees	Add'l out-of-state/ district tuition	Books and supplies	Costs for campus residents			Costs for students at home		
				Room and board	Trans-portation	Other costs	Board only	Trans-portation	Other costs
Kentucky College of Business	4,160		450						
† Kentucky State University	1,432	2,600/—	510	2,468	300	800		350	800
‡ Kentucky Wesleyan College	6,100		350	3,400	350	750	800	700	600
Lees College	3,600		400	2,500	300	650	800	720	400
‡ Lexington Community College	1,710	3,000/—	350	2,892					
Lindsey Wilson College	5,168		450	3,280	210	960	1,600	910	960
Louisville Technical Institute	5,980		450			1,650		750	
Madisonville Community College	680	1,360/—	425				1,650	460	150
Maysville Community College	680	1,360/—	450				1,500	405	745
† Mid-Continent Baptist Bible College	1,550		200	2,684	200	600		810	600
Midway College	5,800		350	3,550	320	500	1,100	640	500
‡ Morehead State University	1,320	2,360/—	400	2,430	200	700	1,500	1,190	700
Murray State University	1,410	2,600/—	500	2,395	350	600	750	480	600
† National Education Center: Kentucky College of Technology Campus	6,800								
Northern Kentucky University	1,410	2,600/—	400		700	500	1,500	700	500
Owensboro Junior College of Business	3,525		450						
Paducah Community College	680	1,360/—	350				1,200	916	350
Pikeville College	4,250		425	2,450	325	750	1,200	750	750
Prestonburg Community College	680	1,360/—	450					400	2,250
RETS Electronic Institute	5,615						2,608	728	896
St. Catharine College	3,700		300	2,490	300	625	600	700	550
Somerset Community College	680	1,360/—	340						
Southeast Community College	680	1,360/—	450				2,850	800	
Spalding University	6,696		265	2,760		1,000	1,280	480	800
‡ Sue Bennett College	3,440		400	2,100	1,000	600	1,700	1,000	700
‡ Thomas More College	7,430		400	3,440	400	500	1,400	500	500
Transylvania University	9,619		400	4,048	200	800	700	600	800
Union College	5,630		450	2,550	900	600	1,500	900	600
† University of Kentucky	1,830	3,240/—	425	3,054	160	570		210	520
University of Louisville	1,620	3,000/—	388	2,994	504	918	1,500	660	918
Watterson College	6,660		450		60	550	1,150	410	550
Western Kentucky University	1,440	2,600/—	400	2,900	300	800	1,300	1,500	1,500

Louisiana

Institution	Tuition and fees	Add'l out-of-state/ district tuition	Books and supplies	Room and board	Trans-portation	Other costs	Board only	Trans-portation	Other costs
Bossier Parish Community College	505		575				1,600	900	1,000
Centenary College of Louisiana	7,210		550	3,060	700	1,200	1,800	900	1,200
† Delgado Community College	980	1,200/—	500				1,500	860	930
Dillard University	9,150		500	3,350	360	875		400	900
† Grambling State University	1,778	1,550/—	500	2,636	353	930	1,500	859	830
† Grantham College of Engineering	1,800								
Jimmy Swaggart Bible College and Seminary	2,620		300	2,600	1,080	1,090	1,800	680	1,090
Louisiana College	4,160		520	2,650	384	1,011		934	1,011
Louisiana State University									
‡ Alexandria	924	1,472/—	520				1,630	934	1,011
† Eunice	888	1,200/—	650						
† Medical Center	1,802	2,400/—	1,658		385		880	979	2,492
‡ Shreveport	1,480	2,190/—	500				1,500	859	930

†Figures are projected for 1991-92.   ‡Figures are for 1990-91.

All aid		Need–based aid		Grants and scholarships								Financial aid deadlines		Inst aid form	Need analysis document
				Need–based				Nonneed–based							
Total freshmen	Percent receiving aid	Freshmen judged to have need	Percent offered aid	Acad	Music/drama	Art	Athl	Acad	Music/drama	Art	Athl	Priority	Closing		
240	71												none		FAF
424	82	340	100					X	X		X	3/15	4/15		FAF
167	85	140	100					X	X	X	X		4/1		FAF*/FFS
237	90	190	100					X			X	4/1	none		FAF
912	5											4/15	none	X	FAF
410	92	390	100	X	X	X	X					4/15	none		FAF
232	82												none		FAF/AFSA
1,666	54			X				X				4/1	none		FAF
255	51			X				X				4/1	none		FAF
14	1	12	100									5/1	none	X	AFSA
186	80							X	X	X	X		3/1		FAF
1,494	68			X				X	X	X	X	4/1	none	X	FAF*/FFS/AFSA
1,383	58	1,000	90					X	X	X	X	4/1	none	X	FAF
													none		AFSA
1,547	21							X	X	X	X	4/1	none	X	FAF
168	95			X									none		FAF/AFSA
		493	100	X				X			X	4/1	none	X	FAF
200	78	142	96	X			X	X			X	3/15	none	X	FAF
1,421	60			X				X				4/1	none	X	FAF
													none	X	AFSA
178	64	134	100	X		X	X	X		X	X	3/1	none	X	FAF+AFSA;FAF/AFSA
1,274	79	1,154	100	X				X				4/15	none	X	FAF;FAF/FFS
534	70			X				X				4/15	none	X	FAF
227	95			X	X	X		X	X	X		3/15	none	X	FAF;FAF*/FFS/SF
232	75	197	100	X	X		X	X					none	X	FAF*/AFSA/AFSSA
318	70	210	100					X	X	X		3/1	none	X	FAF;FAF*/AFSA
307	83	151	100					X	X	X	X	4/1	8/1	X	FAF;FAF*/FFS/AFSA/ CSS SAAC/ACT SAAC/ AFSSA/APSGFSA/SF
332	83	147	100					X	X		X	4/1	none		FAF;FAF*/FFS/AFSA
2,592	48			X				X	X	X	X	4/1	none		FAF
2,292	50	1,815	72					X	X	X	X	4/15	none		FAF
													none		FAF/AFSA*
2,625	41	993	94					X	X	X	X	4/1	none	X	FAF*/FFS/AFSA; FAF*/FFS
552	10	150	100	X		X		X			X	6/1	none		SF
206	82	82	100	X				X	X	X	X	3/15	none		FAF*/FFS/AFSA; FAF*/FFS/AFSA/SF
														X	FAF*/FFS
619	85	436	92	X		X		X			X	4/15	6/1		FFS
1,251	95												none		AFSA
				X				X					none		FAF
238	75			X				X			X		5/15		FFS
614	43			X				X	X	X		6/15	none		FAF/FFS/AFSA/SF*
602	60			X				X				7/1	none	X	FFS
				X				X				5/1	none		FFS
								X					none	X	AFSA

*Preferred need analysis document.

Institution	Tuition and fees	Add'l out-of-state/district tuition	Books and supplies	Costs for campus residents			Costs for students at home		
				Room and board	Transportation	Other costs	Board only	Transportation	Other costs
† Louisiana State University and Agricultural and Mechanical College	2,017	3,200/—	520	2,600		1,395			1,395
† Louisiana Tech University	1,841	1,155/—	500	2,115	340	900	1,100	340	660
Loyola University	8,698		500	5,334	800	750	1,100	300	750
† McNeese State University	1,626	1,550/—	500	2,100	353	930	1,500	875	930
New Orleans Baptist Theological Seminary	1,000								
† Nicholls State University	1,591	1,800/—	400	2,350	400	1,000		859	930
† Northeast Louisiana University	1,613	1,584/—	500	1,950	353	930	1,500	859	930
† Northwestern State University	1,749	1,800/—	550	2,024	875	950	1,500	600	
‡ Our Lady of Holy Cross College	4,600		406				1,500	500	1,000
Phillips Junior College: New Orleans	4,600								
St. Bernard Parish Community College	290		300						
St. Joseph Seminary College	5,570		780	3,500	680				
‡ Southeastern Louisiana University	1,703	1,800/—	500	2,280	898	972	295	898	972
Southern University									
New Orleans	1,451	1,558/—	400						
Shreveport	830	1,030/—	400				1,100	720	1,280
† Southern University and Agricultural and Mechanical College	1,576	1,522/—	500	2,551	375	500	700	150	275
Tulane University	16,980		350	5,505		800	735	650	555
† University of New Orleans	1,924	2,692/—	543	2,368		1,055	900	975	1,055
† University of Southwestern Louisiana	1,565	1,750/—	500	1,952	353	930	1,500	859	930
Xavier University of Louisiana	5,905		500	3,200	369	971	1,566	897	971

Maine

Institution	Tuition and fees	Add'l out-of-state/district tuition	Books and supplies	Room and board	Transportation	Other costs	Board only	Transportation	Other costs
Andover College	4,100		485				2,860	1,035	980
Beal College	3,610		750		350	1,400	1,200	1,500	700
Bowdoin College	16,380		540	5,590		870			870
‡ Casco Bay College	4,650		500	3,040			800	400	800
Central Maine Medical Center School of Nursing	2,370		790			700	1,500	405	700
‡ Central Maine Technical College	1,475	1,200/—	500	2,400	800	800	2,300	850	850
Colby College	16,460		500	5,350	200	800	400	600	600
‡ College of the Atlantic	10,485		400	3,000		650	800		650
† Eastern Maine Technical College	1,330	1,200/—	600	2,400	250	900	1,100	846	825
‡ Husson College	7,135		350	3,630	650	1,100		1,200	1,400
‡ Kennebec Valley Vocational Technical Institute	1,267	1,000/—	400						
Maine Maritime Academy	3,900	2,440/830	400	4,000	200	1,000	600		1,000
‡ Northern Maine Vocational Technical Institute	1,550	1,200/—	500	3,150	500	900	1,500	800	900
Portland School of Art	9,145		1,500	4,212	700	1,210		700	1,210
St. Joseph's College	8,500		550	4,300	300	1,500		1,000	1,500
† Southern Maine Technical College	1,380	1,200/—	680	2,500	500	800	1,600	850	900
Thomas College	8,050		750	4,150	800	1,000	1,600	1,700	1,200
Unity College	7,150	1,150/—	450	4,400	400	600		225	600

†Figures are projected for 1991-92.   ‡Figures are for 1990-91.

All aid		Need-based aid		Grants and scholarships								Financial aid deadlines		Inst aid form	Need analysis document
				Need-based				Nonneed-based							
Total freshmen	Percent receiving aid	Freshmen judged to have need	Percent offered aid	Acad	Music/drama	Art	Athl	Acad	Music/drama	Art	Athl	Priority	Closing		
3,409	50			X				X	X		X	4/1	none	X	FFS
1,911	52	842	100	X				X	X	X	X	4/1	none	X	FAF/FFS/AFSA/SF*
		349	99					X	X	X		5/1	8/1		FAF
1,475	49			X				X	X	X	X	5/1	none	X	FFS
1,297	60	756	100	X				X	X		X		6/1	X	FAF/FFS/AFSA/AFSSA/SF*
1,667	65	1,000	100	X				X	X	X	X	4/1	none		AFSA/SF
1,930	70	1,027	99	X	X		X	X	X	X	X	4/1	none		FAF/FFS/AFSA/AFSSA/SF*
58	48	41	100	X				X				3/18	6/1	X	AFSA
														X	AFSA
272	5			X			X						6/30		FAF/AFSA
17	72	5	100										none		AFSA
2,304	55	520	100	X	X			X	X		X	4/20	none	X	FAF*/FFS/AFSA/SF
300	80												5/1		FFS
197	90			X	X	X		X					none	X	FAF/FFS*
1,723	90			X	X		X	X			X		none	X	FAF/FFS*/AFSA/SF; FAF/FFS*/AFSA/CSS SAAC/ACT SAAC/SF
1,329	50	709	100	X				X			X		2/1		FAF
1,745	51	488	87	X	X		X	X	X		X	5/1	none		FFS*/AFSA
2,519	75	1,208	82					X	X	X	X	3/1	none		FAF/FFS*
595	90							X	X	X	X	7/21	none	X	FAF*/FFS/AFSA/AFSSA/SF;FAF*/FFS/AFSA/CSS SAAC/ACT
216	60	105	100										none		FAF*/AFSA
190	70	69	100	X				X				5/1	none		FAF*/AFSA
406	60	163	100										3/1	X	FAF
270	70	130	100										none	X	FAF*/FFS
53	62	34	97									3/15	9/7		FAF
341	70	175	100	X				X				4/1	none	X	FAF;FAF*/FFS
422	75	160	100	X								1/15	2/1	X	FAF
35	66	23	100									2/15	5/1		FAF
406	76			X								4/1	none		FAF
314	88	224	100	X			X	X				3/15	none		FAF
															FAF*/FFS
202	82	154	97					X				4/15	none		FAF
													none	X	FAF
69	68	52	100			X		X		X		3/1	none	X	FAF
187	88	151	100	X				X				3/15	none	X	FAF
776	70			X								4/15	8/15		FAF
185	90	162	100	X				X				2/1	8/1		FAF*/FFS/AFSA
135	73	93	100					X			X	4/15	none	X	FAF

*Preferred need analysis document.

Institution	Tuition and fees	Add'l out-of-state/ district tuition	Books and supplies	Costs for campus residents			Costs for students at home		
				Room and board	Trans-portation	Other costs	Board only	Trans-portation	Other costs
University of Maine									
‡ Augusta	1,965	2,730/—	500					1,100	700
‡ Farmington	2,070	2,730/—	450	3,388	500	1,400	1,600	1,100	100
‡ Fort Kent	2,025	2,625/—	440	3,395	700	900		900	800
‡ Machias	2,005	2,645/—	440	3,090	350	1,000		750	900
‡ Orono	2,470	3,780/—	450	3,945	350	1,130	1,350	1,000	630
‡ Presque Isle	2,000	2,730/—	400	3,284	600	900	1,500	1,050	800
University of New England	9,770		500	4,525	265	450		600	1,000
‡ University of Southern Maine	2,214	3,630/—	500	3,844	330	1,533	1,500	900	1,533
† Westbrook College	9,800		600	4,650	300	750		300	750
Maryland									
† Allegany Community College	1,349	1,500/540	438				1,500	846	950
Anne Arundel Community College	1,320	3,780/1,260	400				1,700	950	1,200
‡ Baltimore Hebrew University	2,430		500					500	100
Baltimore International Culinary College	7,394		550		510		3,312	510	
† Bowie State University	2,254	1,925/—	450	3,427	650	900	1,500	650	900
† Capitol College	6,965		535		800	1,175	1,475	1,575	1,175
Catonsville Community College	1,022	2,192/696	500					1,500	900
Cecil Community College	1,110	2,100/1,050	600				2,000	1,200	1,000
Charles County Community College	1,422	2,640/1,320	350				2,000	600	400
Chesapeake College	904	2,880/1,080	500					950	1,000
College of Notre Dame of Maryland	9,500		450	4,800	250	700	1,600	300	700
‡ Columbia Union College	7,930		400	3,690	400	750	1,800	450	750
† Coppin State College	2,241	1,764/—	600				1,803	1,211	1,549
‡ Dundalk Community College	1,082	2,292/730	500				1,200	1,500	900
‡ Eastern Christian College	2,290		450	2,250	400	300	1,100	800	300
Essex Community College	1,080	2,292/730	500					1,500	
Frederick Community College	1,553	4,140/1,380	450				1,575	1,050	750
† Frostburg State University	2,068	1,912/—	500	3,910	200	750	1,700	600	600
Garrett Community College	1,020	2,040/480	375				1,430	810	700
Goucher College	12,885		400	5,700	300	1,000	1,500	600	400
Hagerstown Business College	3,560		650		325	325	925	725	325
Hagerstown Junior College	1,764	1,680/848	550				1,300	550	
Harford Community College	1,230	2,310/1,020	600		1,700		1,800	1,200	800
Hood College	12,208		400	5,675		717	2,192	717	
‡ Howard Community College	1,355	2,880/728	450				1,500	675	700
Johns Hopkins University									
Peabody Conservatory of Music	11,950		200	5,100	630	700		630	700
School of Arts and Sciences and Engineering	16,000		450	6,120		800	1,500	650	800
School of Nursing	11,900		610		600	800			
‡ Loyola College in Maryland	9,810		500	5,379	200	650	1,500	650	650
‡ Maryland College of Art and Design	6,156		700				1,360	1,150	1,150
‡ Maryland Institute College of Art	10,640		1,100	3,960	500	600	600	1,000	600
Montgomery College									
† Germantown Campus	1,510	2,410/1,350	475				580	2,000	1,050
† Rockville Campus	1,510	2,410/1,350	475				580	2,000	1,050
† Takoma Park Campus	1,510	2,410/1,350	475				580	2,000	1,050
‡ Morgan State University	2,124	1,924/—	800	4,380	450	1,500	750	450	2,250

†Figures are projected for 1991-92. ‡Figures are for 1990-91.

Total freshmen	Percent receiving aid	Freshmen judged to have need	Percent offered aid	Acad	Music/ drama	Art	Athl	Acad	Music/ drama	Art	Athl	Priority	Closing	Inst aid form	Need analysis document
All aid		**Need–based aid**		**Grants and scholarships**								**Financial aid deadlines**			
				Need–based				Nonneed–based							
542	50	225	100					X	X	X		4/1	none		FAF
487	65			X				X				3/15	none	X	FAF
121	95	49	100					X				4/1	none		FAF
193	79	185	98	X	X	X	X					5/1	none		FAF
1,990	57			X				X	X	X	X		3/1		FAF
420	90	128	100	X	X			X					none	X	FAF
161	92			X			X	X			X	3/1	none	X	FAF
												4/1	none		FAF
164	80	124	100	X			X	X			X	3/15	none		FAF
678	54			X			X	X				3/15	none	X	FAF*/FFS/AFSA
				X		X	X	X			X	4/15	none		FAF*/FFS/AFSA
												7/1		X	FAF
84	92	84	100					X					none	X	FAF/FFS/AFSA;FAF/ FFS/AFSA/CSS SAAC/ ACT SAAC/AFSSA
451	70			X				X			X	7/1	none	X	FAF
55	32	31	100	X				X				3/15	none		FAF
2,450	10			X				X			X	6/1	none	X	FAF
				X	X	X	X	X	X	X	X	8/1	none		FAF
													none	X	FAF*/FFS/AFSA/SF
703	3	18	100	X				X				6/1	none	X	FAF*/FFS/AFSA
215	90	109	100	X				X	X	X		2/15	none		FAF
188	74	100	100					X	X		X	3/31	5/31	X	FAF;FFS
414	48	197	100	X							X		5/1	X	FAF*/FFS
				X		X	X	X			X		none	X	FAF*/FFS/AFSA
5	100			X	X			X	X			8/1	none		FAF
								X	X		X	7/1	none		AFSA
1,194	10			X				X			X	6/15	none	X	FAF*/AFSA;FAF/ AFSA*
872	34	300	100	X				X	X	X		4/1	none	X	FAF*/AFSA;FAF*/ AFSA/APSGFSA
175	56			X		X	X	X		X	X	4/1	5/1	X	FAF
142	77	110	100					X	X	X		2/15	none	X	FAF;FAF*/CSS SAAC
174	92	160	100					X				10/3	none	X	FAF/AFSA*
2,075	50	530	95	X			X	X			X	6/15	7/1	X	FAF
				X				X	X		X	5/1	none	X	FAF*/FFS/AFSA
148	80	115	100	X				X				3/31	none		FAF
				X	X			X				3/1	none	X	FAF*/AFSA
					X				X				2/1		FAF
839	60	366	100					X	X		X		1/15	X	FAF*/AFSA
				X				X					none	X	FAF
833	57	346	97					X			X	2/15	3/1		FAF
33	82	26	100			X				X		4/1	none	X	FAF
169	54	91	100	X		X		X		X		3/1	none	X	FAF*/FFS
												2/15	none	X	FAF*/FFS/AFSA
												2/15	none	X	FAF*/FFS/AFSA
												2/15	none	X	FAF*/FFS/AFSA
				X				X			X	4/1	none	X	FAF

*Preferred need analysis document.

Institution	Tuition and fees	Add'l out-of-state/district tuition	Books and supplies	Costs for campus residents			Costs for students at home		
				Room and board	Transportation	Other costs	Board only	Transportation	Other costs
Mount St. Mary's College	9,875		500	5,700	300	1,000	2,825	200	500
Ner Israel Rabbinical College	2,850		180	3,500					
† New Community College of Baltimore	1,090	3,150/1,050	600					650	1,050
Prince George's Community College	1,740	4,490/2,040	440					800	800
St. John's College	14,262		275	4,696	350	600	2,000	200	600
St. Mary's College of Maryland	2,760	1,800/—	500	4,100	150	900	1,650	500	900
† Salisbury State University	2,444	2,054/—	450	3,890	400	800	950	850	800
Sojourner-Douglass College	4,525		400				1,400	578	1,400
‡ Towson State University	2,409	1,922/—	530	4,510	310	925	1,920	310	615
† University of Baltimore	2,120	1,713/—	400				1,500	1,000	1,500
University of Maryland									
‡ Baltimore	2,152	3,948/—	615		125	150		350	1,200
‡ Baltimore County	2,390	3,950/—	450	3,784	300	930	1,600	1,500	930
‡ College Park	2,267	4,056/—	395	4,712	275	650	1,250	865	
‡ Eastern Shore	2,114	3,650/—	450	3,534	400	1,000	1,100	1,000	1,000
‡ University College	3,540		720				2,596	738	1,061
‡ Villa Julie College	5,440		400				1,100	900	900
‡ Washington Bible College	4,889		300	3,070	500	700			
‡ Washington College	11,400		500	4,700	300	500			
Western Maryland College	12,505		400	4,740	400	500	2,580	600	500
Wor-Wic Tech Community College	1,130	3,330/1,470	400				1,700	1,000	400

Massachusetts

Institution	Tuition and fees	Add'l out-of-state/district tuition	Books and supplies	Room and board	Transportation	Other costs	Board only	Transportation	Other costs
‡ American International College	7,731		500	3,750	400	800	1,400	600	500
Amherst College	16,945		660	4,600		1,285			
† Anna Maria College for Men and Women	9,620		450	4,380	500	950	1,600	1,200	980
Aquinas College at Milton	7,100		400				1,900	2,450	1,000
‡ Aquinas College at Newton	6,750		350				1,900	1,000	1,600
‡ Assumption College	9,210		400	4,700	400	600		600	600
† Atlantic Union College	9,996		450	3,250	600	900		700	900
‡ Babson College	13,853		500	5,476		1,000		1,000	1,000
Bay Path College	8,500		400	5,600	500	600	500	700	1,400
Bay State College	6,825		500	5,700	630	1,460	2,115	810	1,235
Becker College									
Leicester Campus	6,925		300	3,925	300	600		700	600
Worcester Campus	6,925		300	3,925	300	600	1,500	700	600
Bentley College	11,390		350	4,768	290	850		1,160	850
Berklee College of Music	9,040		550	6,190	200	800	2,500	500	800
‡ Berkshire Community College	1,238	3,040/—	434				1,500	400	850
‡ Boston Architectural Center	2,480		1,210				1,800	1,430	935
† Boston College	14,084		450	6,150	500	800	1,500	1,300	690
Boston Conservatory	10,350		475	5,300	350	800	1,500	350	800
Boston University	16,190		410	6,320	270	710	875	1,015	710
Bradford College	11,885		425	5,875	450	950	1,650	550	950
‡ Brandeis University	15,320		410	5,960		1,000	1,500	3,120	1,000
‡ Bridgewater State College	2,108	3,075/—	455	3,720	403	1,091	2,140	1,119	1,091
‡ Bristol Community College	1,604	3,040/—	400				1,500	1,124	965
‡ Bunker Hill Community College	1,226	3,040/—	400				1,000	500	1,000
‡ Cape Cod Community College	1,462	3,040/—	450				1,500	1,400	850
‡ Clark University	14,380		450	4,500	100	650	2,200	250	650

†Figures are projected for 1991-92.   ‡Figures are for 1990-91.

All aid		Need-based aid		Grants and scholarships								Financial aid deadlines		Inst aid form	Need analysis document
				Need-based				Nonneed-based							
Total freshmen	Percent receiving aid	Freshmen judged to have need	Percent offered aid	Acad	Music/drama	Art	Athl	Acad	Music/drama	Art	Athl	Priority	Closing		
356	57	146	100	X				X			X		3/15		FAF
45	28	13	100	X				X					5/15	X	FFS
1,515	75							X			X	6/1	none	X	FAF/FFS*/AFSA
													none		AFSA
109	48	52	100									3/1	none	X	FAF
210	23	52	94					X	X			3/1	3/15	X	FAF*/AFSA
700	16	200	55	X								3/1	none	X	FAF
89	48	43	100	X				X					none	X	FAF
1,440	22	353	90	X	X	X	X	X	X	X	X	3/15	none	X	FAF*/AFSA
								X				3/15	none	X	FAF*/FFS
												2/15	3/1	X	FAF
1,102	46			X	X		X	X	X	X	X	3/1	none		FAF
				X	X	X	X	X	X	X	X	2/15	none		FAF
505	80							X	X	X	X	4/1	none		FAF*/FFS
				X		X		X					5/1	X	FAF
399	68	224	92	X				X				3/1	none		FAF*/FFS/AFSA
101	30				X		X	X	X		X	6/1	none	X	FAF
236	53	145	100	X				X				2/15	none	X	FAF*/FFS
261	66	205	94	X	X	X		X				3/1	none	X	FAF*/FFS/AFSA
387	30	115	100					X					none		FAF
313	71	205	96				X	X			X	4/15	none		FAF*/FFS
401	59	191	100									2/1		X	FAF
112	73	82	100	X	X			X	X			3/1	none	X	FAF*/FFS;FAF*/FFS/APSGFSA
117	72	90	100	X				X				3/1	none		FAF
90	62	44	100	X				X					3/15		FAF
459	56	255	96	X				X			X		2/1	X	FAF*/FFS
196	90	150	100	X	X		X	X	X		X	6/1	none	X	FAF
422	45	194	100	X				X					2/1	X	FAF
261	77	186	100					X	X			2/28	none		FAF
554	75	300	83					X				3/1	none		FAF
255	61	120	94								X	2/15	none	X	FAF*/FFS
332	64	210	93			X		X			X	2/15	none	X	FAF*/FFS
911	59	468	100	X		X		X			X		2/1		FAF*/FFS/AFSA; FAF*/FFS/AFSA/CSS SAAC/ACT SAAC
745	62	423	88	X	X			X	X			3/31	none	X	FAF*/FFS
511	33	316	100									5/1	none		FAF
													none		FAF
2,127	61	861	100	X				X			X		2/1	X	FAF
61	80				X				X				3/1	X	FAF
3,397	69	1,752	98	X	X	X		X	X	X	X	3/1	none		FAF;FAF*/CSS SAAC
98	49							X				3/1	none	X	FAF
715	48	327	100	X				X				2/15	4/15	X	FAF*/FFS/AFSA
950	52							X				5/1	none	X	FAF
1,262	48			X	X	X		X		X		4/15	none	X	FAF
												5/1	none	X	FAF*/FFS
872	47	186	96					X	X	X	X	3/15	5/1		FAF
459	51	233	100	X	X	X							2/1		FAF

*Preferred need analysis document.

Institution	Tuition and fees	Add'l out-of-state/district tuition	Books and supplies	Costs for campus residents			Costs for students at home		
				Room and board	Transportation	Other costs	Board only	Transportation	Other costs
College of the Holy Cross	15,530		400	5,700	100	960	1,500	300	660
‡ Curry College	11,470		600	5,250	300	800		1,400	800
Dean Junior College	8,860		400	5,800	500	500	1,000	1,000	500
Eastern Nazarene College	7,660		350	3,200	300	660		300	660
Elms College	9,650		450	4,400	400	800	1,500	700	850
† Emerson College	13,072		500	7,121	500	932	1,500	1,000	1,615
‡ Emmanuel College	9,685		500	5,065		900			900
Endicott College	9,640		400	5,310	600	800	1,600	850	800
† Essex Agricultural and Technical Institute	1,304	—/2,796	500				1,700	1,500	
‡ Fisher College	8,590		400	5,800	500	900	1,500	500	550
‡ Fitchburg State College	2,058	3,075/—	450	3,104	350	1,000	1,600	1,000	1,000
† Forsyth School for Dental Hygienists	11,355		400	6,680	175	450		675	450
† Framingham State College	2,879	3,075/—	450	3,300	550	1,200	1,500	1,310	1,200
Franklin Institute of Boston	7,790		600	6,320	225	525	1,650	625	600
Gordon College	11,400		400	3,630	400	400	1,300		400
† Greenfield Community College	1,765	3,396/—	500				1,960	938	1,230
Hampshire College	17,785		300	4,560		450	1,665		450
‡ Harvard and Radcliffe Colleges	15,530		400	5,125	350	1,105			3,665
‡ Hellenic College	5,845		458		636	1,060		318	1,060
‡ Holyoke Community College	1,390	3,040/—	400				100	700	200
† Katharine Gibbs School	7,400		425						
‡ Laboure College	6,650		800		360	900	1,200	960	675
† Lasell College	9,850		600	5,500	250	2,000	1,700	250	2,000
‡ Lesley College	10,710		470	4,770	325	720	1,700	730	720
Marian Court Junior College	6,180		400				750	1,054	1,393
‡ Massachusetts Bay Community College	1,370	3,040/—	400				2,015	800	860
‡ Massachusetts College of Art	1,845	3,780/—	1,700	5,300	600			600	2,200
‡ Massachusetts College of Pharmacy and Allied Health Sciences	9,316		350	5,995	320	1,600	1,700	750	1,600
Massachusetts Institute of Technology	16,900		575	5,330	400	1,325	1,900	360	1,825
‡ Massachusetts Maritime Academy	1,592	3,780/—	500	3,598	350	200			300
‡ Massasoit Community College	1,520	3,040/—	400				2,250	900	900
Merrimack College	10,350		550	5,700	1,000	450	1,600	1,000	450
‡ Middlesex Community College	1,211	3,040/—	405				1,500	1,677	936
† Montserrat College of Art	7,700		800				1,700	800	600
Mount Holyoke College	16,050		600	4,900		700			2,700
Mount Ida College	9,140		650	6,245	500	600		850	600
‡ Mount Wachusett Community College	1,382	3,040/—	400				1,200	1,140	1,000
‡ New England Banking Institute	1,476		300						
New England Conservatory of Music	13,350		400	6,150	550	1,800		800	1,800
‡ Newbury College	8,200		350	5,260	250	400		225	425
Nichols College	7,867		400	4,480	250	650		500	650
† North Adams State College	2,500	3,075/—	350	3,460	200	1,100		950	1,100
‡ North Shore Community College	1,404	3,040/—	600				1,630	924	906
‡ Northeastern University	9,968		480	6,375	150	540	1,455	675	540
‡ Northern Essex Community College	1,370	3,040/—	500				1,700	1,175	1,400
Pine Manor College	14,000		300	5,700	350	540	1,200	100	540
‡ Quincy College	1,880		400				500	200	400
‡ Quinsigamond Community College	1,212	3,040/—	500				1,100	700	1,100
Regis College	10,550		380	5,200		700	1,575	885	700
‡ Roxbury Community College	1,423	3,040/—	500				1,500	1,000	1,400
St. Hyacinth College and Seminary	3,685		375	4,000	400	700	1,100	800	700

†Figures are projected for 1991-92.   ‡Figures are for 1990-91.

All aid		Need–based aid		Grants and scholarships								Financial aid deadlines		Inst aid form	Need analysis document
				Need–based				Nonneed–based							
Total freshmen	Percent receiving aid	Freshmen judged to have need	Percent offered aid	Acad	Music/ drama	Art	Athl	Acad	Music/ drama	Art	Athl	Priority	Closing		
627	60	347	100					X				2/1	none		FAF*/FFS
211	45												4/15	X	FAF*/FFS
650	42	300	92									3/15	none	X	FAF*/FFS
182	85			X	X			X	X			3/1	none	X	FAF
121	80			X				X				2/15	none	X	FAF
358	80			X	X				X			2/1	none	X	FAF
158	71	102	100	X	X			X				3/15	none		FAF
401	53	340	100	X		X	X					3/15	none		FAF
132	25	65	100									5/1	none		FAF
160	72	137	100									3/1	none		FAF*/FFS
545	53	139	100	X				X	X	X		3/30	none	X	FAF
57	55	50	96	X				X				3/1	none	X	FAF
483	32	183	100	X				X				3/1	none	X	FAF
213	75			X								4/1	none	X	FAF
225	90			X	X								3/15		FAF
524	76	236	100	X			X					4/15	none		FAF*/FFS/AFSA
310	48	199	95					X				2/15	none	X	FAF
1,609	60											2/15		X	FAF
															FAF
				X				X	X	X	X	5/15	none	X	FAF*/AFSA
													none	X	
														X	FAF
184	55	101	100									5/1	none		FAF
134	56	121	100	X				X				3/1	none	X	FAF
78	60	54	100					X				4/1	none		FAF
2,738	12	467	100	X				X	X	X	X		5/1		FAF/FFS
127	46	62	100									5/1	none		FAF/FFS
													none	X	FAF
1,084	56	607	100									2/1	none	X	FAF
180	77	58	100	X				X				5/1	none	X	FAF
1,189	65			X			X	X			X	4/15	none	X	FAF
556	66	401	91	X			X				X		3/1		FAF
1,948	39											3/31	none		FAF
65	71	43	100	X		X				X		4/15	none		FAF
453	57	244	100										2/1	X	FAF
750	50	488	100	X			X					5/1	none	X	FAF
1,190	63	850	88										none	X	FAF
99	75				X				X				3/1	X	FAF
542	60	182	100									8/1	none	X	FAF
220	65	92	100	X				X				4/1	none		FAF
447	36	230	95									5/1	none	X	FAF
962	30											3/1	none		FAF
2,711	81	2,373	94	X				X			X	3/1	none		FAF
1,484	50			X				X			X	4/1	none	X	FAF
160	26	46	100	X				X				3/15	none	X	FAF
1,098	75											5/1	none	X	FAF
2,760	25							X	X	X	X		none	X	FAF
197	69			X								2/15	none	X	FAF
434	85											5/1	none		FAF
													6/15		FAF

*Preferred need analysis document.

Institution	Tuition and fees	Add'l out-of-state/district tuition	Books and supplies	Costs for campus residents			Costs for students at home		
				Room and board	Transportation	Other costs	Board only	Transportation	Other costs
St. John's Seminary College	3,600		400	3,000	400	600			
‡ Salem State College	1,980	3,095/—	420	3,425	430	855	2,070	1,170	855
‡ School of the Museum of Fine Arts	10,351		925					550	890
Simmons College	14,074		400	6,000		1,000	1,650	520	1,350
‡ Simon's Rock College of Bard	14,450		400	4,810	400	450	1,925	250	400
Smith College	15,770		400	6,100		550			550
‡ Southeastern Massachusetts University	2,160	3,885/—	500	4,000	400	1,000	1,500	1,250	1,000
Springfield College	9,441		400	4,376		1,000		350	1,000
‡ Springfield Technical Community College	1,406	3,040/207	400				2,060	800	1,500
Stonehill College	10,285		480	5,366	430	834	2,650	1,280	800
Suffolk University	8,531		450	5,500			1,500	700	2,450
‡ Tufts University	15,917		625	5,170	100	700	2,360	500	700
‡ University of Lowell	2,711	3,910/—	400	3,990	200	1,160	1,440	900	1,380
University of Massachusetts									
‡ Amherst	3,476	4,853/—	500	3,694	300	1,000	1,800	700	1,000
‡ Boston	2,702	4,853/—	520				1,830	936	1,132
Wellesley College	16,271		475	5,657	340	625	900		625
Wentworth Institute of Technology	8,220		600	5,950	200	400		600	400
Western New England College	7,967		475	4,900	300	840	1,500	925	1,140
‡ Westfield State College	1,941	3,075/—	400	3,598	360	1,280	750	1,350	1,280
Wheaton College	15,760		585	5,480		775	2,810		775
‡ Wheelock College	10,528		300	4,926	150	600	2,500	350	600
‡ Williams College	15,785		500	4,975	200	800			
Worcester Polytechnic Institute	14,125		450	4,590		700	1,500		700
‡ Worcester State College	1,812	2,513/—	500	3,630	300	1,125	1,680	900	1,250

Michigan

Institution	Tuition and fees	Add'l out-of-state/district tuition	Books and supplies	Room and board	Transportation	Other costs	Board only	Transportation	Other costs
Adrian College	9,390		400	3,000	300	694	1,650	300	694
Albion College	11,134		500	4,064	400	400	2,122		
‡ Alma College	9,852		500	3,626		600	1,060	650	600
Alpena Community College	1,220	1,320/510	300				1,600	840	600
Andrews University	8,985		560	3,675					
‡ Aquinas College	8,296		305	3,726	438	601	1,636	788	601
Baker College									
Flint	4,560		650		1,000	2,500	1,500	900	2,494
Owosso	4,560		700	1,500		400			
‡ Baker College of Muskegon	4,295		600		425	923	1,200	900	1,650
† Bay de Noc Community College	1,316	1,554/488	450		818	586	1,500	818	586
Calvin College	8,100		365	3,350	520	610	1,660	970	610
Center for Creative Studies: College of Art and Design	9,495		1,926	4,100	530	636	2,332	1,484	477
‡ Central Michigan University	2,129	3,460/—	450	3,350	500	700		500	700
Charles Stewart Mott Community College	1,240	1,050/480	500					500	560
Cleary College	5,025		750				1,600	1,200	1,000
‡ Concordia College	7,102		400	3,456	268	1,032	2,074	268	1,032
Davenport College of Business	7,236		600		489	729		589	729
‡ Delta College	1,300	1,410/540	416	3,072			2,500	750	540
‡ Detroit College of Business	5,310		500				2,400	900	750
† Eastern Michigan University	2,104	3,055/—	450	3,581	100	1,000	1,751	668	1,114
‡ Ferris State University	2,412	2,589/—	390	3,018	333	597	1,696	474	185
Glen Oaks Community College	1,020	420/120	438				1,000	760	773
GMI Engineering and Management Institute	7,490		450	2,450					

†Figures are projected for 1991-92.   ‡Figures are for 1990-91.

All aid		Need–based aid		Grants and scholarships								Financial aid deadlines		Inst aid form	Need analysis document
				Need–based				Nonneed–based							
Total fresh-men	Percent receiving aid	Freshmen judged to have need	Percent offered aid	Acad	Music/ drama	Art	Athl	Acad	Music/ drama	Art	Athl	Priority	Closing		
8	60	7	100										7/1		FAF
1,260	52	366	88	X	X	X		X	X	X		4/15	none		FAF
208	44	51	100			X						3/15	none	X	FAF*/AFSA
285	56	161	100					X					2/1	X	FAF
		90	100										none		FAF
615	55	276	100										1/15	X	FAF
864	40			X				X				5/1	none	X	FAF
523	80			X									4/1	X	FAF
								X	X	X	X	4/1	none	X	FAF
510	57	275	97	X			X	X	X		X	2/15	none		FAF
441	60	400	94	X				X					3/1	X	FAF
1,115	36	368	100	X				X					2/1	X	FAF;FAF*/CSS SAAC
1,360	40						X						5/1		FAF
3,589	65			X	X	X	X	X	X	X	X	3/1	none		FAF
751	50	333	93	X				X				3/15	none		FAF
584	44	258	100										2/1	X	FAF
1,255	39							X				3/1	none		FAF
531	49			X									none	X	FAF
824	55							X				4/1	none		FAF
372	52	199	100	X									2/1	X	FAF*/FFS
179	71	128	100										3/1	X	FAF
506	35	178	100	X	X	X	X						2/1	X	FAF
703	85	512	100										3/1	X	FAF
477	42							X				4/13	none		FAF
290	85	212	100	X	X			X	X			5/1	none		FAF*/FFS
417	70	215	100					X	X			3/1	none		FAF*/FFS
290	95	184	100	X	X	X		X	X	X		2/15	5/1		FAF*/FFS/AFSA
750	55	475	100	X				X			X	5/15	none		FAF/FFS/AFSA*
426	90			X				X					1/31	X	FAF*/FFS
265	91	219	100	X	X	X	X	X	X	X	X	2/15	none		FAF*/FFS
1,254	63			X				X				2/15	none	X	FAF*/FFS/AFSA
								X				5/1	none	X	FAF*/FFS/AFSA
754	78							X				9/1	none	X	FAF*/FFS/AFSA/ AFSSA/SF
570	75							X				4/15	none		FAF/FFS*
964	88	602	100	X	X	X		X	X	X		2/15	none		FAF*/FFS
96	58			X	X					X		2/15	none	X	FAF/FFS*/AFSA
2,686	55	1,275	99	X				X	X	X	X	3/1	none		FAF*/FFS/AFSA/SF
								X	X	X	X		5/31	X	AFSA
391	64	248	94	X				X				3/1	8/31	X	FAF*/FFS/AFSA
139	85	90	100	X			X	X	X	X	X		5/31		FAF*/FFS
1,244	75							X				3/15	none		FAF*/FFS
													none		AFSA
1,719	37	813	98					X			X	2/15	none	X	FAF
2,465	60	1,275	100	X	X	X		X	X	X	X	4/1	none	X	FAF/FFS
2,810	65			X				X	X		X	4/1	none	X	FAF*/FFS
913	25	150	80					X	X	X	X	5/15	none	X	FAF*/FFS/AFSA
													none	X	FAF

*Preferred need analysis document.

Institution	Tuition and fees	Add'l out-of-state/district tuition	Books and supplies	Costs for campus residents			Costs for students at home		
				Room and board	Transportation	Other costs	Board only	Transportation	Other costs
Gogebic Community College	720	—/360	350		750	750	800	750	750
Grace Bible College	3,860		250	2,750	600	500	1,200	500	500
‡ Grand Rapids Baptist College and Seminary	5,386		400	3,460	474	850	1,200	800	850
Grand Rapids Junior College	1,220	1,050/630	420					720	460
‡ Grand Valley State University	2,132	2,778/—	400	3,300	350	500	1,100	900	500
Great Lakes Bible College	3,695		500	2,580	215	600		800	600
Great Lakes Junior College of Business	4,080		450					818	490
Henry Ford Community College	1,230	—/540	250				1,100	740	630
Highland Park Community College	1,270	450/—	250				1,650	675	1,300
Hillsdale College	9,610		500	4,000	500	600	2,220	700	700
‡ Hope College	9,426		350	3,610	250	750	1,500	100	750
‡ Jackson Community College	1,170	540/300	332				2,154	788	584
Jordan College	5,280		975				2,325	850	
Kalamazoo College	12,669		450	4,053	180	450	598	600	450
Kalamazoo Valley Community College	750	1,260/630	360				1,500	800	800
Kellogg Community College	930	1,500/600	420				2,200	840	1,376
Kendall College of Art and Design	8,250		2,000				2,700	765	800
‡ Kirtland Community College	1,320	1,200/495	360					820	680
Lake Michigan College	1,080	600/300	385				1,500	750	950
‡ Lake Superior State University	2,040	2,079/—	420	3,454	350	550		300	500
Lansing Community College	1,065	1,080/540	600				2,270	1,100	800
‡ Lawrence Technological University	4,500		1,000		600	665	1,800	1,200	665
Lewis College of Business	4,700		500						
‡ Macomb Community College	1,208	1,116/713	400				2,000	2,372	2,250
Madonna University	4,050		396	3,200	500	638	1,210	899	638
‡ Marygrove College	6,050		460	3,200	560	1,304		1,178	1,304
‡ Michigan Christian College	4,200		300	3,030	455	640	1,500	1,000	640
‡ Michigan State University	3,272	4,872/—	450	3,168			1,240		932
‡ Michigan Technological University	2,541	3,471/—	500	3,186	400	450	1,100	400	450
† Mid Michigan Community College	1,130	870/510	520				1,700	2,050	2,000
Monroe County Community College	830	—/370	700				2,200	1,100	650
‡ Montcalm Community College	984	810/480	350				1,700	1,200	750
‡ Muskegon Community College	1,000	810/420	350				1,500	1,000	750
‡ Nazareth College in Kalamazoo	7,724		300	3,174	400	550		600	610
‡ North Central Michigan College	1,110	600/300	400	2,976	405	630	1,940	730	630
Northern Michigan University	2,120	1,920/—	400	4,721	400	595	1,500	400	595
† Northwestern Michigan College	1,461	1,152/888	450	3,020	400	600		850	800
Northwood Institute	8,220		525	3,720	455	650	1,784	455	650
Oakland Community College	1,160	1,530/720	400				1,500	1,900	360
‡ Oakland University	2,166	3,720/—	350	3,257	435	600	1,500	785	600
Olivet College	7,890		500	2,860	460	490		460	490
Reformed Bible College	5,236		365	2,960	475	610		475	610
Sacred Heart Major Seminary	3,020		750	2,600	500	750			
‡ Saginaw Valley State University	2,131	2,511/—	450	3,212		500		450	500
‡ St. Clair County Community College	1,240	1,457/713	400				2,500	1,000	800
St. Mary's College	4,170		500	3,000					
‡ Schoolcraft College	1,165	1,080/305	300				1,500	800	800
‡ Siena Heights College	6,600		350	3,380	455	590		455	590
Southwestern Michigan College	1,080	600/300	500				1,500	1,200	800

†Figures are projected for 1991-92.   ‡Figures are for 1990-91.

Total freshmen	Percent receiving aid	Freshmen judged to have need	Percent offered aid	Acad	Music/drama	Art	Athl	Acad	Music/drama	Art	Athl	Priority	Closing	Inst aid form	Need analysis document
All aid		**Need-based aid**		**Grants and scholarships** Need-based				Nonneed-based				**Financial aid deadlines**			
326	75			X			X	X			X	3/15	none		FAF*/FFS/AFSA
32	74							X	X			7/15	none		FAF*/FFS/AFSA; FAF*/FFS/AFSA/CSS SAAC
198	73	147	100					X	X		X	3/1	9/1		FAF*/FFS
8,461	40	1,600	100	X				X	X	X	X	4/1	8/1		FAF*/FFS/AFSA
1,586	70	910	100	X				X	X	X	X	2/15	none		FAF*/FFS
44	80	38	92					X	X			8/1	none		FFS+FAF
847	69	834	99					X					none	X	FAF
5,114	33	1,903	100	X	X	X	X	X	X	X	X	4/1	none		FAF*/FFS/AFSA
1,475	95												none	X	FFS
302	70	191	100	X	X	X	X	X	X	X	X	3/15	none		FAF*/FFS
590	73	371	100	X				X	X	X		2/15	none		FAF*/FFS
		1,600	100	X				X	X			4/1	none		FAF*/FFS/AFSA
1,029	99	959	100					X			X		none		FAF*/FFS/AFSA
321	88	179	100	X	X	X		X	X	X		2/15	5/1	X	FAF*/FFS
1,699	20			X				X			X		none	X	FAF/FFS*/AFSA
985	60			X	X	X	X	X	X	X	X	6/1	none		FAF/FFS/AFSA*
111	70			X	X			X			X	2/15	none		FAF*/FFS/AFSA/SF
356	68	170	99	X				X				5/15	none	X	FAF*/FFS/AFSA
768	30			X	X		X	X	X	X	X	6/1	none		FAF/FFS/AFSA*
492	70			X				X			X	4/1	none		FAF*/FFS/AFSA
4,706	35	3,000	100	X	X	X	X	X	X	X	X	7/1	none	X	FAF/FFS/AFSA
339	60			X				X				6/1	9/1		FAF/FFS* FAF
4,793	15			X	X		X	X	X		X	5/1	none	X	FAF/FFS/AFSA*
232	24	40	100	X	X	X	X	X	X	X	X	2/15	none	X	FAF*/FFS
93	92			X	X	X		X	X	X		3/15	none	X	FAF*/FFS/AFSA
								X	X		X	8/1	none		FAF/FFS*;FAF/FFS/AFSA*
6,558	50	3,215	100	X	X		X	X	X	X	X		none		FAF/FFS*
1,156	68	414	86	X				X			X		3/1	X	FAF*/FFS
403	34	343	100	X				X				5/1	none		FAF/FFS*/AFSA
911	43			X		X		X	X	X		6/1	none		AFSA
400	60			X				X	X			6/30	none		FAF
1,804	60			X				X	X	X	X	6/1	none	X	FAF*/FFS/AFSA
96	98	74	100					X			X	4/30	none		FAF*/FFS
												4/15	none		AFSA
1,480	63	829	100	X	X	X	X	X				2/1	none		FAF*/FFS
1,315	30	1,083	75	X	X	X		X	X	X		5/1	none		AFSA
511	89	284	100	X			X	X			X		none		FAF*/FFS
												7/1	none		AFSA
1,217	35	260	97	X				X	X		X	3/1	none	X	FAF*/FFS
161	98			X	X			X	X			4/15	8/1		FAF*/FFS
32	88	27	100	X								5/15	none		FAF
6	100	2	100									4/1	none		FAF
662	70	462	100					X	X	X	X	4/1	none		FAF/FFS/AFSA/SF*
1,526	45	900	92	X	X	X		X	X	X	X	6/1	none		FAF*/FFS/AFSA
131	60			X		X		X			X		3/15		FAF
1,211	25			X	X	X	X	X	X	X	X	3/31	none	X	AFSA
220	87	181	100				X	X	X	X		4/1	none		FAF*/FFS/AFSA
1,725	45	800	100	X	X	X	X	X	X	X	X	6/1	none	X	FAF/FFS*/AFSA

*Preferred need analysis document.

Institution	Tuition and fees	Add'l out-of-state/district tuition	Books and supplies	Costs for campus residents			Costs for students at home		
				Room and board	Trans-portation	Other costs	Board only	Trans-portation	Other costs
Spring Arbor College	7,556		350	3,100	475	625	1,665	475	625
Suomi College	7,400		500	2,780	700	800	1,800	1,125	600
‡ University of Detroit Mercy	8,890		400	3,466	475	950	1,100		1,682
University of Michigan									
‡ Ann Arbor	3,502	8,508/—	424	3,856	195	1,184		195	1,184
‡ Dearborn	2,526	5,434/—	400	2,980		2,190		780	1,040
‡ Flint	2,240	5,204/—	440					1,000	796
‡ Walsh College of Accountancy and Business Administration	3,860							765	880
Washtenaw Community College	1,035	1,020/540	500				2,000	600	600
Wayne County Community College	1,014	900/450	400				2,200	800	1,000
‡ Wayne State University	2,403	2,835/—	430	4,860	1,080	700	1,700	1,080	700
West Shore Community College	1,044	1,050/600	600				1,350	850	950
‡ Western Michigan University	2,276	3,090/—	400	3,375	200	900	1,700	500	900
William Tyndale College	4,580		450	3,210	425	480		810	480
Minnesota									
‡ Alexandria Technical College	1,838	1,785/—	400				1,500	900	900
‡ Anoka-Ramsey Community College	1,474	743/—	450				1,500	800	500
Augsburg College	10,245		400	3,832	100	650	1,700	100	650
‡ Austin Community College	1,474	743/—	400				500	800	800
‡ Bemidji State University	1,884	1,170/—	500	2,384	525	1,000	1,100	800	1,000
† Bethany Lutheran College	6,400		350	2,800	150	750	1,600		750
Bethel College	9,950		370	3,590	800	1,500	1,000	680	1,500
‡ Brainerd Community College	1,474	743/—	500				1,700	720	800
Carleton College	16,296		475	3,324	500				
College of Associated Arts	6,650		1,600				2,043	275	1,143
College of St. Benedict	10,135		500	3,850	100	500	1,350	100	500
‡ College of St. Catherine: St. Catherine Campus	9,416		450	3,140	300	900		360	630
‡ College of St. Scholastica	9,192		405	3,018	387	609	1,638	387	609
Concordia College: Moorhead	8,690		400	2,710	200	600	2,710	200	600
Concordia College: St. Paul	8,268		390	2,910	100	750	1,700	100	750
† Dakota County Technical College	1,727	1,701/—	600				1,800	1,500	1,700
Dr. Martin Luther College	3,419		560	1,770	600	600	1,770	330	600
‡ Fergus Falls Community College	1,474	743/—	450			450		500	450
‡ Gustavus Adolphus College	11,000		350	2,750		550			
Hamline University	11,550		350	3,631		675			675
‡ Hibbing Community College	1,474	743/—	385					700	700
‡ Inver Hills Community College	1,474	743/—	450		700	3,500	2,100	700	750
† Itasca Community College: Arrowhead Region	1,474	743/—	375				1,500	460	895
‡ Lakewood Community College	1,474	743/—	500					360	750
‡ Macalester College	12,471		350	3,714		650	1,784		650
‡ Mankato State University	1,868	1,170/—	425	2,388	245	1,250	720	710	1,125
‡ Mesabi Community College: Arrowhead Region	1,474	743/—	460					300	900
‡ Metropolitan State University	1,654	1,170/—	450					960	1,800

†Figures are projected for 1991-92.   ‡Figures are for 1990-91.

All aid		Need–based aid		Grants and scholarships								Financial aid deadlines		Inst aid form	Need analysis document
Total freshmen	Percent receiving aid	Freshmen judged to have need	Percent offered aid	Need–based				Nonneed–based							
				Acad	Music/drama	Art	Athl	Acad	Music/drama	Art	Athl	Priority	Closing		
168	90							X	X	X	X	2/15	none		FAF*/FFS
286	94			X	X	X		X	X	X		5/1	8/15		FAF
401	70			X				X			X	6/1	none	X	FAF*/FFS
4,631	32	1,850	100	X				X	X	X	X	2/1	9/30		FAF*/FFS
680	46	348	78	X				X			X	4/1	none	X	FAF/FFS*
578	37	213	100	X	X			X	X				4/15	X	FAF/FFS*
								X				8/1	none	X	FAF*/FFS/AFSA
													none	X	FAF
1,699	42											8/1	none	X	FAF/FFS/AFSA*
1,797	75	760	100	X	X	X	X	X	X	X	X		5/1		FAF*/FFS
775	50	355	100	X				X	X			5/1	none	X	FAF/FFS*/AFSA
2,858	82	1,210	100					X	X	X	X	3/1	none		FAF/FFS*
130	60	72	100	X	X			X	X			2/15	5/1		FAF*/FFS
1,102	95	933	100					X				5/1	none		FAF/FFS*
2,107	40			X				X				5/15	none		FAF/FFS*
292	90							X				6/1	8/1	X	FAF/FFS*
287	79							X	X		X	3/15	none		FFS
630	80							X	X	X	X	5/15	none	X	FFS
158	88	100	100					X	X	X	X	5/1	none		FFS;FAF/FFS*
398	87	280	99	X	X	X		X	X	X		4/15	none	X	FFS;FAF/FFS*
1,400	79	650	92	X	X	X	X	X	X	X	X	7/1	none		FFS
465	76	231	100	X				X					3/1		FFS;FAF
48	80	16	100					X		X		4/1	none		FAF/FFS*/AFSA/AFSSA;FAF/FFS*/AFSA
430	85	352	100	X				X	X	X		6/1	none		FFS;FAF/FFS*/AFSA
248	85	177	100	X	X			X	X			4/1	none	X	FFS;FAF/FFS*
324	95	315	100	X	X			X	X			3/1	none		FAF/FFS*
		636	100	X	X			X	X			4/1	7/1	X	FFS;FAF/FFS*/AFSA/AFSSA/SF
180	90	142	100	X	X	X	X	X	X	X	X	5/1	none		FAF/FFS*/AFSA/AFSSA;FAF/FFS*/AFSA/CSS SAAC/ACT
1,209	80	960	100										none		FAF/FFS*/AFSA
119	96	91	100	X	X			X	X			5/15	none	X	FFS;FAF/FFS*/AFSA/CSS SAAC/ACT SAAC/AFSSA/APSGFSA/SF
661	89	432	100	X	X	X	X	X	X	X	X	6/1	none		FFS;FAF/FFS*
556	76	376	100	X				X				3/1	5/1	X	FFS;FAF/FFS
312	80			X	X	X	X					5/1	none		FFS;FAF/FFS*
954	64			X	X		X	X				9/1	none	X	FFS
								X	X	X	X	6/1	none		FFS
771	65	320	100	X				X				5/1			FAF/FFS*
2,132	40	560	100					X					none	X	FFS
434	65	237	100	X				X				3/1		X	FFS;FAF*/FFS
2,106	65	1,105	98	X				X	X	X	X	7/1	none		FFS
								X				4/22	none		FFS
				X									none		FFS

*Preferred need analysis document.

Institution	Tuition and fees	Add'l out-of-state/district tuition	Books and supplies	Costs for campus residents			Costs for students at home		
				Room and board	Transportation	Other costs	Board only	Transportation	Other costs
‡ Minneapolis College of Art and Design	9,640		1,000	2,800	300	500	1,600	300	500
‡ Minneapolis Community College	1,476	720/—	450				1,100	390	850
Minnesota Bible College	2,925		300		250	1,000		500	1,000
† Moorhead State University	1,975	1,170/—	450	2,350	150	1,200	850	500	800
National College	4,179		350						
National Education Center: Brown Institute Campus	5,750						1,200	850	875
‡ Normandale Community College	1,474	743/—	450	2,912	400	900	1,100	400	900
‡ North Central Bible College	4,690		450				1,900	1,500	200
‡ North Hennepin Community College	1,474	743/—	500				1,500	500	1,200
† Northland Community College	1,474	743/—	450						
Northwest Technical Institute	6,505		275						
‡ Northwestern College	8,310		390	2,595	450	975	750	1,000	575
† Northwestern Electronics Institute	3,604		525				2,616	1,346	1,464
Oak Hills Bible College	3,945		450	2,340					
Pillsbury Baptist Bible College	3,650		840	2,572	735	1,575	2,575	735	1,050
† Rainy River Community College	1,474	743/—	480	2,500	650	1,200	1,500	400	900
‡ Rochester Community College	1,474	743/—	450		650	950	2,000	750	950
‡ St. Cloud State University	1,868	1,170/—	525	2,379	700	798	800	825	700
St. John's University	10,085		500	3,675	100	500	1,925	100	500
St. Mary's Campus of the College of St. Catherine	7,530		500		500	900	900	600	600
St. Mary's College at Minnesota	9,225		300	3,150	405	675	1,500		
St. Olaf College	12,080		525	3,345		500	1,835	275	500
‡ St. Paul Bible College	6,390		450	3,160	500	700	1,700	500	1,000
‡ St. Paul Technical College	1,530	1,485/—	600					600	
‡ Southwest State University	1,874	1,170/—	500	2,400	200	1,000	1,500	400	600
University of Minnesota									
‡ Crookston	2,435	3,354/—	425	3,089		900	1,500		900
‡ Duluth	2,501	3,354/—	420	3,000	540	1,610		540	1,380
‡ Morris	2,412	3,355/—	500	2,835	500	1,200	1,200	350	1,200
‡ Twin Cities	2,587	3,354/—	512	3,132			1,650	550	1,460
‡ Waseca	2,416	3,354/—	450	2,430		900			
‡ University of St. Thomas	9,772		400	3,500	200	600	1,500	500	600
‡ Vermilion Community College	1,474	743/—	400	2,590	200			200	
‡ Willmar Community College	1,572	786/—	475				1,600	375	275
‡ Willmar Technical College	1,474	743/—	300				1,170	1,200	800
‡ Winona State University	1,884	1,170/—	300	2,450	300	600		300	600
‡ Worthington Community College	1,474	743/—	400				1,260	1,200	850

Mississippi

Institution	Tuition and fees	Add'l out-of-state/district tuition	Books and supplies	Room and board	Transportation	Other costs	Board only	Transportation	Other costs
‡ Alcorn State University	1,750	1,182/—	400	1,925	500	900		900	900
‡ Belhaven College	6,030		300	2,100					
‡ Blue Mountain College	3,248		500	2,030	300	1,500	1,300		
Clarke College	3,520		500	2,390	600	1,200	1,100	900	1,200
‡ Coahoma Community College	700	1,400/400	500	1,897	300	500	1,500	300	500
Copiah-Lincoln Community College	850	980/—	300	1,800					
‡ Delta State University	1,706	1,182/—	500	1,690		3,090			3,000
East Central Community College	800	1,200/—	350	1,750				500	
‡ East Mississippi Junior College	760	1,000/—	300	1,740					

†Figures are projected for 1991-92.   ‡Figures are for 1990-91.

Total fresh-men	Percent receiving aid	Freshmen judged to have need	Percent offered aid	Acad	Music/ drama	Art	Athl	Acad	Music/ drama	Art	Athl	Priority	Closing	Inst aid form	Need analysis document
				Need-based				Nonneed-based							
87	72	81	95			X		X		X		3/1	none		FFS
2,702	50	600	83	X				X				6/1	none		FAF/FFS*
24	84	7	100					X	X			6/1	none		FFS
1,904	67	971	100	X				X	X	X	X	4/15	none	X	FFS
												8/1	none	X	FFS*/AFSA
498	80												none	X	FAF
2,463	33			X	X							5/1	none		FAF/FFS*
								X	X	X		4/30	none		FAF/FFS*
3,500	26	625	100	X	X	X			X	X		8/15	none		FAF/FFS*/AFSA
259	75	190	100	X	X	X	X	X	X	X	X	5/1	none		FFS*/AFSA
280	87	274	100	X	X	X	X	X	X	X	X		none		FFS
												3/1	none		FFS;FAF/FFS*/AFSA/SF
124	62							X					none	X	FFS*/AFSA
46	80											7/1	none		FFS
95	77	79	100					X	X	X			none		FFS
408	82			X	X	X	X	X	X	X	X	8/1	none		FFS*/AFSA
1,422	50	950	95	X				X					none		FAF/FFS*
2,365	42	982	100	X	X	X	X	X	X	X	X		none		FFS
475	70	313	100	X	X	X		X	X	X		3/1	none		FFS;FAF/FFS*
380	77	369	100	X								6/1	none	X	FFS;FAF/FFS*/AFSA
304	70	224	100	X	X	X		X	X	X		3/15	none	X	FFS;FAF/FFS*
756	57	447	100	X								2/15	none	X	FFS;FAF/FFS
89	96	87	100					X	X			4/1	none	X	FFS;FAF/FFS*
													none	X	FFS
556	82			X	X	X	X	X	X		X	4/14	none	X	FFS
412	80			X				X				4/30	none		FFS;FAF/FFS*
2,462	94	1,575	98	X	X	X	X	X				3/31	none		FFS
499	89	279	100	X	X			X	X			5/1	none		FFS
3,700	41	1,185	97	X	X	X	X	X	X	X	X	4/1	none		FFS
381	80	270	100	X				X				4/15	none		FFS
831	75	600	100	X				X				4/1	none		FAF/FFS*
300	93			X				X					none		FAF/FFS*
													none		FAF/FFS*
				X								5/1	none		FFS;FAF/FFS
1,380	70	840	100	X	X	X	X	X	X	X	X	4/1	none		FFS
341	40	200	100	X	X			X	X			5/1	none		FAF/FFS*
701	92			X	X		X	X	X		X	4/14	none	X	FAF
118	60			X	X	X	X	X	X	X	X	4/15	6/15		FAF*/FFS
60	90			X	X		X	X	X		X	5/1	7/1		FAF
													none	X	FAF
															FAF*/FFS/AFSA/SF
1,516	42	578	100					X	X	X	X	4/1	none	X	FAF*/FFS/AFSA/AFSSA/SF
586	68	511	100				X	X	X	X	X	6/1	none		FFS
452	50	232	100					X	X		X	6/1	none		FAF/FFS*/AFSA
749	76			X				X	X		X	6/30			FAF/FFS*

*Preferred need analysis document.

Institution	Tuition and fees	Add'l out-of-state/district tuition	Books and supplies	Costs for campus residents			Costs for students at home		
				Room and board	Transportation	Other costs	Board only	Transportation	Other costs
‡ Hinds Community College	740	1,470/—	400	1,554	426	1,296	1,720	1,682	1,181
Holmes Community College	804	1,000/—	400	1,400					
Itawamba Community College	800	880/—	300	1,710					
‡ Jackson State University	1,786	1,182/—	500	2,488	600	1,018	1,774	500	500
† Jones County Junior College	606	1,000/—	300	1,668	180	275		180	400
Magnolia Bible College	2,260								
† Mary Holmes College	4,100		700	3,800	500	700	1,000	1,500	500
† Meridian Community College	720	840/—	400	1,050				360	
‡ Millsaps College	9,170		650	3,280	500	1,500	2,200	650	1,500
Mississippi College	5,010		600	2,550	700	1,500	1,500	1,500	1,500
† Mississippi Delta Community College	670	1,000/90	400	1,380		400	1,410	250	240
Mississippi Gulf Coast Community College									
Jackson County Campus	760	900/—						500	
Jefferson Davis Campus	760	900/—	150				2,500	1,100	260
Perkinston	760	900/—		1,318					
‡ Mississippi State University	2,061	3,116/—	400	2,784			1,450		
‡ Mississippi University for Women	1,840	1,182/—	500	2,092	400	800	1,350	400	800
‡ Mississippi Valley State University	1,725	1,182/—	450	1,925	400	740	1,500	400	740
Northeast Mississippi Community College	770	880/20	400	1,690	600	600	1,100	600	600
‡ Northwest Mississippi Community College	834	1,000/90	200	1,690		375			375
Pearl River Community College	710	906/—	200	1,540	300	1,085		550	1,085
Phillips Junior College									
‡ Jackson	3,725		200				660	1,040	1,612
Mississippi Gulf Coast	4,450		250						
Rust College	4,152		225	1,948	225	150	1,050	300	
Southeastern Baptist College	2,220		250	1,700	175	325	200	200	300
Southwest Mississippi Community College	750	1,050/—	1,700	1,550			1,100		
‡ Tougaloo College	4,310		500	1,550	300	500	1,300	300	500
University of Mississippi									
‡ Medical Center	1,700	1,182/—	600		450	3,770		900	900
‡ University	2,059	1,182/—	325	2,865	350	750		420	763
‡ University of Southern Mississippi	1,948	1,182/—		2,150					
Wesley College	1,800		350	2,200	300	650		500	1,150
‡ William Carey College	4,000		500	2,120	500	500	1,250	1,000	500
† Wood Junior College	2,400		400	2,500	100	1,000		1,100	1,000
Missouri									
Avila College	7,380		500	3,200	400	1,500		1,200	900
‡ Baptist Bible College	1,570		300	548	400	1,300	1,000	480	1,300
Basic Institute of Technology	5,175		360						
Berean College	1,770								
‡ Calvary Bible College	3,100		350	2,480		350	1,500	374	800
Central Bible College	3,240		500	2,750	400	400	560	500	500
‡ Central Christian College of the Bible	2,349		300	2,120	300	1,512	1,272	150	2,500
Central Methodist College	6,710		400	3,270	400	1,800	1,770	400	1,800

†Figures are projected for 1991-92.   ‡Figures are for 1990-91.

All aid		Need–based aid		Grants and scholarships								Financial aid deadlines		Inst aid form	Need analysis document
				Need–based				Nonneed–based							
Total fresh–men	Percent receiving aid	Freshmen judged to have need	Percent offered aid	Acad	Music/ drama	Art	Athl	Acad	Music/ drama	Art	Athl	Priority	Closing		
2,787	40							X	X		X	4/1	none	X	FAF*/FFS/AFSA/ AFSSA/SF;FAF*/FFS
													none		FFS
													none		FAF/FFS/AFSA*/SF
1,494	76			X	X	X	X	X	X	X	X	4/1			FAF*/FFS/AFSA
				X	X		X	X	X	X	X	5/1	none		FAF/FFS*
6	100	6	100	X				X				8/1	none		FFS
342	98			X	X		X					7/1	none	X	FAF/FFS/AFSA*
1,953	45							X	X	X	X	3/1	none		FAF/FFS/AFSA*
260	68	177	100	X	X	X	X	X	X	X		3/1	none	X	FAF*/FFS/AFSA/ AFSSA/SF;FAF*/FFS/ AFSA/CSS SAAC/ACT
237	75	182	100	X	X	X	X	X	X	X	X	4/1	none	X	FAF
1,574	90							X	X	X	X		none	X	FFS;FAF/FFS*
2,019	50							X				6/1	none		FFS/AFSA*
2,195	70	1,708	100	X				X	X		X	6/1	none	X	FAF/FFS/AFSA*
603	60							X	X	X	X	6/1	none	X	AFSA
		1,367	100					X	X		X	4/1	none	X	FFS
406	76							X	X	X	X	6/1	none		FAF/FFS*/AFSA/ AFSSA/SF
													none	X	FAF/FFS/AFSA*/SF
1,700	75							X	X	X	X	4/1		X	FAF/FFS/AFSA
2,594	80	1,200	100	X	X		X					3/15		X	FAF
1,812	70	825	100	X				X	X		X	5/1	none		FAF/FFS/AFSA*/ AFSSA
4,300	85												none		AFSA
323	87												none	X	AFSA
380	98	380	79	X	X		X	X	X		X	5/1	7/15	X	FFS
22	90				X							7/1	none		AFSA
488	45											8/5	none		FFS
324	92	202	100	X	X		X	X	X		X	4/15	none	X	FAF*/FFS
				X				X				4/1	none	X	FFS*/AFSA/AFSSA
2,259	56			X				X	X	X	X	4/1	none		FAF*/FFS/AFSA/ AFSSA/SF
1,773	60			X				X	X	X	X	3/15	none	X	FAF/FFS*
35	53							X				7/1	none		FAF*/FFS
106	95			X				X	X		X	5/15		X	FAF*/FFS
202	85			X	X	X						6/1	none		FFS
105	90							X	X	X	X	7/1	none	X	FAF/FFS*/AFSA/ AFSSA/SF
															AFSA
															FAF
													none		
70	77	44	100	X				X				7/15	8/15		FAF/FFS/AFSA*
208	69	218	95	X			X	X	X				none		FAF*/FFS
44	78	14	100	X	X			X	X			4/1		X	FAF/FFS/AFSA
239	82	156	100	X	X			X	X		X	4/1	none		FAF/FFS*/AFSSA

*Preferred need analysis document.

Institution	Tuition and fees	Add'l out-of-state/district tuition	Books and supplies	Costs for campus residents			Costs for students at home		
				Room and board	Transportation	Other costs	Board only	Transportation	Other costs
‡ Central Missouri State University	1,680	1,380/—	250	2,616	300	600	500	1,000	150
College of the Ozarks	100		400	1,600	800	1,200	2,000	800	1,200
Columbia College	6,824		600	3,082	500	800		500	800
‡ Conception Seminary College	4,344		350	2,736	550	800	1,710	550	800
Cottey College	4,500		390	2,600	900	500	1,500	250	
‡ Crowder College	780	1,050/240	200	2,120	250	500		1,700	500
Culver-Stockton College	6,650		400	2,600	500	1,200	1,500	500	1,200
‡ Deaconess College of Nursing	5,110		400	2,400	250	200	1,600	360	200
DeVry Institute of Technology: Kansas City	5,015		500				1,839	2,538	1,302
Drury College	7,510		700	3,184	1,000	750	2,000	1,000	750
East Central College	765	690/300	400				1,538	1,120	492
Evangel College	6,178		600	2,880	833	2,184	1,680	896	532
Fontbonne College	7,470		550	3,500	500	1,250	1,350	1,300	1,250
Hannibal-LaGrange College	4,650		300	2,000	300	1,000		300	1,000
Harris Stowe State College	1,490	1,410/—	650				2,100	1,500	1,200
‡ ITT Technical Institute: St. Louis	5,145		800					1,000	
† Jefferson College	720	720/360	300				1,600	700	1,070
Kansas City Art Institute	10,315		800	4,590	600	400	2,700	600	400
Kemper Military School and College	7,600		1,800	2,200	900	1,080			
Lincoln University	1,340	1,320/—	480	2,728	926	1,496	2,057	843	1,531
Lindenwood College	8,180		1,000	4,400	1,050	2,625		1,840	2,635
† Longview Community College	1,050	1,470/630	500				1,989	1,989	1,597
Maple Woods Community College	1,050	1,470/630	500				1,989	1,989	1,597
† Maryville College—St. Louiss	7,750		400	3,800	250	600	2,500	1,450	600
Mineral Area College	750	600/360	440					1,300	1,300
Missouri Baptist College	5,670		600	2,500	275	1,500	1,800	1,500	1,500
Missouri Southern State College	1,532	1,182/—	400	2,340	460	900	1,500	600	600
Missouri Valley College	7,479		990	4,356	1,200	2,700	1,500	1,200	3,000
‡ Missouri Western State College	1,446	1,260/—	500	2,052	600	1,500	1,600	500	1,500
‡ Moberly Area Community College	570	1,710/570	400					500	1,025
National College	5,835		600					500	
North Central Missouri College	825	1,035/383	400			700	1,100	1,000	700
Northeast Missouri State University	1,800	1,704/—	400	2,584	640	1,690		640	2,475
Northwest Missouri State University	1,590	1,290/—	250	2,645	630	1,000	1,560	630	1,000
‡ Ozark Christian College	2,981		450	2,600					
Park College	6,820		450	3,300	425	950	900	800	800
Penn Valley Community College	1,050	1,470/630	500				1,989	1,989	1,597
Phillips Junior College	4,498		250				1,600	400	500
Platt Junior College	4,750		250						
Ranken Technical College	7,675		1,500						
‡ Research College of Nursing	7,700		400	3,500	150	1,100	1,900	1,500	1,190
Rockhurst College	8,400		510	3,600	600	1,373	1,630	1,635	1,373
St. Charles Community College	832	1,200/420	500				1,900	800	1,000
‡ St. Louis Christian College	3,030		300	2,000	400	600	1,500	405	1,200

†Figures are projected for 1991-92.   ‡Figures are for 1990-91.

Total freshmen	Percent receiving aid	Freshmen judged to have need	Percent offered aid	Need-based Acad	Need-based Music/drama	Need-based Art	Need-based Athl	Nonneed Acad	Nonneed Music/drama	Nonneed Art	Nonneed Athl	Priority	Closing	Inst aid form	Need analysis document
2,087	60			X	X	X	X	X	X	X	X	3/1	none		FAF/FFS/AFSA*/AFSSA;FAF/FFS/AFSA*/CSS SAAC/
451	100			X			X	X			X		none		AFSA/AFSSA*
		144	100	X				X	X	X	X	3/15	8/22		FAF/FFS*/AFSA
25	100	24	100									7/31	none		FFS
210	98	107	100					X	X	X	X	3/1	none	X	FAF/FFS*/AFSA
538	60												none		FAF/FFS*
296	85	170	100	X				X	X	X	X	3/15	none	X	FAF/FFS*
93	85			X				X				4/15	7/1	X	FAF/FFS*
439	85							X					none		FAF
286	76	221	100	X	X	X	X	X	X	X	X	4/1	6/15	X	FAF/FFS*/AFSA/AFSSA
1,307	50	421	100					X	X	X		7/1	none		FFS
405	90	331	100	X				X					none		FAF*/FFS/AFSA
102	82	99	100	X	X	X		X	X	X		4/1	none	X	FAF*/FFS
139	89											6/1	none	X	FFS
150	75												none		FAF
								X					none		AFSA
1,838	37							X	X	X	X		none	X	AFSA
198	68										X	2/15	none	X	FAF
													none		FAF*/FFS
								X	X	X	X	3/1	none	X	FAF*/FFS/AFSA
709	89				X	X		X	X	X	X	4/30	none		FAF/FFS*/AFSA
2,200	16							X	X	X	X	5/30	none	X	FAF/FFS*/AFSA
1,023	16							X	X	X	X	6/30	none	X	FAF/FFS*/AFSA*
108	80	110	100	X				X				3/1	none	X	FAF*/FFS
775	46	718	100	X	X	X	X	X	X	X	X	4/30	none		FAF*/FFS
													none	X	FAF/FFS/AFSA/AFSSA*/SF
982	75	715	100					X	X	X	X	2/15	none	X	FAF/FFS/AFSA/AFSSA*
													none		FAF*/FFS/AFSA
				X	X	X	X	X	X		X	4/1	none		FAF/FFS*
334	30	251	100	X				X	X		X		6/30		FAF/FFS*
25	100	22	100	X				X					none		AFSA
388	75					X		X			X	8/1	none		FAF/FFS*
1,310	88			X	X	X	X	X	X	X	X	4/1	none		FAF/FFS*/AFSA/AFSSA/SF;FAF/FFS*/AFSA/CSS SAAC/ACT
1,393	78	865	100	X				X				4/1	none	X	FAF/FFS*/AFSA/AFSSA/SF
147	64											7/1	none		FAF/FFS*/AFSA/SF
98	97	56	100					X	X	X	X	4/1	9/1		FFS
1,039	29							X			X	5/30	none	X	FAF/FFS/AFSA*
													none		AFSA
													none	X	AFSA
															AFSA
31	92	23	100	X	X		X	X	X		X	4/1	none		FAF*/FFS/AFSA/SF
275	98	200	100	X	X		X	X	X		X	4/1	none		FAF*/FFS/AFSA/SF
															FAF/FFS/AFSA/AFSSA/SF
28	69	26	100	X	X			X	X			7/1	none	X	FAF*/FFS/AFSA

*Preferred need analysis document.

Institution	Tuition and fees	Add'l out-of-state/ district tuition	Books and supplies	Costs for campus residents			Costs for students at home		
				Room and board	Trans-portation	Other costs	Board only	Trans-portation	Other costs
‡ St. Louis College of Pharmacy	5,375		300	3,500	350	1,350		1,000	2,000
St. Louis Community College									
Florissant Valley	930	630/300					1,200	700	1,500
Forest Park	1,020	630/300	500				1,200	770	1,400
Meramec	1,020	630/300	500				1,300	750	1,600
St. Louis University	9,160		500	4,242	4,150	3,330	3,780	4,150	3,330
Southeast Missouri State University	1,786	1,440/—	210	2,825	460	1,350		1,800	1,150
Southwest Baptist University	6,192		450	2,340		600			
‡ Southwest Missouri State University	1,790	1,740/—	500	2,830	1,000	1,550	1,560	1,000	1,700
State Fair Community College	720	1,530/420	300				1,550	950	500
Stephens College	11,475		420	4,500	430	930	2,100	630	730
Three Rivers Community College	750	960/300	240				1,300	1,200	600
University of Missouri									
‡ Columbia	1,928	3,591/—	400	2,831		1,200			1,600
† Kansas City	2,277	3,995/—	514	3,065	640	5,440	1,500	1,820	1,490
† Rolla	2,340	3,798/—	400	3,100	500	578	1,500	900	600
‡ St. Louis	2,154	3,798/—	500					1,400	1,525
Washington University	16,110		702	5,187	650	1,475	1,210	1,157	3,223
Webster University	7,300		500	3,650	500	1,500	2,500	500	1,500
Westminster College	8,400		500	3,350	450	850		450	800
‡ William Jewell College	7,450		450	2,560	650	1,450	1,450	650	1,450
William Woods College	8,140		470	3,560	700	1,800	1,850	530	950
Montana									
Blackfeet Community College	1,281		200				900	450	450
‡ Carroll College	6,570		350	3,230	300	600	1,872	300	600
‡ College of Great Falls	4,015		300		300	600	730	200	600
Dawson Community College	774	864/288	450		805	1,000	1,500	250	600
Dull Knife Memorial College	765								
‡ Eastern Montana College	1,389	1,683/—	525	3,300	280	700	1,500	280	700
Flathead Valley Community College	936	666/162	500				1,170	900	600
‡ Fort Belknap College	1,431		450		3,000			750	1,200
Fort Peck Community College	990		400						
Little Big Horn College	975		400					1,050	450
Miles Community College	864	696/276	500	2,200	550	630	900	550	630
‡ Montana College of Mineral Science and Technology	1,306	2,073/—	400	3,094	650	550		400	550
‡ Montana State University	1,390	1,989/—	470	3,276	520	1,400	990	520	1,400
‡ Northern Montana College	1,272	1,683/—	450	2,919	522	450	630	522	450
Rocky Mountain College	7,212		500	3,250		500	983	250	500
Salish Kootenai College	1,302	—/576	600				500	600	1,200
† Stone Child College	1,400								
‡ University of Montana	1,474	2,073/—	300	3,212		855			1,372
‡ Western Montana College of the University of Montana	1,274	1,683/—	350	2,770	125	1,000		500	900

†Figures are projected for 1991-92.   ‡Figures are for 1990-91.

All aid		Need–based aid		Grants and scholarships								Financial aid deadlines		Inst aid form	Need analysis document
				Need–based				Nonneed–based							
Total freshmen	Percent receiving aid	Freshmen judged to have need	Percent offered aid	Acad	Music/drama	Art	Athl	Acad	Music/drama	Art	Athl	Priority	Closing		
126	69			X				X				5/31	none	X	FAF
7,255	18							X	X	X	X		8/1		FFS
4,892	39	1,782	22					X	X	X	X	3/19	none		FAF/FFS*/AFSA/SF
2,520	25	700	100	X	X	X	X	X	X	X	X		none		SF
869	85			X	X	X	X	X	X	X	X	4/1	none	X	FAF/FFS/AFSA/SF*
1,673	45			X	X	X	X	X	X	X	X	3/31	none		FAF/FFS*/AFSA/SF
870	90							X				4/30	none	X	FAF/FFS*
3,571	46	1,575	93	X	X	X	X	X	X	X	X	3/31	none		FAF/FFS*
527	63			X				X	X	X		7/1	none		FAF/FFS*/AFSA
243	43	100	100	X	X	X		X	X			3/15	8/15		FAF*/FFS/AFSA
													none		FAF/FFS/AFSA*
3,851	63	1,466	99					X	X	X		3/1	none		FAF/FFS*/SF
649	38	347	100	X	X	X		X	X	X	X	3/31	none	X	FFS
761	51	560	93					X	X		X	3/31	none		FFS*/AFSA
941	54	215	86	X				X				4/1	none		FAF/FFS*
1,227	62	604	100	X		X		X		X			2/15		FAF
226	70	172	91	X	X	X		X	X	X		4/1	none		FAF*/FFS/AFSA/SF
246	75	108	100					X	X	X	X	3/31	none		FAF*/FFS/AFSA
357	88	208	100					X	X	X	X	3/15	none		FAF/FFS/AFSA/AFSSA*
274	81	88	100	X				X	X	X	X	4/30	7/1	X	FAF*/FFS/AFSA/AFSSA/SF
													none		FAF/AFSA*
227	80			X				X	X		X	3/1	none		FAF*/FFS
227	86			X				X				4/1	none	X	FAF/FFS/AFSA/AFSSA/SF*;FAF/FFS/AFSA/AFSSA
283	70	190	100					X	X	X	X		none		FAF*/FFS/AFSA/SF
582	67	292	100					X	X	X	X	3/1	none	X	FAF/FFS/AFSA/SF; FAF/FFS/AFSA
				X			X	X			X	5/1	none	X	FAF*/FFS/AFSA
														X	FAF*/AFSA AFSA;SF+AFSA
													none		AFSA
145	77	103	100	X	X		X	X	X		X	3/1	none		FAF*/FFS/AFSA/SF
336	68	166	100					X			X	4/1	none		FAF*/FFS
													none	X	FAF/FFS/AFSA*
													none		FAF/FFS/AFSA/SF
228	80	167	100					X	X	X	X	4/1	none		FAF*/FFS/AFSA/AFSSA/SF;FAF*/FFS/AFSA/CSS SAAC/
													none		FAF*/AFSA FAF/FFS
1,203	60	555	97	X	X	X	X	X	X	X	X	3/1	none		FAF*/FFS
													none		FAF*/FFS

*Preferred need analysis document.

Institution	Tuition and fees	Add'l out-of-state/district tuition	Books and supplies	Costs for campus residents			Costs for students at home		
				Room and board	Trans-portation	Other costs	Board only	Trans-portation	Other costs
Nebraska									
Bellevue College	2,805		400		1,000	1,400	2,170	1,000	1,800
‡ Bishop Clarkson College	3,080		382		989	1,206	1,568	1,685	1,014
Central Community College	960	420/—	400	1,500	483	1,444		685	420
‡ Chadron State College	1,376	765/—	500	2,196	400	500	1,032		900
‡ College of St. Mary	7,250		400	2,960	1,030	1,039	1,100	2,059	1,123
Concordia College	7,110		450	2,790	900	1,200	1,800	300	1,200
Creighton University	8,996		575	3,798	300	1,370	1,500	890	1,370
Dana College	7,370		450	2,770	300	1,000	1,610	300	1,000
‡ Doane College	7,830		300	2,465	400	1,005	1,590	300	550
Grace College of the Bible	3,740		200	2,400	275	600		275	660
Hastings College	8,090		500	2,910	350	450		350	450
Lincoln School of Commerce	5,250		425		428	770	1,490	428	770
*‡ McCook Community College	750	150/—	300	1,800	375	600	550	900	600
Metropolitan Community College	878	878/—	450				1,500	600	600
† Mid Plains Community College	760	150/—	400		450	400	1,890	600	
Midland Lutheran College	8,100		350	2,550	400	900	1,000	400	900
Nebraska Christian College	2,440		300	2,460	360	1,505	1,100	360	1,505
† Nebraska Indian Community College	1,680	1,450/—	400	2,700				375	350
† Nebraska Methodist College of Nursing and Allied Health	3,160		500		504	900	1,000	1,008	900
Nebraska Wesleyan University	8,228		450	2,950		1,600		300	1,600
‡ Northeast Community College	846	135/—	300		375	900	1,260	375	900
‡ Peru State College	1,380	765/—	300	2,430	150	650		900	650
Southeast Community College									
Beatrice Campus	1,034	315/—	450		450	500		750	500
Lincoln Campus	1,004	315/—	450				1,500	450	900
Milford Campus	1,004	315/—	472	1,710	210	630	735	945	630
† Union College	7,650		500	2,355					
University of Nebraska									
‡ Medical Center	1,731	2,760/—	450					475	1,500
‡ Lincoln	1,915	2,760/—	400	2,625		1,780	1,600		1,550
‡ Omaha	1,530	2,423/—	600				1,000	600	650
‡ University of Nebraska at Kearney	1,420	765/—	450	2,108	500	1,200	1,700	500	1,200
‡ Wayne State College	1,421	765/—	600	2,290	250	2,500	480	2,000	1,000
Western Nebraska Community College									
Scottsbluff Campus	1,035	60/—	440	2,150	400	700	1,700	500	1,000
Sidney Campus	1,035	60/—	400	2,150	400	700	1,700	700	1,000
York College	3,380		365	2,600	750	925	715	75	50
Nevada									
Clark County Community College	810	3,000/—	700				1,100	906	1,215
‡ Northern Nevada Community College	740	3,000/—	440				1,500	960	1,195
Sierra Nevada College	6,750		450				1,400	500	600
† Truckee Meadows Community College	780	3,000/—	440				1,575	525	470

†Figures are projected for 1991-92.   ‡Figures are for 1990-91.

All aid		Need-based aid		Grants and scholarships								Financial aid deadlines		Inst aid form	Need analysis document
				Need-based				Nonneed-based							
Total freshmen	Percent receiving aid	Freshmen judged to have need	Percent offered aid	Acad	Music/drama	Art	Athl	Acad	Music/drama	Art	Athl	Priority	Closing		
147	38	78	100	X			X	X			X	3/15	6/15		FAF*/FFS/AFSA
133	75	79	100					X				5/30	none		FAF*/FFS
		750	100	X	X	X	X	X	X	X	X	7/1	none		FAF
366	90	290	100					X	X	X	X	7/1	none		FAF/FFS/AFSA*
185	97	135	100	X	X	X	X	X	X	X	X	4/15	none	X	FAF*/FFS
198	99							X	X	X	X	5/1	none	X	FAF*/FFS/AFSA
836	60	495	99	X				X			X	4/1	none		FAF*/FFS/AFSA/SF; FAF*/FFS/AFSA/CSS SAAC/ACT SAAC/SF
141	97	114	100		X	X		X			X	4/1	none	X	FAF*/FFS/AFSA/SF
233	94	170	100	X				X	X	X	X	3/15	none		FAF*/FFS/AFSA
45	70	45	100	X	X			X					none	X	FAF*/FFS/AFSA*
296	91	256	100					X	X	X	X	5/1	none		FAF*/FFS
212	95			X				X					none		FAF*/FFS/AFSA*
237	64	179	100	X	X	X	X	X	X	X	X	4/1	5/1	X	FAF*/FFS
2,813	31	402	100					X					none	X	FAF*/FFS/AFSA
515	60			X				X	X	X	X	4/1	4/15		AFSA
													none	X	FAF*/FFS
46	98	35	100	X				X				6/1	none	X	FAF*/FFS/AFSA
													none		FAF/AFSA*
								X				4/1	none		FAF*/FFS
351	93	249	100					X	X	X			8/15		FAF*/FFS/AFSA
599	41			X	X	X	X	X	X	X	X	5/1	none		FAF*/FFS
		210	90	X	X	X	X	X	X	X	X	4/1	none		FAF*/FFS;FAF/FFS
306	56	108	95	X	X	X	X	X	X	X	X	6/1	none		FAF*/FFS/AFSA
2,148	50	575	96	X				X					none		FAF*/FFS/AFSA/SF
149	56			X				X				4/1	none	X	FAF*/FFS
172	71	103	100	X	X			X	X				none		FAF/FFS/AFSA*/AFSSA;FAF/FFS/AFSA*/CSS SAAC/
				X				X					none		FAF
3,686	47			X	X		X	X	X		X	3/1	none		FAF/FFS*/AFSA
1,770	55	815	92	X	X	X	X	X	X	X	X	3/1	none		FAF/FFS*/AFSA/SF; FAF/FFS*/AFSA/CSS SAAC/ACT SAAC/SF
1,522	76	876	100					X	X	X	X	3/1	none	X	FAF/FFS*/AFSA/SF; FAF/FFS*/AFSA
625	70	500	100					X	X	X	X	5/15	none	X	FAF*/FFS
275	75			X	X		X	X			X	4/1	none		FAF/FFS/AFSA*/SF
94	75							X			X		none	X	FAF*/FFS/AFSA/SF
197	76							X	X	X	X	7/15	none		FFS
													none		FAF/FFS*
1,167	20	270	100	X		X		X				5/1	none		FAF/FFS/AFSA*
100	53							X	X	X	X		none	X	FAF
													none	X	AFSA

*Preferred need analysis document.

Institution	Tuition and fees	Add'l out-of-state/ district tuition	Books and supplies	Costs for campus residents			Costs for students at home		
				Room and board	Trans-portation	Other costs	Board only	Trans-portation	Other costs
University of Nevada									
† Las Vegas	1,470	3,600/—	500	4,438	500	500	1,700	500	500
† Reno	1,470	3,600/—	500	3,720	607	1,725	1,757	821	382
Western Nevada Community College	720	3,000/—	550					500	500
New Hampshire									
Castle Junior College	4,050		400					1,382	1,080
Colby-Sawyer College	12,185		400	4,715	100	1,000			
‡ Daniel Webster College	9,830		500	4,140	300	500	1,500	500	500
Dartmouth College	16,335		1,500	5,160					
Franklin Pierce College	11,190		450	4,160	400	700		500	700
† Hesser College	5,600		500	3,500	500	1,000	900	500	800
‡ Keene State College	2,539	3,860/—	500	3,430	350	800	1,500	600	525
‡ McIntosh College	3,200		363					400	100
‡ New England College	10,570		400	4,420	150	1,000		400	1,000
‡ New Hampshire College	9,408		400	4,500	300	900	1,500	700	900
New Hampshire Technical College									
‡ Berlin	1,890	2,550/—	450				1,575	1,000	1,800
‡ Claremont	1,930	2,776/—	450				1,675	1,600	900
‡ Laconia	1,925	2,550/—	500				1,750	1,200	800
‡ Manchester	1,920	2,550/—	500				1,700	1,000	1,770
‡ Nashua	1,900	2,550/—	450				1,100	1,000	500
‡ Stratham	1,895	2,550/—	500				1,300	1,000	2,000
‡ New Hampshire Technical Institute	2,000	2,550/—	400	2,950	750	1,600	1,500	1,500	1,600
‡ Notre Dame College	7,630		600	4,290	350	850	1,200	850	850
‡ Plymouth State College of the University System of New Hampshire	2,574	3,860/—	450	3,441	225	775		925	600
Rivier College	8,750		400	4,310	200	800	2,100	200	800
St. Anselm College	10,460		400	5,000	200	1,000	1,400	1,400	1,000
‡ School for Lifelong Learning	2,870	300/—	500						
University of New Hampshire									
‡ Durham	3,558	6,080/—	500	3,456	300	1,100	1,200	600	1,100
‡ Manchester	2,570	4,720/—	400				1,500	1,000	900
‡ White Pines College	5,950		440	3,600	220	900		1,320	990
New Jersey									
Assumption College for Sisters	1,200		400	1,100					
‡ Atlantic Community College	1,224	2,476/1,076	500				1,500	1,360	360
Bergen Community College	1,380	3,600/1,200	650				2,250	1,015	950
Berkeley College of Business	8,115		675		1,335	1,044		1,335	1,044
‡ Beth Medrash Govoha	3,000		425	3,500					
Bloomfield College	7,475		400	3,700	300	1,390	1,500	1,100	1,225
† Brookdale Community College	1,352	3,528/1,176	500				1,313	1,056	859
‡ Burlington County College	1,125	2,010/90	500					900	400
† Caldwell College	7,600		375	4,000	300	700		900	700
Camden County College	1,280	—/60	500				1,050	525	825
Centenary College	10,540		500	4,890	518	500		1,987	500
College of St. Elizabeth	9,550		350	4,000	350	650	1,700	850	650

†Figures are projected for 1991-92. ‡Figures are for 1990-91.

All aid		Need–based aid		Grants and scholarships								Financial aid deadlines		Inst aid form	Need analysis document
				Need–based				Nonneed–based							
Total freshmen	Percent receiving aid	Freshmen judged to have need	Percent offered aid	Acad	Music/drama	Art	Athl	Acad	Music/drama	Art	Athl	Priority	Closing		
				X	X	X	X	X	X	X	X	4/1	none	X	FAF/FFS*/SF*;FAF/FFS/SF*
1,377	65							X	X		X	4/1	none	X	FFS
2,240	25	395	100	X				X				5/1	none	X	FAF*/FFS/AFSA
134	48	70	100					X				3/15	none	X	FAF*/AFSA
236	45	107	100					X	X			2/15	none	X	FAF
128	59	104	89					X				3/1	none	X	FAF
1,068	37	443	100					X				2/1		X	FAF
430	64	297	94	X	X		X	X	X		X	2/28	none		FAF*/FFS/AFSA/AFSSA/SF;FAF*/FFS/AFSA/CSS SAAC/ACT
500	70			X		X		X			X		none		FAF*/FFS/AFSA
726	54	430	94					X	X	X	X	3/1	none		FAF*/FFS FAF/AFSA
344	36	155	100	X	X	X		X				3/1	none		FAF
375	73	226	100	X			X	X			X	3/15	none		FAF
															FAF
322	76	128	100	X				X				5/1	none	X	FAF
313	52	135	100	X				X				3/1	5/1	X	FAF
256	25	113	96	X				X				5/1	none		FAF
354	28	107	100	X				X					5/1	X	FAF
399	54	86	100	X								5/1	none		FAF
771	45	187	100	X				X				5/1	none	X	FAF*/FFS/AFSA
117	90	93	100	X				X				3/15	none	X	FAF
781	60	312	99					X	X			3/1	none		FAF
105	79			X				X				3/1	none	X	FAF*/FFS
506	54	290	88	X							X	3/1	4/15	X	FAF
													none		AFSA
2,241	49	2,037	96	X		X		X	X	X	X	2/15	none		FAF
86	35	19	100	X				X				5/1	none		FAF
38	66	18	100	X				X				3/15	5/1	X	FAF
													none		FAF
												5/1	none		FAF*/AFSA;FAF
1,726	25	925	100	X				X			X	6/15	none		FAF
453	75	295	100	X				X					none	X	FAF;AFSA
															FAF
273	80			X		X		X			X	5/1	none		FAF
3,628	43	512	46	X				X			X	6/1	none	X	FAF
1,389	50	271	100	X		X		X			X		none		FAF
195	69	65	100	X		X	X	X		X	X		7/15		FAF
3,610	10							X				7/1	none	X	FAF*/AFSA/SF;FAF*/AFSA/APSGFSA/SF
389	80	80	100	X	X			X				4/1	none	X	FAF*/FFS
138	75	82	100	X				X		X		4/1	none		FAF*/FFS/AFSA; FAF*/FFS/AFSA/CSS SAAC/ACT SAAC

*Preferred need analysis document.

Institution	Tuition and fees	Add'l out-of-state/district tuition	Books and supplies	Costs for campus residents			Costs for students at home		
				Room and board	Transportation	Other costs	Board only	Transportation	Other costs
† County College of Morris	1,330	2,204/1,180	500				1,800	1,000	900
‡ Cumberland County College	1,205	3,960/1,065	450				1,590	1,474	414
‡ Drew University	14,926		480	4,475	180	295	1,500	500	100
‡ Essex County College	1,733	3,000/1,500	550				1,500	500	850
Fairleigh Dickinson University									
‡ Edward Williams College	8,275		400	5,091	480	900	898	1,830	900
‡ Florham-Madison Campus	8,862		400	5,091	480	870	898	1,830	870
Rutherford Campus	9,916		400	5,166	480		898	1,830	
‡ Teaneck-Hackensack Campus	8,862		400	5,091	480	870	898	1,830	870
Felician College	6,950		400				1,500	1,500	3,500
Georgian Court College	7,300		500	3,750	800	800	1,700	1,600	800
† Glassboro State College	2,452	900/—	400	4,300	200	700	1,500	800	700
Gloucester County College	1,470	3,960/30	400					1,000	800
‡ Hudson County Community College	1,240	—/1,080	681					704	950
‡ Jersey City State College	2,212	690/—	398	5,250	400	1,400	1,500	850	1,040
Katharine Gibbs School	7,345		500						
‡ Kean College of New Jersey	2,010	690/—	500	3,020	650	800	900	875	700
‡ Mercer County Community College	1,210	2,400/1,200	400				1,360	1,350	350
Middlesex County College	1,484	—/1,200	624				1,200	1,256	
Monmouth College	10,700		480	4,330	330	1,230	2,100	600	1,230
‡ Montclair State College	2,255	930/—	500	4,132	428	700	1,500	1,332	700
‡ New Jersey Institute of Technology	4,000	3,520/—	700	4,300	450	750		850	750
‡ Ocean County College	1,226	1,066/130	500				1,300	1,350	800
† Passaic County Community College	1,643	1,440/—	700				2,385	795	848
Princeton University	16,570		600	5,311	500	1,389			
‡ Rabbinical College of America	5,500		500	4,500	400	1,000		400	1,000
‡ Ramapo College of New Jersey	2,505	600/—	500	3,950	400	650	1,000	1,100	600
‡ Raritan Valley Community College	1,242	3,240/1,080	550				1,500	1,080	1,000
‡ Rider College	10,120		600	4,330		1,050		1,050	1,650
Rutgers—The State University of New Jersey									
‡ Camden College of Arts and Sciences	3,279	2,958/—	500	3,826		2,093			3,819
‡ College of Engineering	3,753	3,286/—	500	3,826		2,093			3,819
‡ College of Nursing	3,274	2,958/—	500	3,826		2,093			3,819
‡ College of Pharmacy	3,753	3,286/—	500	3,826		2,093			3,819
‡ Cook College	3,766	3,286/—	500	3,826		2,093			3,819
‡ Douglass College	3,424	2,958/—	500	3,826		2,093			3,819
‡ Livingston College	3,444	2,958/—	500	3,826		2,093			3,819
‡ Mason Gross School of the Arts	3,437	2,958/—	500			2,093			3,819
‡ Newark College of Arts and Sciences	3,281	2,958/—	500	3,826		2,093			3,819
‡ Rutgers College	3,432	2,958/—	500	3,826		2,093			3,819
† St. Peter's College	7,343		450		450	400	1,600	530	520
‡ Salem Community College	1,227	610/310	600					1,100	775
Seton Hall University	10,450		500	5,520	530	650	1,950	2,200	1,400
Stevens Institute of Technology	15,030		450	4,830	170	700	1,500	1,200	300
‡ Stockton State College	2,100	640/—	650	3,750	785	1,050	1,500	1,050	950
‡ Sussex County Community College	1,296	2,352/1,176	500				1,700	732	960
† Trenton State College	3,040	1,075/—	600	4,750	100	1,000	1,600	900	600
‡ Union County College	1,306	3,240/1,080	450				1,500	700	800

†Figures are projected for 1991-92.   ‡Figures are for 1990-91.

Total freshmen	Percent receiving aid	Freshmen judged to have need	Percent offered aid	NB Acad	NB Music/drama	NB Art	NB Athl	NNB Acad	NNB Music/drama	NNB Art	NNB Athl	Priority	Closing	Inst aid form	Need analysis document
3,452	25			X	X	X		X			X	4/15	none		FAF*/AFSA
												7/1	none		FAF*/AFSA
320	74	167	99	X				X				3/1		X	FAF
													none	X	FAF
512	90			X	X	X	X	X				3/15	none		FAF
283	90			X	X	X	X	X			X	3/15	none		FAF
136	90			X	X	X	X	X			X	3/15	none		FAF
226	90			X	X	X	X	X			X	3/15	none		FAF
105	51							X				6/1	none	X	FAF
161	81	117	100	X	X	X	X	X	X	X	X	3/1	10/1	X	FAF*/AFSA
962	69			X	X	X		X	X	X			4/15	X	FAF;FAF*/FFS/AFSA/
															CSS SAAC/ACT SAAC/
															AFSSA/APSGFSA/SF
1,459	25			X				X				5/15	none		FAF
703	48			X				X					none		FAF/AFSA;FAF/
															AFSA*
946	82	363	100	X				X	X			4/15	none		FAF*/AFSA
													none		AFSA
1,156	55	600	100	X				X				4/1	none		FAF
1,507	12	600	96	X	X	X	X	X	X		X	5/1	none	X	FAF/FFS/AFSA*/
															AFSSA/SF;FAF/FFS/
															AFSA*/AFSSA/
														none		FAF
497	76	361	97	X				X			X	3/1	none		FAF
1,438	50	713	77										3/1		FAF
551	75	318	100	X				X				3/15	none	X	FAF
								X				5/31	none		
1,194	55	717	70	X			X	X			X		none		FAF;AFSA
1,175	70	498	100										2/1	X	FAF
												10/2	none		FAF/FFS*/AFSA
447	38			X									5/1		FAF
		350	100	X								4/1	none		FAF
679	70			X			X	X	X		X	3/1	none		FAF
282	42	223	95	X	X		X	X				3/1	none		FAF
622	38	271	98	X	X		X	X			X	3/1	none		FAF
45	52	24	100	X	X		X	X				3/1	none		FAF
158	28	49	92	X	X		X	X			X	3/1	none		FAF
479	36	195	95	X	X		X	X			X	3/1	none		FAF
654	41	274	99	X	X		X	X	X		X	3/1	close		FAF
696	44	428	97	X	X		X	X	X		X	3/1	none		FAF
96	40	41	95	X	X		X	X	X	X	X	3/1	none		FAF
498	47	411	96	X	X		X	X				3/1	none		FAF
1,651	39	682	98	X	X		X	X	X		X	3/1	none		FAF
409	75	295	93					X			X	2/15	none		FAF
				X				X			X	3/1	none	X	FAF
966	75	740	98	X				X			X	4/1	none		FAF
383	70	265	100					X				2/1	none		FAF
706	82	506	97	X				X				3/1	none		FAF/AFSA/SF
								X				3/1	8/1		FAF/AFSA
1,025	50	558	100	X				X	X				5/1		FAF
1,783	17	1,500	100					X			X	4/15	none	X	FAF

*Preferred need analysis document.

Institution	Tuition and fees	Add'l out-of-state/district tuition	Books and supplies	Costs for campus residents			Costs for students at home		
				Room and board	Trans-portation	Other costs	Board only	Trans-portation	Other costs
Upsala College	10,050		600	4,528	375	6,072		670	2,375
‡ Warren County Community College	1,150	2,120/1,060	500				1,080	864	900
‡ Westminster Choir College	10,600		500	4,550	150	700	2,050	1,000	700
‡ William Paterson College of New Jersey	2,190	600/—	400	3,630	900	1,500	1,500	900	1,500

New Mexico

Institution	Tuition and fees	Add'l out-of-state/district tuition	Books and supplies	Room and board	Trans-portation	Other costs	Board only	Trans-portation	Other costs
Albuquerque Technical-Vocational Institute	843	1,404/—	321				2,894	987	1,896
‡ College of Santa Fe	7,656		450	2,510	480	1,200	1,500	950	1,200
† College of the Southwest	2,250		400		500	590	1,620	1,380	590
‡ Dona Ana Branch Community College of New Mexico State University	576	1,224/120	250						
Eastern New Mexico University									
‡ Clovis Community College	520	1,008/24	400				1,500	500	
‡ Portales	1,230	3,018/—	450	2,188	700	800		700	800
‡ Roswell Campus	552	1,008/24	500	3,000	800	600	825	1,000	500
Institute of American Indian Arts	2,365		1,100	3,166	400	900		400	900
National College	5,472								
† New Mexico Highlands University	1,179	2,952/—	400	2,250	775	725	2,000	600	775
‡ New Mexico Institute of Mining and Technology	1,392	3,868/—	500	3,027	250	900	1,200	500	900
New Mexico Junior College	385	480/360	450	2,800	600	1,050	900	675	800
New Mexico Military Institute	1,215	1,425/—	300	2,300	1,500	1,000			
New Mexico State University									
‡ Alamogordo	600	1,224/120	310						
‡ Carlsbad	600	1,224/120	420					550	700
‡ Grants	552	1,224/—	380				1,214	754	780
‡ Las Cruces	1,488	3,696/—	450	2,578	816	915	1,500	1,100	915
Northern New Mexico Community College	468	948/—	460	2,728	785	1,025	2,128	935	1,025
Parks College	4,320		300						
St. John's College	14,262		275	4,696	600	500	1,700	100	
† San Juan College	360	240/—	340					800	750
‡ Santa Fe Community College	435	645/72	450				2,320	630	440
Southwestern Indian Polytechnic Institute	90								
University of New Mexico									
‡ Albuquerque	1,453	3,699/—	420	2,990	750	950	1,500	750	950
‡ Gallup	552	816/—	550				1,800	950	980
‡ Western New Mexico University	1,034	4,300/—	400	2,200	700	1,000	800	700	900

†Figures are projected for 1991-92.   ‡Figures are for 1990-91.

All aid		Need-based aid		Grants and scholarships								Financial aid deadlines		Inst aid form	Need analysis document
				Need-based				Nonneed-based							
Total freshmen	Percent receiving aid	Freshmen judged to have need	Percent offered aid	Acad	Music/drama	Art	Athl	Acad	Music/drama	Art	Athl	Priority	Closing		
157	98	112	100	X				X				3/1	none		FAF
340	8	55	75	X				X					none	X	FAF
51	79	39	100	X	X			X	X			3/1	none		FAF*/FFS
1,166	42			X	X			X	X			5/1	none		FAF
				X								3/1	none		FAF*/FFS/AFSA/SF; FAF*/FFS/AFSA/CSS SAAC/ACT SAAC/SF
115	90			X	X	X		X	X	X		3/1	none		FAF
24	87	15	100					X			X	4/1	6/1		FAF/FFS/AFSA*
1,935	21	386	100									3/1	none		FAF*/FFS/AFSA
170	30	90	100	X				X					none		FAF*/FFS/AFSA/ AFSSA
604	80			X	X	X	X	X	X	X	X	3/1	none		FAF*/FFS/AFSA/SF; FAF*/FFS/AFSA/CSS SAAC/ACT SAAC/SF
250	70			X				X				5/1	none	X	FAF*/FFS/AFSA/SF
81	77	75	100										4/15		FAF/FFS/AFSA*/ AFSSA
20	25			X				X					none	X	FAF/FFS/AFSA*/ AFSSA
397	73	285	95	X				X	X	X	X	3/1	none	X	FAF*/FFS
161	74	74	100					X				3/1	none		FAF*/FFS/SF;FAF*/ FFS
634	37			X	X	X	X	X	X		X	4/1	none		FAF*/FFS/AFSA
217	74	70	100	X				X			X	5/1	none	X	FAF*/FFS/AFSA/ AFSSA/SF;FAF*/FFS/ AFSA/CSS SAAC/
				X									3/1	X	FAF/FFS/AFSA/SF*
				X								3/1	none		SF FAF*/FFS
				X				X	X		X		3/1	X	FAF/FFS/AFSA/ AFSSA/SF*
247	85			X				X				5/1	none		FAF
								X					5/31		FAF/FFS/AFSA/SF
79	65											2/25	none		FAF*/FFS
1,589	62	211	100	X	X			X	X			5/1	none		FAF*/FFS/AFSA; FAF*/FFS/AFSA/CSS SAAC/ACT SAAC
486	20	280	63	X				X	X			3/1	none		FAF*/FFS/AFSA/SF; FAF*/FFS/AFSA/CSS SAAC/ACT SAAC/SF FAF
1,811	60	700	100					X	X		X	3/1	none		FAF/FFS/AFSA*
		216	93	X				X				3/1	none	X	FAF/FFS/AFSA*
277	43	170	95					X	X	X	X	4/1	none	X	FAF/FFS*

*Preferred need analysis document.

Institution	Tuition and fees	Add'l out-of-state/district tuition	Books and supplies	Costs for campus residents			Costs for students at home		
				Room and board	Transportation	Other costs	Board only	Transportation	Other costs
New York									
† Adelphi University	10,380		468	5,457	351	821		1,605	680
‡ Adirondack Community College	1,417	1,300/—	475				830	900	750
Albany College of Pharmacy	7,375		425	4,000	300	700	1,500	700	700
Alfred University	14,110		500	4,470	400	525	2,200	1,300	550
American Academy of Dramatic Arts	7,175		500				2,800	900	1,000
American Academy McAllister Institute of Funeral Service	4,885		700						
‡ Bard College	15,710		450	5,160	300	500	1,600	600	500
‡ Barnard College	14,890		500	6,454		830	580	340	830
Berkeley College	8,025		660	4,350	250	650		660	660
‡ Berkeley School: New York City	7,455		550						
‡ Beth Hatalmud Rabbinical College	3,000			1,300					
‡ Beth Medrash Emek Halacha Rabbinical College	2,600			2,600					
‡ Boricua College	4,929		400				2,000	360	900
Bramson ORT Technical Institute	5,152		240					475	1,300
Briarcliffe: The College for Business	6,475		400				1,300	1,500	1,500
‡ Broome Community College	1,450	1,350/—	425				1,500	490	500
Bryant and Stratton Business Institute: Buffalo	4,992		450				1,584	720	1,203
Bryant-Stratton Business Institute Albany	5,142		600				1,500	500	1,053
Rochester	5,142		450						
Syracuse	5,032		450					540	360
Canisius College	8,902		400	4,650	430	700	750	430	630
‡ Catholic Medical Center of Brooklyn and Queens School of Nursing	3,000		500		275	1,000	1,100	500	1,000
‡ Cayuga County Community College	1,452	1,350/—	400				940	500	840
† Cazenovia College	8,224		400	4,100	200	350	750	300	750
Central City Business Institute	4,670		500	2,900	1,173	700	1,500	642	800
‡ Central Yeshiva Tomchei Tmimim Lubavitz	4,400			2,300					
City University of New York									
† Baruch College	1,550	2,600/—	300				1,500	540	1,242
† Borough of Manhattan Community College	1,530	575/—	300				1,750	580	780
† Bronx Community College	1,550	575/—	350				1,100	540	1,050
† Brooklyn College	1,555	2,600/—	250				1,100	540	1,103
† City College	1,545	2,600/—	360				1,500	621	1,359
† College of Staten Island	1,556	2,600/—	300				1,500	540	1,277
† Hostos Community College	1,524	575/—	300				1,500	540	1,242
† Hunter College	1,542	2,600/—	300		621	2,069	1,500	621	1,359
† John Jay College of Criminal Justice	1,550	2,600/—	325					260	225
† Kingsborough Community College	1,540	575/—	300				1,120	540	1,173
† La Guardia Community College	1,551	575/—	360				1,425	720	1,508
† Lehman College	1,540	2,600/—	500				1,500	675	1,415
† Medgar Evers College	1,502	575/—	300					540	503
† New York City Technical College	1,499	2,600/—	400				1,500	540	1,242
† Queens College	1,632	2,600/—	400					600	600
† Queensborough Community College	1,545	575/—	300				1,100	540	1,173
† York College	1,532	2,600/—	360				1,500	828	2,267
‡ Clarkson University	12,895		400	4,482	300	733			700
‡ Clinton Community College	1,403	1,300/—	400				1,150	700	750

†Figures are projected for 1991-92.   ‡Figures are for 1990-91.

Total freshmen	Percent receiving aid	Freshmen judged to have need	Percent offered aid	Acad	Music/drama	Art	Athl	Acad	Music/drama	Art	Athl	Priority	Closing	Inst aid form	Need analysis document
					Need-based				Nonneed-based			Financial aid deadlines			
866	69	546	100					X	X	X	X	5/1	none		FAF
957	40			X	X			X				6/1	none	X	FAF/FFS/AFSA*
110	81	95	98									2/15	4/15		FFS
399	80	325	99	X	X	X		X		X			none	X	FAF
134	65	92	95	X	X							7/1	none	X	FAF
51	65	50	100					X					none		AFSA
290	53	146	100	X	X	X		X	X	X		2/15	none		FAF
529	55	254	100										2/1	X	FAF
													none	X	FAF
													none	X	
															AFSA
600	87	280	93	X				X				5/2	7/15		FAF
													none	X	AFSA
370	80			X									none		FAF/SF
2,007	50			X			X	X			X	4/1	none	X	FAF/FFS*/AFSA
													none	X	FAF/FFS*/AFSA
													none		AFSA
													none		
													none		FAF/FFS
537	80	460	100	X			X	X			X	2/1	none		FAF
													none		FAF
892	75			X				X				5/1	none	X	FAF*/FFS/AFSA/ AFSA
604	87	525	100	X				X		X	X	3/1	none		FAF*/FFS/AFSA
216	85			X				X				6/1	none	X	FAF/FFS/AFSA/ AFSSA*/SF
															AFSA
1,755	70	1,500	93	X				X				4/15	5/30		AFSSA
3,062	90												none		
													none		
2,779	35	808	89	X	X	X	X	X	X	X		5/1	none		
1,283	78	1,050	100	X								5/1	none		
1,476	24											5/25	9/30		AFSSA
1,000	95												none		
1,122	72			X				X				5/13	none		
1,523	70	900	100					X				6/1	none		
2,345	90											8/1	none		
2,200	83											7/1	none		AFSSA
967	90							X				5/30	none		AFSSA
568	90											6/1	8/31		AFSSA
2,290	83											6/30	10/1		
1,933	60							X				5/31	8/1		AFSSA
2,314	92											5/1	none		
685	70	390	90									4/1	8/1		
566	87	420	100	X	X	X	X	X	X	X	X	2/1	2/15		FAF*/FFS
726	80	275	100	X									4/15		AFSA

*Preferred need analysis document.

Institution	Tuition and fees	Add'l out-of-state/ district tuition	Books and supplies	Costs for campus residents			Costs for students at home		
				Room and board	Trans-portation	Other costs	Board only	Trans-portation	Other costs
† Cochran School of Nursing-St. John's Riverside Hospital	7,420		425				2,200	946	2,037
Colgate University	16,240		540	5,070	90	770	2,590	90	770
‡ College of Aeronautics	5,400		600		300	200		450	
College for Human Services	9,180		300				1,000	690	640
College of Insurance	8,574		500	6,300	400	800	1,000	550	800
‡ College of Mount St. Vincent	8,940		400	4,550	150	850	1,500	600	850
College of New Rochelle									
New Rochelle	9,750		500	4,640	150	250	1,500	500	250
‡ School of New Resources	4,530		350					350	350
College of St. Rose	8,510		550	5,010	325	1,439	1,886	375	1,199
Columbia University									
Columbia College	15,858		650	6,122		900	1,680	400	990
‡ School of Engineering and Applied Science	14,902		550	5,725		900			900
† School of General Studies	14,850		900	9,540			2,375	414	400
‡ School of Nursing	14,340		1,400		800	1,200	3,000	1,000	1,200
‡ Columbia-Greene Community College	1,396	1,240/—	400				1,500	500	500
‡ Community College of the Finger Lakes	1,470	1,350/—	400				1,700	600	330
Concordia College	8,370		400	4,200	350	800	550	350	800
Cooper Union	300		745		500	1,260	1,350	500	1,260
Cornell University	16,214		465	5,336		1,000			
‡ Corning Community College	1,455	1,350/—	400				1,040	750	300
‡ Culinary Institute of America	9,890				500	1,200		500	1,200
‡ Daemen College	7,570		500	3,750	600	650		600	650
‡ Darkei No'Am Rabbinical College	4,000		300						
Dominican College of Blauvelt	6,890		500	5,150	450	900	1,650	1,000	900
‡ Dowling College	7,130		450		800	1,413	1,260	1,106	1,413
‡ Dutchess Community College	1,445	1,350/—	450				1,000	700	500
† D'Youville College	7,920		580	3,730	650	650	1,555	650	650
† Eastman School of Music of the University of Rochester	14,300		500	5,717	650	600	2,000	650	600
Elmira College	11,330		450	3,900	450	750	1,500	450	750
Erie Community College									
‡ City Campus	1,424	—/1,350	400				1,800	700	700
‡ North Campus	1,424	—/1,350	400				1,800	700	700
‡ South Campus	1,424	—/1,350	400				1,800	700	700
Eugene Lang College/New School for Social Research	11,944		680	7,346			2,886	600	975
† Fashion Institute of Technology	1,860	2,400/—	1,000	4,555	550	850		650	850
Five Towns College	5,600		475				4,465	2,432	1,700
‡ Fordham University	10,350		375	6,400	375	1,025	1,550	375	950
‡ Friends World College	9,000								
‡ Fulton-Montgomery Community College	1,445	1,350/—	350					450	400
‡ Genesee Community College	1,350	1,250/—	475				1,400	800	525
Hamilton College	16,650		300	4,550	200	600			
Hartwick College	13,450		450	4,350	350	400	1,300	1,100	400
Helene Fuld School of Nursing	5,538		900				2,500	404	1,524
‡ Herkimer County Community College	1,470	1,350/—	400				500	600	500
† Hilbert College	5,810		400	4,110	500	660	1,800	500	660
Hobart College	16,277		600	5,166	200	600			
‡ Hofstra University	9,090		600	4,980	580	1,174	1,500	1,130	640
Holy Trinity Orthodox Seminary	900		100	900					

†Figures are projected for 1991-92.   ‡Figures are for 1990-91.

| All aid | | Need–based aid | | Grants and scholarships | | | | | | | | Financial aid deadlines | | Inst aid form | Need analysis document |
Total freshmen	Percent receiving aid	Freshmen judged to have need	Percent offered aid	Need–based Acad	Music/drama	Art	Athl	Nonneed–based Acad	Music/drama	Art	Athl	Priority	Closing		
59	90	45	100	X									none	X	FAF
685	63	292	100										2/1	X	FAF
342	84	282	100	X				X				5/1	none	X	FAF
141	85			X									none	X	AFSA
127	95			X				X					none		FAF
178	75	111	100	X				X				3/15	none	X	FAF
185	95	141	100					X	X	X			none	X	FAF
869	96	767	100										none		FAF
206	85			X	X	X		X	X	X			3/1	X	FAF
783	46	360	100										2/1	X	FAF
244	59	136	100					X					2/1	X	FAF
132	50			X									7/1	X	FAF
													none		FAF
476	75							X				5/1	none	X	FAF
945	75							X	X	X	X	5/1	none	X	FAF
90	82							X	X		X		3/31		FAF*/FFS
241	40	76	100	X				X				2/15	5/1		FAF
2,919	70	1,334	100	X									2/15	X	FAF;FAF*/CSS SAAC
980	85	800	100	X								7/1	none		FAF
1,152	80			X				X					none		FAF*/FFS
277	91	243	100	X		X	X	X			X	2/15	none	X	FAF
116	75	56	100	X			X	X			X	3/1	none	X	FAF*/AFSA
392	70	254	100	X	X		X	X			X		8/1	X	FAF*/FFS/AFSA/AFSSA/SF
1,501	50	1,401	66	X				X				5/1	none		FAF/FFS/AFSA
158	94							X			X	4/15	none		FAF
125	89	73	100		X			X	X			2/1	none	X	FAF
247	80	188	100					X	X	X		3/1	none		FAF
984	82											4/30	none	X	FAF
				X								4/30	none		FAF*/FFS/AFSA
998	53			X								4/30	none		FAF
130	60	100	100	X				X				3/1	none	X	FAF*/FFS
1,694	47	860	90										3/15	X	FAF/FFS
163	60	64	100		X			X	X			5/15	8/21		FAF
1,061	80			X	X		X	X	X		X		2/15	X	FAF
44	67	26	100									4/1	6/15	X	FAF*/FFS
617	75			X				X				4/1	none	X	FAF
1,323	75	350	100	X	X	X	X	X	X	X			6/1		FAF
448	63	203	100										2/1	X	FAF*/FFS
		213	100	X	X		X	X	X		X	4/1	none	X	FAF
33	84			X				X					none	X	AFSA
903	84	700	100	X			X	X			X		4/1		FAF
313	82			X			X	X				3/1	none		FAF*/FFS/AFSA
290	38	116	100	X	X	X							2/15	X	FAF
1,377	82	1,225	90	X				X				3/1	none		FAF*/FFS

*Preferred need analysis document.

Institution	Tuition and fees	Add'l out-of-state/ district tuition	Books and supplies	Costs for campus residents			Costs for students at home		
				Room and board	Trans-portation	Other costs	Board only	Trans-portation	Other costs
Houghton College	8,676		500	3,134	550	600	800	250	600
‡ Hudson Valley Community College	1,299	1,380/—	425				1,700	900	800
Institute of Design and Construction	2,740		400					200	400
‡ Interboro Institute	4,828		450				1,100	400	1,000
‡ Iona College	8,270		450	5,600	450	1,300	700	600	1,900
Ithaca College	11,946		500	5,104	240	910	2,604	1,240	910
Jamestown Business College	4,625		400				800	700	725
‡ Jamestown Community College	1,468	1,350/—	400				1,300	600	400
‡ Jefferson Community College	1,491	1,350/—	600				1,500	310	500
Jewish Theological Seminary of America	5,950		400		400	2,300		400	
Juilliard School	10,350		2,325	7,700		6,400	2,200	1,200	
Katharine Gibbs School									
‡ Melville	7,045		550				1,100	1,315	1,053
‡ New York	7,020		500					1,300	
Kehilath Yakov Rabbinical Seminary	3,900			2,000					
Keuka College	8,120		500	3,850	500	500	1,500	500	500
King's College	8,310		400	3,820	300	500	425	300	500
Kol Yaakov Torah Center	3,000		50	1,950	150	150		100	100
Laboratory Institute of Merchandising	8,450		300				1,500	1,500	1,000
Le Moyne College	9,290		300	4,020	230	625	700	250	1,025
† Long Island College Hospital School of Nursing	4,037		800				1,200	570	400
Long Island University									
‡ Brooklyn Campus	8,350		425	4,000	450	900		450	900
‡ C. W. Post Campus	9,170		450	4,360	500	1,150	1,700	900	770
† Southampton Campus	9,810		525	5,110	400	550	2,499	500	550
‡ Machzikei Hadath Rabbinical College	4,200			1,800					
Manhattan College	11,100		500	5,750	500	1,000	1,800	800	1,000
Manhattan School of Music	10,250		525		650	900	2,500	650	900
‡ Manhattanville College	11,660		350	5,250	375	725		750	825
Mannes College of Music	10,180		450			650		400	650
† Maria College	3,960		500					500	500
† Marist College	8,835		500	5,150	250	600	1,500	600	500
Marymount College	10,200		500	5,750	400	600		1,000	600
† Marymount Manhattan College	8,800		300		400	1,000	1,600	400	1,000
‡ Mater Dei College	4,255		550	2,850	150	600	1,500	300	600
Medaille College	7,180		500					550	600
‡ Mercy College	6,600		500				1,500	625	800
‡ Mesivta Eastern Parkway Rabbinical Seminary	3,800			2,200					
‡ Mesivta Tifereth Jerusalem of America	3,000		300	2,300					
‡ Mesivta Torah Vodaath Seminary	4,465		200	4,500			2,175		
Mirrer Yeshiva Central Institute	2,250		400	2,000			1,000		
‡ Mohawk Valley Community College	1,451	1,350/—	600	3,100				500	700
† Molloy College	8,200		700				1,800	1,200	1,100
‡ Monroe College	4,390		450				1,500	520	680
‡ Monroe Community College	1,437	1,350/—	350				1,500	600	880
‡ Mount St. Mary College	6,940		300	4,000	500	600	600	500	600
‡ Nassau Community College	1,440	1,350/—	600					1,200	850
† Nazareth College of Rochester	8,950		450	4,270	150	800	1,500	550	800
‡ New York Institute of Technology	6,530		410	4,620	320	1,040		1,000	2,640
New York School of Interior Design	9,200		900				4,000	700	700
‡ New York University	14,520		350	6,880		1,000		320	1,000

†Figures are projected for 1991-92.   ‡Figures are for 1990-91.

All aid		Need–based aid		Grants and scholarships								Financial aid deadlines		Inst aid form	Need analysis document
				Need–based				Nonneed–based							
Total freshmen	Percent receiving aid	Freshmen judged to have need	Percent offered aid	Acad	Music/ drama	Art	Athl	Acad	Music/ drama	Art	Athl	Priority	Closing		
278	94	227	100	X	X	X	X	X	X	X	X	3/15	none		FAF
3,954	60			X								5/30	none		FAF/FFS
30	60												none		AFSA
													none	X	AFSA
1,308	89			X				X		X	X	4/1	none	X	FAF*/FFS/AFSA
1,676	51	755	100	X	X				X				3/1		FAF
165	89	152	100	X				X					none		FAF/AFSA*
1,676	80	1,487	100	X			X	X	X		X	5/1	none		FAF
750	86			X			X	X			X	4/1	none	X	FAF*/FFS
26	60							X				2/15	3/14	X	FAF
79	75	71	100	X	X								2/15	X	FAF
													none		AFSA
													none	X	FAF*/AFSA
														X	AFSA
137	96	116	100	X				X				3/15	none	X	FAF
104	85	78	100	X	X		X	X	X		X	3/15	none	X	FAF*/AFSA
													none	X	AFSA
48	80			X									none		FAF
377	70	316	96	X	X	X	X	X			X	2/15	7/1	X	FAF
													none		FAF
623	90	322	77	X	X	X	X	X	X	X	X		none	X	FAF
789	77	490	92	X	X	X	X	X	X	X	X	3/1	none		FAF
273	85	193	79					X		X	X		none	X	FAF*/FFS/AFSA
													none	X	AFSA
646	88	450	100	X				X			X	2/15	none	X	FAF
100	69	40	100						X			3/1	7/15	X	FAF
252	67	187	100	X	X	X		X	X	X		3/1	none		FAF*/FFS
24	81				X				X			5/15	none	X	FAF
119	55											8/1	none		FAF
770	71			X	X	X	X	X	X		X	3/15	none		FAF*/FFS
171	63	128	100	X		X		X	X	X	X	3/1	none		FAF*/FFS
143	100			X	X	X		X	X	X		3/1	4/1	X	FAF
179	90	170	100	X			X	X			X	5/1	none		FAF/FFS*/AFSA
		83	100	X				X				5/1	none		FAF
830	80	470	92					X			X	3/1	none		FAF
													none		FAF
															FAF/FFS/AFSA*
															AFSA
1,561	85			X				X				5/1	none	X	FAF
162	75	73	100				X	X	X	X	X	3/1	4/15	X	FAF
977	98	854	99										3/31		FAF*/FFS/AFSA
3,929	70											5/1	none		FAF
263	64	168	100	X				X				3/15	none		FAF
				X				X	X	X	X	5/1	none	X	AFSSA
270	78	154	100	X	X	X		X	X	X		3/30	none		FAF
													none		FAF
19	35	9	100	X		X						7/1	none		FAF
2,508	82	1,594	100	X	X			X	X				2/15	X	FAF/FFS*/AFSA

*Preferred need analysis document.

Institution	Tuition and fees	Add'l out-of-state/ district tuition	Books and supplies	Costs for campus residents			Costs for students at home		
				Room and board	Trans-portation	Other costs	Board only	Trans-portation	Other costs
‡ Niagara County Community College	1,350	—/1,280	350				750	650	600
‡ Niagara University	8,240		500	3,886	300	650	1,500	500	650
‡ North Country Community College	1,485	1,350/—	500				950	625	600
Nyack College	7,430		500	3,440	300	600		600	900
Ohr Somayach Institutions	3,000			3,000	150	725	1,300	150	725
Olean Business Institute	4,080		400				1,600		
‡ Onondaga Community College	1,434	2,700/1,350	350				600	650	450
‡ Orange County Community College	1,435	1,350/—	300				1,100	685	778
Pace University									
† College of White Plains	9,368		500	4,530	500	800	1,600	500	800
† New York	9,368		500	4,530	500	800	1,600	500	800
† Pleasantville/Briarcliff	9,368		500	4,530	500	800	1,600	500	800
‡ Parsons School of Design	11,190		1,400	5,880		1,000	1,800	700	1,000
Paul Smith's College	8,320		591	3,950	200	600	1,500	600	600
Phillips Beth Israel School of Nursing	4,745		760		520	950	1,400	640	950
Plaza Business Institute	5,005		600					720	1,080
Polytechnic University									
Brooklyn	14,100		400	4,000	640	1,130	1,000	640	1,130
Long Island Campus	14,100		400	4,000	640	1,130	1,000	640	1,130
Pratt Institute	11,406		1,200	5,600	345	630	1,685	345	630
‡ Rabbinical College Bobover Yeshiva B'nei Zion	3,600		400	2,600		350			350
‡ Rabbinical College Ch'san Sofer of New York	4,400		600	2,800					
‡ Rabbinical College of Long Island	6,300			3,300					
Rabbinical Seminary Adas Yereim	3,500			2,000					
Rabbinical Seminary of America	3,000		1,100	2,000	150	1,000			
Rabbinical Seminary M'Kor Chaim	3,600		400	2,200					
Rensselaer Polytechnic Institute	15,625		475	5,150		600			600
Rika Breuer Teachers Seminary	1,600			3,000					
Roberts Wesleyan College	8,510		519	2,976	467	950		467	3,450
Rochester Business Institute	4,800		600					3,459	1,100
Rochester Institute of Technology	12,018		500	5,034	300	575	1,500	300	575
† Rockland Community College	1,651	1,550/—	400				1,700	800	600
‡ Russell Sage College	9,500		400	4,000	200	650	1,500	300	700
Sage Junior College of Albany, A Division of Russell Sage College	6,120		400	4,240	300	550	3,300	300	800
St. Bonaventure University	9,067		450	4,594	400	650	1,500	600	650
‡ St. Francis College	5,500		400				2,050	450	1,200
‡ St. John Fisher College	8,500		300	4,480	200	600	800	600	600
‡ St. John's University	7,000		400				1,800	500	1,000
St. Joseph's College									
Brooklyn	6,290		475				1,500	500	600
Suffolk Campus	6,506		450				1,500	900	600
St. Joseph's School of Nursing	3,948								
St. Lawrence University	15,735		500	5,050	300	800		300	1,000
St. Thomas Aquinas College	6,750		500		500	1,000	3,100	1,000	1,000
‡ Sarah Lawrence College	16,750		500	6,400		600		450	
‡ Schenectady County Community College	1,453	1,350/—	375				1,550	500	500
School of Visual Arts	10,810		1,265		675	1,580		675	1,580

†Figures are projected for 1991-92.   ‡Figures are for 1990-91.

All aid		Need–based aid		Grants and scholarships								Financial aid deadlines		Inst aid form	Need analysis document
				Need–based				Nonneed–based							
Total freshmen	Percent receiving aid	Freshmen judged to have need	Percent offered aid	Acad	Music/drama	Art	Athl	Acad	Music/drama	Art	Athl	Priority	Closing		
1,590	70	978	64					X				4/15	none		FAF*/FFS/AFSA
530	75			X			X	X			X	2/15	none		FAF
													none		FAF/FFS/AFSA
104	87			X	X		X	X				3/1	none	X	FAF
													none	X	AFSA
															FAF
2,000	80							X					4/15		FFS
2,250	60			X				X				5/1	none		FAF
176	61			X				X				3/15	7/1		FAF*/FFS
667	76			X	X		X	X	X		X	3/15	7/1		FAF*/FFS
555	58			X			X	X	X		X	3/15	7/1		FAF*/FFS
345	85	245	98	X		X						3/1	7/1	X	FAF*/FFS
486	82	451	100	X			X				X	2/28	none		FAF*/FFS/AFSA
														X	FAF*/AFSA
152	94	152	100	X				X					none	X	AFSA
236	93			X				X				2/1	3/1	X	FAF
111	80			X				X				2/1	3/1	X	FAF
343	74	241	100	X		X		X		X		3/1	none		FAF*/FFS
															AFSA
															AFSA
															AFSA
													none		FAF/FFS;FAF/FFS/ CSS SAAC/AFSSA
															AFSA
989	74	740	100					X			X	2/15	none		FAF
													none		AFSA
203	92	140	100	X	X	X	X	X	X	X	X	5/15	none	X	FAF*/FFS/AFSA/SF; FAF*/FFS/AFSA/CSS SAAC/ACT SAAC/SF
													none	X	AFSA
1,113	70	958	100	X		X		X				3/1	none		FAF*/FFS
2,265	58	1,900	100	X				X				6/15	none		FAF/AFSA*
200	85	160	100	X				X				3/1	none		FAF
437	77	328	100	X				X		X	X	3/15	none	X	FAF
517	79	322	100	X				X	X		X		3/1		FAF*/FFS/AFSA/ AFSSA
331	80	261	93	X			X	X			X	2/15	none	X	FAF
366	83	268	100	X				X				3/1	none		FAF
2,697	75	1,984	86	X				X	X		X	4/1	none		FAF
65	87	34	100	X				X				2/25	none	X	FAF
177	86	99	100	X				X				2/25	none		FAF
															FAF
534	46	284	98										2/15	X	FAF
228	65	180	100	X		X		X		X	X		3/1	X	FAF*/AFSA/SF
238	43	102	100	X	X			X					2/1	X	FAF
892	70			X			X	X				5/1	none	X	FAF/FFS/AFSA
337	70	320	100	X		X		X		X		2/28	none	X	FAF

*Preferred need analysis document.

Institution	Tuition and fees	Add'l out-of-state/ district tuition	Books and supplies	Costs for campus residents			Costs for students at home		
				Room and board	Trans-portation	Other costs	Board only	Trans-portation	Other costs
Siena College....................	9,060		425	4,465	310	510	1,500	505	535
Skidmore College.................	16,000		500	5,090	250	700			
State University of New York									
† Albany....................	1,785	3,050/—	500	3,422	250	650	1,600	250	650
† Binghamton	1,853	3,050/—	500	4,152	400	700	1,890	600	765
† Buffalo....................	1,825	3,050/—	730	4,132	779	835	1,904	779	835
‡ Purchase....................	1,805	3,350/—	336	3,740	315	845	1,500	609	845
† Stony Brook	1,795	3,050/—	500	3,894	400	675		900	675
† College of Agriculture and Technology at Cobleskill	1,805	3,350/—	400	3,700	200	600	1,500	550	600
† College of Agriculture and Technology at Morrisville	1,845	3,050/—	600	3,550	450	700	1,000	1,500	800
† College at Brockport	1,911	3,050/—	480	3,795	400	775	1,500	700	775
† College at Buffalo	1,765	3,050/—	450	3,690	450	600	1,570	450	600
† College at Cortland	1,832	3,050/—	500	3,560	300	900	2,250	600	600
† College of Environmental Science and Forestry	1,937	3,050/—	600	5,565	200	450	1,700	600	300
† College at Fredonia	1,893	3,050/—	510	3,840	583	882	1,670	503	728
† College at Geneseo	1,875	3,050/—	500	3,267	450	700	1,200	600	700
† College at New Paltz	1,831	3,050/—	500	3,720	500	750	1,620	500	750
† College at Old Westbury	1,825	3,050/—	600	3,578	650	1,250		1,450	900
† College at Oneonta	1,870	3,050/—	400	3,795	300	950	1,600	300	600
† College at Plattsburgh	1,785	3,050/—	520	3,416	466	750	750	400	750
† College at Potsdam	1,790	3,050/—	450	3,550	300	675	950	600	675
† College of Technology at Alfred.....................	1,825	3,050/—	450	3,845	300	600	1,260	600	600
† College of Technology at Canton	1,830	3,050/—	550	3,610	400	600	1,630	830	600
† College of Technology at Delhi.....................	1,785	3,050/—	450	3,710	330	640	1,440	800	650
† College of Technology at Farmingdale	1,907	3,050/—	475	3,680	500	800	2,000	950	800
† Empire State College.....................	1,887	3,050/—	600				2,730	405	1,500
† Health Science Center at Brooklyn	1,750	3,050/—	575		575	575	1,155	575	690
† Health Science Center at Syracuse	1,775	3,050/—	500	4,025	460	810	1,500	975	810
† Health Sciences Center at Stony Brook.....................	1,795	3,050/—	600	3,894	1,540	1,300	1,500	1,540	1,300
† Institute of Technology at Utica/Rome	1,809	3,050/—	480				750	870	1,340
† Maritime College	1,915	3,050/—	500	3,816	400	1,200			
† Oswego	1,775	3,050/—	425	3,600	500	1,125		500	1,125
† Stenotype Academy	6,500								
Suffolk County Community College									
‡ Eastern Campus	1,395	—/1,350	400				2,000	1,240	940
‡ Selden.....................	1,458	—/1,350	400				2,000	1,240	940
‡ Western Campus	1,500	—/1,350	400				2,000	1,240	940
‡ Sullivan County Community College.....................	1,486	1,350/—	600				900	600	1,264
Syracuse University.....................	12,957		530	5,860	250	535	2,730	530	535
‡ Talmudical Institute of Upstate New York	3,500			2,200					
Talmudical Seminary Oholei Torah	4,400			1,800					
Technical Career Institutes.....................	5,450		450				2,000	487	1,430
Tobe-Coburn School for Fashion Careers...............	8,975		300				2,100	1,250	1,550
‡ Tompkins-Cortland Community College	1,518	1,350/—	450				1,100	900	900
‡ Touro College	6,415		500		375	600	8,000	375	600
‡ Trocaire College.....................	4,850		600				1,500	700	600
† Ulster County Community College.....................	1,749	1,650/—	500				1,491	700	600
‡ Union College	14,578		400	5,065	250	807	1,500	250	572

†Figures are projected for 1991-92.   ‡Figures are for 1990-91.

| All aid | | Need–based aid | | Grants and scholarships | | | | | | | | Financial aid deadlines | | Inst aid form | Need analysis document |
| Total freshmen | Percent receiving aid | Freshmen judged to have need | Percent offered aid | Need–based | | | | Nonneed–based | | | | Priority | Closing | | |
				Acad	Music/drama	Art	Athl	Acad	Music/drama	Art	Athl				
602	77	315	100	X			X	X			X		2/1		FAF/FFS
587	40	198	100						X				2/1	X	FAF
2,095	76	1,300	92	X				X				4/25	none	X	FAF
1,705	70	1,100	100	X	X	X		X	X	X		2/15	none		FAF
2,538	75	1,645	83	X	X	X	X	X	X	X		3/16	none		FAF
393	55	197	100	X	X	X		X	X	X		2/15	none	X	FAF*/FFS
								X				2/15	none	X	FAF
1,152	65	830	100	X				X				4/1	none	X	FAF*/FFS
1,473	90	1,110	73					X					4/1		FAF
964	84	645	84					X	X	X	X	5/1	none	X	FAF*/FFS/AFSA
1,446	85	1,085	95					X				3/1	none		FAF*/FFS/AFSA
981	74	535	100	X				X	X			5/1	none	X	FAF*/FFS
		20	100	X				X				3/15	none		FFS
829	70	712	98	X									none		FAF
1,135	88	1,008	95	X				X	X			3/1	4/1		FAF
1,161	65	447	100										2/15		FAF
		485	100	X								5/1	none	X	FAF*/FFS/AFSA/ AFSSA
941	71	576	75	X				X				5/1	none		FAF*/FFS
942	50	413	97	X	X	X		X	X	X		4/15	none		FAF
892	80	445	100	X	X			X	X			3/1	none		FAF*/FFS/AFSA
1,628	75							X				2/1	6/30		FAF
1,111	80			X				X				3/1	none		FAF/FFS*/AFSA
1,158	79			X			X	X				4/1	none	X	FAF
2,543	72	2,243	100	X				X				4/15	none	X	FAF*/FFS/AFSA
				X									5/1	X	FAF*/FFS/AFSA
															FAF
													none	X	FAF/FFS*
				X								3/15	none		FAF
				X				X				5/1	none		FAF*/FFS/AFSA
215	81	110	100	X				X				4/1	none	X	FAF
1,370	80	623	100	X	X			X	X			3/1	none		FAF
													none		FAF
								X				6/1	none	X	FAF/FFS
3,288	65							X				6/1	none		FAF/FFS
1,877	65							X				6/1	none	X	FAF/FFS
530	70			X				X		X		5/15	none	X	FAF/FFS/AFSA*
2,769	60	1,420	100	X	X	X			X	X	X		2/1		FAF
													none		AFSA
													none		AFSA
													none		AFSA
													none		AFSA
682	75	460	100	X				X					none		FAF*/FFS
2,913	85			X				X				5/15	none		FAF
154	86			X				X				3/15	none		FAF
661	80							X				6/1	none	X	FAF
443	51	184	100										2/1	X	FAF

*Preferred need analysis document.

Institution	Tuition and fees	Add'l out-of-state/district tuition	Books and supplies	Costs for campus residents			Costs for students at home		
				Room and board	Transportation	Other costs	Board only	Transportation	Other costs
‡ United States Merchant Marine Academy	2,859								
United States Military Academy	0								
United Talmudical Academy	4,000		500	4,000					
‡ University of Rochester	14,555		450	5,470	200	806	1,500	579	806
‡ University of the State of New York: Regents College	425								
† Utica College of Syracuse University	10,446		450	4,549	300	400		400	600
† Utica School of Commerce	4,080		600						
‡ Vassar College	16,510		550	5,260		600	2,460	300	600
‡ Villa Maria College of Buffalo	4,860		400				1,700	350	650
Wadhams Hall Seminary-College	3,650		500	3,400	300	700	1,700	300	700
‡ Wagner College	9,280		500	4,700	320	1,000	1,200	850	1,000
Wells College	12,750		450	4,600	300	500			500
Westchester Business Institute	8,205		540				2,200	950	
‡ Westchester Community College	1,564	2,025/—	400				500	1,000	700
‡ William Smith College	15,296		550	4,899	200	600			
Wood School	8,035		700				2,490	1,200	2,800
Yeshiva Derech Chaim	4,000		400	1,500		955			955
Yeshiva Gedolah Zichron Moshe	4,800		275	2,300	100	400		100	
Yeshiva Karlin Stolin Beth Aron Y'Israel Rabbinical Institute	3,000		400	2,000			1,000		
† Yeshiva of Nitra Rabbinical College	3,000		400	2,300		400			
‡ Yeshiva University	10,330		325	5,130	600	600	1,000	500	600

North Carolina

Institution	Tuition and fees	Add'l out-of-state/district tuition	Books and supplies	Room and board	Transportation	Other costs	Board only	Transportation	Other costs
Alamance Community College	333	2,628/—	450				1,200	600	650
Anson Community College	448	3,504/—	650				1,500	1,300	900
‡ Appalachian State University	1,160	4,573/—	300	2,450	450	450	1,000	1,000	500
‡ Asheville Buncombe Technical Community College	336	2,628/—	600				788	891	1,014
‡ Barber-Scotia College	4,000		700	2,487	1,000	1,000	1,500	800	1,000
Barton College	6,173		500	2,814	900	1,200	822	1,000	1,200
‡ Beaufort County Community College	333	2,628/—	441				1,330	1,323	484
Belmont Abbey College	7,870		500	3,804	800	1,120		1,200	960
‡ Bennett College	5,230		600	2,250	1,500	1,000		400	1,000
‡ Bladen Community College	341	2,628/—	290				450	710	1,504
Blanton's Junior College	4,025		750						
† Blue Ridge Community College	336	2,628/—	450				1,500	989	487
Brevard College	4,700		400	3,500	700	900	2,000	700	600
‡ Brunswick Community College	339	2,628/—	390				1,500	1,089	900
† Caldwell Community College and Technical Institute	330	2,628/—	400				1,620	900	1,350
‡ Campbell University	6,844		400	2,584	535	1,350	1,465	1,500	1,000
‡ Cape Fear Community College	342	2,628/—	600				1,800	1,200	816
‡ Carteret Community College	331	2,628/—	425				1,500	800	700
‡ Catawba College	7,300		300	3,500	450	625	1,800	550	625
‡ Catawba Valley Community College	333	2,628/—	800					900	800
Cecils College	3,760		400				1,503	911	1,080
‡ Central Carolina Community College	336	2,628/—	350				1,550	1,400	850
‡ Central Piedmont Community College	323	2,628/—	500				1,700	1,500	875

†Figures are projected for 1991-92.   ‡Figures are for 1990-91.

| All aid | | Need–based aid | | Grants and scholarships | | | | | | | | Financial aid deadlines | | Inst aid form | Need analysis document |
Total freshmen	Percent receiving aid	Freshmen judged to have need	Percent offered aid	Need–based Acad	Music/ drama	Art	Athl	Nonneed–based Acad	Music/ drama	Art	Athl	Priority	Closing		
284	20	63										1/15	1/30		FAF
															AFSA
1,189	76	760	100	X	X			X	X			2/1	none	X	FAF*/FFS
													7/1	X	FAF/FFS
362	68	273	92	X				X				3/15	none		FAF
345	85							X					none		FAF
568	50	247	96									1/15		X	FAF
170	65	170	100	X				X	X	X	X		none		FAF*/FFS/AFSA
7	78	5	100					X				8/1	none		FAF/FFS/AFSA/ AFSSA*
308	70	191	100	X	X		X	X	X		X	4/1	5/1	X	FAF
79	78							X				2/15	none		FAF*/FFS
													none		FAF
				X				X	X	X			none	X	FAF*/AFSA/AFSSA
228	43	105	100	X	X	X							2/15	X	FAF
335	93	312	100					X					none	X	FAF*/AFSA
													none		AFSA
															FAF
													none		AFSA
													none		FAF/FFS*
603	75	270	100					X					4/15	X	FAF
925	18	205	100	X				X				5/15	none	X	FAF/FFS*
294	29	74	100	X									none		FAF*/FFS/AFSA
1,829	48	907	98					X	X	X	X	3/15	none	X	FAF*/FFS/AFSA
1,730	27	224	100	X				X				3/1	none		FFS
241	95	219	100					X			X	3/15	none	X	FAF/FFS*
281	80	200	100	X	X	X	X	X	X	X	X	4/15	none		FAF/FFS*
306	26			X				X				6/1	none		FAF/FFS/AFSA*
203	74	118	100					X			X	4/1	none		FAF*/FFS
188	80			X			X	X			X		4/15		FAF*/FFS
274	40	105	100									8/15	none	X	FAF/AFSA*
													none		FFS
504	15	198	100	X				X				8/15	none		FAF*/FFS/AFSA
418	74	165	100					X	X	X	X	4/1	none		FAF*/FFS
322	38			X				X				8/1	none	X	FAF*/FFS/AFSA/SF
820	25	300	100					X				5/1	none		FAF/FFS*/AFSA
934	85							X	X		X	3/15	none		FAF/FFS*
682	45							X				3/15	none	X	FAF*/FFS/AFSA
690	60	150	100	X								8/1	none	X	FAF/FFS/AFSA/SF; FAF/FFS/AFSA
219	85	95	100					X	X		X	3/30	none		FAF*/FFS
													none		FFS
201	80			X									none	X	FAF*/FFS
930	30	185	100	X								5/15	none		FAF*/FFS
													none	X	FAF*/FFS/AFSA/SF

*Preferred need analysis document.

Institution	Tuition and fees	Add'l out-of-state/ district tuition	Books and supplies	Costs for campus residents			Costs for students at home		
				Room and board	Transportation	Other costs	Board only	Transportation	Other costs
Chowan College	5,380		550	2,600	475	1,300		1,500	1,300
Cleveland Community College	339	2,628/—	450				2,000	750	1,175
‡ Coastal Carolina Community College	336	2,628/—	400				1,600	450	800
‡ College of the Albemarle	345	2,628/—	325				1,500	783	735
‡ Craven Community College	342	2,628/—	500				2,000	700	500
Davidson College	13,680		400	4,160		800	2,100	250	800
‡ Davidson County Community College	338	2,628/—	500				1,500	1,030	470
† Duke University	15,101		544	4,960	800	985	2,650	600	1,000
‡ Durham Technical Community College	330	2,628/—	400				1,100	1,200	750
‡ East Carolina University	1,140	4,490/—	360	2,673	130	650	1,305	185	650
‡ East Coast Bible College	3,005		400	1,950					
‡ Edgecombe Community College	333	2,628/—	375				2,350	850	1,500
‡ Elizabeth City State University	1,077	4,029/—	300	2,464	490	810	2,000	600	810
† Elon College	7,150		400	3,350	570	1,050	1,620	800	1,050
‡ Fayetteville State University	981	4,573/—	325	2,150	250	500		250	500
‡ Fayetteville Technical Community College	324	2,628/—	600				1,200		600
† Forsyth Technical Community College	445	3,944/—	500				2,000	650	700
Gardner-Webb College	6,720		500	3,200	550	625		1,500	1,000
Gaston College	345	2,628/—	1,000					1,000	1,000
Greensboro College	6,830		450	3,280	650	650	1,500	650	650
‡ Guilford College	9,540		425	3,929	460	608	1,700	460	608
‡ Guilford Technical Community College	338	2,628/—	650				1,800	300	450
Halifax Community College	333	2,628/—	377				1,500	1,031	896
‡ Haywood Community College	335	2,628/—	400				1,000	1,200	870
High Point College	6,710		540	3,200	550	900	1,500	1,070	1,100
‡ Isothermal Community College	345	2,628/—	377				2,900	700	400
† James Sprunt Community College	339	2,628/—	400				1,163	1,237	600
John Wesley College	3,569		300		100	1,500	1,500	765	1,500
‡ Johnson C. Smith University	5,671		400	2,158	910	1,560	1,072	950	1,560
† Johnston Community College	336	2,628/—	475				1,600	1,250	900
† Lees-McRae College	5,506		400	2,844	350	700	1,330	700	700
‡ Lenoir Community College	342	2,628/—	450				1,500	680	540
Lenoir-Rhyne College	8,584		500	3,326	300	600	1,860	300	600
‡ Livingstone College	3,784		675	2,494	700	750	1,354	700	750
Louisburg College	5,639		450	2,840	500	1,000	1,500	700	1,000
‡ Mars Hill College	6,250		500	2,850	1,000	800	1,800	800	200
‡ Martin Community College	330	2,628/—	400				3,024	990	400
‡ Mayland Community College	333	2,628/—	600				980	893	1,087
† McDowell Technical Community College	333	2,628/—	400				1,700	619	450
Meredith College	5,720		400	2,820	250	900	2,000	450	700
Methodist College	7,700		600	3,100	400	1,360	2,050	600	1,360
‡ Mitchell Community College	342	2,628/—	375				1,575	772	1,334
† Montgomery Community College	327	2,628/—	600				1,500	1,936	1,885
Montreat-Anderson College	5,832		500	3,118	500	900	1,768	600	500
Mount Olive College	6,600		400	2,550	300	600	1,350		
‡ Nash Community College	333	2,628/—	600					600	400
‡ North Carolina Agricultural and Technical State University	1,113	4,573/—	495	2,344	380	967	1,500	412	1,083
‡ North Carolina Central University	1,054	4,573/—	290	2,764	246	630	1,100		630

†Figures are projected for 1991-92.   ‡Figures are for 1990-91.

All aid		Need–based aid		Grants and scholarships								Financial aid deadlines		Inst aid form	Need analysis document
				Need–based				Nonneed–based							
Total fresh–men	Percent receiving aid	Freshmen judged to have need	Percent offered aid	Acad	Music/drama	Art	Athl	Acad	Music/drama	Art	Athl	Priority	Closing		
354	80	364	98	X	X	X	X	X	X	X	X	3/1	none		FAF*/FFS/AFSA/AFSSA
648	10			X									none		FFS
1,311	75	493	82	X			X					7/15	none	X	AFSA
377	28	107	100	X	X								3/1		FAF/FFS*/AFSA/SF
				X			X	X				4/1	none	X	FAF/FFS*/AFSA
426	61	130	100	X				X	X	X	X		2/1	X	FAF
1,268	20	365	100	X									none	X	FAF/FFS*/AFSA
1,750	38	664	97					X	X		X	2/15	none		FAF
1,674	50	512	100	X									none	X	FFS
				X	X	X	X	X	X	X	X	4/15	none		FAF/FFS/AFSA/SF*
45	56			X	X								5/15		FFS
666	42	151	100	X				X			X		7/15		FAF*/FFS/AFSA/AFSSA
309	91							X	X		X	5/1	none	X	FAF/FFS*
709	40	184	100	X	X		X	X	X		X	5/1	none	X	FAF
													none	X	FAF*/FFS
2,532	69	1,723	98	X				X				6/1	none		FFS
				X				X				5/1	none	X	FFS
300	65	178	100	X	X		X	X	X		X	4/1	none		FAF/FFS*/AFSA
1,355	39	172	100	X				X					none	X	FAF*/FFS/AFSA; FAF*/FFS
222	59	104	100	X	X	X		X	X	X		3/15	none		FAF
333	63	174	98	X	X	X		X	X	X			3/1		FAF
													none		FAF/FFS*
													none		FFS
544	27			X								4/1	none		FAF/FFS*
391	56	119	100	X				X			X	3/1	none	X	FAF*/FFS/SF
													none	X	FAF/FFS*/AFSA
222	45	153	100	X				X				7/1	none		FAF/FFS*/AFSA
													none		FAF
322	90			X	X		X					5/15	none		FAF/FFS*
721	45			X				X				6/1	none	X	FAF*/FFS
397	87	149	100	X	X		X	X	X		X	3/15	none	X	FAF*/FFS
													none	X	FAF/FFS/AFSA*
305	57	201	100	X	X		X	X	X		X	3/1	none		FAF/FFS/SF*
302	84			X	X		X	X	X		X	5/1	5/15		FAF*/FFS
450	85	195	100	X	X		X	X	X		X	3/1	none	X	FAF*/FFS
291	72	198	100					X			X	5/1	none		FAF*/FFS/AFSA
115	50			X				X				8/1	none		FAF/FFS/AFSA*
304	52	112	100	X								4/30	none	X	FFS*/AFSA
300	34			X								8/1	none		AFSA
383	47	181	100	X	X	X		X	X	X		2/15	none	X	FAF
241	81	216	100	X				X				5/1	none		FAF/FFS/AFSA/SF*
392	14	39	92	X	X	X		X	X	X		7/1	none		FAF/FFS*/AFSA
324	52	175	94									7/15	none		FAF/FFS*
145	85	87	100	X				X		X	X	3/1	none		FAF*/FFS
148	95	120	100					X	X	X	X	3/1	5/1		FAF
		148	95									3/15	none		FAF/FFS/AFSA*
				X	X	X		X	X	X	X	5/15	none		FAF/FFS*
794	69							X				4/14	none		FAF/FFS*

*Preferred need analysis document.

Institution	Tuition and fees	Add'l out-of-state/district tuition	Books and supplies	Costs for campus residents			Costs for students at home		
				Room and board	Transportation	Other costs	Board only	Transportation	Other costs
† North Carolina School of the Arts	1,551	5,086/—	500	2,999		1,200	1,500		900
‡ North Carolina State University	1,109	4,709/—	500	3,030		1,000	2,000	300	1,000
‡ North Carolina Wesleyan College	6,730		400	3,250	400	1,525	1,500	500	600
† Pamlico Community College	330	2,628/—	340				3,165	1,356	1,623
Peace College	4,545		500	3,875	600	1,000	1,500	500	1,600
‡ Pembroke State University	841	4,029/—	400	2,070	300	500		620	500
‡ Pfeiffer College	6,620		650	2,960	1,700	1,200	1,360	1,200	1,500
Phillips Junior College									
Fayetteville	4,498						2,000	400	500
Greensboro	4,598							400	500
Hardbarger Campus	4,498		400						
‡ Winston-Salem	4,498							400	500
Piedmont Bible College	3,190		450	2,500	500	550	1,200	800	550
‡ Piedmont Community College	333	2,628/—	800				1,800	1,800	850
‡ Pitt Community College	333	2,628/—	400				1,100	1,260	400
Queens College	9,300		450	4,400	975	850	1,700	1,375	850
‡ Randolph Community College	337	2,628/—	1,000					800	850
‡ Richmond Community College	342	2,628/—	400				1,500	700	500
Roanoke Bible College	2,800		280	2,400	350	200	1,900	950	200
† Roanoke-Chowan Community College	339	2,628/—	300					906	150
‡ Robeson Community College	333	2,628/—	250						
† Rockingham Community College	342	2,628/—	350					700	
‡ Rowan-Cabarrus Community College	339	2,628/—	255				1,100	500	500
‡ St. Andrews Presbyterian College	8,150		400	3,670	300	350			
St. Augustine's College	4,950		500	3,200	600	550		270	200
St. Mary's College	6,265		550	5,320	575	1,400	1,300	575	1,000
‡ Salem College	9,075		600	5,600	500	800	1,200	500	800
‡ Sampson Community College	345	2,628/—	500				1,700	700	900
† Sandhills Community College	339	2,628/—	400				1,100	1,260	581
‡ Shaw University	4,530		850	3,190	1,000	1,000			1,000
Southeastern Baptist Theological Seminary	975			945					
‡ Southeastern Community College	344	2,628/—	388				1,500	1,247	846
‡ Southwestern Community College	339	2,628/—	300				1,500	760	550
‡ Stanly Community College	333	2,628/—	500				1,500	825	
‡ Surry Community College	333	2,628/—	400				1,500	940	350
‡ Tri-County Community College	328	2,628/—	259				562	1,185	450
University of North Carolina									
‡ Asheville	1,043	4,029/—	350	2,900	900	700	1,170	800	700
‡ Chapel Hill	1,059	4,709/—	450	3,390	50	930	1,500	110	612
‡ Charlotte	1,032	4,573/—	375	2,592	555	675	1,350	1,130	675
‡ Greensboro	1,363	4,709/—	425	3,345	300	750	800	750	750
‡ Wilmington	1,187	4,573/—	444	3,034	277	1,303	800	804	1,303
† Vance-Granville Community College	342	2,628/—	475				1,500	900	400
† Wake Forest University	10,670		400	3,960	450	700	500	600	1,500
‡ Wake Technical Community College	324	2,628/—	350				1,300	1,500	1,000
Warren Wilson College	8,515		400	2,852	540	718	1,500	900	718
Wayne Community College	342	2,628/—	450				1,500	500	400

†Figures are projected for 1991-92. ‡Figures are for 1990-91.

All aid		Need–based aid		Grants and scholarships								Financial aid deadlines		Inst aid form	Need analysis document
				Need–based				Nonneed–based							
Total freshmen	Percent receiving aid	Freshmen judged to have need	Percent offered aid	Acad	Music/drama	Art	Athl	Acad	Music/drama	Art	Athl	Priority	Closing		
107	66	72	100		X	X		X	X	X		4/1	none		FAF
3,377	52	1,537	68	X				X			X	3/15	none	X	FAF*/FFS
211	70			X				X				3/1	none		FAF*/FFS
102	80												none		FAF/FFS;FFS
201	69	58	100	X	X	X	X	X	X	X	X	4/1	none		FAF*/FFS
				X	X	X	X		X	X	X	4/15	none		FAF
209	84							X	X		X	5/1	none		FAF/FFS*
													none	X	AFSA
													none		AFSA
													none	X	AFSA
240	90			X									none		AFSA
62	100	62	100					X	X				1/1		FAF/FFS/AFSA*
538	50											4/15	none		FAF/FFS*/AFSA
								X				5/1	8/24	X	FAF/FFS/AFSA*
215	80	82	100					X	X	X	X	3/1	none	X	FAF*/FFS/AFSA
														X	FAF/FFS*
249	65			X				X				8/1	none		FAF*/FFS/AFSA
														X	FAF/FFS/AFSA*
296	62	125	100	X				X					none		FFS
													none		FAF
1,133	25	330	100	X				X				5/1	none		FAF*/AFSA
690	40	199	85	X				X				8/1	none		FAF/FFS*
145	80	110	100					X	X	X	X	4/1	7/1		FAF*/FFS
687	88			X	X		X						4/15	X	FAF
151	28	42	100	X				X	X	X		4/1	none	X	FAF*/FFS
73	77	49	100					X	X			3/1	8/1	X	FAF*/FFS;FAF*/FFS/ CSS SAAC/ACT SAAC/ APSGFSA
317	24	255	100	X				X				7/1	none		FAF/FFS*/AFSA/SF
1,123	26	577	71	X				X				6/1	none	X	FAF/FFS*
													none		FAF/FFS*
811	32	330	73	X				X			X	4/1	none		FAF*/FFS
													none		FAF/FFS
				X				X				5/1	none		FAF*/FFS/AFSA; FAF*/FFS
713	50			X				X				6/1	none	X	FAF*/FFS/AFSA
317	38			X								5/31	none		FAF*/FFS
383	52	147	86	X			X	X	X	X	X	3/1	none	X	FAF
3,260	35	850	88	X	X	X	X	X	X		X	3/1	none		FAF
1,847	42	830	100	X				X			X	4/15	none		FAF
1,513	42	576	89	X	X	X	X	X	X		X	3/1	none		FAF
1,120	38	412	95	X	X	X	X	X	X	X	X	3/15	none		FAF*/FFS/AFSA
480	45	375	100	X				X					7/1		FAF/FFS*/AFSA
923	67	220	100	X			X	X	X	X	X	3/1	none	X	FAF
1,965	10	850	53									8/31	none	X	FAF*/FFS
103	80	51	100	X				X				5/1	none		FAF/FFS*/AFSA/ AFSSA/SF;FAF/FFS*/ AFSA/AFSSA/
603	16	296	87	X								4/15	none	X	FAF*/FFS/AFSA

*Preferred need analysis document.

Institution	Tuition and fees	Add'l out-of-state/ district tuition	Books and supplies	Costs for campus residents			Costs for students at home		
				Room and board	Trans-portation	Other costs	Board only	Trans-portation	Other costs
‡ Western Carolina University	1,114	4,573/—	200	2,230	500	720	1,500	800	720
† Western Piedmont Community College	337	2,628/—	450				1,500	700	1,200
† Wilkes Community College	335	2,628/—	350				1,500	400	1,125
‡ Wilson Technical Community College	330	2,628/—	550				1,700	680	1,800
Wingate College	6,120		500	2,750	680	800	650	680	800
‡ Winston-Salem State University	987	4,029/—	600	2,630	551	2,100	1,100	476	2,100

North Dakota

Institution	Tuition and fees	Add'l out-of-state/ district tuition	Books and supplies	Room and board	Trans-portation	Other costs	Board only	Trans-portation	Other costs
‡ Bismarck State College	1,596	2,424/—	420	1,928	330	945	1,575	565	660
‡ Dickinson State University	1,659	2,472/—	400	1,750		1,200			1,200
Fort Bethold Community College	1,340		300				1,800	600	800
Jamestown College	6,670		400	2,980	250	450	775	450	450
Little Hoop Community College	1,130		175					650	875
‡ Mayville State University	1,684	2,472/—	400	2,079	360	1,140		360	1,140
Medcenter One College of Nursing	5,110								
‡ Minot State University	1,653	2,476/—	525	1,746	430	1,221	1,020	426	801
‡ North Dakota State College of Science	1,560	2,424/—	400	1,695	500	1,255	1,500	500	500
North Dakota State University									
‡ Bottineau and Institute of Forestry	1,615	2,430/—	375	1,980	525	900	1,000	525	900
‡ Fargo	2,040	3,156/—	475	1,924	270	1,350		500	1,200
Standing Rock College	1,720		200				700	1,000	748
Trinity Bible College	4,608		400	3,138	530	850	2,000	530	430
† Turtle Mountain Community College	1,152		360	3,000			1,200	900	1,320
United Tribes Technical College	2,375		175	2,200	400	1,500	700	600	1,500
University of Mary	5,650		500	2,400	300	700	1,000	900	700
University of North Dakota									
‡ Grand Forks	2,040	3,018/—	400	2,190		1,618	1,500		1,626
Lake Region	1,632	2,424/—	580	2,010	540	1,030	900	540	1,030
† Williston	1,658	2,424/—	500	1,000		400		300	300
‡ Valley City State University	1,638	2,472/—	450	1,920	450	1,050		540	749

Ohio

Institution	Tuition and fees	Add'l out-of-state/ district tuition	Books and supplies	Room and board	Trans-portation	Other costs	Board only	Trans-portation	Other costs
‡ Antioch College	12,960		400	3,490	400	700		400	700
‡ Antioch School for Adult and Experiential Learning	7,650		400						
Antonelli Institute of Art and Photography	7,990		1,200	3,750				1,350	
Art Academy of Cincinnati	7,200		1,000				2,000	1,140	590
Ashland University	9,966		450	4,119	150	900	1,688	518	900
‡ Baldwin-Wallace College	9,225		375	3,675				300	
‡ Belmont Technical College	1,020	525/—	450				1,668	1,230	4,507
† Bliss College	5,900		400						
‡ Bluffton College	7,650		300	3,135		700		600	700
Bowling Green State University									
‡ Bowling Green	2,808	3,350/—	420	2,514	400	1,202		820	1,196
‡ Firelands College	2,166	3,350/—	400					720	1,413
Bradford School	7,520		600						
Bryant and Stratton Business Institute, Great Northern	4,729		600						
‡ Capital University	10,360		400	3,490	110	740	440	480	1,470
Case Western Reserve University	13,710		470	4,930		1,070			1,070

†Figures are projected for 1991-92.   ‡Figures are for 1990-91.

All aid		Need–based aid		Grants and scholarships — Need–based				Nonneed–based				Financial aid deadlines		Inst aid form	Need analysis document
Total freshmen	Percent receiving aid	Freshmen judged to have need	Percent offered aid	Acad	Music/drama	Art	Athl	Acad	Music/drama	Art	Athl	Priority	Closing		
1,000	35			X	X		X	X	X		X	4/1	none	X	FAF
1,644	40	350	99					X				4/15	none		FAF/FFS*
640	22	345	80	X	X	X		X	X	X			4/1		FAF/FFS*/AFSA*/SF
384	40	380	79	X									none		FAF/FFS*
374	75	245	100					X	X		X	3/1	none		FAF
400	86			X	X		X	X	X	X	X	6/1	none	X	FAF/FFS*/AFSA;FAF/FFS*/AFSA/APSGFSA
774	80	597	93					X	X		X	5/1	none		FAF/FFS*/AFSA/SF
309	65	300	100					X	X		X		none		FAF/FFS*/AFSA
								X						X	FAF/FFS
289	95			X	X		X	X	X		X		none		FAF/FFS*
														X	FAF/FFS
185	81	125	100	X							X	4/15	none		FAF/FFS*
650	66	371	98	X	X	X	X	X	X		X	4/15	none		FAF/FFS*/AFSA;FAF/FFS*/CSS SAAC/ACT SAAC/APSGFSA
733	81			X	X		X	X	X		X	4/15	none		FAF/FFS*
193	75			X	X		X	X			X		none		FAF/FFS*
1,359	62	840	100	X	X		X	X				3/15	4/15	X	FAF/FFS*
													none		FAF/FFS*
183	99	100	100	X	X		X	X	X		X	3/15	none		FAF/FFS*/AFSA;FAF/FFS*/AFSA/ACT SAAC
													5/1		FFS
														X	FAF/CSS SAAC
317	90	200	100	X	X	X		X	X		X	3/15	none		FAF/FFS*
1,596	51	1,003	100					X	X	X	X	3/15	none		FAF/FFS*/AFSA
188	85			X			X	X			X	3/15	none		FAF/FFS*/AFSA
				X			X	X			X	3/15	none	X	FFS
196	85	126	100	X	X	X	X	X	X	X	X	4/15	none		FAF/FFS*/AFSA
119	66	75	100					X					5/1	X	FAF*/FFS
													none		FAF
													none		FAF/AFSA
57	90				X			X		X		3/15	none	X	FAF/AFSA/SF*
727	95	382	100	X	X	X	X	X	X	X	X	3/15	none		FAF
513	95	495	100	X				X	X			5/1	none	X	FAF
								X					none		FAF/AFSA*
													none	X	AFSA
171	100			X	X	X		X				5/15	none		FAF*/FFS
2,864	55	1,632	100	X				X	X	X	X	2/15	4/1		FAF*/AFSA/SF
								X				4/1	none		FAF
169	85												none		FAF/AFSA*
160	70												none		FAF/FFS/AFSA*
267	90	200	100	X				X	X			3/1	7/15		FAF
653	80	400	100	X				X	X	X		2/1	none		FAF*/FFS

*Preferred need analysis document.

Institution	Tuition and fees	Add'l out-of-state/district tuition	Books and supplies	Costs for campus residents			Costs for students at home		
				Room and board	Trans-portation	Other costs	Board only	Trans-portation	Other costs
Cedarville College	5,709		525	3,390		900	1,785		1,050
† Central Ohio Technical College	1,822	720/—	550				2,000	1,020	700
‡ Central State University	2,247	2,541/—	360	3,753	240	300		650	300
‡ Chatfield College	3,570		340				675	755	1,075
Cincinnati Bible College and Seminary	3,420		500	2,966	750	1,500	1,536	1,200	1,500
Cincinnati College of Mortuary Science	6,010		550					750	900
Cincinnati Metropolitan College	4,670		500				1,962	210	2,000
† Cincinnati Technical College	2,200	1,400/—	600				1,700	450	900
Circleville Bible College	3,825		250	3,000	325	750	1,230	450	2,000
‡ Clark State Community College	1,737	1,575/—	585				1,500	330	750
Cleveland College of Jewish Studies	3,015		150						
† Cleveland Institute of Art	10,500		1,000	4,310	520	800	1,500	1,560	800
‡ Cleveland Institute of Music	11,005		600	4,735	650	500		425	500
‡ Cleveland State University	2,397	2,397/—	475	3,069		700	1,500	350	700
College of Mount St. Joseph	8,170		400	3,810	400	600	1,830	650	600
College of Wooster	13,410		400	4,240	150	480	1,500		
Columbus College of Art and Design	8,200		900	4,500	300	750		300	750
Columbus State Community College	1,656	1,944/—	390				1,782	612	988
Cuyahoga Community College									
‡ Eastern Campus	1,293	2,025/405	575				825	450	450
‡ Metropolitan Campus	1,293	2,025/405	450				1,590	725	775
‡ Western Campus	1,293	2,025/405	525				1,503	330	1,053
Davis Junior College of Business	4,776		550					1,000	600
Defiance College	8,690		400	3,160	200	1,000	1,800	1,020	1,000
Denison University	14,700		450	3,980		600	1,500		600
DeVry Institute of Technology: Columbus	5,015		500				1,839	2,382	1,357
‡ Dyke College	4,500		450				1,200	700	900
‡ Edison State Community College	1,575	1,440/—	535				1,500	638	400
ETI Technical College	3,885		1,450						500
Franciscan University of Steubenville	7,190		500	3,900	1,200	800	1,700	1,200	800
‡ Franklin University	3,630		425				4,000	600	480
God's Bible School and College	2,720		295	2,140	425	545	650	1,050	950
Heidelberg College	11,680		400	3,730	400	400	1,760	500	
Hiram College	12,165		400	3,780		900	1,790	500	900
Hocking Technical College	1,563	1,548/—	525		312	1,089	940	1,760	489
ITT Technical Institute									
‡ Dayton	7,225		1,200				2,000	500	1,400
‡ Youngstown	6,923							740	
Jefferson Technical College	1,148	675/135	500				1,700	360	400
John Carroll University	9,600		600	5,050	800	450	3,050	1,875	575
Kent State University									
‡ Ashtabula Regional Campus	2,445	3,000/—	375				900	636	2,004
‡ East Liverpool Regional Campus	2,445	3,000/—	400					462	600
‡ Kent	3,006	3,000/—	450	3,008	518	1,266		836	1,266
‡ Salem Regional Campus	2,445	3,000/—	400				1,500	720	1,100
‡ Stark Campus	2,445	3,000/—	400				1,500	720	1,100
‡ Trumbull Regional Campus	2,445	3,000/—	450					300	250
‡ Tuscarawas Campus	2,445	3,000/2	375						
Kenyon College	16,050		650	3,376	150	400			

†Figures are projected for 1991-92.   ‡Figures are for 1990-91.

| All aid | | Need-based aid | | Grants and scholarships | | | | | | | | Financial aid deadlines | | Inst aid form | Need analysis document |
| | | | | Need-based | | | | Nonneed-based | | | | | | | |
Total freshmen	Percent receiving aid	Freshmen judged to have need	Percent offered aid	Acad	Music/drama	Art	Athl	Acad	Music/drama	Art	Athl	Priority	Closing		
481	74	348	87	X				X	X		X	4/1	none	X	FAF*/FFS
458	45	215	100	X				X				4/15	none		FAF/FFS
947	70			X	X	X		X	X	X		5/15	8/1		FAF
35	55	24	100	X								7/15	none		FAF*/AFSA;FAF
173	95	159	100	X				X	X			4/1	none	X	FAF*/FFS/AFSA
10	50	2	100										none		AFSA
150	98												none	X	FAF/FFS
		1,023	80	X				X			X	3/15	none	X	FAF*/AFSA
64	95			X	X								none	X	FAF/FFS
529	35			X			X						none	X	FAF*/AFSA/SF
													none		
98	60			X		X		X		X		4/20	none	X	FAF
33	90			X	X			X	X				3/1		FAF
1,531	33	525	90	X				X	X	X	X	4/15	none	X	FAF
246	94	192	100	X				X		X	X	4/15	none		FAF*/FFS/AFSA
496	64	255	100	X				X	X			2/15	none		FAF*/FFS
319	85	245	100							X			5/1	X	FAF
														X	FAF*/FFS
4,353	26			X	X	X	X	X				5/31	none		FAF
													none		FAF/FFS/AFSA
				X	X	X	X	X	X	X	X		none	X	FAF/FFS
359	80			X				X					none		AFSA
192	96	161	100	X	X		X	X	X		X	3/1	none		FAF*/FFS
555	54	213	100	X	X	X		X	X	X		4/1	none		FAF*/FFS
910	81							X					none		FAF
194	80			X			X	X			X	8/15	none		FAF*/FFS
								X			X		4/1		AFSA
													none	X	AFSA
248	80	191	100	X				X				3/1	5/1		FAF*/FFS/AFSA
177	57	46	100	X				X				5/30	none	X	FAF
64	73			X	X			X	X			7/15	none		AFSSA
270	82	208	100					X	X			4/1	none		FAF*/FFS/AFSA; FAF*/FFS/AFSA/ AFSSA/APSGFSA
189	85	175	100					X	X			3/1	8/1		FAF*/FFS
3,600	60			X								4/29	none	X	FAF*/FFS
279	89											8/1	none		SF
146	90											9/29	none	X	AFSA
1,254	55							X				6/1	none	X	AFSA
795	70	510	100	X				X				3/1	6/1		FAF
208	51			X				X				4/1	8/1		FAF
157	63			X				X				4/1	none		FAF
3,290	70			X				X	X	X	X	2/14	4/1		FAF
								X				4/1	none		FAF
								X				3/15	none	X	FAF*/AFSA
657	70			X	X	X	X	X				4/1	none	X	FAF*/FFS/AFSA/SF; FAF*/FFS/AFSA/ APSGFSA/SF
								X					7/15		FAF*/FFS/AFSA
								X					2/15		FAF

*Preferred need analysis document.

Institution	Tuition and fees	Add'l out-of-state/district tuition	Books and supplies	Costs for campus residents			Costs for students at home		
				Room and board	Trans-portation	Other costs	Board only	Trans-portation	Other costs
Kettering College of Medical Arts	3,840		600	2,867	333	325	840	185	300
Lake Erie College	7,950		425	4,000	700	950	4,000	700	900
‡ Lakeland Community College	1,536	2,086/263	435				1,503	933	1,053
‡ Lima Technical College	1,575	1,586/—	600				2,000	775	450
‡ Lorain County Community College	1,704	2,925/450	500				1,350	400	900
Lourdes College	5,750		440				1,685	700	505
Malone College	7,860		400	3,000	424	1,030	800	880	940
Marietta College	11,800		425	3,460	500	500		600	
Marion Technical College	1,956	1,764/—	460					1,000	
Miami University									
‡ Hamilton Campus	2,468	3,980/—	450				1,700	720	772
Middletown Campus	478	3,980/—	400					650	750
‡ Oxford Campus	3,388	3,980/—	450	3,100	280	1,280	1,700	720	972
Miami-Jacobs College	3,645		795				1,881	1,062	2,043
‡ Mount Union College	10,680		400	3,100	800	550	1,500	900	550
Mount Vernon Nazarene College	6,070		400	3,030	400	900	900	500	700
Muskingum Area Technical College	1,965	1,350/—	450						
Muskingum College	11,855		450	3,510	400	700		400	700
‡ North Central Technical College	2,268	1,998/—	358				1,500	753	935
‡ Northwest Technical College	1,935	2,880/—	600				750	990	450
‡ Northwestern College	2,655		500		225	1,000		900	675
‡ Notre Dame College of Ohio	6,270		450	3,200	425	625	1,600	775	625
Oberlin College	16,817		475	5,155		450	2,575		450
‡ Ohio Dominican College	6,660		310	3,680	290	725	1,500	735	725
‡ Ohio Northern University	10,845		600	3,195	275	520			
Ohio State University									
‡ Agricultural Technical Institute	2,253	4,375/—	420		670	2,921	528	1,274	2,338
‡ Columbus Campus	2,343	4,599/—	420	3,690	390	1,476	528	708	2,352
‡ Lima Campus	2,253	4,599/—	420				528	1,262	2,338
‡ Mansfield Campus	2,253	4,599/—	420				528	1,262	2,338
‡ Marion Campus	2,253	4,599/—	420				528	1,262	2,338
‡ Newark Campus	2,253	4,599/—	420				528	1,262	2,338
Ohio University									
† Athens	2,946	3,345/—	425	3,633	425	1,200		1,800	
Belmont Campus	2,199	3,084/—	390					1,995	
‡ Chillicothe Campus	2,199	3,084/—	500					1,842	
‡ Ironton Campus	2,199	3,084/—	450				1,728	1,842	
‡ Lancaster Campus	2,199	3,084/—	450					400	
‡ Zanesville Campus	2,199	3,084/—	480					2,019	549
Ohio Valley Business College	2,810		625			75			
Ohio Wesleyan University	13,610		450	4,884	200	650	1,500	100	650
Otterbein College	10,800		315	3,912	210	720	1,600	1,250	550
Owens Technical College									
‡ Findlay Campus	1,615	1,285/—	400		1,000	800	1,700	1,000	800
‡ Toledo	1,580	1,320/—	670				1,700	1,000	
‡ Pontifical College Josephinum	4,270		300	2,800	1,000	300			
‡ Rabbinical College of Telshe	1,610		250	2,400					
RETS Technical Center	6,600		700				1,100	900	945
‡ Shawnee State University	1,893	804/—	420		500	700	2,100	520	720
† Sinclair Community College	1,305	1,350/450	475				1,500	360	1,000

†Figures are projected for 1991-92.   ‡Figures are for 1990-91.

All aid		Need–based aid		Grants and scholarships								Financial aid deadlines		Inst aid form	Need analysis document
				Need–based				Nonneed–based							
Total freshmen	Percent receiving aid	Freshmen judged to have need	Percent offered aid	Acad	Music/drama	Art	Athl	Acad	Music/drama	Art	Athl	Priority	Closing		
108	33			X									none		FAF/FFS*
68	93	65	100	X	X		X	X	X	X	X	4/1	8/22	X	FAF*/FFS
				X	X	X	X	X	X	X	X	3/1	none	X	FAF/FFS/AFSA*
														X	FAF*/FFS
													none	X	AFSA
130	26	44	100	X									none		FAF/SF
285	90	267	100	X	X		X	X	X		X	3/15	4/15	X	FAF
315	82	199	99					X	X	X		5/1	none		FAF*/FFS;FAF*/FFS/ CSS SAAC
1,148	60	320	94	X				X				7/1	9/15		FAF/FFS/AFSA*/SF
926	16	161	76	X				X				2/15	none	X	FAF
													none	X	FAF*/FFS/AFSA/SF; FAF*/FFS/AFSA/ AFSSA/APSGFSA/SF
3,381	35	1,112	86	X				X	X	X	X	2/15	none	X	FAF*/FFS
221	85	204	69	X									none		AFSA
427	90	339	100					X	X	X		4/1	none		FAF
365	87	231	100	X	X			X	X		X	4/30	none	X	FAF
															AFSA
346	88	211	100	X				X	X	X		3/1	8/1		FAF*/FFS
685	51	429	100	X				X				4/1	none		FAF/SF
								X					none		FAF/AFSA/SF
243	63	274	100	X				X					none		FAF/FFS/AFSA
73	95	40	100	X			X	X				3/1	none	X	FAF
571	44	254	100					X	X				2/1	X	FAF
187	82							X			X	3/1	none		FAF
525	92							X	X	X		5/1	7/31	X	FAF*/FFS/AFSA
				X				X					none		FAF*/FFS
6,072	65			X	X	X		X	X	X	X	3/1	none		FAF*/FFS
451	45			X	X	X		X	X	X		4/1	none		FAF*/FFS
348	40			X	X	X	X	X	X	X	X	4/1	none	X	FAF*/FFS
				X	X	X		X				4/1	none		FAF*/FFS
444	30			X				X				4/1	none		FAF*/FFS
3,050	65							X	X	X	X	2/15	3/15		FAF
															FAF
492	40												4/1	X	FAF
													none		FAF
												2/15	none		FAF
								X				2/15	none		FAF
150	80	84	89								X		none		AFSA
571	80	348	100					X	X	X		3/1	none		FAF
399	90	330	100					X	X	X		3/1	4/15		FAF*/FFS/AFSA
													none		FAF
2,062	40						X	X				3/15	none	X	FAF
12	95	3	100					X				6/30	none		FAF*/FFS
															FAF
													none	X	AFSA
670	85			X	X	X	X	X	X	X	X	6/15	none		FAF*/FFS
4,196	6			X				X	X	X	X	4/15	none		FAF*/AFSA;FAF

*Preferred need analysis document.

Institution	Tuition and fees	Add'l out-of-state/district tuition	Books and supplies	Costs for campus residents			Costs for students at home		
				Room and board	Trans-portation	Other costs	Board only	Trans-portation	Other costs
Southern Ohio College	5,530		500				1,250	600	
Southern State Community College	1,869	1,599/—	400				1,500	750	
‡ Stark Technical College	1,858	900/—	672				1,500	1,050	1,475
Terra Technical College	1,596	2,226/—	500					750	400
Tiffin University	6,100		500	3,380	350	980	1,600	450	850
‡ Union Institute	5,463		300						
University of Akron									
‡ Akron	2,820	2,985/—	350	3,200	490	933	1,500	1,000	803
‡ Wayne College	2,278	3,315/—	350				1,500	960	720
University of Cincinnati									
‡ Access Colleges	2,838	3,936/—	426	3,948	516	1,149	1,974	894	1,026
‡ Cincinnati	2,838	3,936/—	399	3,948	487	1,084	1,860	842	970
‡ Clermont College	2,706	3,936/—	400				1,300		
‡ Raymond Walters College	2,706	3,936/—	400				1,200	300	1,200
University of Dayton	9,410		500	3,760	300	900	1,700	300	600
University of Findlay	9,064		500	3,960	400	600	1,000	800	500
University of Rio Grande	1,890	3,171/810	550	3,000	325	1,450	1,500	1,485	1,350
‡ University of Toledo	2,526	3,255/—	500	2,805	380	919	800	664	917
Urbana University	7,476		500	3,880	150	600	1,500	150	600
‡ Ursuline College	6,600		392	3,380	376	790	2,000	635	790
Virginia Marti College of Fashion and Art	6,940		600				2,700	368	1,512
Walsh College	6,220		300	3,350	350	400		600	1,400
Washington State Community College	1,944	1,836/—	500				1,200	500	500
‡ West Side Institute of Technology	5,900		782				2,043	936	1,353
‡ Wilberforce University	5,816		500	3,200	820	1,392	1,644	820	1,658
Wilmington College	8,680		495	3,200	795	1,140	1,560	1,145	1,200
† Wittenberg University	13,400		350	4,000		900			
Wright State University									
† Dayton	2,649	2,649/—	450	3,360	553	912		1,310	912
‡ Lake Campus	2,196	2,469/—	420					1,200	
Xavier University	9,700		500	4,110	450	700	1,940	450	700
† Youngstown State University	2,304	1,440/—	480	3,405	390	930	1,800	900	930
Oklahoma									
‡ Bacone College	2,660		500	2,900					
† Bartlesville Wesleyan College	5,650		250	2,900	500	600	700	500	600
‡ Cameron University	1,270	1,757/—	500	2,200		900	1,500	250	800
‡ Carl Albert State College	864	1,478/—	450		300	400		700	900
‡ Central State University	1,160	1,757/—	450	1,992	500	1,500		600	1,000
‡ Connors State College	882	1,478/—	385	1,840	350	1,000	650	700	340
‡ East Central University	1,190	1,757/—	350	1,988	400	1,200	900	600	1,200
‡ Eastern Oklahoma State College	864	1,478/—	500	1,994	250	500	1,250	900	500
‡ El Reno Junior College	864	1,478/—	465					473	1,176
Flaming Rainbow University	3,500		400				700	880	1,700
Hillsdale Free Will Baptist College	2,617		400	2,540	400	700	300	1,000	2,000
‡ Langston University	1,233	1,757/—	368	2,100					
† Mid-America Bible College	3,872		400	3,480	1,060	1,155	1,350	660	2,100
‡ Murray State College	879	1,478/—	400	2,130					
‡ Northeastern Oklahoma Agricultural and Mechanical College	819	1,478/—	330	1,877	300	638			638
‡ Northeastern State University	1,190	1,757/—	350	2,088	540	625		440	625

†Figures are projected for 1991-92.   ‡Figures are for 1990-91.

Total fresh-men	Percent receiving aid	Freshmen judged to have need	Percent offered aid	Need-based Acad	Music/drama	Art	Athl	Nonneed-based Acad	Music/drama	Art	Athl	Priority	Closing	Inst aid form	Need analysis document
551	30							X	X	X		7/1	none		AFSA
													none		FAF/FFS/AFSA/SF*;
															FAF/FFS/AFSA/ AFSSA/APSGFSA/SF*
				X				X				5/1	none		FAF
731	60							X				8/20	none		FAF/FFS/AFSA/SF*
215	77	167	100	X			X	X			X	3/31	none		FAF*/FFS/AFSA/SF
													none		FAF
4,006	50	1,500	100	X				X	X	X	X	2/1	4/1		FAF
															FAF
												3/1	none		FAF*/FFS
2,322	52			X	X			X	X		X	3/1	none		FAF*/FFS
				X	X			X	X	X		3/1	none		FAF*/FFS
													none		FAF*/FFS/AFSA
1,475	89	1,072	100					X	X	X	X	3/31	none	X	FAF*/FFS/SF
373	85	345	93	X	X		X	X	X		X	4/1	8/1		FAF*/FFS
581	66	349	100	X	X	X	X	X	X		X	4/15	none	X	FAF
4,122	65			X	X	X	X	X	X	X	X	4/1	none	X	FAF*/FFS
163	100	128	100	X				X	X		X	5/1	none		FAF*/FFS/AFSA/SF
120	90			X		X		X				3/15	none	X	FAF
													none	X	AFSA
394	94	191	100	X			X	X			X	3/1	8/1	X	FAF*/FFS/AFSA
322	79			X				X					none		FAF/FFS/AFSA*
													none	X	AFSA
243	95	231	100	X				X				4/30	6/1	X	FAF
230	88	171	100					X	X			3/31	none	X	FAF
622	50	321	100	X	X	X		X	X	X		2/15	3/15	X	FAF
2,476	53	1,172	100	X				X	X	X	X	4/19	none	X	FAF*/FFS
203	70			X				X				3/31	none		FAF
646	85	383	100					X	X	X	X	4/15	none		FAF*/FFS/AFSA/SF
2,262	60			X	X			X	X		X	4/1	none		FAF*/FFS
													none	X	FAF/FFS*
143	81	55	100	X	X		X	X	X		X	5/1	none	X	FFS
848	42	406	100	X	X	X	X	X	X	X	X	5/15	none	X	FAF/FFS*/AFSA
													none		FFS
1,300	30	308	96	X	X	X	X	X	X	X	X	6/1	none		FAF/FFS*
1,192	68			X			X	X			X	3/31	none	X	FAF/FFS/AFSA*
499	59			X	X	X	X	X	X	X	X	4/1	none	X	FFS
1,450	70			X				X	X		X	3/1	none	X	FFS
443	22	175	100	X			X	X			X	3/30	4/15		FAF/FFS*/SF
42	100			X				X				3/30	none		FAF
51	68	42	100					X	X				none		FFS
379	38							X	X		X	3/1	none	X	FAF*/FFS
110	75							X				5/1	none	X	FAF
															FFS*/AFSSA
									X				3/1	X	FAF/FFS*
												4/1	none		FAF*/FFS

*Preferred need analysis document.

Institution	Tuition and fees	Add'l out-of-state/district tuition	Books and supplies	Costs for campus residents			Costs for students at home		
				Room and board	Trans-portation	Other costs	Board only	Trans-portation	Other costs
‡ Northern Oklahoma College	810	1,470/—	450	1,844	200	500	954	500	450
‡ Northwestern Oklahoma State University	1,187	1,757/—	450	1,648	600	1,000	824	500	1,100
Oklahoma Baptist University	4,664		400	2,800	225	1,000		1,000	1,000
† Oklahoma Christian University of Science and Arts	4,700		440	2,660	800	800	1,300	1,000	400
‡ Oklahoma City Community College	927	1,478/—	600					800	500
† Oklahoma City University	4,858		325	3,380	640	800	750	785	800
‡ Oklahoma Panhandle State University	1,261	1,757/—		1,800	400	1,000	1,500	1,000	1,000
‡ Oklahoma State University	1,523	2,751/—	405	2,744	512	1,567	850	936	716
‡ Oklahoma State University: Oklahoma City	1,103	2,790/—	550					380	900
‡ Oklahoma State University Technical Branch: Okmulgee	1,133	2,790/—	500	1,950	300	900	400	300	900
Oral Roberts University	6,025		450	3,495	1,000	1,116	1,500	1,000	1,116
† Phillips University	8,530		550	2,766	640	960	1,500	480	640
‡ Rogers State College	917	1,478/—	500	2,400	700	1,200		1,000	1,200
‡ Rose State College	782	1,478/—	600					200	100
† St. Gregory's College	3,700		420	2,660	250	700	1,500	500	700
‡ Seminole Junior College	894	1,478/—	260	1,880	86	162	960	480	826
‡ Southeastern Oklahoma State University	1,175	1,757/—	400	2,080	709	945	1,500	825	1,158
‡ Southern Nazarene University	5,070		300	3,092	350	800	1,500	550	
Southwestern College of Christian Ministries	2,960		350	2,070	600	1,000	800	600	1,000
‡ Southwestern Oklahoma State University	1,160	1,757/—	350	1,430	400	850	1,425	600	800
‡ Tulsa Junior College	864	1,478/—	335				1,100	632	466
University of Oklahoma									
‡ Health Sciences Center	1,465	3,162/—	820				1,575	800	1,400
‡ Norman	1,527	2,760/—	556	3,127	1,077	1,691	1,909	1,077	1,691
‡ University of Science and Arts of Oklahoma	1,197	1,757/—	600	1,820	250	1,200		350	1,200
University of Tulsa	7,950		500	3,300	900	900	700	1,700	900
‡ Western Oklahoma State College	819	1,478/—	450					900	400
Oregon									
Bassist College	8,400		1,700		560	1,200	1,800	600	1,200
Blue Mountain Community College	792	1,440/72	330					600	900
Central Oregon Community College	780	2,760/390	600	2,996	700	700	1,600	700	700
‡ Chemeketa Community College	828	2,160/—	510					1,060	1,060
† Clackamas Community College	795	2,055/—	475				1,500	850	750
Clatsop Community College	756	2,952/—	600				1,830	1,000	500
Columbia Christian College	6,443		375	2,872	500	625	1,728	450	750
Concordia College	8,070		400	2,550	300	500	1,350	300	500
‡ Eastern Oregon State College	1,764		450	2,910	600	900	1,600	600	900
‡ Eugene Bible College	3,307		600	2,250		900	1,400		1,500
‡ George Fox College	8,185		400	3,230	300	800	1,615	350	800
‡ Lane Community College	858	2,484/—	564				1,500	990	850
‡ Lewis and Clark College	12,588		250	4,386		700	1,500	270	700
† Linfield College	11,057		500	3,484	350	850	1,575	75	850

†Figures are projected for 1991-92.   ‡Figures are for 1990-91.

All aid		Need-based aid		Grants and scholarships								Financial aid deadlines		Inst aid form	Need analysis document
				Need-based				Nonneed-based							
Total freshmen	Percent receiving aid	Freshmen judged to have need	Percent offered aid	Acad	Music/drama	Art	Athl	Acad	Music/drama	Art	Athl	Priority	Closing		
323	65	242	100	X	X	X		X	X	X		8/1	none	X	FAF/FFS*/AFSA
													none		FAF/FFS/AFSA/ AFSSA
548	85	274	100	X	X	X	X	X	X	X	X	4/15	none		FFS
349	80	234	100					X	X	X	X	3/1	none	X	FFS
													none	X	FAF/FFS*
288	85	87	100	X	X	X	X	X	X	X	X	3/1	none		FAF*/FFS
													none		FAF/FFS*
2,319	73	928	91	X	X	X	X	X	X	X	X	3/1	none		FFS
2,685	30	750	100	X				X				7/1	none		FFS
770	60			X									none		FFS
568	91			X				X	X	X	X	4/1	none		FAF/FFS/AFSA/SF*
155	85	126	100					X	X	X	X	5/1	none		FAF/FFS/SF*
2,052	46			X				X	X	X		4/15	none		FFS
2,500	30			X	X	X	X	X	X	X	X	6/1	none		FAF/FFS*
162	78			X	X	X	X	X	X	X	X	6/1	none		FFS
													none		FAF/FFS*/AFSA/SF; FAF/FFS*/AFSA/CSS SAAC/ACT SAAC/SF
633	48			X	X		X	X	X		X	4/1	none		FFS
287	77							X	X	X	X	3/1	none	X	FAF/FFS*/AFSA
17	80							X	X			5/15	7/15		FFS
1,192	42			X	X	X	X	X	X	X	X		none		FAF/FFS*
												5/1	none		FFS
				X								3/1	none		FAF
2,576	34	1,090	95					X	X	X	X	3/1	11/1		FAF/FFS*
214	79	135	100					X	X	X	X	3/15	none		FAF/FFS*
725	74	324	100	X				X	X	X	X	3/1	none	X	FAF/FFS/AFSA/SF*
													none	X	FAF/FFS*
49	60	48	100					X				6/1			FAF*/FFS
													none		FAF
				X				X	X	X	X	4/1	none		FAF
															FAF
5,157	45				X	X	X		X	X	X	4/30	none		FAF
233	63			X				X				5/1	none		FAF*/FFS/AFSA/ AFSSA/SF;FAF*/FFS/ AFSA/CSS SAAC/ACT
79	80	56	100	X	X		X	X	X		X	4/15	none	X	FAF
70	90	60	100					X	X		X	5/1	none		FAF*/FFS/AFSA/ AFSSA/SF;FAF*/FFS/ AFSA/CSS SAAC/ACT
332	80			X	X			X	X			3/1	none		FAF*/FFS
65	80	28	100	X	X							4/15	9/1	X	FAF
187	86	168	100	X			X	X	X		X	3/1	8/1		FAF*/FFS/AFSA
5,504	22	1,480	100					X	X		X	3/15	none		FAF
437	76	240	100	X	X		X	X	X			2/15	none		FAF*/FFS;FAF*/FFS/ CSS SAAC/ACT SAAC
382	88	210	100	X	X	X	X	X	X			3/1	none	X	FAF/FFS/AFSA/ AFSSA/SF;FAF/FFS

*Preferred need analysis document.

Institution	Tuition and fees	Add'l out-of-state/district tuition	Books and supplies	Costs for campus residents			Costs for students at home		
				Room and board	Transportation	Other costs	Board only	Transportation	Other costs
‡ Linn-Benton Community College	864	2,700/—	350				1,760	600	1,688
‡ Marylhurst College	6,780		500						
Mount Angel Seminary	3,200		225	3,000		1,000			
‡ Mount Hood Community College	810	1,980/—	520				2,000	726	500
‡ Multnomah School of the Bible	4,950		360	2,900	480	800	1,670	700	600
‡ Northwest Christian College	5,264		405	3,072		1,446			1,446
‡ Oregon Health Sciences University	2,729	3,627/—	705	3,618	1,407	675	2,016	1,407	675
‡ Oregon Institute of Technology	1,890	3,702/—	500	3,180	600	1,750	1,200	200	1,750
‡ Oregon Polytechnic Institute	4,650		675				1,700	450	675
‡ Oregon State University	1,878	3,759/—	513	2,879	450	1,644	1,925	450	1,644
Pacific Northwest College of Art	6,690		700					500	2,000
Pacific University	10,477		350	3,145	100	570	1,200	100	570
Portland Community College	972	2,943/780	540				1,575	708	705
‡ Portland State University	1,917	3,759/—	600		603	1,008	585	603	774
Reed College	16,700		450	4,640		450	1,200		450
Rogue Community College	968	2,052/504	450		350		1,600	350	825
‡ Southern Oregon State College	1,824	3,174/—	500	3,050	310	1,383		618	765
‡ Southwestern Oregon Community College	792	1,584/—	350				1,500	816	380
Treasure Valley Community College	894	864/—	350	2,160	700	750		700	750
Umpqua Community College	1,053	4,032/—	450					650	600
‡ University of Oregon	1,965	3,759/—	425	2,806	250	1,145	1,575	250	1,145
University of Portland	9,080			3,500	550	550	1,880	550	550
Warner Pacific College	7,511		400	3,228	300	900	1,500	300	600
Western Baptist College	7,150		375	3,350	550	864	1,610	690	864
‡ Western Oregon State College	1,812	3,174/—	570	3,090	630	1,040	1,155	630	1,040
Willamette University	11,480		350	3,950	400	670	1,400	1,000	670
Pennsylvania									
Academy of the New Church	3,483			3,039		1,200			
Albright College	13,560		500	4,015	325	700	1,830	340	700
Allegheny College	14,850		450	4,120	330	600	750	600	600
Allentown College of St. Francis de Sales	8,000		425	4,150	500		1,985	500	
Alvernia College	6,958		450	3,630	300	400	1,500	500	400
American Institute of Design	15,315		928						
Antonelli Institute of Art and Photography	7,225		1,320	3,500			1,500	1,225	1,320
Art Institute of Philadelphia	8,170		1,600				1,200	810	1,100
Art Institute of Pittsburgh	8,040		1,073	5,279			2,166	623	1,212

†Figures are projected for 1991-92.   ‡Figures are for 1990-91.

All aid		Need-based aid		Grants and scholarships								Financial aid deadlines		Inst aid form	Need analysis document
				Need-based				Nonneed-based							
Total freshmen	Percent receiving aid	Freshmen judged to have need	Percent offered aid	Acad	Music/drama	Art	Athl	Acad	Music/drama	Art	Athl	Priority	Closing		
1,613	51			X				X	X	X	X	4/1	none		FAF
15	60	7	100	X	X	X			X	X		5/1	none		FAF*/FFS/AFSA/SF; FAF*/FFS/AFSA/CSS SAAC/ACT SAAC/SF
													none		FAF
													none	X	FAF*/FFS
75	70			X	X			X	X			3/1	5/1	X	FAF
66	95			X				X				4/15	none		FAF
		69	100									3/1	none		FAF*/FFS/AFSA/SF
359	70			X			X	X				3/1	none		FAF/FFS/AFSA/AFSSA/SF;FAF/FFS/AFSA/CSS SAAC/ACT
													none		AFSA
2,289	60			X	X			X	X		X	3/1	none		FAF/FFS/AFSA/SF; FAF/FFS/AFSA/CSS SAAC/ACT SAAC/SF
		41	100					X		X		5/1	none		FAF
309	80	162	100	X	X	X	X	X	X	X		3/15	none		FAF*/FFS;FAF*/FFS/AFSA/CSS SAAC/ACT SAAC/AFSSA/
		2,123	89	X			X				X	3/31	none		FAF/FFS/AFSA/AFSSA/SF
663	48	620	84	X				X	X	X	X	3/1	none		FAF/FFS/AFSA/AFSSA/SF*;FAF/FFS/AFSA/CSS SAAC/ACT
288	42	149	79										3/1	X	FAF
264	70			X								5/1			FAF/FFS/AFSA/AFSSA/SF;FAF/FFS/AFSA/CSS SAAC/ACT
752	60			X			X	X	X	X		3/1	none		FAF
302	45			X				X	X	X	X	3/1	none		FAF*/AFSA/SF
2,516	80			X				X	X	X	X	4/1	none		FAF*/FFS
1,410	60	250	100	X	X	X	X					3/1	none	X	FAF*/AFSA/SF
3,337	55			X				X	X	X	X	3/1	none		FAF
638	70	207	100	X				X	X		X	3/15	none	X	FAF
72	95							X	X		X	5/1	8/15		FAF
153	92	78	88					X	X		X	3/1	none		FAF
684	65	340	85	X	X		X	X	X	X		3/1	none		FAF*/AFSA/SF
388	78	342	100	X	X	X	X	X	X	X		2/15	none		FAF*/FFS/SF;FAF*/FFS/CSS SAAC/ACT SAAC/SF
												3/1	8/15		
302	65	197	100	X				X					4/1		FAF
384	75	263	100	X				X				2/15	none		FAF
236	85			X	X			X	X			2/15	5/1		APSGFSA
289	85	120	100	X	X		X	X			X	4/1			FAF
													none		APSGFSA;APSGFSA+ AFSA
155	86			X		X						7/31	8/15		AFSA/APSGFSA
													none	X	APSGFSA;FAF
1,032	85										X	3/1	none	X	FAF/FFS/AFSA/APSGFSA*

*Preferred need analysis document.

Institution	Tuition and fees	Add'l out-of-state/district tuition	Books and supplies	Costs for campus residents			Costs for students at home		
				Room and board	Trans-portation	Other costs	Board only	Trans-portation	Other costs
Baptist Bible College of Pennsylvania	4,979		450	2,971	500	600	1,931	1,650	600
Beaver College	10,960		400	4,750	250	550	1,500	450	550
Berean Institute	2,610		300				1,500	500	500
‡ Bloomsburg University of Pennsylvania	2,518	2,034/—	400	2,466	385	1,400		935	1,400
Bryn Mawr College	15,600		450	5,850	300	700	2,450	400	700
Bucknell University	15,650		650	3,825	150	1,785	1,825	2,475	1,785
† Bucks County Community College	1,524	3,600/1,800	275					1,125	875
‡ Butler County Community College	1,182	2,238/1,140	525				1,500	835	900
‡ Cabrini College	7,740		580	4,790	375	1,116	1,500	1,550	1,150
‡ California University of Pennsylvania	2,648	2,034/—	400	2,680	225	1,275	900	1,005	1,275
† Carlow College	8,753		400	4,000		1,200	1,500	240	1,000
Carnegie Mellon University	15,350		450	5,110	700	1,000	800	450	1,000
‡ Cedar Crest College	11,130		500	4,556	350	350	1,500	350	350
Central Pennsylvania Business School	4,750		800	4,550	550	1,000	1,500	1,000	1,000
‡ Chatham College	10,160		400	4,490	200	800	750	450	800
‡ Chestnut Hill College	7,550		650	3,800	450	300	1,500	800	300
‡ Cheyney University of Pennsylvania	2,488	2,034/—	350	2,956	675	1,000	1,500	675	686
‡ CHI Institute	5,630								
Churchman Business School	3,970		650					600	
‡ Clarion University of Pennsylvania	2,728	2,034/—	450	2,550	500	600	1,350	600	650
‡ College Misericordia	7,900		400	4,034	500	500	1,500	700	500
Community College of Allegheny County									
Allegheny Campus	1,398	2,544/1,272	450				1,500	650	950
Boyce Campus	1,398	2,544/1,272	450				1,500	650	950
North Campus	1,398	2,544/1,272	450				1,500	650	950
South Campus	1,398	2,544/1,272	450				1,500	650	950
Community College of Beaver County	1,460	3,420/1,710	420				1,700	1,000	700
‡ Community College of Philadelphia	1,690	3,300/1,650	400				1,500	360	530
Dean Institute of Technology	4,860		500					1,000	
‡ Delaware County Community College	1,120	2,160/1,080	300				2,000	600	1,030
‡ Delaware Valley College of Science and Agriculture	8,705		400	3,695	300	1,200		700	1,200
Dickinson College	15,550		410	4,530	290	710	1,400	200	710
‡ Drexel University	10,119		500	4,616	350	1,500		780	1,480
DuBois Business College	4,450		400						
‡ Duquesne University	8,850		350	4,317	584	450	1,500	510	450
‡ East Stroudsburg University of Pennsylvania	2,642	2,034/—	450	2,706	250	750		900	1,350
‡ Eastern College	8,925		400	3,470	200	900	1,400	900	800
‡ Edinboro University of Pennsylvania	2,590	2,034/—	400	2,904	180	898		1,280	898
Electronic Institutes									
Middletown	3,950		140				1,886	2,832	1,350
Pittsburgh	5,850		450						
‡ Elizabethtown College	10,700		500	3,750	100	600	1,500	350	600

†Figures are projected for 1991-92.   ‡Figures are for 1990-91.

All aid		Need-based aid		Grants and scholarships								Financial aid deadlines		Inst aid form	Need analysis document
				Need-based				Nonneed-based							
Total freshmen	Percent receiving aid	Freshmen judged to have need	Percent offered aid	Acad	Music/ drama	Art	Athl	Acad	Music/ drama	Art	Athl	Priority	Closing		
273	58	99	93	X				X				3/1	4/15		APSGFSA FAF
1,128	80			X	X		X	X				3/13	none	X	APSGFSA APSGFSA
331	48	141	95	X									1/15	X	FAF/APSGFSA*;FAF
891	60	415	100	X	X	X	X						2/15		FAF
				X	X	X		X	X	X		5/1	none	X	APSGFSA;FAF/ APSGFSA*
2,172	55			X			X	X					5/1		FAF/APSGFSA*
114	75	140	100	X				X				4/1	none	X	APSGFSA
1,047	72	611	95	X				X	X		X	4/1	none		APSGFSA
93	85	85	100	X			X	X		X	X	3/15	none	X	APSGFSA;FAF/AFSA/ APSGFSA*
1,152	75	712	100	X	X	X		X	X	X			2/15	X	FAF*/FFS
106	80	77	100					X				3/1	none		FAF+APSGFSA;FAF
365	83			X				X				5/1	none	X	APSGFSA
97	94	82	100					X	X			3/15	5/1	X	FAF*/FFS
133	68	85	100	X				X				3/15	none	X	APSGFSA;FAF/ APSGFSA
				X				X	X		X	3/15	4/30		FAF/FFS/AFSA/ APSGFSA;FAF/FFS/ AFSA
325	85												8/15		FAF/FFS FAF
1,207	65			X	X	X	X	X	X	X	X	3/15			FAF/APSGFSA*
300	95	201	100	X			X	X			X	3/1	4/1	X	APSGFSA
													none		FAF
													none		FAF
													none		FAF
													none		FAF
858	61			X				X				5/1	none		FAF/FFS/AFSA/ AFSSA/APSGFSA*
4,407	47							X					5/1	X	FAF/FFS/AFSA/ APSGFSA*
55	85	26	100										8/1	X	AFSA/APSGFSA*/SF
2,973	30			X								5/1	none	X	FAF/FFS/AFSA;FAF/ FFS/AFSA/APSGFSA*
426	76	288	87	X				X				3/1	4/1		APSGFSA
556	59	246	100	X	X	X		X					2/15		FAF
1,687	76							X	X	X	X	5/1	none	X	APSGFSA;FAF/ APSGFSA*
152	90												8/1		APSGFSA
				X				X	X		X		5/1	X	APSGFSA;FAF*/FFS/ APSGFSA
781	77	468	100					X			X	3/15		X	APSGFSA
155	80							X			X	4/15	none		APSGFSA
1,706	78			X				X				3/15	none		FAF
								X					none		APSGFSA;FAF/AFSA*
												8/1	none		APSGFSA;AFSA
718	80	229	100	X	X	X		X				3/1	4/1	X	APSGFSA

*Preferred need analysis document.

Institution	Tuition and fees	Add'l out-of-state/district tuition	Books and supplies	Costs for campus residents			Costs for students at home		
				Room and board	Trans-portation	Other costs	Board only	Trans-portation	Other costs
† Gannon University	8,680		400	3,500	300				
‡ Geneva College	7,184		450	3,480		1,100			1,500
Gettysburg College	16,500		300	3,470	200	500	1,580	500	300
† Gratz College	3,500		600					370	
‡ Grove City College	4,390		325	2,390	200	325	1,620	800	325
‡ Gwynedd-Mercy College	7,900		500	4,000	300	500	900	500	500
‡ Hahnemann University School of Health Sciences and Humanities	7,150		500		765	2,000		765	1,500
‡ Harcum Junior College	6,008		400	3,900		1,500			1,500
Harrisburg Area Community College	1,368	2,626/1,338	500				1,500	650	600
Haverford College	16,150		550	5,400		775			
Holy Family College	7,000		500				1,500	600	850
Hussian School of Art	5,635		700				1,907	700	1,300
Immaculata College	8,300		500	4,410	750	750		1,500	750
‡ Indiana University of Pennsylvania	2,611	2,034/—	500	2,476			1,100		1,350
‡ Johnson Technical Institute	3,995		400				1,962	765	1,098
Juniata College	12,470		450	3,690	250	420	1,940	600	420
Keystone Junior College	7,410		500	4,440	200	800		850	800
King's College	8,740		470	4,100	475	1,600	1,500	600	1,600
‡ Kutztown University of Pennsylvania	2,552	2,034/—	500	2,548		1,000		800	1,000
‡ La Roche College	6,711		630	3,590	210	1,350	1,700		1,350
La Salle University	10,250		500	4,500			1,015	1,500	
‡ Lackawanna Junior College	5,400		540				2,250	400	675
‡ Lafayette College	14,000		500	4,600	100	900	2,250	100	1,500
‡ Lancaster Bible College	6,160		400	2,820	350	1,225	1,500	650	1,225
‡ Lansdale School of Business	4,320		350						
‡ Lebanon Valley College of Pennsylvania	10,650		425	4,240	200	780	1,960	800	780
† Lehigh County Community College	1,455	3,060/1,530	500				680	1,000	400
Lehigh University	15,650		600	4,940	150	1,150	2,070	450	900
Lincoln Technical Institute	5,272		750						
‡ Lincoln University	2,400	900/—	450	2,600	425	900	900	650	900
‡ Lock Haven University of Pennsylvania	2,588	2,034/—	400	2,676	200	1,000		400	1,000
Luzerne County Community College	1,470	2,640/1,320	375				725	500	625
Lycoming College	11,200		500	3,975	300	600	1,800	300	600
‡ Manor Junior College	5,860		400	3,000	600	1,450	1,500	800	1,200
‡ Mansfield University of Pennsylvania	2,628	2,034/—	600	2,490	750	750	1,500	750	750
‡ Marywood College	7,300		400	3,500	200	700	750	500	700
† Mercyhurst College	8,700		400	3,175	250	800		450	
Messiah College	8,700		450	4,380	400	800	750	400	800
‡ Millersville University of Pennsylvania	2,636	2,034/—	402	2,810	300	967	1,056	600	1,010
Montgomery County Community College	1,580	4,500/3,000	350					1,000	
‡ Moore College of Art and Design	10,000		800	4,600	500	900	1,500	600	700
‡ Moravian College	11,660		400	3,780	260	900	1,720	1,100	1,580
‡ Mount Aloysius Junior College	6,400		500	2,990		1,000			1,000

†Figures are projected for 1991-92.   ‡Figures are for 1990-91.

All aid		Need–based aid		Grants and scholarships								Financial aid deadlines		Inst aid form	Need analysis document
				Need–based				Nonneed–based							
Total freshmen	Percent receiving aid	Freshmen judged to have need	Percent offered aid	Acad	Music/drama	Art	Athl	Acad	Music/drama	Art	Athl	Priority	Closing		
801	80			X				X			X	3/1		X	APSGFSA
244	91			X			X	X	X			4/15	none	X	APSGFSA;FAF/FFS/ APSGFSA
572	42	244	100	X	X								2/15		APSGFSA;FAF
													none	X	FAF/AFSSA
550	54	210	96	X	X			X					5/1	X	FAF*/FFS
129	67			X			X	X			X	3/1	4/15	X	FAF+APSGFSA+FFS/ AFSA
				X				X				5/1	5/31	X	APSGFSA
302	74							X		X		3/15	none		APSGFSA
		896	100	X		X		X		X		6/1		X	APSGFSA
287	45	108	100										1/31	X	FAF
198	88	149	100					X			X	2/15	none		APSGFSA+AFSA
60	80					X				X		8/1	none	X	SF
4,908	64	142	91	X	X		X	X	X		X	3/1	5/1		APSGFSA
2,392	83			X	X	X		X	X	X	X	5/1	none		APSGFSA
212	80	160	100	X				X				8/1	none		FAF/AFSA/APSGFSA*
275	80	201	100	X	X	X		X	X	X			3/1		FAF+APSGFSA;FAF
584	50	373	85	X	X	X		X	X	X		5/1	none	X	APSGFSA
378	80	323	96	X				X				3/1	4/1	X	FAF/AFSA/APSGFSA*
1,310	85	1,231	97	X	X	X	X	X		X	X		2/15	X	APSGFSA
121	72	80	100					X			X	5/1	none		APSGFSA;FAF/ APSGFSA
760	70	527	83	X				X			X		2/15		FAF/APSGFSA*
													none	X	APSGFSA+FAF/FFS/ AFSA/AFSSA; APSGFSA+FAF/FFS/
501	56	223	97	X	X	X	X					2/15	none	X	FAF
73	93	50	100					X	X			6/1	none	X	FAF/FFS/AFSA/ AFSSA/APSGFSA*
150	65	38	100	X								7/1	8/16		APSGFSA
242	78	158	100	X	X			X				3/1	none	X	APSGFSA
1,107	21							X				3/31	none	X	FAF/AFSA/APSGFSA*
1,138	48	480	100	X	X		X	X					2/8	X	FAF
															FAF/AFSA/APSGFSA*; FAF/AFSA*
317	91	301	100	X	X			X	X			3/1	3/15		APSGFSA;FAF
724	80	470	100	X	X		X	X	X		X	4/15	none	X	APSGFSA;FAF
2,253	75	675	93	X				X					none		APSGFSA
375	65	264	100	X	X	X		X	X	X		5/1	none	X	FAF
228	79	160	94	X			X	X				3/15	8/15	X	APSGFSA
638	75			X				X	X	X	X		4/15	X	APSGFSA
400	80	356	94	X	X	X		X	X	X			2/15		FAF
395	100	331	100	X				X	X	X	X	3/15	none	X	APSGFSA;FAF/ APSGFSA*
524	84	312	98	X				X				4/1	8/1		APSGFSA;FAF*/FFS
1,089	70	495	93				X	X	X		X		5/1	X	APSGFSA
1,762	40	730	67									5/1	none	X	APSGFSA+FAF/FFS/ AFSA
121	88										X	4/1	none	X	FAF
271	71	162	100	X	X			X				3/1	none	X	FAF*/FFS
537	89	506	94	X				X			X	5/1	8/1	X	APSGFSA

*Preferred need analysis document.

Institution	Tuition and fees	Add'l out-of-state/ district tuition	Books and supplies	Costs for campus residents			Costs for students at home		
				Room and board	Trans-portation	Other costs	Board only	Trans-portation	Other costs
Muhlenberg College 15,115			450	4,260	200	700	1,030	400	1,500
National Education Center: Vale Tech Campus..... 5,333			581		406	938	1,673	406	938
‡ Neumann College 7,560			500				1,700	1,000	500
Northampton County Area Community College.... 1,650	3,450/1,740		500	3,125		1,200		500	1,200
‡ Northeastern Christian Junior College..................... 5,658			320	3,634	700	2,540	550	850	2,808
‡ Peirce Junior College 5,360			500		425	2,090	1,500	425	2,240
Penn State									
‡ Allentown Campus 3,922	4,522/—		400				1,500	900	1,530
‡ Altoona Campus 3,922	4,522/—		400	3,510	297	1,665	1,500	900	1,530
‡ Beaver Campus 3,922	4,522/—		400	3,510	297	1,665	1,500	900	1,530
‡ Berks Campus 3,922	4,522/—		400				1,500	900	1,530
‡ Delaware County Campus 3,922	4,522/—		400				1,500	900	1,530
‡ Du Bois Campus 3,922	4,522/—		400				1,500	900	1,530
‡ Erie Behrend College 4,048	4,396/—		400	3,510	297	1,665	1,500	900	1,530
‡ Fayette Campus 3,922	4,522/—		400				1,500	900	1,530
‡ Harrisburg Capital College 4,048	4,396/—		400	3,510	297	1,665	1,500	900	1,530
‡ Hazleton Campus.. 3,922	4,522/—		400	3,510	297	1,665	1,500	900	1,530
‡ McKeesport Campus 3,922	4,522/—		400	3,510	297	1,665	1,500	900	1,530
‡ Mont Alto Campus.. 3,922	4,522/—		400	3,510	297	1,665	1,500	900	1,530
‡ New Kensington Campus 3,922	4,522/—		400				1,500	900	1,530
‡ Ogontz Campus 3,922	4,522/—		400				1,500	900	1,530
‡ Schuylkill Campus 3,922	4,522/—		400	3,510	297	1,665	1,500	900	1,530

†Figures are projected for 1991-92.   ‡Figures are for 1990-91.

All aid		Need-based aid		Grants and scholarships								Financial aid deadlines		Inst aid form	Need analysis document
				Need-based				Nonneed-based							
Total fresh-men	Percent receiving aid	Freshmen judged to have need	Percent offered aid	Acad	Music/ drama	Art	Athl	Acad	Music/ drama	Art	Athl	Priority	Closing		
415	57	239	95	X	X			X					3/15	X	FAF
													none		APSGFSA
217	79	78	100	X				X			X	3/15	4/30		APSGFSA
1,452	36	814	97					X			X	3/31	none		FAF/FFS/AFSA/ APSGFSA*/SF;FAF/ FFS/APSGFSA/SF
99	95							X	X	X	X	5/1	none		FAF/AFSA/APSGFSA*
599	80			X				X				4/15	6/1	X	APSGFSA
															FAF/FFS/AFSA/ APSGFSA*/SF;FAF/ AFSA/APSGFSA/SF
															FAF/FFS/AFSA/ APSGFSA*/SF;FAF/ AFSA/APSGFSA/SF
															FAF/FFS/AFSA/ APSGFSA*/SF;FAF/ AFSA/APSGFSA/SF
															FAF/FFS/AFSA/ APSGFSA*/SF;FAF/ AFSA/APSGFSA/SF
															FAF/FFS/AFSA/ APSGFSA*/SF;FAF/ AFSA/APSGFSA/SF
643	79											3/15	none		APSGFSA;FAF/AFSA/ APSGFSA/SF
															FAF/FFS/AFSA/ APSGFSA*/SF;FAF/ AFSA/APSGFSA/SF
												3/15	none		FAF/FFS/AFSA/ APSGFSA*/SF;FAF/ AFSA/APSGFSA/SF
															FAF/FFS/AFSA/ APSGFSA*/SF;FAF/ AFSA/APSGFSA/SF
															FAF/FFS/AFSA/ APSGFSA*/SF;FAF/ AFSA/APSGFSA/SF
															FAF/FFS/AFSA/ APSGFSA*/SF;FAF/ AFSA/APSGFSA/SF
															FAF/FFS/AFSA/ APSGFSA*/SF;FAF/ AFSA/APSGFSA/SF
															FAF/FFS/AFSA/ APSGFSA*/SF;FAF/ AFSA/APSGFSA/SF
															FAF/FFS/AFSA/ APSGFSA*/SF;FAF/ AFSA/APSGFSA/SF

*Preferred need analysis document.

Institution	Tuition and fees	Add'l out-of-state/district tuition	Books and supplies	Costs for campus residents			Costs for students at home		
				Room and board	Transportation	Other costs	Board only	Transportation	Other costs
‡ Shenango Campus	3,922	4,522/—	400				1,500	900	1,530
‡ University Park Campus	4,048	4,396/—	400	3,510	297	1,665	1,500	900	1,530
‡ Wilkes-Barre Campus	3,922	4,522/—	400				1,500	900	1,530
‡ Worthington-Scranton Campus	3,922	4,522/—	400				1,500	900	1,530
‡ York Campus	3,922	4,522/—	400				1,500	900	1,530
Penn Technical Institute	6,250		600					350	1,000
‡ Pennsylvania College of Technology	4,290	2,160/—	500				1,500	750	1,000
† Pennsylvania Institute of Technology	6,413		700				600		
Philadelphia College of Bible	6,245		500	3,400	500	790	1,275	880	790
‡ Philadelphia College of Pharmacy and Science	8,580		300	4,375	300	900	850	600	900
‡ Philadelphia College of Textiles and Science	8,866		500	4,204	450	855		700	855
Pinebrook Junior College	6,096		540	3,388	400	1,242	1,560	890	1,242
‡ Pittsburgh Institute of Mortuary Science	6,660								
Pittsburgh Technical Institute	15,730		690			1,952		2,338	
‡ Point Park College	7,122		400	3,800	300	500		400	500
Reading Area Community College	1,560	3,000/1,500	450					600	1,200
Robert Morris College	5,400		450	3,500	400	500	1,700	400	500
‡ Rosemont College	8,610		500	5,160	300	700		650	700
† St. Charles Borromeo Seminary	4,500		700	3,000	700	2,100	2,000	700	2,100
‡ St. Francis College	8,758		420	4,120	300	720	1,500	300	7,200
‡ St. Joseph's University	9,600		450	4,500	535	1,155		1,050	1,940
St. Vincent College	8,990		400	3,520		1,600	1,920		1,600
Seton Hill College	9,000		500	3,760	500	1,500	1,500	1,000	1,500
‡ Shippensburg University of Pennsylvania	2,694	2,034/—	350	2,594	200	1,100		800	1,300
‡ Slippery Rock University of Pennsylvania	2,668	2,034/—	400	2,794		800		400	800
Spring Garden College	8,480		440	4,000	880	2,211	1,650	1,320	1,870
Susquehanna University	13,950		400	4,030	200	600	1,500	200	600
‡ Swarthmore College	15,490		750	5,220		650			650
‡ Talmudical Yeshiva of Philadelphia	3,250		50	3,250					
‡ Temple University	4,354	3,598/—	450	4,484			1,600	450	550
Thaddeus Stevens State School of Technology	3,400		200	3,110	200		700	350	
† Thiel College	9,196		500	4,310		1,230	1,600	500	580
‡ Thomas Jefferson University: College of Allied Health Sciences	10,600		900		500	600	1,600	1,000	600
‡ Tracey-Warner School	5,385		200				1,600	924	1,500

†Figures are projected for 1991-92.   ‡Figures are for 1990-91.

All aid		Need–based aid		Grants and scholarships								Financial aid deadlines		Inst aid form	Need analysis document
				Need–based				Nonneed–based							
Total freshmen	Percent receiving aid	Freshmen judged to have need	Percent offered aid	Acad	Music/drama	Art	Athl	Acad	Music/drama	Art	Athl	Priority	Closing		
4,489	61			X	X	X	X	X	X	X	X	3/15	none		FAF/FFS/AFSA/APSGFSA*/SF;FAF/AFSA/APSGFSA/SF FAF/FFS/AFSA/APSGFSA*/SF;FAF/AFSA/APSGFSA/SF FAF/FFS/AFSA/APSGFSA*/SF;FAF/AFSA/APSGFSA/SF FAF/FFS/AFSA/APSGFSA*/SF;FAF/AFSA/APSGFSA/SF FAF/FFS/AFSA/APSGFSA*/SF;FAF/AFSA/APSGFSA/SF
1,973	62			X				X					none	X	APSGFSA
				X				X				3/1	none	X	APSGFSA
													8/1	X	AFSA/APSGFSA*;FAF*/APSGFSA
133	72	102	96	X	X		X	X	X			5/1	none		FAF
348	75	230	100	X				X			X	3/1	3/15	X	APSGFSA
361	73	201	100					X			X		4/15	X	APSGFSA;FAF/APSGFSA*
60	72	48	100					X	X	X	X	4/1	none		APSGFSA;FAF
				X				X					none		FAF
								X					none	X	APSGFSA;AFSA
256	81			X	X			X	X	X	X	5/1	none	X	APSGFSA;FAF/APSGFSA*
													none	X	APSGFSA
662	68	480	93	X			X	X			X	5/1	none	X	APSGFSA
126	40	63	100	X		X		X			X	3/1	none		FAF/APSGFSA;FAF
12	100	6	100									4/1	8/1	X	APSGFSA
329	85	227	100	X			X	X			X		5/1		FAF/FFS/AFSA/APSGFSA*;FAF/FFS/AFSA/APSGFSA
686	91	366	100	X				X			X	1/1	2/15	X	FAF*/APSGFSA;FAF
261	82	182	100					X	X		X	3/1	5/1		APSGFSA;FAF
214	85	168	100	X	X	X	X	X	X	X	X	5/1	8/1	X	FAF/FFS/AFSA/APSGFSA*
1,139	57	825	100	X			X	X			X	5/1	none	X	APSGFSA;FAF/AFSA
				X	X		X	X	X	X	X		5/1		APSGFSA
190	70			X				X					5/1	X	APSGFSA
353	63	206	100					X	X			3/1	5/1		FAF*/APSGFSA;FAF
363	47	174	100					X					2/1	X	APSGFSA;FAF
													none		AFSA
2,835	61	1,898	100	X				X	X	X	X		5/1	X	APSGFSA;FAF
246	94	230	100	X				X				4/1	none	X	FAF/FFS/AFSA/APSGFSA*;AFSA
														X	FAF
58	98	40	100										none	X	FAF/FFS*/AFSA

*Preferred need analysis document.

Institution	Tuition and fees	Add'l out-of-state/ district tuition	Books and supplies	Costs for campus residents			Costs for students at home		
				Room and board	Trans-portation	Other costs	Board only	Trans-portation	Other costs
Triangle Tech									
‡ Greensburg School	5,112		750					720	825
Pittsburgh Campus	5,705		1,400				1,100	904	952
‡ University of the Arts	10,070		1,000		450	550	800	835	295
University of Pennsylvania	15,894		440	6,030		1,120	1,110		1,120
University of Pittsburgh									
‡ Bradford	4,298	4,572/—	400	3,460	600	500		1,200	500
‡ Greensburg	4,278	4,572/—	500	3,120	450	850	1,660	1,000	850
‡ Johnstown	4,262	4,572/—	500	3,186	420	1,080		1,370	940
‡ Pittsburgh	4,314	4,572/—	400	3,514	400	900	1,500	600	900
‡ Titusville	4,190	4,390/—	400	3,370	400	500	1,500	900	450
‡ University of Scranton	8,756		400	4,088	300	500	1,300	500	500
‡ Ursinus College	11,520		400	4,250	300	700	1,500	450	650
‡ Valley Forge Christian College	4,498		350	2,640	500	500	1,400	500	500
‡ Villanova University	10,850		450	5,220	300	850		450	800
Washington and Jefferson College	12,850		150	3,290	100	600	850	250	350
‡ Waynesburg College	7,220		500	2,900	350	699	1,783	1,000	993
‡ West Chester University of Pennsylvania	2,528	2,034/—	450	3,194	514	1,000	1,200	870	1,000
‡ Westminster College	9,620		425	2,730		575	1,440		575
† Westmoreland County Community College	1,193	2,490/1,320	400				1,500	420	100
† Widener University	10,500		500	4,610	450	900	1,500	900	900
Wilkes University	9,275		500	4,250	675	725	1,500	675	660
‡ Wilson College	10,076		450	4,263	125	350	1,500	300	350
York College of Pennsylvania	4,448		450	2,972	400	850		750	500
Puerto Rico									
American University of Puerto Rico	2,100		400					780	
Bayamon Central University	2,200		400				600	400	800
Caribbean University	2,400		600				1,125	900	1,825
Catholic University of Puerto Rico	2,457		300	2,265	340	1,000		510	1,000
Columbia College	3,150		400						300
Conservatory of Music of Puerto Rico	450		400				2,268	650	450
Electronic Data Processing College of Puerto Rico	2,529		465				900	600	1,015
Escuela De Artes Plasticas	700		2,000				600		
Huertas Junior College	2,985		300					300	
ICPR Junior College	2,523		465				1,020	270	875
Instituto Tecnico Comercial Junior College	2,380		400					400	600
Inter American University of Puerto Rico									
‡ Arecibo University College	2,380		590	2,816			1,200		880
‡ Metropolitan Campus	2,400		590				1,200	504	880
San German Campus	2,500		600	2,050	100	600	1,400	400	800
Puerto Rico Junior College	2,650		250					150	900
Ramirez College of Business and Technology	2,833		180						
Technological College of the Municipality of San Juan	620		465				440	315	900
Turabo University	2,670		300				1,800	306	
Universidad Adventista de las Antillas	2,470		300	2,300	300	540	1,060	500	540

†Figures are projected for 1991-92.   ‡Figures are for 1990-91.

212

| All aid | | Need–based aid | | Grants and scholarships | | | | | | | | Financial aid deadlines | | Inst aid form | Need analysis document |
Total freshmen	Percent receiving aid	Freshmen judged to have need	Percent offered aid	Need–based Acad	Music/ drama	Art	Athl	Nonneed–based Acad	Music/ drama	Art	Athl	Priority	Closing		
106	90	71	100										none		AFSA
								X					none	X	AFSA
223	98	288	100	X	X	X		X	X	X		2/15	none		APSGFSA;FAF
2,231	53	980	100									2/15	none	X	FAF
264	58	143	100	X			X						3/1	X	FAF/FFS/APSGFSA*; FAF*/FFS
539	70	370	100	X								4/1	5/1	X	FAF
				X				X			X	4/1	none		APSGFSA
3,084	74	2,192	100	X				X			X	3/1	none	X	APSGFSA+FAF
346	78	186	96					X				3/1	none	X	FAF/APSGFSA*;FAF
891	82	530	96	X				X				2/15	none		FAF/APSGFSA*;FAF/APSGFSA
275	68	160	100	X				X					2/15		FAF/APSGFSA;FAF
													none		FAF/AFSSA*
1,767	50	623	100	X				X			X	2/15	3/15	X	FAF*/APSGFSA;FAF
293	70	198	91	X				X				3/15	none		FAF
331	90			X				X				3/15	none	X	FAF/FFS/AFSA/ AFSSA/SF;FAF+FFS/ AFSA/CSS SAAC/ACT
1,511	65	1,000	95					X	X		X	3/1	none		APSGFSA
343	70							X	X		X	5/1	none		APSGFSA;FAF
1,562	60	530	100	X								5/1	none		APSGFSA
467	87	357	99	X	X			X	X			3/1	4/1	X	APSGFSA;FAF/ APSGFSA*
618	82	319	99	X	X	X	X	X	X	X	X	6/1	none	X	APSGFSA
66	74	45	100	X				X			X		5/1		APSGFSA+FAF/FFS; FAF/FFS/APSGFSA*
723	62	330	100	X	X	X		X	X	X		4/15	none	X	FAF/FFS/APSGFSA*
1,310	72	1,179	80	X	X							5/31	6/30	X	AFSA
443	94			X	X			X			X		8/1	X	AFSA
792	50			X						X	X	7/30	none		AFSA
2,776	88	1,656	100	X					X	X	X	5/17	none	X	AFSA
															AFSA
56	64	26	100		X			X				6/30	none		FAF/FFS*/AFSA
440	85			X									9/30	X	FAF*/AFSA;AFSA
															AFSA
723	95	622	100										4/15	X	AFSA
													none		AFSA
971	85					X							4/27	X	FAF/AFSA* AFSA*/AFSSA
967	23												4/27	X	AFSA
														X	FAF*/FFS/AFSA
														X	AFSA
															FAF/FFS/AFSA*
													none	X	AFSA
													5/31		FAF/FFS/AFSA*

*Preferred need analysis document.

Institution	Tuition and fees	Add'l out-of-state/district tuition	Books and supplies	Costs for campus residents			Costs for students at home		
				Room and board	Trans-portation	Other costs	Board only	Trans-portation	Other costs
Universidad Metropolitana	2,642		300				720	720	1,380
‡ Universidad Politecnica de Puerto Rico	2,740		850				1,600	516	812
University of Puerto Rico									
‡ Aguadilla	492		800				1,000	700	600
‡ Arecibo Campus	492		325					700	600
‡ Bayamon Technological University College	492		800				1,890	700	600
‡ Carolina Regional College	717		800	2,950			1,950	700	600
‡ Cayey University College	492		800				1,200	600	600
‡ Humacao University College	492		800				1,950	700	600
La Montana Regional College	520		800				1,500	700	600
‡ Mayaguez Campus	492		900				1,500	700	600
‡ Medical Sciences Campus	717		250				2,700	680	525
‡ Ponce Technological University College	492		800				1,500	700	600
‡ Rio Piedras Campus	492		800	3,350	700	600	1,890	700	600
‡ University of the Sacred Heart	2,650		450		664	600	1,500	475	495
Rhode Island									
Brown University	16,860		591	5,219		960	1,780	315	885
Bryant College	10,993		450	5,935	350	900	1,800	1,120	900
‡ Community College of Rhode Island	1,100	1,030/—	450				1,780	1,350	701
Johnson & Wales University	8,517		500	3,999	400	500	1,100	500	400
New England Institute of Technology	7,980		600				1,890	900	1,000
‡ Providence College	12,065		400	5,300		900	1,400	1,400	900
† Rhode Island College	1,990	3,120/—	500	5,210	300	1,000	1,500	850	1,000
‡ Rhode Island School of Design	13,210		1,000	5,520	300	765		1,000	765
‡ Roger Williams College	9,765		500	4,750	500	260	2,000	500	200
† Salve Regina College	11,740		500	5,500	600	1,250	2,250	1,200	1,250
† University of Rhode Island	2,791	4,910/—	600	4,423	183	1,450	1,884	1,840	1,282
South Carolina									
‡ Aiken Technical College	600	285/—	450				1,800	1,000	750
Allen University	3,720		300	2,900					
Anderson College	5,850		400	3,820	750	1,400	2,000	1,000	900
‡ Benedict College	4,571		600	2,418	600	750		900	850
Bob Jones University	3,880		500	3,360					
Central Wesleyan College	7,090		550	2,980	600	500	2,000	750	500
† Charleston Southern University	6,430		600	2,906	765	1,125	1,500	990	500
‡ Chesterfield-Marlboro Technical College	744	400/100	600				2,000	1,694	1,884
‡ The Citadel	2,513	3,163/—	630	2,276		850			
† Claflin College	4,018		350	1,980	500	500	780		500
† Clemson University	2,623	4,378/—	486	3,153	469	927		1,500	927
Clinton Junior College	1,220		225	1,890					
‡ Coker College	7,715		600	3,552		750			750
† College of Charleston	2,300	2,250/—	476	3,000	303	1,684	1,850	1,480	1,684
Columbia Bible College and Seminary	5,085		350	2,850	550	410		400	
Columbia College	8,725		500	3,255	650	1,250		950	1,000
‡ Columbia Junior College of Business	2,585		225		150	500			
Converse College	10,368		500	3,240	300	600		150	600
‡ Denmark Technical College	1,000	1,000/—	500	3,044	700	1,600	1,500	800	1,600

†Figures are projected for 1991-92.   ‡Figures are for 1990-91.

All aid		Need–based aid		Grants and scholarships								Financial aid deadlines		Inst aid form	Need analysis document
				Need–based				Nonneed–based							
Total freshmen	Percent receiving aid	Freshmen judged to have need	Percent offered aid	Acad	Music/ drama	Art	Athl	Acad	Music/ drama	Art	Athl	Priority	Closing		
1,100	76			X								5/31	6/30	X	AFSA AFSA
425	68	388	74	X	X		X						6/29	X	AFSA
651	67	496	88	X			X	X					6/15		AFSA
618	55			X				X			X		6/28		AFSA
472	64	300	100					X	X		X	6/15	6/30	X	FFS
754	25			X								5/31	6/28	X	AFSSA
782	79	685	89	X									6/30	X	AFSA AFSA
1,890	73	1,412	100					X	X		X		7/15	X	AFSA
				X								4/30	none	X	FAF
485	80	420	100	X				X	X		X		6/28	X	AFSA
														X	AFSA
		573	84										6/30	X	AFSA
1,386	36	514	100										1/1	X	FAF
657	58	402	84					X			X		3/1	X	FAF
2,519	40												none		FAF
													none		FAF*/AFSA
692	80											6/1	none		FAF/AFSA*
936	45	416	100	X			X	X			X		2/15		FAF
1,167	53	400	100	X				X	X	X			3/1		FAF
376	63			X		X		X		X			2/15		FAF
682	44	310	100	X				X				3/1	none	X	FAF
416	45											3/1	none		FAF
2,162	60	1,296	100	X	X	X	X					3/1	none	X	FAF
465	39	193	75					X				5/1	none		FAF
52	100											5/15	none		FAF*/FFS
431	82			X	X	X	X	X	X	X	X	4/1	none		FAF*/FFS
395	89			X	X		X	X			X	1/1	none	X	FAF*/FFS/AFSA/ AFSSA;FAF*/FFS/ AFSA/AFSSA/
1,238	50	551	100	X									none		
121	96	102	100					X	X		X	4/15	none	X	FAF/FFS/SF*
702	90				X			X		X	X		none	X	FAF
293	58	250	100										none		FAF
591	73	439	92					X			X	3/15			FAF
426	94	326	100	X	X	X	X						6/1		FAF*/FFS
2,513	59	654	95	X				X	X		X		4/1		FAF FAF
90	75			X	X	X	X	X	X	X	X	3/31	8/1		FAF*/AFSA/SF;FAF*/ AFSA/APSGFSA/SF
1,159	61			X	X	X		X	X	X	X	4/15	none	X	FAF/FFS/AFSA/SF*; FAF/FFS/AFSA/ APSGFSA/SF*
				X								5/1	none		FFS
267	92	225	100	X				X	X	X	X	4/1	none	X	FAF*/FFS
144	76			X			X	X			X	5/30	none		FAF
190	77	95	75					X	X		X	3/15	none		FAF
454	95			X				X				5/1	8/15	X	FAF*/AFSA/AFSSA

*Preferred need analysis document.

Institution	Tuition and fees	Add'l out-of-state/ district tuition	Books and supplies	Costs for campus residents			Costs for students at home		
				Room and board	Trans-portation	Other costs	Board only	Trans-portation	Other costs
‡ Erskine College	8,760		475	3,105	325	625	1,500	600	1,100
† Florence-Darlington Technical College	865	495/180	700				1,200		700
‡ Francis Marion College	1,800	1,800/—	400	3,010	300	700	1,500	1,165	640
† Furman University	10,566		425	3,771	500	1,000		750	750
‡ Greenville Technical College	672	477/63	350				2,500	1,500	1,000
‡ Horry-Georgetown Technical College	750	750/—	300						
‡ Lander College	2,390	1,000/—	300	2,380	200	550		750	550
Limestone College	6,464		375	3,100	225	700	700	260	650
Midlands Technical College	750	750/195	300					900	600
‡ Morris College	3,717		670	2,255	825	975	1,500	1,200	975
Newberry College	7,400		350	3,000	350	300		500	900
Nielsen Electronics Institute	3,000		300						
† North Greenville College	5,600		500	3,140	350	500	1,600	300	1,000
‡ Orangeburg-Calhoun Technical College	600	300/150	250				800	275	250
Phillips Junior College									
Columbia	4,165							400	500
Greenville	4,600							400	500
North Charleston	4,498							400	500
Spartanburg	4,498							400	500
‡ Piedmont Technical College	750	450/150	400					800	800
Presbyterian College	10,326		511	3,184	461	912	1,598	796	1,004
‡ South Carolina State College	2,340	1,690/—	400	2,376	300	600		200	600
† Spartanburg Methodist College	5,500		400	3,300	500	500		500	1,500
‡ Spartanburg Technical College	540	540/164	450					1,100	600
‡ Sumter Area Technical College	659	405/117	400				1,500	500	800
‡ Technical College of the Lowcountry	750	330/150	400					1,000	1,500
‡ Tri-County Technical College	675	663/—	464				1,500	1,021	971
† Trident Technical College	1,060	944/212	650					1,584	1,000
University of South Carolina									
‡ Aiken	1,800	2,700/—	425		1,440	6,120	1,500	1,440	1,035
‡ Beaufort	1,164	1,836/—	425				1,500	1,090	675
‡ Coastal Carolina College	1,920	2,880/—	400	2,200			1,500	1,090	675
‡ Columbia	2,560	3,840/—	384	2,928	672	1,413	1,500	670	1,413
‡ Lancaster	1,164	1,836/—	400				1,500	1,090	675
‡ Salkehatchie University Campus	1,164	1,836/—	400				1,500	1,090	675
‡ Spartanburg	1,920	2,880/—	500		1,000	675	1,500	500	400
‡ Sumter	1,164	1,836/—	400				1,500	1,090	675
‡ Union	1,164	1,836/—	400				1,500	1,090	675
Voorhees College	3,340		500	2,522	1,000	700		1,000	700
‡ Williamsburg Technical College	800		400						
‡ Winthrop College	2,326	1,802/—	300	2,124	300	600	800	500	725
‡ Wofford College	9,015		565	3,950	480	880	705	630	880
‡ York Technical College	495	495/99	450					1,155	

†Figures are projected for 1991-92.   ‡Figures are for 1990-91.

All aid		Need–based aid		Grants and scholarships								Financial aid deadlines		Inst aid form	Need analysis document
				Need–based				Nonneed–based							
Total freshmen	Percent receiving aid	Freshmen judged to have need	Percent offered aid	Acad	Music/drama	Art	Athl	Acad	Music/drama	Art	Athl	Priority	Closing		
127	79	100	100	X			X	X	X		X	3/15	none	X	FAF*/FFS
536	52											5/1	none		FAF*/FFS/AFSA
				X				X	X	X	X	3/1	none		FAF*/FFS/AFSA/SF
666	65	260	100	X				X	X	X	X	2/1		X	FAF
				X				X		X		5/1	none	X	FAF/FFS/AFSA*
485	49	228	89	X				X	X	X	X	4/15	none		FAF*/AFSA FAF*/FFS/AFSA; FAF*/FFS/AFSA/CSS SAAC
310	98			X	X	X	X	X	X		X	3/30	none	X	FAF
2,746	45							X				6/1	none		FAF*/FFS
217	88	207	100	X	X		X					3/1	none	X	FAF*/FFS/AFSA/SF
177	70	134	100	X				X	X		X	5/1	none		FAF
														X	AFSA
214	94			X	X	X	X	X	X	X	X	6/1	none	X	FAF
591	70							X					none	X	FFS
37	90	85	100										none	X	AFSA
													none		AFSA
															AFSA
													none		FAF/FFS*/AFSA
514	67							X				6/1	none		FAF/FFS*
302	46	136	100	X	X		X	X	X		X	3/15	6/1	X	FAF*/FFS
1,562	82			X				X			X		6/1		FAF*/FFS/AFSA
433	92	415	100	X	X		X	X	X		X	6/1	none	X	FAF*/FFS
															FAF
816	50			X								8/1	none		FAF/FFS/AFSA/SF*
468	55	98	100										5/1		FFS
				X				X				6/1	none	X	FAF/FFS/AFSA/ AFSSA/SF*
				X				X				5/1	none	X	AFSSA
461	40	175	86	X				X	X		X	3/15	none		FAF*/FFS/SF
200	80			X				X				4/15	none		FAF/FFS*
605	52							X			X		4/1	X	FAF/FFS*
2,457	25	831	76	X				X	X	X	X	4/15	none		FFS
217	35	54	100					X				4/15	none		FAF/FFS*
207	44			X				X			X	4/15	none		FAF/FFS*/AFSA
490	43			X			X	X	X		X	4/15	none		FAF/FFS*
210	33							X				4/15	none		FAF/FFS*/AFSA;FAF/ FFS*
210	70	100	100					X				5/15	8/15		FAF/FFS*
233	98			X				X				5/1	7/30		FAF*/FFS
				X									5/1	X	FAF/FFS/AFSA*;FAF/ FFS
		342	89					X	X	X	X	4/1	none		FAF
262	70	131	100	X	X		X	X	X		X	3/1	none		FAF*/FFS/AFSA/ AFSSA/SF;FAF*/FFS/ AFSA/AFSSA/
853	38			X				X				3/31	none		FFS*/AFSA

*Preferred need analysis document.

Institution	Tuition and fees	Add'l out-of-state/district tuition	Books and supplies	Costs for campus residents			Costs for students at home		
				Room and board	Transportation	Other costs	Board only	Transportation	Other costs
South Dakota									
Augustana College	9,330		400	2,860	225	675		500	400
‡ Black Hills State University	1,712	1,274/—	400	2,200	540	1,250	1,051	615	540
† Dakota State University	1,866		400	2,020	350	800	1,300	600	800
Dakota Wesleyan University	6,250		450	2,550	450	850	1,500	450	850
† Huron University	5,775		500	2,816	200	1,500	1,800	900	945
‡ Kilian Community College	3,185		400				1,780	640	400
† Mitchell Vocational Technical Institute	1,600		700				750	300	750
Mount Marty College	6,590		500	2,660	540	900	1,800	540	900
† National College	5,760		600	3,000	750	900	1,600	900	600
† Northern State University	1,700	1,338/—	450	2,544	630	950	1,500	630	950
Oglala Lakota College	1,590		200					162	450
Presentation College	5,740		600	2,466	550	850	750	550	850
Sinte Gleska College	1,580		200					900	400
Sioux Falls College	7,496		600	2,950	700	900	1,750	650	650
Sisseton-Wahpeton Community College	2,070		360					489	
‡ South Dakota School of Mines and Technology	1,899	1,503/—	425	1,980	485	893	1,500	485	893
‡ South Dakota State University	1,824	1,503/—	400	2,341	550	900	950	440	1,000
Southeast Vo-Tech Institute	1,550								
‡ University of South Dakota	1,869	1,503/—	500	2,116	530	920	750	500	900
Western Dakota Vocational Technical Institute	2,040		500		600		900	600	
Tennessee									
American Baptist College of ABT Seminary	2,000		400	1,984					
† American Technical Institute	1,000								
‡ Aquinas Junior College	3,090		450						
‡ Austin Peay State University	1,442	3,204/—	450	2,550	696	1,500	1,500	1,266	1,500
Belmont College	5,900		450	3,150	600	750	1,500	600	750
Bethel College	4,350		350	2,400		900	650	700	
Bristol University	5,450								
‡ Carson-Newman College	6,000		350	2,560	750	550	1,300	1,050	700
‡ Chattanooga State Technical Community College	844	2,430/—	440				1,900	1,600	1,700
‡ Christian Brothers University	6,960		600	3,070					
‡ Cleveland State Community College	848	2,430/—	450				1,500	576	750
‡ Columbia State Community College	844	2,430/—	420				1,200	820	610
Crichton College	3,896		400	1,450		2,000	1,500	300	2,000
Cumberland University	4,400		450	2,720					
David Lipscomb University	5,670		450	3,020	500	650	1,570	500	650
Draughons Junior College	5,696		50					360	
Draughons Junior College of Business									
‡ Knoxville	4,196								
Nashville	3,830		370						
Draughon's Junior College: Johnson City	4,407								
‡ Dyersburg State Community College	850	2,430/—	400				1,500	1,225	480

†Figures are projected for 1991-92.   ‡Figures are for 1990-91.

| All aid | | Need–based aid | | Grants and scholarships | | | | | | | | Financial aid deadlines | | Inst aid form | Need analysis document |
| Total freshmen | Percent receiving aid | Freshmen judged to have need | Percent offered aid | Need–based | | | | Nonneed–based | | | | | | | |
				Acad	Music/ drama	Art	Athl	Acad	Music/ drama	Art	Athl	Priority	Closing		
503	85	324	100	X	X		X	X	X		X	4/15	none		FAF/FFS*
551	70	310	100	X				X	X	X	X	4/1	none		FAF/FFS
198	70	154	100	X			X	X	X		X	4/1	none		FAF/FFS;FAF/FFS/ CSS SAAC
168	86	160	100	X	X	X	X	X	X	X	X	4/1	none	X	FAF/FFS*/AFSA
134	97	74	100	X			X	X			X	4/15	none		FAF/FFS*
													none	X	FFS
													none		FAF/FFS/AFSA
135	94			X	X		X	X	X		X	3/1	none		FAF/FFS
258	94			X				X				3/15	none	X	FAF/FFS/AFSA/ AFSSA;FAF/FFS/ AFSA/CSS SAAC/ACT
564	73	385	100	X	X			X	X	X	X	3/1	none		FAF/FFS/AFSA/SF; FAF/AFSA/SF
													none		FFS
209	89							X				3/1	none		FFS
													none	X	FAF
169	90	130	100	X	X		X	X	X		X	4/1	none		FAF/FFS*/AFSA
													none		FFS
385	43	204	100					X			X	5/1	none		FAF/FFS
1,506	82	950	100					X	X	X	X	3/15	none	X	FAF/FFS*/AFSA
													none		FFS
1,175	80			X	X	X	X	X	X	X	X	2/15	none		FAF/FFS*
		250	100				X				X	7/1	none		FAF/AFSA;FAF/AFSA/ ACT SAAC
													none		FAF
				X				X						X	FFS
1,239	70							X	X	X	X	4/1	none		FAF/FFS*/AFSA
701	70			X				X	X		X	4/15	none	X	FAF*/FFS
130	90							X	X		X	5/1	none		FAF/FFS*
95	60												none	X	FFS
400	89			X	X	X	X	X	X	X	X	5/1	6/30	X	FAF*/FFS
1,135	39						X	X	X	X	X	4/1	none		FFS
263	81	186	100	X	X		X	X	X		X	5/1	none		FAF/FFS*
1,559	30	535	89	X			X	X				5/15	none		FAF
													none	X	FAF/FFS
60	89			X	X			X	X			7/15	none	X	FFS
260	70			X				X			X	3/1	none	X	FAF/FFS*
								X	X	X	X	4/15	none		FAF*/FFS;FAF*/FFS/ AFSA/AFSSA/ APSGFSA
															FAF
													none		FAF
200	82												none		FAF/AFSA/AFSSA*; FAF
															FAF
407	50			X			X	X	X		X	3/15	none		FAF/FFS*/AFSA

*Preferred need analysis document.

Institution	Tuition and fees	Add'l out-of-state/district tuition	Books and supplies	Costs for campus residents			Costs for students at home		
				Room and board	Transportation	Other costs	Board only	Transportation	Other costs
‡ East Tennessee State University	1,396	3,204/—	400		400	600		420	600
Fisk University	5,010		500	3,050		2,349			2,349
Free Will Baptist Bible College	3,174		350	2,880	225	500		275	500
Freed-Hardeman University	5,080		500	2,810	550	750	1,500	750	808
Hiwassee College	3,800		300	2,600	150	900			
‡ Jackson State Community College	850	2,430/—	400						
John A. Gupton College	6,263		600						
Johnson Bible College	3,350		600	2,645	500	700	1,600	1,200	800
King College	6,650		400	3,050	600	1,200		320	3,000
† Knoxville Business College	3,600		425					1,200	1,000
‡ Knoxville College	5,190		300	3,600					
‡ Lambuth College	4,392		300	2,858	500	1,200		800	1,000
‡ Lane College	4,187		400	2,355	200	900	1,500	800	300
Lee College	4,379		420	2,774	650	650	855	835	340
LeMoyne-Owen College	3,650		400					500	900
† Lincoln Memorial University	4,700		300	2,600	200	600	900	750	750
Martin Methodist College	4,500		250	2,600					
‡ Maryville College	7,750		450	3,550	600	500	1,500	600	500
† McKenzie College	4,000		300				700	500	
Memphis College of Art	8,180		800	4,500	700	435	1,650	650	435
‡ Memphis State University	1,564	3,204/—	600		400	700			
Mid-America Baptist Theological Seminary	800		300						
‡ Middle Tennessee State University	1,348	3,204/—	175	1,822					
‡ Milligan College	6,196		500	2,736	1,190	1,140	900	1,040	1,300
‡ Motlow State Community College	854	2,430/—	330						3,171
‡ Nashville State Technical Institute	848	2,430/—	400						
‡ Northeast State Technical Community College	850	2,430/—	500					750	890
O'More College of Design	5,935		600		1,500			1,500	
‡ Pellissippi State Technical Community College	850	2,430/—	400	2,430			1,800	1,900	1,300
Phillips Junior College: Memphis	4,448							400	500
Rhodes College	12,958		500	4,516	600	790	1,898	600	790
Roane State Community College	915	2,430/—	400				1,500	360	750
‡ Shelby State Community College	846	2,430/—	400				1,500	540	675
† Southern College of Seventh-day Adventists	7,160		450	3,040	500	575		500	550
‡ State Technical Institute at Memphis	842	2,430/—	360						
‡ Tennessee Institute of Electronics	3,045		325				1,890		1,143
‡ Tennessee State University	1,396	3,204/—	375	2,284	450	700	1,500	450	700
‡ Tennessee Technological University	1,430	3,204/—	600	2,900	642	600		642	600
Tennessee Temple University	3,970		450	3,180	800	900		400	900
Tennessee Wesleyan College	5,564		400	3,144	1,000	1,200	1,500	1,200	900
Tomlinson College	3,640		300	2,700	500	700	1,000	600	600
‡ Trevecca Nazarene College	5,136		450	2,580	540	650	1,500	540	600
Tusculum College	6,000		550	3,100	400	800	1,700	700	900
Union University	4,550		400	2,260		300		300	300
† University of the South	13,500		425	3,510	320	860	1,760		860

†Figures are projected for 1991-92.   ‡Figures are for 1990-91.

Total freshmen	Percent receiving aid	Freshmen judged to have need	Percent offered aid	Acad	Music/drama	Art	Athl	Acad	Music/drama	Art	Athl	Priority	Closing	Inst aid form	Need analysis document
All aid		**Need–based aid**		**Grants and scholarships**								**Financial aid deadlines**			
				Need–based				**Nonneed–based**							
1,575	33							X	X	X	X	4/15	none		FFS;FAF/FFS*
304	80			X				X				4/20	none	X	FAF
70	45	15	100	X				X	X	X		5/15	none	X	FFS
264	84	200	100	X				X	X	X	X	5/15	none		FAF/FFS*
276	75											5/1	none	X	FAF*/FFS
1,507	52							X			X	4/1	none	X	FAF/FFS*/AFSA
													none		FFS
92	80	85	100					X	X			7/1	none	X	FAF/FFS*/AFSA/
															AFSSA
142	90	108	100	X			X	X			X	3/15	none	X	FAF
													none	X	FFS
690	98							X	X				none		FAF*/FFS
159	75			X	X	X	X	X	X	X	X	3/15	none		FAF/FFS*
														X	FAF*/FFS
653	90	460	100	X	X		X	X	X		X	4/15	none	X	FFS
184	88											4/15	none		FFS
486	70			X			X	X	X		X	6/1	none		FAF*/FFS
														X	FFS
163	87	109	100					X	X	X		3/1	none	X	FAF*/FFS
57	80	50	100										none		FAF/FFS*/AFSA/
															AFSSA
89	84					X		X		X		6/1	none	X	FAF/FFS*
1,688	50							X	X	X	X	4/1	none		FAF/FFS*
1,830	60			X	X	X	X	X			X	3/15	5/15		FAF/FFS
190	90			X	X	X	X	X	X	X	X	4/1	none	X	FAF/FFS*/AFSA
600	62			X			X	X			X	5/1	8/14		FAF/FFS*
				X				X				5/1	none		FAF/FFS*/AFSA
638	36			X				X				8/1	none		FFS
50	30	19	100									5/1	7/30	X	FFS
3,865	29	600	100					X	X	X			7/1		FAF/FFS*/AFSA
													none		FAF/FFS/AFSA*
388	67	208	100	X	X	X		X	X	X		3/1	none	X	FAF*/FFS
													none		FAF/FFS*/AFSA/
															AFSSA
668	42							X	X	X	X	5/1	none	X	FFS
374	76	276	61	X	X			X	X			5/1	none		FAF/FFS
				X				X				5/15	7/1	X	FFS
													none		AFSA
716	80			X	X		X	X	X		X	4/1	none	X	FAF*/FFS
1,398	65	843	100	X				X	X		X	4/15	none		FAF/FFS*/AFSA/SF
212	60							X	X		X	3/31	none		FFS
96	95	88	80					X	X		X	4/15	7/31	X	FAF
92	86							X	X			4/1	none		FAF/FFS*/AFSA/
															AFSSA;FAF/FFS*/
															AFSA/ACT SAAC/
200	95			X	X		X					4/15	none		FFS
76	94	59	100	X			X	X			X	4/1	none	X	FAF*/FFS
439	79	294	94					X	X	X	X	5/15	8/1	X	FFS
288	71	125	100	X				X				3/1	none	X	FAF*/FFS/SF;FAF*/
															FFS/CSS SAAC/ACT
															SAAC/AFSSA/

*Preferred need analysis document.

Institution	Tuition and fees	Add'l out-of-state/district tuition	Books and supplies	Costs for campus residents			Costs for students at home		
				Room and board	Trans-portation	Other costs	Board only	Trans-portation	Other costs
University of Tennessee									
‡ Chattanooga	1,488	3,204/—	500		434	800	1,388	1,130	800
‡ Knoxville	1,712	3,204/—	591	3,044	435	1,125	1,487	1,702	1,125
‡ Martin	1,546	3,204/—	500	2,670	427	1,576	580	577	1,576
‡ Memphis	1,486	3,204/—	1,045	3,780	1,305	1,455		1,305	1,455
Vanderbilt University	15,234		575	5,420		575			
‡ Volunteer State Community College	850	2,430/—	400				1,250	1,300	420
† Walters State Community College	910	2,430/—	500				1,500	1,200	900
William Jennings Bryan College	6,370		450	3,520	600	700	1,125	805	1,350
Texas									
† Abilene Christian University	6,480		420	3,050	700	1,155	1,180	700	1,155
Alvin Community College	360	900/150	385				1,500	625	1,017
† Amarillo College	479	1,207/247					1,160	1,136	851
Amber University	3,750		300						
Angelina College	562	290/158	550	2,440	275	550	825	1,600	550
Angelo State University	1,070	3,240/—	380	3,356	550	1,300		1,220	1,300
Arlington Baptist College	2,450		500	2,944	600	720	1,100	600	800
Austin College	9,465		630	3,605	570	1,085	1,930	570	1,085
† Austin Community College	680	2,520/270	400				1,540	700	1,074
Baptist Missionary Association Theological Seminary	1,110		400	5,350	560	1,000	3,570	560	1,000
Bauder Fashion College	5,690		800	3,790					
Bay Ridge Christian College	1,800		160	1,880	25	65			
Baylor College of Dentistry	1,425		2,400						
Baylor University	6,110		560	3,654	772	1,252	1,868	1,502	1,310
† Bee County College	356	3,300/300	400	2,110	176	605	1,500	396	605
‡ Blinn College	670	1,500/—	471	2,150	360	925		224	925
Brazosport College	250	300/60	516				1,474	630	800
Brookhaven College	420	1,490/380	390					1,560	1,245
Cedar Valley College	424	1,490/440	600				1,500	1,330	1,045
† Central Texas College	408	870/—	475	2,610	447	874		485	1,036
Cisco Junior College	530	400/120	500	1,900	200	600	1,100	500	800
‡ Clarendon College	410	130/30	300	1,470		900	900	290	800
College of the Mainland	186	600/33	385					875	900
† Collin County Community College District	450	1,050/150	416				850	1,328	1,044
Commonwealth Institute of Funeral Service	4,900						150	250	100
Concordia Lutheran College	6,090		430	3,200	750	1,050	1,500	620	1,050
Cooke County College	440	390/60	450	2,150	800	1,075	1,620	950	1,075
Corpus Christi State University	910	3,120/—	400	3,042	630	1,100	1,500	1,100	900
† Criswell College	2,650		200						
‡ Dallas Baptist University	5,650		572	2,928	117	1,036	1,700	1,304	1,036
† Dallas Christian College	2,350		650	2,600	160	625	3,200	650	625
Del Mar College	480	900/—	400				1,500	630	810
DeVry Institute of Technology: Irving	5,015	1,902/—	500				1,839	2,894	2,691
East Texas Baptist University	4,350		470	2,760	465	895	1,500	540	895
East Texas State University									
† Commerce	1,022	3,060/—	600	3,082	840	930	1,500	840	930
Texarkana	930	3,660/—	600				1,530	840	930

†Figures are projected for 1991-92. ‡Figures are for 1990-91.

Total freshmen	Percent receiving aid	Freshmen judged to have need	Percent offered aid	Need-based Acad	Need-based Music/drama	Need-based Art	Need-based Athl	Nonneed-based Acad	Nonneed-based Music/drama	Nonneed-based Art	Nonneed-based Athl	Priority	Closing	Inst aid form	Need analysis document
830	70							X	X	X	X	3/1	none		FAF/FFS*
3,418	50	1,841	92	X	X	X	X	X	X	X	X	3/1	none		FAF/FFS
1,229	65			X				X	X		X	3/1	none		FAF/FFS*
				X				X				2/15	none	X	FAF*/FFS
1,397	38	475	100	X				X	X		X	2/15	none	X	FAF
								X			X	4/15	none		FAF/FFS*/AFSA/ AFSSA
780	15	325	98	X				X	X		X	3/31	none		FAF/FFS*/AFSA
107	85	72	100					X	X		X	5/1	none	X	FAF/FFS*/AFSSA; FAF/FFS*
749	75	458	100					X	X	X	X	4/1	none	X	FFS
646	23	322	100					X	X	X	X	6/15	none	X	FAF/FFS/AFSA*
1,132	38							X				6/1	none		FFS
												7/1			FAF
953	21	290	100	X	X	X	X	X	X	X	X	6/15	none	X	FAF/FFS/AFSA*
				X				X				7/15	none		FAF/FFS*
48	95	24	100	X	X			X				8/15	none	X	FAF/FFS/AFSA*
322	80	159	100	X				X	X	X		5/1	7/1	X	FAF*/FFS
								X				2/15	4/1	X	FAF
												8/1	9/6		FAF
250	40	125	100	X				X					7/1	X	FAF
6	100			X				X					none		FAF/FFS/AFSA/ AFSSA;FAF/FFS/ AFSA/AFSSA/ FAF
												6/1			
2,435	60	943	100	X	X	X	X	X	X	X	X	3/1	none	X	FAF
708	50			X				X	X	X		4/1	none	X	FAF*/FFS/AFSA
3,790	30			X			X	X	X		X	7/1	none	X	FFS
2,078	21							X				8/1	none	X	FAF/FFS/AFSA*
6,725	68			X		X		X				7/1	none		FAF
				X	X	X		X	X	X			none		FAF*/FFS
1,300	21											7/1	none		FAF/FFS*
657	50							X	X		X	8/15	none		FAF/FFS*
													none		FFS
391	92	131	100					X	X	X			none		FAF*/FFS/AFSA
1,729	10	682	100	X	X	X	X	X	X	X	X		none		FAF*/FFS/AFSA
		62	100										none		FFS
148	80	92	100	X	X		X	X	X		X		7/1	X	FFS
1,201	30							X	X		X		6/1		FFS
													4/1		FAF*/FFS
121	20	25	100										7/15		
124	87							X	X	X	X	5/1	none	X	FAF/FFS*
24	78	21	100	X	X			X	X			7/15	8/15		FFS
2,053	40			X	X	X		X	X	X		5/1	none		FAF/FFS/AFSA/SF
650	81							X					none		FAF
214	96							X	X		X	7/15	none	X	FAF*/FFS/AFSA
				X	X	X	X					3/1	10/1	X	FFS
				X				X				5/1	none		FFS

*Preferred need analysis document.

Institution	Tuition and fees	Add'l out-of-state/district tuition	Books and supplies	Costs for campus residents			Costs for students at home		
				Room and board	Transportation	Other costs	Board only	Transportation	Other costs
Eastfield College	420	1,490/380	350				1,100	1,170	935
El Centro College	420	1,490/380	570					400	600
El Paso Community College	532	1,372/—	412						915
‡ Frank Phillips College	430	120/60	412	1,490	475	811	1,500	874	811
Galveston College	522	438/—	400					700	1,000
‡ Grayson County College	510	1,200/120	285	3,000	572	592		762	592
‡ Hardin-Simmons University	5,432		411	2,612	676	1,092	989	676	1,092
† Hill College	615	200/—	466	2,500	639	853		1,063	853
Houston Baptist University	8,175		490	2,880	1,260	1,370	1,700	1,260	1,370
† Houston Community College	750	1,410/150	600				1,977	330	989
Howard College	468	500/50	300	2,052	800	1,175	750	800	1,175
Howard Payne University	4,162		350	2,470	650	1,650		700	1,650
Huston-Tillotson College	4,440		490	3,290	540	980		520	520
† Incarnate Word College	7,000		500	3,230	1,000	1,600	1,700	1,300	1,700
† Institute for Christian Studies	910			1,500					
‡ ITT Technical Institute: Arlington	6,875		525						1,398
† Jacksonville College	2,220		400	2,200				1,000	
† Jarvis Christian College	3,522		377	2,999	750	900		750	900
† Kilgore College	330	480/—	450	2,000		1,000			1,000
Lamar University	1,102	3,238/—	450	2,762	1,042	1,210	1,500	1,736	1,114
† Laredo Junior College	570	1,560/780	450	2,781				1,800	934
Laredo State University	870	3,120/—	486	2,901			1,622	1,287	1,014
Lee College	390	900/60	350				1,768	657	917
LeTourneau University	7,350		600	3,640	500	900		843	1,021
Lon Morris College	4,004		450	3,186	974	1,510	1,150	974	1,510
† Lubbock Christian University	6,020		300	2,330	550	1,000	1,400	630	1,200
McLennan Community College	460	1,980/120	320				1,275	1,500	1,365
‡ McMurry University	5,250		250	2,710	475	1,318	1,100	650	1,318
† Midland College	457	550/20	400				1,500	990	1,210
Midwestern State University	1,110	3,120/—	600	2,918	500	900	700	500	480
Miss Wade's Fashion Merchandising College	4,515		535		1,160	936	1,440	1,160	936
Mountain View College	420	1,490/380	600				1,500	1,330	1,045
Navarro College	680	156/120	416	2,575	644	811	1,500	807	811
North Harris County College	324	660/600	400				1,560	1,200	900
North Lake College	420	1,490/380	400						
Northeast Texas Community College	570	760/240	490				1,638	1,081	1,255
† Northwood Institute: Texas Campus	7,545		500	3,711		550			
Odessa College	457	273/40	400	2,626	490	3,635	1,500	660	760
‡ Our Lady of the Lake University of San Antonio	5,992		690	2,860	638	1,354	1,500	638	1,204
† Palo Alto College	500	780/—							
‡ Panola College	300	250/20	400	1,990	100	300		900	300
Paris Junior College	2,070	5,250/1,350	400	2,584	600			600	700
Paul Quinn College	3,635		400	2,975	600	700	1,500		
† Prairie View A&M University	991	3,240/—	533	2,938	1,620	1,352	1,500	1,918	1,491
Ranger Junior College	540	240/20	360	2,241	661	661		771	661
Rice University	8,017		425	4,900	300	1,300	1,500	700	825

†Figures are projected for 1991-92. ‡Figures are for 1990-91.

Total freshmen	Percent receiving aid	Freshmen judged to have need	Percent offered aid	Need-based Acad	Need-based Music/drama	Need-based Art	Need-based Athl	Nonneed-based Acad	Nonneed-based Music/drama	Nonneed-based Art	Nonneed-based Athl	Priority	Closing	Inst aid form	Need analysis document
3,046	24			X	X	X		X	X	X			6/1		FAF*/FFS
3,397	65							X				7/1	none	X	FAF/FFS/AFSA*
300	42	31	100					X	X		X	7/1	none	X	FAF/FFS*/AFSA
310	18	203	74					X	X			6/1	none		AFSA
													none	X	FAF*/FFS
364	87	225	99	X				X	X	X	X	3/15	none	X	FAF/FFS*/AFSA
482	60			X	X	X	X	X	X		X	8/1	none	X	FAF/FFS*/AFSA
213	70							X	X	X	X		5/1		FAF*/FFS
5,424	45	1,940	100	X								4/15	none		AFSSA
684	60			X	X	X	X	X	X	X	X	4/1	none	X	FAF/FFS*
351	71	240	88									5/1	none	X	FFS
290	95			X	X		X						5/1		FAF/FFS*/AFSA*
603	62	203	100					X	X	X	X	4/1	none		FAF
				X									6/15		FAF
								X	X		X		none		FAF
130	94							X	X		X		5/15	X	FFS*/AFSA
327	97			X	X		X	X	X			7/30	none	X	FFS
2,400	13							X				8/1	none		FAF*/AFSA
1,922	31							X	X	X	X	4/1	none	X	FAF*/FFS
997	61			X	X		X	X	X		X		none	X	FAF*/FFS
													none		FAF*/FFS
3,598	15	76	96					X	X	X	X	7/1	none	X	FAF/FFS/AFSA*
167	78	137	100	X				X				2/15	none		FAF*/FFS/AFSA; FAF*/FFS/AFSA/CSS SAAC/ACT SAAC
250	90	200	100	X	X	X	X	X	X	X	X	6/1	none	X	FAF*/FFS
275	90			X	X		X					7/1	8/1	X	FFS
4,230	34			X	X		X	X			X	6/1	none	X	FFS/AFSA
307	88	217	100					X	X	X		3/15	none	X	FAF/FFS*
2,750	24							X	X	X	X	6/1	none		FFS
													none	X	FAF*/FFS
148	80	115	100										none	X	AFSA
4,721	12											6/1	none		FAF*/FFS
2,057	30							X	X	X	X	6/1	none		FAF/FFS*/AFSA
10,707	15			X	X	X						4/15	none	X	FAF/FFS/AFSA*
				X				X				7/1	none		FAF
								X	X	X		5/1	none	X	FAF/FFS*/AFSA
													none		FAF*/FFS
1,526	30	308	100					X	X	X	X	6/1	none	X	FAF/FFS*/AFSA
371	60								X			4/15	7/15		FAF/FFS*
													6/1		FAF
538	40	174	98	X	X			X	X		X	6/1	none		FAF/FFS*
735	44											4/1	none		FFS
													none	X	FAF*/FFS
813	85							X	X	X	X	4/16	none	X	FAF*/FFS/AFSA/AFSSA;FAF*/FFS/AFSA/CSS SAAC/ACT
				X	X		X	X	X		X	8/1	none		AFSA
622	91	259	100	X				X	X		X	3/1	6/1	X	FAF

*Preferred need analysis document.

Institution	Tuition and fees	Add'l out-of-state/district tuition	Books and supplies	Costs for campus residents			Costs for students at home		
				Room and board	Trans-portation	Other costs	Board only	Trans-portation	Other costs
Richland College	420	1,490/380	350					1,170	935
† St. Edward's University	7,750		450	3,450	550	1,520		450	500
St. Mary's University	7,320		500	3,450	250	1,000	1,620	648	788
‡ St. Philip's College	480	780/—	225				1,700	450	500
Sam Houston State University	1,060	3,660/—	400	2,730	700	900	1,330	1,500	500
San Antonio Art Institute	8,840								
† San Antonio College	484	960/384	420				1,600	1,216	1,550
San Jacinto College									
Central Campus	310	960/300	350					1,000	1,209
North	334	1,024/320	400				1,584	778	1,295
Schreiner College	7,425		346	4,990	346	1,036	1,500	464	1,036
South Plains College	560	540/—	300	2,100	800	900		900	900
Southern Methodist University	11,768		550	4,832		1,030	1,500	820	927
Southwest Texas Junior College	650	1,248/96	325	2,360	634	411	900	430	773
Southwest Texas State University	1,122	3,240/—	500	2,060	1,116	1,970	700	1,116	1,970
‡ Southwestern Adventist College	6,552		387	3,242	698	988	1,560	820	988
‡ Southwestern Assemblies of God College	3,540		400	2,750	800	1,080	1,500	650	1,080
Southwestern Christian College	3,640		300	2,307		400			400
Southwestern University	9,400		500	4,281	230	770	1,500	500	750
Stephen F. Austin State University	825	3,660/—	500	2,994	900	900	1,750	1,167	800
Sul Ross State University	985	3,120/—	450	2,860	588	1,100	1,500	839	1,100
Tarleton State University	1,220	3,300/—	425	2,930	404	1,266	1,500	506	1,094
Tarrant County Junior College	330	3,300/90	475					1,265	1,090
‡ Temple Junior College	568	1,140/300	500	3,000	630	868	1,500	863	842
Texarkana College	480	440/150	475					550	1,200
Texas A&I University	1,184	2,592/—	484	2,624	1,200	1,714		1,496	1,296
Texas A&M University									
College Station	1,324	3,060/—	530	3,884	658	1,124			
Galveston	1,225	3,120/—	400	3,124	600	725	950	525	650
Texas Christian University	8,130		584	3,058		1,718		522	1,718
† Texas College	3,605		400	2,430	500	925	2,500	575	975
‡ Texas Lutheran College	5,870		450	2,820	650	900	1,170	1,000	1,000
Texas Southern University	1,030	3,240/—	500	3,320	1,400	1,700	1,500	1,400	1,700
Texas Southmost College	601	1,680/180	350				1,633	824	412
Texas State Technical Institute									
† Amarillo	816	3,360/—	720	2,780	400	4,524	900	800	1,900
† Harlingen	900	3,150/—	600	3,080			369		
† Sweetwater	1,014	3,840/—	800	3,420	1,412	736	1,514	1,412	736
† Waco	816	3,360/—	650	3,272	300	1,200	1,820	1,500	1,200
Texas Tech University	1,198	3,060/—	300	3,348					
† Texas Wesleyan University	5,600		350	3,080	450	900		1,200	900
Trinity University	10,340		400	4,060	460	500	2,000		
Trinity Valley Community College	336	1,560/240	440	2,350	165	605	692	528	605
‡ Tyler Junior College	470	690/300	500	2,100	500	750	1,000	1,000	750
† University of Central Texas	3,660		783	3,142	400	1,200	2,000	500	1,200
University of Dallas	8,600		450	4,170	750	800	1,500	600	800
University of Houston									
† Clear Lake	1,030	3,120/—	540					1,779	1,669
Downtown	1,010	3,300/—	331	3,034	414	731	1,560	993	703

†Figures are projected for 1991-92.   ‡Figures are for 1990-91.

| All aid | | Need–based aid | | Grants and scholarships | | | | | | | | Financial aid deadlines | | Inst aid form | Need analysis document |
Total freshmen	Percent receiving aid	Freshmen judged to have need	Percent offered aid	Need-based Acad	Music/ drama	Art	Athl	Nonneed-based Acad	Music/ drama	Art	Athl	Priority	Closing		
9,387	10	500	60	X				X				6/1	none		FAF*/FFS/AFSA/ AFSSA/SF;FAF*/FFS/ AFSA/CSS SAAC/ACT
334	61	208	100					X			X	3/1	8/15	X	FAF
536	77	305	100	X				X	X		X	4/1	none		FAF*/FFS/AFSA/SF
2,279	34			X				X	X			6/1		X	AFSA
2,367	29	862	100					X	X	X	X		none		FAF/FFS*
													3/1		
3,786	40			X	X	X		X	X		X	5/1	none	X	FAF/FFS/AFSA/SF*
															AFSA
2,279	15	274	100	X	X	X	X	X	X	X	X	7/1	none		FAF/FFS/AFSA
182	83	124	100	X	X	X	X	X	X	X	X	4/15	none		FAF*/FFS
													none		FAF/FFS*
1,101	60			X	X	X	X	X	X	X	X	3/1	6/1		FAF
													none		FAF*/FFS/AFSA
2,922	26							X	X		X	4/1	none		FAF/FFS*/AFSA
152	68	104	100	X	X			X	X			5/15	7/15		FAF
135	75	82	100					X	X			5/1	none	X	FFS
															FAF*/FFS/AFSA
311	66	178	100	X				X	X	X			3/15	X	FAF*/FFS
3,945	45							X	X		X	4/1	6/1	X	FFS
		250	100	X				X	X			4/1	none		FAF/FFS*
937	14	857						X	X			6/1	none		FAF
4,999	10			X				X	X			5/15	none	X	AFSA
1,542	45			X	X	X	X	X	X		X	8/1	none		FFS
889	85			X				X	X	X	X	6/1	7/15		FAF/FFS/AFSA*
													4/15	X	FAF*/FFS
6,100	58	2,565	96	X				X				4/15	none		FAF*/FFS/AFSA
												4/1	none		FAF
1,140	53	442	98	X				X	X	X	X	5/1	none		FAF*/FFS
156	90	156	100	X	X	X	X	X	X	X	X		none	X	FAF/FFS/AFSA;FAF/ FFS
222	87	106	100					X	X	X	X	5/1	none		FAF*/FFS
1,059	80											5/1	none		FAF*/FFS
															FFS
207	51	135	100	X								7/1	none		FAF/FFS*/AFSA/ AFSSA/SF
1,293	80			X								5/5	6/15		FFS
532	60	304	100	X								7/15	none	X	FAF/FFS*/AFSA
1,412	52	1,116	100	X				X				5/31	none	X	FAF
3,527	30	1,284	75	X	X	X		X	X	X	X	4/1	none		FFS
164	82			X				X	X	X	X	4/15	none	X	FAF*/FFS/AFSA
601	78			X	X	X		X					2/1		FAF
1,177	65	911	100					X	X	X	X	7/1	none		FAF/FFS/AFSA*
1,698	28	437	100	X	X	X	X	X	X	X	X		5/1	X	AFSA
				X								7/1	9/7		FFS
276	77	175	100					X	X	X		3/1	none		FAF*/FFS
								X				5/1	none	X	FAF
1,450	70	790	100	X		X		X		X		6/1	none		FAF/FFS*

*Preferred need analysis document.

Institution	Tuition and fees	Add'l out-of-state/ district tuition	Books and supplies	Costs for campus residents			Costs for students at home		
				Room and board	Trans-portation	Other costs	Board only	Trans-portation	Other costs
† Houston	1,140	3,120/—	400	3,770	1,000	1,500		1,000	1,500
‡ Victoria	960	3,120/—	400				1,560	1,315	1,315
University of Mary Hardin-Baylor	4,450		450	2,970	800	1,200	1,500	688	982
University of North Texas	1,036	3,120/—	300	3,304	550	750			750
University of St. Thomas	6,830		425	3,360	660	1,050	850	1,025	1,050
University of Texas									
Arlington	1,000	3,120/—	416	2,800	594	900	1,100	1,314	900
Austin	1,100	3,120/—	500	3,400	530	1,300	1,500	530	1,300
Dallas	1,010	3,060/—	553				1,500	1,237	490
‡ El Paso	930	3,120/—	340	2,600	1,306	1,056	1,500	1,286	1,088
Health Science Center at Houston	890	3,060/—	450		1,449	168	2,340	1,449	1,728
Health Science Center at San Antonio	733	3,120/—	300				1,890	1,809	2,853
Medical Branch at Galveston	711	3,600/—	702	4,158	1,665	6,120			
Pan American	918	3,120/ 2,288	375	7,288	380	1,685	825		1,279
Permian Basin	1,005	3,240/—	525		970	630	975	970	630
San Antonio	1,290	4,200/—	500		1,763	1,439	1,560	1,763	1,439
Southwestern Medical Center at Dallas									
Southwestern Allied Health Sciences School	825	3,240/—	560				3,344	1,760	4,304
Tyler	980	3,300/—	400				1,620	580	934
† Vernon Regional Junior College	500	150/20	500	1,700	2,000	2,500		2,000	2,500
Victoria College	390	810/320	350				1,500	450	781
† Wayland Baptist University	4,137		475	2,735	530	938	1,600	530	848
‡ Weatherford College	450	2,100/120	450	2,500	450	1,000	1,300	1,200	1,000
West Texas State University	1,070	3,000/—	500	2,794	580	1,040	1,560	1,100	770
‡ Western Texas College	540	150/60	350	1,920	512	720	1,500	704	720
Wharton County Junior College	990	900/—	500	1,900	500	1,100	1,300	850	1,100
Wiley College	3,946		200	2,544	600	900	1,500	600	595
Utah									
Brigham Young University	2,000		600	3,200	880	1,080	1,600	880	1,080
‡ College of Eastern Utah	1,005	1,704/—	800	2,520				1,000	
‡ Dixie College	1,156	1,989/—	350	2,430	425	690		200	200
LDS Business College	1,790		525		555	888	1,500	585	786
† Phillips Junior College: Salt Lake City Campus	9,450								
‡ Salt Lake Community College	1,239	2,199/—	630				1,575	450	1,020
‡ Snow College	1,005	1,674/—	475	2,355	500	900	1,500	600	700
Southern Utah University	1,410	3,441/—	300	2,370					
Stevens-Henager College of Business	7,500		500						
‡ University of Utah	1,884	3,426/—		3,939					
‡ Utah State University	1,596	2,814/—	600	2,592	1,000	1,200	2,000	450	700
‡ Utah Valley Community College	1,194	2,106/—	558				1,500	630	630
‡ Weber State University	1,398	2,355/—	450	3,100	775	975	1,600	775	975
‡ Westminster College of Salt Lake City	6,540		500	3,400	950	1,650	668	950	1,650
Vermont									
Bennington College	19,400		400	3,800		600	1,830	930	
‡ Burlington College	6,030		550				1,800	1,080	2,090
† Castleton State College	3,319	2,931/—	600	4,300	300	600	1,200	600	600
Champlain College	6,995		350	4,945	200	600	1,500	650	500

†Figures are projected for 1991-92.   ‡Figures are for 1990-91.

| All aid | | Need–based aid | | Grants and scholarships | | | | | | | | Financial aid deadlines | | Inst aid form | Need analysis document |
| | | | | Need–based | | | | Nonneed–based | | | | | | | |
Total freshmen	Percent receiving aid	Freshmen judged to have need	Percent offered aid	Acad	Music/drama	Art	Athl	Acad	Music/drama	Art	Athl	Priority	Closing		
2,559	35			X	X	X		X	X	X	X	4/3	none		FAF/FFS*
				X				X				5/15	none		FAF
254	80							X	X		X	5/1	none	X	FAF/FFS*
2,301	27			X	X	X	X	X	X	X	X	6/1	none		FAF
217	50							X	X			3/1	none		FAF
1,881	25	883	54					X	X	X	X	6/1	none	X	FAF/FFS
5,573	27	1,850	92	X	X	X	X	X	X	X	X	3/1	none		FAF/FFS*
				X				X				5/1	11/1	X	FAF*/FFS
2,367	55			X	X		X	X	X		X	3/15	none	X	FAF/FFS*/AFSA
				X				X				3/1	12/2		FAF
				X				X				3/12	none		FAF*/FFS
				X								3/15	none		FAF*/AFSA/AFSSA; FAF*/AFSA/CSS SAAC/ACT SAAC/ AFSA
														X	FAF/FFS*/AFSA
1,745	76	1,006	100	X				X			X	3/31	none	X	FAF/SF
								X				4/15	10/3		FAF
				X	X	X	X	X	X	X		6/1	7/1	X	FAF/FFS*
350	35	240	100	X	X		X	X	X	X	X	7/15	none		AFSA
				X	X			X	X				none		FAF
													none		FAF/FFS*/AFSA
502	20	250	80	X	X		X	X	X		X		6/1		FAF/FFS*
976	55							X	X	X	X	7/15	none		FAF/FFS*
851	44							X	X	X	X	7/1	none		FAF/FFS*/AFSA
		410	100					X	X		X	6/1	none		FAF/FFS*/AFSA
164	55	102	100	X	X		X	X	X		X	6/1	9/1	X	FAF/FFS/AFSA*
4,493	53							X	X	X	X		2/15		AFSA
				X	X	X		X	X	X	X	6/1	none	X	FAF*/AFSA
1,267	45							X	X	X	X	6/1	none	X	FFS/AFSA*;AFSA+ FFS
216	50	100	89					X					none		FAF/FFS*/AFSA
				X									none		AFSA
2,979	44							X		X	X	4/1	none	X	FAF/FFS*
														X	FAF*/FFS
													none	X	FFS
														X	AFSA
				X	X	X	X	X	X	X	X	3/1	none		FFS
1,973	61	840	100					X	X	X	X	3/15	none		FAF/FFS/AFSA*
5,950	65							X				7/1	none	X	FFS
1,951	32							X	X	X	X	5/1	none		FAF/FFS/AFSA*
193	80			X				X				3/1	none	X	FAF/FFS*/AFSA
153	58	100	100										3/1	X	FAF
47	80	36	100	X								6/1	none	X	FAF/FFS;FAF/FFS/ AFSA
369	57	219	100	X		X		X				3/15	none		FAF*/FFS
873	70	568	100	X			X					5/1	none		FAF*/FFS/AFSA

*Preferred need analysis document.

Institution	Tuition and fees	Add'l out-of-state/ district tuition	Books and supplies	Costs for campus residents			Costs for students at home		
				Room and board	Transportation	Other costs	Board only	Transportation	Other costs
‡ College of St. Joseph in Vermont	6,570		400	3,840	450	900	1,600	650	900
‡ Community College of Vermont	2,010	1,950/—	350					600	
Goddard College	12,330		400	4,120	400	800			
Green Mountain College	7,890		400	4,880	400	125	1,500	400	125
‡ Johnson State College	3,060	3,312/—	400	4,086	300	600	921	400	600
Landmark College	20,100		500	5,000	1,200	1,000			
‡ Lyndon State College	3,070	3,312/—	400	4,086	300	400		300	400
Marlboro College	15,390		400	5,150	200	320	2,020	50	320
New England Culinary Institute	12,875		450	2,325					
‡ Norwich University	11,800		450	4,500	400	750	1,800	400	750
St. Michael's College	11,265		350	5,090	250	600	2,070	200	400
School for International Training	9,820		350	3,585	400	800	3,000	400	800
Southern Vermont College	7,430		500	3,820	400	550	1,000	600	550
Sterling College	10,480		525	4,400	300	200			
‡ Trinity College of Vermont	8,770		550	4,450	250	250	1,500	250	250
‡ University of Vermont	4,590	8,600/—	400	4,026		840	1,640	984	840
‡ Vermont Technical College	3,670	3,072/—	600	4,086	350	550	1,700	600	550

Virginia

Institution	Tuition and fees	Add'l out-of-state/ district tuition	Books and supplies	Room and board	Transportation	Other costs	Board only	Transportation	Other costs
Averett College	8,750		350	4,200	500	600		400	500
‡ Blue Ridge Community College	863	3,402/—	500				1,500	1,000	500
Bluefield College	5,400		400	3,620	778	830	1,280	1,361	830
Bridgewater College	9,195		475	4,295	150	825	2,280	500	825
‡ Central Virginia Community College	858	3,402/—	400				600	500	2,800
Christendom College	7,650		400	3,400	500	300	1,400	600	300
‡ Christopher Newport College	2,010	2,450/—	350				1,500	650	625
† Clinch Valley College of the University of Virginia	2,356	2,060/—	550	3,050	600	660	1,550	1,000	660
College of Health Sciences	2,328		699		872	4,332	2,376	1,872	2,033
‡ College of William and Mary	3,396	5,850/—	500	3,746	350	800	1,200	400	800
Commonwealth College	5,260		750	3,000	350	300		350	300
‡ Dabney S. Lancaster Community College	870	3,402/—	400				900	840	1,410
Danville Community College	862	3,402/—	400				1,600	800	1,000
Eastern Mennonite College	7,900		600	3,300	500	1,300	1,000	500	1,300
‡ Eastern Shore Community College	873	3,402/—	400				1,000		
Emory and Henry College	7,270		600	3,956	500	1,000	1,500	1,000	800
Ferrum College	7,400		400	3,400	400	1,200	2,200	600	1,000
‡ George Mason University	2,496	3,456/—	500	4,470	500	900	1,200	1,200	900
‡ Germanna Community College	867	3,402/—	300				1,000	1,440	1,274
Hampden-Sydney College	11,017		300	3,354	150	500			
‡ Hampton University	6,263		450	2,723	1,100	500	1,500	1,100	500
‡ Hollins College	10,810		400	4,350	350	550		300	1,000
‡ J. Sargeant Reynolds Community College	858	3,402/—	400				1,200	850	800
‡ James Madison University	3,062	3,083/—	500	3,908	562	700	1,860	562	700
‡ John Tyler Community College	858	3,402/—	600				1,800	950	900
Liberty University	5,850		500	3,700	600	500	1,500	700	1,500
‡ Longwood College	2,880	2,736/—	400	3,428	500	894		1,000	
‡ Lord Fairfax Community College	874	3,402/—	400				1,500	950	990

†Figures are projected for 1991-92.   ‡Figures are for 1990-91.

| All aid | | Need-based aid | | Grants and scholarships | | | | | | | | Financial aid deadlines | | Inst aid form | Need analysis document |
| Total freshmen | Percent receiving aid | Freshmen judged to have need | Percent offered aid | Need-based | | | | Nonneed-based | | | | Priority | Closing | | |
				Acad	Music/ drama	Art	Athl	Acad	Music/ drama	Art	Athl				
60	66			X				X				3/1	5/1		FAF*/FFS
394	86							X					none	X	FFS
43	55	21	100									5/15	6/15	X	FAF*/FFS
219	38	80	100	X				X		X	X	4/1	none		FAF
561	35			X	X			X				3/1	none		FAF*/FFS
8	8	2	100	X									8/1	X	FAF
309	59	211	94	X				X				3/15	none	X	FAF*/FFS
82	57			X								3/1	5/1	X	FAF*/FFS
216	90	180	100										none	X	FAF*/FFS
702	72	350	100	X				X				3/1	none		FAF
360	62	198	100	X	X	X	X	X			X	3/15	none	X	FAF
								X					9/1		FAF*/FFS
132	70	69	100	X								4/15	none		FAF*/FFS/AFSA/ AFSSA/SF;FAF*/FFS/ AFSA/CSS SAAC/ACT
53	49	31	100									3/15	none	X	FAF*/FFS/AFSA; FAF*/FFS/AFSA/CSS SAAC/ACT SAAC/
274	65	74	100	X				X				3/1	none		FAF*/FFS;FAF*/FFS/ CSS SAAC/ACT SAAC
1,906	42	793	100	X	X	X	X	X	X	X	X	3/1	none		FAF*/FFS
277	66	228	100	X				X				3/1	none	X	FAF*/FFS
136	82	112	100	X	X			X				4/1	none	X	FAF*/FFS/AFSA
				X								5/15	none		FAF*/AFSA
176	85	124	100					X	X	X	X	3/1	none		FAF
282	96	181	100					X	X				3/15		FAF*/FFS
714	20			X				X				5/15	none	X	FAF/AFSA*
36	63	23	100					X				5/1	6/1	X	FAF*/FFS
504	73	417	88	X				X	X			4/1	none	X	FAF
308	62	239	80	X			X	X			X	4/1	none	X	FAF
42	59			X				X				7/1	none		FAF/AFSA*/SF
1,236	23	290	100	X	X	X	X	X			X	2/15	none		FAF
566	98	206	100	X				X					none	X	AFSA
677	15	100	100	X				X				7/1	none	X	FAF/AFSA
				X				X				4/30	none	X	FAF/AFSA*
193	71	137	100	X	X			X				4/15	none	X	FAF
191	66	126	100	X								6/1	none		FAF
168	93	75	100					X					4/1		FAF*/FFS
394	60	235	100	X				X				6/1	none	X	FAF*/FFS
1,814	32	587	100					X			X	3/1	none		FAF
								X					none	X	FAF*/AFSA
245	60	85	100	X				X				3/1	none		FAF*/FFS/AFSA
1,200	70							X	X		X	3/31	6/1	X	FAF
226	42	94	100	X	X			X	X	X			3/31		FAF
														X	FAF/AFSA
1,912	46	870	100	X	X	X	X	X	X	X	X	2/15	3/19		FAF
								X				6/30	none	X	FAF/AFSA*
2,195	875	711	98					X	X		X	4/15	none		FAF/FFS/AFSA/SF*
603	62			X				X	X	X	X	3/1	4/1	X	FAF
688	44	331	91	X								5/1	none	X	FAF/AFSA

*Preferred need analysis document.

Institution	Tuition and fees	Add'l out-of-state/district tuition	Books and supplies	Costs for campus residents			Costs for students at home		
				Room and board	Trans-portation	Other costs	Board only	Trans-portation	Other costs
Lynchburg College	10,330		450	5,050	430	440	1,500	390	
Mary Baldwin College	9,165		450	6,175	250	800	1,700	360	600
‡ Mary Washington College	2,362	2,956/—	450	3,994	615	1,048	1,686	925	1,200
Marymount University	9,707		350	4,650	450	600	1,800	600	600
‡ Mountain Empire Community College	875	3,402/—	400				500	1,000	
National Business College	4,326								
‡ New River Community College	882	3,402/—	250					1,500	950
‡ Norfolk State University	2,180	2,430/—	550	3,200	700	300	1,250	750	500
‡ Northern Virginia Community College	858	3,402/1,980	470				1,640	980	730
‡ Old Dominion University	2,510	3,264/—	400	4,164	564	1,000	1,500	992	1,000
‡ Patrick Henry Community College	864	3,402/—	400				1,100	970	600
‡ Paul D. Camp Community College	858	3,402/—	300				1,500	800	650
‡ Piedmont Virginia Community College	868	3,402/—	350				750	1,000	2,100
‡ Radford University	2,178	2,528/—	400	3,568	300	600		500	600
‡ Randolph-Macon College	10,810		350	4,600	250	550	1,770	650	550
Randolph-Macon Woman's College	11,680		350	5,140	265	550	1,500	225	550
‡ Rappahannock Community College	870	3,402/—	500				1,100	1,000	600
‡ Richard Bland College	1,260	2,300/—	400				1,500	750	1,500
‡ Roanoke College	10,200		400	3,800	600	600	1,950	600	600
‡ St. Paul's College	4,556		450	3,010	350	650	1,500	300	750
‡ Shenandoah University	7,400		500	3,500	600			600	900
‡ Southside Virginia Community College	864	3,402/—	400				1,350	1,200	700
‡ Southwest Virginia Community College	863	3,402/—	400				1,800	1,600	800
† Strayer College	4,950		450				2,500	1,092	2,000
Sweet Briar College	12,625		500	4,850	500	600		500	600
‡ Thomas Nelson Community College	866	3,402/—	400				1,550	700	650
‡ Tidewater Community College	858	3,402/—	400				1,500	750	810
University of Richmond	11,695		550	2,840		1,270	1,600		910
‡ University of Virginia	2,966	5,170/—	525	3,150		1,050			
‡ Virginia Commonwealth University	2,719	3,980/—	500	3,532	1,330	1,620	1,500	1,330	1,620
‡ Virginia Highlands Community College	858	3,402/—	420				1,575	840	680
† Virginia Intermont College	6,570		400	3,930	900	1,400	1,400	900	1,200
† Virginia Military Institute	3,965	5,380/—	500	3,525	400	500			
‡ Virginia Polytechnic Institute and State University	2,846	3,384/—	560	2,672	210	950	4,088	500	950
Virginia State University	2,668	3,240/—	450	3,977	400	475	1,350	500	525
‡ Virginia Union University	5,840		250	3,010	260	400	1,480	260	400
Virginia Wesleyan College	8,790		500	4,425	1,000	1,500	500	1,500	1,500
‡ Virginia Western Community College	862	3,402/—	450				1,200	750	750
‡ Washington and Lee University	10,970		500	3,900	400	910	2,000	50	910
Wytheville Community College	1,065	3,210/—	500				1,575	1,300	630

Washington

Institution	Tuition and fees	Add'l out-of-state/district tuition	Books and supplies	Room and board	Trans-portation	Other costs	Board only	Trans-portation	Other costs
Antioch University Seattle	7,575		350						
‡ Art Institute of Seattle	7,555		1,022	3,880	1,694	1,143	2,043	944	1,143
† Bellevue Community College	945	2,772/—	600				1,800	900	700

†Figures are projected for 1991-92.   ‡Figures are for 1990-91.

| All aid | | Need-based aid | | Grants and scholarships | | | | | | | | Financial aid deadlines | | Inst aid form | Need analysis document |
| Total freshmen | Percent receiving aid | Freshmen judged to have need | Percent offered aid | Need-based | | | | Nonneed-based | | | | | | | |
				Acad	Music/drama	Art	Athl	Acad	Music/drama	Art	Athl	Priority	Closing		
380	37	141	100	X				X	X			4/1	none	X	FAF*/FFS
148	93	98	100	X	X	X		X	X	X		3/1	4/15		FAF
752	35	210	88					X					3/1		FAF
283	45	128	100	X		X		X				3/1	none	X	FAF*/FFS/AFSA/AFSSA/SF;FAF*/FFS/AFSA/AFSSA/
2,125	28	525	100	X				X				5/1	none	X	FAF/FFS/AFSA*/SF
443	92	400	100	X				X					none	X	AFSA
366	35			X				X				6/1	none		FAF*/FFS/AFSA
1,600	85											4/15	none		FAF*/FFS
3,780	21	836	97					X				4/1	none	X	FAF
1,558	63	1,104	89	X	X	X	X	X	X	X	X		2/15		FAF
				X				X				6/15	none	X	FAF/AFSA*
623	48	300	100	X				X				8/7	8/14	X	AFSA
1,850	14											4/15	none	X	FAF*/FFS
1,661	35	850	68					X	X	X	X		3/15		FAF
318	68	104	100					X				3/1	none	X	FAF*/FFS
183	71	75	100					X	X				3/1	X	FAF*/FFS/AFSA/AFSSA/SF;FAF*/FFS/AFSA/CSS SAAC/ACT
591	25	60	100	X				X				6/1	none		FAF
412	48	213	92	X				X				4/1	6/1	X	FAF
396	78	161	100	X	X	X		X	X	X		3/1	none		FAF*/FFS/AFSA
201	80	161	100					X				6/1	none	X	FAF
199	88	176	100	X	X			X	X			3/15	4/1	X	FAF
310	52							X				5/1	none	X	FAF/AFSA*
1,414	91	1,300	100	X				X				5/30	none	X	FAF/AFSA
391	64			X				X				7/1	none		FAF/FFS/AFSA*
		59	100	X	X			X	X			4/1	none	X	FAF
													none	X	FAF/FFS/AFSA/AFSSA/SF
								X				8/1	none		FAF
786	53	183	93	X	X	X	X	X	X		X	2/15	2/25		FAF
2,568	35	850	89								X		3/1		FAF
1,612	60	850	100					X	X	X	X	5/1	none		FAF*/FFS/AFSA/SF
363	35	335	95	X				X					none		FAF
138	62			X				X				3/1	none	X	FAF/FFS*
431	34	150	99	X				X			X	3/1	none	X	FAF*/FFS/AFSA/AFSSA/SF;FAF*/FFS/AFSA/AFSSA/
4,259	27	1,348	85	X	X	X	X	X	X	X	X		3/15		FAF
990	85	879	98	X			X	X				3/31	5/1	X	FAF
357	87			X	X			X	X		X	6/15	none		FAF
338	57	194	100	X	X	X		X	X	X			3/1		FAF
3,387	15			X									none		AFSA
386	28	107	100	X	X			X				2/1	none		FAF
													none	X	FAF
													none		FAF
478	90	340	50			X							none		FAF
													none	X	FAF

*Preferred need analysis document.

Institution	Tuition and fees	Add'l out-of-state/district tuition	Books and supplies	Costs for campus residents			Costs for students at home		
				Room and board	Trans-portation	Other costs	Board only	Trans-portation	Other costs
† Big Bend Community College	945	2,772/—	530	3,200	840	1,200	1,200	500	600
† Central Washington University	1,698	4,272/—	450	3,143	660	1,100			
† Centralia College	945	2,772/—	405					720	1,020
City University	6,030		450				1,000	814	862
† Clark College	945	2,772/—	498				1,560	762	570
† Cogswell College North	6,480		550						
† Columbia Basin College	945	2,772/—	550				700	840	600
Cornish College of the Arts	7,479		1,100				1,650	840	600
† Eastern Washington University	1,698	4,272/—	500	3,150	800	1,160	1,570	800	570
† Edmonds Community College	945	2,772/—	560		890	1,220	1,740	890	600
† Everett Community College	945	2,772/—	500					900	1,000
† Evergreen State College	1,698	4,272/—	564	3,400	798	1,212	1,740	798	1,212
Gonzaga University	10,335		560	3,700	880	1,240	1,760	880	630
† Grays Harbor College	945	2,772/—	500				1,570	800	570
† Green River Community College	945	2,772/—	480				1,800	800	600
Griffin College	6,400		900				1,800	800	1,200
Heritage College	4,450		514				1,570	800	570
Highline Community College	945	2,772/—	560				1,740	880	630
† Lower Columbia College	945	2,772/—	540				1,650	750	600
Lutheran Bible Institute of Seattle	2,440		480	3,240	760	350		1,060	440
† North Seattle Community College	945	2,772/—	500				1,570	800	1,000
Northwest College of the Assemblies of God	5,816		560	2,900	840	1,200	1,650	840	600
Northwest Indian College	843	2,535/—	500				1,570	800	570
† Olympic College	945	2,772/—	480				1,800	760	500
Pacific Lutheran University	11,075		560	3,890	500	1,250	1,600	900	600
† Peninsula College	945	2,772/—	500	3,050	800	1,050	810	800	1,000
† Pierce College	945	2,772/—.	560				1,740	880	630
† Puget Sound Christian College	4,650		525	3,000	300	1,305	1,950	932	945
‡ St. Martin's College	9,070		500	3,500	700	1,010		700	500
† Seattle Central Community College	945	2,772/—	600				1,540	825	935
Seattle Pacific University	10,581		525	3,969	375	1,500	1,839	375	745
Seattle University	10,710		500	3,900	700	500		700	500
‡ Shoreline Community College	858	2,535/—	501				1,600	798	570
† Skagit Valley College	945	2,772/—	530				1,749	869	965
† South Puget Sound Community College	945	2,772/—	550				1,800	960	800
† South Seattle Community College	945	2,772/—	530				1,650	840	600
† Spokane Community College	945	2,772/—	540				1,650	840	510
† Spokane Falls Community College	945	2,772/—	540				1,620	840	500
† Tacoma Community College	945	2,772/—	530				1,650	840	600
‡ University of Puget Sound	11,420			3,800	300	900	1,500	800	900
† University of Washington	2,178	3,970/—	492	3,510	606	1,335	1,500	576	996
Walla Walla College	9,083		550	2,955	220	450	1,600	700	450
† Walla Walla Community College	945	2,772/—	510				1,650	825	600
† Washington State University	2,178	3,897/—	605	3,300	800	1,160	1,500	760	1,160
† Wenatchee Valley College	945	2,772/—	500	3,400	800	1,160	1,100	800	570

†Figures are projected for 1991-92.   ‡Figures are for 1990-91.

Total freshmen	Percent receiving aid	Freshmen judged to have need	Percent offered aid	Need-based Acad	Music/drama	Art	Athl	Nonneed-based Acad	Music/drama	Art	Athl	Priority	Closing	Inst aid form	Need analysis document
690	50							X	X		X	7/1	none	X	FAF
1,133	35	488	84	X				X	X			3/15	none		FAF
													none	X	FAF
															FAF
													none	X	FAF
23	26	10	100										8/15	X	FAF
1,013	33	380	87					X	X	X	X	4/1	none	X	FAF*/FFS
194	70	143	100	X	X	X		X	X	X		2/28	none	X	FAF
805	50	426	95	X	X		X	X	X	X	X	2/15	none		FAF
4,221	22	500	70	X	X		X	X	X	X	X	7/1	none		FAF
1,077	20	690	71	X	X		X	X		X	X	5/1	none	X	FAF
				X				X			X	3/15	none		FAF
480	79	381	100	X	X		X	X	X		X	2/1	none		FAF
1,913	66							X	X	X	X	5/15	none		FAF
4,300	17							X	X	X	X	5/1	none	X	FAF
24	69			X				X					none	X	AFSA
												4/10	none		FAF*/AFSA;FAF*/FFS/AFSA/CSS SAAC
													none	X	AFSA
800	35			X	X	X	X	X	X		X	7/1	none	X	FAF/FFS/AFSA*/AFSSA/SF;FAF/FFS/AFSA*/CSS SAAC/
41	73	35	86	X	X			X	X			5/1	none	X	FAF
3,000	30	912	99	X	X	X		X	X	X		5/1	8/31	X	FAF/FFS/AFSA*;FAF/FFS/AFSA*/CSS SAAC/ACT SAAC
143	50							X	X			5/1	none		FAF*/FFS
														X	FAF/AFSA*
2,000	28	564	100	X				X	X	X	X	6/1	none	X	FAF
501	79	324	100	X	X	X	X	X	X	X		3/1	5/1		FAF
476	50	300	97	X				X	X	X		6/1	none	X	FAF
2,801	18	515	100					X			X	4/1	none	X	FAF
12	85	7	100	X				X	X			5/1	9/1	X	FAF
37	85							X			X	3/1	none	X	FAF
3,278	41							X				5/15	8/15	X	FAF
				X	X	X		X	X	X	X	3/1	none		FAF
387	72	300	93				X	X	X	X	X	3/1	none		FAF*/FFS;FAF*/FFS/CSS SAAC/ACT SAAC
													none		FAF*/FFS
1,500	246	450	98	X	X	X	X	X	X	X	X	5/1	none	X	FAF
978	45											5/1	7/31	X	FAF/FFS*/AFSA
													none	X	FAF
1,893	73	1,390	100	X			X				X	3/15	none	X	FAF/FFS*
1,291	85	1,100	100	X			X				X	4/1	none	X	FAF
1,690	20			X				X	X	X	X		4/1	X	FAF
701	70	350	100	X	X	X	X	X	X	X	X	2/1	3/1		FAF
3,579	30	1,072	87	X	X		X	X			X	3/1	none		FAF
345	54	200	100	X				X	X	X		4/1	none	X	FAF*/FFS/AFSA/SF
				X				X	X		X	6/1	none	X	FAF*/FFS/AFSA;FAF*/FFS
2,526	40	1,000	90	X	X	X	X	X	X	X	X	3/1	none	X	FAF; FAF*/FFS

*Preferred need analysis document.

Institution	Tuition and fees	Add'l out-of-state/ district tuition	Books and supplies	Costs for campus residents			Costs for students at home		
				Room and board	Trans-portation	Other costs	Board only	Trans-portation	Other costs
† Western Washington University	1,698	4,272/—	550	3,143	900	1,200	1,700	900	600
† Whatcom Community College	945	2,772/—	500				1,520	800	570
Whitman College	13,210		750	4,340		500	2,400		500
‡ Whitworth College	9,615		500	3,600	700	1,200	1,500	300	1,200
† Yakima Valley Community College	945	2,772/—	500	3,200	800	1,100	1,600	850	600

West Virginia

Institution	Tuition and fees	Add'l out-of-state/ district tuition	Books and supplies	Room and board	Trans-portation	Other costs	Board only	Trans-portation	Other costs
‡ Alderson-Broaddus College	7,950		550	2,665	300	300	1,200	300	300
‡ Appalachian Bible College	3,390		510	2,600	685	580	1,500	830	580
Beckley College	2,520		625				2,000	800	700
† Bethany College	11,650		350	4,022	595	750	1,744	1,135	1,000
‡ Bluefield State College	1,316	1,870/—	800				1,600	900	900
‡ Concord College	1,416	2,060/—	366	2,698	548	918	750	664	918
Davis and Elkins College	7,710		400	3,930		400	2,100		400
† Fairmont State College	1,360	1,970/—	500	2,620		500		600	500
‡ Glenville State College	1,280	1,870/—	350	2,590	200	1,000		900	1,000
Huntington Junior College of Business	3,375								
‡ Marshall University	1,538	2,238/1,070	400	3,436	429	524	1,500	451	212
National Education Center: National Institute of Technology Campus	10,760								
† Ohio Valley College	4,650		300	2,950	400	600		800	600
‡ Potomac State College of West Virginia University	1,256	2,028/—	350	2,650	1,200	640	1,900	800	640
‡ Salem-Teikyo University	6,740		350	3,760	200	250	1,980	200	250
‡ Shepherd College	1,494	2,050/—	400	3,360	110	800	1,500	810	800
† Southern West Virginia Community College	844	1,684/—	400		850	1,850	1,500		900
University of Charleston	7,950		400	3,500	250	500			1,500
‡ West Liberty State College	1,320	1,850/—	500	2,600	150	650		800	650
‡ West Virginia Institute of Technology	1,422	2,070/—	400	3,250	400	700	1,200	700	700
‡ West Virginia Northern Community College	942	1,776/—	400				1,500	800	1,007
‡ West Virginia State College	1,432	2,110/—	420	2,800	368	920	1,260	920	1,000
West Virginia University									
‡ Morgantown	1,777	2,869/—	350	3,612	285	1,625	1,500	1,050	400
Parkersburg	760	1,760/—	300				1,600	990	1,175
West Virginia Wesleyan College	11,830		450	3,150	1,000	850	1,500	1,000	850
‡ Wheeling Jesuit College	7,970		600	3,730	500	500		500	500

Wisconsin

Institution	Tuition and fees	Add'l out-of-state/ district tuition	Books and supplies	Room and board	Trans-portation	Other costs	Board only	Trans-portation	Other costs
‡ Alverno College	6,390		500	2,850	400	1,650	1,100	400	1,262
‡ Bellin College of Nursing	5,622		380				878	459	743
Beloit College	13,050		350	3,300	400	700	1,500	600	700
† Blackhawk Technical College	1,136	7,730/63	400				1,250	375	725

†Figures are projected for 1991-92.   ‡Figures are for 1990-91.

| All aid | | Need–based aid | | Grants and scholarships | | | | | | | | Financial aid deadlines | | Inst aid form | Need analysis document |
| | | | | Need–based | | | | Nonneed–based | | | | | | | |
Total fresh–men	Percent receiving aid	Freshmen judged to have need	Percent offered aid	Acad	Music/drama	Art	Athl	Acad	Music/drama	Art	Athl	Priority	Closing		
1,260	63			X	X	X		X	X	X	X	3/31	none	X	FAF
		591	72					X				6/1	none	X	FAF
346	74	195	100	X	X	X	X	X	X	X			2/15		FAF*/FFS/SF;FAF*/ FFS/CSS SAAC/ACT SAAC/SF
268	88	236	100	X	X	X	X	X	X	X		2/15	none		FAF*/FFS/AFSA; FAF*/FFS/AFSA/CSS SAAC
977	51	500	100	X	X		X					5/1	none	X	FAF
263	91	167	100	X	X		X	X	X		X	5/1	none		FAF*/FFS
55	91			X									6/1		FAF
732	30			X				X				6/1	none		FAF*/FFS
270	75	169	100	X				X				4/1	none		FAF
488	60	244	100	X			X	X			X	3/1	none	X	FAF
816	70	350	100	X	X	X	X	X	X	X	X	4/15	none		FAF*/AFSA
321	65	160	100	X	X	X	X	X	X	X	X	3/1	none		FAF*/FFS
1,693	60			X	X		X	X	X		X		3/1	X	FAF
386	73	231	87	X	X	X	X	X	X	X	X		3/1		FAF*/FFS/AFSA/ AFSSA/SF;FAF*/FFS/ AFSA/AFSSA/
													none		AFSA
2,200	44	1,800	100					X	X	X	X	3/1	none	X	FAF*/FFS/AFSA/SF; FAF*/FFS/AFSA/ APSGFSA/SF
													none		AFSA
116	93	100	100	X	X	X	X	X	X	X	X	6/1	none		FAF
				X	X		X	X				3/31	none		FAF
				X			X	X			X	4/15	none		FAF*/FFS
860	30	196	100					X	X	X	X	3/1	none		FAF*/FFS/AFSA/SF
														X	FAF
258	70	258	100	X			X	X	X		X	3/1	none	X	FAF
460	60	200	100	X	X	X	X	X	X	X	X	3/1	none		FAF
615	40	334	88	X	X		X	X	X		X	1/31	4/1	X	FAF*/AFSA;FAF*/ FFS/AFSA
615	40			X				X				7/1	none	X	FAF
939	55			X	X	X	X	X	X	X	X	3/1	8/10		FAF*/FFS
3,114	44	1,273	93	X				X	X	X	X	3/1	none	X	FAF
														X	FAF
416	67	241	100	X			X	X	X	X	X	3/1	none		FAF*/FFS/AFSA/ AFSSA/SF;FAF*/FFS/ AFSA/AFSSA/
213	87	165	100					X	X		X	3/1	none		FAF*/FFS/SF;FAF*/ FFS/APSGFSA/SF
606	75	236	100	X	X	X		X	X	X		3/15	none	X	FAF*/FFS/AFSA/ AFSSA
												3/1	none	X	FAF
252	76	162	100	X	X			X	X			4/15	none	X	FAF*/FFS/SF
1,050	40											4/1	none		FAF/FFS*

*Preferred need analysis document.

Institution	Tuition and fees	Add'l out-of-state/ district tuition	Books and supplies	Costs for campus residents			Costs for students at home		
				Room and board	Trans-portation	Other costs	Board only	Trans-portation	Other costs
† Cardinal Stritch College	6,960		490	3,260	350	1,200	1,700	800	1,200
Carroll College	11,068		400	3,460	200	900		900	
Carthage College	10,640		500	3,350	500	500	500	500	600
† Chippewa Valley Technical College	1,230	7,730/—	375					450	800
Columbia College of Nursing	11,068		350	3,560	275	850		900	850
Concordia University Wisconsin	7,400		410	3,100	120	1,260	1,550	500	1,170
Edgewood College	6,990		500	3,330	450	1,125	950	450	1,125
Fox Valley Technical College	1,280	8,010/—	500					600	800
Gateway Technical College	1,290	8,010/—	538				1,545	562	937
‡ Lac Courte Oreilles Ojibwa Community College	2,425								
Lakeland College	8,050		500	3,250	700	750	900	700	750
Lakeshore Technical College	1,432	7,800/—	570				1,690	615	1,020
‡ Lawrence University	13,710		375	3,237		660			660
‡ Madison Area Technical College	1,106	7,730/—	600				1,600	600	950
‡ Madison Business College	3,115		400				1,135	196	906
Maranatha Baptist Bible College	4,150		400	2,200					
Marian College of Fond du Lac	7,550		350	3,500	130	700	1,300	370	700
Marquette University	9,034		550	4,040		1,220	1,764	880	1,220
Mid-State Technical College	1,315	8,116/—	600				1,700	600	1,000
Milwaukee Area Technical College	1,375	7,730/—	600		610	1,018	1,680	610	1,018
‡ Milwaukee Institute of Art & Design	7,120		900				1,900	324	1,020
Milwaukee School of Engineering	9,150		720	3,225	820	1,060	1,500	820	1,060
‡ Moraine Park Technical College	1,151	7,730/—	538				1,545	562	937
Mount Mary College	6,950		400	2,447	420	900	1,500	420	900
† Mount Senario College	6,340		420	2,625	450	1,350	1,600	400	1,350
Nicolet Area Technical College	1,167	8,055/—	450				1,000	600	1,320
Northcentral Technical College	1,390	8,590/—	440	2,700			1,650	550	1,100
Northeast Wisconsin Technical College	1,167	8,055/—	540				1,600	585	975
Northland College	8,380		400	3,450	450	1,000	1,960	400	1,000
Northwestern College	3,174		180	1,770	550	1,145		550	
Ripon College	12,900		350	3,100		650	1,900		650
St. Norbert College	10,225		425	3,955	350	750	900	450	750
† Silver Lake College	7,480		450	2,910	1,000	850	1,560	1,000	850
Southwest Wisconsin Technical College	1,267	6,888/—	538				1,190	300	685
Stratton College	5,470						2,320	520	1,542
University of Wisconsin									
‡ Eau Claire	1,760	3,647/—	150	2,420	600	1,100	950	650	1,050
‡ Green Bay	1,753	3,647/—	450		350	830	900	400	545
‡ La Crosse	1,984	3,830/—	200	2,180	220	1,630	750	100	730
‡ Madison	2,107	4,724/—	490	3,620	250	1,110	1,500	160	1,110
‡ Milwaukee	2,156	4,724/—	509	3,188	519	1,532	1,650	519	1,030
‡ Oshkosh	1,764	3,647/—	350	1,990	260	1,050		450	900
‡ Parkside	1,780	3,647/—	453	3,076	609	1,066		605	906
‡ Platteville	1,797	3,647/—	295	2,260	300	900	1,100	425	900
‡ River Falls	1,771	3,647/—	160	2,308	456	1,100	1,700	676	1,100

†Figures are projected for 1991-92.   ‡Figures are for 1990-91.

Total fresh-men	Percent receiving aid	Freshmen judged to have need	Percent offered aid	Acad	Music/ drama	Art	Athl	Acad	Music/ drama	Art	Athl	Priority	Closing	Inst aid form	Need analysis document
All aid		*Need-based aid*		*Grants and scholarships* — *Need-based*				*Nonneed-based*				*Financial aid deadlines*			
122	79	71	100	X				X		X		4/1	none	X	FAF*/FFS/AFSA/ AFSSA/SF;FAF*/FFS/ AFSA/CSS SAAC/ACT
466	93	285	100	X	X	X		X	X	X		4/15	none	X	FAF*/FFS
324	85	295	100					X	X	X		3/1	none	X	FAF*/FFS
													none	X	FFS
													none		FAF*/FFS
282	90	235	100					X	X		X	5/1	none	X	FAF*/FFS
115	95	41	100	X	X	X	X	X	X	X		4/15	none	X	FAF*/FFS
1,750	75			X				X					none	X	FFS;FAF/FFS*/AFSA/ AFSSA
												3/1	7/1	X	FAF
															FAF/FFS;FFS
270	95							X				5/1	none	X	FAF*/FFS/AFSA/ AFSSA
1,065	65	622	98										none		FFS
318	83	203	100	X	X			X	X			3/1	none	X	FAF*/FFS;FAF*/FFS/ CSS SAAC/ACT SAAC
		3,195						X				6/1	none		FAF
131	48							X					none	X	FFS
111	44	62	100	X				X				6/30	none		FAF/FFS*/AFSA
180	90	100	100	X	X	X	X	X	X	X	X	3/1	none	X	FAF*/FFS/AFSA; FAF*/FFS/AFSA/ AFSSA
1,650	83	884	100	X				X	X		X		none		FAF*/FFS
1,379	70			X			X	X					5/1		FFS
1,194	70							X				3/15	none		FFS
143	64	81	100								X	4/15	none	X	FAF
528	85							X				4/1	none	X	FAF*/FFS
1,211	40	800	100					X				5/1	none	X	FAF*/FFS/AFSA
103	82	55	100	X	X	X		X	X	X		3/15	none	X	FAF*/FFS/AFSA
145	96			X	X	X	X	X	X	X		4/1	none		FAF*/FFS/AFSA
349	70			X				X				3/15	none		FFS*/AFSA
													none		FFS
									X				5/1	none		FAF*/FFS
208	80			X	X		X	X	X		X	5/1	none		FAF*/FFS
58	90	42	95	X				X				5/1	none	X	FAF*/FFS/AFSA
232	85	175	100	X	X			X	X			3/1	none		FAF*/FFS
460	89	355	100	X	X			X	X	X		3/1	none	X	FAF*/FFS
43	95	34	100	X	X	X		X	X	X		3/15	none	X	FAF
													none	X	FAF*/FFS
246	76	185	100					X					none	X	AFSA
1,736	74	743	100	X	X			X	X				2/28	X	FAF/FFS/AFSA*
746	60			X			X	X	X	X	X	4/1	none		FAF/FFS
1,622	45	800	100	X				X	X			3/15	none	X	FAF*/FFS/AFSA
4,699	41	2,155	100					X	X	X	X	3/1	none	X	FAF*/FFS
2,446	38	648	92	X			X					3/1	none		FAF/FFS*/AFSA
1,617	45	636	100	X				X	X				none		FAF*/FFS;FAF
782	35			X	X	X	X	X	X	X	X	4/15	6/15	X	FAF/FFS/AFSA*;FAF/ FFS*/AFSA
940	75			X				X				3/15	none	X	FAF/FFS*
938	72							X	X	X		3/18	none		FAF*/FFS

*Preferred need analysis document.

239

Institution	Tuition and fees	Add'l out-of-state/ district tuition	Books and supplies	Costs for campus residents			Costs for students at home		
				Room and board	Trans-portation	Other costs	Board only	Trans-portation	Other costs
‡ Stevens Point	1,813	3,647/—	150	2,614	280	920	1,500	220	920
‡ Stout	1,793	3,647/—	320	2,269	368	1,248		420	1,034
‡ Superior	1,753	3,647/—	450	2,206	600	1,200		600	1,200
‡ Whitewater	1,810	3,647/—	420	2,150	500	1,040	1,925	855	1,040
University of Wisconsin Center									
‡ Baraboo/Sauk County	1,348	2,884/—	375				1,175	650	700
‡ Barron County	1,421	2,884/—	100				1,140	600	940
‡ Fond du Lac	1,401	2,884/—	380				360	610	670
‡ Fox Valley	1,384	2,884/—	300				1,700	1,200	1,000
‡ Manitowoc County	1,354	2,884/—	360				1,200	580	940
‡ Marathon County	1,361	2,884/—	320	2,052	550	900	1,140	550	940
‡ Marinette County	1,363	2,884/—	380				1,140	610	670
‡ Marshfield/Wood County	1,396	2,884/—	250				1,100	600	800
‡ Richland	1,473	2,884/—	380		610	1,030	1,140	610	670
‡ Rock County	1,357	2,884/—	360				1,140	580	640
‡ Sheboygan County	1,364	2,884/—	380				1,140	610	670
‡ Washington County	1,389	2,884/—	300				1,100	600	850
‡ Waukesha	1,352	2,884/—	375				1,140	580	640
Viterbo College	7,960		400	3,090	250	1,000	1,500	250	750
‡ Waukesha County Technical College	1,256	7,730/—	600					700	850
Western Wisconsin Technical College	1,375	7,525/—	550	2,200	590	975	2,000	590	975
† Wisconsin Indianhead Technical College	1,239	8,244/—	535					590	945
Wisconsin Lutheran College	7,578		500	3,200	300	990	1,500	250	810
Wisconsin School of Electronics	5,520		500						
Wyoming									
Casper College	672	556/—	400	2,150	200	1,200	900	300	800
‡ Central Wyoming College	652	532/—	400	2,338	500	750	1,560	500	750
Eastern Wyoming College	626	556/—	450	2,000	300	350	925	325	350
Laramie County Community College	664	556/—	400	2,956	250	400		650	600
† Northwest College	808	556/—	500	2,464	700	1,000	800	600	600
† Sheridan College	688	688/—	420	2,250	500	800	1,000	650	800
‡ University of Wyoming	1,200	2,500/—	400	3,100	500	750		200	750
Western Wyoming Community College	676	616/—	400	2,300	500	950	1,500	250	950
American Samoa, Caroline Islands, Guam, Marianas, Virgin Islands									
† American Samoa Community College	154	144/—	500					360	1,100
† Community College of Micronesia	2,385		300	2,912	420	1,000		420	1,000
Guam Community College	322		420				1,210	825	1,118
† Micronesian Occupational College	2,200		200	2,352	871	300	1,764		
Northern Marianas College	1,250		400				900	540	1,200
‡ University of Guam	1,500	780/—	300	2,905	880	875		550	900
‡ University of the Virgin Islands	970	1,670/—	400	3,024	650	800	2,370	600	750
Canada									
McGill University	6,600		1,000	5,300		1,400		300	1,400
France									
† American University of Paris	12,775		750		300			300	

†Figures are projected for 1991-92.   ‡Figures are for 1990-91.

All aid		Need–based aid		Grants and scholarships								Financial aid deadlines		Inst aid form	Need analysis document
				Need-based				Nonneed-based							
Total freshmen	Percent receiving aid	Freshmen judged to have need	Percent offered aid	Acad	Music/drama	Art	Athl	Acad	Music/drama	Art	Athl	Priority	Closing		
1,578	60							X	X	X		3/15	7/15		FFS
1,140	59	563	95	X				X	X	X	X	4/15	none		FFS
653	68	450	76	X	X	X		X				5/1	none	X	FAF/FFS/AFSA/SF
				X	X			X	X			4/15	none		FFS
315	48	147	100	X				X				4/15	none	X	FAF*/FFS
				X	X	X		X	X	X		3/1	none	X	FAF*/FFS
													none	X	FAF/FFS/AFSA
				X				X				4/15	none	X	FAF*/FFS
167	40	100	100	X				X				3/1	none	X	FAF*/FFS
398	71	282	100					X	X	X		4/15	none		FAF*/FFS
282	60			X				X				3/1	none	X	FAF*/FFS
391	46			X	X	X		X	X	X	X	4/15	none	X	FAF*/FFS
178	60			X	X	X		X	X	X		4/15	none	X	FAF*/FFS
605	50			X	X			X	X			3/1	none	X	FAF/FFS
267	22			X				X				4/15	none	X	FAF*/FFS
								X	X			3/1	none	X	FAF*/FFS
578	16			X				X	X			3/1	none	X	FAF*/FFS
236	92			X	X	X		X	X	X		3/15	none		FAF*/FFS
1,307	15			X				X					none		FAF/FFS/AFSA*
1,946	60							X				3/1	none	X	FAF
1,747	75			X				X					none		FAF/FFS*
66	90	55	100	X				X	X	X	X	4/1	none	X	FAF*/FFS
													none		FAF
726	70			X	X	X	X	X	X	X	X	4/1	none	X	FAF*/FFS/AFSA
265	43	115	100	X	X	X	X	X	X	X	X	4/15	none		FAF*/FFS/AFSA
391	75	267	100					X	X	X	X	4/1	none		FAF/FFS/AFSA*
956	75			X	X	X	X	X	X	X	X	4/1	none		FAF
798	78	600	100					X	X	X	X		none	X	FAF/FFS*/AFSA/ AFSSA/SF
572	35	310	93					X	X	X	X	3/1	none		FAF/FFS/AFSA*
1,306	55	426	94	X				X	X	X	X		3/1	X	FAF*/FFS
991	49	196	41					X	X	X	X	4/1	none		FAF*/FFS/AFSA/SF
													none		FAF/FFS/AFSA
															FAF/AFSA
394	9	104	85	X									5/1	X	AFSA;FAF/FFS/ AFSA*
109	98	172	97	X								6/1	none	X	FAF
434	30	30	100										none	X	AFSA
															FAF/FFS
579	80							X					4/15		FAF
													none		FAF
143	11	38	100	X				X				5/1	7/15	X	FAF*/FFS/AFSA/ AFSSA/SF;FAF*/FFS/ AFSA/CSS SAAC/ACT

*Preferred need analysis document.

Institution	Tuition and fees	Add'l out-of-state/ district tuition	Books and supplies	Costs for campus residents			Costs for students at home		
				Room and board	Trans-portation	Other costs	Board only	Trans-portation	Other costs
Mexico									
‡ Instituto Tecnologico y de Estudios Superiores de Monterrey 3,500			500						
Switzerland									
American College of Switzerland 15,486				3,829					
‡ Franklin College: Switzerland 13,153			400		1,000	3,600			
Arab Republic of Egypt									
American University in Cairo.................................... 6,860			500			1,000			

†Figures are projected for 1991-92.   ‡Figures are for 1990-91.

All aid		Need-based aid		Grants and scholarships									Financial aid deadlines		Inst aid form	Need analysis document
Total freshmen	Percent receiving aid	Freshmen judged to have need	Percent offered aid	Need-based				Nonneed-based					Priority	Closing		
				Acad	Music/ drama	Art	Athl	Acad	Music/ drama	Art	Athl					
															X	
63	35			X									4/1	none	X	FAF
		9	100	X										3/15	X	FAF*/FFS
765	66							X	X	X	X					

*Preferred need analysis document.

2. Institutions listed alphabetically

Abilene Christian University, Abilene, TX 79699-8481
Abraham Baldwin Agricultural College, Tifton, GA 31794-2693
Academy of Art College, San Francisco, CA 94108
Academy of the New Church, Bryn Athyn, PA 19009
Adams State College, Alamosa, CO 81102
Adelphi University, Garden City, NY 11530
Adirondack Community College, Queensbury, NY 12804-1498
Adrian College, Adrian, MI 49221-2575
Aero-Space Institute, Chicago, IL 60605-1025
Agnes Scott College, Decatur, GA 30030
Aiken Technical College, Aiken, SC 29802-0696
Aims Community College, Greeley, CO 80632
Alabama Agricultural and Mechanical University, Normal, AL 35762
Alabama Aviation and Technical College, Ozark, AL 36361
Alabama Christian School of Religion, Montgomery, AL 36117-3553
Alabama State University, Montgomery, AL 36101-0271
Alamance Community College, Haw River, NC 27258
Alaska Bible College, Glennallen, AK 99588
Alaska Pacific University, Anchorage, AK 99508-4672
Albany College of Pharmacy, Albany, NY 12208
Albany State College, Albany, GA 31705-2796
Albertus Magnus College, New Haven, CT 06511-1189
Albion College, Albion, MI 49224
Albright College, Reading, PA 19612-5234
Albuquerque Technical-Vocational Institute, Albuquerque, NM 87106
Alcorn State University, Lorman, MS 39096
Alderson-Broaddus College, Philippi, WV 26416
Alexandria Technical College, Alexandria, MN 56308
Alfred University, Alfred, NY 14802
Alice Lloyd College, Pippa Passes, KY 41844
Allan Hancock College, Santa Maria, CA 93454
Allegany Community College, Cumberland, MD 21502
Allegheny College, Meadville, PA 16335
Allen County Community College, Iola, KS 66749
Allen University, Columbia, SC 29204
Allentown College of St. Francis de Sales, Center Valley, PA 18034
Alma College, Alma, MI 48801-1599
Alpena Community College, Alpena, MI 49707
Alvernia College, Reading, PA 19607
Alverno College, Milwaukee, WI 53215-4020
Alvin Community College, Alvin, TX 77511
Amarillo College, Amarillo, TX 79178
Amber University, Garland, TX 75041-5595
American Academy of Art, Chicago, IL 60603
American Academy of Dramatic Arts
   New York, New York, NY 10016
   West, Pasadena, CA 91107
American Academy McAllister Institute of Funeral Service, New York, NY
   10019
American Armenian International College, LaVerne, CA 91750
American Baptist College of ABT Seminary, Nashville, TN 37207
American College for the Applied Arts, Atlanta, GA 30326
American College of Switzerland, Leysin, Switzerland 02140
American Conservatory of Music, Chicago, IL 60602-4792
American Indian Bible College, Phoenix, AZ 85021-2199
American Institute of Business, Des Moines, IA 50321
American Institute of Commerce, Davenport, IA 52807
American Institute of Design, Philadelphia, PA 19124
American International College, Springfield, MA 01109-3184
American River College, Sacramento, CA 95841

American Samoa Community College, Pago Pago, AS 96799
American Technical Institute, Brunswick, TN 38014
American University, Washington, DC 20016-8001
American University in Cairo, Cairo, Arab Republic of Egypt 10017-1889
American University of Paris, Paris, France
American University of Puerto Rico, Bayamon, PR 00619-2037
Amherst College, Amherst, MA 01002
Ancilla College, Donaldson, IN 46513
Anderson College, Anderson, SC 29621
Anderson University, Anderson, IN 46012-3462
Andover College, Portland, ME 04103
Andrew College, Cuthbert, GA 31740-1395
Andrews University, Berrien Springs, MI 49104
Angelina College, Lufkin, TX 75902-1768
Angelo State University, San Angelo, TX 76909
Anna Maria College for Men and Women, Paxton, MA 01612
Anne Arundel Community College, Arnold, MD 21012
Anoka-Ramsey Community College, Coon Rapids, MN 55433
Anson Community College, Ansonville, NC 28007
Antelope Valley College, Lancaster, CA 93536-5426
Antioch College, Yellow Springs, OH 45387
Antioch School for Adult and Experiential Learning, Yellow Springs, OH
   45387
Antioch Southern California
   Los Angeles, Marina Del Rey, CA 90292
   Santa Barbara, Santa Barbara, CA 93101
Antioch University Seattle, Seattle, WA 98121
Antonelli Institute of Art and Photography, Plymouth Meeting, PA 19462
Antonelli Institute of Art and Photography, Cincinnati, OH 45202
Appalachian Bible College, Bradley, WV 25818-0353
Appalachian State University, Boone, NC 28608
Aquinas College, Grand Rapids, MI 49506-1799
Aquinas College at Milton, Milton, MA 02186
Aquinas College at Newton, Newton, MA 02158
Aquinas Junior College, Nashville, TN 37205
Arapahoe Community College, Littleton, CO 80160-9002
Arizona College of the Bible, Phoenix, AZ 85021-5197
Arizona State University, Tempe, AZ 85287-0112
Arizona Western College, Yuma, AZ 85366-0929
Arkansas Baptist College, Little Rock, AR 72202
Arkansas College, Batesville, AR 72503
Arkansas State University
   Beebe Branch, Beebe, AR 72012-1008
   Jonesboro, Jonesboro, AR 72467-1630
Arkansas Tech University, Russellville, AR 72801-2222
Arlington Baptist College, Arlington, TX 76012-3425
Armstrong College, Berkeley, CA 94704
Armstrong State College, Savannah, GA 31419-1997
Art Academy of Cincinnati, Cincinnati, OH 45202-1597
Art Center College of Design, Pasadena, CA 91103
Art Institute of Atlanta, Atlanta, GA 30326
Art Institute of Fort Lauderdale, Fort Lauderdale, FL 33316-3000
Art Institute of Philadelphia, Philadelphia, PA 19103
Art Institute of Pittsburgh, Pittsburgh, PA 15222
Art Institute of Seattle, Seattle, WA 98121
Art Institute of Southern California, Laguna Beach, CA 92651
Asbury College, Wilmore, KY 40390
Asheville Buncombe Technical Community College, Asheville, NC 28801
Ashland Community College, Ashland, KY 41101
Ashland University, Ashland, OH 44805

Asnuntuck Community College, Enfield, CT 06082
Assumption College, Worcester, MA 01615-0005
Assumption College for Sisters, Mendham, NJ 07945-9998
Athens Area Technical Institute, Athens, GA 30610-0399
Athens State College, Athens, AL 35611
Atlanta Christian College, East Point, GA 30344
Atlanta College of Art, Atlanta, GA 30309
Atlanta Metropolitan College, Atlanta, GA 30310
Atlantic Community College, Mays Landing, NJ 08330-9888
Atlantic Union College, South Lancaster, MA 01561
Auburn University
    Auburn, Auburn, AL 36849-5145
    Montgomery, Montgomery, AL 36117-3596
Augsburg College, Minneapolis, MN 55454
Augusta College, Augusta, GA 30910
Augusta Technical Institute, Augusta, GA 30906
Augustana College, Rock Island, IL 61201-2296
Augustana College, Sioux Falls, SD 57197-9990
Aurora University, Aurora, IL 60506
Austin College, Sherman, TX 75091-1177
Austin Community College, Austin, MN 55912
Austin Community College, Austin, TX 78714
Austin Peay State University, Clarksville, TN 37044
Averett College, Danville, VA 24541
Avila College, Kansas City, MO 64145-9990
Azusa Pacific University, Azusa, CA 91702-7000
Babson College, Wellesley, MA 02157-0901
Bacone College, Muskogee, OK 74403-1597
Bainbridge College, Bainbridge, GA 31717-0953
Baker College
    Flint, Flint, MI 48507
    Owosso, Owosso, MI 48867
Baker College of Muskegon, Muskegon, MI 49442
Baker University, Baldwin City, KS 66006
Bakersfield College, Bakersfield, CA 93305
Baldwin-Wallace College, Berea, OH 44017
Ball State University, Muncie, IN 47306-0855
Baltimore Hebrew University, Baltimore, MD 21215-3996
Baltimore International Culinary College, Baltimore, MD 21202
Baptist Bible College, Springfield, MO 65803
Baptist Bible College of Pennsylvania, Clarks Summit, PA 18411
Baptist Missionary Association Theological Seminary, Jacksonville, TX 75766
Barat College, Lake Forest, IL 60045
Barber-Scotia College, Concord, NC 28025
Barclay College, Haviland, KS 67059
Bard College, Annandale-on-Hudson, NY 12504
Barnard College, New York, NY 10027-6598
Barry University, Miami Shores, FL 33161
Barstow College, Barstow, CA 92311-9984
Bartlesville Wesleyan College, Bartlesville, OK 74006
Barton College, Wilson, NC 27893
Barton County Community College, Great Bend, KS 67530-9283
Basic Institute of Technology, St. Louis, MO 63116
Bassist College, Portland, OR 97201
Bauder Fashion College, Atlanta, GA 30326-9975
Bauder Fashion College, Arlington, TX 76010
Bay de Noc Community College, Escanaba, MI 49829
Bay Path College, Longmeadow, MA 01106
Bay Ridge Christian College, Kendleton, TX 77451
Bay State College, Boston, MA 02116
Bayamon Central University, Bayamon, PR 00621
Baylor College of Dentistry, Dallas, TX 75246
Baylor University, Waco, TX 76798-7056
Beal College, Bangor, ME 04401
Beaufort County Community College, Washington, NC 27889
Beaver College, Glenside, PA 19038-3295
Becker College
    Leicester Campus, Leicester, MA 01524
    Worcester Campus, Worcester, MA 01609
Beckley College, Beckley, WV 25802-2830
Bee County College, Beeville, TX 78102
Belhaven College, Jackson, MS 39202
Bellarmine College, Louisville, KY 40205-0671
Belleville Area College, Belleville, IL 62221-9989
Bellevue College, Bellevue, NE 68005
Bellevue Community College, Bellevue, WA 98007-6484
Bellin College of Nursing, Green Bay, WI 54301
Belmont Abbey College, Belmont, NC 28012-2795
Belmont College, Nashville, TN 37212-3757
Belmont Technical College, St. Clairsville, OH 43950
Beloit College, Beloit, WI 53511-5595

Bel-Rea Institute of Animal Technology, Denver, CO 80231
Bemidji State University, Bemidji, MN 56601
Benedict College, Columbia, SC 29204
Benedictine College, Atchison, KS 66002-1499
Bennett College, Greensboro, NC 27401-3239
Bennington College, Bennington, VT 05201
Bentley College, Waltham, MA 02154-4705
Berea College, Berea, KY 40404
Berean College, Springfield, MO 65802
Berean Institute, Philadelphia, PA 19130
Bergen Community College, Paramus, NJ 07652-1595
Berkeley College, White Plains, NY 10604-9990
Berkeley College of Business, West Paterson, NJ 07424
Berkeley School: New York City, New York, NY 10017
Berklee College of Music, Boston, MA 02215
Berkshire Community College, Pittsfield, MA 01201-5786
Berry College, Rome, GA 30149
Bessemer State Technical College, Bessemer, AL 35021
Beth Hatalmud Rabbinical College, Brooklyn, NY 11214
Beth Medrash Emek Halacha Rabbinical College, Brooklyn, NY 11204
Beth Medrash Govoha, Lakewood, NJ 08701
Bethany Bible College, Scotts Valley, CA 95066-2898
Bethany College, Bethany, WV 26032
Bethany College, Lindsborg, KS 67456-1897
Bethany Lutheran College, Mankato, MN 56001-4490
Bethel College, McKenzie, TN 38201
Bethel College, Mishawaka, IN 46545
Bethel College, North Newton, KS 67117-9899
Bethel College, St. Paul, MN 55112
Beth-El College of Nursing, Colorado Springs, CO 80909
Bethune-Cookman College, Daytona Beach, FL 32115
Big Bend Community College, Moses Lake, WA 98837
Biola University, La Mirada, CA 90639
Birmingham-Southern College, Birmingham, AL 35254
Bishop Clarkson College, Omaha, NE 68131-7999
Bishop State Community College, Mobile, AL 36603-5898
Bismarck State College, Bismarck, ND 58501
Black Hawk College
    East Campus, Kewanee, IL 61443-0489
    Moline, Moline, IL 61265
Black Hills State University, Spearfish, SD 57799-9502
Blackburn College, Carlinville, IL 62626
Blackfeet Community College, Browning, MT 59417
Blackhawk Technical College, Janesville, WI 53547
Bladen Community College, Dublin, NC 28332
Blair Junior College, Colorado Springs, CO 80915
Blanton's Junior College, Asheville, NC 28801
Blessing-Reiman College of Nursing, Quincy, IL 62301
Blinn College, Brenham, TX 77833
Bliss College, Columbus, OH 43214
Bloomfield College, Bloomfield, NJ 07003
Bloomsburg University of Pennsylvania, Bloomsburg, PA 17815
Blue Mountain College, Blue Mountain, MS 38610
Blue Mountain Community College, Pendleton, OR 97801
Blue Ridge Community College, Flat Rock, NC 28731-9624
Blue Ridge Community College, Weyers Cave, VA 24486-9989
Bluefield College, Bluefield, VA 24605-1799
Bluefield State College, Bluefield, WV 24701
Bluffton College, Bluffton, OH 45817
Bob Jones University, Greenville, SC 29614
Boise Bible College, Boise, ID 83714-1220
Boise State University, Boise, ID 83725
Boricua College, New York, NY 10032
Bossier Parish Community College, Bossier City, LA 71111
Boston Architectural Center, Boston, MA 02115-2795
Boston College, Chestnut Hill, MA 02167-3804
Boston Conservatory, Boston, MA 02215
Boston University, Boston, MA 02215
Bowdoin College, Brunswick, ME 04011
Bowie State University, Bowie, MD 20715
Bowling Green State University
    Bowling Green, Bowling Green, OH 43403-0080
    Firelands College, Huron, OH 44839
Bradford College, Bradford, MA 01835-7393
Bradford School, Columbus, OH 43229
Bradley University, Peoria, IL 61625
Brainerd Community College, Brainerd, MN 56401
Bramson ORT Technical Institute, Forest Hills, NY 11375
Brandeis University, Waltham, MA 02254-9110
Brazosport College, Lake Jackson, TX 77566
Brenau Women's College, Gainesville, GA 30501-3697
Brescia College, Owensboro, KY 42301

Brevard College, Brevard, NC 28712
Brevard Community College, Cocoa, FL 32922-9987
Brewer State Junior College, Fayette, AL 35555
Brewton-Parker College, Mount Vernon, GA 30445
Briar Cliff College, Sioux City, IA 51104-2100
Briarcliffe: The College for Business, Hicksville, NY 11801
Briarwood College, Southington, CT 06489
Bridgeport Engineering Institute, Fairfield, CT 06430
Bridgewater College, Bridgewater, VA 22812
Bridgewater State College, Bridgewater, MA 02325
Brigham Young University, Provo, UT 84602
Brigham Young University-Hawaii, Laie, HI 96762-1294
Bristol Community College, Fall River, MA 02720
Bristol University, Bristol, TN 37621
Brookdale Community College, Lincroft, NJ 07738
Brookhaven College, Farmers Branch, TX 75244
Brooks College, Long Beach, CA 90804
Brooks Institute of Photography, Santa Barbara, CA 93108
Broome Community College, Binghamton, NY 13902
Broward Community College, Fort Lauderdale, FL 33301
Brown Mackie College, Salina, KS 67401
Brown University, Providence, RI 02912
Brunswick College, Brunswick, GA 31523
Brunswick Community College, Supply, NC 28462
Bryant College, Smithfield, RI 02917-1285
Bryant and Stratton Business Institute: Buffalo, Buffalo, NY 14202
Bryant and Stratton Business Institute, Great Northern, North Olmsted, OH 44070
Bryant-Stratton Business Institute
    Albany, Albany, NY 12205
    Rochester, Rochester, NY 14604-1381
    Syracuse, Syracuse, NY 13202
Bryn Mawr College, Bryn Mawr, PA 19010
Bucknell University, Lewisburg, PA 17837-9988
Bucks County Community College, Newtown, PA 18940
Buena Vista College, Storm Lake, IA 50588
Bunker Hill Community College, Boston, MA 02129
Burlington College, Burlington, VT 05401
Burlington County College, Pemberton, NJ 08068-1599
Butler County Community College, Butler, PA 16003-1203
Butler County Community College, Eldorado, KS 67042-3280
Butler University, Indianapolis, IN 46208
Butte College, Oroville, CA 95965
Cabrillo College, Aptos, CA 95003
Cabrini College, Radnor, PA 19087-3699
Caldwell College, Caldwell, NJ 07006-6195
Caldwell Community College and Technical Institute, Hudson, NC 28638
California Baptist College, Riverside, CA 92504-3297
California College of Arts and Crafts, Oakland, CA 94618-1487
California College for Respiratory Therapy, National City, CA 92050
California Institute of the Arts, Valencia, CA 91355
California Institute of Technology, Pasadena, CA 91125
California Lutheran University, Thousand Oaks, CA 91360-2787
California Maritime Academy, Vallejo, CA 94590-0644
California Polytechnic State University: San Luis Obispo, San Luis Obispo, CA 93407
California State Polytechnic University: Pomona, Pomona, CA 91768-4019
California State University
    Bakersfield, Bakersfield, CA 93311-1099
    Chico, Chico, CA 95929-0720
    Dominguez Hills, Carson, CA 90747-9960
    Fresno, Fresno, CA 93740-0057
    Fullerton, Fullerton, CA 92634
    Hayward, Hayward, CA 94542-3035
    Long Beach, Long Beach, CA 90840-0108
    Los Angeles, Los Angeles, CA 90032
    Northridge, Northridge, CA 91330
    Sacramento, Sacramento, CA 95819
    San Bernardino, San Bernardino, CA 92407
    San Marcos, San Marcos, CA 92069
    Stanislaus, Turlock, CA 95380-0283
California University of Pennsylvania, California, PA 15419
Calumet College of St. Joseph, Hammond, IN 46394-2195
Calvary Bible College, Kansas City, MO 64147-1341
Calvin College, Grand Rapids, MI 49546
Camden County College, Blackwood, NJ 08012
Cameron University, Lawton, OK 73505
Campbell University, Buies Creek, NC 27506
Campbellsville College, Campbellsville, KY 42718
Canada College, Redwood City, CA 94061
Canisius College, Buffalo, NY 14208-9989

Cannon's International Business College of Honolulu, Honolulu, HI 96814-3715
Cape Cod Community College, West Barnstable, MA 02668
Cape Fear Community College, Wilmington, NC 28401
Capital City Junior College, Little Rock, AR 72204
Capital University, Columbus, OH 43209-2394
Capitol College, Laurel, MD 20708
Cardinal Stritch College, Milwaukee, WI 53217
CareerCom Junior College of Business, Hopkinsville, KY 42240
Caribbean University, Bayamon, PR 00619
Carl Albert State College, Poteau, OK 74953-5208
Carl Sandburg College, Galesburg, IL 61401
Carleton College, Northfield, MN 55057
Carlow College, Pittsburgh, PA 15213
Carnegie Mellon University, Pittsburgh, PA 15213-3890
Carroll College, Waukesha, WI 53186
Carroll College, Helena, MT 59625
Carson-Newman College, Jefferson City, TN 37760
Carteret Community College, Morehead City, NC 28557-2989
Carthage College, Kenosha, WI 53140
Casco Bay College, Portland, ME 04101-3483
Case Western Reserve University, Cleveland, OH 44106-1712
Casper College, Casper, WY 82601
Castle Junior College, Windham, NH 03087-1297
Castleton State College, Castleton, VT 05735
Catawba College, Salisbury, NC 28144-2488
Catawba Valley Community College, Hickory, NC 28602
Catholic Medical Center of Brooklyn and Queens School of Nursing, Woodhaven, NY 11421
Catholic University of America, Washington, DC 20064
Catholic University of Puerto Rico, Ponce, PR 00732
Catonsville Community College, Catonsville, MD 21228
Cayuga County Community College, Auburn, NY 13021
Cazenovia College, Cazenovia, NY 13035-9989
Cecil Community College, North East, MD 21901-1999
Cecils College, Asheville, NC 28816
Cedar Crest College, Allentown, PA 18104-6196
Cedar Valley College, Lancaster, TX 75134
Cedarville College, Cedarville, OH 45314-0601
Centenary College, Hackettstown, NJ 07840-9989
Centenary College of Louisiana, Shreveport, LA 71134-1188
Center for Creative Studies: College of Art and Design, Detroit, MI 48202
Central Alabama Community College
    Alexander City Campus, Alexander City, AL 35010
    Childersburg Campus, Childersburg, AL 35044
Central Arizona College, Coolidge, AZ 85228
Central Baptist College, Conway, AR 72032
Central Bible College, Springfield, MO 65803
Central California Commercial College, Fresno, CA 93704-1706
Central Carolina Community College, Sanford, NC 27330
Central Christian College of the Bible, Moberly, MO 65270-1997
Central City Business Institute, Syracuse, NY 13203
Central College, Pella, IA 50219-9989
Central College, McPherson, KS 67460-5740
Central Community College, Grand Island, NE 68802-4903
Central Connecticut State University, New Britain, CT 06050
Central Florida Community College, Ocala, FL 32678
Central Maine Medical Center School of Nursing, Lewiston, ME 04240-9986
Central Maine Technical College, Auburn, ME 04210-6498
Central Methodist College, Fayette, MO 65248-1198
Central Michigan University, Mount Pleasant, MI 48859
Central Missouri State University, Warrensburg, MO 64093
Central Ohio Technical College, Newark, OH 43055
Central Oregon Community College, Bend, OR 97701-5998
Central Pennsylvania Business School, Summerdale, PA 17093-0309
Central Piedmont Community College, Charlotte, NC 28235
Central State University, Wilberforce, OH 45384
Central State University, Edmond, OK 73034-0151
Central Texas College, Killeen, TX 76541
Central Virginia Community College, Lynchburg, VA 24502
Central Washington University, Ellensburg, WA 98926
Central Wesleyan College, Central, SC 29630-1020
Central Wyoming College, Riverton, WY 82501
Central Yeshiva Tomchei Tmimim Lubavitz, Brooklyn, NY 11230
Centralia College, Centralia, WA 98531
Centre College, Danville, KY 40422
Cerritos Community College, Norwalk, CA 90650
Cerro Coso Community College, Ridgecrest, CA 93555-7777
Chabot College, Hayward, CA 94545
Chadron State College, Chadron, NE 69337
Chaffey Community College, Rancho Cucamonga, CA 91701-3002

Chaminade University of Honolulu, Honolulu, HI 96816-1578
Champlain College, Burlington, VT 05402
Chapman College, Orange, CA 92666
Charles County Community College, La Plata, MD 20646
Charles R. Drew University: College of Allied Health, Los Angeles, CA 90059
Charles Stewart Mott Community College, Flint, MI 48502
Charleston Southern University, Charleston, SC 29411
Chatfield College, St. Martin, OH 45118
Chatham College, Pittsburgh, PA 15232
Chattahoochee Technical Institute, Marietta, GA 30060
Chattahoochee Valley Community College, Phenix City, AL 36869
Chattanooga State Technical Community College, Chattanooga, TN 37406
Chemeketa Community College, Salem, OR 97309-7070
Chesapeake College, Wye Mills, MD 21679
Chesterfield-Marlboro Technical College, Cheraw, SC 29520
Chestnut Hill College, Philadelphia, PA 19118-2695
Cheyney University of Pennsylvania, Cheyney, PA 19319
CHI Institute, Southampton, PA 18966
Chicago State University, Chicago, IL 60628
Chipola Junior College, Marianna, FL 32446
Chippewa Valley Technical College, Eau Claire, WI 54701
Chowan College, Murfreesboro, NC 27855
Christ College Irvine, Irvine, CA 92715
Christendom College, Front Royal, VA 22630
Christian Brothers University, Memphis, TN 38104-5581
Christian Heritage College, El Cajon, CA 92019
Christopher Newport College, Newport News, VA 23606-2998
Churchman Business School, Easton, PA 18042
Cincinnati Bible College and Seminary, Cincinnati, OH 45204-3200
Cincinnati College of Mortuary Science, Cincinnati, OH 45212
Cincinnati Metropolitan College, St. Bernard, OH 45217
Cincinnati Technical College, Cincinnati, OH 45223
Circleville Bible College, Circleville, OH 43113
Cisco Junior College, Cisco, TX 76437
The Citadel, Charleston, SC 29409
Citrus College, Glendora, CA 91740-1899
City College of San Francisco, San Francisco, CA 94112
City Colleges of Chicago
    Chicago City-Wide College, Chicago, IL 60606-6997
    Harold Washington College, Chicago, IL 60601
    Harry S. Truman College, Chicago, IL 60640
    Kennedy-King College, Chicago, IL 60621
    Malcolm X College, Chicago, IL 60612
    Olive-Harvey College, Chicago, IL 60628
    Richard J. Daley College, Chicago, IL 60652
    Wright College, Chicago, IL 60634-4276
City University, Bellevue, WA 98008
City University of New York
    Baruch College, New York, NY 10010
    Borough of Manhattan Community College, New York, NY 10007-1097
    Bronx Community College, New York, NY 10453
    Brooklyn College, Brooklyn, NY 11210
    City College, New York, NY 10031
    College of Staten Island, Staten Island, NY 10301-4547
    Hostos Community College, Bronx, NY 10451
    Hunter College, New York, NY 10021
    John Jay College of Criminal Justice, New York, NY 10019
    Kingsborough Community College, Brooklyn, NY 11235
    La Guardia Community College, Long Island City, NY 11101
    Lehman College, Bronx, NY 10468
    Medgar Evers College, Brooklyn, NY 11225-2201
    New York City Technical College, Brooklyn, NY 11201-2983
    Queens College, Flushing, NY 11367
    Queensborough Community College, Bayside, NY 11364
    York College, Jamaica, NY 11451-9989
Clackamas Community College, Oregon City, OR 97045
Claflin College, Orangeburg, SC 29115
Claremont McKenna College, Claremont, CA 91711-6420
Clarendon College, Clarendon, TX 79226
Clarion University of Pennsylvania, Clarion, PA 16214
Clark Atlanta University, Atlanta, GA 30314
Clark College, Vancouver, WA 98663
Clark County Community College, North Las Vegas, NV 89030
Clark State Community College, Springfield, OH 45501
Clark University, Worcester, MA 01610-1477
Clarke College, Newton, MS 39345
Clarke College, Dubuque, IA 52001-3198
Clarkson University, Potsdam, NY 13676
Clatsop Community College, Astoria, OR 97103
Clayton State College, Morrow, GA 30260-1221

Clear Creek Baptist Bible College, Pineville, KY 40977
Clearwater Christian College, Clearwater, FL 34619-9997
Cleary College, Ypsilanti, MI 48197
Clemson University, Clemson, SC 29634-4024
Cleveland College of Jewish Studies, Beachwood, OH 44122
Cleveland Community College, Shelby, NC 28150
Cleveland Institute of Art, Cleveland, OH 44106
Cleveland Institute of Music, Cleveland, OH 44106
Cleveland State Community College, Cleveland, TN 37320-3570
Cleveland State University, Cleveland, OH 44115-2403
Clinch Valley College of the University of Virginia, Wise, VA 24293
Clinton Community College, Plattsburgh, NY 12901-4297
Clinton Community College, Clinton, IA 52732-6299
Clinton Junior College, Rock Hill, SC 29731
Cloud County Community College, Concordia, KS 66901-1002
Coahoma Community College, Clarksdale, MS 38614
Coastal Carolina Community College, Jacksonville, NC 28540-6877
Coastline Community College, Fountain Valley, CA 92708
Cochise College, Douglas, AZ 85607
Cochran School of Nursing-St. John's Riverside Hospital, Yonkers, NY 10701
Coe College, Cedar Rapids, IA 52402-9983
Coffeyville Community College, Coffeyville, KS 67337
Cogswell College North, Kirkland, WA 98033
Cogswell Polytechnical College, Cupertino, CA 95014
Coker College, Hartsville, SC 29550
Colby College, Waterville, ME 04901-4799
Colby Community College, Colby, KS 67701
Colby-Sawyer College, New London, NH 03257
Coleman College, La Mesa, CA 92042-1532
Colgate University, Hamilton, NY 13346-1383
College of Aeronautics, Flushing, NY 11371
College of Alameda, Alameda, CA 94501
College of the Albemarle, Elizabeth City, NC 27906-2327
College of Associated Arts, St. Paul, MN 55102-2199
College of the Atlantic, Bar Harbor, ME 04609
College of Boca Raton, Boca Raton, FL 33431-5598
College of the Canyons, Valencia, CA 91355
College of Charleston, Charleston, SC 29424
College of the Desert, Palm Desert, CA 92260
College of DuPage, Glen Ellyn, IL 60137
College of Eastern Utah, Price, UT 84501
College of Great Falls, Great Falls, MT 59405
College of Health Sciences, Roanoke, VA 24031-3186
College of the Holy Cross, Worcester, MA 01610
College for Human Services, New York, NY 10014
College of Idaho, Caldwell, ID 83605
College of Insurance, New York, NY 10007-2132
College of Lake County, Grayslake, IL 60030-1198
College of the Mainland, Texas City, TX 77591
College of Marin: Kentfield, Kentfield, CA 94904
College Misericordia, Dallas, PA 18612-9984
College of Mount St. Joseph, Cincinnati, OH 45051
College of Mount St. Vincent, Riverdale, NY 10471
College of New Rochelle
    New Rochelle, New Rochelle, NY 10805-2308
    School of New Resources, New Rochelle, NY 10805-2308
College of Notre Dame, Belmont, CA 94002
College of Notre Dame of Maryland, Baltimore, MD 21210
College of the Ozarks, Point Lookout, MO 65726
College of the Redwoods, Eureka, CA 95501-9302
College of St. Benedict, St. Joseph, MN 56374-2099
College of St. Catherine: St. Catherine Campus, St. Paul, MN 55105
College of St. Elizabeth, Morris Township, NJ 07961
College of St. Francis, Joliet, IL 60435-6188
College of St. Joseph in Vermont, Rutland, VT 05701
College of St. Mary, Omaha, NE 68124
College of St. Rose, Albany, NY 12203
College of St. Scholastica, Duluth, MN 55811-4199
College of San Mateo, San Mateo, CA 94402
College of Santa Fe, Santa Fe, NM 87501-5634
College of the Sequoias, Visalia, CA 93277
College of the Siskiyous, Weed, CA 96094
College of Southern Idaho, Twin Falls, ID 83303-1238
College of the Southwest, Hobbs, NM 88240-9987
College of William and Mary, Williamsburg, VA 23185
College of Wooster, Wooster, OH 44691-2363
Collin County Community College District, McKinney, TX 75070-2906
Colorado Christian University, Denver, CO 80226
Colorado College, Colorado Springs, CO 80903
Colorado Institute of Art, Denver, CO 80203

Colorado Mountain College
    Alpine Campus, Steamboat Springs, CO 80477
    Spring Valley Campus, Glenwood Springs, CO 81601
    Timberline Campus, Leadville, CO 80461
Colorado Northwestern Community College, Rangely, CO 81648-9988
Colorado School of Mines, Golden, CO 80401
Colorado State University, Fort Collins, CO 80523-0015
Colorado Technical College, Colorado Springs, CO 80907-3896
Columbia Basin College, Pasco, WA 99301
Columbia Bible College and Seminary, Columbia, SC 29230-3122
Columbia Christian College, Portland, OR 97216-1515
Columbia College, Chicago, IL 60605-1996
Columbia College, Columbia, CA 95310
Columbia College, Columbia, SC 29203
Columbia College, Columbia, MO 65216
Columbia College, Caguas, PR 00626
Columbia College: Hollywood, Los Angeles, CA 90038
Columbia College of Nursing, Milwaukee, WI 53186
Columbia Junior College of Business, Columbia, SC 29203
Columbia State Community College, Columbia, TN 38401
Columbia Union College, Takoma Park, MD 20912
Columbia University
    Columbia College, New York, NY 10027
    School of Engineering and Applied Science, New York, NY 10027
    School of General Studies, New York, NY 10027
    School of Nursing, New York, NY 10032
Columbia-Greene Community College, Hudson, NY 12534
Columbus College, Columbus, GA 31993-2399
Columbus College of Art and Design, Columbus, OH 43215-3875
Columbus State Community College, Columbus, OH 43216-1609
Columbus Technical Institute, Columbus, OH 43995
Commonwealth College, Virginia Beach, VA 23452
Commonwealth Institute of Funeral Service, Houston, TX 77090-5913
Community College of Allegheny County
    Allegheny Campus, Pittsburgh, PA 15212
    Boyce Campus, Monroeville, PA 15146
    North Campus, Pittsburgh, PA 15237
    South Campus, West Mifflin, PA 15122
Community College of Aurora, Aurora, CO 80011
Community College of Beaver County, Monaca, PA 15061
Community College of Denver, Denver, CO 80204
Community College of the Finger Lakes, Canandaigua, NY 14424-8399
Community College of Micronesia, Kolonia, Ponape Island, TT 96941
Community College of Philadelphia, Philadelphia, PA 19130-3991
Community College of Rhode Island, Warwick, RI 02886-1805
Community College of Vermont, Waterbury, VT 05676
Compton Community College, Compton, CA 90221
Conception Seminary College, Conception, MO 64433
Concord College, Athens, WV 24712
Concordia College, Ann Arbor, MI 48105
Concordia College, Selma, AL 36701
Concordia College, Bronxville, NY 10708
Concordia College, Portland, OR 97211-6099
Concordia College, Seward, NE 68434-9989
Concordia College: Moorhead, Moorhead, MN 56562-9981
Concordia College: St. Paul, St. Paul, MN 55104-5494
Concordia Lutheran College, Austin, TX 78705-2799
Concordia University, River Forest, IL 60305-1499
Concordia University Wisconsin, Mequon, WI 53092-9650
Connecticut College, New London, CT 06320
Connors State College, Warner, OK 74469-0389
Conservatory of Music of Puerto Rico, Hato Rey, PR 00918
Contra Costa College, San Pablo, CA 94806
Converse College, Spartanburg, SC 29302-0006
Cooke County College, Gainesville, TX 76240
Cooper Union, New York, NY 10003-7183
Copiah-Lincoln Community College, Wesson, MS 39191
Coppin State College, Baltimore, MD 21216
Corcoran School of Art, Washington, DC 20006
Cornell College, Mount Vernon, IA 52314-1098
Cornell University, Ithaca, NY 14850
Corning Community College, Corning, NY 14830
Cornish College of the Arts, Seattle, WA 98102
Corpus Christi State University, Corpus Christi, TX 78412
Cosumnes River College, Sacramento, CA 95823-5799
Cottey College, Nevada, MO 64772
County College of Morris, Randolph, NJ 07869
Covenant College, Lookout Mountain, GA 30750
Cowley County Community College, Arkansas City, KS 67005
Crafton Hills College, Yucaipa, CA 92399-1799
Crandall Junior College, Macon, GA 31204
Craven Community College, New Bern, NC 28560

Creighton University, Omaha, NE 68178
Crichton College, Memphis, TN 38175-7830
Criswell College, Dallas, TX 75246
Crowder College, Neosho, MO 64850
Crowley's Ridge College, Paragould, AR 72450
Cuesta College, San Luis Obispo, CA 93403-8106
Culinary Institute of America, Hyde Park, NY 12538-1499
Culver-Stockton College, Canton, MO 63435
Cumberland College, Williamsburg, KY 40769-6178
Cumberland County College, Vineland, NJ 08360
Cumberland University, Lebanon, TN 37087
Curry College, Milton, MA 02186-9984
Cuyahoga Community College
    Eastern Campus, Highland Hills, OH 44122
    Metropolitan Campus, Cleveland, OH 44115-2878
    Western Campus, Parma, OH 44130
Cuyamaca College, El Cajon, CA 92019-4304
Cypress College, Cypress, CA 90630
Dabney S. Lancaster Community College, Clifton Forge, VA 24422-1000
Daemen College, Amherst, NY 14226
Dakota County Technical College, Rosemount, MN 55068
Dakota State University, Madison, SD 57042
Dakota Wesleyan University, Mitchell, SD 57301
Dallas Baptist University, Dallas, TX 75211-9800
Dallas Christian College, Dallas, TX 75234
Dalton College, Dalton, GA 30720
Dana College, Blair, NE 68008-9905
Daniel Webster College, Nashua, NH 03063-1699
Danville Area Community College, Danville, IL 61832
Danville Community College, Danville, VA 24541
Darkei No'Am Rabbinical College, Brooklyn, NY 11210
Darton College, Albany, GA 31707-3098
Davenport College of Business, Grand Rapids, MI 49503
David Lipscomb University, Nashville, TN 37204-3951
Davidson College, Davidson, NC 28036
Davidson County Community College, Lexington, NC 27293-1287
Davis and Elkins College, Elkins, WV 26241
Davis Junior College of Business, Toledo, OH 43623
Dawson Community College, Glendive, MT 59330
Daytona Beach Community College, Daytona Beach, FL 32115-2811
De Anza College, Cupertino, CA 95014
De Paul University, Chicago, IL 60604
Deaconess College of Nursing, St. Louis, MO 63139
Dean Institute of Technology, Pittsburgh, PA 15226
Dean Junior College, Franklin, MA 02038-1994
Defiance College, Defiance, OH 43512-1695
DeKalb College, Decatur, GA 30034
DeKalb Technical Institute, Clarkston, GA 30021
Del Mar College, Corpus Christi, TX 78404-3897
Delaware County Community College, Media, PA 19063
Delaware State College, Dover, DE 19901
Delaware Technical and Community College
    Southern Campus, Georgetown, DE 19947
    Stanton/Wilmington Campus, Wilmington, DE 19850
    Terry Campus, Dover, DE 19903
Delaware Valley College of Science and Agriculture, Doylestown, PA 18901
Delgado Community College, New Orleans, LA 70119-4399
Delta College, University Center, MI 48710
Delta State University, Cleveland, MS 38733
Denison University, Granville, OH 43023
Denmark Technical College, Denmark, SC 29042-0327
Denver Technical College, Denver, CO 80222-1658
DePauw University, Greencastle, IN 46135-0037
Des Moines Area Community College, Ankeny, IA 50021
Detroit College of Business, Dearborn, MI 48126-3799
DeVry Institute of Technology
    Chicago, Chicago, IL 60618-5994
    City of Industry, City of Industry, CA 91746-3495
    Columbus, Columbus, OH 43209-2764
    Decatur, Decatur, GA 30030-2198
    Irving, Irving, TX 75038-4299
    Kansas City, Kansas City, MO 64131-3626
    Lombard, Lombard, IL 60148-4892
    Phoenix, Phoenix, AZ 85021-2995
Diablo Valley College, Pleasant Hill, CA 94523
Dickinson College, Carlisle, PA 17013-2896
Dickinson State University, Dickinson, ND 58601
Dillard University, New Orleans, LA 70122-3097
Divine Word College, Epworth, IA 52045
Dixie College, St. George, UT 84770
Doane College, Crete, NE 68333

Dodge City Community College, Dodge City, KS 67801-2399
Dominican College of Blauvelt, Orangeburg, NY 10962
Dominican College of San Rafael, San Rafael, CA 94901-8008
Dominican School of Philosophy and Theology, Berkeley, CA 94709
Don Bosco Technical Institute, Rosemead, CA 91770-4299
Dona Ana Branch Community College of New Mexico State University, Las Cruces, NM 88003
Donnelly College, Kansas City, KS 66102
Dordt College, Sioux Center, IA 51250
Douglas MacArthur State Technical College, Opp, AL 36467
Dowling College, Oakdale, NY 11769-1999
D-Q University, Davis, CA 95617
Dr. Martin Luther College, New Ulm, MN 56073-3347
Drake University, Des Moines, IA 50311-4505
Draughons Junior College, Montgomery, AL 36104
Draughons Junior College, Memphis, TN 38186-9930
Draughons Junior College of Business
    Knoxville, Knoxville, TN 37919
    Nashville, Nashville, TN 37217
Draughon's Junior College: Johnson City, Johnson City, TN 37601
Drew University, Madison, NJ 07940
Drexel University, Philadelphia, PA 19104
Drury College, Springfield, MO 65802-9977
DuBois Business College, DuBois, PA 15801
Duke University, Durham, NC 27706
Dull Knife Memorial College, Lame Deer, MT 59043
Dundalk Community College, Baltimore, MD 21222-4692
Duquesne University, Pittsburgh, PA 15282-0201
Durham Technical Community College, Durham, NC 27703
Dutchess Community College, Poughkeepsie, NY 12601-1595
Dyersburg State Community College, Dyersburg, TN 38025-0648
Dyke College, Cleveland, OH 44115
D'Youville College, Buffalo, NY 14201
Earlham College, Richmond, IN 47374
East Arkansas Community College, Forrest City, AR 72335-9598
East Carolina University, Greenville, NC 27858-4353
East Central College, Union, MO 63084
East Central Community College, Decatur, MS 39327
East Central University, Ada, OK 74820-6899
East Coast Bible College, Charlotte, NC 28214
East Georgia College, Swainsboro, GA 30401-2699
East Los Angeles College, Monterey Park, CA 91754
East Mississippi Junior College, Scooba, MS 39358
East Stroudsburg University of Pennsylvania, East Stroudsburg, PA 18301
East Tennessee State University, Johnson City, TN 37614-0002
East Texas Baptist University, Marshall, TX 75670-1498
East Texas State University
    Commerce, Commerce, TX 75429
    Texarkana, Texarkana, TX 75505-0518
Eastern Arizona College, Thatcher, AZ 85552-0769
Eastern Christian College, Bel Air, MD 21014-0629
Eastern College, St. Davids, PA 19087-3696
Eastern Connecticut State University, Willimantic, CT 06226-2295
Eastern Illinois University, Charleston, IL 61920
Eastern Kentucky University, Richmond, KY 40475
Eastern Maine Technical College, Bangor, ME 04401
Eastern Mennonite College, Harrisonburg, VA 22801-9980
Eastern Michigan University, Ypsilanti, MI 48197-2260
Eastern Montana College, Billings, MT 59101-0298
Eastern Nazarene College, Quincy, MA 02170
Eastern New Mexico University
Clovis Community College, Clovis, NM 88101
    Portales, Portales, NM 88130
    Roswell Campus, Roswell, NM 88202-6000
Eastern Oklahoma State College, Wilburton, OK 74578-4999
Eastern Oregon State College, LaGrande, OR 97850
Eastern Shore Community College, Melfa, VA 23410-9755
Eastern Washington University, Cheney, WA 99004-2496
Eastern Wyoming College, Torrington, WY 82240
Eastfield College, Mesquite, TX 75150
Eastman School of Music of the University of Rochester, Rochester, NY 14604
East-West University, Chicago, IL 60605
Eckerd College, St. Petersburg, FL 33733-9979
Edgecombe Community College, Tarboro, NC 27886
Edgewood College, Madison, WI 53711
Edinboro University of Pennsylvania, Edinboro, PA 16444
Edison Community College, Fort Myers, FL 33906-6210
Edison State Community College, Piqua, OH 45356
Edmonds Community College, Lynnwood, WA 98036
Edward Waters College, Jacksonville, FL 32209
El Camino College, Torrance, CA 90506

El Centro College, Dallas, TX 75202
El Paso Community College, El Paso, TX 79998
El Reno Junior College, El Reno, OK 73036
Electronic Data Processing College of Puerto Rico, Hato Rey, PR 00918
Electronic Institutes
    Middletown, Middletown, PA 17057
    Pittsburgh, Pittsburgh, PA 15217
Elgin Community College, Elgin, IL 60123
Elizabeth City State University, Elizabeth City, NC 27909
Elizabethtown College, Elizabethtown, PA 17022-2298
Elizabethtown Community College, Elizabethtown, KY 42701
Ellsworth Community College, Iowa Falls, IA 50126
Elmhurst College, Elmhurst, IL 60126-3296
Elmira College, Elmira, NY 14901-2345
Elms College, Chicopee, MA 01013-2839
Elon College, Elon College, NC 27244-2010
Embry-Riddle Aeronautical University
    Daytona Beach, Daytona Beach, FL 32114-9970
    Prescott Campus, Prescott, AZ 86301
Emerson College, Boston, MA 02116
Emmanuel College, Boston, MA 02115
Emmanuel College, Franklin Springs, GA 30639-0129
Emmanuel College School of Christian Ministries, Franklin Springs, GA 30639
Emmaus Bible College, Dubuque, IA 52001
Emory and Henry College, Emory, VA 24327
Emory University, Atlanta, GA 30322
Emporia State University, Emporia, KS 66801-5087
Endicott College, Beverly, MA 01915-9985
Enterprise State Junior College, Enterprise, AL 36331
Erie Community College
    City Campus, Buffalo, NY 14203-2601
    North Campus, Williamsville, NY 14127
    South Campus, Orchard Park, NY 14127-2199
Erskine College, Due West, SC 29639-0176
Escuela De Artes Plasticas, San Juan, PR 00905
Essex Agricultural and Technical Institute, Hathorne, MA 01937
Essex Community College, Baltimore, MD 21237-3899
Essex County College, Newark, NJ 07102
ETI Technical College, Cleveland, OH 44103
Eugene Bible College, Eugene, OR 97405
Eugene Lang College/New School for Social Research, New York, NY 10114-0059
Eureka College, Eureka, IL 61530
Evangel College, Springfield, MO 65802
Everett Community College, Everett, WA 98201
Evergreen State College, Olympia, WA 98505
Evergreen Valley College, San Jose, CA 95135
Fairfield University, Fairfield, CT 06430
Fairleigh Dickinson University
    Edward Williams College, Hackensack, NJ 07601
    Florham-Madison Campus, Madison, NJ 07070
    Rutherford Campus, Rutherford, NJ 07070
    Teaneck-Hackensack Campus, Teaneck, NJ 07070
Fairmont State College, Fairmont, WV 26554
Faith Baptist Bible College and Theological Seminary, Ankeny, IA 50021
Fashion Institute of Design and Merchandising
    Los Angeles, Los Angeles, CA 90015
    San Francisco, San Francisco, CA 94108-5805
Fashion Institute of Technology, New York, NY 10001-5992
Faulkner University, Montgomery, AL 36193
Fayetteville State University, Fayetteville, NC 28301-4298
Fayetteville Technical Community College, Fayetteville, NC 28303-0236
Feather River College, Quincy, CA 95971
Felician College, Lodi, NJ 07644-2198
Fergus Falls Community College, Fergus Falls, MN 56537
Ferris State University, Big Rapids, MI 49307
Ferrum College, Ferrum, VA 24088
Fisher College, Boston, MA 02116
Fisk University, Nashville, TN 37208
Fitchburg State College, Fitchburg, MA 01420
Five Towns College, Seaford, NY 11783-9800
Flagler College, St. Augustine, FL 32084
Flaming Rainbow University, Stilwell, OK 74960
Flathead Valley Community College, Kalispell, MT 59901
Florence-Darlington Technical College, Florence, SC 29501
Florida Agricultural and Mechanical University, Tallahassee, FL 32307
Florida Atlantic University, Boca Raton, FL 33431
Florida Baptist Theological College, Graceville, FL 32440-1830
Florida Bible College, Kissimmee, FL 34758
Florida Christian College, Kissimmee, FL 34744-4402
Florida College, Temple Terrace, FL 33617

Florida Community College at Jacksonville, Jacksonville, FL 32202-4030
Florida Institute of Technology, Melbourne, FL 32901
Florida International University, Miami, FL 33199
Florida Keys Community College, Key West, FL 33040
Florida Memorial College, Miami, FL 33054
Florida Southern College, Lakeland, FL 33801-5698
Florida State University, Tallahassee, FL 32306-1009
Floyd College, Rome, GA 30163-1801
Fontbonne College, St. Louis, MO 63105
Foothill College, Los Altos Hills, CA 94022-4599
Fordham University, Bronx, NY 10458
Forsyth School for Dental Hygienists, Boston, MA 02115
Forsyth Technical Community College, Winston-Salem, NC 27103
Fort Belknap College, Harlem, MT 59526-0159
Fort Bethold Community College, New Town, ND 58763
Fort Hays State University, Hays, KS 67601-4099
Fort Lauderdale College, Fort Lauderdale, FL 33301
Fort Lewis College, Durango, CO 81301
Fort Peck Community College, Poplar, MT 59255
Fort Scott Community College, Fort Scott, KS 66701
Fort Valley State College, Fort Valley, GA 31030
Fox Valley Technical College, Appleton, WI 54913-2277
Framingham State College, Framingham, MA 01701
Francis Marion College, Florence, SC 29501-0547
Franciscan University of Steubenville, Steubenville, OH 43952
Frank Phillips College, Borger, TX 79008-5118
Franklin College, Franklin, IN 46131-2598
Franklin College, Paducah, KY 42001
Franklin College: Switzerland, Lugano, Switzerland
Franklin Institute of Boston, Boston, MA 02116
Franklin Pierce College, Rindge, NH 03461-0060
Franklin University, Columbus, OH 43215-5399
Frederick Community College, Frederick, MD 21701
Free Will Baptist Bible College, Nashville, TN 37205-0117
Freed-Hardeman University, Henderson, TN 38340
Fresno City College, Fresno, CA 93741
Fresno Pacific College, Fresno, CA 93702
Friends University, Wichita, KS 67213
Friends World College, Huntington, NY 11743-9820
Front Range Community College, Westminster, CO 80030
Frostburg State University, Frostburg, MD 21532-1099
Fullerton College, Fullerton, CA 92634
Fulton-Montgomery Community College, Johnstown, NY 12095
Furman University, Greenville, SC 29613
Gadsden State Community College, Gadsden, AL 35902-0227
Gainesville College, Gainesville, GA 30503
Gallaudet University, Washington, DC 20002
Galveston College, Galveston, TX 77550
Gannon University, Erie, PA 16541
Garden City Community College, Garden City, KS 67846
Gardner-Webb College, Boiling Springs, NC 28017
Garland County Community College, Hot Springs, AR 71913-9120
Garrett Community College, McHenry, MD 21541
Gaston College, Dallas, NC 28034-1499
Gateway Community College, Phoenix, AZ 85034
Gateway Technical College, Kenosha, WI 53141-1582
Gavilan Community College, Gilroy, CA 95020
Gem City College, Quincy, IL 62306
Genesee Community College, Batavia, NY 14020
Geneva College, Beaver Falls, PA 15010
George C. Wallace State Community College
      Dothan, Dothan, AL 36303-9234
      Selma, Selma, AL 36701-1049
George Fox College, Newberg, OR 97132-9987
George Mason University, Fairfax, VA 22030-4444
George Rogers Clark College, Indianapolis, IN 46202
George Washington University, Washington, DC 20052
Georgetown College, Georgetown, KY 40324-1696
Georgetown University, Washington, DC 20057
Georgia College, Milledgeville, GA 31061
Georgia Institute of Technology, Atlanta, GA 30332-0320
Georgia Military College, Milledgeville, GA 31061
Georgia Southern University, Statesboro, GA 30460-8024
Georgia Southwestern College, Americus, GA 31709-4693
Georgia State University, Atlanta, GA 30303-3083
Georgian Court College, Lakewood, NJ 08701-9972
Germanna Community College, Locust Grove, VA 22508
Gettysburg College, Gettysburg, PA 17325-1484
Glassboro State College, Glassboro, NJ 08028
Glen Oaks Community College, Centreville, MI 49032
Glendale Community College, Glendale, CA 91208
Glendale Community College, Glendale, AZ 85302-3090

Glenville State College, Glenville, WV 26351-1292
Gloucester County College, Sewell Post Office, NJ 08080
GMI Engineering and Management Institute, Flint, MI 48504-4898
Goddard College, Plainfield, VT 05667
God's Bible School and College, Cincinnati, OH 45210
Gogebic Community College, Ironwood, MI 49938
Golden Gate University, San Francisco, CA 94105-2968
Golden West College, Huntington Beach, CA 92647-0592
Goldey-Beacom College, Wilmington, DE 19808
Gonzaga University, Spokane, WA 99258-0001
Gordon College, Wenham, MA 01984
Gordon College, Barnesville, GA 30204
Goshen College, Goshen, IN 46526-9988
Goucher College, Baltimore, MD 21204
Governors State University, University Park, IL 60466
Grace Bible College, Grand Rapids, MI 49509
Grace College, Winona Lake, IN 46590
Grace College of the Bible, Omaha, NE 68108
Graceland College, Lamoni, IA 50140
Grambling State University, Grambling, LA 71245
Grand Canyon University, Phoenix, AZ 85061-1097
Grand Rapids Baptist College and Seminary, Grand Rapids, MI 49505
Grand Rapids Junior College, Grand Rapids, MI 49503
Grand Valley State University, Allendale, MI 49401-9403
Grand View College, Des Moines, IA 50316
Grantham College of Engineering, Slidell, LA 70469-5700
Gratz College, Melrose Park, PA 19126
Grays Harbor College, Aberdeen, WA 98520-7599
Grayson County College, Denison, TX 75020
Great Lakes Bible College, Lansing, MI 48901
Great Lakes Junior College of Business, Saginaw, MI 48607
Greater Hartford Community College, Hartford, CT 06105-2354
Greater New Haven State Technical College, North Haven, CT 06473
Green Mountain College, Poultney, VT 05764
Green River Community College, Auburn, WA 98002
Greenfield Community College, Greenfield, MA 01301
Greensboro College, Greensboro, NC 27401-1875
Greenville College, Greenville, IL 62246
Greenville Technical College, Greenville, SC 29606
Griffin College, Seattle, WA 98121
Grinnell College, Grinnell, IA 50112-0807
Grossmont Community College, El Cajon, CA 92020
Grove City College, Grove City, PA 16127-2197
Guam Community College, Guam, GU 96921
Guilford College, Greensboro, NC 27410
Guilford Technical Community College, Jamestown, NC 27282
Gulf Coast Community College, Panama City, FL 32401-1041
Gustavus Adolphus College, St. Peter, MN 56082
Gwynedd-Mercy College, Gwynedd Valley, PA 19437
Hagerstown Business College, Hagerstown, MD 21740
Hagerstown Junior College, Hagerstown, MD 21740-6590
Hahnemann University School of Health Sciences and Humanities,
      Philadelphia, PA 19102-1192
Halifax Community College, Weldon, NC 27890
Hamilton College, Clinton, NY 13323-1293
Hamilton Technical College, Davenport, IA 52807
Hamline University, St. Paul, MN 55104-1284
Hampden-Sydney College, Hampden-Sydney, VA 23943
Hampshire College, Amherst, MA 01002
Hampton University, Hampton, VA 23668
Hannibal-LaGrange College, Hannibal, MO 63401
Hanover College, Hanover, IN 47243
Harcum Junior College, Bryn Mawr, PA 19010-3476
Harding University, Searcy, AR 72143
Hardin-Simmons University, Abilene, TX 79698
Harford Community College, Bel Air, MD 21014
Harrington Institute of Interior Design, Chicago, IL 60605
Harris Stowe State College, St. Louis, MO 63103
Harrisburg Area Community College, Harrisburg, PA 17110-2999
Harry M. Ayers State Technical College, Anniston, AL 36202
Hartford College for Women, Hartford, CT 06105
Hartford State Technical College, Hartford, CT 06106
Hartnell College, Salinas, CA 93901
Hartwick College, Oneonta, NY 13820-9989
Harvard and Radcliffe Colleges, Cambridge, MA 02138
Harvey Mudd College, Claremont, CA 91711-5990
Haskell Indian Junior College, Lawrence, KS 66046
Hastings College, Hastings, NE 68901
Haverford College, Haverford, PA 19041-1392
Hawaii Loa College, Kaneohe, HI 96744
Hawaii Pacific University, Honolulu, HI 96813
Hawkeye Institute of Technology, Waterloo, IA 50704

Haywood Community College, Clyde, NC 28721
Hazard Community College, Hazard, KY 41701
Heald Business College
    Rohnert Park, Rohnert Park, CA 94928
    San Jose, San Jose, CA 95130
    Walnut Creek, Walnut Creek, CA 94596
Heald College: Sacramento, Rancho Cordova, CA 95670
Heald Institute of Technology, Martinez, CA 94553
Hebrew Theological College, Skokie, IL 60077
Hebrew Union College: Jewish Institute of Religion, Los Angeles, CA 90007
Heidelberg College, Tiffin, OH 44883
Helene Fuld School of Nursing, New York, NY 10035
Hellenic College, Brookline, MA 02146
Henderson Community College, Henderson, KY 42420
Henderson State University, Arkadelphia, AR 71923
Hendrix College, Conway, AR 72032-3080
Henry Ford Community College, Dearborn, MI 48128
Heritage College, Toppenish, WA 98948
Herkimer County Community College, Herkimer, NY 13350-1598
Hesser College, Manchester, NH 03103-9969
Hesston College, Hesston, KS 67062-3000
Hibbing Community College, Hibbing, MN 55746
High Point College, High Point, NC 27261-1949
Highland Community College, Freeport, IL 61032-9341
Highland Community College, Highland, KS 66035-0068
Highland Park Community College, Highland Park, MI 48203
Highline Community College, Des Moines, WA 98198-9800
Hilbert College, Hamburg, NY 14075
Hill College, Hillsboro, TX 76645
Hillsborough Community College, Tampa, FL 33631-3127
Hillsdale College, Hillsdale, MI 49242
Hillsdale Free Will Baptist College, Moore, OK 73153-1208
Hinds Community College, Raymond, MS 39154-9799
Hiram College, Hiram, OH 44234
Hiwassee College, Madisonville, TN 37354
Hobart College, Geneva, NY 14456
Hobe Sound Bible College, Hobe Sound, FL 33475-1065
Hobson State Technical College, Thomasville, AL 36784
Hocking Technical College, Nelsonville, OH 45764
Hofstra University, Hempstead, NY 11550
Hollins College, Roanoke, VA 24020-1707
Holmes Community College, Goodman, MS 39079
Holy Apostles College and Seminary, Cromwell, CT 06416
Holy Cross College, Notre Dame, IN 46556-0308
Holy Family College, Philadelphia, PA 19114-2094
Holy Names College, Oakland, CA 94619-1699
Holy Trinity Orthodox Seminary, Jordanville, NY 13361
Holyoke Community College, Holyoke, MA 01040
Hood College, Frederick, MD 21701-9988
Hope College, Holland, MI 49423-3698
Hopkinsville Community College, Hopkinsville, KY 42241-2100
Horry-Georgetown Technical College, Conway, SC 29526-1966
Houghton College, Houghton, NY 14744-9989
Housatonic Community College, Bridgeport, CT 06608
Houston Baptist University, Houston, TX 77074
Houston Community College, Houston, TX 77270
Howard College, Big Spring, TX 79720
Howard Community College, Columbia, MD 21044
Howard Payne University, Brownwood, TX 76801-2794
Howard University, Washington, DC 20059
Hudson County Community College, Jersey City, NJ 07306
Hudson Valley Community College, Troy, NY 12180
Huertas Junior College, Caguas, PR 00625
Humboldt State University, Arcata, CA 95521
Humphreys College, Stockton, CA 95207-3896
Huntingdon College, Montgomery, AL 36106-2148
Huntington College, Huntington, IN 46750
Huntington Junior College of Business, Huntington, WV 25701
Huron University, Huron, SD 57350
Hussian School of Art, Philadelphia, PA 19107
Husson College, Bangor, ME 04401
Huston-Tillotson College, Austin, TX 78702
Hutchinson Community College, Hutchinson, KS 67501
ICPR Junior College, Hato Rey, PR 00919
Idaho State University, Pocatello, ID 83209
Illinois Benedictine College, Lisle, IL 60532-0900
Illinois Central College, East Peoria, IL 61635
Illinois College, Jacksonville, IL 62650-9990

Illinois Eastern Community Colleges
    Frontier Community College, Fairfield, IL 62837-9801
    Lincoln Trail College, Robinson, IL 62454-9803
    Olney Central College, Olney, IL 62450
    Wabash Valley College, Mount Carmel, IL 62863-2657
Illinois Institute of Technology, Chicago, IL 60616
Illinois State University, Normal, IL 61761
Illinois Technical College, Chicago, IL 60605
Illinois Valley Community College, Oglesby, IL 61348-1099
Illinois Wesleyan University, Bloomington, IL 61702-9965
Immaculata College, Immaculata, PA 19345
Imperial Valley College, Imperial, CA 92251-0158
Incarnate Word College, San Antonio, TX 78209-6397
Independence Community College, Independence, KS 67301
Indian Hills Community College, Ottumwa, IA 52501
Indian River Community College, Fort Pierce, FL 34981-5599
Indiana Institute of Technology, Fort Wayne, IN 46803
Indiana State University, Terre Haute, IN 47809
Indiana University
    Bloomington, Bloomington, IN 47405
    East, Richmond, IN 47374-1289
    Kokomo, Kokomo, IN 46904-9003
    Northwest, Gary, IN 46408
    South Bend, South Bend, IN 46634-7111
    Southeast, New Albany, IN 47150
Indiana University of Pennsylvania, Indiana, PA 15705-1088
Indiana University—Purdue University
    Fort Wayne, Fort Wayne, IN 46805
    Indianapolis, Indianapolis, IN 46202-5143
Indiana Vocational Technical College
    Central Indiana, Indianapolis, IN 46206-1763
    Columbus, Columbus, IN 47203
    Eastcentral, Muncie, IN 47307
    Kokomo, Kokomo, IN 46901
    Lafayette, Lafayette, IN 47903
    Northcentral, South Bend, IN 46619
    Northeast, Fort Wayne, IN 46805
    Northwest, Gary, IN 46409-1499
    Southcentral, Sellersburg, IN 47172
    Southeast, Madison, IN 47250
    Southwest, Evansville, IN 47710
    Wabash Valley, Terre Haute, IN 47802
    Whitewater, Richmond, IN 47374
Indiana Wesleyan University, Marion, IN 46953
Institute of American Indian Arts, Santa Fe, NM 87504
Institute for Christian Studies, Austin, TX 78705
Institute of Design and Construction, Brooklyn, NY 11201-5380
Institute of Electronic Technology, Paducah, KY 42001
Instituto Tecnico Comercial Junior College, San Juan, PR 00936
Instituto Tecnologico y de Estudios Superiores de Monterrey, Monterrey,
    Neuvo Leon, Mexico 64849
Inter American University of Puerto Rico
    Arecibo University College, Arecibo, PR 00613
    Metropolitan Campus, San Juan, PR 00919
    San German Campus, San German, PR 00753
Interboro Institute, New York, NY 10019
International Academy of Merchandising and Design, Chicago, IL 60654-
    1596
International Bible College, Florence, AL 35630
International Business College, Fort Wayne, IN 46804
International Fine Arts College, Miami, FL 33132
Inver Hills Community College, Inver Grove Heights, MN 55076-3209
Iona College, New Rochelle, NY 10801
Iowa Central Community College, Fort Dodge, IA 50501
Iowa Lakes Community College, Estherville, IA 51334
Iowa State University, Ames, IA 50011-2010
Iowa Wesleyan College, Mount Pleasant, IA 52641
Iowa Western Community College, Council Bluffs, IA 51502
Irvine Valley College, Irvine, CA 92720
Isothermal Community College, Spindale, NC 28160
Itasca Community College: Arrowhead Region, Grand Rapids, MN 55744
Itawamba Community College, Fulton, MS 38843
Ithaca College, Ithaca, NY 14850

ITT Technical Institute
    Arlington, Arlington, TX 76011
    Aurora, Aurora, CO 80014
    Dayton, Dayton, OH 45414
    Phoenix, Phoenix, AZ 85008
    Sacramento, Sacramento, CA 95827
    St. Louis, St. Louis, MO 63045
    Schaumburg, Schaumburg, IL 60173
    Tucson, Tucson, AZ 85714
    Youngstown, Youngstown, OH 44501-0779
J. F. Drake State Technical College, Huntsville, AL 35811
J. Sargeant Reynolds Community College, Richmond, VA 23261-2040
Jackson Community College, Jackson, MI 49201
Jackson State Community College, Jackson, TN 38301-3797
Jackson State University, Jackson, MS 39217
Jacksonville College, Jacksonville, TX 75766
Jacksonville State University, Jacksonville, AL 36265
Jacksonville University, Jacksonville, FL 32211
James H. Faulkner State Junior College, Bay Minette, AL 36507
James Madison University, Harrisonburg, VA 22807
James Sprunt Community College, Kenansville, NC 28349-0398
Jamestown Business College, Jamestown, NY 14701
Jamestown College, Jamestown, ND 58401
Jamestown Community College, Jamestown, NY 14701
Jarvis Christian College, Hawkins, TX 75765
Jefferson College, Hillsboro, MO 63050-1000
Jefferson Community College, Louisville, KY 40202
Jefferson Community College, Watertown, NY 13601
Jefferson Davis State Junior College, Brewton, AL 36426
Jefferson State Community College, Birmingham, AL 35215-3098
Jefferson Technical College, Steubenville, OH 43952
Jersey City State College, Jersey City, NJ 07305
Jewish Theological Seminary of America, New York, NY 10027
Jimmy Swaggart Bible College and Seminary, Baton Rouge, LA 70828-8000
John A. Gupton College, Nashville, TN 37203
John A. Logan College, Carterville, IL 62918
John Brown University, Siloam Springs, AR 72761
John C. Calhoun State Community College, Decatur, AL 35609-2216
John Carroll University, University Heights, OH 44118-4581
John F. Kennedy University, Orinda, CA 94563
John M. Patterson State Technical College, Montgomery, AL 36116
John Tyler Community College, Chester, VA 23831-5399
John Wesley College, High Point, NC 27265
John Wood Community College, Quincy, IL 62301
Johns Hopkins University
    Peabody Conservatory of Music, Baltimore, MD 21202
    School of Arts and Sciences and Engineering, Baltimore, MD 21218
    School of Nursing, Baltimore, MD 21205
Johnson Bible College, Knoxville, TN 37998
Johnson C. Smith University, Charlotte, NC 28216-5398
Johnson County Community College, Overland Park, KS 66210-1299
Johnson State College, Johnson, VT 05656
Johnson Technical Institute, Scranton, PA 18508
Johnson & Wales University, Providence, RI 02903
Johnston Community College, Smithfield, NC 27577-2350
Joliet Junior College, Joliet, IL 60436-9985
Jones College, Jacksonville, FL 32211
Jones County Junior College, Ellisville, MS 39437
Jordan College, Cedar Springs, MI 49319
Judson College, Marion, AL 36756
Judson College, Elgin, IL 60123
Juilliard School, New York, NY 10023-6590
Juniata College, Huntingdon, PA 16652
KAES College, Chicago, IL 60646
Kalamazoo College, Kalamazoo, MI 49007-3295
Kalamazoo Valley Community College, Kalamazoo, MI 49009
Kankakee Community College, Kankakee, IL 60901
Kansas City Art Institute, Kansas City, MO 64111
Kansas City College and Bible School, Overland Park, KS 66204
Kansas City Kansas Community College, Kansas City, KS 66112
Kansas Newman College, Wichita, KS 67213-2097
Kansas State University, Manhattan, KS 66506
Kansas Wesleyan University, Salina, KS 67401-6196
Kaskaskia College, Centralia, IL 62801
Katharine Gibbs School, Boston, MA 02116
Katharine Gibbs School, Montclair, NJ 07042
Katharine Gibbs School
    Melville, Melville, NY 11747
    New York, New York, NY 10166
Kean College of New Jersey, Union, NJ 07083
Keene State College, Keene, NH 03431
Kehilath Yakov Rabbinical Seminary, Brooklyn, NY 11211

Kellogg Community College, Battle Creek, MI 49016-3397
Kelsey-Jenney Business College, San Diego, CA 92101
Kemper Military School and College, Boonville, MO 65233
Kendall College, Evanston, IL 60201
Kendall College of Art and Design, Grand Rapids, MI 49503-3194
Kennebec Valley Vocational Technical Institute, Fairfield, ME 04937
Kennesaw State College, Marietta, GA 30061
Kent State University
    Ashtabula Regional Campus, Ashtabula, OH 44004
    East Liverpool Regional Campus, East Liverpool, OH 43920
    Kent, Kent, OH 44242
    Salem Regional Campus, Salem, OH 44460
    Stark Campus, Canton, OH 44720
    Trumbull Regional Campus, Warren, OH 44483
    Tuscarawas Campus, New Philadelphia, OH 44663
Kentucky Christian College, Grayson, KY 41143-1199
Kentucky College of Business, Lexington, KY 40508
Kentucky State University, Frankfort, KY 40601
Kentucky Wesleyan College, Owensboro, KY 42301-1039
Kenyon College, Gambier, OH 43022-9623
Kettering College of Medical Arts, Kettering, OH 45429
Keuka College, Keuka Park, NY 14478-0098
Keystone Junior College, La Plume, PA 18440-0200
Kilgore College, Kilgore, TX 75662-3299
Kilian Community College, Sioux Falls, SD 57105
King College, Bristol, TN 37620
King's College, Briarcliff Manor, NY 10510-9985
King's College, Wilkes-Barre, PA 18711
Kings River Community College, Reedley, CA 93654
Kirkwood Community College, Cedar Rapids, IA 52406
Kirtland Community College, Roscommon, MI 48653
Kishwaukee College, Malta, IL 60150-9699
Knox College, Galesburg, IL 61401
Knoxville Business College, Knoxville, TN 37927-3670
Knoxville College, Knoxville, TN 37921
Kol Yaakov Torah Center, Monsey, NY 10952
Kutztown University of Pennsylvania, Kutztown, PA 19530
La Roche College, Pittsburgh, PA 15237
La Salle University, Philadelphia, PA 19141
La Sierra University, Riverside, CA 92515
Labette Community College, Parsons, KS 67357
Laboratory Institute of Merchandising, New York, NY 10022
Laboure College, Boston, MA 02124
Lac Courte Oreilles Ojibwa Community College, Hayward, WI 54843
Lackawanna Junior College, Scranton, PA 18505
Lafayette College, Easton, PA 18042-1770
LaGrange College, LaGrange, GA 30240
Lake City Community College, Lake City, FL 32055
Lake Erie College, Painesville, OH 44077
Lake Forest College, Lake Forest, IL 60045
Lake Land College, Mattoon, IL 61938
Lake Michigan College, Benton Harbor, MI 49022-1899
Lake Superior State University, Sault Ste. Marie, MI 49783
Lake Tahoe Community College, South Lake Tahoe, CA 95702
Lakeland College, Sheboygan, WI 53082-0359
Lakeland Community College, Mentor, OH 44060-7594
Lakeshore Technical College, Cleveland, WI 53015-9761
Lake-Sumter Community College, Leesburg, FL 34788
Lakeview College of Nursing, Danville, IL 61832
Lakewood Community College, White Bear Lake, MN 55110
Lamar Community College, Lamar, CO 81052
Lamar University, Beaumont, TX 77710
Lambuth College, Jackson, TN 38301
Lamson Junior College, Phoenix, AZ 85017
Lancaster Bible College, Lancaster, PA 17601
Lander College, Greenwood, SC 29646
Landmark College, Putney, VT 05346
Lane College, Jackson, TN 38301
Lane Community College, Eugene, OR 97405
Langston University, Langston, OK 73050
Lansdale School of Business, North Wales, PA 19436
Lansing Community College, Lansing, MI 48901
Laramie County Community College, Cheyenne, WY 82007
Laredo Junior College, Laredo, TX 78040
Laredo State University, Laredo, TX 78040-9960
Lasell College, Newton, MA 02166
Lassen College, Susanville, CA 96130
Lawrence Technological University, Southfield, MI 48075-1058
Lawrence University, Appleton, WI 54912-9986
Lawson State Community College, Birmingham, AL 35221
LDS Business College, Salt Lake City, UT 84111-1392

Le Moyne College, Syracuse, NY 13214-1399
Lebanon Valley College of Pennsylvania, Annville, PA 17003-0501
Lee College, Cleveland, TN 37311
Lee College, Baytown, TX 77520-4703
Lees College, Jackson, KY 41339
Lees-McRae College, Banner Elk, NC 28604
Lehigh County Community College, Schnecksville, PA 18078
Lehigh University, Bethlehem, PA 18015-3094
LeMoyne-Owen College, Memphis, TN 38126
Lenoir Community College, Kinston, NC 28501
Lenoir-Rhyne College, Hickory, NC 28603
Lesley College, Cambridge, MA 02138-2790
LeTourneau University, Longview, TX 75607-7001
Lewis and Clark College, Portland, OR 97219
Lewis and Clark Community College, Godfrey, IL 62035-2466
Lewis Clark State College, Lewiston, ID 83501-2698
Lewis College of Business, Detroit, MI 48235
Lewis University, Romeoville, IL 60441-2298
Lexington Community College, Lexington, KY 40506
Lexington Institute of Hospitality Careers, Chicago, IL 60643
Liberty Christian College, Pensacola, FL 32516
Liberty University, Lynchburg, VA 24506-8001
LIFE Bible College, San Dimas, CA 91773-3298
Lima Technical College, Lima, OH 45804
Limestone College, Gaffney, SC 29340
Lincoln Christian College and Seminary, Lincoln, IL 62656
Lincoln College, Lincoln, IL 62656
Lincoln Land Community College, Springfield, IL 62794-9256
Lincoln Memorial University, Harrogate, TN 37752
Lincoln School of Commerce, Lincoln, NE 68508
Lincoln Technical Institute, Allentown, PA 18104
Lincoln University, Lincoln University, PA 19352-0999
Lincoln University, San Francisco, CA 94118
Lincoln University, Jefferson City, MO 65101
Lindenwood College, St. Charles, MO 63301-1695
Lindsey Wilson College, Columbia, KY 42728
Linfield College, McMinnville, OR 97128-6894
Linn-Benton Community College, Albany, OR 97321-3779
Little Big Horn College, Crow Agency, MT 59022
Little Hoop Community College, Fort Totten, ND 58335
Livingston University, Livingston, AL 35470
Livingstone College, Salisbury, NC 28144-5213
Lock Haven University of Pennsylvania, Lock Haven, PA 17745
Lockyear College, Evansville, IN 47706-0923
Lon Morris College, Jacksonville, TX 75766
Long Beach City College, Long Beach, CA 90808
Long Island College Hospital School of Nursing, Brooklyn, NY 11201
Long Island University
    Brooklyn Campus, Brooklyn, NY 11201
    C. W. Post Campus, Brookville, NY 11548
    Southampton Campus, Southampton, NY 11968
Longview Community College, Lee's Summit, MO 64081
Longwood College, Farmville, VA 23901
Lorain County Community College, Elyria, OH 44035-1697
Loras College, Dubuque, IA 52001
Lord Fairfax Community College, Middletown, VA 22645
Los Angeles City College, Los Angeles, CA 90029
Los Angeles Harbor College, Wilmington, CA 90744
Los Angeles Mission College, San Fernando, CA 91340
Los Angeles Pierce College, Woodland Hills, CA 91371
Los Angeles Southwest College, Los Angeles, CA 90047
Los Angeles Trade and Technical College, Los Angeles, CA 90015-4181
Los Angeles Valley College, Van Nuys, CA 91401-4096
Los Medanos College, Pittsburg, CA 94565
Louisburg College, Louisburg, NC 27549
Louise Salinger Academy of Fashion, San Francisco, CA 94105
Louisiana College, Pineville, LA 71359-0560
Louisiana State University
    Alexandria, Alexandria, LA 71302-9633
    Eunice, Eunice, LA 70535
    Medical Center, New Orleans, LA 70112-2223
    Shreveport, Shreveport, LA 71115
Louisiana State University and Agricultural and Mechanical College, Baton Rouge, LA 70803-2750
Louisiana Tech University, Ruston, LA 71272
Louisville Technical Institute, Louisville, KY 40205
Lourdes College, Sylvania, OH 43560
Lower Columbia College, Longview, WA 98632
Loyola College in Maryland, Baltimore, MD 21210-2699
Loyola Marymount University, Los Angeles, CA 90045
Loyola University, New Orleans, LA 70118
Loyola University of Chicago, Chicago, IL 60611

Lubbock Christian University, Lubbock, TX 79407
Lurleen B. Wallace State Junior College, Andalusia, AL 36420-1418
Luther College, Decorah, IA 52101-1042
Lutheran Bible Institute of Seattle, Issaquah, WA 98027
Lutheran College of Health Professions, Fort Wayne, IN 46807-1698
Luzerne County Community College, Nanticoke, PA 18634
Lycoming College, Williamsport, PA 17701
Lynchburg College, Lynchburg, VA 24501-9986
Lyndon State College, Lyndonville, VT 05851
Macalester College, St. Paul, MN 55105-1899
MacCormac Junior College, Chicago, IL 60604-3395
Machzikei Hadath Rabbinical College, Brooklyn, NY 11204
MacMurray College, Jacksonville, IL 62650-2590
Macomb Community College, Warren, MI 48093-3896
Macon College, Macon, GA 31297
Madison Area Technical College, Madison, WI 53704-2599
Madison Business College, Madison, WI 53705-1399
Madisonville Community College, Madisonville, KY 42431
Madonna University, Livonia, MI 48150-1173
Magnolia Bible College, Kosciusko, MS 39090
Maharishi International University, Fairfield, IA 52556-2091
Maine Maritime Academy, Castine, ME 04420-5000
Malone College, Canton, OH 44709
Manatee Community College, Bradenton, FL 34206-1849
Manchester College, North Manchester, IN 46962-0365
Manchester Community College, Manchester, CT 06040
Manhattan Christian College, Manhattan, KS 66502
Manhattan College, Riverdale, NY 10471
Manhattan School of Music, New York, NY 10027-4698
Manhattanville College, Purchase, NY 10577
Mankato State University, Mankato, MN 56002
Mannes College of Music, New York, NY 10024
Manor Junior College, Jenkintown, PA 19046-3399
Mansfield University of Pennsylvania, Mansfield, PA 16933
Maple Woods Community College, Kansas City, MO 64156-1299
Maranatha Baptist Bible College, Watertown, WI 53094
Maria College, Albany, NY 12208
Marian College, Indianapolis, IN 46222
Marian College of Fond du Lac, Fond du Lac, WI 54935-4699
Marian Court Junior College, Swampscott, MA 01907-2896
Marietta College, Marietta, OH 45750-9982
Marion Military Institute, Marion, AL 36756-0420
Marion Technical College, Marion, OH 43302-5694
Marist College, Poughkeepsie, NY 12601
Marlboro College, Marlboro, VT 05344
Marquette University, Milwaukee, WI 53233-9988
Mars Hill College, Mars Hill, NC 28754
Marshall University, Huntington, WV 25755-2020
Marshalltown Community College, Marshalltown, IA 50158
Martin Community College, Williamston, NC 27892-9988
Martin Methodist College, Pulaski, TN 38478
Martin University, Indianapolis, IN 46218
Mary Baldwin College, Staunton, VA 24401
Mary Holmes College, West Point, MS 39773-1257
Mary Washington College, Fredericksburg, VA 22401-5358
Marygrove College, Detroit, MI 48221
Maryland College of Art and Design, Silver Spring, MD 20902
Maryland Institute College of Art, Baltimore, MD 21217
Marylhurst College, Marylhurst, OR 97036
Marymount College, Tarrytown, NY 10591-3796
Marymount College, Rancho Palos Verdes, CA 90274
Marymount Manhattan College, New York, NY 10021
Marymount University, Arlington, VA 22207-4299
Maryville College, Maryville, TN 37801
Maryville College—St. Louis, St. Louis, MO 63141
Marywood College, Scranton, PA 18509-9989
Massachusetts Bay Community College, Wellesley Hills, MA 02181
Massachusetts College of Art, Boston, MA 02115-5882
Massachusetts College of Pharmacy and Allied Health Sciences, Boston, MA 02115
Massachusetts Institute of Technology, Cambridge, MA 02139
Massachusetts Maritime Academy, Buzzards Bay, MA 02532-1803
Massasoit Community College, Brockton, MA 02402
Master's College, Santa Clarita, CA 91322-0878
Mater Dei College, Ogdensburg, NY 13669
Mattatuck Community College, Waterbury, CT 06708
Mayland Community College, Spruce Pine, NC 28777
Maysville Community College, Maysville, KY 41056
Mayville State University, Mayville, ND 58257
McCook Community College, McCook, NE 69001
McDowell Technical Community College, Marion, NC 28752
McGill University, Montreal, Quebec, Canada H3A 2T5

McHenry County College, Crystal Lake, IL 60012
McIntosh College, Dover, NH 03820
McKendree College, Lebanon, IL 62254
McKenzie College, Chattanooga, TN 37402
McLennan Community College, Waco, TX 76708
McMurry University, Abilene, TX 79697-0001
McNeese State University, Lake Charles, LA 70609-2495
McPherson College, McPherson, KS 67460
Meadows College of Business, Columbus, GA 31906
Medaille College, Buffalo, NY 14214
Medcenter One College of Nursing, Bismarck, ND 58501
Medical College of Georgia, Augusta, GA 30912
Memphis College of Art, Memphis, TN 38112
Memphis State University, Memphis, TN 38152
Mendocino College, Ukiah, CA 95482
Menlo College, Atherton, CA 94027-4301
Mennonite College of Nursing, Bloomington, IL 61701
Merced College, Merced, CA 95348-2898
Mercer County Community College, Trenton, NJ 08690-1099
Mercer University
    Atlanta, Atlanta, GA 30341-4115
    Macon, Macon, GA 31207-0001
Mercy College, Dobbs Ferry, NY 10522
Mercyhurst College, Erie, PA 16546
Meredith College, Raleigh, NC 27607-5298
Meridian Community College, Meridian, MS 39307
Merrimack College, North Andover, MA 01845
Merritt College, Oakland, CA 94619
Mesa Community College, Mesa, AZ 85202
Mesa State College, Grand Junction, CO 81502
Mesabi Community College: Arrowhead Region, Virginia, MN 55792
Mesivta Eastern Parkway Rabbinical Seminary, Brooklyn, NY 11218
Mesivta Tifereth Jerusalem of America, New York, NY 10002
Mesivta Torah Vodaath Seminary, Brooklyn, NY 11218
Messiah College, Grantham, PA 17027-0800
Methodist College, Fayetteville, NC 28311-1499
Metropolitan Community College, Omaha, NE 68103-3777
Metropolitan State College of Denver, Denver, CO 80217-3362
Metropolitan State University, St. Paul, MN 55101-2189
Miami Christian College, Miami, FL 33167-9972
Miami University
    Hamilton Campus, Hamilton, OH 45011
    Middletown Campus, Middletown, OH 45042
    Oxford Campus, Oxford, OH 45056
Miami-Dade Community College, Miami, FL 33132-2297
Miami-Jacobs College, Dayton, OH 45401
Michigan Christian College, Rochester Hills, MI 48307-2764
Michigan State University, East Lansing, MI 48824-1046
Michigan Technological University, Houghton, MI 49931
Micronesian Occupational College, Koror, TT 96940-9999
Mid Michigan Community College, Harrison, MI 48625
Mid Plains Community College, North Platte, NE 69101-0001
Mid-America Baptist Theological Seminary, Memphis, TN 38104-7250
Mid-America Bible College, Oklahoma City, OK 73170
Mid-America Nazarene College, Olathe, KS 66061-1776
Mid-Continent Baptist Bible College, Mayfield, KY 42066-0357
Middle Georgia College, Cochran, GA 31014
Middle Tennessee State University, Murfreesboro, TN 37132
Middlesex Community College, Middletown, CT 06457
Middlesex Community College, Bedford, MA 01730
Middlesex County College, Edison, NJ 08818-3050
Midland College, Midland, TX 79705
Midland Lutheran College, Fremont, NE 68025
Midlands Technical College, Columbia, SC 29202
Midstate College, Peoria, IL 61602-9990
Mid-State Technical College, Wisconsin Rapids, WI 54494
Midway College, Midway, KY 40347-1120
Midwestern State University, Wichita Falls, TX 76308
Miles College, Fairfield, AL 35064
Miles Community College, Miles City, MT 59301
Millersville University of Pennsylvania, Millersville, PA 17551
Milligan College, Milligan College, TN 37682
Millikin University, Decatur, IL 62522-9982
Mills College, Oakland, CA 94613
Millsaps College, Jackson, MS 39210
Milwaukee Area Technical College, Milwaukee, WI 53233
Milwaukee Institute of Art & Design, Milwaukee, WI 53202
Milwaukee School of Engineering, Milwaukee, WI 53201-0644
Mineral Area College, Flat River, MO 63601
Minneapolis College of Art and Design, Minneapolis, MN 55404
Minneapolis Community College, Minneapolis, MN 55403
Minnesota Bible College, Rochester, MN 55902

Minot State University, Minot, ND 58702-5002
MiraCosta College, Oceanside, CA 92056-3899
Mirrer Yeshiva Central Institute, Brooklyn, NY 11223
Miss Wade's Fashion Merchandising College, Dallas, TX 75258
Mission College, Santa Clara, CA 95054-1897
Mississippi College, Clinton, MS 39058
Mississippi County Community College, Blytheville, AR 72316-1109
Mississippi Delta Community College, Moorhead, MS 38761
Mississippi Gulf Coast Community College
    Jackson County Campus, Gautier, MS 39553
    Jefferson Davis Campus, Gulfport, MS 39507-3894
    Perkinston, Perkinston, MS 39573
Mississippi State University, Mississippi State, MS 39762
Mississippi University for Women, Columbus, MS 39701
Mississippi Valley State University, Itta Bena, MS 38941
Missouri Baptist College, St. Louis, MO 63141
Missouri Southern State College, Joplin, MO 64801-1595
Missouri Valley College, Marshall, MO 65340
Missouri Western State College, St. Joseph, MO 64507-2294
Mitchell College, New London, CT 06320
Mitchell Community College, Statesville, NC 28677
Mitchell Vocational Technical Institute, Mitchell, SD 57301
Moberly Area Community College, Moberly, MO 65270
Mobile College, Mobile, AL 36613
Modesto Junior College, Modesto, CA 95350
Mohave Community College, Kingman, AZ 86401
Mohawk Valley Community College, Utica, NY 13501-9979
Mohegan Community College, Norwich, CT 06360-2479
Molloy College, Rockville Centre, NY 11570
Monmouth College, Monmouth, IL 61462
Monmouth College, West Long Branch, NJ 07764-1898
Monroe College, Bronx, NY 10468
Monroe Community College, Rochester, NY 14623
Monroe County Community College, Monroe, MI 48161
Montana College of Mineral Science and Technology, Butte, MT 59701
Montana State University, Bozeman, MT 59717-0016
Montay College, Chicago, IL 60659-3115
Montcalm Community College, Sidney, MI 48885-9746
Montclair State College, Upper Montclair, NJ 07043-1624
Monterey Institute of International Studies, Monterey, CA 93940
Monterey Peninsula College, Monterey, CA 93940
Montgomery College
    Germantown Campus, Germantown, MD 20876
    Rockville Campus, Rockville, MD 20850
    Takoma Park Campus, Takoma Park, MD 20912
Montgomery Community College, Troy, NC 27371-0787
Montgomery County Community College, Blue Bell, PA 19422
Montreat-Anderson College, Montreat, NC 28757
Montserrat College of Art, Beverly, MA 01915
Moody Bible Institute, Chicago, IL 60610
Moore College of Art and Design, Philadelphia, PA 19103-1179
Moorhead State University, Moorhead, MN 56563
Moorpark College, Moorpark, CA 93021
Moraine Park Technical College, Fond du Lac, WI 54935
Moraine Valley Community College, Palos Hills, IL 60465
Moravian College, Bethlehem, PA 18018
Morehead State University, Morehead, KY 40351
Morehouse College, Atlanta, GA 30314
Morgan Community College, Fort Morgan, CO 80701
Morgan State University, Baltimore, MD 21239
Morningside College, Sioux City, IA 51106-9989
Morris Brown College, Atlanta, GA 30314
Morris College, Sumter, SC 29150
Morrison Institute of Technology, Morrison, IL 61270-0410
Morton College, Cicero, IL 60650
Motlow State Community College, Tullahoma, TN 37388-8100
Mount Aloysius Junior College, Cresson, PA 16630
Mount Angel Seminary, St. Benedict, OR 97373
Mount Holyoke College, South Hadley, MA 01075-1488
Mount Hood Community College, Gresham, OR 97030
Mount Ida College, Newton Centre, MA 02159
Mount Marty College, Yankton, SD 57078
Mount Mary College, Milwaukee, WI 53222-4597
Mount Mercy College, Cedar Rapids, IA 52402
Mount Olive College, Mount Olive, NC 28365
Mount St. Clare College, Clinton, IA 52732
Mount St. Mary College, Newburgh, NY 12550
Mount St. Mary's College, Los Angeles, CA 90049-1597
Mount St. Mary's College, Emmitsburg, MD 21727-7796
Mount San Antonio College, Walnut, CA 91789
Mount San Jacinto College, San Jacinto, CA 92383-2399
Mount Senario College, Ladysmith, WI 54848

Mount Union College, Alliance, OH 44601-3993
Mount Vernon College, Washington, DC 20007
Mount Vernon Nazarene College, Mount Vernon, OH 43050
Mount Wachusett Community College, Gardner, MA 01440
Mountain Empire Community College, Big Stone Gap, VA 24219
Mountain View College, Dallas, TX 75211-6599
Muhlenberg College, Allentown, PA 18104
Multnomah School of the Bible, Portland, OR 97220-5898
Mundelein College, Chicago, IL 60660
Murray State College, Tishomingo, OK 73460
Murray State University, Murray, KY 42071
Muscatine Community College, Muscatine, IA 52761-5396
Muskegon Community College, Muskegon, MI 49442
Muskingum Area Technical College, Zanesville, OH 43701
Muskingum College, New Concord, OH 43762
NAES College, Chicago, IL 60659
Napa Valley College, Napa, CA 94558
Naropa Institute, Boulder, CO 80302
Nash Community College, Rocky Mount, NC 27804
Nashville State Technical Institute, Nashville, TN 37209
Nassau Community College, Garden City, NY 11530
National Business College, Roanoke, VA 24017-0400
National College, Denver, CO 80222
National College, Kansas City, MO 64111
National College, St. Paul, MN 55108
National College, Albuquerque, NM 87110
National College, Rapid City, SD 57709-1780
National College of Chiropractic, Lombard, IL 60148
National Education Center
    Arizona Automotive Institute, Glendale, AZ 85301
    Arkansas College of Technology, Little Rock, AR 72207-9979
    Bauder Campus, Fort Lauderdale, FL 33334
    Brown Institute Campus, Minneapolis, MN 55407
    Kentucky College of Technology Campus, Louisville, KY 40213
    National Institute of Technology Campus, Birmingham, AL 35209
    National Institute of Technology Campus, West Des Moines, IA 50265
    National Institute of Technology Campus, Cross Lanes, WV 25313
    Vale Tech Campus, Blairsville, PA 15717
National Hispanic University, San Jose, CA 95122
National University, San Diego, CA 92108-4194
National-Louis University, Evanston, IL 60201-1796
Navajo Community College, Tsaile, AZ 86556
Navarro College, Corsicana, TX 75110
Nazarene Bible College, Colorado Springs, CO 80935
Nazareth College in Kalamazoo, Kalamazoo, MI 49001-1282
Nazareth College of Rochester, Rochester, NY 14618-3790
Nebraska Christian College, Norfolk, NE 68701
Nebraska Indian Community College, Winnebago, NE 68071
Nebraska Methodist College of Nursing and Allied Health, Omaha, NE 68114
Nebraska Wesleyan University, Lincoln, NE 68504
Neosho County Community College, Chanute, KS 66720
Ner Israel Rabbinical College, Baltimore, MD 21208-9964
Neumann College, Aston, PA 19014
New College of California, San Francisco, CA 94102
New College of the University of South Florida, Sarasota, FL 34243-2197
New Community College of Baltimore, Baltimore, MD 21215
New England Banking Institute, Boston, MA 02111
New England College, Henniker, NH 03242-0792
New England Conservatory of Music, Boston, MA 02115
New England Culinary Institute, Montpelier, VT 05602
New England Institute of Technology, West Palm Beach, FL 33407
New England Institute of Technology, Warwick, RI 02886
New Hampshire College, Manchester, NH 03104-1394
New Hampshire Technical College
    Berlin, Berlin, NH 03570
    Claremont, Claremont, NH 03743-9968
    Laconia, Laconia, NH 03246
    Manchester, Manchester, NH 03102-8518
    Nashua, Nashua, NH 03061-2052
    Stratham, Stratham, NH 03885-0365
New Hampshire Technical Institute, Concord, NH 03301
New Jersey Institute of Technology, Newark, NJ 07102-9938
New Mexico Highlands University, Las Vegas, NM 87701
New Mexico Institute of Mining and Technology, Socorro, NM 87801
New Mexico Junior College, Hobbs, NM 88240
New Mexico Military Institute, Roswell, NM 88201-5173
New Mexico State University
    Alamogordo, Alamogordo, NM 88310
    Carlsbad, Carlsbad, NM 88220
    Grants, Grants, NM 87020
    Las Cruces, Las Cruces, NM 88003-0001

New Orleans Baptist Theological Seminary, New Orleans, LA 70126-4858
New River Community College, Dublin, VA 24084
New York Institute of Technology, Old Westbury, NY 11568
New York School of Interior Design, New York, NY 10022
New York University, New York, NY 10011-9108
Newberry College, Newberry, SC 29108
Newbury College, Brookline, MA 02146
Niagara County Community College, Sanborn, NY 14132
Niagara University, Niagara Falls, NY 14109
Nicholls State University, Thibodaux, LA 70310
Nichols College, Dudley, MA 01570-5000
Nicolet Area Technical College, Rhinelander, WI 54501
Nielsen Electronics Institute, Charleston, SC 29405
Norfolk State University, Norfolk, VA 23504
Normandale Community College, Bloomington, MN 55431
North Adams State College, North Adams, MA 01247
North Arkansas Community College, Harrison, AR 72601
North Carolina Agricultural and Technical State University, Greensboro, NC 27411
North Carolina Central University, Durham, NC 27707
North Carolina School of the Arts, Winston-Salem, NC 27117-2189
North Carolina State University, Raleigh, NC 27695-7103
North Carolina Wesleyan College, Rocky Mount, NC 27804
North Central Bible College, Minneapolis, MN 55404
North Central College, Naperville, IL 60566-7063
North Central Michigan College, Petoskey, MI 49770
North Central Missouri College, Trenton, MO 64683
North Central Technical College, Mansfield, OH 44901
North Country Community College, Saranac Lake, NY 12983
North Dakota State College of Science, Wahpeton, ND 58076
North Dakota State University
    Bottineau and Institute of Forestry, Bottineau, ND 58318-1198
    Fargo, Fargo, ND 58105
North Florida Junior College, Madison, FL 32340
North Georgia College, Dahlonega, GA 30597
North Greenville College, Tigerville, SC 29688-1892
North Harris County College, Houston, TX 77073
North Hennepin Community College, Minneapolis, MN 55445
North Idaho College, Coeur d'Alene, ID 83814
North Iowa Area Community College, Mason City, IA 50401
North Lake College, Irving, TX 75038-3899
North Park College and Theological Seminary, Chicago, IL 60625-4987
North Seattle Community College, Seattle, WA 98103-3599
North Shore Community College, Beverly, MA 01915
Northampton County Area Community College, Bethlehem, PA 18017
Northcentral Technical College, Wausau, WI 54401
Northeast Alabama State Junior College, Rainsville, AL 35986
Northeast Community College, Norfolk, NE 68702-0469
Northeast Iowa Community College, Calmar, IA 52132
Northeast Louisiana University, Monroe, LA 71209-0730
Northeast Mississippi Community College, Booneville, MS 38829
Northeast Missouri State University, Kirksville, MO 63501-9980
Northeast State Technical Community College, Blountville, TN 37617
Northeast Texas Community College, Mount Pleasant, TX 75455-1307
Northeast Wisconsin Technical College, Green Bay, WI 54307-9042
Northeastern Christian Junior College, Villanova, PA 19085
Northeastern Illinois University, Chicago, IL 60625
Northeastern Junior College, Sterling, CO 80751
Northeastern Oklahoma Agricultural and Mechanical College, Miami, OK 74354-6497
Northeastern State University, Tahlequah, OK 74464
Northeastern University, Boston, MA 02115-9959
Northern Arizona University, Flagstaff, AZ 86011-4082
Northern Essex Community College, Haverhill, MA 01830-2399
Northern Illinois University, DeKalb, IL 60115-2854
Northern Kentucky University, Highland Heights, KY 41076
Northern Maine Vocational Technical Institute, Presque Isle, ME 04769
Northern Marianas College, Saipan, CM 96950
Northern Michigan University, Marquette, MI 49855
Northern Montana College, Havre, MT 59501
Northern Nevada Community College, Elko, NV 89801
Northern New Mexico Community College, Espanola, NM 87532
Northern Oklahoma College, Tonkawa, OK 74653-0310
Northern State University, Aberdeen, SD 57401
Northern Virginia Community College, Annandale, VA 22003
Northland College, Ashland, WI 54806
Northland Community College, Thief River Falls, MN 56701
Northland Pioneer College, Holbrook, AZ 86025
Northrop University, Los Angeles, CA 90045-0065
Northwest Alabama Community College, Phil Campbell, AL 35581
Northwest Christian College, Eugene, OR 97401-9983
Northwest College, Powell, WY 82435

Northwest College of the Assemblies of God, Kirkland, WA 98083-0579
Northwest Indian College, Bellingham, WA 98226
Northwest Iowa Technical College, Sheldon, IA 51201
Northwest Mississippi Community College, Senatobia, MS 38668
Northwest Missouri State University, Maryville, MO 64468-6001
Northwest Nazarene College, Nampa, ID 83686
Northwest Technical College, Archbold, OH 43502
Northwest Technical Institute, Eden Prairie, MN 55344-5351
Northwestern College, Watertown, WI 53094
Northwestern College, Lima, OH 45805
Northwestern College, Roseville, MN 55113
Northwestern College, Orange City, IA 51041
Northwestern Connecticut Community College, Winsted, CT 06098
Northwestern Electronics Institute, Minneapolis, MN 55421-9990
Northwestern Michigan College, Traverse City, MI 49684
Northwestern Oklahoma State University, Alva, OK 73717
Northwestern State University, Natchitoches, LA 71497
Northwestern University, Evanston, IL 60204-3060
Northwood Institute, Midland, MI 48640
Northwood Institute: Texas Campus, Cedar Hill, TX 75104
Norwalk Community College, Norwalk, CT 06854
Norwalk State Technical College, Norwalk, CT 06854
Norwich University, Northfield, VT 05663
Notre Dame College, Manchester, NH 03104-2299
Notre Dame College of Ohio, Cleveland, OH 44121
Nova University, Fort Lauderdale, FL 33314
Nyack College, Nyack, NY 10960
Oak Hills Bible College, Bemidji, MN 56601
Oakland City College, Oakland City, IN 47660
Oakland Community College, Bloomfield Hills, MI 48303-0812
Oakland University, Rochester, MI 48309-4401
Oakton Community College, Des Plaines, IL 60016
Oakwood College, Huntsville, AL 35896
Oberlin College, Oberlin, OH 44074
Oblate College, Washington, DC 20017-1587
Occidental College, Los Angeles, CA 90041-3393
Ocean County College, Toms River, NJ 08753-2001
Odessa College, Odessa, TX 79764-7127
Oglala Lakota College, Kyle, SD 57752
Oglethorpe University, Atlanta, GA 30319-9985
Ohio Dominican College, Columbus, OH 43219-2099
Ohio Northern University, Ada, OH 45810-1599
Ohio State University
    Agricultural Technical Institute, Wooster, OH 44691-4099
    Columbus Campus, Columbus, OH 43210-1200
    Lima Campus, Lima, OH 45804-3596
    Mansfield Campus, Mansfield, OH 44906
    Marion Campus, Marion, OH 43302
    Newark Campus, Newark, OH 43055
Ohio University
    Athens, Athens, OH 45701-2979
    Belmont Campus, St. Clairsville, OH 43950
    Chillicothe Campus, Chillicothe, OH 45601
    Ironton Campus, Ironton, OH 45638
    Lancaster Campus, Lancaster, OH 43130
    Zanesville Campus, Zanesville, OH 43701
Ohio Valley Business College, East Liverpool, OH 43920
Ohio Valley College, Parkersburg, WV 26101-9975
Ohio Wesleyan University, Delaware, OH 43015
Ohlone College, Fremont, CA 94539-0390
Ohr Somayach Institutions, Monsey, NY 10952
Okaloosa-Walton Community College, Niceville, FL 32578
Oklahoma Baptist University, Shawnee, OK 74801
Oklahoma Christian University of Science and Arts, Oklahoma City, OK 73136-1100
Oklahoma City Community College, Oklahoma City, OK 73159
Oklahoma City University, Oklahoma City, OK 73106
Oklahoma Panhandle State University, Goodwell, OK 73939-0430
Oklahoma State University, Stillwater, OK 74078
Oklahoma State University: Oklahoma City, Oklahoma City, OK 73107
Oklahoma State University Technical Branch: Okmulgee, Okmulgee, OK 74447-3901
Old Dominion University, Norfolk, VA 23529-0050
Olean Business Institute, Olean, NY 14760
Olivet College, Olivet, MI 49076
Olivet Nazarene University, Kankakee, IL 60901
Olympic College, Bremerton, WA 98310-1699
O'More College of Design, Franklin, TN 37065
Onondaga Community College, Syracuse, NY 13215
Oral Roberts University, Tulsa, OK 74171
Orange Coast College, Costa Mesa, CA 92626
Orange County Community College, Middletown, NY 10940

Orangeburg-Calhoun Technical College, Orangeburg, SC 29115
Oregon Health Sciences University, Portland, OR 97201
Oregon Institute of Technology, Klamath Falls, OR 97601-8801
Oregon Polytechnic Institute, Portland, OR 97214
Oregon State University, Corvallis, OR 97331-2130
Orlando College, Orlando, FL 32810
Otero Junior College, La Junta, CO 81050
Otis Art Institute of Parsons School of Design, Los Angeles, CA 90057
Ottawa University, Ottawa, KS 66067
Otterbein College, Westerville, OH 43081
Ouachita Baptist University, Arkadelphia, AR 71923-4099
Our Lady of Holy Cross College, New Orleans, LA 70131-7399
Our Lady of the Lake University of San Antonio, San Antonio, TX 78207-4666
Owens Technical College
    Findlay Campus, Findlay, OH 45840
    Toledo, Toledo, OH 43699-1947
Owensboro Junior College of Business, Owensboro, KY 42303
Oxford College of Emory University, Oxford, GA 30267-1328
Oxnard College, Oxnard, CA 93033
Ozark Christian College, Joplin, MO 64801
Pace University
    College of White Plains, White Plains, NY 10603-3796
    New York, New York, NY 10038
    Pleasantville/Briarcliff, Pleasantville, NY 10570
Pacific Christian College, Fullerton, CA 92631
Pacific Lutheran University, Tacoma, WA 98447-0003
Pacific Northwest College of Art, Portland, OR 97205
Pacific Oaks College, Pasadena, CA 91103
Pacific Union College, Angwin, CA 94508
Pacific University, Forest Grove, OR 97116-1797
Paducah Community College, Paducah, KY 42002-7380
Paier College of Art, Hamden, CT 06517
Paine College, Augusta, GA 30910-2799
Palm Beach Atlantic College, West Palm Beach, FL 33401-3353
Palm Beach Community College, Lake Worth, FL 33461
Palo Alto College, San Antonio, TX 78224
Palo Verde College, Blythe, CA 92225
Palomar College, San Marcos, CA 92069
Pamlico Community College, Grantsboro, NC 28529
Panola College, Carthage, TX 75633
Paradise Valley Community College, Phoenix, AZ 85032
Paris Junior College, Paris, TX 75460
Park College, Parkville, MO 64152-9970
Parkland College, Champaign, IL 61821-1899
Parks College, Albuquerque, NM 87102
Parks College of St. Louis University, Cahokia, IL 62206
Parsons School of Design, New York, NY 10011
Pasadena City College, Pasadena, CA 91106
Pasco-Hernando Community College, Dade City, FL 34654-5199
Passaic County Community College, Paterson, NJ 07509
Patrick Henry Community College, Martinsville, VA 24115-5311
Patrick Henry State Junior College, Monroeville, AL 36461-2000
Patten College, Oakland, CA 94601-2699
Paul D. Camp Community College, Franklin, VA 23851
Paul Quinn College, Waco, TX 76704
Paul Smith's College, Paul Smiths, NY 12970-0265
Peace College, Raleigh, NC 27604
Pearl River Community College, Poplarville, MS 39470
Peirce Junior College, Philadelphia, PA 19102
Pellissippi State Technical Community College, Knoxville, TN 37933-0990
Pembroke State University, Pembroke, NC 28372
Peninsula College, Port Angeles, WA 98362

Penn State
Allentown Campus, Fogelsville, PA 18051-9733
Altoona Campus, Altoona, PA 16601-3760
Beaver Campus, Monaca, PA 15061
Berks Campus, Reading, PA 19610-6009
Delaware County Campus, Media, PA 19063
Du Bois Campus, Du Bois, PA 15801
Erie Behrend College, Erie, PA 16563
Fayette Campus, Uniontown, PA 15401
Harrisburg Capital College, Middletown, PA 17057
Hazleton Campus, Hazleton, PA 18201
McKeesport Campus, McKeesport, PA 15132
Mont Alto Campus, Mont Alto, PA 17237
New Kensington Campus, New Kensington, PA 15068
Ogontz Campus, Abington, PA 19001
Schuylkill Campus, Schuylkill Haven, PA 17972
Shenango Campus, Sharon, PA 16146
University Park Campus, University Park, PA 16802
Wilkes-Barre Campus, Wilkes-Barre, PA 18627
Worthington-Scranton Campus, Dunmore, PA 18512
York Campus, York, PA 17403
Penn Technical Institute, Pittsburgh, PA 15222
Penn Valley Community College, Kansas City, MO 64111
Pennsylvania College of Technology, Williamsport, PA 17701-5799
Pennsylvania Institute of Technology, Media, PA 19063-4098
Pensacola Junior College, Pensacola, FL 32504
Pepperdine University, Malibu, CA 90263
Peru State College, Peru, NE 68421
Pfeiffer College, Misenheimer, NC 28109
Philadelphia College of Bible, Langhorne, PA 19047-2992
Philadelphia College of Pharmacy and Science, Philadelphia, PA 19104
Philadelphia College of Textiles and Science, Philadelphia, PA 19144
Philander Smith College, Little Rock, AR 72202
Phillips Beth Israel School of Nursing, New York, NY 10010
Phillips College of Chicago, Chicago, IL 60606
Phillips College: Columbus, Columbus, GA 31901
Phillips County Community College, Helena, AR 72342
Phillips Junior College
Augusta, Augusta, GA 30901
Columbia, Columbia, SC 29201
Fayetteville, Fayetteville, NC 28301
Fresno Campus, Clovis, CA 93612
Greensboro, Greensboro, NC 27401
Greenville, Greenville, SC 29601
Hardbarger Campus, Raleigh, NC 27604
Jackson, Jackson, MS 39216
Melbourne, Melbourne, FL 32935
Memphis, Memphis, TN 38134
Mississippi Gulf Coast, Gulfport, MS 39507
New Orleans, New Orleans, LA 70121
North Charleston, North Charleston, SC 29405
Salt Lake City Campus, Salt Lake City, UT 84106
San Fernando Valley Campus, Northridge, CA 91325
Spartanburg, Spartanburg, SC 29301
Springfield, Springfield, MO 65806
Winston-Salem, Winston-Salem, NC 27106
Phillips University, Enid, OK 73701
Phoenix College, Phoenix, AZ 85013
Piedmont Bible College, Winston-Salem, NC 27101-5197
Piedmont College, Demorest, GA 30535
Piedmont Community College, Roxboro, NC 27573
Piedmont Technical College, Greenwood, SC 29648
Piedmont Virginia Community College, Charlottesville, VA 22901-8714
Pierce College, Tacoma, WA 98498-1999
Pikes Peak Community College, Colorado Springs, CO 80906-5498
Pikeville College, Pikeville, KY 41501-1194
Pillsbury Baptist Bible College, Owatonna, MN 55060
Pima Community College, Tucson, AZ 85709-3010
Pine Manor College, Chestnut Hill, MA 02167
Pinebrook Junior College, Coopersburg, PA 18036
Pitt Community College, Greenville, NC 27835-7007
Pittsburg State University, Pittsburg, KS 66762
Pittsburgh Institute of Mortuary Science, Pittsburgh, PA 15206
Pittsburgh Technical Institute, Pittsburgh, PA 15222
Pitzer College, Claremont, CA 91711-6114
Platt Junior College, St. Joseph, MO 64506-2911
Plaza Business Institute, Jackson Heights, NY 11372
Plymouth State College of the University System of New Hampshire, Plymouth, NH 03264
Point Loma Nazarene College, San Diego, CA 92106-2899
Point Park College, Pittsburgh, PA 15222
Polk Community College, Winter Haven, FL 33881-4299

Polytechnic University
Brooklyn, Brooklyn, NY 11201
Long Island Campus, Farmingdale, NY 11735-3995
Pomona College, Claremont, CA 91711-6312
Pontifical College Josephinum, Columbus, OH 43085
Porterville College, Porterville, CA 93257
Portland Community College, Portland, OR 97219-0990
Portland School of Art, Portland, ME 04101-3987
Portland State University, Portland, OR 97207-0751
Potomac State College of West Virginia University, Keyser, WV 26726
Prairie State College, Chicago Heights, IL 60411
Prairie View A&M University, Prairie View, TX 77446
Pratt Community College, Pratt, KS 67124
Pratt Institute, Brooklyn, NY 11205
Presbyterian College, Clinton, SC 29325-9989
Prescott College, Prescott, AZ 86301
Presentation College, Aberdeen, SD 57401
Prestonburg Community College, Prestonburg, KY 41653
Prince George's Community College, Largo, MD 20772-2199
Prince William Sound Community College, Valdez, AK 99686
Princeton University, Princeton, NJ 08544-0430
Principia College, Elsah, IL 62028-9799
Providence College, Providence, RI 02918-0001
Pueblo Community College, Pueblo, CO 81004
Puerto Rico Junior College, Rio Piedras, PR 00928
Puget Sound Christian College, Edmonds, WA 98020-3171
Purdue University
Calumet, Hammond, IN 46323-2094
North Central Campus, Westville, IN 46391
West Lafayette, West Lafayette, IN 47907
Queen of the Holy Rosary College, Fremont, CA 94539
Queens College, Charlotte, NC 28274
Quincy College, Quincy, IL 62301-2699
Quincy College, Quincy, MA 02169
Quinebaug Valley Community College, Danielson, CT 06239-1699
Quinnipiac College, Hamden, CT 06518-0569
Quinsigamond Community College, Worcester, MA 01606
Rabbinical College of America, Morristown, NJ 07960
Rabbinical College Bobover Yeshiva B'nei Zion, Brooklyn, NY 11219
Rabbinical College Ch'san Sofer of New York, Brooklyn, NY 11204
Rabbinical College of Long Island, Long Beach, NY 11561
Rabbinical College of Telshe, Wickliffe, OH 44092-2584
Rabbinical Seminary Adas Yereim, Brooklyn, NY 11211
Rabbinical Seminary of America, Forest Hills, NY 11375
Rabbinical Seminary M'Kor Chaim, Brooklyn, NY 11219
Radford University, Radford, VA 24142-5430
Rainy River Community College, International Falls, MN 56649
Ramapo College of New Jersey, Mahwah, NJ 07430-1680
Ramirez College of Business and Technology, Santurce, PR 00910-8340
Rancho Santiago Community College, Santa Ana, CA 92706
Randolph Community College, Asheboro, NC 27204-1009
Randolph-Macon College, Ashland, VA 23005-1697
Randolph-Macon Woman's College, Lynchburg, VA 24503
Ranger Junior College, Ranger, TX 76470
Ranken Technical College, St. Louis, MO 63113
Rappahannock Community College, Glenns, VA 23149
Raritan Valley Community College, Somerville, NJ 08876-1265
Ray College of Design, Chicago, IL 60611
Reading Area Community College, Reading, PA 19603
Red Rocks Community College, Lakewood, CO 80401
Reed College, Portland, OR 97202-8199
Reformed Bible College, Grand Rapids, MI 49505-9749
Regis College, Weston, MA 02193
Regis University, Denver, CO 80221-1099
Reid State Technical College, Evergreen, AL 36401
Reinhardt College, Waleska, GA 30183
Rend Lake College, Ina, IL 62846
Rensselaer Polytechnic Institute, Troy, NY 12181-3590
Research College of Nursing, Kansas City, MO 64110-2508
RETS Electronic Institute, Louisville, KY 40219
RETS Electronics Institute, Birmingham, AL 35234
RETS Technical Center, Centerville, OH 45459
Rhode Island College, Providence, RI 02908
Rhode Island School of Design, Providence, RI 02903
Rhodes College, Memphis, TN 38112
Rice University, Houston, TX 77251
Rich Mountain Community College, Mena, AR 71953
Richard Bland College, Petersburg, VA 23805
Richland College, Dallas, TX 75243-2199
Richland Community College, Decatur, IL 62521
Richmond Community College, Hamlet, NC 28345
Ricks College, Rexburg, ID 83460-4104

Rider College, Lawrenceville, NJ 08648-3099
Rika Breuer Teachers Seminary, New York, NY 10033
Ringling School of Art and Design, Sarasota, FL 34234
Rio Hondo College, Whittier, CA 90608
Rio Salado Community College, Phoenix, AZ 85003
Ripon College, Ripon, WI 54971
Riverside Community College, Riverside, CA 92506-1299
Rivier College, Nashua, NH 03060-5086
Roane State Community College, Harriman, TN 37748
Roanoke Bible College, Elizabeth City, NC 27909
Roanoke College, Salem, VA 24153-3794
Roanoke-Chowan Community College, Ahoskie, NC 27910
Robert Morris College, Coraopolis, PA 15108-1189
Robert Morris College: Chicago, Chicago, IL 60601
Roberts Wesleyan College, Rochester, NY 14624-1997
Robeson Community College, Lumberton, NC 28359
Rochester Business Institute, Rochester, NY 14604
Rochester Community College, Rochester, MN 55904-4999
Rochester Institute of Technology, Rochester, NY 14623-0887
Rock Valley College, Rockford, IL 61111
Rockford College, Rockford, IL 61108-2393
Rockhurst College, Kansas City, MO 64110-2508
Rockingham Community College, Wentworth, NC 27375-0038
Rockland Community College, Suffern, NY 10901
Rocky Mountain College, Billings, MT 59102-1796
Rocky Mountain College of Art and Design, Denver, CO 80224-2359
Roger Williams College, Bristol, RI 02809-2923
Rogers State College, Claremore, OK 74017
Rogue Community College, Grants Pass, OR 97527
Rollins College, Winter Park, FL 32789-4499
Roosevelt University, Chicago, IL 60605-1394
Rosary College, River Forest, IL 60305-1099
Rose State College, Midwest City, OK 73110-2799
Rose-Hulman Institute of Technology, Terre Haute, IN 47803-9989
Rosemont College, Rosemont, PA 19010
Rowan-Cabarrus Community College, Salisbury, NC 28145-1595
Roxbury Community College, Boston, MA 02120-3400
Rush University, Chicago, IL 60612
Russell Sage College, Troy, NY 12180
Rust College, Holly Springs, MS 38635-2328
Rutgers—The State University of New Jersey
    Camden College of Arts and Sciences, Camden, NJ 08101-2740
    College of Engineering, New Brunswick, NJ 08903-2101
    College of Nursing, Newark, NJ 07102-1896
    College of Pharmacy, New Brunswick, NJ 08903-2101
    Cook College, New Brunswick, NJ 08903-2101
    Douglass College, New Brunswick, NJ 08903-2101
    Livingston College, New Brunswick, NJ 08903-2101
    Mason Gross School of the Arts, New Brunswick, NJ 08903-2101
    Newark College of Arts and Sciences, Newark, NJ 07102-1896
    Rutgers College, New Brunswick, NJ 08903-2101
Sacramento City College, Sacramento, CA 95822
Sacred Heart Major Seminary, Detroit, MI 48206
Sacred Heart University, Fairfield, CT 06432-1000
Saddleback College, Mission Viejo, CA 92692
Sage Junior College of Albany, A Division of Russell Sage College, Albany, NY 12208
Saginaw Valley State University, University Center, MI 48710-0001
St. Ambrose University, Davenport, IA 52803
St. Andrews Presbyterian College, Laurinburg, NC 28352-9151
St. Anselm College, Manchester, NH 03102-9001
St. Augustine College, Chicago, IL 60640
St. Augustine's College, Raleigh, NC 27610-2298
St. Basil's College, Stamford, CT 06902
St. Bernard Parish Community College, Chalmette, LA 70043
St. Bonaventure University, Olean, NY 14778-9985
St. Catharine College, St. Catharine, KY 40061
St. Charles Borromeo Seminary, Overbrook, PA 19096-3099
St. Charles Community College, St. Charles, MO 63301
St. Clair County Community College, Port Huron, MI 48061-5015
St. Cloud State University, St. Cloud, MN 56301-4498
St. Edward's University, Austin, TX 78704
St. Francis College, Fort Wayne, IN 46808
St. Francis College, Brooklyn Heights, NY 11201
St. Francis College, Loretto, PA 15940
St. Francis Medical Center College of Nursing, Peoria, IL 61603
St. Gregory's College, Shawnee, OK 74801
St. Hyacinth College and Seminary, Granby, MA 01033
St. John Fisher College, Rochester, NY 14618
St. John Vianney College Seminary, Miami, FL 33165
St. John's College, Santa Fe, NM 87501-4599
St. John's College, Annapolis, MD 21404-2800

St. Johns River Community College, Palatka, FL 32177-3897
St. John's Seminary College, Brighton, MA 02135
St. John's Seminary College, Camarillo, CA 93010
St. John's University, Jamaica, NY 11439
St. John's University, Collegeville, MN 56321
St. Joseph College, West Hartford, CT 06117
St. Joseph College of Nursing, Joliet, IL 60435
St. Joseph Seminary College, St. Benedict, LA 70457-9990
St. Joseph's College, Rensselaer, IN 47978
St. Joseph's College, Windham, ME 04062-1198
St. Joseph's College
    Brooklyn, Brooklyn, NY 11205-3688
    Suffolk Campus, Patchogue, NY 11772-2603
St. Joseph's School of Nursing, Syracuse, NY 13203
St. Joseph's University, Philadelphia, PA 19131
St. Lawrence University, Canton, NY 13617-1447
St. Leo College, St. Leo, FL 33574
St. Louis Christian College, Florissant, MO 63033
St. Louis College of Pharmacy, St. Louis, MO 63110
St. Louis Community College
    Florissant Valley, St. Louis, MO 63135
    Forest Park, St. Louis, MO 63110
    Meramec, Kirkwood, MO 63122-5799
St. Louis University, St. Louis, MO 63103-2097
St. Martin's College, Lacey, WA 98503
St. Mary College, Leavenworth, KS 66048-5082
St. Mary of the Plains College, Dodge City, KS 67801
St. Mary-of-the-Woods College, St. Mary-of-the-Woods, IN 47876
St. Mary's Campus of the College of St. Catherine, Minneapolis, MN 55454
St. Mary's College, Notre Dame, IN 46556
St. Mary's College, Orchard Lake, MI 48324
St. Mary's College, Raleigh, NC 27603-1689
St. Mary's College of California, Moraga, CA 94575-9988
St. Mary's College of Maryland, St. Mary's City, MD 20686-9990
St. Mary's College at Minnesota, Winona, MN 55987-0857
St. Mary's University, San Antonio, TX 78228-8503
St. Meinrad College, St. Meinrad, IN 47577-1030
St. Michael's College, Colchester, VT 05439
St. Norbert College, De Pere, WI 54115-2099
St. Olaf College, Northfield, MN 55057
St. Paul Bible College, St. Bonifacius, MN 55375-9001
St. Paul Technical College, St. Paul, MN 55102-9913
St. Paul's College, Lawrenceville, VA 23868
St. Peter's College, Jersey City, NJ 07306-5944
St. Petersburg Junior College, St. Petersburg, FL 33733
St. Philip's College, San Antonio, TX 78203
St. Thomas Aquinas College, Sparkill, NY 10976
St. Thomas University, Miami, FL 33054
St. Vincent College, Latrobe, PA 15650-2690
St. Xavier College, Chicago, IL 60655
Salem College, Winston-Salem, NC 27108
Salem Community College, Carneys Point, NJ 08069-2799
Salem State College, Salem, MA 01970
Salem-Teikyo University, Salem, WV 26426
Salisbury State University, Salisbury, MD 21801-6862
Salish Kootenai College, Pablo, MT 59855
Salt Lake Community College, Salt Lake City, UT 84130-0808
Salve Regina College, Newport, RI 02840-4192
Sam Houston State University, Huntsville, TX 77341-2418
Samford University, Birmingham, AL 35229
Sampson Community College, Clinton, NC 28328
Samuel Merritt College, Oakland, CA 94609-9954
San Antonio Art Institute, San Antonio, TX 78209-0092
San Antonio College, San Antonio, TX 78212
San Bernardino Valley College, San Bernardino, CA 92410
San Diego City College, San Diego, CA 92101
San Diego Mesa College, San Diego, CA 92111
San Diego Miramar College, San Diego, CA 92126-2999
San Diego State University, San Diego, CA 92182-0771
San Francisco Art Institute, San Francisco, CA 94133-2299
San Francisco College of Mortuary Science, San Francisco, CA 94115-3912
San Francisco Conservatory of Music, San Francisco, CA 94122
San Francisco State University, San Francisco, CA 94132
San Jacinto College
    Central Campus, Pasadena, TX 77505-2007
    North, Houston, TX 77049
San Joaquin Delta College, Stockton, CA 95207
San Jose Christian College, San Jose, CA 95108-1090
San Jose City College, San Jose, CA 95128-2798
San Jose State University, San Jose, CA 95192-0009
San Juan College, Farmington, NM 87402
Sandhills Community College, Pinehurst, NC 28374

Sangamon State University, Springfield, IL 62794-9243
Santa Barbara City College, Santa Barbara, CA 93109-2394
Santa Clara University, Santa Clara, CA 95053
Santa Fe Community College, Santa Fe, NM 87502-4187
Santa Fe Community College, Gainesville, FL 32601
Santa Monica College, Santa Monica, CA 90405-1628
Santa Rosa Junior College, Santa Rosa, CA 95401
Sarah Lawrence College, Bronxville, NY 10708
Sauk Valley Community College, Dixon, IL 61021-9110
Savannah College of Art and Design, Savannah, GA 31401-3146
Savannah State College, Savannah, GA 31404
Savannah Technical Institute, Savannah, GA 31499
Schenectady County Community College, Schenectady, NY 12305
School of the Art Institute of Chicago, Chicago, IL 60603
School for International Training, Brattleboro, VT 05301
School for Lifelong Learning, Durham, NH 03824-3545
School of the Museum of Fine Arts, Boston, MA 02115
School of Visual Arts, New York, NY 10010-3994
Schoolcraft College, Livonia, MI 48152-2696
Schreiner College, Kerrville, TX 78028
Scott Community College, Bettendorf, IA 52722-5649
Scottsdale Community College, Scottsdale, AZ 85253
Scripps College, Claremont, CA 91711-3948
Seattle Central Community College, Seattle, WA 98122
Seattle Pacific University, Seattle, WA 98119-1997
Seattle University, Seattle, WA 98122
Selma University, Selma, AL 36701
Seminole Community College, Sanford, FL 32773-6199
Seminole Junior College, Seminole, OK 74868
Seton Hall University, South Orange, NJ 07079-2689
Seton Hill College, Greensburg, PA 15601-1599
Seward County Community College, Liberal, KS 67901
Shasta College, Redding, CA 96099
Shaw University, Raleigh, NC 27611
Shawnee Community College, Ullin, IL 62992
Shawnee State University, Portsmouth, OH 45662
Shelby State Community College, Memphis, TN 38174-0568
Sheldon Jackson College, Sitka, AK 99835
Shelton State Community College, Tuscaloosa, AL 35405
Shenandoah University, Winchester, VA 22601
Shepherd College, Shepherdstown, WV 25443-1569
Sheridan College, Sheridan, WY 82801
Shimer College, Waukegan, IL 60079
Shippensburg University of Pennsylvania, Shippensburg, PA 17257
Shoals Community College, Muscle Shoals, AL 35662
Shoreline Community College, Seattle, WA 98133
Shorter College, Rome, GA 30161
Shorter College, North Little Rock, AR 72114
Siena College, Loudonville, NY 12211
Siena Heights College, Adrian, MI 49221-9937
Sierra College, Rocklin, CA 95677
Sierra Nevada College, Incline Village, NV 89450-4269
Silver Lake College, Manitowoc, WI 54220-9391
Simmons College, Boston, MA 02115-5898
Simon's Rock College of Bard, Great Barrington, MA 01230
Simpson College, Redding, CA 96003-8606
Simpson College, Indianola, IA 50125-1299
Sinclair Community College, Dayton, OH 45402
Sinte Gleska College, Rosebud, SD 57570
Sioux Falls College, Sioux Falls, SD 57105
Sisseton-Wahpeton Community College, Sisseton, SD 57262-0689
Skagit Valley College, Mount Vernon, WA 98273
Skidmore College, Saratoga Springs, NY 12866
Skyline College, San Bruno, CA 94066-1698
Slippery Rock University of Pennsylvania, Slippery Rock, PA 16057
Smith College, Northampton, MA 01063
Snead State Junior College, Boaz, AL 35957
Snow College, Ephraim, UT 84627
Sojourner-Douglass College, Baltimore, MD 21205
Solano Community College, Suisun City, CA 94585
Somerset Community College, Somerset, KY 42501
Sonoma State University, Rohnert Park, CA 94928
South Carolina State College, Orangeburg, SC 29117
South Central Community College, New Haven, CT 06511-5970
South College, Savannah, GA 31406
South College: Palm Beach Campus, West Palm Beach, FL 33409
South Dakota School of Mines and Technology, Rapid City, SD 57701-3995
South Dakota State University, Brookings, SD 57007-1198
South Florida Community College, Avon Park, FL 33825
South Georgia College, Douglas, GA 31533
South Mountain Community College, Phoenix, AZ 85040
South Plains College, Levelland, TX 79336

South Puget Sound Community College, Olympia, WA 98502
South Seattle Community College, Seattle, WA 98106
South Suburban College of Cook County, South Holland, IL 60473
Southeast Community College, Cumberland, KY 40823
Southeast Community College
    Beatrice Campus, Beatrice, NE 68310
    Lincoln Campus, Lincoln, NE 68520
    Milford Campus, Milford, NE 68405
Southeast Missouri State University, Cape Girardeau, MO 63701
Southeast Vo-Tech Institute, Sioux Falls, SD 57107
Southeastern Baptist College, Laurel, MS 39441-8000
Southeastern Baptist Theological Seminary, Wake Forest, NC 27587
Southeastern Bible College, Birmingham, AL 35243-4181
Southeastern College of the Assemblies of God, Lakeland, FL 33801
Southeastern Community College, Whiteville, NC 28472
Southeastern Community College
    North Campus, West Burlington, IA 52655-0605
    South Campus, Keokuk, IA 52632-1088
Southeastern Illinois College, Harrisburg, IL 62946
Southeastern Louisiana University, Hammond, LA 70402-0752
Southeastern Massachusetts University, North Dartmouth, MA 02747
Southeastern Oklahoma State University, Durant, OK 74701
Southeastern University, Washington, DC 20024
Southern Arkansas University
    El Dorado Branch, El Dorado, AR 71730
    Magnolia, Magnolia, AR 71753
    Technical Branch, Camden, AR 71701
Southern California College, Costa Mesa, CA 92626-9601
Southern California Institute of Architecture, Santa Monica, CA 90404
Southern College, Orlando, FL 32807
Southern College of Seventh-day Adventists, Collegedale, TN 37315
Southern College of Technology, Marietta, GA 30060-2896
Southern Connecticut State University, New Haven, CT 06515
Southern Illinois University
    Carbondale, Carbondale, IL 62901
    Edwardsville, Edwardsville, IL 62026-1600
Southern Junior College, Birmingham, AL 35203
Southern Maine Technical College, South Portland, ME 04106
Southern Methodist University, Dallas, TX 75275
Southern Nazarene University, Bethany, OK 73008-2694
Southern Ohio College, Cincinnati, OH 45237
Southern Oregon State College, Ashland, OR 97520-5032
Southern State Community College, Hillsboro, OH 45133
Southern Union State Junior College, Wadley, AL 36276
Southern University
    New Orleans, New Orleans, LA 70126
    Shreveport, Shreveport, LA 71107
Southern University and Agricultural and Mechanical College, Baton Rouge, LA 70813
Southern Utah University, Cedar City, UT 84720
Southern Vermont College, Bennington, VT 05201
Southern West Virginia Community College, Logan, WV 25601
Southside Virginia Community College, Alberta, VA 23821
Southwest Baptist University, Bolivar, MO 65613-2496
Southwest Mississippi Community College, Summit, MS 39666
Southwest Missouri State University, Springfield, MO 65804-0094
Southwest State Technical College, Mobile, AL 36605
Southwest State University, Marshall, MN 56258
Southwest Texas Junior College, Uvalde, TX 78801
Southwest Texas State University, San Marcos, TX 78666
Southwest Virginia Community College, Richlands, VA 24641-1510
Southwest Wisconsin Technical College, Fennimore, WI 53809
Southwestern Adventist College, Keene, TX 76059
Southwestern Assemblies of God College, Waxahachie, TX 75165
Southwestern Christian College, Terrell, TX 75160
Southwestern College, Chula Vista, CA 92010
Southwestern College, Phoenix, AZ 85032
Southwestern College, Winfield, KS 67156
Southwestern College of Christian Ministries, Bethany, OK 73008
Southwestern Community College, Sylva, NC 28779
Southwestern Community College, Creston, IA 50801
Southwestern Indian Polytechnic Institute, Albuquerque, NM 87184
Southwestern Michigan College, Dowagiac, MI 49047
Southwestern Oklahoma State University, Weatherford, OK 73096
Southwestern Oregon Community College, Coos Bay, OR 97420
Southwestern University, Georgetown, TX 78626
Spalding University, Louisville, KY 40203
Spartanburg Methodist College, Spartanburg, SC 29301
Spartanburg Technical College, Spartanburg, SC 29305
Spelman College, Atlanta, GA 30314-4399
Spokane Community College, Spokane, WA 99207-5399
Spokane Falls Community College, Spokane, WA 99204-5288

Spoon River College, Canton, IL 61520
Spring Arbor College, Spring Arbor, MI 49283
Spring Garden College, Philadelphia, PA 19119-1651
Spring Hill College, Mobile, AL 36608
Springfield College, Springfield, MA 01109
Springfield College in Illinois, Springfield, IL 62702-2694
Springfield Technical Community College, Springfield, MA 01105
Standing Rock College, Fort Yates, ND 58538
Stanford University, Stanford, CA 94305
Stanly Community College, Albemarle, NC 28001
Stark Technical College, Canton, OH 44720
State Community College, East St. Louis, IL 62201
State Fair Community College, Sedalia, MO 65301-2199
State Technical Institute at Memphis, Memphis, TN 38134
State University of New York
    Albany, Albany, NY 12222
    Binghamton, Binghamton, NY 13902-6001
    Buffalo, Buffalo, NY 14214
    Purchase, Purchase, NY 10577-1400
    Stony Brook, Stony Brook, NY 11794-1901
    College of Agriculture and Technology at Cobleskill, Cobleskill, NY 12043
    College of Agriculture and Technology at Morrisville, Morrisville, NY 13408
    College at Brockport, Brockport, NY 14420
    College at Buffalo, Buffalo, NY 14222-1095
    College at Cortland, Cortland, NY 13045
    College of Environmental Science and Forestry, Syracuse, NY 13210-2779
    College at Fredonia, Fredonia, NY 14063
    College at Geneseo, Geneseo, NY 14454-1471
    College at New Paltz, New Paltz, NY 12561
    College at Old Westbury, Old Westbury, NY 11568-0210
    College at Oneonta, Oneonta, NY 13820-4016
    College at Plattsburgh, Plattsburgh, NY 12901
    College at Potsdam, Potsdam, NY 13676-2294
    College of Technology at Alfred, Alfred, NY 14802-1196
    College of Technology at Canton, Canton, NY 13617
    College of Technology at Delhi, Delhi, NY 13753-1190
    College of Technology at Farmingdale, Farmingdale, NY 11735
    Empire State College, Saratoga Springs, NY 12866
    Health Science Center at Brooklyn, Brooklyn, NY 11203
    Health Science Center at Syracuse, Syracuse, NY 13210
    Health Sciences Center at Stony Brook, Stony Brook, NY 11794-8276
    Institute of Technology at Utica/Rome, Utica, NY 13504-3050
    Maritime College, Throggs Neck, NY 10465-4198
    Oswego, Oswego, NY 13126-3599
Stenotype Academy, New York, NY 10007
Stephen F. Austin State University, Nacogdoches, TX 75962
Stephens College, Columbia, MO 65215-9986
Sterling College, Craftsbury Common, VT 05827-0072
Sterling College, Sterling, KS 67579-9989
Stetson University, DeLand, FL 32720
Stevens Institute of Technology, Hoboken, NJ 07030
Stevens-Henager College of Business, Provo, UT 84606-6157
Stillman College, Tuscaloosa, AL 35403
Stockton State College, Pomona, NJ 08240
Stone Child College, Box Elder, MT 59521
Stonehill College, North Easton, MA 02357
Stratton College, Milwaukee, WI 53202-2608
Strayer College, Arlington, VA 22204
Sue Bennett College, London, KY 40741
Suffolk County Community College
    Eastern Campus, Riverhead, NY 11901
    Selden, Selden, NY 11784
    Western Campus, Brentwood, NY 11717
Suffolk University, Boston, MA 02108-2772
Sul Ross State University, Alpine, TX 79832
Sullivan County Community College, Loch Sheldrake, NY 12759
Summit Christian College, Fort Wayne, IN 46807
Sumter Area Technical College, Sumter, SC 29150
Suomi College, Hancock, MI 49930
Surry Community College, Dobson, NC 27017
Susquehanna University, Selinsgrove, PA 17870-1001
Sussex County Community College, Newton, NJ 07860
Swarthmore College, Swarthmore, PA 19081-1397
Sweet Briar College, Sweet Briar, VA 24595
Syracuse University, Syracuse, NY 13244-1120
Tabor College, Hillsboro, KS 67063
Tacoma Community College, Tacoma, WA 98465-9971
Taft College, Taft, CA 93268
Talladega College, Talladega, AL 35160

Tallahassee Community College, Tallahassee, FL 32304-2895
Talmudic College of Florida, Miami Beach, FL 33140
Talmudical Institute of Upstate New York, Rochester, NY 14607
Talmudical Seminary Oholei Torah, Brooklyn, NY 11213-3397
Talmudical Yeshiva of Philadelphia, Philadelphia, PA 19131
Tampa College, Tampa, FL 33614
Tarleton State University, Stephenville, TX 76402
Tarrant County Junior College, Fort Worth, TX 76102-6599
Taylor University, Upland, IN 46989
Technical Career Institutes, New York, NY 10001
Technical College of the Lowcountry, Beaufort, SC 29902-1288
Technological College of the Municipality of San Juan, Hato Rey, PR 00918
Teikyo Marycrest University, Davenport, IA 52804-4096
Teikyo Westmar University, Le Mars, IA 51031
Teikyo-Post University, Waterbury, CT 06723-2540
Telshe Yeshiva-Chicago, Chicago, IL 60625
Temple Junior College, Temple, TX 76504-7435
Temple University, Philadelphia, PA 19122-1803
Tennessee Institute of Electronics, Knoxville, TN 37918
Tennessee State University, Nashville, TN 37203
Tennessee Technological University, Cookeville, TN 38505
Tennessee Temple University, Chattanooga, TN 37404
Tennessee Wesleyan College, Athens, TN 37303-9988
Terra Technical College, Fremont, OH 43420
Texarkana College, Texarkana, TX 75501
Texas A&I University, Kingsville, TX 78363-8201
Texas A&M University
    College Station, College Station, TX 77843-0100
    Galveston, Galveston, TX 77553-1675
Texas Christian University, Fort Worth, TX 76129
Texas College, Tyler, TX 75702-2404
Texas Lutheran College, Seguin, TX 78155
Texas Southern University, Houston, TX 77004
Texas Southmost College, Brownsville, TX 78520
Texas State Technical Institute
    Amarillo, Amarillo, TX 79111
    Harlingen, Harlingen, TX 78550-3697
    Sweetwater, Sweetwater, TX 79556
    Waco, Waco, TX 76705
Texas Tech University, Lubbock, TX 79409
Texas Wesleyan University, Fort Worth, TX 76105-1536
Thaddeus Stevens State School of Technology, Lancaster, PA 17602
Thames Valley State Technical College, Norwich, CT 06360
Thiel College, Greenville, PA 16125
Thomas Aquinas College, Santa Paula, CA 93060
Thomas College, Waterville, ME 04901-9986
Thomas College, Thomasville, GA 31792-7499
Thomas Jefferson University: College of Allied Health Sciences, Philadelphia, PA 19107
Thomas More College, Crestview Hills, KY 41017
Thomas Nelson Community College, Hampton, VA 23670
Three Rivers Community College, Poplar Bluff, MO 63901-1308
Tidewater Community College, Portsmouth, VA 23703
Tiffin University, Tiffin, OH 44883
Tobe-Coburn School for Fashion Careers, New York, NY 10012
Toccoa Falls College, Toccoa Falls, GA 30598-0368
Tomlinson College, Cleveland, TN 37320-3030
Tompkins-Cortland Community College, Dryden, NY 13053-0139
Tougaloo College, Tougaloo, MS 39174
Touro College, New York, NY 10036
Towson State University, Towson, MD 21204-7097
Tracey-Warner School, Philadelphia, PA 19108-1084
Transylvania University, Lexington, KY 40508
Treasure Valley Community College, Ontario, OR 97914
Trenholm State Technical College, Montgomery, AL 36108
Trenton State College, Trenton, NJ 08650-4700
Trevecca Nazarene College, Nashville, TN 37203
Triangle Tech
    Greensburg School, Greensburg, PA 15601
    Pittsburgh Campus, Pittsburgh, PA 15214
Tri-County Community College, Murphy, NC 28906
Tri-County Technical College, Pendleton, SC 29670
Trident Technical College, Charleston, SC 29411
Trinidad State Junior College, Trinidad, CO 81082
Trinity Bible College, Ellendale, ND 58436-1001
Trinity Christian College, Palos Heights, IL 60463
Trinity College, Deerfield, IL 60015
Trinity College, Hartford, CT 06106
Trinity College, Washington, DC 20017-1094
Trinity College of Vermont, Burlington, VT 05401
Trinity University, San Antonio, TX 78212
Trinity Valley Community College, Athens, TX 75751

Tri-State University, Angola, IN 46703-0307
Triton College, River Grove, IL 60171
Trocaire College, Buffalo, NY 14220
Troy State University
    Dothan, Dothan, AL 36304-0368
    Montgomery, Montgomery, AL 36103-4419
    Troy, Troy, AL 36082
Truckee Meadows Community College, Reno, NV 89512
Truett-McConnell College, Cleveland, GA 30528
Tufts University, Medford, MA 02155
Tulane University, New Orleans, LA 70118-5680
Tulsa Junior College, Tulsa, OK 74135-6101
Tunxis Community College, Farmington, CT 06032
Turabo University, Caguas, PR 00658
Turtle Mountain Community College, Belcourt, ND 58316-0340
Tusculum College, Greeneville, TN 37743
Tuskegee University, Tuskegee, AL 36088
Tyler Junior College, Tyler, TX 75711-9020
Ulster County Community College, Stone Ridge, NY 12484
Umpqua Community College, Roseburg, OR 97470
Union College, Barbourville, KY 40906
Union College, Schenectady, NY 12308-2311
Union College, Lincoln, NE 68506-4300
Union County College, Cranford, NJ 07016-1599
Union Institute, Cincinnati, OH 45206-1947
Union University, Jackson, TN 38305
United Electronics Institute, Tampa, FL 33619
United States International University, San Diego, CA 92131-1799
United States Merchant Marine Academy, Kings Point, NY 11024
United Talmudical Academy, Brooklyn, NY 11211
United Tribes Technical College, Bismarck, ND 58504
Unity College, Unity, ME 04988
Universidad Adventista de las Antillas, Mayaguez, PR 00709-0118
Universidad Metropolitana, Rio Piedras, PR 00928
Universidad Politecnica de Puerto Rico, San Juan, PR 00918
University of Akron
    Akron, Akron, OH 44325-2001
    Wayne College, Orrville, OH 44667
University of Alabama
    Birmingham, Birmingham, AL 35294
    Huntsville, Huntsville, AL 35899
    Tuscaloosa, Tuscaloosa, AL 35487-0132
University of Alaska
    Anchorage, Anchorage, AK 99508-4675
    Fairbanks, Fairbanks, AK 99775-0060
    Southeast, Juneau, AK 99801
University of Arizona, Tucson, AZ 85721
University of Arkansas
    Fayetteville, Fayetteville, AR 72701
    Little Rock, Little Rock, AR 72204
    Medical Sciences, Little Rock, AR 72205-7199
    Monticello, Monticello, AR 71655
    Pine Bluff, Pine Bluff, AR 71601
University of the Arts, Philadelphia, PA 19102
University of Baltimore, Baltimore, MD 21201-5779
University of Bridgeport, Bridgeport, CT 06602
University of California
    Berkeley, Berkeley, CA 94720
    Davis, Davis, CA 95616
    Irvine, Irvine, CA 92717
    Los Angeles, Los Angeles, CA 90024
    Riverside, Riverside, CA 92521
    San Diego, La Jolla, CA 92093-0337
    San Francisco, San Francisco, CA 94143-0244
    Santa Barbara, Santa Barbara, CA 93106
    Santa Cruz, Santa Cruz, CA 95064
University of Central Arkansas, Conway, AR 72032
University of Central Florida, Orlando, FL 32816
University of Central Texas, Killeen, TX 76540-1416
University of Charleston, Charleston, WV 25304-1099
University of Chicago, Chicago, IL 60637
University of Cincinnati
    Access Colleges, Cincinnati, OH 45221
    Cincinnati, Cincinnati, OH 45221-0091
    Clermont College, Batavia, OH 45103
    Raymond Walters College, Cincinnati, OH 45236
University of Colorado
    Boulder, Boulder, CO 80309-0007
    Colorado Springs, Colorado Springs, CO 80933-7150
    Denver, Denver, CO 80217-3364
    Health Sciences Center, Denver, CO 80262
University of Connecticut, Storrs, CT 06269-3088

University of Dallas, Irving, TX 75062
University of Dayton, Dayton, OH 45469-1611
University of Delaware, Newark, DE 19716
University of Denver, Denver, CO 80208-0132
University of Detroit Mercy, Detroit, MI 48221
University of the District of Columbia, Washington, DC 20008
University of Dubuque, Dubuque, IA 52001
University of Evansville, Evansville, IN 47722
University of Findlay, Findlay, OH 45840
University of Florida, Gainesville, FL 32611
University of Georgia, Athens, GA 30602
University of Guam, Mangilao, Guam, GU 96923
University of Hartford, West Hartford, CT 06117-0395
University of Hawaii
    Hilo, Hilo, HI 96720-4091
    Honolulu Community College, Honolulu, HI 96817
    Kapiolani Community College, Honolulu, HI 96816
    Kauai Community College, Lihue, HI 96766
    Leeward Community College, Pearl City, HI 96782
    Manoa, Honolulu, HI 96822
    Maui Community College, Kahului, HI 96732
    West Oahu, Pearl City, HI 96782
    Windward Community College, Kaneohe, HI 96817
University of Health Sciences: The Chicago Medical School, North Chicago, IL 60064
University of Houston
    Clear Lake, Houston, TX 77058-1080
    Downtown, Houston, TX 77002
    Houston, Houston, TX 77204-2161
    Victoria, Victoria, TX 77901
University of Idaho, Moscow, ID 83843
University of Illinois
    Chicago, Chicago, IL 60680
    Urbana-Champaign, Urbana, IL 61801
University of Indianapolis, Indianapolis, IN 46227-3697
University of Iowa, Iowa City, IA 52242
University of Judaism, Los Angeles, CA 90077
University of Kansas
    Lawrence, Lawrence, KS 66045-0215
    Medical Center, Kansas City, KS 66103
University of Kentucky, Lexington, KY 40506-0054
University of La Verne, La Verne, CA 91750-4443
University of Louisville, Louisville, KY 40292
University of Lowell, Lowell, MA 01854
University of Maine
    Augusta, Augusta, ME 04330
    Farmington, Farmington, ME 04938
    Fort Kent, Fort Kent, ME 04743-1292
    Machias, Machias, ME 04654
    Orono, Orono, ME 04469-0113
    Presque Isle, Presque Isle, ME 04769-2888
University of Mary, Bismarck, ND 58504-9652
University of Mary Hardin-Baylor, Belton, TX 76513
University of Maryland
    Baltimore, Baltimore, MD 21201
    Baltimore County, Catonsville, MD 21228
    College Park, College Park, MD 20742-5235
    Eastern Shore, Princess Anne, MD 21853-1299
    University College, College Park, MD 20742-1672
University of Massachusetts
    Amherst, Amherst, MA 01003
    Boston, Boston, MA 02125
University of Miami, Coral Gables, FL 33124
University of Michigan
    Ann Arbor, Ann Arbor, MI 48109-1316
    Dearborn, Dearborn, MI 48128-1491
    Flint, Flint, MI 48502-2186
University of Minnesota
    Crookston, Crookston, MN 56716
    Duluth, Duluth, MN 55812
    Morris, Morris, MN 56267
    Twin Cities, Minneapolis-St. Paul, MN 55455
    Waseca, Waseca, MN 56093
University of Mississippi
    Medical Center, Jackson, MS 39216
    University, University, MS 38677
University of Missouri
    Columbia, Columbia, MO 65211
    Kansas City, Kansas City, MO 64110-2944
    Rolla, Rolla, MO 65401
    St. Louis, St. Louis, MO 63121
University of Montana, Missoula, MT 59812

University of Montevallo, Montevallo, AL 35115-6030
University of Nebraska
    Medical Center, Omaha, NE 68198-4230
    Lincoln, Lincoln, NE 68588-0417
    Omaha, Omaha, NE 68182-0005
University of Nebraska at Kearney, Kearney, NE 68849
University of Nevada
    Las Vegas, Las Vegas, NV 89154
    Reno, Reno, NV 89557-0002
University of New England, Biddeford, ME 04005
University of New Hampshire
    Durham, Durham, NH 03824
    Manchester, Manchester, NH 03102
University of New Haven, West Haven, CT 06516
University of New Mexico
    Albuquerque, Albuquerque, NM 87131
    Gallup, Gallup, NM 87301
University of New Orleans, New Orleans, LA 70148
University of North Alabama, Florence, AL 35632-0001
University of North Carolina
    Asheville, Asheville, NC 28804-3299
    Chapel Hill, Chapel Hill, NC 27599-2200
    Charlotte, Charlotte, NC 28223
    Greensboro, Greensboro, NC 27412-5001
    Wilmington, Wilmington, NC 28403-3297
University of North Dakota
    Grand Forks, Grand Forks, ND 58202
    Lake Region, Devils Lake, ND 58301
    Williston, Williston, ND 58801-1326
University of North Florida, Jacksonville, FL 32216
University of North Texas, Denton, TX 76203-3797
University of Northern Colorado, Greeley, CO 80639
University of Northern Iowa, Cedar Falls, IA 50614-0018
University of Notre Dame, Notre Dame, IN 46556
University of Oklahoma
    Health Sciences Center, Oklahoma City, OK 73190
    Norman, Norman, OK 73069-0520
University of Oregon, Eugene, OR 97403-1217
University of Osteopathic Medicine and Health Sciences, Des Moines, IA 50312
University of the Ozarks, Clarksville, AR 72830
University of the Pacific, Stockton, CA 95211
University of Pennsylvania, Philadelphia, PA 19104-6376
University of Phoenix, Phoenix, AZ 85040
University of Pittsburgh
    Bradford, Bradford, PA 16701-2898
    Greensburg, Greensburg, PA 15601-5898
    Johnstown, Johnstown, PA 15904
    Pittsburgh, Pittsburgh, PA 15260
    Titusville, Titusville, PA 16354
University of Portland, Portland, OR 97203-5798
University of Puerto Rico
    Aguadilla, Aguadilla, PR 00604
    Arecibo Campus, Arecibo, PR 00613
    Bayamon Technological University College, Bayamon, PR 00619-1919
    Carolina Regional College, Carolina, PR 00628-4800
    Cayey University College, Cayey, PR 00633
    Humacao University College, Humacao, PR 00661
    La Montana Regional College, Utuado, PR 00761
    Mayaguez Campus, Mayaguez, PR 00709
    Medical Sciences Campus, Rio Piedras, PR 00936
    Ponce Technological University College, Ponce, PR 00732
    Rio Piedras Campus, Rio Piedras, PR 00931
University of Puget Sound, Tacoma, WA 98416
University of Redlands, Redlands, CA 92373-0999
University of Rhode Island, Kingston, RI 02881-0806
University of Richmond, Richmond, VA 23173
University of Rio Grande, Rio Grande, OH 45674
University of Rochester, Rochester, NY 14627-9998
University of the Sacred Heart, Santurce, PR 00914
University of St. Thomas, St. Paul, MN 55105-1096
University of St. Thomas, Houston, TX 77006
University of San Diego, San Diego, CA 92110
University of San Francisco, San Francisco, CA 94117-1080
University of Science and Arts of Oklahoma, Chickasha, OK 73018
University of Scranton, Scranton, PA 18510-2192
University of the South, Sewanee, TN 37375-4004
University of South Alabama, Mobile, AL 36688

University of South Carolina
    Aiken, Aiken, SC 29801
    Beaufort, Beaufort, SC 29902
    Coastal Carolina College, Conway, SC 29526
    Columbia, Columbia, SC 29208
    Lancaster, Lancaster, SC 29721
    Salkehatchie University Campus, Allendale, SC 29810
    Spartanburg, Spartanburg, SC 29303
    Sumter, Sumter, SC 29150
    Union, Union, SC 29379
University of South Dakota, Vermillion, SD 57069-2390
University of South Florida, Tampa, FL 33620-6900
University of Southern California, Los Angeles, CA 90089-0911
University of Southern Colorado, Pueblo, CO 81001
University of Southern Indiana, Evansville, IN 47712
University of Southern Maine, Portland, ME 04103
University of Southern Mississippi, Hattiesburg, MS 39406
University of Southwestern Louisiana, Lafayette, LA 70504
University of the State of New York: Regents College, Albany, NY 12203
University of Tampa, Tampa, FL 33606
University of Tennessee
    Chattanooga, Chattanooga, TN 37403
    Knoxville, Knoxville, TN 37996-0230
    Martin, Martin, TN 38238
    Memphis, Memphis, TN 38163
University of Texas
    Arlington, Arlington, TX 76019
    Austin, Austin, TX 78712-1159
    Dallas, Richardson, TX 75083-0688
    El Paso, El Paso, TX 79968
    Health Science Center at Houston, Houston, TX 77225
    Health Science Center at San Antonio, San Antonio, TX 78284-7702
    Medical Branch at Galveston, Galveston, TX 77550-2764
    Pan American, Edinburg, TX 78539
    Permian Basin, Odessa, TX 79762
    San Antonio, San Antonio, TX 78285
    Southwestern Medical Center at Dallas Southwestern Allied Health Sciences School, Dallas, TX 75235-9024
    Tyler, Tyler, TX 75701-6699
University of Toledo, Toledo, OH 43606-3398
University of Tulsa, Tulsa, OK 74104
University of Utah, Salt Lake City, UT 84112
University of Vermont, Burlington, VT 05401-3596
University of the Virgin Islands, Charlotte Amalie, VI 00802
University of Virginia, Charlottesville, VA 22906
University of Washington, Seattle, WA 98195
University of West Florida, Pensacola, FL 32514-5750
University of West Los Angeles, Los Angeles, CA 90066
University of Wisconsin
    Eau Claire, Eau Claire, WI 54701
    Green Bay, Green Bay, WI 54311-7001
    La Crosse, La Crosse, WI 54601
    Madison, Madison, WI 53706-1490
    Milwaukee, Milwaukee, WI 53201
    Oshkosh, Oshkosh, WI 54901
    Parkside, Kenosha, WI 53141-2000
    Platteville, Platteville, WI 53818
    River Falls, River Falls, WI 54022
    Stevens Point, Stevens Point, WI 54481
    Stout, Menomonie, WI 54751
    Superior, Superior, WI 54880
    Whitewater, Whitewater, WI 53190-1791
University of Wisconsin Center
    Baraboo/Sauk County, Baraboo, WI 53913-1098
    Barron County, Rice Lake, WI 54868
    Fond du Lac, Fond du Lac, WI 54935-2998
    Fox Valley, Menasha, WI 54952
    Manitowoc County, Manitowoc, WI 54220-6699
    Marathon County, Wausau, WI 54401-5396
    Marinette County, Marinette, WI 54143
    Marshfield/Wood County, Marshfield, WI 54449
    Richland, Richland Center, WI 53581
    Rock County, Janesville, WI 53546
    Sheboygan County, Sheboygan, WI 53081-4789
    Washington County, West Bend, WI 53095
    Waukesha, Waukesha, WI 53188-1628
University of Wyoming, Laramie, WY 82071-3435
Upper Iowa University, Fayette, IA 52142-1859
Upsala College, East Orange, NJ 07019
Urbana University, Urbana, OH 43078
Ursinus College, Collegeville, PA 19426
Ursuline College, Pepper Pike, OH 44124-4398

Utah State University, Logan, UT 84322-1600
Utah Valley Community College, Orem, UT 84058
Utica College of Syracuse University, Utica, NY 13502-4892
Utica School of Commerce, Utica, NY 13501
Valdosta State College, Valdosta, GA 31698
Valencia Community College, Orlando, FL 32802-3028
Valley City State University, Valley City, ND 58072
Valley Forge Christian College, Phoenixville, PA 19460
Valparaiso University, Valparaiso, IN 46383-9978
Vance-Granville Community College, Henderson, NC 27536
Vanderbilt University, Nashville, TN 37212-9976
VanderCook College of Music, Chicago, IL 60616
Vassar College, Poughkeepsie, NY 12601
Vennard College, University Park, IA 52595
Ventura College, Ventura, CA 93003
Vermilion Community College, Ely, MN 55731-9989
Vermont Technical College, Randolph Center, VT 05061
Vernon Regional Junior College, Vernon, TX 76384-4092
Victor Valley College, Victorville, CA 92392-9699
Victoria College, Victoria, TX 77901
Villa Julie College, Stevenson, MD 21153
Villa Maria College of Buffalo, Buffalo, NY 14225-3999
Villanova University, Villanova, PA 19085-1672
Vincennes University, Vincennes, IN 47591
Virginia Commonwealth University, Richmond, VA 23284
Virginia Highlands Community College, Abingdon, VA 24210
Virginia Intermont College, Bristol, VA 24201-4298
Virginia Marti College of Fashion and Art, Lakewood, OH 44107
Virginia Military Institute, Lexington, VA 24450-9967
Virginia Polytechnic Institute and State University, Blacksburg, VA 24061-0202
Virginia State University, Petersburg, VA 23803
Virginia Union University, Richmond, VA 23220
Virginia Wesleyan College, Norfolk, VA 23502
Virginia Western Community College, Roanoke, VA 24038
Vista Community College, Berkeley, CA 94704
Viterbo College, La Crosse, WI 54601
Volunteer State Community College, Gallatin, TN 37066-3188
Voorhees College, Denmark, SC 29042
Wabash College, Crawfordsville, IN 47933-0352
Wadhams Hall Seminary-College, Ogdensburg, NY 13669-9308
Wagner College, Staten Island, NY 10301-4495
Wake Forest University, Winston-Salem, NC 27109
Wake Technical Community College, Raleigh, NC 27603
Waldorf College, Forest City, IA 50436
Walker College, Jasper, AL 35501
Walker State Technical College, Sumiton, AL 35148
Walla Walla College, College Place, WA 99324-1198
Walla Walla Community College, Walla Walla, WA 99362-9267
Wallace State Community College at Hanceville, Hanceville, AL 35077-9080
Walsh College, North Canton, OH 44720
Walsh College of Accountancy and Business Administration, Troy, MI 48007-7006
Walters State Community College, Morristown, TN 37813-6899
Warner Pacific College, Portland, OR 97215
Warner Southern College, Lake Wales, FL 33853
Warren County Community College, Washington, NJ 07882-9605
Warren Wilson College, Swannanoa, NC 28778-2099
Wartburg College, Waverly, IA 50677
Washburn University of Topeka, Topeka, KS 66621
Washington Bible College, Lanham, MD 20706
Washington College, Chestertown, MD 21620
Washington and Jefferson College, Washington, PA 15301
Washington and Lee University, Lexington, VA 24450
Washington State Community College, Marietta, OH 45750
Washington State University, Pullman, WA 99164-1036
Washington University, St. Louis, MO 63130
Washtenaw Community College, Ann Arbor, MI 48106-0978
Waterbury State Technical College, Waterbury, CT 06708-3089
Watterson College, Louisville, KY 40218
Waubonsee Community College, Sugar Grove, IL 60554
Waukesha County Technical College, Pewaukee, WI 53072
Waycross College, Waycross, GA 31501
Wayland Baptist University, Plainview, TX 79072
Wayne Community College, Goldsboro, NC 27533-8002
Wayne County Community College, Detroit, MI 48226
Wayne State College, Wayne, NE 68787
Wayne State University, Detroit, MI 48202
Waynesburg College, Waynesburg, PA 15370
Weatherford College, Weatherford, TX 76086
Webber College, Babson Park, FL 33827
Weber State University, Ogden, UT 84408-1015

Webster University, Webster Groves, MO 63119-3194
Wellesley College, Wellesley, MA 02181
Wells College, Aurora, NY 13026
Wenatchee Valley College, Wenatchee, WA 98801
Wentworth Institute of Technology, Boston, MA 02115
Wesley College, Florence, MS 39073-0070
Wesley College, Dover, DE 19901-3875
Wesleyan College, Macon, GA 31297-4299
Wesleyan University, Middletown, CT 06457
West Chester University of Pennsylvania, West Chester, PA 19383
West Coast Christian College, Fresno, CA 93710
West Coast University, Los Angeles, CA 90020-1765
West Georgia College, Carrollton, GA 30118-0001
West Hills College, Coalinga, CA 93210
West Liberty State College, West Liberty, WV 26074
West Los Angeles College, Culver City, CA 90230
West Shore Community College, Scottville, MI 49454-0277
West Side Institute of Technology, Cleveland, OH 44102
West Suburban College of Nursing, Oak Park, IL 60302
West Texas State University, Canyon, TX 79016
West Valley College, Saratoga, CA 95070
West Virginia Institute of Technology, Montgomery, WV 25136-2436
West Virginia Northern Community College, Wheeling, WV 26003
West Virginia State College, Institute, WV 25112-0335
West Virginia University
    Morgantown, Morgantown, WV 26506-6009
    Parkersburg, Parkersburg, WV 26101-9577
West Virginia Wesleyan College, Buckhannon, WV 26201-2998
Westark Community College, Fort Smith, AR 72913-3649
Westbrook College, Portland, ME 04103
Westchester Business Institute, White Plains, NY 10602
Westchester Community College, Valhalla, NY 10595
Western Baptist College, Salem, OR 97301
Western Carolina University, Cullowhee, NC 28723
Western Connecticut State University, Danbury, CT 06810
Western Dakota Vocational Technical Institute, Rapid City, SD 57701
Western Illinois University, Macomb, IL 61455
Western International University, Phoenix, AZ 85021
Western Iowa Tech Community College, Sioux City, IA 51102
Western Kentucky University, Bowling Green, KY 42101
Western Maryland College, Westminster, MD 21157
Western Michigan University, Kalamazoo, MI 49008
Western Montana College of the University of Montana, Dillon, MT 59725
Western Nebraska Community College
    Scottsbluff Campus, Scottsbluff, NE 69361
    Sidney Campus, Sidney, NE 69162
Western Nevada Community College, Carson City, NV 89703
Western New England College, Springfield, MA 01119-2688
Western New Mexico University, Silver City, NM 88062
Western Oklahoma State College, Altus, OK 73521
Western Oregon State College, Monmouth, OR 97361-1394
Western Piedmont Community College, Morganton, NC 28655
Western State College of Colorado, Gunnison, CO 81231
Western State University College of Law
    Orange County, Fullerton, CA 92631
    San Diego, San Diego, CA 92110
Western Texas College, Snyder, TX 79549
Western Washington University, Bellingham, WA 98225
Western Wisconsin Technical College, La Crosse, WI 54602-0908
Western Wyoming Community College, Rock Springs, WY 82901
Westfield State College, Westfield, MA 01086
Westminster Choir College, Princeton, NJ 08540
Westminster College, New Wilmington, PA 16172-0001
Westminster College, Fulton, MO 65251-1299
Westminster College of Salt Lake City, Salt Lake City, UT 84105
Westmont College, Santa Barbara, CA 93108-1099
Westmoreland County Community College, Youngwood, PA 15697
Wharton County Junior College, Wharton, TX 77488-0080
Whatcom Community College, Bellingham, WA 98226
Wheaton College, Wheaton, IL 60187
Wheaton College, Norton, MA 02766
Wheeling Jesuit College, Wheeling, WV 26003
Wheelock College, Boston, MA 02215
White Pines College, Chester, NH 03036
Whitman College, Walla Walla, WA 99362-2085
Whittier College, Whittier, CA 90608
Whitworth College, Spokane, WA 99251-0002
Wichita State University, Wichita, KS 67208-1595
Widener University, Chester, PA 19013
Wilberforce University, Wilberforce, OH 45384-1091
Wiley College, Marshall, TX 75670
Wilkes Community College, Wilkesboro, NC 28697-0120

Wilkes University, Wilkes-Barre, PA 18766
Willamette University, Salem, OR 97301-3922
William Carey College, Hattiesburg, MS 39401
William Jennings Bryan College, Dayton, TN 37321-7000
William Jewell College, Liberty, MO 64068
William Paterson College of New Jersey, Wayne, NJ 07470
William Penn College, Oskaloosa, IA 52577
William Rainey Harper College, Palatine, IL 60067-7398
William Smith College, Geneva, NY 14456-3381
William Tyndale College, Farmington Hills, MI 48331-9985
William Woods College, Fulton, MO 65251-1098
Williams Baptist College, Walnut Ridge, AR 72476
Williams College, Williamstown, MA 01267
Williamsburg Technical College, Kingstree, SC 29556
Willmar Community College, Willmar, MN 56201
Willmar Technical College, Willmar, MN 56201
Wilmington College, Wilmington, OH 45177
Wilmington College, New Castle, DE 19720
Wilson College, Chambersburg, PA 17201-1285
Wilson Technical Community College, Wilson, NC 27893
Wingate College, Wingate, NC 28174-0157
Winona State University, Winona, MN 55987
Winston-Salem State University, Winston-Salem, NC 27110
Winthrop College, Rock Hill, SC 29733
Wisconsin Indianhead Technical College, Shell Lake, WI 54871
Wisconsin Lutheran College, Milwaukee, WI 53226
Wisconsin School of Electronics, Madison, WI 53704
Wittenberg University, Springfield, OH 45501
Wofford College, Spartanburg, SC 29303-3840
Wood Junior College, Mathiston, MS 39752
Wood School, New York, NY 10016-0190
Woodbury University, Burbank, CA 91510-7846
Worcester Polytechnic Institute, Worcester, MA 01609-2280
Worcester State College, Worcester, MA 01602-2597
World College West, Petaluma, CA 94952
Worthington Community College, Worthington, MN 56187
Wor-Wic Tech Community College, Salisbury, MD 21801
Wright State University
        Dayton, Dayton, OH 45435
        Lake Campus, Celina, OH 45822
Wytheville Community College, Wytheville, VA 24382
Xavier University, Cincinnati, OH 45207
Xavier University of Louisiana, New Orleans, LA 70125
Yakima Valley Community College, Yakima, WA 98907
Yale University, New Haven, CT 06520
Yavapai College, Prescott, AZ 86301
Yeshiva Derech Chaim, Brooklyn, NY 11218
Yeshiva Gedolah Zichron Moshe, South Fallsburg, NY 12779
Yeshiva Karlin Stolin Beth Aron Y'Israel Rabbinical Institute, Brooklyn, NY
    11204-9961
Yeshiva of Nitra Rabbinical College, Mt. Kisco, NY 11211
Yeshiva Ohr Elchonon Chabad/West Coast Talmudical Seminary, Los
    Angeles, CA 90046
Yeshiva Toras Chaim Talmudical Seminary, Denver, CO 80204
Yeshiva University, New York, NY 10033-3299
York College, York, NE 68467-2699
York College of Pennsylvania, York, PA 17403-3426
York Technical College, Rock Hill, SC 29730
Young Harris College, Young Harris, GA 30582-0116
Youngstown State University, Youngstown, OH 44555-0001
Yuba College, Marysville, CA 95901

3. Colleges that offer tuition and/or fee waivers and special tuition payment plans

Tuition and/or fee waiver for adult students

Alabama
Birmingham-Southern College
Community College of the Air Force
Faulkner University

Arizona
Rio Salado Community College
Western International University

Arkansas
John Brown University
North Arkansas Community College

California
California State University: Dominguez Hills
City College of San Francisco
Compton Community College
Cosumnes River College
D-Q University
Feather River College
Fresno City College
Fullerton College
Napa Valley College
Orange Coast College
Oxnard College
Porterville College

Colorado
Aims Community College
Regis University

Connecticut
Teikyo-Post University
Trinity College

District of Columbia
Mount Vernon College

Florida
Webber College

Georgia
Wesleyan College

Hawaii
University of Hawaii at Manoa

Idaho
College of Idaho

Illinois
KAES College
Northeastern Illinois University

Shimer College
South Suburban College of Cook County
Springfield College in Illinois

Indiana
Anderson University
Calumet College of St. Joseph
Huntington College
Indiana Vocational Technical College: Columbus
St. Francis College

Iowa
Coe College
Northwestern College
St. Ambrose University
Simpson College

Kansas
Fort Hays State University
Kansas Newman College
Kansas Wesleyan University
St. Mary College
Sterling College
Tabor College

Kentucky
Brescia College
Campbellsville College
Kentucky State University
University of Kentucky

Maryland
Harford Community College
Ner Israel Rabbinical College
Western Maryland College

Massachusetts
Atlantic Union College
Bay Path College
Berkshire Community College
Massasoit Community College
Middlesex Community College
Pine Manor College
Simmons College
Wheaton College

Michigan
Aquinas College
Lake Michigan College
Mid Michigan Community College

Minnesota
Austin Community College
Concordia College: Moorhead
Fergus Falls Community College
St. Olaf College
University of Minnesota: Crookston
Worthington Community College

Missouri
St. Louis University
William Jewell College

Nebraska
Chadron State College
College of St. Mary
Hastings College
Metropolitan Community College

New Jersey
Felician College

New York
Long Island University: Southampton Campus
Nyack College

North Carolina
Campbell University
Salem College

Ohio
Cleveland College of Jewish Studies
Cleveland Institute of Electronics
Urbana University

Oklahoma
Cameron University
Central State University
Flaming Rainbow University
Oklahoma State University: Oklahoma City
Phillips University
Southeastern Oklahoma State University

Oregon
Central Oregon Community College

Pennsylvania
Chatham College
Eastern College
Immaculata College
Juniata College
Keystone Junior College
Mercyhurst College
Messiah College
Rosemont College
St. Charles Borromeo Seminary
St. Francis College
Seton Hill College
Thiel College

South Carolina
Coker College
Spartanburg Methodist College

Tennessee
Carson-Newman College
Freed-Hardeman University
Jackson State Community College
Lambuth College
William Jennings Bryan College

Texas
Concordia Lutheran College

Virginia
Bluefield College
Randolph-Macon Woman's College
Sweet Briar College

Washington
Gonzaga University
Lower Columbia College
North Seattle Community College

West Virginia
Fairmont State College

Wisconsin
Mount Senario College
Viterbo College

Wyoming
Eastern Wyoming College

Tuition and/or fee waiver for children of alumni

Arkansas
Arkansas State University

California
Brooks Institute of Photography
California Baptist College
Compton Community College
D-Q University
LIFE Bible College
Mount St. Mary's College
Porterville College
University of La Verne

Florida
Florida Bible College
Webber College

Georgia
Shorter College
Wesleyan College

Idaho

College of Idaho

Illinois

Chicago State University
Illinois Benedictine College
Lewis University
MacMurray College
Mundelein College
Rockford College

Indiana

Indiana State University
Indiana Vocational Technical
    College: Columbus
Manchester College
Marian College
Valparaiso University

Iowa

Clarke College
Morningside College
Northwestern College
St. Ambrose University
Teikyo Marycrest University
Teikyo Westmar University
Upper Iowa University

Kansas

Kansas Newman College
Kansas Wesleyan University

Kentucky

Brescia College
Cumberland College
Thomas More College
Union College
University of Kentucky
Western Kentucky University

Louisiana

Grambling State University
Louisiana State University
    Medical Center
    Shreveport
Louisiana State University and
    Agricultural and Mechanical
    College
Louisiana Tech University
McNeese State University
University of New Orleans

Maine

University of New England

Maryland

Ner Israel Rabbinical College

Massachusetts

Curry College
Eastern Nazarene College
Pine Manor College
Wheelock College

Michigan

Aquinas College
Concordia College
Detroit College of Business
Michigan Christian College
Michigan Technological University
University of Detroit Mercy
Wayne State University

Mississippi

Delta State University
Mississippi State University
Mississippi University for Women
University of Mississippi

Missouri

Avila College
Columbia College

Harris Stowe State College
Northwest Missouri State
    University
University of Missouri: Rolla
Westminster College
William Jewell College

Nebraska

College of St. Mary
Concordia College

Nevada

University of Nevada: Reno

New Hampshire

Rivier College
White Pines College

New Jersey

Bloomfield College

New Mexico

College of the Southwest

New York

Adelphi University
Boricua College
Daemen College
Dowling College
Iona College
Long Island University: Brooklyn
    Campus
St. Joseph's College

Ohio

Ashland University
Cedarville College
Cincinnati Technical College
College of Mount St. Joseph
Defiance College
Kent State University
Malone College
University of Findlay
Walsh College
Wilmington College

Oklahoma

Central State University
Hillsdale Free Will Baptist College
Oklahoma Baptist University
Oklahoma Christian University of
    Science and Arts
Southeastern Oklahoma State
    University

Oregon

Bassist College
Warner Pacific College

Pennsylvania

Eastern College
Keystone Junior College
Lancaster Bible College
Mercyhurst College
Peirce Junior College
Philadelphia College of Bible
Pinebrook Junior College
Point Park College
University of the Arts
Wilkes University
Wilson College

Puerto Rico

ICPR Junior College

Rhode Island

Salve Regina College

South Carolina

North Greenville College
Spartanburg Methodist College
University of South Carolina

South Dakota

Black Hills State University
Northern State University
South Dakota School of Mines and
    Technology

Tennessee

Crichton College
Johnson Bible College
William Jennings Bryan College

Texas

Dallas Baptist University
University of Mary Hardin-Baylor
University of St. Thomas

Virginia

Marymount University

Washington

Gonzaga University
Pacific Lutheran University

West Virginia

Appalachian Bible College
Fairmont State College

Wisconsin

Concordia University Wisconsin

Wyoming

Eastern Wyoming College
University of Wyoming

Tuition and/or fee waiver
for senior citizens

Alabama

Alabama Agricultural and
    Mechanical University
Alabama Aviation and Technical
    College
Athens State College
Bessemer State Technical College
Bishop State Community College
Brewer State Junior College
Central Alabama Community
    College: Alexander City Campus
Douglas MacArthur State Technical
    College
Enterprise State Junior College
Faulkner University
Gadsden State Community College
J. F. Drake State Technical College
James H. Faulkner State Junior
    College
Jefferson Davis State Junior College
Jefferson State Community College
John C. Calhoun State Community
    College
Lawson State Community College
Lurleen B. Wallace State Junior
    College
Northeast Alabama State Junior
    College
Northwest Alabama Community
    College
Patrick Henry State Junior College
Reid State Technical College
Shelton State Community College
Shoals Community College
Snead State Junior College
Southern Union State Junior
    College
Trenholm State Technical College
Walker State Technical College
Wallace State Community College
    at Hanceville

Alaska

Alaska Pacific University
Prince William Sound Community
    College
Sheldon Jackson College
University of Alaska
    Anchorage
    Fairbanks
    Southeast

Arizona

Central Arizona College
Cochise College
Gateway Community College
Mohave Community College
Rio Salado Community College
Southwestern College
Yavapai College

Arkansas

Arkansas Baptist College
Arkansas State University
    Beebe Branch
    Jonesboro
Arkansas Tech University
East Arkansas Community College
Garland County Community
    College
Harding University
Henderson State University
John Brown University
Mississippi County Community
    College
North Arkansas Community College
Phillips County Community College
Southern Arkansas University
    El Dorado Branch
    Magnolia
    Technical Branch
University of Arkansas
    Fayetteville
    Little Rock
    Medical Sciences
    Monticello
    Pine Bluff
University of Central Arkansas
Westark Community College
Williams Baptist College

California

Azusa Pacific University
California Polytechnic State
    University: San Luis Obispo
California State Polytechnic
    University: Pomona
California State University
    Bakersfield
    Chico
    Dominguez Hills
    Fresno
    Fullerton
    Hayward
    Long Beach
    Los Angeles
    Northridge
    Sacramento
    San Bernardino
    San Marcos
    Stanislaus
City College of San Francisco
Coastline Community College
College of Notre Dame
Compton Community College
De Anza College
D-Q University
Fullerton College
Humboldt State University
Los Angeles Harbor College
Pacific Christian College
Point Loma Nazarene College
Porterville College
San Diego State University

San Jose State University
Sonoma State University
University of California: Santa Cruz
West Coast Christian College
West Valley College
Whittier College

Colorado

Adams State College
Aims Community College
Arapahoe Community College
Colorado Northwestern Community
College
Community College of Denver
Front Range Community College
Lamar Community College
Metropolitan State College of
Denver
Morgan Community College
Naropa Institute
Pikes Peak Community College
Pueblo Community College
Red Rocks Community College
University of Colorado at Boulder
University of Northern Colorado

Connecticut

Asnuntuck Community College
Central Connecticut State
University
Eastern Connecticut State
University
Greater Hartford Community
College
Greater New Haven State Technical
College
Hartford College for Women
Hartford State Technical College
Housatonic Community College
Mattatuck Community College
Middlesex Community College
Mohegan Community College
Northwestern Connecticut
Community College
Norwalk Community College
Norwalk State Technical College
Quinebaug Valley Community
College
Quinnipiac College
South Central Community College
Southern Connecticut State
University
Teikyo-Post University
Thames Valley State Technical
College
Tunxis Community College
University of Connecticut
Waterbury State Technical College
Western Connecticut State
University

Delaware

Delaware State College
Delaware Technical and
Community College
Southern Campus
Stanton/Wilmington Campus
Terry Campus

Florida

Brevard Community College
Broward Community College
Daytona Beach Community College
Edison Community College
Florida Agricultural and Mechanical
University
Florida Atlantic University
Florida Institute of Technology
Florida International University
Florida State University
Hillsborough Community College
Lake City Community College

Lake-Sumter Community College
North Florida Junior College
Palm Beach Atlantic College
Palm Beach Community College
St. Petersburg Junior College
Santa Fe Community College
Seminole Community College
Tallahassee Community College
University of Central Florida
University of North Florida
University of South Florida
Valencia Community College
Webber College

Georgia

Abraham Baldwin Agricultural
College
Albany State College
Armstrong State College
Atlanta Metropolitan College
Augusta College
Bainbridge College
Berry College
Brunswick College
Chattahoochee Technical Institute
Clayton State College
Columbus College
Darton College
DeKalb College
DeKalb Technical Institute
Floyd College
Fort Valley State College
Georgia College
Georgia Southwestern College
Georgia State University
Gordon College
Kennesaw State College
LaGrange College
Macon College
Middle Georgia College
North Georgia College
Savannah State College
Shorter College
Southern College of Technology
Thomas College
Toccoa Falls College
University of Georgia
Valdosta State College
Waycross College
Wesleyan College
West Georgia College

Hawaii

University of Hawaii
Kauai Community College
Leeward Community College
Manoa
Maui Community College
West Oahu
Windward Community College

Idaho

Boise Bible College
College of Idaho
College of Southern Idaho
Idaho State University
Lewis Clark State College
North Idaho College
Northwest Nazarene College

Illinois

American Academy of Art
Aurora University
Belleville Area College
Black Hawk College
East Campus
Moline
Bradley University
Carl Sandburg College
Chicago State University

City Colleges of Chicago
Chicago City-Wide College
Harold Washington College
Richard J. Daley College
Wright College
College of DuPage
College of Lake County
Eastern Illinois University
Elgin Community College
Elmhurst College
Governors State University
Greenville College
Highland Community College
Illinois Central College
Illinois College
Illinois Eastern Community
Colleges
Frontier Community College
Lincoln Trail College
Olney Central College
Wabash Valley College
Illinois State University
Joliet Junior College
KAES College
Kankakee Community College
Kaskaskia College
Kendall College
Kishwaukee College
Lake Land College
Lewis and Clark Community
College
Loyola University of Chicago
MacMurray College
McHenry County College
Moraine Valley Community College
Morton College
Northeastern Illinois University
Northern Illinois University
Oakton Community College
Parkland College
Prairie State College
Quincy College
Rend Lake College
Richland Community College
Roosevelt University
Sangamon State University
Sauk Valley Community College
South Suburban College of Cook
County
Southeastern Illinois College
Southern Illinois University
Carbondale
Edwardsville
Spoon River College
Springfield College in Illinois
State Community College
Trinity Christian College
University of Illinois
Chicago
Urbana-Champaign
Waubonsee Community College
Western Illinois University
William Rainey Harper College

Indiana

Anderson University
Ball State University
Calumet College of St. Joseph
Franklin College
Huntington College
Indiana State University
Indiana Vocational Technical
College
Columbus
Eastcentral
Northwest
Marian College
Martin University
Oakland City College
Purdue University: North Central
Campus
St. Francis College

University of Evansville
University of Indianapolis
University of Southern Indiana
Vincennes University

Iowa

Clarke College
Des Moines Area Community
College
Drake University
Emmaus Bible College
Graceland College
Indian Hills Community College
Iowa Wesleyan College
Iowa Western Community College
Kirkwood Community College
Maharishi International University
Morningside College
Mount St. Clare College
Muscatine Community College
St. Ambrose University
Simpson College
Teikyo Westmar University

Kansas

Barton County Community College
Brown Mackie College
Butler County Community College
Cowley County Community College
Donnelly College
Emporia State University
Garden City Community College
Hesston College
Hutchinson Community College
Independence Community College
Johnson County Community
College
Kansas Newman College
Kansas Wesleyan University
Labette Community College
Manhattan Christian College
Mid-America Nazarene College
Neosho County Community College
St. Mary College
St. Mary of the Plains College
Southwestern College
Sterling College
Tabor College
Washburn University of Topeka
Wichita State University

Kentucky

Asbury College
Bellarmine College
Brescia College
Campbellsville College
Cumberland College
Eastern Kentucky University
Elizabethtown Community College
Jefferson Community College
Kentucky State University
Kentucky Wesleyan College
Lees College
Lexington Community College
Madisonville Community College
Maysville Community College
Mid-Continent Baptist Bible College
Midway College
Morehead State University
Murray State University
Northern Kentucky University
Paducah Community College
Pikeville College
Prestonburg Community College
St. Catharine College
Somerset Community College
Southeast Community College
Spalding University
Sue Bennett College
Union College
University of Kentucky
University of Louisville

Western Kentucky University

Louisiana

Bossier Parish Community College
Grambling State University
Louisiana College
Louisiana State University
    Alexandria
    Eunice
    Medical Center
    Shreveport
Louisiana State University and
   Agricultural and Mechanical
   College
Louisiana Tech University
Loyola University
McNeese State University
Nicholls State University
Northeast Louisiana University
Northwestern State University
Our Lady of Holy Cross College
St. Bernard Parish Community
   College
Southeastern Louisiana University
Southern University in Shreveport
Southern University and
   Agricultural and Mechanical
   College
University of New Orleans
University of Southwestern
   Louisiana
Xavier University of Louisiana

Maine

Colby College
Eastern Maine Technical College
Husson College
Unity College
University of Maine
    Augusta
    Farmington
    Fort Kent
    Machias
    Orono
    Presque Isle
University of Southern Maine

Maryland

Allegany Community College
Anne Arundel Community College
Baltimore Hebrew University
Bowie State University
Catonsville Community College
Cecil Community College
Chesapeake College
Coppin State College
Dundalk Community College
Essex Community College
Frederick Community College
Frostburg State University
Garrett Community College
Hagerstown Junior College
Harford Community College
Hood College
Howard Community College
Maryland Institute College of Art
Montgomery College
   Germantown Campus
   Rockville Campus
   Takoma Park Campus
Morgan State University
Mount St. Mary's College
New Community College of
   Baltimore
St. Mary's College of Maryland
Salisbury State University
Towson State University
University of Baltimore

University of Maryland
   Baltimore County
   College Park
   Eastern Shore
   University College
Wor-Wic Tech Community College

Massachusetts

American International College
Anna Maria College for Men and
   Women
Atlantic Union College
Becker College
    Leicester Campus
    Worcester Campus
Bentley College
Berkshire Community College
Boston University
Bridgewater State College
Bristol Community College
Bunker Hill Community College
Cape Cod Community College
Eastern Nazarene College
Elms College
Fitchburg State College
Framingham State College
Greenfield Community College
Holyoke Community College
Massachusetts Bay Community
   College
Massachusetts College of Art
Massasoit Community College
Merrimack College
Mount Wachusett Community
   College
Nichols College
North Adams State College
North Shore Community College
Northeastern University
Northern Essex Community College
Quincy College
Quinsigamond Community College
Salem State College
Southeastern Massachusetts
   University
Springfield Technical Community
   College
Stonehill College
Suffolk University
University of Lowell
University of Massachusetts
    Amherst
    Boston
Western New England College
Westfield State College
Worcester State College

Michigan

Alpena Community College
Aquinas College
Bay de Noc Community College
Charles Stewart Mott Community
   College
Delta College
Glen Oaks Community College
Gogebic Community College
Henry Ford Community College
Highland Park Community College
Jackson Community College
Jordan College
Kalamazoo Valley Community
   College
Kellogg Community College
Kirtland Community College
Lake Michigan College
Lake Superior State University
Madonna University
Marygrove College
Michigan Christian College
Michigan Technological University
Mid Michigan Community College

Monroe County Community
   College
Montcalm Community College
Muskegon Community College
North Central Michigan College
Northern Michigan University
Reformed Bible College
Saginaw Valley State University
St. Clair County Community
   College
Schoolcraft College
Southwestern Michigan College
University of Michigan
   Dearborn
   Flint
Wayne County Community College
Wayne State University
West Shore Community College
Western Michigan University
William Tyndale College

Minnesota

Alexandria Technical College
Augsburg College
Austin Community College
Bemidji State University
Bethel College
Brainerd Community College
College of St. Catherine: St.
   Catherine Campus
College of St. Scholastica
Concordia College: St. Paul
Dakota County Technical College
Fergus Falls Community College
Itasca Community College:
   Arrowhead Region
Lakewood Community College
Mankato State University
Mesabi Community College:
   Arrowhead Region
Metropolitan State University
Minneapolis Community College
Minnesota Bible College
Moorhead State University
Normandale Community College
North Central Bible College
North Hennepin Community
   College
Northwestern College
Rainy River Community College
Rochester Community College
St. Olaf College
St. Paul Technical College
Southwest State University
University of Minnesota
   Duluth
   Twin Cities
University of St. Thomas
Winona State University
Worthington Community College

Mississippi

Belhaven College
Copiah-Lincoln Community College
Delta State University
East Central Community College
Hinds Community College
Jones County Junior College
Meridian Community College
Mississippi Gulf Coast Community
   College
    Jackson County Campus
    Jefferson Davis Campus
    Perkinston
Northeast Mississippi Community
   College
Northwest Mississippi Community
   College
Pearl River Community College
Southeastern Baptist College
Southwest Mississippi Community
   College

University of Mississippi
Wood Junior College

Missouri

Avila College
Central Methodist College
Columbia College
Culver-Stockton College
East Central College
Fontbonne College
Lincoln University
Lindenwood College
Longview Community College
Maple Woods Community College
Maryville College—St. Louis
Missouri Southern State College
Missouri Western State College
Moberly Area Community College
North Central Missouri College
Northeast Missouri State University
Northwest Missouri State
   University
Park College
Penn Valley Community College
St. Louis Community College
   Forest Park
   Meramec
Southeast Missouri State University
Southwest Missouri State University
State Fair Community College
William Jewell College

Montana

Carroll College
College of Great Falls
Dawson Community College
Eastern Montana College
Flathead Valley Community College
Miles Community College
Montana College of Mineral
   Science and Technology
University of Montana

Nebraska

Chadron State College
Doane College
Grace College of the Bible
McCook Community College
Metropolitan Community College
Mid Plains Community College
Nebraska Wesleyan University
Southeast Community College
   Beatrice Campus
   Lincoln Campus
Western Nebraska Community
   College
    Scottsbluff Campus
    Sidney Campus

Nevada

Northern Nevada Community
   College
University of Nevada
   Las Vegas
   Reno
Western Nevada Community
   College

New Hampshire

Franklin Pierce College
Hesser College
Keene State College
New England College
New Hampshire College
New Hampshire Technical College
   Claremont
   Laconia
   Manchester
   Nashua
   Stratham
New Hampshire Technical Institute
Notre Dame College

Plymouth State College of the
University System of New
Hampshire
Rivier College
St. Anselm College
University of New Hampshire
Durham
Manchester
White Pines College

New Jersey

Atlantic Community College
Bergen Community College
Bloomfield College
Brookdale Community College
Burlington County College
Caldwell College
Camden County College
Centenary College
College of St. Elizabeth
County College of Morris
Cumberland County College
Drew University
Fairleigh Dickinson University
Edward Williams College
Florham-Madison Campus
Rutherford Campus
Teaneck-Hackensack Campus
Felician College
Georgian Court College
Gloucester County College
Hudson County Community College
Jersey City State College
Kean College of New Jersey
Monmouth College
Montclair State College
Ocean County College
Passaic County Community College
Raritan Valley Community College
Rutgers—The State University of
New Jersey
Camden College of Arts and
Sciences
College of Engineering
College of Nursing
College of Pharmacy
Cook College
Douglass College
Livingston College
Mason Gross School of the
Arts
Newark College of Arts and
Sciences
Rutgers College
University College Camden
University College New
Brunswick
University College Newark
Salem Community College
Stockton State College
Sussex County Community College
Trenton State College
Union County College
Upsala College
Warren County Community College
William Paterson College of New
Jersey

New Mexico

College of Santa Fe
College of the Southwest
Dona Ana Branch Community
College of New Mexico State
University
Eastern New Mexico University
Clovis Community College
Roswell Campus
National College
New Mexico Highlands University
New Mexico Institute of Mining
and Technology

New Mexico State University
Alamogordo
Carlsbad
Las Cruces
Northern New Mexico Community
College
San Juan College
Santa Fe Community College
University of New Mexico: Gallup
Western New Mexico University

New York

Adelphi University
Adirondack Community College
Broome Community College
Cayuga County Community College
Central City Business Institute
City University of New York
Baruch College
Borough of Manhattan
Community College
Brooklyn College
City College
College of Staten Island
Hunter College
John Jay College of Criminal
Justice
Lehman College
Medgar Evers College
New York City Technical
College
Queens College
York College
Clinton Community College
College of Mount St. Vincent
College of New Rochelle
College of St. Rose
Columbia-Greene Community
College
Community College of the Finger
Lakes
Concordia College
Daemen College
Dominican College of Blauvelt
Dowling College
D'Youville College
Erie Community College: North
Campus
Five Towns College
Fulton-Montgomery Community
College
Hofstra University
Houghton College
Iona College
Jamestown Community College
Jefferson Community College
Jewish Theological Seminary of
America
Long Island University
C. W. Post Campus
Southampton Campus
Maria College
Mercy College
Mohawk Valley Community College
Niagara County Community College
Nyack College
Orange County Community College
Pace University
College of White Plains
New York
Pleasantville/Briarcliff
Roberts Wesleyan College
Rockland Community College
Russell Sage College
Sage Junior College of Albany, A
Division of Russell Sage College
St. Bonaventure University
St. John Fisher College
St. John's University
St. Joseph's College: Suffolk
Campus
St. Thomas Aquinas College

Schenectady County Community
College
State University of New York
Albany
Binghamton
Purchase
College of Agriculture and
Technology at Cobleskill
College at Cortland
College at Old Westbury
Institute of Technology at
Utica/Rome
Suffolk County Community College
Eastern Campus
Selden
Western Campus
Sullivan County Community
College
Tompkins-Cortland Community
College
Trocaire College
Ulster County Community College
Utica College of Syracuse
University
Villa Maria College of Buffalo
Wagner College

North Carolina

Alamance Community College
Anson Community College
Appalachian State University
Asheville Buncombe Technical
Community College
Beaufort County Community
College
Belmont Abbey College
Bladen Community College
Blue Ridge Community College
Brunswick Community College
Caldwell Community College and
Technical Institute
Cape Fear Community College
Carteret Community College
Central Carolina Community
College
Cleveland Community College
Coastal Carolina Community
College
College of the Albemarle
Craven Community College
Davidson County Community
College
Durham Technical Community
College
East Carolina University
Edgecombe Community College
Fayetteville Technical Community
College
Forsyth Technical Community
College
Gaston College
Haywood Community College
James Sprunt Community College
Johnston Community College
Lenoir-Rhyne College
Martin Community College
Mayland Community College
McDowell Technical Community
College
Methodist College
Mitchell Community College
Montgomery Community College
Montreat-Anderson College
Nash Community College
North Carolina Agricultural and
Technical State University
North Carolina State University
Pamlico Community College
Pembroke State University
Piedmont Community College
Pitt Community College
Richmond Community College

Roanoke-Chowan Community
College
Rockingham Community College
Rowan-Cabarrus Community
College
Sampson Community College
Sandhills Community College
Southeastern Community College
Stanly Community College
Surry Community College
Tri-County Community College
University of North Carolina
Asheville
Chapel Hill
Charlotte
Greensboro
Wilmington
Vance-Granville Community
College
Wake Technical Community
College
Wayne Community College
Western Carolina University
Western Piedmont Community
College
Wilkes Community College
Wilson Technical Community
College
Winston-Salem State University

North Dakota

Bismarck State College
Fort Berthold Community College
Mayville State University
North Dakota State University:
Bottineau and Institute of
Forestry
University of Mary
University of North Dakota
Valley City State University

Ohio

Belmont Technical College
Bowling Green State University
Bowling Green
Firelands College
Cedarville College
Central Ohio Technical College
Central State University
Chatfield College
Cincinnati Bible College and
Seminary
Cincinnati Technical College
Clark State Community College
Cleveland College of Jewish Studies
Cleveland State University
Cuyahoga Community College
Eastern Campus
Western Campus
Defiance College
Denison University
Edison State Community College
Hiram College
Jefferson Technical College
Kent State University
East Liverpool Regional
Campus
Trumbull Regional Campus
Tuscarawas Campus
Lake Erie College
Lakeland Community College
Lourdes College
Malone College
Marion Technical College
Miami University: Hamilton
Campus
Mount Union College
Mount Vernon Nazarene College
North Central Technical College
Northwest Technical College
Ohio Dominican College
Ohio Northern University

Ohio State University
    Mansfield Campus
    Marion Campus
    Newark Campus
Ohio University
    Chillicothe Campus
    Zanesville Campus
Shawnee State University
Sinclair Community College
Stark Technical College
Terra Technical College
University of Akron
University of Dayton
University of Findlay
University of Rio Grande
University of Toledo
Urbana University
Walsh College
Washington State Community
    College
Wittenberg University
Wright State University
    Dayton
    Lake Campus
Xavier University
Youngstown State University

Oklahoma

Bartlesville Wesleyan College
Cameron University
Central State University
Connors State College
East Central University
El Reno Junior College
Northeastern State University
Northwestern Oklahoma State
    University
Oklahoma Baptist University
Oklahoma City University
Oklahoma State University
Oklahoma State University:
    Oklahoma City
Phillips University
Rogers State College
Rose State College
Southeastern Oklahoma State
    University
Southern Nazarene University
Southwestern Oklahoma State
    University
Tulsa Junior College
University of Science and Arts of
    Oklahoma

Oregon

Central Oregon Community College
Clackamas Community College
Clatsop Community College
Concordia College
George Fox College
Lane Community College
Linfield College
Linn-Benton Community College
Portland Community College
Portland State University
Rogue Community College
Southwestern Oregon Community
    College
Treasure Valley Community College
Umpqua Community College
Western Oregon State College

Pennsylvania

Academy of the New Church
Albright College
Alvernia College
Beaver College
Bucks County Community College
Butler County Community College
California University of
    Pennsylvania
Chestnut Hill College

Clarion University of Pennsylvania
College Misericordia
Community College of Beaver
    County
Community College of Philadelphia
Delaware County Community
    College
Delaware Valley College of Science
    and Agriculture
Duquesne University
East Stroudsburg University of
    Pennsylvania
Eastern College
Edinboro University of
    Pennsylvania
Gannon University
Gwynedd-Mercy College
Holy Family College
Immaculata College
Indiana University of Pennsylvania
Juniata College
Keystone Junior College
King's College
Lancaster Bible College
Lehigh County Community College
Lock Haven University of
    Pennsylvania
Luzerne County Community
    College
Manor Junior College
Marywood College
Messiah College
Montgomery County Community
    College
Northampton County Area
    Community College
Point Park College
Robert Morris College
Rosemont College
Seton Hill College
Shippensburg University of
    Pennsylvania
Spring Garden College
Temple University
University of Pittsburgh at Bradford
University of Scranton
Villanova University
West Chester University of
    Pennsylvania
Westmoreland County Community
    College
Wilkes University

Rhode Island

Community College of Rhode
    Island
Rhode Island College
Salve Regina College
University of Rhode Island

South Carolina

Aiken Technical College
Benedict College
Central Wesleyan College
Chesterfield-Marlboro Technical
    College
The Citadel
Clemson University
College of Charleston
Denmark Technical College
Florence-Darlington Technical
    College
Francis Marion College
Furman University
Greenville Technical College
Lander College
Midlands Technical College
Newberry College
Orangeburg-Calhoun Technical
    College
Piedmont Technical College
South Carolina State College

Spartanburg Methodist College
Sumter Area Technical College
Technical College of the
    Lowcountry
Tri-County Technical College
Trident Technical College
University of South Carolina
    Aiken
    Beaufort
    Coastal Carolina College
    Columbia
    Lancaster
    Salkehatchie University
        Campus
    Spartanburg
    Sumter
    Union
Williamsburg Technical College
Winthrop College
York Technical College

South Dakota

Augustana College
Black Hills State University
Dakota State University
National College
Northern State University
Presentation College
Sioux Falls College
South Dakota School of Mines and
    Technology

Tennessee

Austin Peay State University
Belmont College
Bethel College
Carson-Newman College
Chattanooga State Technical
    Community College
Cleveland State Community College
Dyersburg State Community
    College
East Tennessee State University
Freed-Hardeman University
Jackson State Community College
King College
Lambuth College
Lee College
Lincoln Memorial University
Memphis College of Art
Memphis State University
Middle Tennessee State University
Motlow State Community College
Nashville State Technical Institute
Pellissippi State Technical
    Community College
Shelby State Community College
Southern College of Seventh-day
    Adventists
State Technical Institute at
    Memphis
Tennessee Technological University
University of Tennessee
    Chattanooga
    Knoxville
    Martin
Volunteer State Community College
Walters State Community College

Texas

Alvin Community College
Angelina College
Bee County College
College of the Mainland
Corpus Christi State University
Del Mar College
East Texas State University
El Paso Community College
Frank Phillips College
Galveston College
Hardin-Simmons University
Hill College

Houston Baptist University
Houston Community College
Howard Payne University
Laredo Junior College
Lee College
McMurry University
Northeast Texas Community
    College
Paris Junior College
St. Philip's College
Southwestern Adventist College
Tarleton State University
Temple Junior College
Texarkana College
Texas A&M University
Texas Christian University
Trinity Valley Community College
Tyler Junior College
Vernon Regional Junior College
Wayland Baptist University
Weatherford College
Western Texas College

Utah

College of Eastern Utah
Dixie College
Salt Lake Community College
University of Utah
Utah Valley Community College
Weber State University

Vermont

Burlington College
Castleton State College
Champlain College
College of St. Joseph in Vermont
Community College of Vermont
Johnson State College
Lyndon State College
Southern Vermont College
University of Vermont

Virginia

Averett College
Blue Ridge Community College
Bluefield College
Bridgewater College
Central Virginia Community College
Christopher Newport College
Clinch Valley College of the
    University of Virginia
College of William and Mary
Dabney S. Lancaster Community
    College
Danville Community College
Eastern Mennonite College
Eastern Shore Community College
Ferrum College
George Mason University
John Tyler Community College
Longwood College
Lord Fairfax Community College
Mary Washington College
Marymount University
Mountain Empire Community
    College
New River Community College
Norfolk State University
Northern Virginia Community
    College
Old Dominion University
Patrick Henry Community College
Paul D. Camp Community College
Piedmont Virginia Community
    College
Radford University
Rappahannock Community College
Richard Bland College
Roanoke College
Southside Virginia Community
    College

Southwest Virginia Community
College
Sweet Briar College
Tidewater Community College
University of Virginia
Virginia Commonwealth University
Virginia Highlands Community
College
Virginia Polytechnic Institute and
State University
Virginia Western Community
College

Washington

Big Bend Community College
Central Washington University
Columbia Basin College
Edmonds Community College
Everett Community College
Grays Harbor College
Green River Community College
Heritage College
Lower Columbia College
North Seattle Community College
Olympic College
Peninsula College
Pierce College
Seattle Central Community College
Seattle Pacific University
Spokane Falls Community College
Tacoma Community College
University of Washington
Walla Walla College
Walla Walla Community College
Whatcom Community College
Whitworth College
Yakima Valley Community College

West Virginia

Appalachian Bible College
Fairmont State College
Wheeling Jesuit College

Wisconsin

Lakeland College
Marian College of Fond du Lac
Milwaukee Area Technical College
Mount Mary College
Northland College
Silver Lake College
University of Wisconsin
Eau Claire
Green Bay
La Crosse
Milwaukee
Oshkosh
River Falls
Stout
Whitewater
University of Wisconsin Center
Baraboo/Sauk County
Fox Valley
Manitowoc County
Marathon County
Richland
Rock County
Washington County
Waukesha
Viterbo College

Wyoming

Casper College
Central Wyoming College
Eastern Wyoming College
Laramie County Community
College
Northwest College
Sheridan College
University of Wyoming
Western Wyoming Community
College

American Samoa, Caroline Islands, Guam, Marianas, Virgin Islands

Guam Community College

Tuition and/or fee waiver for minority students

Alabama

Faulkner University

Alaska

Prince William Sound Community
College
University of Alaska Southeast

Arizona

Northern Arizona University
Rio Salado Community College
University of Arizona

California

California Baptist College
City College of San Francisco
Coastline Community College
Compton Community College
Fresno City College
Fullerton College
Napa Valley College
Orange Coast College
Oxnard College
Porterville College
University of California
Davis
Santa Cruz
University of La Verne

Colorado

Aims Community College
Colorado State University
Metropolitan State College of
Denver
Red Rocks Community College

Connecticut

Albertus Magnus College
Fairfield University
Sacred Heart University
Teikyo-Post University
University of Hartford

Florida

Brevard Community College
Central Florida Community College
Florida Atlantic University
Florida International University
Lake City Community College
Rollins College
University of Florida

Hawaii

University of Hawaii at Manoa

Idaho

University of Idaho

Illinois

KAES College
Loyola University of Chicago
Northern Illinois University
University of Illinois at Chicago

Indiana

Indiana University at Kokomo
Indiana Vocational Technical
College
Columbus
Southwest

Purdue University: North Central
Campus
St. Mary's College

Iowa

St. Ambrose University

Kansas

Kansas Wesleyan University
Labette Community College

Kentucky

Bellarmine College
Murray State University
Transylvania University
University of Kentucky

Louisiana

Bossier Parish Community College
Grambling State University
Louisiana State University and
Agricultural and Mechanical
College
University of New Orleans

Maine

Central Maine Technical College
Eastern Maine Technical College
University of Maine
Farmington
Machias
Orono
Presque Isle
University of New England

Maryland

University of Maryland: Eastern
Shore

Massachusetts

Greenfield Community College
Massasoit Community College
Merrimack College
Regis College
St. John's Seminary College
Stonehill College
Western New England College

Michigan

Concordia College
Northwestern Michigan College

Minnesota

University of Minnesota
Morris
Twin Cities

Mississippi

Mississippi University for Women
University of Mississippi

Missouri

North Central Missouri College
St. Louis University
University of Missouri: Rolla
William Woods College

Montana

Eastern Montana College
University of Montana

Nebraska

Chadron State College
College of St. Mary

Nevada

University of Nevada: Reno

New York

Canisius College
Hobart College
Iona College

St. Bonaventure University
State University of New York at
Buffalo
William Smith College

North Carolina

Western Carolina University

Ohio

Cleveland Institute of Electronics
Hiram College
Northwestern College
Walsh College
Wilmington College

Oklahoma

Central State University
Oklahoma State University
Oklahoma State University:
Oklahoma City
Southeastern Oklahoma State
University
University of Oklahoma Health
Sciences Center

Oregon

Eastern Oregon State College
George Fox College
Oregon Health Sciences University
Oregon Institute of Technology
Southern Oregon State College
University of Oregon
Eugene
Robert Donald Clark Honors
College

Pennsylvania

Bloomsburg University of
Pennsylvania
California University of
Pennsylvania
Chatham College
Cheyney University of Pennsylvania
Clarion University of Pennsylvania
Eastern College
Edinboro University of
Pennsylvania
Immaculata College
Kutztown University of
Pennsylvania
Lock Haven University of
Pennsylvania
Lycoming College
Manor Junior College
Mansfield University of
Pennsylvania
Millersville University of
Pennsylvania
St. Charles Borromeo Seminary
University of Pittsburgh at Bradford
West Chester University of
Pennsylvania

Puerto Rico

American University of Puerto Rico
Caribbean University

Rhode Island

Providence College
Salve Regina College

South Carolina

Furman University
Greenville Technical College
Spartanburg Methodist College
University of South Carolina at
Lancaster

Tennessee

Carson-Newman College
Jackson State Community College
Johnson Bible College

Northeast State Technical
  Community College
University of Tennessee: Memphis
Volunteer State Community College
Walters State Community College

Texas

Dallas Baptist University
El Centro College
Hardin-Simmons University
Lon Morris College
Texas Southern University
University of Mary Hardin-Baylor

Vermont

Lyndon State College

Virginia

Eastern Mennonite College
Norfolk State University
St. Paul's College
Virginia State University

Washington

Cornish College of the Arts
Edmonds Community College
Gonzaga University
Grays Harbor College
Skagit Valley College
Western Washington University

West Virginia

Fairmont State College

Wisconsin

University of Wisconsin
  La Crosse
  Superior
University of Wisconsin Center:
  Baraboo/Sauk County

**American Samoa, Caroline
Islands, Guam, Marianas,
Virgin Islands**

Northern Marianas College

Tuition and/or fee waiver
for family members
enrolled simultaneously

Alabama

RETS Electronics Institute
Tuskegee University

Arizona

Arizona College of the Bible

Arkansas

East Arkansas Community College
Philander Smith College

California

American Armenian International
  College
Azusa Pacific University
Bethany Bible College
California Baptist College
California Lutheran University
City College of San Francisco
Compton Community College
LIFE Bible College
Monterey Institute of International
  Studies
Pacific Christian College
Porterville College
Riverside Community College
St. Mary's College of California
San Jose Christian College

Santa Clara University
Southern California College
University of La Verne
University of San Francisco
West Coast Christian College

Colorado

Colorado Christian University
Denver Institute of Technology

Connecticut

Albertus Magnus College
Briarwood College
Fairfield University
Hartford College for Women
Sacred Heart University
Teikyo-Post University
University of Hartford
University of New Haven

Delaware

Goldey-Beacom College

District of Columbia

George Washington University
Trinity College

Florida

Barry University
Florida Bible College
Florida Christian College
Florida Southern College
Jacksonville University
St. Leo College
Santa Fe Community College

Georgia

Atlanta Christian College
Berry College
Oglethorpe University
Paine College
Shorter College
Toccoa Falls College
Truett-McConnell College
Wesleyan College

Hawaii

Chaminade University of Honolulu

Idaho

Northwest Nazarene College

Illinois

Augustana College
College of St. Francis
Illinois Benedictine College
KAES College
Kendall College
Lewis University
Lincoln Christian College and
  Seminary
MacCormac Junior College
Mundelein College
Olivet Nazarene University
Quincy College
Rockford College
Rosary College

Indiana

Bethel College
Grace College
Huntington College
Indiana Institute of Technology
Indiana State University
Indiana Vocational Technical
  College: Columbus
Manchester College
Marian College
St. Joseph's College
St. Mary's College
Summit Christian College
Vincennes University

Iowa

American Institute of Business
Clarke College
Ellsworth Community College
Faith Baptist Bible College and
  Theological Seminary
Mount St. Clare College
Northwestern College
St. Ambrose University
Simpson College
Teikyo Marycrest University
Teikyo Westmar University
University of Dubuque
Upper Iowa University
Vennard College

Kansas

Benedictine College
Brown Mackie College
Colby Community College
Kansas Newman College
Kansas Wesleyan University
Ottawa University
St. Mary College
Southwestern College

Kentucky

Asbury College
Clear Creek Baptist Bible College
Spalding University

Maine

St. Joseph's College
University of New England

Maryland

College of Notre Dame of
  Maryland
Coppin State College
Eastern Christian College
Hood College
Loyola College in Maryland
Mount St. Mary's College
Ner Israel Rabbinical College
Western Maryland College

Massachusetts

Atlantic Union College
Bay Path College
Becker College
  Leicester Campus
  Worcester Campus
Elms College
Lasell College
Merrimack College
Nichols College
Pine Manor College
Stonehill College
Suffolk University
Wheelock College

Michigan

Andrews University
Great Lakes Bible College
Marygrove College
Michigan Christian College
North Central Michigan College
Northwood Institute
Reformed Bible College
Saginaw Valley State University
Siena Heights College
West Shore Community College

Minnesota

College of St. Scholastica
North Central Bible College
Northwestern College
University of St. Thomas

Mississippi

Blue Mountain College
Delta State University

Magnolia Bible College
Rust College

Missouri

Avila College
Calvary Bible College
Central Bible College
Central Methodist College
Columbia College
Fontbonne College
Maryville College—St. Louis
National College
Research College of Nursing
Rockhurst College
Stephens College
William Woods College

Montana

Carroll College
College of Great Falls

Nebraska

College of St. Mary
Creighton University
Grace College of the Bible
Hastings College
Nebraska Christian College
York College

Nevada

Sierra Nevada College

New Hampshire

Hesser College
Notre Dame College
Rivier College
St. Anselm College

New Jersey

Bloomfield College
Caldwell College
Centenary College
College of St. Elizabeth
Fairleigh Dickinson University
  Edward Williams College
  Florham-Madison Campus
  Rutherford Campus
  Teaneck-Hackensack Campus
Felician College
Georgian Court College
Monmouth College

New Mexico

National College

New York

Canisius College
College of Mount St. Vincent
College of New Rochelle
  New Rochelle
  School of New Resources
Daemen College
D'Youville College
Elmira College
Hartwick College
Houghton College
Iona College
King's College
Long Island University: Brooklyn
  Campus
Manhattan College
Marymount College
Molloy College
Nazareth College of Rochester
Nyack College
Russell Sage College
Sage Junior College of Albany, A
  Division of Russell Sage College
St. Bonaventure University
St. John's University

St. Joseph's College
  Brooklyn
  Suffolk Campus
St. Thomas Aquinas College
Villa Maria College of Buffalo
Wagner College

North Carolina

Belmont Abbey College
East Coast Bible College
Greensboro College
Lenoir-Rhyne College
Livingstone College
Peace College
Pfeiffer College
Piedmont Bible College
Queens College

North Dakota

Jamestown College
University of Mary

Ohio

Antioch College
Ashland University
Capital University
Cincinnati Bible College and
  Seminary
Defiance College
Franciscan University of
  Steubenville
Hiram College
Lake Erie College
Malone College
Mount Union College
Mount Vernon Nazarene College
Muskingum College
Ohio Northern University
Otterbein College
Terra Technical College
University of Dayton
University of Findlay
Ursuline College
Walsh College
Wilmington College
Xavier University

Oklahoma

Central State University
Hillsdale Free Will Baptist College
Northeastern Oklahoma
  Agricultural and Mechanical
  College
Oklahoma Christian University of
  Science and Arts
Southeastern Oklahoma State
  University

Oregon

Bassist College
Clatsop Community College
Eugene Bible College
George Fox College
Linfield College
Linn-Benton Community College
Multnomah School of the Bible

Pennsylvania

Allentown College of St. Francis de
  Sales
Carlow College
Eastern College
Elizabethtown College
Gannon University
Immaculata College
La Roche College
Lancaster Bible College
Lycoming College
Marywood College
Mercyhurst College
Messiah College
Moore College of Art and Design

Northeastern Christian Junior
  College
Peirce Junior College
Philadelphia College of Bible
Pinebrook Junior College
Point Park College
Robert Morris College
Rosemont College
St. Francis College
Seton Hill College
Thiel College
University of the Arts
University of Scranton
Ursinus College
Valley Forge Military Junior
  College
Villanova University
Waynesburg College
Wilkes University

Puerto Rico

Caribbean University
ICPR Junior College
Universidad Adventista de las
  Antillas

Rhode Island

Bryant College
Providence College
Salve Regina College

South Carolina

Central Wesleyan College
Erskine College
Limestone College
North Greenville College
Spartanburg Methodist College

South Dakota

Mount Marty College
National College

Tennessee

Belmont College
Carson-Newman College
Free Will Baptist Bible College
Johnson Bible College
Knoxville College
Lee College
Southern College of Seventh-day
  Adventists
Tennessee Temple University
Tennessee Wesleyan College
Tomlinson College
Union University

Texas

Arlington Baptist College
Dallas Baptist University
Lon Morris College
Lubbock Christian University
Southwestern Adventist College
Southwestern Assemblies of God
  College
University of Dallas

Utah

Westminster College of Salt Lake
  City

Vermont

Champlain College
Green Mountain College
Johnson State College
Lyndon State College
St. Michael's College

Virginia

Averett College
Christendom College
Ferrum College
Mary Baldwin College

Marymount University
Randolph-Macon College

Washington

Gonzaga University
Heritage College
Northwest College of the
  Assemblies of God
Puget Sound Christian College
Seattle University

West Virginia

Appalachian Bible College

Wisconsin

Alverno College
Cardinal Stritch College
Marian College of Fond du Lac
Marquette University
Mount Mary College
St. Norbert College
Viterbo College
Wisconsin Lutheran College

Wyoming

Northwest College

Tuition and/or fee waiver for unemployed or children of unemployed workers

Alabama

Bessemer State Technical College
Faulkner University

Arizona

Mohave Community College

Arkansas

Williams Baptist College

California

City College of San Francisco
Coastline Community College
Compton Community College
D-Q University
Feather River College
Fresno City College
Fullerton College
Moorpark College
Orange Coast College
Oxnard College
Pasadena City College
Porterville College
Riverside Community College
San Diego City College
Santa Barbara City College
Santa Monica College
Sierra College
University of La Verne
West Los Angeles College
West Valley College

Connecticut

Teikyo-Post University

Idaho

Northwest Nazarene College

Illinois

Lincoln Christian College and
  Seminary

Indiana

Indiana Vocational Technical
  College: Southwest

Iowa

Drake University

Kansas

Cowley County Community College
Kansas Wesleyan University
Labette Community College
Neosho County Community College

Louisiana

Northeast Louisiana University

Maine

University of New England

Maryland

Ner Israel Rabbinical College

Massachusetts

Atlantic Union College
Bridgewater State College
Bristol Community College
Bunker Hill Community College
Greenfield Community College
Massachusetts Bay Community
  College
Massachusetts College of Art
Massasoit Community College
Middlesex Community College
Mount Wachusett Community
  College
North Adams State College
Quinsigamond Community College
Regis College
Salem State College
University of Massachusetts at
  Amherst

Michigan

St. Mary's College
Wayne State University

Minnesota

Gustavus Adolphus College
Rainy River Community College

Mississippi

Rust College

Missouri

Lindenwood College

Nebraska

Metropolitan Community College

New Jersey

Camden County College
County College of Morris
Cumberland County College
Passaic County Community College
Raritan Valley Community College
Sussex County Community College
Warren County Community College
William Paterson College of New
  Jersey

New York

Herkimer County Community
  College
Mannes College of Music
Plaza Business Institute
William Smith College

North Carolina

Chowan College

Ohio

Belmont Technical College
Cincinnati Technical College
Cleveland Institute of Electronics
Hiram College

Oregon

Linn-Benton Community College
Marylhurst College
Rogue Community College
Southwestern Oregon Community
 College

Pennsylvania

Bucks County Community College
Chatham College
Eastern College
King's College
La Roche College
Mercyhurst College
Point Park College
St. Charles Borromeo Seminary
University of the Arts

Rhode Island

Salve Regina College

South Carolina

Greenville Technical College
Spartanburg Methodist College

Texas

El Centro College

Washington

Big Bend Community College
Columbia Basin College
Cornish College of the Arts
Edmonds Community College
Everett Community College
Lower Columbia College
North Seattle Community College
Peninsula College
Pierce College
Seattle Central Community College
Skagit Valley College
South Puget Sound Community
 College
Tacoma Community College
Walla Walla Community College
Whatcom Community College
Yakima Valley Community College

West Virginia

Alderson-Broaddus College

Tuition payment by credit card

Alabama

Alabama Agricultural and
 Mechanical University
Alabama State University
Bessemer State Technical College
Birmingham-Southern College
Bishop State Community College
Brewer State Junior College
Central Alabama Community
 College: Alexander City Campus
Enterprise State Junior College
Faulkner University
Gadsden State Community College
Huntingdon College
J. F. Drake State Technical College
Jacksonville State University
Jefferson Davis State Junior College
Jefferson State Community College
John C. Calhoun State Community
 College
Judson College
Northwest Alabama Community
 College
Patrick Henry State Junior College
Samford University

Shelton State Community College
Southeastern Bible College
Talladega College
Trenholm State Technical College
Troy State University
 Dothan
 Montgomery
University of Alabama
 Birmingham
 Tuscaloosa
University of South Alabama
Walker College

Alaska

Alaska Pacific University
Prince William Sound Community
 College
Sheldon Jackson College
University of Alaska
 Anchorage
 Fairbanks
 Southeast

Arizona

Arizona College of the Bible
Arizona State University
Central Arizona College
Cochise College
DeVry Institute of Technology:
 Phoenix
Eastern Arizona College
Embry-Riddle Aeronautical
 University: Prescott Campus
Gateway Community College
Glendale Community College
Grand Canyon University
ITT Technical Institute: Tucson
Mesa Community College
Mohave Community College
Northern Arizona University
Paradise Valley Community College
Phoenix College
Rio Salado Community College
South Mountain Community
 College
University of Arizona
University of Phoenix
Western International University
Yavapai College

Arkansas

East Arkansas Community College
Garland County Community
 College
Henderson State University
Mississippi County Community
 College
North Arkansas Community College
Southern Arkansas University
 El Dorado Branch
 Magnolia
 Technical Branch
University of Arkansas
 Fayetteville
 Little Rock
 Monticello
University of Central Arkansas
Westark Community College

California

Academy of Art College
Allan Hancock College
American Armenian International
 College
Armstrong College
Azusa Pacific University
Bethany Bible College
Biola University
Brooks College
Brooks Institute of Photography
California Baptist College

California College of Arts and
 Crafts
California Lutheran University
California State University
 Bakersfield
 Dominguez Hills
 Fresno
 Hayward
 Los Angeles
 Sacramento
 San Bernardino
 Stanislaus
Canada College
Chaffey Community College
Chapman College
Christian Heritage College
Coastline Community College
Cogswell Polytechnical College
Coleman College
College of Alameda
College of Notre Dame
College of Oceaneering
College of the Sequoias
Compton Community College
Cosumnes River College
Crafton Hills College
De Anza College
DeVry Institute of Technology: City
 of Industry
Diablo Valley College
Dominican College of San Rafael
Evergreen Valley College
Fashion Institute of Design and
 Merchandising
Feather River College
Fresno Pacific College
Golden Gate University
Heald Business College: San Jose
Holy Names College
Humboldt State University
Humphreys College
ITT Technical Institute
 La Mesa
 Van Nuys
John F. Kennedy University
Lake Tahoe Community College
Lincoln University
Long Beach City College
Los Medanos College
Marymount College
Master's College
MiraCosta College
Modesto Junior College
Monterey Institute of International
 Studies
Moorpark College
Mount St. Mary's College
Northrop University
Otis Art Institute of Parsons School
 of Design
Oxnard College
Pacific Christian College
Pacific Oaks College
Palomar College
Patten College
Pepperdine University
Phillips Junior College
 Condie Campus
 San Fernando Valley Campus
Point Loma Nazarene College
Riverside Community College
Sacramento City College
Saddleback College
St. Mary's College of California
Samuel Merritt College
San Diego City College
San Diego Mesa College
San Diego Miramar College
San Diego State University
San Francisco Conservatory of
 Music
San Francisco State University

San Jose City College
San Jose State University
Santa Clara University
Santa Monica College
Scripps College
Simpson College
Skyline College
Sonoma State University
Southern California College
Southern California Institute of
 Architecture
University of California: Los
 Angeles
University of Judaism
University of La Verne
University of the Pacific
University of Redlands
University of San Francisco
University of Southern California
University of West Los Angeles
West Valley College
Western State University College of
 Law: San Diego
Woodbury University
World College West

Colorado

Aims Community College
Arapahoe Community College
Colorado Christian University
Colorado Institute of Art
Colorado Northwestern Community
 College
Colorado State University
Colorado Technical College
Community College of Denver
Denver Institute of Technology
Fort Lewis College
Front Range Community College
ITT Technical Institute: Aurora
Lamar Community College
Metropolitan State College of
 Denver
Morgan Community College
Naropa Institute
Pikes Peak Community College
Pueblo Community College
Red Rocks Community College
Regis University
Rocky Mountain College of Art and
 Design
University of Colorado
 Colorado Springs
 Denver
University of Denver
University of Northern Colorado
University of Southern Colorado
Western State College of Colorado

Connecticut

Asnuntuck Community College
Briarwood College
Bridgeport Engineering Institute
Central Connecticut State
 University
Greater Hartford Community
 College
Hartford College for Women
Housatonic Community College
Middlesex Community College
Mitchell College
Mohegan Community College
Norwalk Community College
Quinebaug Valley Community
 College
Quinnipiac College
Sacred Heart University
St. Joseph College
South Central Community College
Teikyo-Post University
Tunxis Community College
University of Hartford

University of New Haven
Yale University

Delaware

Delaware State College
Delaware Technical and
  Community College
    Southern Campus
    Stanton/Wilmington Campus
    Terry Campus
Goldey-Beacom College
Wesley College
Wilmington College

District of Columbia

Corcoran School of Art
Georgetown University
Howard University
Mount Vernon College
Trinity College
University of the District of
  Columbia

Florida

Art Institute of Fort Lauderdale
Barry University
Bethune-Cookman College
Brevard Community College
Daytona Beach Community College
Edison Community College
Embry-Riddle Aeronautical
  University
Florida Agricultural and Mechanical
  University
Florida Community College at
  Jacksonville
Florida Institute of Technology
Florida Memorial College
Florida State University
Gulf Coast Community College
Hillsborough Community College
Hobe Sound Bible College
Indian River Community College
International Fine Arts College
Jacksonville University
Jones College
Keiser College of Technology
Lake-Sumter Community College
Manatee Community College
Miami-Dade Community College
Nova University
Okaloosa-Walton Community
  College
Orlando College
Palm Beach Atlantic College
Phillips Junior College: Melbourne
Ringling School of Art and Design
Rollins College
St. Petersburg Junior College
St. Thomas University
Santa Fe Community College
Seminole Community College
South Florida Community College
Southeastern College of the
  Assemblies of God
Southern College
Tallahassee Community College
Tampa College
University of Central Florida
University of Florida
University of Miami
University of North Florida
University of Tampa
University of West Florida
Valencia Community College
Warner Southern College
Webber College

Georgia

Abraham Baldwin Agricultural
  College
Albany State College

Atlanta Christian College
Augusta College
Augusta Technical Institute
Brenau Women's College
Brunswick College
Columbus College
Covenant College
Darton College
DeVry Institute of Technology:
  Decatur
Gainesville College
Georgia College
Georgia Southern University
Georgia Southwestern College
Gordon College
LaGrange College
Macon College
Meadows College of Business
Mercer University Atlanta
Morris Brown College
North Georgia College
Oglethorpe University
Piedmont College
Savannah College of Art and
  Design
Savannah Technical Institute
Shorter College
South College
Southern College of Technology
Wesleyan College
West Georgia College

Hawaii

Cannon's International Business
  College of Honolulu
Chaminade University of Honolulu
Hawaii Loa College
Hawaii Pacific University
University of Hawaii
    Kauai Community College
    Leeward Community College
    Manoa
    West Oahu
    Windward Community College

Idaho

College of Idaho
College of Southern Idaho
Lewis Clark State College
North Idaho College
Ricks College

Illinois

American Academy of Art
American Conservatory of Music
Aurora University
Belleville Area College
Black Hawk College
    East Campus
    Moline
Blackburn College
Bradley University
Carl Sandburg College
Chicago State University
City Colleges of Chicago
    Chicago City-Wide College
    Harold Washington College
    Richard J. Daley College
    Wright College
College of DuPage
College of Lake County
College of St. Francis
Columbia College
Concordia University
De Paul University
DeVry Institute of Technology
    Chicago
    Lombard
Elgin Community College
Elmhurst College
Eureka College
Governors State University

Illinois Benedictine College
Illinois Central College
Illinois Institute of Technology
Illinois Technical College
International Academy of
  Merchandising and Design
ITT Technical Institute:
  Schaumburg
Joliet Junior College
Kankakee Community College
Kendall College
Kishwaukee College
Lake Land College
Lewis and Clark Community
  College
Lewis University
Loyola University of Chicago
MacMurray College
McHenry County College
Midstate College
Moraine Valley Community College
Morton College
Mundelein College
National-Louis University
North Central College
Northeastern Illinois University
Oakton Community College
Olivet Nazarene University
Parkland College
Prairie State College
Quincy College
Ray College of Design
Richland Community College
Rock Valley College
Rockford College
Roosevelt University
Rosary College
St. Xavier College
Sangamon State University
Sauk Valley Community College
School of the Art Institute of
  Chicago
Shimer College
South Suburban College of Cook
  County
Southern Illinois University at
  Edwardsville
Spoon River College
Springfield College in Illinois
University of Chicago
VanderCook College of Music
Waubonsee Community College
William Rainey Harper College

Indiana

Butler University
Calumet College of St. Joseph
Goshen College
Huntington College
Indiana Institute of Technology
Indiana State University
Indiana University
    Bloomington
    East
    Kokomo
    Northwest
    South Bend
    Southeast
Indiana University—Purdue
  University
    Fort Wayne
    Indianapolis

Indiana Vocational Technical
  College
    Central Indiana
    Columbus
    Kokomo
    Lafayette
    Northcentral
    Northeast
    Northwest
    Southcentral
    Southwest
    Whitewater
International Business College
Lutheran College of Health
  Professions
Marian College
Purdue University
    Calumet
    North Central Campus
Rose-Hulman Institute of
  Technology
St. Francis College
St. Mary-of-the-Woods College
Tri-State University
University of Evansville
University of Indianapolis
University of Southern Indiana
Valparaiso University
Vincennes University

Iowa

American Institute of Business
Briar Cliff College
Central College
Clarke College
Clinton Community College
Coe College
Des Moines Area Community
  College
Drake University
Hamilton Technical College
Hawkeye Institute of Technology
Indian Hills Community College
Iowa Lakes Community College
Iowa Western Community College
Kirkwood Community College
Luther College
Maharishi International University
Morningside College
Muscatine Community College
North Iowa Area Community
  College
Northeast Iowa Community College
St. Ambrose University
Scott Community College
Simpson College
Teikyo Marycrest University
Teikyo Westmar University
University of Dubuque
William Penn College

Kansas

Barton County Community College
Benedictine College
Bethany College
Brown Mackie College
Butler County Community College
Cloud County Community College
Colby Community College
Emporia State University
Fort Hays State University
Fort Scott Community College
Highland Community College
Hutchinson Community College
Johnson County Community
  College
Kansas Newman College
Kansas State University
Labette Community College
Mid-America Nazarene College
Pittsburg State University
St. Mary College

Southwestern College
Tabor College
University of Kansas
    Lawrence
    Medical Center
Washburn University of Topeka
Wichita State University

Kentucky

Bellarmine College
Campbellsville College
Eastern Kentucky University
Elizabethtown Community College
Georgetown College
Jefferson Community College
Kentucky State University
Louisville Technical Institute
Maysville Community College
Midway College
Morehead State University
Murray State University
Northern Kentucky University
Pikeville College
Prestonburg Community College
Somerset Community College
Spalding University
Sullivan College
Thomas More College
University of Louisville
Western Kentucky University

Louisiana

Dillard University
Grambling State University
Jimmy Swaggart Bible College and
    Seminary
Louisiana Tech University
Loyola University
McNeese State University
Northeast Louisiana University
Our Lady of Holy Cross College
Southeastern Louisiana University
Southern University in Shreveport
Southern University and
    Agricultural and Mechanical
    College

Maine

Andover College
Beal College
Central Maine Technical College
College of the Atlantic
Husson College
St. Joseph's College
Southern Maine Technical College
Thomas College
Unity College
University of Maine
    Augusta
    Fort Kent
    Machias
    Orono
    Presque Isle
University of New England
University of Southern Maine

Maryland

Allegany Community College
Anne Arundel Community College
Baltimore Hebrew University
Bowie State University
Capitol College
Catonsville Community College
Cecil Community College
Chesapeake College
College of Notre Dame of
    Maryland
Coppin State College
Dundalk Community College
Essex Community College
Frederick Community College
Frostburg State University

Hagerstown Business College
Hagerstown Junior College
Harford Community College
Hood College
Howard Community College
Loyola College in Maryland
Maryland College of Art and
    Design
Montgomery College
    Germantown Campus
    Rockville Campus
    Takoma Park Campus
Morgan State University
Mount St. Mary's College
New Community College of
    Baltimore
St. Mary's College of Maryland
Towson State University
University of Baltimore
University of Maryland
    Baltimore
    Baltimore County
    College Park
    Eastern Shore
    University College
Villa Julie College
Washington College
Western Maryland College
Wor-Wic Tech Community College

Massachusetts

Anna Maria College for Men and
    Women
Atlantic Union College
Babson College
Bentley College
Berklee College of Music
Berkshire Community College
Boston University
Bradford College
Bridgewater State College
Bristol Community College
Cape Cod Community College
Clark University
Elms College
Emerson College
Emmanuel College
Endicott College
Fisher College
Framingham State College
Greenfield Community College
Hebrew College
Holyoke Community College
Marian Court Junior College
Massachusetts Bay Community
    College
Massasoit Community College
Mount Holyoke College
Mount Ida College
Mount Wachusett Community
    College
New England Conservatory of
    Music
Newbury College
Nichols College
North Shore Community College
Northeastern University
Northern Essex Community College
Quincy College
Quinsigamond Community College
School of the Museum of Fine Arts
Southeastern Massachusetts
    University
Suffolk University
Tufts University
Western New England College
Wheaton College
Wheelock College
Worcester State College

Michigan

Alma College
Alpena Community College
Andrews University
Aquinas College
Baker College
    Flint
    Owosso
Center for Creative Studies: College
    of Art and Design
Charles Stewart Mott Community
    College
Cleary College
Concordia College
Delta College
Detroit College of Business
Eastern Michigan University
Glen Oaks Community College
Grace Bible College
Grand Rapids Baptist College and
    Seminary
Grand Rapids Junior College
Grand Valley State University
Great Lakes Bible College
Great Lakes Junior College of
    Business
Henry Ford Community College
Highland Park Community College
Jackson Community College
Jordan College
Kalamazoo Valley Community
    College
Kellogg Community College
Kendall College of Art and Design
Kirtland Community College
Lake Michigan College
Macomb Community College
Madonna University
Marygrove College
Michigan Christian College
Michigan State University
Mid Michigan Community College
Monroe County Community
    College
Montcalm Community College
Muskegon Community College
Nazareth College in Kalamazoo
Northwestern Michigan College
Oakland Community College
Olivet College
Saginaw Valley State University
St. Clair County Community
    College
St. Mary's College
Schoolcraft College
Southwestern Michigan College
Spring Arbor College
Suomi College
University of Detroit Mercy
University of Michigan
    Dearborn
    Flint
Walsh College of Accountancy and
    Business Administration
Wayne County Community College
Wayne State University
West Shore Community College
Western Michigan University

Minnesota

Augsburg College
Austin Community College
Bethany Lutheran College
Bethel College
College of St. Catherine: St.
    Catherine Campus
College of St. Scholastica
Concordia College: St. Paul
Dakota County Technical College
Lakewood Community College
Minneapolis Community College
Normandale Community College

North Central Bible College
North Hennepin Community
    College
Northwestern College
Rochester Community College

Mississippi

Alcorn State University
Belhaven College
Blue Mountain College
Hinds Community College
Jackson State University
Magnolia Bible College
Millsaps College
Mississippi Gulf Coast Community
    College
    Jackson County Campus
    Jefferson Davis Campus
    Perkinston
Mississippi State University
Mississippi University for Women
Northeast Mississippi Community
    College
Northwest Mississippi Community
    College
Pearl River Community College
Tougaloo College
University of Mississippi
University of Southern Mississippi
William Carey College

Missouri

Avila College
Calvary Bible College
Central Methodist College
Central Missouri State University
Columbia College
DeVry Institute of Technology:
    Kansas City
East Central College
Evangel College
Fontbonne College
Harris Stowe State College
ITT Technical Institute: St. Louis
Jefferson College
Lincoln University
Lindenwood College
Longview Community College
Maple Woods Community College
Maryville College—St. Louis
Missouri Southern State College
Missouri Western State College
Moberly Area Community College
North Central Missouri College
Northeast Missouri State University
Northwest Missouri State
    University
Park College
Penn Valley Community College
Research College of Nursing
Rockhurst College
St. Louis College of Pharmacy
St. Louis Community College
    Florissant Valley
    Forest Park
    Meramec
Southeast Missouri State University
Southwest Baptist University
Southwest Missouri State University
State Fair Community College
Stephens College
University of Missouri
    Columbia
    Kansas City
    Rolla
    St. Louis
Webster University
William Jewell College

Montana

College of Great Falls

Nebraska

Bellevue College
Bishop Clarkson College
Central Community College
Chadron State College
College of St. Mary
Concordia College
Creighton University
Dana College
Doane College
Lincoln School of Commerce
Metropolitan Community College
Nebraska Methodist College of
Nursing and Allied Health
Nebraska Wesleyan University
Northeast Community College
Peru State College
Southeast Community College
Beatrice Campus
Lincoln Campus
Milford Campus
Union College
Wayne State College
Western Nebraska Community
College
Scottsbluff Campus
Sidney Campus
York College

Nevada

Northern Nevada Community
College
Sierra Nevada College
University of Nevada
Las Vegas
Reno
Western Nevada Community
College

New Hampshire

Daniel Webster College
Franklin Pierce College
Hesser College
Keene State College
New England College
New Hampshire Technical College
Claremont
Laconia
Manchester
Nashua
Stratham
New Hampshire Technical Institute
Notre Dame College
Rivier College
University of New Hampshire at
Manchester

New Jersey

Atlantic Community College
Bergen Community College
Bloomfield College
Brookdale Community College
Burlington County College
Caldwell College
Camden County College
Centenary College
Cumberland County College
Drew University
Fairleigh Dickinson University
Edward Williams College
Florham-Madison Campus
Rutherford Campus
Teaneck-Hackensack Campus
Glassboro State College
Gloucester County College
Hudson County Community College
Kean College of New Jersey
Mercer County Community College
Monmouth College
Montclair State College
New Jersey Institute of Technology
Passaic County Community College

Ramapo College of New Jersey
Raritan Valley Community College
Rider College
St. Peter's College
Salem Community College
Seton Hall University
Stockton State College
Thomas A. Edison State College
Union County College
Upsala College
William Paterson College of New
Jersey

New Mexico

Albuquerque Technical-Vocational
Institute
College of Santa Fe
College of the Southwest
Dona Ana Branch Community
College of New Mexico State
University
Eastern New Mexico University
Clovis Community College
Portales
Roswell Campus
New Mexico Highlands University
New Mexico Institute of Mining
and Technology
New Mexico Junior College
New Mexico Military Institute
New Mexico State University
Northern New Mexico Community
College
Parks College
San Juan College
Santa Fe Community College
University of New Mexico
Albuquerque
Gallup
Western New Mexico University

New York

Adelphi University
Adirondack Community College
Barnard College
Briarcliffe: The College for Business
Broome Community College
Canisius College
Cayuga County Community College
Cazenovia College
Central City Business Institute
City University of New York
Borough of Manhattan
Community College
City College
John Jay College of Criminal
Justice
Queens College
Queensborough Community
College
Clinton Community College
Cochran School of Nursing-St.
John's Riverside Hospital
Colgate University
College for Human Services
College of Insurance
College of Mount St. Vincent
College of New Rochelle
New Rochelle
School of New Resources
College of St. Rose
Columbia University
Columbia College
School of Engineering and
Applied Science
School of General Studies
Columbia-Greene Community
College
Corning Community College
Daemen College
Dominican College of Blauvelt
Dowling College

Dutchess Community College
D'Youville College
Eastman School of Music of the
University of Rochester
Elmira College
Erie Community College
North Campus
South Campus
Eugene Lang College/New School
for Social Research
Fashion Institute of Technology
Fordham University
Fulton-Montgomery Community
College
Genesee Community College
Herkimer County Community
College
Hilbert College
Hofstra University
Hudson Valley Community College
Iona College
Ithaca College
Jamestown Community College
Jefferson Community College
Keuka College
King's College
Long Island University
Brooklyn Campus
C. W. Post Campus
Southampton Campus
Manhattan College
Manhattanville College
Marist College
Marymount Manhattan College
Mater Dei College
Medaille College
Mercy College
Mohawk Valley Community College
Molloy College
Monroe Community College
Mount St. Mary College
Nazareth College of Rochester
New York School of Interior
Design
New York University
Niagara County Community College
Niagara University
Nyack College
Onondaga Community College
Orange County Community College
Pace University
College of White Plains
New York
Pleasantville/Briarcliff
Paul Smith's College
Plaza Business Institute
Polytechnic University
Pratt Institute
Rensselaer Polytechnic Institute
Roberts Wesleyan College
Rochester Institute of Technology
Rockland Community College
Russell Sage College
Sage Junior College of Albany, A
Division of Russell Sage College
St. Francis College
St. John Fisher College
St. John's University
St. Joseph's College
Brooklyn
Suffolk Campus
St. Thomas Aquinas College
Schenectady County Community
College
School of Visual Arts
Siena College

State University of New York
Albany
Binghamton
Buffalo
Stony Brook
College of Agriculture and
Technology at Cobleskill
College of Agriculture and
Technology at Morrisville
College at Brockport
College at Buffalo
College at Cortland
College at Fredonia
College at Geneseo
College at New Paltz
College at Old Westbury
College at Plattsburgh
College at Potsdam
College of Technology at
Alfred
College of Technology at
Canton
College of Technology at
Farmingdale
Institute of Technology at
Utica/Rome
Oswego
Suffolk County Community College
Selden
Western Campus
Sullivan County Community
College
Taylor Business Institute
Tompkins-Cortland Community
College
Trocaire College
Ulster County Community College
University of Rochester
University of the State of New
York: Regents College
Utica College of Syracuse
University
Utica School of Commerce
Wagner College
Wells College
Westchester Community College
William Smith College
Wood School

North Carolina

Alamance Community College
Anson Community College
Appalachian State University
Belmont Abbey College
Bennett College
Brunswick Community College
Campbell University
Catawba College
East Carolina University
East Coast Bible College
Elon College
Fayetteville Technical Community
College
Gaston College
Greensboro College
Johnson C. Smith University
Louisburg College
Methodist College
Mount Olive College
North Carolina Agricultural and
Technical State University
North Carolina Central University
Piedmont Bible College
Queens College
Roanoke-Chowan Community
College
University of North Carolina
Chapel Hill
Charlotte
Greensboro
Wilmington
Warren Wilson College

North Dakota

Trinity Bible College
University of North Dakota

Ohio

Art Academy of Cincinnati
Ashland University
Baldwin-Wallace College
Bluffton College
Bowling Green State University
    Bowling Green
    Firelands College
Bradford School
Bryant and Stratton Business
    Institute, Great Northern
Capital University
Cedarville College
Central Ohio Technical College
Central State University
Chatfield College
Cincinnati Bible College and
    Seminary
Cincinnati Technical College
Circleville Bible College
Clark State Community College
Cleveland Institute of Electronics
Cleveland Institute of Music
College of Mount St. Joseph
Columbus College of Art and
    Design
Cuyahoga Community College
    Eastern Campus
    Western Campus
Davis Junior College of Business
Defiance College
DeVry Institute of Technology:
    Columbus
Dyke College
Edison State Community College
Franciscan University of
    Steubenville
Franklin University
God's Bible School and College
Heidelberg College
Hiram College
Hocking Technical College
ITT Technical Institute: Dayton
John Carroll University
Kent State University
    Ashtabula Regional Campus
    East Liverpool Regional
        Campus
    Kent
    Salem Regional Campus
    Stark Campus
    Trumbull Regional Campus
    Tuscarawas Campus
Lake Erie College
Lakeland Community College
Lourdes College
Malone College
Marietta College
Marion Technical College
Miami University: Hamilton
    Campus
Miami-Jacobs College
Mount Union College
Muskingum College
North Central Technical College
Northwest Technical College
Ohio Dominican College
Ohio Northern University
Ohio State University
    Agricultural Technical Institute
    Columbus Campus
    Lima Campus
    Mansfield Campus
    Marion Campus
    Newark Campus

Ohio University
    Athens
    Chillicothe Campus
    Ironton Campus
    Zanesville Campus
Ohio Valley Business College
Ohio Wesleyan University
Otterbein College
Owens Technical College: Findlay
    Campus
Shawnee State University
Sinclair Community College
Southern State Community College
Stark Technical College
Terra Technical College
Tiffin University
Union Institute
University of Akron
University of Cincinnati
    Cincinnati
    Clermont College
University of Dayton
University of Toledo
Urbana University
Ursuline College
Washington State Community
    College
Wilberforce University
Wilmington College
Wright State University
    Dayton
    Lake Campus
Xavier University
Youngstown State University

Oklahoma

Bartlesville Wesleyan College
Cameron University
Connors State College
East Central University
Langston University
Northeastern Oklahoma
    Agricultural and Mechanical
    College
Oklahoma Junior College
Oklahoma State University
Oklahoma State University:
    Oklahoma City
Oral Roberts University
Phillips University
Rogers State College
Rose State College
Southeastern Oklahoma State
    University
Southern Nazarene University
Tulsa Junior College
University of Oklahoma
University of Science and Arts of
    Oklahoma
University of Tulsa

Oregon

Bassist College
Central Oregon Community College
Clackamas Community College
Clatsop Community College
Columbia Christian College
Concordia College
George Fox College
ITT Technical Institute: Portland
Lane Community College
Linfield College
Linn-Benton Community College
Marylhurst College
Oregon Health Sciences University
Oregon Institute of Technology
Portland Community College
Portland State University
Rogue Community College
Southern Oregon State College
Southwestern Oregon Community
    College

Treasure Valley Community College
University of Portland
Warner Pacific College
Western Baptist College
Western Oregon State College

Pennsylvania

Albright College
Alvernia College
Art Institute of Pittsburgh
Beaver College
Bucks County Community College
Cabrini College
Carlow College
Cedar Crest College
Chatham College
Chestnut Hill College
Cheyney University of Pennsylvania
Clarion University of Pennsylvania
Community College of Beaver
    County
Community College of Philadelphia
Delaware County Community
    College
Delaware Valley College of Science
    and Agriculture
Duquesne University
Eastern College
Elizabethtown College
Gannon University
Gwynedd-Mercy College
Holy Family College
Hussian School of Art
ICS Center for Degree Studies
Johnson Technical Institute
King's College
Kutztown University of
    Pennsylvania
La Roche College
La Salle University
Lansdale School of Business
Lebanon Valley College of
    Pennsylvania
Lehigh County Community College
Lincoln University
Luzerne County Community
    College
Manor Junior College
Marywood College
Millersville University of
    Pennsylvania
Montgomery County Community
    College
Moore College of Art and Design
Mount Aloysius Junior College
Northampton County Area
    Community College
Northeastern Christian Junior
    College
Peirce Junior College
Pennsylvania Institute of
    Technology
Philadelphia College of Textiles and
    Science
Pinebrook Junior College
Pittsburgh Institute of Mortuary
    Science
Point Park College
Robert Morris College
St. Joseph's University
Seton Hill College
Spring Garden College
Temple University
Triangle Tech: Pittsburgh Campus
University of the Arts
University of Pittsburgh
    Bradford
    Greensburg
University of Scranton
Villanova University
West Chester University of
    Pennsylvania

Widener University
Wilkes University
Wilson College

Puerto Rico

American University of Puerto Rico
Caribbean University
Catholic University of Puerto Rico
Electronic Data Processing College
    of Puerto Rico
Inter American University of Puerto
    Rico
    Arecibo University College
    San German Campus
Universidad Politecnica de Puerto
    Rico
University of Puerto Rico: Cayey
    University College
University of the Sacred Heart

Rhode Island

Bryant College
Community College of Rhode
    Island
New England Institute of
    Technology
Rhode Island College
Roger Williams College
Salve Regina College

South Carolina

Central Wesleyan College
Chesterfield-Marlboro Technical
    College
The Citadel
Claflin College
Clemson University
Coker College
College of Charleston
Columbia Junior College of Business
Florence-Darlington Technical
    College
Francis Marion College
Furman University
Greenville Technical College
Lander College
Limestone College
Midlands Technical College
Newberry College
North Greenville College
Orangeburg-Calhoun Technical
    College
Piedmont Technical College
Sumter Area Technical College
Technical College of the
    Lowcountry
Tri-County Technical College
Trident Technical College
University of South Carolina
    Aiken
    Beaufort
    Coastal Carolina College
    Columbia
    Lancaster
    Salkehatchie University
        Campus
    Spartanburg
    Sumter
    Union
Winthrop College
York Technical College

South Dakota

Augustana College
Black Hills State University
Dakota State University
Dakota Wesleyan University
National College
Northern State University
Sioux Falls College
South Dakota State University
University of South Dakota

Tennessee

Austin Peay State University
Belmont College
Carson-Newman College
Chattanooga State Technical
  Community College
Christian Brothers University
Cleveland State Community College
Crichton College
Draughons Junior College of
  Business: Nashville
Dyersburg State Community
  College
East Tennessee State University
Fisk University
Freed-Hardeman University
Lee College
LeMoyne-Owen College
Lincoln Memorial University
Maryville College
McKenzie College
Memphis College of Art
Memphis State University
Middle Tennessee State University
Milligan College
Nashville State Technical Institute
Northeast State Technical
  Community College
Pellissippi State Technical
  Community College
Shelby State Community College
Southern College of Seventh-day
  Adventists
State Technical Institute at
  Memphis
Tennessee State University
Tennessee Technological University
Tennessee Temple University
Tennessee Wesleyan College
Tomlinson College
Tusculum College
University of the South
University of Tennessee
  Chattanooga
  Knoxville
  Martin
  Memphis
Volunteer State Community College
Walters State Community College

Texas

Amarillo College
Angelina College
Arlington Baptist College
Brazosport College
Brookhaven College
Cedar Valley College
Cisco Junior College
Collin County Community College
  District
Concordia Lutheran College
Corpus Christi State University
Dallas Baptist University
Dallas Christian College
Del Mar College
DeVry Institute of Technology:
  Irving
East Texas Baptist University
Eastfield College
El Centro College
El Paso Community College
Hardin-Simmons University
Houston Community College
Howard College
Huston-Tillotson College
Incarnate Word College
Jarvis Christian College
Lamar University
Lee College
Lubbock Christian University
McLennan Community College
Mountain View College

Navarro College
North Lake College
Odessa College
Our Lady of the Lake University of
  San Antonio
Prairie View A&M University
Richland College
St. Edward's University
St. Mary's University
St. Philip's College
Sam Houston State University
San Antonio College
San Jacinto College North
Southwest Texas State University
Southwestern Assemblies of God
  College
Temple Junior College
Texas A&I University
Texas College
Texas Southern University
Texas Tech University
Texas Wesleyan University
Texas Woman's University
Tyler Junior College
University of Dallas
University of Houston: Downtown
University of Mary Hardin-Baylor
University of St. Thomas
University of Texas
  Arlington
  Dallas
  San Antonio
  Tyler
Wayland Baptist University
Western Texas College

Utah

LDS Business College
Phillips Junior College: Salt Lake
  City Campus
University of Utah
Utah Valley Community College
Weber State University

Vermont

Burlington College
College of St. Joseph in Vermont
Community College of Vermont
Lyndon State College
Norwich University
St. Michael's College
School for International Training
Southern Vermont College
Trinity College of Vermont
University of Vermont

Virginia

Blue Ridge Community College
Central Virginia Community College
Christopher Newport College
College of Health Sciences
College of William and Mary
Commonwealth College
Dabney S. Lancaster Community
  College
Danville Community College
Eastern Shore Community College
Ferrum College
George Mason University
Hampton University
James Madison University
John Tyler Community College
Liberty University
Longwood College
Lord Fairfax Community College
Mary Baldwin College
Mary Washington College
Marymount University
Mountain Empire Community
  College
New River Community College
Norfolk State University

Northern Virginia Community
  College
Old Dominion University
Patrick Henry Community College
Paul D. Camp Community College
Piedmont Virginia Community
  College
Rappahannock Community College
Richard Bland College
St. Paul's College
Southside Virginia Community
  College
Southwest Virginia Community
  College
Strayer College
Tidewater Community College
Virginia Commonwealth University
Virginia Highlands Community
  College
Virginia Intermont College
Virginia Polytechnic Institute and
  State University
Virginia State University
Virginia Union University
Virginia Wesleyan College
Virginia Western Community
  College

Washington

Art Institute of Seattle
Big Bend Community College
Cogswell College North
Columbia Basin College
Cornish College of the Arts
Eastern Washington University
Edmonds Community College
Everett Community College
Gonzaga University
Green River Community College
Heritage College
Lower Columbia College
North Seattle Community College
Northwest College of the
  Assemblies of God
Olympic College
Pacific Lutheran University
Peninsula College
Pierce College
St. Martin's College
Seattle Central Community College
Seattle Pacific University
Seattle University
Skagit Valley College
South Puget Sound Community
  College
Spokane Community College
Spokane Falls Community College
Tacoma Community College
Walla Walla College
Walla Walla Community College
Western Washington University
Whatcom Community College
Whitworth College

West Virginia

Alderson-Broaddus College
Bluefield State College
Davis and Elkins College

Wisconsin

Alverno College
Carroll College
Fox Valley Technical College
Lakeland College
Lakeshore Technical College
Madison Area Technical College
Madison Business College
Mount Senario College
Northeast Wisconsin Technical
  College
Northland College
St. Norbert College

Stratton College
University of Wisconsin: Stout
Waukesha County Technical
  College

Wyoming

Casper College
Central Wyoming College
Northwest College

American Samoa, Caroline Islands, Guam, Marianas, Virgin Islands

Guam Community College

France

American University of Paris

Tuition payment by installments

Alabama

Alabama State University
Birmingham-Southern College
Concordia College
Faulkner University
Huntingdon College
Judson College
Livingston University
Miles College
RETS Electronics Institute
Selma University
Southeastern Bible College
Stillman College
Talladega College
Trenholm State Technical College
Tuskegee University
University of Alabama
University of Montevallo
Walker College

Alaska

Alaska Bible College
University of Alaska
  Fairbanks
  Southeast

Arizona

American Indian Bible College
Arizona College of the Bible
DeVry Institute of Technology:
  Phoenix
Gateway Community College
Grand Canyon University
ITT Technical Institute: Phoenix
Prescott College
South Mountain Community
  College
Southwestern College
Western International University

Arkansas

Arkansas Baptist College
Arkansas College
Arkansas State University
Arkansas Tech University
Crowley's Ridge College
Harding University
Hendrix College
John Brown University
Mississippi County Community
  College
National Education Center:
  Arkansas College of Technology
North Arkansas Community College
Ouachita Baptist University
Philander Smith College
Phillips County Community College

Shorter College
Southern Arkansas University
  Magnolia
  Technical Branch
University of Arkansas
  Fayetteville
  Little Rock
  Pine Bluff
University of the Ozarks
Westark Community College
Williams Baptist College

California

Academy of Art College
American Armenian International
  College
Antelope Valley College
Antioch Southern California
  Los Angeles
  Santa Barbara
Armstrong College
Art Center College of Design
Azusa Pacific University
Bethany Bible College
Biola University
Brooks College
Brooks Institute of Photography
California Baptist College
California College of Arts and
  Crafts
California Institute of Technology
California Lutheran University
California State Polytechnic
  University: Pomona
California State University
  Bakersfield
  Chico
  Stanislaus
Canada College
Cerro Coso Community College
Chabot College
Chapman College
Charles R. Drew University: College
  of Allied Health
Christian Heritage College
Claremont McKenna College
Cogswell Polytechnical College
College of Alameda
College of the Canyons
College of Notre Dame
College of Oceaneering
College of the Sequoias
Compton Community College
Cosumnes River College
De Anza College
DeVry Institute of Technology: City
  of Industry
Dominican College of San Rafael
Dominican School of Philosophy
  and Theology
Fashion Institute of Design and
  Merchandising
Feather River College
Fresno Pacific College
Golden Gate University
Harvey Mudd College
Heald Business College: San Jose
Heald College: Sacramento
Hebrew Union College: Jewish
  Institute of Religion
Holy Names College
Humphreys College
ITT Technical Institute: Van Nuys
John F. Kennedy University
LIFE Bible College
Loyola Marymount University
Marymount College
Mendocino College
Menlo College
Mills College
Mission College

Monterey Institute of International
  Studies
Monterey Peninsula College
Mount St. Mary's College
Mount San Jacinto College
Napa Valley College
New College of California
Northrop University
Occidental College
Otis Art Institute of Parsons School
  of Design
Oxnard College
Pacific Christian College
Pacific Oaks College
Pacific Union College
Patten College
Pepperdine University
Phillips Junior College
  Condie Campus
  Fresno Campus
  San Fernando Valley Campus
Pitzer College
Point Loma Nazarene College
Pomona College
Porterville College
Sacramento City College
St. John's Seminary College
St. Mary's College of California
Samuel Merritt College
San Diego State University
San Francisco Art Institute
San Francisco Conservatory of
  Music
San Jose Christian College
Santa Clara University
Scripps College
Sierra College
Simpson College
Southern California College
Southern California Institute of
  Architecture
Stanford University
Taft College
Thomas Aquinas College
United States International
  University
University of California at Berkeley
University of Judaism
University of La Verne
University of the Pacific
University of San Diego
University of San Francisco
University of Southern California
University of West Los Angeles
Victor Valley College
West Coast Christian College
Western State University College of
  Law: San Diego
Westmont College
Woodbury University
Yuba College

Colorado

Adams State College
Arapahoe Community College
Bel-Rea Institute of Animal
  Technology
Blair Junior College
Colorado Christian University
Colorado College
Colorado Institute of Art
Colorado Northwestern Community
  College
Colorado School of Mines
Colorado State University
Colorado Technical College
Denver Institute of Technology
Fort Lewis College
ITT Technical Institute: Aurora
Lamar Community College
Metropolitan State College of
  Denver

Otero Junior College
Regis University
Rocky Mountain College of Art and
  Design
University of Colorado
  Colorado Springs
  Denver
University of Denver
University of Northern Colorado
Western State College of Colorado

Connecticut

Albertus Magnus College
Briarwood College
Bridgeport Engineering Institute
Connecticut College
Eastern Connecticut State
  University
Hartford College for Women
Holy Apostles College and
  Seminary
Mitchell College
Paier College of Art
Quinnipiac College
Sacred Heart University
St. Joseph College
Teikyo-Post University
Trinity College
University of Hartford
University of New Haven
Wesleyan University
Yale University

Delaware

Delaware State College
Delaware Technical and
  Community College: Southern
  Campus
Goldey-Beacom College
University of Delaware
Wesley College
Wilmington College

District of Columbia

American University
Catholic University of America
Corcoran School of Art
Gallaudet University
George Washington University
Mount Vernon College
University of the District of
  Columbia

Florida

Art Institute of Fort Lauderdale
Barry University
Florida Atlantic University
Florida Baptist Theological College
Florida Bible College
Florida Christian College
Florida College
Florida Memorial College
Florida Southern College
Florida State University
Hobe Sound Bible College
International Fine Arts College
Jacksonville University
Keiser College of Technology
New England Institute of
  Technology
North Florida Junior College
Nova University
Okaloosa-Walton Community
  College
Orlando College
Palm Beach Atlantic College
Phillips Junior College: Melbourne
Rollins College
St. John Vianney College Seminary
Southeastern College of the
  Assemblies of God
Southern College

Tampa College
University of Miami
University of Tampa
University of West Florida
Warner Southern College
Webber College

Georgia

Agnes Scott College
Atlanta Christian College
Atlanta College of Art
Augusta Technical Institute
Bauder Fashion College
Berry College
Brenau Women's College
Clark Atlanta University
Covenant College
DeVry Institute of Technology:
  Decatur
Emory University
Georgia Institute of Technology
LaGrange College
Meadows College of Business
Morris Brown College
Oglethorpe University
Paine College
Piedmont College
Reinhardt College
Savannah College of Art and
  Design
Shorter College
South College
Thomas College
Toccoa Falls College
Truett-McConnell College
Wesleyan College
Young Harris College

Hawaii

Cannon's International Business
  College of Honolulu
Hawaii Loa College
Hawaii Pacific University

Idaho

Boise Bible College
College of Idaho

Illinois

American Conservatory of Music
Augustana College
Aurora University
Barat College
Belleville Area College
Black Hawk College
Blackburn College
Bradley University
Carl Sandburg College
City Colleges of Chicago
  Chicago City-Wide College
  Harold Washington College
  Wright College
College of Lake County
College of St. Francis
Columbia College
Concordia University
De Paul University
DeVry Institute of Technology
  Chicago
  Lombard
Eastern Illinois University
East-West University
Elgin Community College
Elmhurst College
Governors State University
Greenville College
Harrington Institute of Interior
  Design
Illinois Benedictine College
Illinois Central College
Illinois College
Illinois Institute of Technology

Illinois State University
Illinois Technical College
Illinois Wesleyan University
International Academy of
  Merchandising and Design
ITT Technical Institute:
  Schaumburg
Kaskaskia College
Kendall College
Kishwaukee College
Knox College
Lake Forest College
Lakeview College of Nursing
Lewis and Clark Community
  College
Lewis University
Lincoln Christian College and
  Seminary
Lincoln College
Loyola University of Chicago
MacCormac Junior College
MacMurray College
McHenry County College
Midstate College
Millikin University
Monmouth College
Moraine Valley Community College
Morrison Institute of Technology
Mundelein College
National College of Chiropractic
National-Louis University
North Central College
North Park College and Theological
  Seminary
Northeastern Illinois University
Northern Illinois University
Northwestern University
Olivet Nazarene University
Parkland College
Parks College of St. Louis
  University
Prairie State College
Principia College
Quincy College
Ray College of Design
Richland Community College
Robert Morris College: Chicago
Rockford College
Roosevelt University
Rosary College
St. Joseph College of Nursing
St. Xavier College
School of the Art Institute of
  Chicago
Shimer College
Southeastern Illinois College
Southern Illinois University at
  Carbondale
Spoon River College
Springfield College in Illinois
State Community College
Trinity Christian College
Trinity College
University of Chicago
University of Illinois
  Chicago
  Urbana-Champaign
VanderCook College of Music
Waubonsee Community College
West Suburban College of Nursing
Western Illinois University
Wheaton College
William Rainey Harper College

Indiana

Anderson University
Ball State University
Bethel College
Butler University
Calumet College of St. Joseph
Earlham College
Franklin College

Goshen College
Grace College
Hanover College
Huntington College
Indiana Institute of Technology
Indiana University
  Kokomo
  Southeast
Indiana Vocational Technical
  College
  Kokomo
  Wabash Valley
  Whitewater
International Business College
Lutheran College of Health
  Professions
Manchester College
Marian College
Martin University
Purdue University
  Calumet
  West Lafayette
St. Francis College
St. Mary-of-the-Woods College
St. Meinrad College
Summit Christian College
University of Evansville
University of Indianapolis
Vincennes University
Wabash College

Iowa

Briar Cliff College
Buena Vista College
Central College
Clarke College
Clinton Community College
Coe College
Cornell College
Des Moines Area Community
  College
Divine Word College
Drake University
Ellsworth Community College
Emmaus Bible College
Faith Baptist Bible College and
  Theological Seminary
Graceland College
Grinnell College
Hamilton Technical College
Hawkeye Institute of Technology
Indian Hills Community College
Iowa Central Community College
Iowa State University
Iowa Western Community College
Kirkwood Community College
Loras College
Luther College
Maharishi International University
Morningside College
Mount Mercy College
Mount St. Clare College
Muscatine Community College
North Iowa Area Community
  College
Northwest Iowa Technical College
Northwestern College
St. Ambrose University
Scott Community College
Simpson College
Southeastern Community College:
  South Campus
Teikyo Marycrest University
Teikyo Westmar University
University of Dubuque
University of Iowa
University of Northern Iowa
Upper Iowa University
Vennard College
Wartburg College
William Penn College

Kansas

Baker University
Barton County Community College
Benedictine College
Bethany College
Bethel College
Brown Mackie College
Central College
Cloud County Community College
Cowley County Community College
Donnelly College
Emporia State University
Fort Scott Community College
Hesston College
Independence Community College
Kansas Newman College
Kansas Wesleyan University
Manhattan Christian College
Mid-America Nazarene College
Neosho County Community College
Ottawa University
Pratt Community College
St. Mary College
Southwestern College
Sterling College
Tabor College
Washburn University of Topeka
Wichita State University

Kentucky

Alice Lloyd College
Asbury College
Bellarmine College
Brescia College
Campbellsville College
Centre College
Clear Creek Baptist Bible College
Cumberland College
Eastern Kentucky University
Georgetown College
Institute of Electronic Technology
Kentucky State University
Kentucky Wesleyan College
Lees College
Lindsey Wilson College
Louisville Technical Institute
Mid-Continent Baptist Bible College
Midway College
Morehead State University
Murray State University
Owensboro Junior College of
  Business
Pikeville College
St. Catharine College
Southeast Community College
Spalding University
Sue Bennett College
Sullivan College
Transylvania University
Union College
University of Louisville

Louisiana

Centenary College of Louisiana
Dillard University
Jimmy Swaggart Bible College and
  Seminary
Louisiana College
Northwestern State University
St. Bernard Parish Community
  College
St. Joseph Seminary College
Southeastern Louisiana University
Southern University in Shreveport
Southern University and
  Agricultural and Mechanical
  College
Xavier University of Louisiana

Maine

Beal College
Bowdoin College

Casco Bay College
Central Maine Technical College
Colby College
College of the Atlantic
Eastern Maine Technical College
Husson College
Maine Maritime Academy
Portland School of Art
Southern Maine Technical College
Thomas College
Unity College
University of Maine
  Augusta
  Farmington
  Fort Kent
  Machias
  Orono
  Presque Isle
University of New England
University of Southern Maine

Maryland

Baltimore International Culinary
  College
Bowie State University
Capitol College
Cecil Community College
Columbia Union College
Dundalk Community College
Garrett Community College
Goucher College
Hagerstown Business College
Harford Community College
Hood College
Johns Hopkins University: School of
  Arts and Sciences and
  Engineering
Montgomery College
  Germantown Campus
  Rockville Campus
  Takoma Park Campus
Mount St. Mary's College
Ner Israel Rabbinical College
New Community College of
  Baltimore
St. John's College
Sojourner-Douglass College
University of Maryland: College
  Park
Villa Julie College
Washington Bible College
Washington College
Western Maryland College

Massachusetts

American International College
Aquinas College at Newton
Assumption College
Atlantic Union College
Bay Path College
Bay State College
Bentley College
Boston College
Boston Conservatory
Boston University
Brandeis University
Bridgewater State College
Clark University
Dean Junior College
Elms College
Emerson College
Emmanuel College
Endicott College
Essex Agricultural and Technical
  Institute
Fisher College
Fitchburg State College
Framingham State College
Gordon College
Hampshire College
Harvard and Radcliffe Colleges
Hebrew College

Marian Court Junior College
Massachusetts Institute of
Technology
Massasoit Community College
Merrimack College
Montserrat College of Art
Mount Holyoke College
Mount Ida College
Newbury College
Nichols College
North Adams State College
Pine Manor College
Regis College
St. Hyacinth College and Seminary
Salem State College
School of the Museum of Fine Arts
Simon's Rock College of Bard
Smith College
Southeastern Massachusetts
University
Springfield College
Suffolk University
Tufts University
University of Lowell
Wellesley College
Western New England College
Wheaton College
Williams College
Worcester Polytechnic Institute

Michigan

Adrian College
Albion College
Alma College
Andrews University
Aquinas College
Baker College
Flint
Owosso
Baker College of Muskegon
Calvin College
Center for Creative Studies: College
of Art and Design
Cleary College
Concordia College
Davenport College of Business
Eastern Michigan University
Grace Bible College
Grand Rapids Baptist College and
Seminary
Grand Rapids Junior College
Grand Valley State University
Great Lakes Bible College
Great Lakes Junior College of
Business
Highland Park Community College
Hillsdale College
Hope College
Jordan College
Kalamazoo College
Kellogg Community College
Kendall College of Art and Design
Lake Superior State University
Lawrence Technological University
Madonna University
Marygrove College
Michigan Christian College
Mid Michigan Community College
Nazareth College in Kalamazoo
Northern Michigan University
Olivet College
Reformed Bible College
Saginaw Valley State University
St. Mary's College
Siena Heights College
Southwestern Michigan College
Spring Arbor College
Suomi College
University of Detroit Mercy

University of Michigan
Ann Arbor
Dearborn
Flint
Walsh College of Accountancy and
Business Administration
Wayne County Community College
William Tyndale College

Minnesota

Augsburg College
Bemidji State University
Bethany Lutheran College
Bethel College
Carleton College
College of St. Catherine: St.
Catherine Campus
College of St. Scholastica
Concordia College: Moorhead
Concordia College: St. Paul
Dr. Martin Luther College
Hamline University
Macalester College
Minneapolis College of Art and
Design
Minnesota Bible College
National College
National Education Center: Brown
Institute Campus
North Central Bible College
Northwestern College
Northwestern Electronics Institute
Oak Hills Bible College
Pillsbury Baptist Bible College
St. John's University
St. Mary's Campus of the College of
St. Catherine
St. Mary's College at Minnesota
St. Olaf College
Southwest State University
University of Minnesota
Crookston
Duluth
Morris
Twin Cities
Waseca
University of St. Thomas

Mississippi

Alcorn State University
Blue Mountain College
Delta State University
East Mississippi Junior College
Jackson State University
Jones County Junior College
Magnolia Bible College
Mary Holmes College
Millsaps College
Mississippi College
Mississippi Gulf Coast Community
College: Perkinston
Mississippi University for Women
Northeast Mississippi Community
College
Northwest Mississippi Community
College
Pearl River Community College
Phillips Junior College
Jackson
Mississippi Gulf Coast
Tougaloo College
University of Mississippi
Medical Center
University
University of Southern Mississippi
Wesley College

Missouri

Avila College
Calvary Bible College
Central Bible College

Central Christian College of the
Bible
Central Methodist College
Central Missouri State University
Conception Seminary College
Culver-Stockton College
DeVry Institute of Technology:
Kansas City
Drury College
East Central College
Evangel College
Fontbonne College
Hannibal-LaGrange College
Harris Stowe State College
ITT Technical Institute: St. Louis
Jefferson College
Kansas City Art Institute
Lincoln University
Lindenwood College
Maryville College—St. Louis
Missouri Southern State College
Missouri Western State College
Moberly Area Community College
National College
North Central Missouri College
Northeast Missouri State University
Northwest Missouri State
University
Park College
Research College of Nursing
Rockhurst College
St. Louis Christian College
St. Louis College of Pharmacy
St. Louis University
Southeast Missouri State University
Stephens College
University of Missouri
Columbia
Kansas City
Rolla
St. Louis
Washington University
Webster University
Westminster College
William Jewell College
William Woods College

Montana

Carroll College
College of Great Falls
Dawson Community College
Eastern Montana College
Flathead Valley Community College
Miles Community College
Rocky Mountain College
University of Montana

Nebraska

Bellevue College
Bishop Clarkson College
Central Community College
College of St. Mary
Concordia College
Creighton University
Dana College
Doane College
Hastings College
Lincoln School of Commerce
McCook Community College
Mid Plains Community College
Nebraska Christian College
Nebraska Methodist College of
Nursing and Allied Health
Nebraska Wesleyan University
Southeast Community College:
Beatrice Campus
Union College
Wayne State College
Western Nebraska Community
College
Scottsbluff Campus
Sidney Campus

York College

Nevada

University of Nevada: Las Vegas

New Hampshire

Castle Junior College
Daniel Webster College
Dartmouth College
Franklin Pierce College
Hesser College
Keene State College
New England College
New Hampshire College
New Hampshire Technical College
Laconia
Manchester
Nashua
Stratham
New Hampshire Technical Institute
Notre Dame College
White Pines College

New Jersey

Assumption College for Sisters
Berkeley College of Business
Bloomfield College
Burlington County College
Caldwell College
College of St. Elizabeth
Drew University
Fairleigh Dickinson University
Edward Williams College
Florham-Madison Campus
Rutherford Campus
Teaneck-Hackensack Campus
Felician College
Georgian Court College
Glassboro State College
Jersey City State College
Monmouth College
New Jersey Institute of Technology
Passaic County Community College
Princeton University
Rabbinical College of America
Ramapo College of New Jersey
Rutgers—The State University of
New Jersey
Camden College of Arts and
Sciences
College of Engineering
College of Nursing
College of Pharmacy
Cook College
Douglass College
Livingston College
Mason Gross School of the
Arts
Newark College of Arts and
Sciences
Rutgers College
University College Camden
University College New
Brunswick
University College Newark
St. Peter's College
Salem Community College
Seton Hall University
Trenton State College
Upsala College
Westminster Choir College
William Paterson College of New
Jersey

New Mexico

College of Santa Fe
College of the Southwest
Dona Ana Branch Community
College of New Mexico State
University
Eastern New Mexico University
National College

New Mexico Highlands University
New Mexico State University
 Alamogordo
 Las Cruces
St. John's College

New York

Adelphi University
Adirondack Community College
Albany College of Pharmacy
Alfred University
American Academy of Dramatic
 Arts
Bard College
Barnard College
Boricua College
Briarcliffe: The College for Business
Canisius College
Catholic Medical Center of
 Brooklyn and Queens School of
 Nursing
Cazenovia College
Central City Business Institute
City University of New York
 Borough of Manhattan
  Community College
 John Jay College of Criminal
  Justice
Clarkson University
Cochran School of Nursing-St.
 John's Riverside Hospital
Colgate University
College of Aeronautics
College for Human Services
College of Insurance
College of Mount St. Vincent
College of New Rochelle
 New Rochelle
 School of New Resources
College of St. Rose
Columbia University
 Columbia College
 School of Engineering and
  Applied Science
Columbia-Greene Community
 College
Concordia College
Cornell University
Daemen College
Dowling College
D'Youville College
Eastman School of Music of the
 University of Rochester
Elmira College
Eugene Lang College/New School
 for Social Research
Fordham University
Friends World College
Hamilton College
Hartwick College
Herkimer County Community
 College
Hilbert College
Hobart College
Houghton College
Hudson Valley Community College
Iona College
Ithaca College
Jewish Theological Seminary of
 America
Juilliard School
King's College
Laboratory Institute of
 Merchandising
Le Moyne College
Long Island University
 Brooklyn Campus
 C. W. Post Campus
 Southampton Campus
Manhattan College
Manhattan School of Music
Manhattanville College

Mannes College of Music
Maria College
Marist College
Marymount College
Marymount Manhattan College
Mater Dei College
Medaille College
Mercy College
Molloy College
Monroe College
Nazareth College of Rochester
New York School of Interior
 Design
New York University
Niagara University
Pace University
 College of White Plains
 New York
 Pleasantville/Briarcliff
Parsons School of Design
Paul Smith's College
Plaza Business Institute
Pratt Institute
Rensselaer Polytechnic Institute
Roberts Wesleyan College
Rochester Institute of Technology
Sage Junior College of Albany, A
 Division of Russell Sage College
St. John Fisher College
St. Joseph's College
 Brooklyn
 Suffolk Campus
St. Thomas Aquinas College
Sarah Lawrence College
School of Visual Arts
Skidmore College
State University of New York
 Albany
 Binghamton
 Buffalo
 Purchase
 College at Brockport
 College at Buffalo
 College at Cortland
 College at Fredonia
 College at New Paltz
 College at Plattsburgh
 College at Potsdam
 College of Technology at
  Alfred
 Institute of Technology at
  Utica/Rome
Sullivan County Community
 College
Syracuse University
Taylor Business Institute
Tompkins-Cortland Community
 College
Touro College
Trocaire College
Ulster County Community College
University of Rochester
Utica School of Commerce
Vassar College
Wadhams Hall Seminary-College
Wagner College
Wells College
William Smith College
Wood School
Yeshiva University

North Carolina

Barber-Scotia College
Barton College
Bennett College
Campbell University
Catawba College
Cecils College
Chowan College
Davidson College
Duke University
Elon College

Gardner-Webb College
Guilford College
Johnson C. Smith University
Lees-McRae College
Lenoir-Rhyne College
Livingstone College
Louisburg College
Mars Hill College
McDowell Technical Community
 College
Meredith College
Methodist College
Montreat-Anderson College
Mount Olive College
North Carolina Agricultural and
 Technical State University
North Carolina Wesleyan College
Peace College
Pfeiffer College
Phillips Junior College: Winston-
 Salem
Piedmont Bible College
Queens College
St. Andrews Presbyterian College
St. Augustine's College
St. Mary's College
Salem College
Wake Forest University
Warren Wilson College
Wingate College
Winston-Salem State University

North Dakota

Fort Bethold Community College
Jamestown College
Mayville State University
Turtle Mountain Community
 College
University of Mary

Ohio

Antioch School for Adult and
 Experiential Learning
Art Academy of Cincinnati
Ashland University
Baldwin-Wallace College
Bluffton College
Bowling Green State University
 Bowling Green
 Firelands College
Bradford School
Capital University
Case Western Reserve University
Cedarville College
Chatfield College
Cincinnati Bible College and
 Seminary
Cincinnati Metropolitan College
Cincinnati Technical College
Circleville Bible College
Cleveland College of Jewish Studies
Cleveland Institute of Art
Cleveland Institute of Electronics
Cleveland State University
College of Mount St. Joseph
College of Wooster
Columbus College of Art and
 Design
Davis Junior College of Business
Defiance College
Denison University
DeVry Institute of Technology:
 Columbus
Dyke College
Franciscan University of
 Steubenville
Franklin University
God's Bible School and College
Hiram College
Hocking Technical College
ITT Technical Institute: Dayton
Jefferson Technical College

John Carroll University
Kent State University
 Ashtabula Regional Campus
 East Liverpool Regional
  Campus
 Kent
 Salem Regional Campus
 Stark Campus
 Trumbull Regional Campus
 Tuscarawas Campus
Kenyon College
Lake Erie College
Lakeland Community College
Lourdes College
Malone College
Marietta College
Miami University
 Hamilton Campus
 Oxford Campus
Miami-Jacobs College
Mount Union College
Mount Vernon Nazarene College
Muskingum College
North Central Technical College
Northwestern College
Notre Dame College of Ohio
Oberlin College
Ohio Dominican College
Ohio Institute of Photography
Ohio Northern University
Ohio University
Ohio Valley Business College
Ohio Wesleyan University
Otterbein College
Pontifical College Josephinum
Stark Technical College
Terra Technical College
Tiffin University
Union Institute
University of Akron
University of Findlay
University of Rio Grande
Urbana University
Ursuline College
Walsh College
Washington State Community
 College
Wilmington College
Wittenberg University
Wright State University
 Dayton
 Lake Campus
Xavier University

Oklahoma

Bartlesville Wesleyan College
Connors State College
Hillsdale Free Will Baptist College
Mid-America Bible College
National Education Center: Spartan
 School of Aeronautics Campus
Northeastern Oklahoma
 Agricultural and Mechanical
 College
Northwestern Oklahoma State
 University
Oklahoma Christian University of
 Science and Arts
Oklahoma City University
Oklahoma Junior College
Oral Roberts University
Phillips University
St. Gregory's College
Southern Nazarene University
Southwestern College of Christian
 Ministries
University of Tulsa

Oregon

Bassist College
Central Oregon Community College
Clackamas Community College

Clatsop Community College
Columbia Christian College
Concordia College
George Fox College
ITT Technical Institute: Portland
Lane Community College
Lewis and Clark College
Linfield College
Northwest Christian College
Oregon Institute of Technology
Oregon State University
Pacific Northwest College of Art
Pacific University
Portland Community College
Reed College
Southern Oregon State College
Southwestern Oregon Community
  College
University of Oregon
  Eugene
    Robert Donald Clark Honors
      College
University of Portland
Warner Pacific College
Western Baptist College
Western Oregon State College
Willamette University

Pennsylvania

Academy of the New Church
Albright College
Allegheny College
Allentown College of St. Francis de
  Sales
Antonelli Institute of Art and
  Photography
Art Institute of Pittsburgh
Bryn Mawr College
Bucknell University
Bucks County Community College
Cabrini College
Carlow College
Carnegie Mellon University
Cedar Crest College
Central Pennsylvania Business
  School
Chatham College
Clarion University of Pennsylvania
College Misericordia
Community College of Beaver
  County
Dean Institute of Technology
Delaware Valley College of Science
  and Agriculture
Dickinson College
Drexel University
East Stroudsburg University of
  Pennsylvania
Eastern College
Elizabethtown College
Franklin and Marshall College
Gannon University
Geneva College
Gettysburg College
Gwynedd-Mercy College
Hahnemann University School of
  Health Sciences and Humanities
Harcum Junior College
Harrisburg Area Community
  College
Haverford College
Holy Family College
Hussian School of Art
ICS Center for Degree Studies
Immaculata College
Indiana University of Pennsylvania
Johnson Technical Institute
Juniata College
Keystone Junior College
King's College
Kutztown University of
  Pennsylvania

La Roche College
La Salle University
Lansdale School of Business
Lebanon Valley College of
  Pennsylvania
Lock Haven University of
  Pennsylvania
Manor Junior College
Marywood College
Mercyhurst College
Messiah College
Millersville University of
  Pennsylvania
Montgomery County Community
  College
Moore College of Art and Design
Neumann College
Northeastern Christian Junior
  College
Peirce Junior College
Pennsylvania Institute of
  Technology
Philadelphia College of Bible
Philadelphia College of Pharmacy
  and Science
Philadelphia College of Textiles and
  Science
Pinebrook Junior College
Pittsburgh Institute of Aeronautics
Pittsburgh Institute of Mortuary
  Science
Pittsburgh Technical Institute
Point Park College
Robert Morris College
St. Charles Borromeo Seminary
St. Francis College
St. Joseph's University
Seton Hill College
Shippensburg University of
  Pennsylvania
Slippery Rock University of
  Pennsylvania
Spring Garden College
Swarthmore College
Thiel College
Tracey-Warner School
Triangle Tech: Pittsburgh Campus
University of the Arts
University of Pennsylvania
University of Pittsburgh
  Bradford
  Greensburg
  Titusville
Ursinus College
Valley Forge Military Junior
  College
Villanova University
West Chester University of
  Pennsylvania
Widener University
Wilkes University

Puerto Rico

American University of Puerto Rico
Catholic University of Puerto Rico
ICPR Junior College
Inter American University of Puerto
  Rico: San German Campus
Universidad Adventista de las
  Antillas
Universidad Politecnica de Puerto
  Rico
University of Puerto Rico
  Mayaguez Campus
  Medical Sciences Campus

Rhode Island

Brown University
Bryant College
New England Institute of
  Technology
Providence College

Rhode Island College
Rhode Island School of Design

South Carolina

Anderson College
Benedict College
Bob Jones University
Central Wesleyan College
Charleston Southern University
Claflin College
Coker College
College of Charleston
Columbia College
Columbia Junior College of Business
Converse College
Erskine College
Greenville Technical College
Limestone College
Morris College
Newberry College
North Greenville College
Phillips Junior College: Columbia
Presbyterian College
Spartanburg Methodist College
University of South Carolina
  Spartanburg
  Union
Voorhees College

South Dakota

Augustana College
Dakota Wesleyan University
Huron University
Mount Marty College
National College
Oglala Lakota College
Presentation College
Sioux Falls College
South Dakota School of Mines and
  Technology
University of South Dakota

Tennessee

Belmont College
Bethel College
Carson-Newman College
Christian Brothers University
David Lipscomb University
Draughons Junior College of
  Business: Nashville
Free Will Baptist Bible College
Freed-Hardeman University
Hiwassee College
King College
Knoxville College
Lambuth College
Lee College
LeMoyne-Owen College
Lincoln Memorial University
Maryville College
McKenzie College
Memphis College of Art
Milligan College
O'More College of Design
Rhodes College
Tennessee Temple University
Tennessee Wesleyan College
Tomlinson College
Trevecca Nazarene College
Union University
University of the South
University of Tennessee
  Chattanooga
  Knoxville
  Memphis
William Jennings Bryan College

Texas

Angelo State University
Arlington Baptist College
Austin College

Baptist Missionary Association
  Theological Seminary
Bauder Fashion College
Bay Ridge Christian College
Commonwealth Institute of Funeral
  Service
Concordia Lutheran College
Corpus Christi State University
Criswell College
Dallas Baptist University
Dallas Christian College
DeVry Institute of Technology:
  Irving
East Texas State University
  Commerce
  Texarkana
Hardin-Simmons University
Howard Payne University
Huston-Tillotson College
Incarnate Word College
Institute for Christian Studies
Jacksonville College
Jarvis Christian College
Lamar University
LeTourneau University
Lon Morris College
Lubbock Christian University
McMurry University
Miss Wade's Fashion
  Merchandising College
Odessa College
Our Lady of the Lake University of
  San Antonio
Prairie View A&M University
Ranger Junior College
Rice University
St. Edward's University
St. Mary's University
Sam Houston State University
Schreiner College
Southern Methodist University
Southwestern Adventist College
Southwestern Assemblies of God
  College
Southwestern University
Stephen F. Austin State University
Sul Ross State University
Tarleton State University
Texas A&I University
Texas A&M University
  College Station
  Galveston
Texas Christian University
Texas College
Texas Lutheran College
Texas State Technical Institute
  Harlingen
  Sweetwater
  Waco
Texas Tech University
Texas Wesleyan University
Texas Woman's University
University of Central Texas
University of Dallas
University of Houston
  Clear Lake
  Downtown
  Houston
  Victoria
University of North Texas

University of Texas
  Arlington
  Austin
  Dallas
  El Paso
  Health Science Center at
    Houston
  Health Science Center at San
    Antonio
  Medical Branch at Galveston
  San Antonio
  Southwestern Medical Center
    at Dallas Southwestern
    Allied Health Sciences
    School
  Tyler
Wayland Baptist University
Wiley College

Utah

LDS Business College
Phillips Junior College: Salt Lake
  City Campus
Westminster College of Salt Lake
  City

Vermont

Bennington College
Burlington College
Champlain College
College of St. Joseph in Vermont
Community College of Vermont
Norwich University
Southern Vermont College
Sterling College
Trinity College of Vermont
University of Vermont
Vermont Technical College

Virginia

Averett College
Bluefield College
Christendom College
Christopher Newport College
Clinch Valley College of the
  University of Virginia
College of William and Mary
Commonwealth College
Eastern Mennonite College
Emory and Henry College
Ferrum College
George Mason University
Hampden-Sydney College
Hollins College
James Madison University
Liberty University
Longwood College
Lord Fairfax Community College
Lynchburg College
Mary Baldwin College
Marymount University
Norfolk State University
Radford University
Randolph-Macon College
Randolph-Macon Woman's College
Richard Bland College
Roanoke College
St. Paul's College
Shenandoah University
Strayer College
Sweet Briar College
Virginia Commonwealth University
Virginia Intermont College
Virginia Polytechnic Institute and
  State University
Virginia State University
Virginia Union University
Virginia Wesleyan College

Washington

Antioch University Seattle
Art Institute of Seattle

Cornish College of the Arts
Evergreen State College
Gonzaga University
Griffin College
Heritage College
Lutheran Bible Institute of Seattle
Northwest College of the
  Assemblies of God
Pacific Lutheran University
Puget Sound Christian College
St. Martin's College
Seattle Pacific University
Seattle University
University of Puget Sound
Walla Walla College
Whitman College
Whitworth College

West Virginia

Appalachian Bible College
Beckley College
Bethany College
Davis and Elkins College
Fairmont State College
Huntington Junior College of
  Business
Ohio Valley College
Shepherd College
University of Charleston
West Virginia University
Wheeling Jesuit College

Wisconsin

Alverno College
Bellin College of Nursing
Beloit College
Carroll College
Carthage College
Concordia University Wisconsin
Edgewood College
Lakeland College
Lawrence University
Maranatha Baptist Bible College
Marian College of Fond du Lac
Marquette University
Milwaukee Institute of Art &
  Design
Milwaukee School of Engineering
Mount Mary College
Mount Senario College
Northland College
Northwestern College
Ripon College
St. Norbert College
Stratton College
University of Wisconsin
  Eau Claire
  Green Bay
  La Crosse
  Milwaukee
  Oshkosh
  Parkside
  Platteville
  River Falls
  Stevens Point
  Stout
  Superior
  Whitewater
University of Wisconsin Center
  Baraboo/Sauk County
  Fox Valley
  Manitowoc County
  Marathon County
  Marinette County
  Marshfield/Wood County
  Richland
  Rock County
  Washington County
  Waukesha
Viterbo College
Wisconsin Lutheran College

Wyoming

Casper College
Central Wyoming College
Eastern Wyoming College
Sheridan College
University of Wyoming

**American Samoa, Caroline
Islands, Guam, Marianas,
Virgin Islands**

Micronesian Occupational College
Northern Marianas College

France

American University of Paris

Switzerland

Franklin College: Switzerland

Tuition discount for
prepayment

Alabama

Faulkner University

California

Azusa Pacific University
Biola University
California Maritime Academy
Christian Heritage College
College of Oceaneering
Compton Community College
LIFE Bible College
Northrop University
Pacific Christian College
Pacific Union College
St. Mary's College of California
Southern California College
University of Redlands
University of San Diego
University of San Francisco
University of Southern California
Westmont College

Colorado

Colorado Technical College

Connecticut

Hartford College for Women

District of Columbia

Catholic University of America
Mount Vernon College

Florida

Hobe Sound Bible College
New College of the University of
  South Florida
University of Miami

Georgia

Augusta Technical Institute
Meadows College of Business
Morris Brown College
Oglethorpe University

Hawaii

Cannon's International Business
  College of Honolulu

Idaho

College of Idaho

Illinois

Barat College
Columbia College
Midstate College
National-Louis University

Quincy College
State Community College
Trinity College
University of Chicago

Indiana

Anderson University
Butler University
Goshen College
Huntington College
Summit Christian College

Iowa

Coe College
Emmaus Bible College
Luther College
Simpson College
Teikyo Westmar University
Vennard College

Kansas

Barclay College
Brown Mackie College
Cowley County Community College
Hesston College
Ottawa University

Kentucky

Centre College

Maine

College of the Atlantic
Unity College
University of New England

Maryland

Eastern Christian College
Johns Hopkins University: School of
  Arts and Sciences and
  Engineering
Mount St. Mary's College
Washington Bible College

Massachusetts

American International College
Atlantic Union College
Boston College
Boston University
Gordon College
Marian Court Junior College
Pine Manor College
Regis College
Wheaton College

Michigan

Alma College
Andrews University
Cleary College
Kendall College of Art and Design
Kirtland Community College
Marygrove College

Minnesota

Bethel College
College of St. Benedict
Concordia College: Moorhead
Hamline University
North Central Bible College
St. John's University
St. Olaf College
University of St. Thomas

Mississippi

Tougaloo College
Wood Junior College

Missouri

Central Bible College
Northeast Missouri State University
Park College
Southeast Missouri State University
University of Missouri: Columbia

Nebraska

Union College

New Hampshire

Colby-Sawyer College
Franklin Pierce College
New England College
Notre Dame College

New Jersey

Berkeley College of Business
Seton Hall University

New Mexico

St. John's College

New York

Alfred University
Barnard College
Canisius College
Colgate University
Columbia University: Columbia
  College
Hobart College
Keuka College
New York University
Nyack College
William Smith College

North Carolina

Duke University
Louisburg College
Pfeiffer College
Piedmont Bible College

North Dakota

Trinity Bible College

Ohio

Cedarville College
Cincinnati Bible College and
  Seminary
Circleville Bible College
Cleveland Institute of Electronics
Hiram College
Kenyon College
Lake Erie College
Malone College
Marietta College
Ohio Northern University
Ohio Wesleyan University
Union Institute

Oklahoma

Oklahoma Christian University of
  Science and Arts

Oregon

Bassist College
Linfield College
Pacific University
Western Baptist College

Pennsylvania

Academy of the New Church
Allegheny College
Duquesne University
Gettysburg College
Harcum Junior College
Lafayette College
Mercyhurst College
Philadelphia College of Bible
Spring Garden College
University of Pennsylvania

Rhode Island

Brown University

South Dakota

Dakota Wesleyan University
Sioux Falls College

Tennessee

Memphis College of Art
Milligan College
Southern College of Seventh-day
  Adventists

Texas

Huston-Tillotson College
Lon Morris College
Schreiner College
Southwestern Adventist College
Southwestern Assemblies of God
  College

Vermont

Lyndon State College
Middlebury College
Norwich University
Southern Vermont College

Virginia

Lynchburg College
Marymount University
Roanoke College

Washington

Griffin College
Lutheran Bible Institute of Seattle
Pacific Lutheran University
Seattle University
Walla Walla College

Wisconsin

Lakeland College
Marquette University

France

American University of Paris

Tuition payment by deferred payments

Alabama

Alabama Agricultural and
  Mechanical University
Alabama State University
Auburn University at Montgomery
Birmingham-Southern College
Bishop State Community College
Huntingdon College
Livingston University
Mobile College
Southern Union State Junior
  College
Spring Hill College
Trenholm State Technical College
Troy State University in
  Montgomery
University of Alabama

Alaska

Prince William Sound Community
  College
Sheldon Jackson College
University of Alaska
    Fairbanks
    Southeast

Arizona

Cochise College
DeVry Institute of Technology:
  Phoenix
Embry-Riddle Aeronautical
  University: Prescott Campus
Gateway Community College
Grand Canyon University
Mohave Community College
Northern Arizona University

Paradise Valley Community College
Phoenix College
Rio Salado Community College
South Mountain Community
  College
Southwestern College
Yavapai College

Arkansas

Arkansas Baptist College
Mississippi County Community
  College
University of Arkansas
    Fayetteville
    Pine Bluff
University of the Ozarks
Westark Community College
Williams Baptist College

California

Academy of Art College
Allan Hancock College
American Academy of Dramatic
  Arts: West
American Armenian International
  College
Antelope Valley College
Antioch Southern California at Los
  Angeles
Armstrong College
Bakersfield College
Biola University
California Lutheran University
Canada College
Chapman College
Charles R. Drew University: College
  of Allied Health
Christian Heritage College
Coastline Community College
Cogswell Polytechnical College
College of Alameda
College of Notre Dame
College of the Redwoods
Compton Community College
Cosumnes River College
DeVry Institute of Technology: City
  of Industry
Dominican College of San Rafael
Evergreen Valley College
Fashion Institute of Design and
  Merchandising
Gavilan Community College
Glendale Community College
Golden Gate University
Golden West College
Holy Names College
Kings River Community College
Long Beach City College
Los Angeles City College
Los Angeles Harbor College
Los Angeles Mission College
Los Angeles Pierce College
Los Angeles Trade and Technical
  College
Loyola Marymount University
Mendocino College
Merced College
Mills College
MiraCosta College
Modesto Junior College
Monterey Institute of International
  Studies
Monterey Peninsula College
Mount St. Mary's College
Mount San Antonio College
Napa Valley College
Northrop University
Ohlone College
Orange Coast College
Otis Art Institute of Parsons School
  of Design
Oxnard College

Pacific Christian College
Pacific Union College
Pasadena City College
Pepperdine University
Pomona College
Rancho Santiago Community
  College
Riverside Community College
Sacramento City College
Samuel Merritt College
San Jose City College
Santa Barbara City College
Santa Clara University
Santa Monica College
Santa Rosa Junior College
Scripps College
Shasta College
Skyline College
Sonoma State University
Stanford University
Taft College
United States International
  University
University of California: Santa
  Barbara
University of Judaism
University of La Verne
University of the Pacific
University of San Francisco
University of Southern California
University of West Los Angeles
Ventura College
Victor Valley College
West Los Angeles College
West Valley College
Western State University College of
  Law: San Diego
Woodbury University

Colorado

Adams State College
Aims Community College
Arapahoe Community College
Blair Junior College
Colorado Christian University
Colorado School of Mines
Fort Lewis College
ITT Technical Institute: Aurora
Metropolitan State College of
  Denver
Morgan Community College
Naropa Institute
Pueblo Community College
Regis University
University of Colorado at Boulder
University of Denver
University of Southern Colorado
Western State College of Colorado

Connecticut

Briarwood College
Central Connecticut State
  University
Connecticut College
Greater Hartford Community
  College
Hartford College for Women
Middlesex Community College
Northwestern Connecticut
  Community College
Norwalk Community College
Quinebaug Valley Community
  College
Quinnipiac College
Sacred Heart University
Tunxis Community College
Wesleyan University

Delaware

Delaware State College
Delaware Technical and
Community College
Stanton/Wilmington Campus
Terry Campus
Goldey-Beacom College

District of Columbia

American University
George Washington University
Georgetown University
Howard University
University of the District of
Columbia

Florida

Art Institute of Fort Lauderdale
Barry University
Bethune-Cookman College
Brevard Community College
Broward Community College
Central Florida Community College
Chipola Junior College
Daytona Beach Community College
Embry-Riddle Aeronautical
University
Florida Atlantic University
Florida Christian College
Florida Community College at
Jacksonville
Florida International University
International Fine Arts College
Jacksonville University
Lake City Community College
Nova University
Okaloosa-Walton Community
College
Phillips Junior College: Melbourne
St. John Vianney College Seminary
St. Thomas University
Tampa College
University of Florida
University of Miami
University of North Florida
Warner Southern College

Georgia

Atlanta Christian College
Clark Atlanta University
Covenant College
DeKalb Technical Institute
DeVry Institute of Technology:
Decatur
Georgia Southern University
LaGrange College
Meadows College of Business
Mercer University Atlanta
Morris Brown College
Oglethorpe University
Piedmont College
Reinhardt College
Spelman College
Thomas College
Toccoa Falls College

Idaho

Boise State University
College of Southern Idaho
Idaho State University
Lewis Clark State College
North Idaho College
University of Idaho

Illinois

Aurora University
Barat College
Belleville Area College
Black Hawk College
East Campus
Moline
Blackburn College

Bradley University
Carl Sandburg College
Chicago State University
City Colleges of Chicago
Chicago City-Wide College
Richard J. Daley College
College of DuPage
College of Lake County
DeVry Institute of Technology
Chicago
Lombard
East-West University
Elgin Community College
Governors State University
Greenville College
Illinois Central College
Illinois Eastern Community
Colleges: Olney Central College
International Academy of
Merchandising and Design
Joliet Junior College
KAES College
Kankakee Community College
Kaskaskia College
Kishwaukee College
Knox College
Lake Land College
Lakeview College of Nursing
Lewis and Clark Community
College
Lewis University
Lexington Institute of Hospitality
Careers
Lincoln Christian College and
Seminary
Lincoln College
Loyola University of Chicago
MacMurray College
McKendree College
Midstate College
Moody Bible Institute
Morrison Institute of Technology
Morton College
National College of Chiropractic
National-Louis University
Parks College of St. Louis
University
Quincy College
Rend Lake College
Richland Community College
Rockford College
Rush University
St. Xavier College
Sangamon State University
Sauk Valley Community College
South Suburban College of Cook
County
Southeastern Illinois College
Southern Illinois University at
Edwardsville
State Community College
Trinity Christian College
Trinity College
University of Health Sciences: The
Chicago Medical School
VanderCook College of Music
Waubonsee Community College
Western Illinois University
Wheaton College

Indiana

Ancilla College
Anderson University
Bethel College
Butler University
DePauw University
Earlham College
Goshen College
Huntington College
Indiana Institute of Technology
Indiana State University

Indiana University
Bloomington
East
Northwest
South Bend
Southeast
Indiana University—Purdue
University at Indianapolis
Indiana Vocational Technical
College
Columbus
Eastcentral
Kokomo
Lafayette
Northcentral
Northwest
Southeast
Southwest
Wabash Valley
Manchester College
Oakland City College
Purdue University: Calumet
St. Mary-of-the-Woods College
St. Meinrad College
Summit Christian College
University of Indianapolis

Iowa

Briar Cliff College
Cornell College
Drake University
Ellsworth Community College
Emmaus Bible College
Indian Hills Community College
Iowa Lakes Community College
Iowa Wesleyan College
Iowa Western Community College
Morningside College
North Iowa Area Community
College
St. Ambrose University
Simpson College
Southeastern Community College:
North Campus
Teikyo Marycrest University
University of Dubuque
University of Northern Iowa
Vennard College
Wartburg College

Kansas

Allen County Community College
Barclay College
Bethel College
Brown Mackie College
Cloud County Community College
Colby Community College
Cowley County Community College
Emporia State University
Fort Hays State University
Fort Scott Community College
Garden City Community College
Independence Community College
Kansas City Kansas Community
College
Manhattan Christian College
Neosho County Community College
Pittsburg State University
Pratt Community College
St. Mary College
St. Mary of the Plains College
Southwestern College
University of Kansas
Washburn University of Topeka
Wichita State University

Kentucky

Asbury College
Berea College
Brescia College
Campbellsville College
Clear Creek Baptist Bible College

Cumberland College
Eastern Kentucky University
Georgetown College
Jefferson Community College
Kentucky State University
Kentucky Wesleyan College
Lindsey Wilson College
Louisville Technical Institute
Maysville Community College
Midway College
Morehead State University
Murray State University
Northern Kentucky University
Somerset Community College
Sullivan College
Transylvania University

Louisiana

Bossier Parish Community College
Dillard University
Jimmy Swaggart Bible College and
Seminary
Louisiana State University
Alexandria
Eunice
Medical Center
Louisiana State University and
Agricultural and Mechanical
College
Northwestern State University
St. Bernard Parish Community
College
Southeastern Louisiana University
Southern University in Shreveport
Southern University and
Agricultural and Mechanical
College
University of New Orleans

Maine

Beal College
Bowdoin College
Casco Bay College
Central Maine Medical Center
School of Nursing
College of the Atlantic
Unity College
University of Maine
Augusta
Fort Kent
University of New England
University of Southern Maine

Maryland

Allegany Community College
Anne Arundel Community College
Bowie State University
Capitol College
Catonsville Community College
Cecil Community College
Coppin State College
Dundalk Community College
Eastern Christian College
Essex Community College
Frostburg State University
Garrett Community College
Hagerstown Junior College
Hood College
Johns Hopkins University: School of
Arts and Sciences and
Engineering
Loyola College in Maryland
Maryland College of Art and
Design
Montgomery College
Germantown Campus
Rockville Campus
Takoma Park Campus
Morgan State University
Mount St. Mary's College
Ner Israel Rabbinical College

New Community College of
    Baltimore
University of Baltimore
University of Maryland: College
    Park
Wor-Wic Tech Community College

Massachusetts

Anna Maria College for Men and
    Women
Atlantic Union College
Boston Conservatory
Boston University
Bristol Community College
Elms College
Emerson College
Emmanuel College
Forsyth School for Dental
    Hygienists
Hampshire College
Massachusetts Bay Community
    College
Merrimack College
Middlesex Community College
Mount Holyoke College
Northeastern University
Quincy College
Quinsigamond Community College
Smith College
Southeastern Massachusetts
    University
Springfield Technical Community
    College
Suffolk University
Wellesley College
Western New England College

Michigan

Albion College
Alma College
Aquinas College
Center for Creative Studies: College
    of Art and Design
Charles Stewart Mott Community
    College
Concordia College
Eastern Michigan University
Glen Oaks Community College
Grand Rapids Junior College
Grand Valley State University
Great Lakes Junior College of
    Business
Highland Park Community College
Jackson Community College
Kalamazoo College
Kalamazoo Valley Community
    College
Kellogg Community College
Kirtland Community College
Lawrence Technological University
Marygrove College
Michigan Christian College
Michigan State University
Mid Michigan Community College
Monroe County Community
    College
Nazareth College in Kalamazoo
North Central Michigan College
Northwestern Michigan College
Sacred Heart Major Seminary
St. Clair County Community
    College
St. Mary's College
Siena Heights College
Spring Arbor College
Suomi College
University of Detroit Mercy
University of Michigan: Dearborn
Walsh College of Accountancy and
    Business Administration
Wayne County Community College
Wayne State University

West Shore Community College
William Tyndale College

Minnesota

Bemidji State University
Brainerd Community College
College of St. Benedict
College of St. Catherine: St.
    Catherine Campus
Lakewood Community College
Mankato State University
Moorhead State University
Rainy River Community College
Southwest State University
University of Minnesota: Morris
University of St. Thomas
Vermilion Community College

Mississippi

Alcorn State University
Belhaven College
Blue Mountain College
Copiah-Lincoln Community College
East Central Community College
Hinds Community College
Jackson State University
Magnolia Bible College
Mary Holmes College
Meridian Community College
Millsaps College
Mississippi College
Mississippi Gulf Coast Community
    College
    Jackson County Campus
    Jefferson Davis Campus
Mississippi State University
Northwest Mississippi Community
    College
Pearl River Community College
Phillips Junior College of the
    Mississippi Gulf Coast
Rust College
Tougaloo College
University of Mississippi
    Medical Center
    University
University of Southern Mississippi
Wesley College
William Carey College
Wood Junior College

Missouri

Avila College
Central Christian College of the
    Bible
Columbia College
Conception Seminary College
Deaconess College of Nursing
DeVry Institute of Technology:
    Kansas City
Drury College
East Central College
Fontbonne College
Harris Stowe State College
Jefferson College
Lincoln University
Lindenwood College
Maryville College—St. Louis
Missouri Western State College
Park College
Research College of Nursing
Rockhurst College
St. Louis University
Southeast Missouri State University
Southwest Baptist University
University of Missouri
    Columbia
    Rolla
Washington University
Webster University
William Jewell College

Montana

College of Great Falls
Dawson Community College
Eastern Montana College
Flathead Valley Community College
Miles Community College
Montana College of Mineral
    Science and Technology

Nebraska

Bellevue College
Central Community College
College of St. Mary
Dana College
Grace College of the Bible
Metropolitan Community College
Nebraska Christian College
Nebraska Methodist College of
    Nursing and Allied Health
Nebraska Wesleyan University
University of Nebraska—Omaha
Western Nebraska Community
    College
    Scottsbluff Campus
    Sidney Campus

Nevada

Northern Nevada Community
    College
University of Nevada
    Las Vegas
    Reno
Western Nevada Community
    College

New Hampshire

Dartmouth College
Franklin Pierce College
Keene State College
New Hampshire Technical College
    Laconia
    Manchester
    Nashua
Rivier College

New Jersey

Bloomfield College
Burlington County College
Camden County College
Fairleigh Dickinson University
    Edward Williams College
    Florham-Madison Campus
    Rutherford Campus
    Teaneck-Hackensack Campus
Hudson County Community College
Jersey City State College
Kean College of New Jersey
Monmouth College
New Jersey Institute of Technology
Ocean County College
Passaic County Community College
Princeton University
Raritan Valley Community College
Rutgers—The State University of
    New Jersey
    Camden College of Arts and
      Sciences
    College of Engineering
    College of Nursing
    College of Pharmacy
    Cook College
    Douglass College
    Livingston College
    Mason Gross School of the
      Arts
    Newark College of Arts and
      Sciences
    Rutgers College
    University College Camden
    University College New
      Brunswick
    University College Newark

Salem Community College
Seton Hall University
Stevens Institute of Technology
Stockton State College
Trenton State College
Union County College
University of Medicine and
    Dentistry of New Jersey: School
    of Health Related Professions
William Paterson College of New
    Jersey

New Mexico

Albuquerque Technical-Vocational
    Institute
College of the Southwest
Dona Ana Branch Community
    College of New Mexico State
    University
Eastern New Mexico University
Clovis Community College
    Roswell Campus
National College
New Mexico Highlands University
New Mexico Institute of Mining
    and Technology
New Mexico Military Institute
New Mexico State University
    Alamogordo
    Carlsbad
    Las Cruces
Northern New Mexico Community
    College
Santa Fe Community College
Western New Mexico University

New York

Adelphi University
Adirondack Community College
Albany College of Pharmacy
American Academy of Dramatic
    Arts
American Academy McAllister
    Institute of Funeral Service
Boricua College
Broome Community College
Catholic Medical Center of
    Brooklyn and Queens School of
    Nursing
Cayuga County Community College
Cazenovia College
Central City Business Institute
City University of New York
    Baruch College
    City College
    College of Staten Island
    Hostos Community College
    John Jay College of Criminal
      Justice
    Lehman College
    Medgar Evers College
    New York City Technical
      College
    Queensborough Community
      College
    York College
Clinton Community College
College of Insurance
College of Mount St. Vincent
College of New Rochelle
    New Rochelle
    School of New Resources
Columbia University: School of
    Engineering and Applied Science
Columbia-Greene Community
    College
Community College of the Finger
    Lakes
Concordia College
Dowling College
Dutchess Community College
Elmira College

Erie Community College: North Campus
Eugene Lang College/New School for Social Research
Five Towns College
Fordham University
Fulton-Montgomery Community College
Genesee Community College
Hilbert College
Hofstra University
Hudson Valley Community College
Ithaca College
Long Island University
   Brooklyn Campus
   C. W. Post Campus
   Southampton Campus
Manhattan College
Manhattan School of Music
Mannes College of Music
Marymount Manhattan College
Mater Dei College
Medaille College
Mercy College
Molloy College
Monroe College
Mount St. Mary College
Nassau Community College
New York School of Interior Design
New York University
Niagara County Community College
Niagara University
Onondaga Community College
Pace University
   College of White Plains
   New York
   Pleasantville/Briarcliff
Paul Smith's College
Plaza Business Institute
Polytechnic University
   Brooklyn
   Long Island Campus
Pratt Institute
Rochester Institute of Technology
Sage Junior College of Albany, A Division of Russell Sage College
St. Bonaventure University
St. John Fisher College
School of Visual Arts
State University of New York
   Albany
   Binghamton
   Stony Brook
   College at Brockport
   College at Buffalo
   College of Environmental Science and Forestry
   College at New Paltz
   College at Potsdam
   College of Technology at Alfred
   College of Technology at Delhi
Tompkins-Cortland Community College
Trocaire College
Ulster County Community College
Utica College of Syracuse University
Vassar College
Villa Maria College of Buffalo
Wadhams Hall Seminary-College
Westchester Community College
Yeshiva University

North Carolina

Anson Community College
Asheville Buncombe Technical Community College
Bladen Community College
Chowan College
East Coast Bible College

Guilford College
Mayland Community College
McDowell Technical Community College
Methodist College
Montgomery Community College
North Carolina Agricultural and Technical State University
Peace College
Pfeiffer College
Queens College
Richmond Community College
St. Andrews Presbyterian College
Warren Wilson College
Wayne Community College
Western Piedmont Community College
Wilson Technical Community College

North Dakota

Fort Bethold Community College
North Dakota State University
Trinity Bible College

Ohio

Antioch School for Adult and Experiential Learning
Art Academy of Cincinnati
Bluffton College
Cedarville College
Chatfield College
Cincinnati Metropolitan College
Circleville Bible College
Clark State Community College
Cleveland Institute of Electronics
Cleveland State University
Cuyahoga Community College
   Eastern Campus
   Western Campus
Davis Junior College of Business
Denison University
DeVry Institute of Technology: Columbus
Edison State Community College
God's Bible School and College
Hiram College
Kent State University
   East Liverpool Regional Campus
   Salem Regional Campus
   Stark Campus
   Trumbull Regional Campus
Malone College
Marietta College
Marion Technical College
Miami-Jacobs College
Mount Vernon Nazarene College
Muskingum College
North Central Technical College
Oberlin College
Ohio Dominican College
Southern State Community College
Terra Technical College
Tiffin University
University of Cincinnati
   Cincinnati
   Clermont College
University of Dayton
University of Toledo
Urbana University
Walsh College
Wilberforce University
Wilmington College
Xavier University

Oklahoma

Bartlesville Wesleyan College
Central State University
Oklahoma Christian University of Science and Arts
Rogers State College

Southeastern Oklahoma State University

Oregon

Bassist College
Central Oregon Community College
Clackamas Community College
Columbia Christian College
Concordia College
Eastern Oregon State College
George Fox College
Lane Community College
Linfield College
Linn-Benton Community College
Marylhurst College
Multnomah School of the Bible
Northwest Christian College
Oregon Health Sciences University
Oregon Institute of Technology
Pacific Northwest College of Art
Pacific University
Portland Community College
Portland State University
Southwestern Oregon Community College
Treasure Valley Community College
University of Portland
Western Baptist College
Western Oregon State College

Pennsylvania

Academy of the New Church
Bloomsburg University of Pennsylvania
Bryn Mawr College
Bucks County Community College
California University of Pennsylvania
Carnegie Mellon University
Central Pennsylvania Business School
Chestnut Hill College
Clarion University of Pennsylvania
College Misericordia
Community College of Beaver County
Delaware County Community College
Delaware Valley College of Science and Agriculture
Drexel University
Duquesne University
East Stroudsburg University of Pennsylvania
Eastern College
Elizabethtown College
Gannon University
Gettysburg College
Harcum Junior College
Haverford College
Holy Family College
Hussian School of Art
ICS Center for Degree Studies
Immaculata College
Kutztown University of Pennsylvania
La Roche College
La Salle University
Lafayette College
Lancaster Bible College
Manor Junior College
Mansfield University of Pennsylvania
Marywood College
Moravian College
Neumann College
Peirce Junior College
Penn State
   Harrisburg Capital College
   University Park Campus
Pennsylvania College of Technology
Pinebrook Junior College

Point Park College
Robert Morris College
St. Charles Borromeo Seminary
St. Vincent College
Spring Garden College
Temple University
University of the Arts
University of Pennsylvania
Ursinus College
Valley Forge Military Junior College
Wilkes University
York College of Pennsylvania

Puerto Rico

Bayamon Central University
Caribbean University
Catholic University of Puerto Rico
Conservatory of Music of Puerto Rico
Electronic Data Processing College of Puerto Rico
ICPR Junior College
Inter American University of Puerto Rico
   Arecibo University College
   San German Campus
Universidad Politecnica de Puerto Rico
University of Puerto Rico
   Aguadilla
   Arecibo Campus
   Bayamon Technological University College
   Humacao University College
   Mayaguez Campus
   Medical Sciences Campus
   Ponce Technological University College
University of the Sacred Heart

Rhode Island

Brown University
Rhode Island School of Design
Salve Regina College

South Carolina

Central Wesleyan College
The Citadel
Columbia Bible College and Seminary
Columbia College
Technical College of the Lowcountry
Trident Technical College
University of South Carolina
   Aiken
   Coastal Carolina College
   Columbia
   Spartanburg
   Union

South Dakota

Black Hills State University
Dakota State University
Huron University
Northern State University
Presentation College
Western Dakota Vocational Technical Institute

Tennessee

Carson-Newman College
Christian Brothers University
Draughons Junior College of Business: Knoxville
Free Will Baptist Bible College
Johnson Bible College
Lee College
Lincoln Memorial University
Memphis College of Art
Tennessee Temple University

Tennessee Wesleyan College
Trevecca Nazarene College
Union University
University of Tennessee: Knoxville

Texas

Abilene Christian University
Amber University
Arlington Baptist College
Concordia Lutheran College
Corpus Christi State University
Dallas Christian College
DeVry Institute of Technology:
 Irving
East Texas State University
  Commerce
  Texarkana
Huston-Tillotson College
Jarvis Christian College
LeTourneau University
North Lake College
Prairie View A&M University
St. Edward's University
St. Mary's University
San Jacinto College North
Southern Methodist University
Southwestern University
Texas College
Texas State Technical Institute:
 Sweetwater
Texas Wesleyan University
University of Houston: Downtown
University of Mary Hardin-Baylor
University of Texas
  El Paso
  Health Science Center at
   Houston
  Medical Branch at Galveston
  Tyler

Utah

University of Utah
Utah State University
Utah Valley Community College

Vermont

Community College of Vermont
Johnson State College
Southern Vermont College
University of Vermont
Vermont Technical College

Virginia

Hampton University
Lord Fairfax Community College
Norfolk State University
Northern Virginia Community
 College
Old Dominion University
Strayer College
Virginia State University
Virginia Union University

Washington

Antioch University Seattle
Art Institute of Seattle
Cornish College of the Arts
Eastern Washington University
Gonzaga University
Grays Harbor College
Heritage College
Lower Columbia College
Northwest College of the
 Assemblies of God
Peninsula College
Pierce College
St. Martin's College
Skagit Valley College
South Puget Sound Community
 College
Tacoma Community College
University of Puget Sound

Western Washington University
Whitman College
Yakima Valley Community College

West Virginia

West Virginia State College

Wisconsin

Blackhawk Technical College
Carroll College
Gateway Technical College
Lakeshore Technical College
Madison Area Technical College
Marquette University
Mid-State Technical College
Milwaukee Area Technical College
Milwaukee Institute of Art &
 Design
Moraine Park Technical College
St. Norbert College
Silver Lake College
University of Wisconsin Center
  Baraboo/Sauk County
  Barron County
  Fox Valley
  Manitowoc County
  Marinette County
  Marshfield/Wood County
  Rock County
  Washington County
  Waukesha
Waukesha County Technical
 College
Western Wisconsin Technical
 College

Wyoming

Central Wyoming College
Sheridan College
Western Wyoming Community
 College

American Samoa, Caroline Islands, Guam, Marianas, Virgin Islands

Guam Community College
Micronesian Occupational College
Northern Marianas College

4. Sources of information about state grant programs and the Stafford Loan Program

State scholarships and grants

The major state scholarship and grant programs are described in the following list. Included in the description of each program are eligibility requirements, average awards, and the address of the administrative agency. Unless otherwise indicated, funds are available to state residents who are enrolled for full-time study at eligible postsecondary institutions in their state of residence.

Alabama

Alabama Student Assistance Program—Variable grants at in-state postsecondary institutions.

Alabama Student Grant Program—Non-need-based grants of up to $1,200 at private nonprofit colleges and universities.

National Guard Educational Assistance Program—Available to members of the Alabama National Guard for college study. Pays for tuition, fees, books, and supplies up to $500 per term or $1,000 per year.

Emergency Secondary Education Scholarship Loan Program—Available to mathematics and science education majors in accredited teacher education programs, up to $4,000 per year.

Teacher Re-Certification Scholarship Loan Program—Available to public school teachers working for their certification in critical-need fields, i.e. mathematics and science. Up to $4,000 per year.

For more information, contact the Alabama Commission on Higher Education, One Court Square, Suite 221, Montgomery, AL 36104-3584.

Alaska

Alaska Student Incentive Grant Program—Grants of up to $1,500 for use at eligible in-state and out-of-state postsecondary institutions.

For more information, contact the Alaska Commission on Postsecondary Education, Box FP, Juneau, AK 99811.

Arizona

Arizona State Student Incentive Grant Program—Need-based grants of $100 to $2,500 at accredited postsecondary institutions.

For more information, contact the financial aid office at the institution you wish to attend.

Arkansas

Arkansas Student Assistance Grant Program—Need-based grants of $200 to $624 at colleges and universities.

Governor's Scholars Program—100 merit-based $2,000 scholarships for attendance at colleges and universities in Arkansas, renewable for four years, awarded to high school seniors.

Emergency Secondary Education Loan Program—Available to secondary school education majors in shortage areas. Must pursue secondary teacher certification in state. Loans up to $2,500.

Paul Douglas Teacher Scholarship Program—Loans up to $5,000 available to education majors. Must pursue teacher certification in state.

For more information, contact the Department of Higher Education, 1220 West Third Street, Little Rock, AR 72201.

California

Three state student aid programs: Cal Grant A—Grants of $500 to $5,250 at independent colleges, $300 to $1,767 at the University of California, and $300 to $953 at California State University. Cal Grant B—Subsistence grants of $300 to $1,410 and in some cases tuition. Cal Grant C—Grants of up to $2,360 for tuition plus $530 for training-related expenses at vocational and technical schools.

For more information, contact the California Student Aid Commission, P.O. Box 510625, Sacramento, CA 94245-0625.

Colorado

Student Grant—Need-based grants of up to $2,000 at eligible postsecondary institutions.

Scholarship Program for Undergraduate Students—Scholarships of up to the amount of resident tuition and mandatory student fees at in-state institutions.

For more information, contact the financial aid office at the institution you wish to attend.

Connecticut

State Scholastic Achievement Grant Program—Grants of up to $2,000 may be taken to Connecticut colleges. Grants of up to

$500 may be taken to colleges located in reciprocal states. Based on academic performance and financial need. February 15 application deadline.

For more information, contact the Department of Higher Education, 61 Woodland Street, Hartford, CT 06105.

Delaware

Delaware Postsecondary Scholarship Fund—Need-based grants of $600 to $1,000 at approved Delaware, Maryland, and Pennsylvania colleges and at colleges in other states if the program of study is not offered at Delaware tax-supported colleges.

For more information, contact the Delaware Postsecondary Education Commission, 820 North French Street, Fourth Floor, Wilmington, DE 19801.

District of Columbia

District of Columbia Student Incentive Grant Program—Grants of $400 to $1,300 for the 1991-92 academic year. Renewable.

Paul Douglas Teacher Scholarship—Scholarships of $5,000 per academic year for up to four years to outstanding high school graduates pursuing teaching careers. Students must rank in top 10 percent of graduating class.

For more information, contact the D.C. Office of Postsecondary Education, Research and Assistance, 2100 Martin Luther King, Jr. Ave., S.E., Suite 401, Washington, DC 20020.

Florida

Florida Student Assistance Grant Program—Grants of $200 to $1,500 at eligible Florida colleges. One-year state residency required.

State Tuition Voucher Fund—Non-need grants of up to $2,000 at eligible private Florida colleges and universities. One-year state residency required.

Florida Undergraduate Scholars' Fund—Scholarships of up to $2,500 at eligible Florida colleges and universities. One-year state residency required.

"Chappie" James Most Promising Teacher Scholarship Loan Program—Loans of up to $4,000 to outstanding seniors chosen by high school principals for use at eligible Florida colleges and universities to pursue teaching careers in Florida. Repaid by teaching service or payments.

For more information, contact the Florida Department of Education, Office of Student Financial Assistance, 1344 Florida Education Center, Tallahassee, FL 32399-0400.

Georgia

Georgia Student Incentive Grant Program—Grants of $300 to $2,500 at nonprofit postsecondary institutions.

Georgia Tuition Equalization Grant Program—Grants of $925 at private colleges. Does not require financial need.

Law Enforcement Personnel Dependents Grant—$2,000 a year for dependents of Georgia Law Enforcement Personnel who have been killed or rendered disabled in the line of duty.

For more information, contact the Georgia Student Finance Authority, 2082 East Exchange Place, Suite 200, Tucker, GA 30084

Hawaii

Tuition Waivers and Pacific-Asian Scholarships—provide for tuition expenses at campuses of the University of Hawaii.

Hawaii Student Incentive Grant Program—Grants covering tuition expenses at nonprofit postsecondary institutions.

For more information, contact the financial aid office at the institution you wish to attend.

Idaho

State of Idaho Scholarship—Grants of up to $2,500 per year at public and private postsecondary institutions. Based on academic ability.

Paul Douglas Teacher Scholarship Program—Federally funded scholarships of $5,000 per year for students pursuing teacher certification.

Governor's Cup Scholarship Program—Grants of $3,000 based on academic ability.

Paul L. Fowler Scholarship Program—Memorial grant of $1,500 per year to Idaho high school graduates. Based on academic ability.

For more information, contact the Office of the State Board of Education, 650 West State Street, Boise, ID 83720.

Illinois

General Assembly Scholarships—Waivers of tuition and fees at public postsecondary institutions. Selection by general assembly members from residents of their districts.

For more information on this program contact your district legislator directly.

Illinois Monetary Award Program—Need-based grants of up to $3,500 at approved postsecondary institutions for half-time (6 hours minimum) and full-time study.

Illinois Merit Recognition Scholarship—$1,000 scholarships to Illinois students who rank in the top 5 percent of their high school classes at the end of the seventh semester. Financial need is not a factor. Not renewable.

Paul Douglas Teacher Scholarship—A federally funded program administered by the Illinois Student Assistance Commission providing scholarships of up to $5,000 per year to outstanding Illinois students who plan to become teachers at the elementary or high school level. Students must rank in the top 10 percent of their high school classes and may receive the award for four years.

For more information, contact the Illinois Student Assistance Commission, 106 Wilmot Road, Deerfield, IL 60015.

Indiana

Higher Education Awards—Grants of $200 to $4,313 for full-time students at private, nonprofit in-state postsecondary institutions and of $200 to $1,854 at state-supported universities. Based on need. Awarded to Indiana residents working on their first undergraduate degree.

Hoosier Scholar Awards—One-time grants of $500 to residents in the top 20 percent of their graduating class who are nominated by their high schools. Financial need is not considered.

Lilly Endowment Educational Awards—Need-based grants of $200 to $1,606 at nonprofit and public postsecondary institutions.

Paul Douglas Teacher Scholarship—Federally funded program providing renewable scholarships of up to $5,000 per year for students committed to a career in teaching who graduated in the top 10 percent of their high school class. Obligation to teach two years for every year scholarship is received.

Minority Teacher Scholarship—Grants of up to $1,000 for black or Hispanic students who want to be teachers. Renewable for up to four out of six years. Obligation to teach in Indiana for three out of five years following certification.

Special Education Teacher Scholarship—Grants of up to $1,000 for students who desire to teach in the field of Special Education. Renewable for up to four out of six years at eligible nonprofit or public postsecondary institutions. Obligation to teach in Indiana for three out of five years after certification.

Nursing Scholarship—Need-based grants for tuition of up to $5,000 for students who attend eligible nonprofit and public postsecondary institutions with nursing programs. Award is renewable.

State Work-Study Program—Summer work available to students who receive the Higher Education Grant or Lilly Grant during the preceding academic year. Funds awarded statewide to employers to reimburse 50 percent of student earnings.

For more information, contact the State Student Assistance Commission of Indiana, 964 North Pennsylvania Street, Indianapolis, IN 46204-1088.

Iowa

Iowa Minority Academic Grants for Economic Success—Need-based grants of up to $3,000 a year at participating colleges for minority students.

Iowa Tuition Grant program—Grants of up to $2,650 at private institutions (including nursing and business schools) for part-time and full-time study.

Iowa Vocational-Technical Tuition Grant Program—Grants of up to $600 at two-year public vocational and technical institutions for full-time study.

State of Iowa Scholarship Program—Grants of $125 to $500 renewable for up to three additional years to Iowa residents who rank in the top 15 percent of senior class. Based on academic ability and curriculum; renewals based on need and grade-point average.

Paul Douglas Teacher Scholarship Program—Federally funded grants of up to $5,000 a year for Iowa students who plan to become teachers. Must rank in the top 10 percent of class and be a State of Iowa Scholarship applicant. Award is renewable for four years.

For more information, contact the Iowa College Student Aid Commission, 201 Jewett Building, Ninth and Grand Avenues, Des Moines, IA 50309.

Kansas

Kansas Tuition Grant Program—Grants of up to $1,700 at private, nonprofit postsecondary institutions.

State Scholarship Program—Stipends of up to $1,000. Based on academic ability and financial need.

For more information, contact the Board of Regents, Capitol Towers, Suite 609, 400 Southwest Eighth, Topeka, KS 66603-3911.

Kentucky

College Access Program Grant—Need-based grants of up to $680 per year for full-time freshmen and sophomores ($29 per semester hour for part-time) who attend public and private colleges and universities. All awards are based upon community college tuition rates.

State Student Incentive Grant Program—Need-based grants of $680 per year for juniors and seniors at eligible postsecondary institutions.

Kentucky Tuition Grant Program—Need-based grants of up to $1,200 per year at eligible private, nonprofit postsecondary institutions.

Paul Douglas Teacher Scholarship Program—Federally funded awards of up to $5,000 per year to students who rank in the top 10 percent of class or on the GED and sign an intent to become a certified teacher and to render teaching service in any state.

Teacher Scholarship Program—Awards up to $5,000 per year to applicants who intend to become teachers in Kentucky. Based on grade-point average, class rank, and test scores. One year in a Kentucky state-accredited school required for each year of award or one semester of teaching in a critical shortage area required for every two semesters of award.

For more information, contact KHEAA Student Aid Program, 1050 U.S. 127 South, Suite 102, Frankfort, KY 40601.

Louisiana

State Student Incentive Grant Program—Grants of $200 to $2,000 at eligible postsecondary institutions.

Rockefeller Scholarship for Wildlife Programs—Up to $1,000 per year for students in forestry, wildlife management, fisheries, and marine science programs. A 2.5 overall grade-point average is required. Does not require financial need.

Education Majors Program—$2,000 per year for students enrolled or planning to enroll in a college of education. ACT composite score of 22 or of 20 with high school average of 3.0 or college average of 3.0 required.

Congressional Teacher's Scholarship Program—$5,000 per year for students with a high school average of 3.0 and ACT composite score of 22 and who rank in the top 10 percent of their high school graduating class or have a college average of 3.2.

For more information, contact the Office of Student Financial Assistance for Louisiana, P.O. Box 91202, Baton Rouge, LA 70821-9202.

Maine

Maine Student Incentive Scholarship Program—Need-based grants of $500 to $1,000 for Maine Students attending eligible postsecondary institutions in New England.

Paul Douglas Teachers Scholarship Program—Federally funded grants of up to $5,000 a year for Maine students who plan to become teachers. Renewable annually.

For more information, contact the Finance Authority of Maine, Maine Education Assistance Division, State House Station 119, Augusta ME 04333.

Maryland

General State Scholarship Program—Grants of $200 to $2,500 at public or private postsecondary institutions. Undergraduate awards based on need.

House of Delegates Grant Program—Grants of $200 to $2,200 to assist with tuition and fees at public and private postsecondary institutions for half-time and full-time study. Undergraduate and graduate students eligible.

Senatorial Scholarship Program—Grants of $200 to $1,500 at postsecondary institutions for half-time and full-time study. Based on academic ability and financial need. Undergraduate, graduate, and non-degree seeking students eligible.

Distinguished Scholar Program—$3,000 undergraduate annual awards based on merit or artistic talent for students nominated by their high schools.

For more information, contact the Maryland Higher Education Commission/State Scholarship Administration, 16 Francis Street, Annapolis, MD 21401-1781.

Massachusetts

General Scholarship Program—Grants of $200 to $3,800 for Massachusetts residents attending full-time eligible in-state postsecondary institutions and approved institutions in Connecticut, the District of Columbia, Maine, Maryland, New Hampshire, Pennsylvania, Rhode Island, and Vermont.

Tuition-Waiver Program—Up to the full cost of tuition waived for students attending a state-supported college or university. Amount of waiver determined by the financial aid office.

For more information, contact the Massachusetts Board of Regents of Higher Education, State Scholarship Office, 330 Stuart Street, Boston, MA 02116

Michigan

Tuition Grant Program—Need-based grants of up to $2,100 at independent nonprofit colleges and universities.

Competitive Scholarship Program—Awards based on ACT scores and financial need.

For more information, contact Michigan Department of Education, Student Financial Assistance Services, P.O. Box 30008, Lansing, MI 48909.

Minnesota

Minnesota State Grant Program—Grants from $100 to $5,564.

Part-Time Student Grant Program—Grants for students attending less than half-time.

Interstate Tuition Reciprocity Programs—Under these programs Minnesota residents pay a tuition rate that is less than the normal out-of-state charges at public collegiate and vocational institutions in Wisconsin, North Dakota, South Dakota, and some Iowa institutions.

For more information, contact the Minnesota Higher Education Coordinating Board, 550 Cedar Street, Suite 400, St. Paul, MN 55101.

Mississippi

State Student Incentive Grant—Grants of $200 to $1,500.

For more information, contact your college financial aid office or the Mississippi Postsecondary Education Financial Assistance Board, 3825 Ridgewood Road, Jackson, MS 39211-6453.

Missouri

Student Grant Program—Grants of up to $1,500 (averaging $1,200) for study at undergraduate nonprofit postsecondary institutions. Divinity, theology, or religion majors are not eligible. Based on need; renewable. Missouri FAF or FFS required.

Missouri Higher Education Academic Scholarship Program—Grants of up to $2,000 for full-time undergraduate students at eligible institutions. Students must have ACT composite scores or SAT combined scores in top 3 percent of all Missouri students taking those tests. Theology or divinity majors are not eligible. State residency required.

For more information, contact the Missouri Coordinating Board for Higher Education, P.O. Box 1438, Jefferson City, MO 65102.

Montana

Montana Student Incentive Grant Program—Grants of up to $900 at public postsecondary institutions and the three private colleges.

Honor Scholarships—Tuition and fee waivers at public postsecondary institutions.

For more information, contact the Montana University System, 33 South Last Chance Gulch, Helena, MT 59620.

Nebraska

For more information about the Scholarship Assistance Program and State Scholarship Award Program, contact a Nebraska postsecondary education institution.

Nevada

Nevada Student Incentive Grant Program—Grants of up to $2,500 for half-time and full-time study.

For more information, contact Nevada Department of Education, Fiscal Services, 400 West King Street, Carson City, NV 89710.

New Hampshire

New Hampshire Incentive Program—Need-based grants of $100 to $1,500 for undergraduate, full-time students. Grants portable by New Hampshire residents to five other New England states. Rank in upper three-fifths of high school graduating class required of first-time freshmen, 2.0 college average required of those with sophomore standing and above.

For more information, contact the New Hampshire Postsecondary Education Commission, 2 Industrial Park Drive, Concord, NH 03301.

New Jersey

Tuition Aid Grant Program—Grants of $400 to $3,700 at in-state colleges only.

Educational Opportunity Fund Grant Program—Grants of $200 to $1,950 at in-state colleges only.

Edward J. Bloustein Distinguished Scholars Program—Grants of $1,000 per year at in-state colleges only. Based on academic ability. Up to an additional $1,000 if student shows need.

Garden State Scholar Program—Grants of $500 per year at in-state colleges only. Based on academic ability. Up to an additional $500 if student shows need.

For more information, contact the Department of Higher Education, Office of Student Assistance, CN 540, Trenton, NJ 08625.

New Mexico

New Mexico Scholars Program—Scholarship provides tuition, required student fees, and books for an academic year for outstanding high school students attending eligible postsecondary institutions as full-time students. Renewable up to four times. Student must have combined family income below $30,000.

New Mexico Student Choice Grant Program—For undergraduates attending an eligible private postsecondary institution and who are enrolled at least half-time.

New Mexico Student Incentive Grant Program—Need-based grants of $200 to $2,500 per year at public and private postsecondary institutions.

New Mexico Vietnam Veterans' Scholarship Program—Tuition grants for undergraduate and graduate students attending postsecondary institutions.

For more information, contact New Mexico Educational Assistance Foundation, P.O. Box 27020, Albuquerque, NM 87125-7020.

New York

New York Tuition Assistance Program—Grants of $350 to $3,650 depending on type of institution and need. Annual; available to undergraduate or graduate students.

New York State Regents College Scholarship Program—Scholarships of $250, based on academic ability.

Empire State Scholarships—Scholarships of up to $2,000 per year to full-time undergraduates.

Empire State Challenger Scholarships and Fellowships for Teachers—Scholarships of up to $3,000 per year for full-time undergraduate study to prospective teachers. Graduate fellowships of up to $4,000 for one year full-time study and up to $1,000 for two years' part-time study; recipients must teach in an elementary or secondary school located in New York State.

Vietnam Veterans Tuition Awards—Grants of $1,000 per semester for full-time study and $500 per semester for part-time study for eligible applicants who served in the U.S. Armed Forces between January 1, 1963, and May 7, 1975.

For more information, contact the Higher Education Services Corporation, Student Information, 99 Washington Avenue, 14th Floor, Albany, NY 12255.

North Carolina

North Carolina Legislative Tuition Grant Program—Grants of up to $1,150 annually at private colleges and universities. Does not require financial need.

North Carolina Student Incentive Grant Program—Grants of up to $1,500 or one-half of unmet need, whichever is less, at colleges, universities, and technical and vocational schools.

North Carolina Student Loan Program for Health, Science, and Mathematics—Scholarships/loans ranging from $2,500 to $7,500 annually depending on degree level, to be repaid through practice service in the state. Available to legal residents in accredited associate, baccalaureate, master's or doctoral programs.

North Carolina Teaching Fellows Program—Grants of up to $5,000 to encourage entry into the elementary and secondary teaching profession. May be used to attend 13 designated constituent institutions of the University of North Carolina. Does not require financial need.

State Contractual Scholarship Fund—Grants at eligible North Carolina private colleges and universities, based on need.

For more information, contact the North Carolina State Education Assistance Authority, Box 2688, Chapel Hill, NC 27515-2688.

North Dakota

Student Financial Assistance Program—Grants of up to $600 for attendance at public and nonprofit postsecondary institutions.

North Dakota Scholars Program—Tuition Scholarships available to students who score at the 95th percentile or above on ACT, and who rank in the top 20 percent of their graduating class.

For more information, contact the Student Financial Assistance Program, State Capitol, Tenth Floor, 600 East Boulevard, Bismarck, ND 58505.

Ohio

Instructional Grant Program—Grants of up to $3,306 at Ohio and Pennsylvania approved private postsecondary institutions and up to $1,326 at Ohio and Pennsylvania approved public postsecondary institutions and up to $2,268 at Ohio and Pennsylvania approved proprietary institutions. For full-time undergraduates enrolled in eligible associate or bachelor's degree or nursing diploma programs.

Ohio Academic Scholarship Program—Scholarships of $1,000 per year at eligible public, private, and proprietary postsecondary Ohio institutions. Based on high school academic ability. For undergraduate students only.

Ohio Student Choice Grant Program—Grants in varying amounts at eligible private postsecondary Ohio institutions. For full-time undergraduates enrolled in a bachelor's degree program who did not attend any institution full-time before July 1, 1984.

For more information, contact the Student Assistance Office, Ohio Board of Regents, 3600 State Office Tower, 30 East Broad Street, Columbus OH 43266-0417.

Oklahoma

Tuition Aid Grant Program—Grants of up to $1,000 or 75 percent of tuition and fees, whichever is less, at eligible colleges, universities, and vocational-technical schools. Based on financial need. Available to undergraduate and graduate students, full-time and part-time.

For more information, contact the Oklahoma State Regents for Tuition Aid Grant Program, P.O. Box 54009, Oklahoma City, OK 73105-2054.

Oregon

Need Grant Program—Need-based grants of up to $1,848 at accredited non-profit postsecondary institutions.

Cash Award Program—Grants of up to $864 at accredited non-profit postsecondary institutions. Based on academic ability and financial need.

For more information, contact the Oregon State Scholarship Commission, 1445 Willamette Street, Eugene, OR 97401-7706.

Pennsylvania

State Higher Education Grant Program—Grants of $100 to $2,200 at in-state postsecondary institutions and lower limits at eligible out-of-state postsecondary institutions.

POW/MIA Grant Program—Grants of $100 to $1,200 for dependents of U.S. Armed Forces veterans who were taken prisoner or declared missing-in-action; for use at in-state postsecondary institutions. Lower limits at eligible out-of-state institutions.

Scholars in Education Award Program—Grants of $1,500 to one-half of tuition costs or $5,000, whichever is less, to high school seniors and college students studying for careers in mathematics or science education.

Veterans Grant Program—Grants of $100 to $2,200 for applicants who served in the U.S. Armed Forces at in-state postsecondary institutions. Lower limits at eligible out-of-state institutions.

For more information, contact the Pennsylvania Higher Education Assistance Agency, 660 Boas Street, Harrisburg, PA 17102.

Puerto Rico

Legislative Scholarship Program—Grants for attendance at the University of Puerto Rico.

Supplemental Aid Program—University of Puerto Rico institutional program for supplemental aid that provides additional aid to needy students.

Legislative Scholarship Program—Grants for attendance at private accredited institutions of higher education.

Educational Fund—Grants for attendance at private accredited institutions of higher education.

Paul Douglas Teacher Scholarship Program—Scholarship to outstanding high school graduates to enable and encourage them to pursue teaching careers at the preschool, elementary, or secondary levels. Grants of up to $5,000 for a maximum of four years.

Robert C. Byrd Honor Scholarship program—Scholarships to promote student excellence and to recognize exceptionally able students. Grants are $1,500 for one academic year.

For more information, contact the Council on Higher Education, Box 23305-UPR Station, Rio Piedras, PR 00931.

Rhode Island

State Grant or Scholarship Program—Scholarships and grants of up to $1,500 at eligible in-state and out-of-state postsecondary institutions. Scholarships based on SAT scores and financial need; grants based on financial need.

For more information, contact the Rhode Island Higher Education Assistance Authority, 560 Jefferson Boulevard, Warwick, RI 02886.

South Carolina

Tuition Grants Program—Need-based grants of $100 to $3,990 at private postsecondary institutions.

For more information, contact the Tuition Grants Commission, First Floor, Keenan Building, P.O. Box 12159, Columbia, SC 29211.

South Dakota

South Dakota Student Incentive Grant Program—Grants of up to $600 at participating postsecondary institutions.

South Dakota Tuition Equalization Grant—Grants of up to $250 at participating in-state private colleges.

South Dakota Superior Scholarship—South Dakota resident students identified as National Merit Scholarship semifinalists pursuant to the October 1982 Preliminary Scholastic Aptitude Test/National Merit Scholarship Qualifying Test (PSAT/NMSQT) testing date, and years following, who attend participating South Dakota colleges and universities are eligible for scholarships of up to $1,500.

National Guard Tuition—Members of the Army or Air National Guard of the state of South Dakota attending any undergraduate-level institution under the control of the Board of Regents or a state vocational institution are entitled to a 50 percent reduction of tuition charges. There is a four-year limit.

Paul Douglas Teacher Scholarship Program—Scholarships to outstanding high school graduates to enable and encourage them to pursue teaching careers at the preschool, elementary, or secondary levels. Grants of up to $5,000 for a maximum of four years.

Robert C. Byrd Honors Scholarship Program—Scholarships to promote student excellence and achievement and to recognize exceptionally able students who show promise of continued excellence. Grants are $1,500 for one academic year.

For more information, contact the Department of Education and Cultural Affairs, Office of the Secretary, 700 Governors Drive, Pierre, SD 57501-2291.

Tennessee

Tennessee Student Assistance Awards Program—Maximum grants of $1,386.

Dependent Children Scholarship—For dependent children of a law enforcement officer, firefighter, or emergency medical service technician in Tennessee who was killed or totally and permanently disabled while performing duties within the scope of his or her employment.

Paul Douglas Teacher Scholarship Program—Federally funded program for students entering the teaching field at the K-12 level. Grants of up to $5,000 for a maximum of four years.

Tennessee Academic Scholars Program—Awards up to $4,000 per academic year for academically superior high school graduates.

Tennessee Teacher Loan/Scholarship Program—For outstanding students who plan to become public school teachers in an academic shortage area designated by the State Board of Education (currently mathematics or science for grades 7-12, or art or music for grades K-8). Award of up to $1,500 per year, for a maximum of $6,000.

Teacher Loan Program for Disadvantaged Areas of Tennessee—For students who plan to become public school teachers at the K-12 level in a geographic area designated by the State Board of Education as disadvantaged at the time the student completes the requirements for teacher certification. Awards of up to $1,500 per year, for a maximum of $6,000.

For more information, contact the Tennessee Student Assistance Corporation, Suite 1950, Parkway Towers, 404 James Robertson Parkway, Nashville, TN 37243-0820.

Texas

Texas Tuition Equalization Grant Program—Grants of up to $1,900 at private, nonprofit postsecondary institutions.

Texas Public Grant Program—Grants of up to $2,500 at public postsecondary institutions.

State Scholarship for Ethnic Recruitment—Scholarships of $500 to $1,000 for eligible minority students attending general academic teaching institutions.

Robert C. Byrd Honors Scholarship Program—Scholarships to promote student excellence and achievement and to recognize exceptionally able students who show promise of continued excellence. Grants are $1,500 for one academic year.

Paul Douglas Teacher Scholarship Program—Loans to outstanding high school graduates to enable and encourage them to pursue teaching careers at the preschool, elementary, or secondary levels. Loans of up to $5,000 per year for a maximum of four years.

For more information, contact the financial aid office at the institution you wish to attend.

Utah

Educational Disadvantaged Fund—Grants of $100 to $2,500 based on need.

Utah Educational Career Teaching Scholarship—Available to students who plan a career teaching in the public educational institutions of Utah. Tuition and fees waived, with additional stipends in some instances awarded on merit. Recipient must teach in the public educational institutions of Utah one year for each year they received the scholarship, for a maximum of five years. This must begin no later than two years after certification.

National Guard State Tuition Assistance—Members of the national guard may receive up to $1,000 per year, not to exceed a $4,000 maximum. Extended service period required.

For more information, contact the financial aid office at the institution you wish to attend.

Vermont

Vermont Incentive Grants Program—Grants of $300 to $3,850 at in-state and out-of-state postsecondary institutions.

Private Tuition Differential Grant Program—Grants of up to an additional $1,200 at in-state private colleges.

Part-Time Student Grant Program—Grants of $75 to $3,790 available to students going less than full-time at in-state and out-of-state postsecondary institutions.

For more information, contact the Vermont Student Assistance Corporation, Champlain Mill, P.O. Box 2000, Winooski, VT 05404-2601.

Virginia

College Scholarship Assistance Program—Grants of $400 to $2,000 at public and private colleges.

Virginia Scholars Program—Merit-based scholarships of $3,000 for outstanding high school students enrolled full-time in a baccalaureate degree program at an accredited, degree-granting, public or private nonprofit institution. Renewable for up to three years. Also available to outstanding graduates of in-state two-year colleges who transfer to a senior in-state college to complete their baccalaureate degree; renewable for up to one year.

Virginia Tuition Assistance Grant—Non-need-based grants of up to $1,375 at private colleges for 1991-92.

Virginia Transfer Grant Program—Full tuition and mandatory fees or remaining need, whichever is lower, awarded to "other race" students who are enrolled in a traditionally white or black four-year public college or university in Virginia. Applicants must meet minimum merit criteria and be first-time transfer students.

Last Dollar Program—Need-based grants for black undergraduates enrolled for the first time in a state-supported college or university.

Paul Douglas Teacher Scholarship Program—Grants of up to $5,000 to undergraduate students matriculating full-time in a program leading to teacher certification and who ranked in the top 10 percent of their high school graduating class. Teaching service required upon completion of the program.

For more information, contact the Virginia Council of Higher Education, James Monroe Building, 101 North 14th Street, Richmond, VA 23219.

Washington

State Need Grant Program—Variable grants for low-income state residents attending in-state postsecondary institutions.

Future Teacher Conditional Scholarship Program—Renewable $3,000 scholarships requiring a 10-year in-state public school teaching commitment.

Paul Douglas Teachers Scholarship Program—Renewable $5,000 scholarships to those graduating in the top 10 percent of their high school class and intending to pursue a teaching career. Recipients must teach two years for each year of scholarship assistance.

Nurses Conditional Scholarship Program—Renewable scholarships of up to $3,000. Recipients agree to nurse in a state-defined shortage area for five years.

Scholars Tuition Waiver and Grant Program—Four-year tuition waivers at public institutions and grants for those attending private institutions. Recipients are high school seniors from the top 1 percent of their class, nominated for academic excellence, leadership, and community service by principals.

For more information, contact the Higher Education Coordinating Board, 917 Lakeridge Way, GV-11, Olympia WA 98504.

West Virginia

Higher Education Grant Program—Grants of up to $1,650 at approved in-state higher education institutions, and up to $600 at approved Pennsylvania institutions for full-time students.

Robert C. Byrd Honors Scholarship Program—Merit scholarships of $1,500 awarded for the first year of study at a nonprofit degree-granting institution of higher education.

Paul Douglas Teacher Scholarship Program—Grants of up to $5,000 to state residents who graduated in the top 10 percent of their high school class; who are enrolled full-time at an in-state college or university in a course of study leading to teacher certification; and who agree to teach in any state for two years for each year of scholarship assistance.

Underwood-Smith Teacher Scholarship Program—Grants of up to $5,000 to state residents who graduated in the top 10 percent of their high school class or scored in the top 10 percent statewide of those students taking the ACT; who are enrolled in a state college or university in a course of study leading to certification as a teacher; and who agree to teach in the state's public school system for two years for each year of scholarship assistance.

For more information, contact the State Colleges and University Systems of West Virginia Central Office, Higher Education Grant Program, P.O. Box 4007, Charleston, WV 25364.

Wisconsin

Wisconsin Higher Education Grants Program—Grants of up to $1,800 at eligible public postsecondary institutions for half-time and full-time study.

Tuition Grant Program—Grants of up to $2,172 at eligible private colleges, universities, and nursing schools for half-time and full-time study.

Interstate Program (Minnesota-Wisconsin)—A reciprocal arrangement paying for Wisconsin resident tuition at public collegiate and vocational institutions in Minnesota.

Minority Grant Program—Grants of up to $2,500 at public VTAE institutions and private nonprofit institutions for full-time study.

Wisconsin Indian Student Grant Program—Grants of up to $1,800 at any eligible public or private institution of higher education in Wisconsin for half-time or full-time students who are of at least 25 percent native American heritage.

For more information, contact the Wisconsin Higher Educational Aids Board, P.O. Box 7885, Madison WI 53707.

Wyoming

State Student Incentive Grants Program—Grants at public non-profit postsecondary institutions averaging $300.

For more information, contact the Wyoming Community College Commission, 122 West 25th, Herschler Building, NW, Cheyenne, WY 82002.

Guam

Government-sponsored scholarships for teaching and nursing programs.

Merit awards available to graduating seniors for attendance at the University of Guam or at an off-island institution if major is not offered at University of Guam.

Need-based aid programs available.

For more information, contact the Student Financial Assistance Program, University of Guam, UOG Station, Mangilao, GU 96923.

Virgin Islands

Student Incentive Grant Program—Grants of up to $2,500 at the College of the Virgin Islands and United States nonprofit postsecondary institutions.

Territorial Scholarship Program—Grants of $1,000 to $3,000 for undergraduate and graduate students at the College of the Virgin Islands and United States nonprofit postsecondary institutions.

For more information, contact the Financial Aid Office, Virgin Islands Board of Education, P.O. Box 11900, St. Thomas, VI 00801.

Sources of information about the Stafford Loan Program

Alabama

Alabama Commission on
    Higher Education
One Court Square, Suite 221
Montgomery, AL 36104-3584
(205) 269-2700

Alaska

United Student Aid Funds
P.O. Box 40529
Indianapolis, IN 46250

Arizona

Arizona Education Loan Program
1400 East Southern Avenue, Suite 200
Tempe, AZ 85282-5679

Arkansas

Student Loan Guarantee
    Foundation of Arkansas
219 South Victory
Little Rock, AR 72201
(501) 372-1491

California

California Student Aid Commission
P.O. Box 510625
Sacramento, CA 94245-0625
(916) 445-0880

Colorado

Colorado Student Loan Program
Denver Place
999 Eighteenth Street, Suite 425
Denver, CO 80202-2440
(303) 294-5050

Connecticut

Connecticut Student Loan
    Foundation
525 Brook Street
Rocky Hill, CT 06067
(203) 257-4001

Delaware

Delaware Higher Education
    Loan Program
Delaware Postsecondary
    Education Commission
820 North French Street
Wilmington, DE 19801
(302) 577-6055

District of Columbia

Higher Education Loan Program of
    Washington, D.C.
1800 K Street NW, Suite 831
Washington, DC 20006

Florida

Office of Student Financial Assistance
Knott Building
Tallahassee, FL 32399
(904) 488-6181

Georgia

Georgia Higher Education Assistance
    Corporation
2082 East Exchange Place, Suite 200
Tucker, GA 30084
(404) 493-5412

Hawaii

Hawaii Educational Loan Program
1314 South King Street, Suite 961
P.O. Box 22187
Honolulu, HI 96814
(808) 536-3731

Idaho

Student Loan Fund of Idaho, Inc.
6905 Highway 95
P.O. Box 730
Fruitland, ID 83619-0730
(208) 452-4058

Illinois

Illinois Student Assistance Commission
Illinois Stafford Loan Program
106 Wilmont Road
Deerfield, IL 60015
(708) 948-8550

Indiana

State Student Assistance Commission of
    Indiana
964 North Pennsylvania Avenue
Indianapolis, IN 46204-1088
(317) 232-2366

Iowa

Iowa College Student Aid Commission
201 Jewett Building
Ninth and Grand Avenues
Des Moines, IA 50309
(515) 281-8537

Kansas

Higher Education Assistance Foundation
6800 College Boulevard, Suite 600
Overland Park, KS 66211
(913) 345-1300

Kentucky

Kentucky Higher Education Assistance
    Authority
1050 U.S. 127 South, Suite 102
Frankfort, KY 40601
(502) 564-7990

Louisiana

Office of Student Financial Assistance
    for Louisiana Student Financial
    Assistance Commission
P.O. Box 91202
Baton Rouge, LA 70821-9202
(504) 922-1011

Maine

Maine Education Assistance Division
    Finance Authority of Maine
State House Station 119
Augusta, ME 04333
(207) 289-2183

Maryland

Maryland Higher Education
    Loan Corporation
2100 Guilford Avenue
Baltimore, MD 21218
(301) 333-6555

Massachusetts

Massachusetts Higher Education
    Assistance Corporation
330 Stuart Street
Boston, MA 02116
(617) 426-9434

Michigan

Michigan Higher Education
    Assistance Authority
Michigan Guaranty Agency
P.O. Box 30047
Lansing, MI 48909
(517) 373-0760

Minnesota

Higher Education Assistance
  Foundation
Hemar Building, Suite 500
85 East Seventh Place
St. Paul, MN 55101
(612) 291-8460

Mississippi

Mississippi Guarantee Student Loan
  Agency
3825 Ridgewood Road
P.O. Box 342
Jackson, MS 39205-0342
(601) 982-6663

Missouri

Missouri Coordinating Board
  for Higher Education
P.O. Box 1438
Jefferson City, MO 65102
(314) 751-3940

Montana

Montana Guaranteed Student
  Loan Program
35 South Last Chance Gulch
Helena, MT 59620
(406) 444-6594

Nebraska

Nebraska Student Loan Program
1300 O Street
P.O. Box 82507
Lincoln, NE 68501-2507
(402) 475-8686

Nevada

United Student Aid Fund, Inc.
1400 East Southern Avenue
Suite 200
Tempe, AZ 85282
(800) 352-3033

New Hampshire

New Hampshire Higher Education
  Assistance Foundation
44 Warren Street
P.O. Box 877
Concord, NH 03302
(603) 225-6612
(800) 235-2577 (New Hampshire)
(800) 525-2577 (elsewhere)

New Jersey

New Jersey Higher Education
  Assistance Authority
4 Quaker Bridge Plaza
CN 540
Trenton, NJ 08625
(609) 588-3200

New Mexico

New Mexico Student Loan Guarantee
  Corporation
P.O. Box 27020
Albuquerque, NM 87125-7020
(505) 345-8821

New York

New York State Higher Education
  Services Corporation
99 Washington Avenue
Albany, NY 12255
(518) 473-1574

North Carolina

North Carolina State Education
  Assistance Authority
P.O. Box 2688
Chapel Hill, NC 27515-2688
(919) 549-8614
            or
College Foundation
P.O. Box 12100
Raleigh, NC 27605
(919) 821-4771

North Dakota

Student Loans of North Dakota
    —Guarantor
Box 5524
Bismarck, ND 58502-5524
(701) 224-5753

Ohio

Ohio Student Loan Commission
P.O. Box 16610
Columbus, OH 43266-0610
(614) 466-3091

Oklahoma

Oklahoma State Regents for
  Higher Education
500 Education Building
State Capitol Complex
Oklahoma City, OK 73105-4503
(405) 524-9100

Oregon

Oregon State Scholarship
  Commission
1445 Willamette Street
Eugene, OR 97401-7707
(503) 346-3200

Pennsylvania

Pennsylvania Higher Education
  Assistance Agency
660 Boas Street, Towne House Apts.
Harrisburg, PA 17102
(717) 257-2860
(800) 692-7392 (Pennsylvania)

Rhode Island

Rhode Island Higher Education
  Assistance Authority
560 Jefferson Boulevard
Warwick, RI 02886
(401) 277-2050

South Carolina

South Carolina Student Loan Corporation
Interstate Center, Suite 210
P.O. Box 21487
Columbia, SC 29221
(803) 798-0916

South Dakota

Education Assistance Corporation
115 First Avenue, S.W.
Aberdeen, SD 57401
(605) 225-6423

Tennessee

Tennessee Student Assistance Corporation
404 James Robertson Parkway
Parkway Towers, Suite 1950
Nashville, TN 37243-0820
(615) 741-1346

Texas

Texas Guaranteed Student Loan
  Corporation
P.O. Box 15996
Austin, TX 78761-5996
(512) 835-1900

Utah

Loan Servicing Corporation of Utah
P.O. Box 30802
Salt Lake City, UT 84130
(801) 975-2200

Vermont

Vermont Student Assistance
    Corporation
Champlain Mill
P.O. Box 2000
Winooski, VT 05404-2601
(802) 655-9602
(800) 642-3177 (Vermont)

Virginia

Virginia State Education Assistance
    Authority/Virginia Education
    Loan Authority
One Franklin Square, 411 East
    Franklin Street
Richmond, VA 23219
(804) 786-2035
(800) 792-LOAN (Virginia)
(800) 937-0032 (National)

Washington

Northwest Education Loan Association
500 Colman Building
811 First Avenue
Seattle, WA 98104
(206) 625-1283

West Virginia

West Virginia Loan Services
P.O. Box 591
Charleston, WV 25322
(304) 345-7211

Wisconsin

Great Lakes Higher Education
    Corporation
2401 International Lane
Madison, WI 53704
(608) 246-1800

Wyoming

United Student Aid Funds
1912 Capitol Avenue, Suite 320
Cheyenne, WY 82001
(307) 635-3259

Puerto Rico

Puerto Rico Higher Education
    Assistance Corporation
P.O. Box 42001
Minillas Station
Santurce, PR 00940-2001
(809) 763-3535

Virgin Islands

Virgin Islands Board of Education
P.O. Box 11900
Charlotte Amalie
St. Thomas, VI 00801
(809) 774-4546

Guam, American Samoa, Northern Marianas, Palau

Hawaii Educational Loan Program
United Student Aid Funds, Inc.
1314 South King Street, Suite 961
Honolulu, HI 96814
(808) 536-3731

USAF, Inc.

United Student Aid Funds, Inc.
Loan Information Services, M372
P.O. Box 6180
Indianapolis, IN 46206
(800) LOAN USA

Appendix. A sample 1992–93 FAF™

The Financial Aid Form (FAF) on the following pages is a draft version. If you file an FAF for the 1992–93 school year, you will fill out an actual FAF very much like this one. This is a sample only, and should not be submitted for analysis.

FAF® Financial Aid Form — School Year 1992-93

(1d) DRAND — May 7, 1991

Warning: If you purposely give false or misleading information, you may be subject to a $10,000 fine, a prison sentence, or both. **Do not write in this space.**

Use only a No. 2 (soft-lead) pencil. Don't write outside of the boxes or answer spaces. "You" and "your" on this form always mean the student who wants aid.

Section A — Student's Identification Information

1. Your name
   Last   First   M.I.

2. Your permanent mailing address (Mail will be sent to this address. See page X for state/country abbreviation.)
   Number, street, and apartment number
   City   State   Zip Code

3. Your title (optional)   1 ☐ Mr.   2 ☐ Miss, Ms., or Mrs.

4. Your state of legal residence

5. Your social security number

6. Your date of birth   Month   Day   Year

7. Are you a U.S. citizen? (Mark only one box.)
   1 ☐ Yes, I am a U.S. citizen.
   2 ☐ No, but I am an eligible noncitizen. (See the instructions on page X.)
   A
   3 ☐ No, neither of the above. (See the instructions on page X.)

8. As of today, are you married? (Mark only one box.)
   1 ☐ I am not married. (I am single, divorced, or widowed.
   2 ☐ I am married.
   3 ☐ I am separated from my spouse.

9. What year will you be in college in 1992-93? (Mark only one box.)
   1 ☐ 1st (never previously attended college)
   2 ☐ 1st (previously attended college)
   3 ☐ 2nd
   4 ☐ 3rd
   5 ☐ 4th
   6 ☐ 5th or more undergraduate
   7 ☐ first year graduate/professional (beyond a bachelor's degree)
   8 ☐ continuing graduate or professional

10. Will you have your first bachelor's degree before July 1, 1992?   Yes ☐1   No ☐2

Section B — Student Status

11. a. Were you born **before** January 1, 1969?   Yes ☐1   No ☐2
    b. Are you a veteran of the U.S. Armed Forces?   Yes ☐1   No ☐2
    c. Are you a ward of the court or are both your parents dead?   Yes ☐1   No ☐2
    d. Do you have legal dependents (other than a spouse) that fit the definition in the instructions on page X?   Yes ☐1   No ☐2

- If you answered "Yes" to any part of question 11, go to Section C and fill in the **GRAY** and the **WHITE** areas on the rest of the form. Some colleges may also ask you to complete the **PURPLE** areas. (Skip questions 12 through 15.)
- If you answered "No" to every part of question 11 and you are:
  —unmarried now (single, divorced, separated, or widowed) **and** will be an undergraduate student in 1992-93, answer question 12. (Skip question 15.)
  —married now or will be a graduate/professional student in 1992-93, answer question 15. (Skip questions 12 through 14f.)

Unmarried Undergraduate Students Only

12. Did your parents claim you as an income tax exemption
    …in 1990?   Yes ☐1   No ☐2
    …in 1991?   Yes ☐1   No ☐2

- If you answered "Yes" to **either** year in question 12, go to Section C and fill in the areas outlined in **PURPLE** and the **WHITE** areas on the rest of the form. (Skip questions 13 through 15.)
- If you answered "No" to **both** years in question 12, answer question 13 below.

13. Beginning with the 1987-88 school year, when did you **first** receive federal student financial aid? (Mark only one box. See instructions on page X.)

    1 ☐ In the 1987-88 school year (Answer 14a only.) → 14. a. Did you have total resources of $4,000 or more, not including parents' support …in 1985? Yes ☐1 No ☐2 …in 1986? Yes ☐1 No ☐2

    2 ☐ In the 1988-89 school year (Answer 14b only.) → 14. b. Did you have total resources of $4,000 or more, not including parents' support …in 1986? Yes ☐1 No ☐2 …in 1987? Yes ☐1 No ☐2

    3 ☐ In the 1989-90 school year (Answer 14c only.) → 14. c. Did you have total resources of $4,000 or more, not including parents' support …in 1987? Yes ☐1 No ☐2 …in 1988? Yes ☐1 No ☐2

    4 ☐ In the 1990-91 school year (Answer 14d only.) → 14. d. Did you have total resources of $4,000 or more, not including parents' support …in 1988? Yes ☐1 No ☐2 …in 1989? Yes ☐1 No ☐2

    5 ☐ In the 1991-92 school year (Answer 14e only.) → 14. e. Did you have total resources of $4,000 or more, not including parents' support …in 1989? Yes ☐1 No ☐2 …in 1990? Yes ☐1 No ☐2

    6 ☐ In none of the above. (Answer 14f only.) → 14. f. Did you have total resources of $4,000 or more, not including parents' support …in 1990? Yes ☐1 No ☐2 …in 1991? Yes ☐1 No ☐2

- If you answered "No" to **either** year in question 14a, 14b, 14c, 14d, 14e, or 14f, go to Section C and fill in the **areas outlined in PURPLE** and the **WHITE** areas on the rest of the form.
- If you answered "Yes" to **both** years in question 14a, 14b, 14c, 14d, 14e, or 14f, go to Section C and fill in the **areas outlined in GRAY** and the **WHITE** areas on the rest of the form. Some colleges may also ask you to complete the **PURPLE** areas.

Married Students or Graduate/Professional Students Only

15. Will your parents claim you as an income tax exemption in 1992?   Yes ☐1   No ☐2

- If you answered "Yes" to question 15, go to Section C and fill in the **areas outlined in PURPLE** and the **WHITE** areas on the rest of the form.
- If you answered "No" to question 15, go to Section C and fill in the **areas outlined in GRAY** and the **WHITE** areas on the rest of the form. Some colleges may also ask you to complete the **PURPLE** areas.

Section C — Household Information

———— Parents ————

16. What is your parents' current marital status? (Mark only one box.)
    1 ☐ single   2 ☐ married   3 ☐ separated   4 ☐ divorced   5 ☐ widowed

17. What is your parents' state of legal residence?

18. Number of family members in 1992-93
    Always include yourself (the student) and your parents. Include your parents' other children and other people only if they meet the definition in the instructions on page X.

19. Number of college students in 1992-93
    Of the number in 18, write in the number of family members who will be in college at least half-time. Include yourself — the student who is applying for aid.

———— Student (and Spouse) ————

20. Number of family members in 1992-93
    Always include yourself and your spouse. Include your children and other people only if they meet the definition in the instructions on page X.

21. Number of college students in 1992-93
    Of the number in 20, write in the number of family members who will be in college at least half-time. Include yourself.

Print your name   Last | | | | | | | | | | | | | | | | | | | | First | | | | | | | | | | | | | | |

Section D — 1991 Income, Earnings, and Benefits (You must see the instructions for income and taxes that you should exclude from questions 24 through 28.)

Everyone must fill out the Student (and Spouse) column below.

	——— Parents ———	——— Student (and Spouse) ———

22. The following 1991 U.S. income tax return figures are (Mark only one box.)

from a completed 1991 IRS Form 1040EZ or 1040A. (Go to 23.)   22. 1 ☐   22. 1 ☐
from a completed 1991 IRS Form 1040. (Go to 23.)   2 ☐   2 ☐
estimated. Will file 1991 IRS Form 1040EZ or 1040A. (Go to 23.)   3 ☐   3 ☐
estimated. Will file 1991 IRS Form 1040. (Go to 23.)   4 ☐   4 ☐
a tax return will not be filed. (Skip to 26.)   5 ☐   5 ☐

Tax Filers Only

23. 1991 total number of exemptions
(IRS Form 1040 — line 6e, 1040A — line 6e, or 1040EZ — see instructions on page X)   23. |_|_| 23. |_|_|

24. 1991 Adjusted Gross Income (AGI) — IRS Form 1040 — line 31, 1040A — line 16, or 1040EZ — line 3. (See instructions on page X.)   24. $ _____.00   24. $ _____.00

25. 1991 U.S. income tax paid (IRS Form 1040 — line 47, 1040A — line 25, or 1040EZ — line 7)   25. $ _____.00   25. $ _____.00

26. 1991 income earned from work by   **Father**   26. $ _____.00   **Student**   26. $ _____.00

27. 1991 income earned from work by   **Mother**   27. $ _____.00   **Spouse**   27. $ _____.00

28. 1991 untaxed income and benefits (yearly totals only)

a. 1991 Social security benefits   28a. $ _____.00   28a. $ _____.00

b. 1991 Aid to Families with Dependent Children (AFDC or ADC)   b. $ _____.00   b. $ _____.00

c. 1991 Child support received for all children   c. $ _____.00   c. $ _____.00

d. Other untaxed 1991 income and benefits from Worksheet II on page X of the instructions   d. $ _____.00   d. $ _____.00

Section E — Stafford Loan Information (formerly Guaranteed Student Loan [GSL])

If you have never received a Stafford Loan (GSL) or a Federally Insured Student Loan (FISL), go to question 34. Skip questions 29 through 33.

29. What is the total unpaid principal balance on all your Stafford Loans (GSLs)? (If you answered "0," go to question 34. Skip questions 30-33.) $ _____.00

30. What is the unpaid total principal balance on your **most recent** Stafford Loan (GSL)? $ _____.00

31. What is the interest rate of your **most recent** Stafford Loan (GSL)?   1 ☐ 7%   2 ☐ 8%   3 ☐ 9%   4 ☐ 8/10%

32. What was the loan period of your **most recent** Stafford Loan (GSL)?   from |_| Month |_| Year   through |_| Month |_| Year

33. What was your class level when you received your **most recent** Stafford Loan (GSL)?

1 ☐ Freshman   5 ☐ 5th-year or more undergraduate
2 ☐ Sophomore   6 ☐ 1st-year graduate/professional (beyond a bachelor's degree)
3 ☐ Junior   7 ☐ Continuing graduate or professional
4 ☐ Senior

Section F — Federal Student Aid Releases and Certification

34. What college(s) do you plan to go to in 1992-93?

	Name	City and State	CSS Code No.
a.			|_|_|_|_|
b.			|_|_|_|_|
c.			|_|_|_|_|

35. Do you give the U.S. Department of Education permission to send information from this form to:
— the financial aid agencies in your state?   Yes ☐1   No ☐2
— the college(s) you named in 34 (or its representative)?   Yes ☐1   No ☐2

Note: By marking "Yes" you are not applying for state and institutional aid in some states. Some agencies and colleges that use the FAF also require that a CSS report be sent to them. See instructions.

36. Are you in default on a federal student loan, or do you owe a refund on a federal student grant? (Mark only one box.)

1 ☐ I am in default on a federal student loan.
2 ☐ I owe a refund on a federal student grant.
3 ☐ Both of the above
4 ☐ None of the above

37. Mark this box if you give Selective Service permission to register you. (See instructions.) ☐

38. Certification: All of the information on this form and the Supplemental Information, if completed, is true and complete to the best of my knowledge. I realize that information from this form will be sent to the U.S. Department of Education for the purpose of determining federal student aid eligibility. If asked by an authorized official, I agree to give proof of the information that I have given on this form and the Supplemental Information, if completed. I realize that this proof may include a copy of my U.S., state, or local income tax return. I also realize that if I don't give proof when asked, the student may be denied aid.

Everyone giving information on this form must sign below. If you don't sign the form, it will be returned unprocessed.

1 _____
Student's signature

2 _____
Student's spouse's signature

3 _____
Father's (Stepfather's) signature

4 _____
Mother's (Stepmother's) signature

Date this form was completed:
Write in the month and day.
Mark the year completed. |_| Month |_| Day   1 ☐1992   2 ☐1993   Year

——— **IMPORTANT:** You must read page X of the instructions to see if you need to fill out Sections G through J. ———

SUPPLEMENTAL INFORMATION

Section G — 1991 Expenses

	——— Parents ———	——— Student (and Spouse) ———

39. 1991 medical and dental expenses not paid by insurance   39. $ _____.00   39. $ _____.00

40. 1991 elementary, junior high, and high school tuition for dependent children
a. Amount paid (Don't include tuition paid for the applicant.)   40a. $ _____.00   40a. $ _____.00
b. For how many dependent children? (Don't include the applicant.)   b. |_| b. |_|

Section H — Asset Information

—————— Parents —————— | —— Student (and Spouse) ——

41. Is either of your parents a displaced homemaker?
(See instructions on page X.)
41. Yes ☐1 No ☐2

41. Are you, or is your spouse, a displaced homemaker? Yes ☐1 No ☐2
(See instructions on page X.)

42. Write in the age of your older parent.
42. ☐☐

42. XXXXXXXXXXXXXXX

	What is it worth today?	What is owed on it?		What is it worth today?	What is owed on it?
43. Cash, savings, and checking accounts	**43.** $ ____ .00	XXXXXXXXXXXXXX	**43.** $ ____ .00	XXXXXXXXXXXXXX	
44. Home (Renters write in "0.")	**44.** $ ____ .00	$ ____ .00	**44.** $ ____ .00	$ ____ .00	
45. Other real estate and investments	**45.** $ ____ .00	$ ____ .00	**45.** $ ____ .00	$ ____ .00	
46. Business and farm	**46.** $ ____ .00	$ ____ .00	**46.** $ ____ .00	$ ____ .00	

47. Does any part of **46** include a farm?
47. Yes ☐1 No ☐2

47. Yes ☐1 No ☐2

Section I — Student's Monthly Veterans Educational Benefits (Expected Amount July 1, 1992 – June 30, 1993) (If you are completing this section, you must

answer question **48**. If you are filling out the gray and white areas, you must also answer question **49**.)

49. Your Veterans Contributory Benefits (VEAP)

48. Your veterans Dependents Educational Assistance Program Benefits

a. Amount per month $ ____ .00   **b.** Number of months ☐☐

49. a. Amount per month $ ____ .00   **b.** Number of months ☐☐

Section J — Expected 1992 Taxable & Nontaxable Income & Benefits

(You must see the instructions for income and taxes that you should exclude from questions **51** through **55**.)

—————— Parents —————— | —— Student (and Spouse) ——

50. Is either parent **certified** as a dislocated worker by the appropriate agency? (See instructions on page X.)
50. Yes ☐1 No ☐2

Are you, or is your spouse, **certified** as a dislocated worker by the appropriate agency? (See instructions on page X.)
50. Yes ☐1 No ☐2

		Parents		Student (and Spouse)
51. 1992 income earned from work by	Father	**51.** $ ____ .00	Student	**51.** $ ____ .00
52. 1992 income earned from work by	Mother	**52.** $ ____ .00	Spouse	**52.** $ ____ .00
53. 1992 other taxable income		**53.** $ ____ .00		**53.** $ ____ .00
54. 1992 U.S. income tax to be paid		**54.** $ ____ .00		**54.** $ ____ .00
55. 1992 nontaxable income and benefits (See instructions on page X.)		**55.** $ ____ .00		**55.** $ ____ .00

IMPORTANT: If your college or state agency needs a CSS report, complete Sections K–Q, and S if applicable, and enclose the correct reporting fee.

Section K — Student's Other Information

56. Your home telephone ☐☐☐ - ☐☐☐ - ☐☐☐☐
Area Code Number

57. Date you began living in your state of legal residence Month ☐☐ Year ☐☐

58. If you have dependents other than a spouse, **how many** will be in each of the following age groups during 1992-93?
Ages 0-5 ☐ Ages 6-12 ☐ Ages 13+ ☐

59. If you are now in high school, give your high school 6-digit code number. ☐☐☐☐☐☐

60. a. List all colleges that you have attended. Always list first the college most recently attended.

Name, city, and state of college	Period of attendance From (mo./yr.)	To (mo./yr.)	CSS Code Number

b. If you have previously attended more than three colleges, write in the total number of colleges you have attended. Give the additional names and CSS code numbers in Section R. ☐

61. Your course of study code (See instructions.) ☐☐

62. Date you expect to complete your current college degree/certificate Month ☐☐ Year ☐☐

63. Your expected enrollment status during the 1992-93 school year (Mark only one box.)
1 ☐ Full-time 2 ☐ Three-quarter time 3 ☐ Half-time 4 ☐ Less than half-time

64. During the 1992-93 school year, you want financial aid from ☐☐ ☐☐ through ☐☐ ☐☐
Month Year Month Year

65. Mark your preference for work or loan assistance.
1 ☐ Part-time job only 3 ☐ Loan only
2 ☐ Part-time job and loan 4 ☐ No preference

66. a. Your occupation/ employer _____

b. Employer's address _____

c. Will you continue to work for this employer during the 1992-93 school year? Yes ☐1 No ☐2

67. a. Your driver's license number ☐☐☐☐☐☐☐☐☐☐☐☐

b. State that issued the above driver's license number State ☐☐

Section L — Student's Expected Summer/School-Year Income

(See instructions for the kinds of income to exclude.)

	Summer 1992 3 months	School Year 1992-93 9 months
68. Income earned from work by you	$ ____ .00	$ ____ .00
69. Income earned from work by your spouse	$ ____ .00	$ ____ .00
70. Other taxable income	$ ____ .00	$ ____ .00
71. Nontaxable income and benefits	$ ____ .00	$ ____ .00

Section M — Student's Expected Other Veterans Benefits

(July 1, 1992 – June 30, 1993)

72. Other benefits administered by the Veterans Administration (See page X of instructions. Don't include any benefits you already reported in **48** or **49**.)

a. Amount per month $ ____ .00   **b.** Number of months ☐☐

Section N — Family Members' Listing
Give information for all family members included in **18** or **20** but don't give information about yourself. List up to seven other family members here. If more than seven, list first those who will be in college at least half-time. List those over seven in Section R.

3.

Full name of family member	Age	Relation-ship (Use code below.)	Will attend college at least half-time in 1992-93 school year? Yes / No	Name of school or college this person will attend in 1992-93 school year	Year in school 1992-93	Occupation/Employer of this person	If attended college in 1991-92, give amount of: 1991-92 Scholarships/Grants	1991-92 Parents' Contribution
1	**You — the Student Applicant**								
2				1 ☐ 2 ☐					
3				1 ☐ 2 ☐					
4				1 ☐ 2 ☐					
5				1 ☐ 2 ☐					
6				1 ☐ 2 ☐					
7				1 ☐ 2 ☐					
8				1 ☐ 2 ☐					

Write in the correct code from the right.

1 = Student's parent   3 = Student's brother or sister   5 = Student's son or daughter   7 = Other (Explain
2 = Student's stepparent   4 = Student's husband or wife   6 = Student's grandparent   in Section R.)

Section O — Parents' Other Information

74. Parents' monthly home mortgage/rental payment (If none, explain in Sect. R.) $ _____ .00

75. If parents own a home, give   **a.** year purchased 1 9 _ _   **b.** purchase price $ _____ .00

76. If parents included non-real estate investments in **45**, give their worth today. $ _____ .00

77. Breakdown of 1991 income in **24** (Tax Filers Only)

a. Wages, salaries, tips (IRS 1040—line 7, 1040A—line 7, or 1040EZ—line 1) **a.** $ _____ .00

b. Interest income (IRS 1040—line 8a, 1040A—line 8a, or 1040EZ—line 2) **b.** $ _____ .00

c. Dividend income (IRS 1040 — line 9, or 1040A — line 9) **c.** $ _____ .00

d. Net income (or loss) from business, farm, rents, royalties, partnerships, estates, trusts, etc. (IRS 1040 — lines 12, 18, and 19) If a loss, enter the amount in (parentheses). **d.** $ _____ .00

e. Other taxable income such as alimony received, capital gains (or losses), pensions, annuities, etc. (IRS 1040—lines 10, 11, 13-15, 16b, 17b, 20, 21b, and 22, or 1040A—lines 10b, 11b, 12, and 13b) **e.** $ _____ .00

f. Adjustments to income (IRS 1040 — line 30, or 1040A — line 15c) **f.** $ _____ .00

g. Total (Add 77a–77e minus 77f.) This is your answer to **24**. **g.** $ _____ .00

Section P — Divorced, Separated, or Remarried Parents
(To be answered by the parent who completes this form, if the student's natural or adoptive parents are divorced or separated.)

78. a. Year of separation ☐☐   Year of divorce ☐☐

b. Other parent's name _____

Home address _____

Occupation/Employer _____

c. According to court order, when will support for the student end? Month ☐☐ Year ☐☐

d. Who claimed the student as a tax exemption for 1991? _____

e. Is there an agreement specifying a contribution for the student's education?   Yes ☐   No ☐

If yes, how much for the 1992-93 school year? $ _____ .00

Section Q — Student's Colleges & Programs

79. List the names and CSS code numbers of the colleges and programs to which you want CSS to send information from this form. Give the correct housing code. Don't list federal student aid programs. Be sure to include the college(s) you listed in **34**. Enclose the right fee. See the instructions and **80**.

Name	City and State	CSS Code No.	Housing Code*

*Housing Codes for 1992-93 (Enter only one code for each college.):
1 = With parents   2 = Campus housing   3 = Off-campus housing   4 = With relatives

80. Fee: Mark the box that tells how many colleges and programs are listed in **79**.

CSS Only

1 ☐ $XX.XX   3 ☐ $XX.XX   5 ☐ $XX.XX   7 ☐ $XX.XX

2 ☐ $XX.XX   4 ☐ $XX.XX   6 ☐ $XX.XX   8 ☐ $XX.XX

CSS Use Only

Mail this form with a check or money order for the right amount made out to CSS.

Section R — Explanations/Special Circumstances
Use this space to explain any unusual expenses, educational and other debts, or special circumstances. Don't send letters, tax forms, or other materials with your FAF as they will be destroyed.

CSS Use Only   5   6

Order Form

Mail order form to: College Board Publications, Department R54, Box 886, New York, New York 10101-0886

Qty.	Item No.	Title	Price	Amount
____	004086	**The College Handbook, 1992**	$ 18.95	$_____
____	004108	**Index of Majors, 1992**	$ 15.95	$_____
____	004094	**The College Cost Book, 1992**	$ 14.95	$_____
____	239348	**3-Book Set: College Handbook, Index of Majors, College Cost Book, 1992**	$ 35.95	$_____
____	004124	**The College Handbook for Transfer Students, 1992**	$ 15.95	$_____
____	004116	**The College Handbook Foreign Student Supplement, 1992**	$ 14.95	$_____
____	003667	**10 SATs. Fourth edition**	$ 11.95	$_____
____	220213	**5 SATs. 1990 edition.**	$ 7.00	$_____
____	003101	**The College Board Guide to Preparing for the PSAT/NMSQT**	$ 8.95	$_____
____	003942	**The College Board Achievement Tests (rev. edition)**	$ 12.95	$_____
____	220220	**Four Popular Achievement Tests**	$ 7.95	$_____
____	003950	**The Revised College Board Guide to the CLEP Examinations**	$ 11.95	$_____
____	003543	**The College Board Guide to Jobs and Career Planning**	$ 12.95	$_____
____	003330	**Choosing a College: The Student's Step-by-Step Decision-Making Workbook**	$ 9.95	$_____
____	002474	**Your College Application**	$ 9.95	$_____
____	003276	**Your College Application video cassette**	$ 29.95	$_____
____	002571	**Writing Your College Application Essay**	$ 9.95	$_____
____	003284	**Writing Your College Application Essay audio cassette**	$ 9.95	$_____
____	002601	**Campus Visits and College Interviews**	$ 9.95	$_____
____	002261	**The College Admissions Organizer**	$ 16.95	$_____
____	003047	**College Bound: Getting Ready, Moving In, and Succeeding on Campus**	$ 9.95	$_____
____	003225	**Summer on Campus: College Experiences for High School Students**	$ 9.95	$_____
____	003357	**Countdown to College: Getting the Most Out of High School**	$ 9.95	$_____
____	004019	**Student Survival Guide (available only if ordered with another item)**	$ 4.95	$_____
____	003179	**Campus Health Guide**	$ 14.95	$_____
____	003349	**Coping with Stress in College**	$ 9.95	$_____
____	003837	**Inside College: New Freedom, New Responsibility**	$ 10.95	$_____
____	003535	**The Student's Guide to Good Writing**	$ 9.95	$_____
____	002598	**Succeed with Math: Every Student's Guide to Conquering Math Anxiety**	$ 12.95	$_____
____	003977	**ABC's of Eligibility for College-Bound Student Athletes video cassette**	$ 49.95	$_____
____	002075	**The College Board Guide to Going to College While Working**	$ 9.95	$_____
____	003055	**How to Help Your Teenager Find the Right Career**	$ 12.95	$_____
____	003160	**The College Guide for Parents**	$ 12.95	$_____
____	**College Explorer, 1992** ___ 004205 (Apple II) ___ 004167 (MS-DOS)		$ 89.95	$_____
____	**College Cost Explorer, 1992** ___ 004221 (Apple II) ___ 004183 (MS-DOS)		$ 89.95	$_____
____	**College Planner** ___ 003675 (Apple 3.5") ___ 003691 (MS-DOS 3.5")		$ 29.95	$_____
____	**College Planner** ___ 003683 (Apple 5.25") ___ 003705 (MS-DOS 5.25")		$ 29.95	$_____
____	**Testwise** ___ 002989 (Apple II) ___ 003071 (MS-DOS)		$ 84.95	$_____
____	**TestSense** ___ 002172 (Apple 5.25")		$ 54.95	$_____

Payment must accompany all orders not submitted on an institutional purchase order or charged to a credit card. The College Board pays 4th class book-rate postage on credit card and prepaid orders. Credit card and purchase orders must be for a minimum of $25. Bookrate postage is charged on all orders received on purchase orders or requesting faster shipment.

CA and PA residents, add 6% sales tax. $_____

Subtotal $_____

Handling Charge $___2.95___

Total $_____

___ Enclosed in my check or money order made payable to the College Board in the amount noted above

___ Enclosed is an institutional purchase order (orders for $25 or more), or

___ Please charge my ___ MasterCard ___ Visa. My credit card number is __ __ __ __/__ __ __ __/__ __ __ __/__ __ __ __

Card expiration date: ___/___ _____

            month/year   Card holder's signature

Credit card holders only can place orders by calling toll-free 1-800-323-7155 Monday through Thursday from 8am to12 midnight; Friday, 8am to 11pm EST. Please have your credit card number ready when you call and give operator the department number R54. For other information or assistance, call (212) 713-8165, Monday through Friday, 9am to 5pm EST, FAX (212) 713-8143.

Ship to:

Name _____ City _____

Street Address (do not use P.O. Box numbers) _____ State _____ Zip _____

Telephone _____

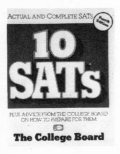

THE RIGHT SOFTWARE FOR COLLEGE PLANNING

College Explorer™ $89.95

Winner of the 1990 Choice Award for Young Adult Software
-- Compute

"...software that expands the things a computer can do."
-- The New York Times

Find out--and compare--what each of the nation's 2,700 two- and four-year colleges has to offer before you decide where to apply. This easy-to-use program with up-to-the-minute data lets you search for colleges using 600 different options, including:

- Degree level, majors, geographic location, tuition
- Admissions rate, application closing date, AP policies
- Enrollment size, coed/single sex, college setting
- Sports, on-campus housing, special programs and services

College Planner™ $29.95

"A must for any student seeking help in organizing college admissions planning." -- Nibble

College Planner will save you much-needed time by helping you keep on top of routine admissions tasks. The program's unique features let you:

- Use electronic calendars and checklists to monitor deadlines
- Compare college information based on your own facts and impressions
- Print customized letters requesting catalogs, interviews, and application forms

College Cost Explorer™ $89.95

"A key resource for college-bound teens and their families."
-- Booklist

Estimate your financial need at 2,700 colleges with this easy-to-use program. You'll find detailed information about 1991-92 costs and financial aid policies at accredited 2- and 4-year institutions and useful information on meeting your share of the costs. The program encourages early planning by showing families how to:

- Calculate what colleges will expect you to pay
- Estimate what you need at individual colleges
- Find out about financial aid availability at each college

Special features include: descriptions of major sources of need and non-need-based financial aid; step-by-step instructions on applying for financial aid; electronic worksheets for calculating expected family contribution; ability to print all calculations and college information; personalized information on the full costs of saving and borrowing.

Apple II version runs on the Apple II family with one 3.5" or two 5.25" disks. For the Apple IIe, an extended 80-column card is required. MS-DOS version runs on IBM and 100% compatibles with at least 256K RAM. PC DOS 2.1 or higher, MS-DOS 3.2 or higher required. All programs can run on a hard drive. To order, use the order form in the back of this book.

GUIDANCE SOFTWARE
FROM
THE COLLEGE BOARD

Order Form

Mail order form to: College Board Publications, Department R54, Box 886, New York, New York 10101-0886

Qty.	Item No.	Title	Price	Amount
____	004086	**The College Handbook, 1992**	$ 18.95	$_____
____	004108	**Index of Majors, 1992**	$ 15.95	$_____
____	004094	**The College Cost Book, 1992**	$ 14.95	$_____
____	239348	**3-Book Set: College Handbook, Index of Majors, College Cost Book, 1992**	$ 35.95	$_____
____	004124	**The College Handbook for Transfer Students, 1992**	$ 15.95	$_____
____	004116	**The College Handbook Foreign Student Supplement, 1992**	$ 14.95	$_____
____	003667	**10 SATs. Fourth edition**	$ 11.95	$_____
____	220213	**5 SATs. 1990 edition.**	$ 7.00	$_____
____	003101	**The College Board Guide to Preparing for the PSAT/NMSQT**	$ 8.95	$_____
____	003942	**The College Board Achievement Tests (rev. edition)**	$ 12.95	$_____
____	220220	**Four Popular Achievement Tests**	$ 7.95	$_____
____	003950	**The Revised College Board Guide to the CLEP Examinations**	$ 11.95	$_____
____	003543	**The College Board Guide to Jobs and Career Planning**	$ 12.95	$_____
____	003330	**Choosing a College: The Student's Step-by-Step Decision-Making Workbook**	$ 9.95	$_____
____	002474	**Your College Application**	$ 9.95	$_____
____	003276	**Your College Application video cassette**	$ 29.95	$_____
____	002571	**Writing Your College Application Essay**	$ 9.95	$_____
____	003284	**Writing Your College Application Essay audio cassette**	$ 9.95	$_____
____	002601	**Campus Visits and College Interviews**	$ 9.95	$_____
____	002261	**The College Admissions Organizer**	$ 16.95	$_____
____	003047	**College Bound: Getting Ready, Moving In, and Succeeding on Campus**	$ 9.95	$_____
____	003225	**Summer on Campus: College Experiences for High School Students**	$ 9.95	$_____
____	003357	**Countdown to College: Getting the Most Out of High School**	$ 9.95	$_____
____	004019	**Student Survival Guide (available only if ordered with another item)**	$ 4.95	$_____
____	003179	**Campus Health Guide**	$ 14.95	$_____
____	003349	**Coping with Stress in College**	$ 9.95	$_____
____	003837	**Inside College: New Freedom, New Responsibility**	$ 10.95	$_____
____	003535	**The Student's Guide to Good Writing**	$ 9.95	$_____
____	002598	**Succeed with Math: Every Student's Guide to Conquering Math Anxiety**	$ 12.95	$_____
____	003977	**ABC's of Eligibility for College-Bound Student Athletes video cassette**	$ 49.95	$_____
____	002075	**The College Board Guide to Going to College While Working**	$ 9.95	$_____
____	003055	**How to Help Your Teenager Find the Right Career**	$ 12.95	$_____
____	003160	**The College Guide for Parents**	$ 12.95	$_____
____		**College Explorer, 1992** ____ 004205 (Apple II) ____ 004167 (MS-DOS)	$ 89.95	$_____
____		**College Cost Explorer, 1992** ____ 004221 (Apple II) ____ 004183 (MS-DOS)	$ 89.95	$_____
____		**College Planner** ____ 003675 (Apple 3.5") ____ 003691 (MS-DOS 3.5")	$ 29.95	$_____
____		**College Planner** ____ 003683 (Apple 5.25") ____ 003705 (MS-DOS 5.25")	$ 29.95	$_____
____		**Testwise** ____ 002989 (Apple II) ____ 003071 (MS-DOS)	$ 84.95	$_____
____		**TestSense** ____ 002172 (Apple 5.25")	$ 54.95	$_____

Payment must accompany all orders not submitted on an institutional purchase order or charged to a credit card. The College Board pays 4th class book-rate postage on credit card and prepaid orders. Credit card and purchase orders must be for a minimum of $25. Bookrate postage is charged on all orders received on purchase orders or requesting faster shipment.

CA and PA residents, add 6% sales tax. $_____
Subtotal $_____
Handling Charge $___ 2.95

Total $_____

___ Enclosed in my check or money order made payable to the College Board in the amount noted above
___ Enclosed is an institutional purchase order (orders for $25 or more), or
___ Please charge my ___ MasterCard ___ Visa. My credit card number is ___ ___ ___ ___/___ ___ ___ ___/___ ___ ___ ___/___ ___ ___ ___

Card expiration date: ___/___ _____
         month/year   Card holder's signature

Credit card holders only can place orders by calling toll-free 1-800-323-7155 Monday through Thursday from 8am to12 midnight; Friday, 8am to 11pm EST. Please have your credit card number ready when you call and give operator the department number R54. For other information or assistance, call (212) 713-8165, Monday through Friday, 9am to 5pm EST, FAX (212) 713-8143.

Ship to:
Name _____ City _____

Street Address (do not use P.O. Box numbers) _____ State _____ Zip _____

_____ Telephone _____